THE INTELLECTUAL CAPITAL *of* MICHAL KALECKI

PHOTOGRAPHER: EWA ULIKOWSKA

THE INTELLECTUAL CAPITAL *of* MICHAŁ KALECKI

A Study in Economic Theory and Policy

GEORGE R. FEIWEL

Foreword by
Lawrence R. Klein

THE UNIVERSITY OF TENNESSEE PRESS
KNOXVILLE

Manufactured in the United States of America.

 First edition.

Library of Congress Cataloging in Publication Data

Feiwel, George R
The intellectual capital of Michal Kalecki.

1. Kalecki, Michal. 2. Economics. I. Title.
HB113.K28F43 330.15'6 74-22487
ISBN 0-87049-161-X

FOREWORD

THERE HAVE BEEN *Festschriften*, short biographical sketches, and obituaries about Michal Kalecki, but no deep and penetrating analyses to compare with George Feiwel's. Kalecki was truly a phenomenon, known well to a select few but with a lasting imprint on the economics of our age. This biography really fills a need. Some scholars generate "fan clubs," and Kalecki had his, although it was reserved, discreet, and not apparent to the outside world, including the bulk of professional economists.

Kalecki's greatest achievement, among many, was undoubtedly his complete anticipation of Keynes' *General Theory*. Keynes had his biographer, and now Kalecki has his. This is a penetrating and fascinating story covering Kalecki in Poland at the beginning, in Europe and England during the late thirties and war years, in North America as an international civil servant, again in Poland, and finally in his last presentations to the Western World.

Not too many know the inside story about Kalecki's "scoop" of the General Theory, including some of the personal details of his relationship to the Cambridge group. Fewer know about his contribution to the economics of rationing and other aspects of the war economy in Britain. His later work in Poland dealing with planning and development was communicated to an enthusiastic group of colleagues and assistants, but not to the economics profession at large.

Now all these strands are pulled together by George Feiwel. The different branches of Kalecki's economics, his views on politics, and many aspects of his personal life are in this book. It is an account of an important economic thinker of our generation. The friends and admirers of Michal Kalecki are deeply indebted to George Feiwel for this painstaking analysis.

LAWRENCE R. KLEIN
Benjamin Franklin
Professor of Economics
University of Pennsylvania

Philadelphia
December, 1973

PREFACE

THIS IS THE STORY OF MICHAL KALECKI'S ECONOMICS, not his life. The profile of the man and the biographical sketches are provided only to the extent that they are necessary to help the reader understand his particular bent of mind and the problems he tried to solve. Clearly, he would not have produced the work he did had he not been the man he was, a fascinating composite of virtues and faults alike. The issues he tackled and his way of approaching them were strongly tinged by his basic concerns as an individual—a profound solicitude for the misery and suffering around him and an overriding desire to help improve the human lot. But leavening the whole, for both the man and the economist, was an underlying strain of pragmatism. Kalecki also was a fiercely independent thinker, bearing the yoke of no political party and standing ready to criticize his adversaries no matter how powerful they were. His views, often unpopular, earned him numerous critics in the major ideological camps.

In a biographical sketch of Alfred Marshall, John Maynard Keynes contemplated the essential qualities of character, understanding, and approach that are the ingredients of greatness in economists:

> The study of economics does not seem to require any specialised gifts of an unusually high order. Is it not, intellectually regarded, a very easy subject compared with the higher branches of philosophy and pure science? Yet good, or even competent, economists are the rarest of birds. An easy subject, at which very few excel! The paradox finds its explanation, perhaps, in that the master-economist must possess a rare *combination* of gifts. He must reach a high standard in several different directions and must combine talents not often found together. He must be mathematician, historian, statesman, philosopher—in some degree. He must understand symbols and speak in words. He must contemplate the particular in terms of the general, and touch abstract and concrete in the same flight of thought. He must study the present in the light of the past for the purposes of the future. No part of man's nature or his institutions must lie entirely outside his regard. He must be purposeful and disinterested in a simultaneous mood; as aloof and incorruptible as an artist, yet sometimes as near the earth as a politician. (Keynes 1963a, pp. 140-41.)

This is a formidable list; and although it is doubtful that all of the requirements have ever been united in one person, some of them were Kalecki's most striking attributes. He did indeed possess a rare combination of gifts. He was not a historian by predisposition, but he had a perception for the economic process in motion and how one sequence develops from the preceding ones. First and foremost he was an essentially original thinker, with an unusual ability to identify and address himself to the most relevant problems. He could forge new tools for the solution of a problem or adapt existing ones. He certainly qualified as a mathematician and philosopher and even as a statesman in the sense that his motivation always was toward solving important public issues. Still another aspect of the Keynes ideal was probably Kalecki's greatest gift: His analytical power and almost a genius for effective simplification permitted him to move easily and quickly from the highly abstract to the earthily practical. In sum, he was a political economist par excellence. And he was absolutely incorruptible, as his life and his former colleagues will attest.

In any assessment of Kalecki's make-up, it is essential to stress his dislike and critique of big monopolies and monopoly motivation as a fairly basic part of his inspiration and shaping. One needs to stress Kalecki's essentially radical reaction to the great crisis and depression of 1929 and the early 1930s, which hit Poland with such severity, to emphasize how much his ideas derive from and were influenced by his experience and painstaking analysis of these events.

Kalecki's work consists of a number of concise and penetrating analyses of various subjects. He refrained from broad and detailed surveys, concentrating on "value added." His major contributions lie primarily in the theory of economic dynamics. More specifically, they include: anticipating, independently discovering, and rigorously constructing all essential ingredients of the Keynesian system and incorporating the forces of market imperfection in his macrodynamic model; supplying the foundation for a modern business cycle theory: constructing a more realistic theory of income distribution based on a plausible theory of the firm; providing a critical starting point for understanding the present problems of the simultaneous occurrence of inflation and unemployment; advancing the political economy of full employment; predicting the regime of the political business cycle; developing the subtle device of general (expenditure) rationing to improve the range of economic choice under trying conditions of a war economy; laying the base for a theory of economic growth under central planning; and contributing to advances in planning methodology, and to advances in investment and foreign trade efficiency calculations. As could be expected, most of these contributions are not tied up in neat packages. There is still much to be done. In this sense, Kalecki has left an "unfinished" legacy, but it is a stimulating legacy and one that embraces a host of conceptual breakthroughs notwithstanding the limitations in the working out of the arguments. Naturally, certain aspects of his work, written at a different time and under different circumstances, may seem somewhat dated. But the close reader will find in his work a wide range of ideas that are particularly topical in the contemporary setting, and in some respects, even ahead of our time. For it is, after all, his mode of thought and his approach to the economic problems that are important.

For a number of reasons, Kalecki's work is not as well known as it deserves to be. In this book I have tried to redress the situation and to provide a commentary on his austere and laconic writings. It would have been awkward to set out in a single volume a detailed treatment of all the multifarious subjects with which Kalecki was concerned and on some of which so many eminent voices have spoken. Thus I have been selective in the choice of topics treated in the following pages. In the future I hope to address myself to some of the other topics in more specialized studies. I have attempted to provide a sympathetic, yet not uncritical, treatment and to recognize not only Kalecki's accomplishments, but also his faults, the flaws in his work, and certain arguments advanced by those who differ from him. In this context, I hope the reader will kindly take into account that the main purpose of this book is to present Kalecki's views on various subjects, rather than to give broad scope to those who differ from him, for their voices are relatively better known and are more likely to be found in the mainstream of economics.

I confess to having known little about Kalecki's contributions when we first met in Cambridge in 1969. It was this meeting, followed by our lively and fascinating discussions, that drove me to study his work. The real stimulation, as is so often the case, came, not from a meeting of minds, but from our differences; and I immediately found it necessary to become much better acquainted with his writings. Although I spent only three months with Kalecki in Cambridge, ours was a very intensive and cordial relationship, in that we saw each other almost daily and often for many hours at a time. I feel not only privileged to have gotten to know him well, but my understanding of certain aspects of his work was enhanced by being able to discuss these matters freely with him. These discussions were particularly beneficial in helping me read between the lines, so to speak. Kalecki's writings were a response to problems of the real world, but he sometimes left the full policy and social implications unstated. This personal contact permitted me to verify some of my interpretations. Obviously, this is not intended to imply that he would have approved of my exposition and conclusions.

The division of the book into three parts is primarily thematic, but to a certain extent also chronological. For example, although during the latter part of his life Kalecki devoted much time to problems of the socialist and mixed economy, discussed in part 3, some of his very last contributions dealt with the theory of dynamics of the capitalist economy and, as such, are found in part 1. Also, although during World War II he was absorbed in the problems of the day, as presented in part 2, he advanced his previous theoretical work and provided some solutions for postwar reconstruction, which are included in part 1.

The first two chapters in part 1 provide a general framework of the Keynesian Revolution and Kalecki's contribution to it. Chapters 3 to 6 are more detailed studies of Kalecki's most important theoretical contributions to modern capitalism. The last three chapters of part 1 deal with the application of theory to policy. Part 2 provides some background of the economic situation in Britain during World War II, shifting from the problems of insufficient effective demand to those of a supply-constrained economy, and concentrates primarily on Kalecki's original rationing scheme and his suggestions on how to finance the war economy. Part 3 opens with a very sketchy background on socialist economics as it took shape in practice, as a contrast to Kalecki's pioneering theory of growth of a socialist (supply-constrained, centrally planned) economy, analyzed in chapters 13, 14, and 15. Chapter 16 shows Kalecki's attempt to apply his knowledge of the dynamics of capitalism and socialism to the problems of a developing mixed economy. Chapters 17 to 19 are concerned with both how a socialist economy should work and how it should not work. In contrast to some other critics of misfired policies, Kalecki not only provided penetrating analyses of the causes of blunders, but time and again offered concrete, positive, and constructive solutions.

I have learned much in writing this book and have come to retract many of my previously held fallacies. Some may still remain. I only ask the reader to remember that, where Feiwel is wrong, Kalecki is probably right; and it certainly would be worth the reader's time to go to the original for the full flavor.

GEORGE R. FEIWEL

Knoxville
January, 1974

ACKNOWLEDGMENTS

WRITING THIS BOOK was a difficult task, but it was a genuinely rewarding experience also, for through this study I found out how many people cared sufficiently about its subject to give generously of precious time in order to support the project and improve the manuscript's contents. It was particularly encouraging that economists of different persuasions and "vested interests" were eager to help. I am grateful not only for valuable information supplied at the initial stages, but also for the constructive criticisms of the various drafts of the manuscript.

No words can express my indebtedness to Professor Joan Robinson for her dedication to the subject of this study, her critical and keen comments, and her unceasing encouragement. Above all this study owes to her a relentless expunging of "nonsense"—to use her favorite expression. Mr. Piero Sraffa, Kalecki's friend of long standing, gave me unstintingly of his time. I have gained immensely from our discussions of the various facets of this study and from his wisdom and deep insight into economics and life. He was also a source of great encouragement. Dr. J. A. Kregel, Université Catholique de Louvain and University of Southampton, gave selflessly of his time. He read a major part of the work, offered critical comments that were most helpful in successive revisions, and with his cheerful spirits he sustained me through the tedious task of rewriting. Mr. G. D. N. Worswick, director of the National Bureau of Economic and Social Research, who worked with Kalecki at the Oxford Institute of Statistics (OIS), read and commented on part 2 of this work and offered much insight into Kalecki's life in Britain. I am particularly grateful to him for his encouragement and firm belief in the need for such a book. Special thanks are due to another friend of Kalecki's, Mr. M. H. Dobb, for constant encouragement, for painstaking reading and criticism of parts of the manuscript, for understanding cooperation and tolerance, and for sharing with me his fond recollections of Kalecki. I benefited greatly from the stimulating discussions, advice, and expertise of Dr. Richard M. Goodwin, also of the University of Cambridge, who kindly commented on some of the chapters. Professor Jan Tinbergen was generous enough to read and advise me on chapters 5 and 6, and to provide encouragement at the time it was most needed. Professor Benjamin Higgins, Université de Montréal, who worked with Kalecki at the International Labour Office (ILO), read and commented on a good part of the manuscript on modern capitalism and the third world. I am also indebted to him for his wholehearted support of this venture and for his advice and insight into Kalecki, the man.

Professor Frank Hahn, University of Cambridge, provided important suggestions and criticisms of chapters 3 and 4, and he was helpful in discussing Kalecki, the economist. I am grateful to Dr. Paul M. Sweezy for pointing out at the embryonic stage of this study the need to stress Kalecki's contribution to income distribution theory—particularly Kalecki's breakthrough in introducing the "degree of monopoly" into his macrodynamic model—and the importance of the nonquantitative aspect of his contribution. He also gave me a better understanding of Kalecki's personality, and he offered warm encouragement. In a similar vein, Professor Abba P. Lerner, then at the University of California, provided illuminating comments about Kalecki in the 1930s, and the value of his contributions in retrospect. Professor G. L. S. Shackle, University of Liverpool, kindly recalled the days when Kalecki first came to the London School of Economics and impressed on me Kalecki's many first-rate qualities. I am also grateful to Professor Josef Steindl, University of Vienna, a collaborator of Kalecki's at the OIS, for lengthy discussions about Kalecki's personality and his work. Professor Kurt W. Rothschild, University of Linz, who also worked with Kalecki during the war, was very helpful, particularly in his comments on chapter 3. Dr. Jozef Goldmann, Institute of Economics, Czechoslovak Academy of Sciences, shared with me many fascinating memories of Kalecki at the OIS. Mr. Stanislaw Braun, who worked with Kalecki at the United Nations, took great pains to elucidate for me that period of Kalecki's activities, and kindly helped me locate Mr. Norman Bay, who knew Kalecki during his student years, to shed some light on the earlier part of Kalecki's life. I am truly grateful for their efforts. Thanks are due to Professor Börje Kragh, University of Stockholm, now with the U. N. Economic Commission for Europe in Geneva, and to Mr. Sidney Glassman, then a young assistant of Kalecki's at the U. N., for insight into Kalecki's personality and the vicissitudes of his life at the U. N.

In tracing Kalecki's life and work after he returned to Poland I profited immensely from numerous discussions with Mr. Jerzy Zachariasz, former Director of the Department of Prices of the Planning Commission, who provided inside information about Kalecki's stand at top level meetings of the Planning Commission and at meetings of the Council for Mutual Economic Assistance (CMEA). I am grateful to Professor Wlodzimierz Brus, formerly of the University of Warsaw, now Visiting Research Fellow, St. Antony's College, University of Oxford, an intimate friend of Kalecki's, for discussing with me certain of Kalecki's personality traits, and for answering some of my queries about Kalecki's theory of a socialist economy. My interesting discussions with Professor Kazimierz Laski, formerly of SGPiS (Central School of Planning and Statistics, Warsaw) now University of Linz, a leading disciple of Kalecki in his work on economic growth in a socialist economy, began in London and continued in Vienna, where I also benefited from his kind hospitality. He shared with me his fond recollections of the man, scholar, and teacher. Professor Ignacy Sachs, formerly Director of the Center for Underdeveloped Economies (Warsaw), now Ecole Pratique des Hautes Etudes (Sorbonne), who collaborated closely with Kalecki in his work on the third world, was kind enough to comment on Chapter 16, and to shed some light on the parts of the book dealing with Kalecki's personality and biography. Dr. Stanislaw Gomulka, a student of Kalecki, now Lecturer at the London School of Economics, recalled for me the exciting atmosphere of Kalecki's Warsaw seminars. He was generous with both his time and his assistance, visiting me in Stockholm in the summer of 1973 to discuss Kalecki's contributions, especially the theory of growth of a socialist economy.

It is a pleasure to thank once again my mentors at McGill University, particularly Professors D. E. Armstrong and E. F. Beach for reading and commenting on parts of this manuscript and for their intellectual and personal support. I wish to record my gratitude to Professor Lawrence R. Klein for the time he spent in reading this text, and for his understanding and encouragement. I would also like to thank my friends Professors Alexander Erlich, Columbia University, and Paolo Sylos-Labini, University of Rome, for taking an active interest in this work and encouraging me every step of the way.

I had the benefit of the cooperation of Mrs. Ada Kalecki, Kalecki's widow. It would be difficult to convey to those who do not know her her unflinching dedication to the "Kalecki message." She very graciously supplied some of the material that I lacked and was untiring in her efforts to do so. Her assistance is greatly appreciated and affectionately acknowledged.

I wish I could be more specific about the help rendered by the many other people who contributed to this study, so as to place their assistance in true perspective. Unfortunately, for the sake of brevity, I have had to resort to the incomplete and impersonal alphabetical listing that follows. Among those who have provided a better understanding of Kalecki, or were good enough to discuss opposite points of view or to clarify some finer points of theory, are: Dr. Krishna Bharadwaj, University of Bombay; Professor William H. Branson, Princeton University; Professor Martin Bronfenbrenner, Duke University; Professor David G. Champernowne, University of Cambridge; Dr. Zofia Dobrska, Center for Underdeveloped Economies (Warsaw); Mr. John L. Eatwell, University of Cambridge; Professor Pierangelo Garegnani, University of Florence; Dr. Sven Grassman, University of Stockholm; Sir Roy Harrod, Christ Church, Oxford; Professor Derek T. Healey, University of Adelaide; Professor Robert L. Heilbroner, New School for Social Research; Mr. K. H. Hennings, University of Reading; Professor Harry G. Johnson, London School of Economics and University of Chicago; Professor Lord Kahn, University of Cambridge; Professor Nicholas Kaldor, University of Cambridge; Academician T. S. Khachaturov, U.S.S.R. Academy of Sciences; Professor Z. A. Konczacki, Dalhousie University; Dr. Tadeusz Kowalik, Polish Academy of Sciences; Professor Simon Kuznets, Harvard University; Professor John M. Letiche, University of California (Berkeley); Professor Assar Lindbeck, University of Stockholm; Professor Siro Lombardini, University of Turin; Professor Eric Lundberg, Stockholm School of Economics; Mr. Aleksander Markowski, formerly of the Planning Commission (Poland), now University of Stockholm; Professor J. E. Meade, University of Cambridge; Professor Michael Michaely, Hebrew University; Professor Franco Modigliani, Massachusetts Institute of Technology; Dr. Donald E. Moggridge, University of Cambridge; Professor Michio Morishima, London School of Economics; Professor Gunnar Myrdal, University of Stockholm; Professor Bruce J. McFarlane, Australian National University; Professor R. R. Neild, University of Cambridge; Dr. D. Mario Nuti, University of Cambridge; Professor Bertil Ohlin, Stockholm School of Economics; Mr. Jerzy Osiatynski, Polish Academy of Sciences; Dr. Luigi L. Pasinetti, University of Cambridge; Professor Mark Perlman, University of Pittsburgh; Mr. Brian Pollitt,

University of Cambridge; Dr. P. A. Riach, Monash University; Professor Paul Rosenstein-Rodan, Massachusetts Institute of Technology and University of Boston; Mr. Robert E. Rowthorn, University of Cambridge; Mr. B. Schefold; Mr. C. T. Taylor, University of Cambridge; Professor Howard M. Wachtel, American University; Professor Stanislaw Wellisz, Columbia University; Professor G. Whittington, University of Edinburgh; and Dr. Alfred Zauberman, London School of Economics.

Many of the ideas expressed in this book were aired at various seminars with my own students and in England, Italy, Sweden, West Germany, and Yugoslavia. The exchange of views was both stimulating and beneficial. I am indebted to Professor Hans E. Jensen, University of Tennessee, not only for his good advice on some aspects of this study, but also for removing institutional obstacles and easing the process of gestation of the study. Similarly, I appreciate the support of Dean John Ross, University of Tennessee, and the expert assistance of the Center for Business and Economic Research, University of Tennessee, in typing a substantial part of the manuscript. The final revision of parts of this manuscript was concluded at the Institute for International Economic Studies, University of Stockholm. I am grateful for its superb facilities and stimulating atmosphere. Thanks are due for innumerable services to the Inter-Library Loan Department of The University of Tennessee; the Marshall Library, University of Cambridge; the British Museum; Library of Congress, and the Library of SGPiS. It was good to have the editorial assistance, interest, and cooperation of Miss Joyce Atwood, who gave unsparingly of her time and effort to improve the presentation of this book. I also wish to thank Professor John Kenneth Galbraith for permission to quote from his letter to Kalecki on the latter's seventieth birthday. I am grateful to the Indian Statistical Institute for making available unpublished material and information in connection with Kalecki's stay in India.

The usual disclaimer is even stronger in the case of this book. For not only did I not always follow the advice received, but I have deliberately sought the opinions of people who differ sharply on many issues. Thus I have had to reconcile for myself the conflicting comments. While some of my informants might approve of some of the ideas expressed here—though differing regarding distribution of emphasis, interpretation, and presentation—I am fully aware that they might censure other ideas and wish to dissociate themselves from them. Some may even object to the main line of reasoning. In drawing the profile of the man and the scholar, I have particularly relied on my own and my wife's observation and judgment of Kalecki. Of course, I bear full responsibility for all parts of this book and absolve anyone mentioned herein from any errors, imperfections, heresies, faults in expression, and other failures remaining.

However, this disclaimer does not apply to my wife, who shared with me in our mutual admiration of Kalecki, in research, in preparation of the several drafts, and through all the toils of the process of gestation of this book. She bore willingly and unfailingly the real costs it entailed, for she believes profoundly in its purpose, whatever our shortcomings in articulating and conveying it.

CONTENTS

THE INTELLECTUAL CAPITAL *of* MICHAL KALECKI

•

PROLOGUE

Portrait of the Man and Scholar

•

Integrity and Independence

Michal Kalecki was a stern moralist whose sense of rectitude and forthrightness permeated his personal and intellectual life. On the conferral of the honorary doctorate degree to Kalecki at Warsaw University, Professor Oskar Lange referred to him as a man and scholar of "inflexible integrity," asserting that

> Michal Kalecki ranks among the world's most distinguished economists; he has always sought bold solutions, never avoiding controversies either in his theoretical work or his practical activity. But these have always been fruitful controversies inspired by his desire to serve social progress.
>
> In this connection his moral attitude should be emphasized, so important in the case of an economist who has decided to serve social practice. He has never been afraid of voicing unpopular views. In his scientific work he has always been guided by only one criterion: that of looking for truth and serving social progress. And these two are inseparably linked together. (Lange 1964, p. 61.)

In the words of Kalecki's students:

> Perhaps his most essential characteristic was the integration of mind, will, and character. His life was another proof that the rank of a scientist and his work is not only decided by intellectual attributes, but also by the will and self-discipline which make it possible to take full advantage of the creative abilities possessed—at the cost of hard work and much self-denial. Moreover—and perhaps above all—it is decided by integrity in conducting research, responsibility in deriving conclusions, and courage in expressing and defending one's opinions. (Dobrska and Szeworski 1970.)

Kalecki exhibited intellectual independence and courage both in his theoretical work and practical advice: He attacked the walls of orthodoxy in the early 1930s. He contended with the seemingly misconceived and inequitable solutions to the problems of a war economy in Britain. At the United Nations his unwillingness to kowtow to authorities, as well as his lack of diplomacy, earned him many enemies, particularly among his superiors. Upon his return to Poland he pitted himself against the orthodoxy and dogma that enshrouded the theorizing about growth in a socialist economy. He suggested that the main ills of the Polish economy stemmed from a misconceived growth strategy. The perspective plan (1961-75) that he elaborated was rejected by the authorities, yet he continued to offer disinterested advice to the increasingly dictatorial Gomulka regime. His championship of realistic planning and of the worker-consumer (as contrasted with the interests of bureaucracy) brought him censure from the top leadership.

Social Concern and Political Position

Kalecki was fond of saying that all human beings could be classified in ascending order according to the amount of time that they spent thinking of some subject other than themselves. He would have ranked among the very top.

On the surface Kalecki's economic writings appear to be dispassionate exercises in economic analyses of a highly technical nature. All of his major contributions, however, have their social underpinning. The sociopolitical aspect is implicit in the economic analysis, often serving as the starting point and initial impetus; and it is sometimes stated explicitly, although in very condensed form. Concern for the common man was the original propelling force behind his studies of such factors as effective demand, income distribution, full employment, the war economy, economic growth under socialism, and developing economies. In the case of economic growth under socialism, for instance, the nature of choice (from a social and political point of view) is actually the main topic of the book. In his later years he devoted increasingly more time directly to sociopolitical questions.

The misery of the Great Depression left an indelible imprint on Kalecki. If I had to identify the main line of his life's work, I would not hesitate to opt for full employment and its content. His concern for this vital economic problem permeated almost all areas of his activity: It was reflected in his studies on capitalist, socialist, and developing economies, and it reverberated through his theoretical and practical-advisory efforts. He would not choose full employment at all costs, however. There were distinct ethical overtones in his work. He was for beneficial full employment whose fruits would be directed to the advancement of living standards of the lower income groups. He was not impressed with huge sacrifices of the present generation for future ones nor even with the sacrifices of a generation for its own long-range benefits. He was outraged at high employment levels and improvement in living standards contrived by means of armaments build-up.[1] He was incensed at the "planned unemployment" in some socialist economies and at the blunders of flimsy plans perpetrated by the planners at the cost of the worker-consumer.

In many ways, Kalecki was extremely sensitive to the problems of the quality of life of the average citizen. He regarded the scope and nature of economic crimes in Poland—namely, their organized nature, often with the participation of managers of state enterprises—as one of the main social and political issues. A new class of criminal "bourgeoisie" had arisen, which participated heavily in the good things of life, i.e., the purchase of automobiles and construction of private villas. Against the backdrop of relatively equalized legal incomes, these peaks of illegal incomes were particularly evident.

As a key to the reasons for economic crimes in a socialist regime, Kalecki cited the phase of development wherein great and often exclusive stress is placed on rapid increase of production. In his view, the following factors, which are instrumental in promoting economic crimes, are characteristic features of this phase: (1) Because the basic task is production plan fulfillment, the problems of costs and quality are of secondary importance; hence, control in these areas is usually neglected. Furthermore, owing to the presence of a sellers' market, the buyers are not overly demanding; as a consequence, any misuse of materials that lowers output quality is not revealed at the time of sale. (2) Also owing to the sellers' market, the disposal of stolen materials at high prices is facilitated. (3) As a result of the large share of investment in national income and the lag of agriculture behind industry, real wages are depressed in relation to the economic potential.

Whereas the first two factors facilitate economic crimes, the third stimulates them. Such crimes, then, are of a rather primitive and individual nature, for the conditions require neither special skills nor organization of those who commit the crimes. For these reasons the scope of economic crimes is very wide. Society tends to regard these crimes indulgently as a source of supplement to generally low incomes. The situation gives rise to a network of middlemen, dealers in stolen goods, who, together with the growing number of others whose practice has inured them to theft and who benefit from society's indulgence, tend to perpetuate the crimes.

In the period that follows the forced growth of industrial production, according to Kalecki, the aforementioned factors are considerably weakened. Increasing attention is paid to costs and quality, the control of which nevertheless remains far behind industry's potential. Inventory control remains rather weak, and quality control by an independent control organ is lacking. However, trade becomes increasingly choosy, in view of the relative expansion of supply, which also adds to the difficulty of disposing of stolen goods. Finally, real wages increase because of a fall in industry's share of investment in national income and because of progress in agriculture.

It might seem that a weakening of factors causing these economic crimes would result in a reduction of the crimes. Instead, new forms of economic crimes arise, adapted to the stronger (but far from adequate) control. The individual dilettante is replaced by a group, much more skilled and better equipped, whose larger turnover compensates for the lower prices obtained for stolen goods in a better-supplied market. The organization of these groups is promoted by middlemen who find it increasingly difficult to deal with individuals. This organization benefits from the general climate of indulgence toward economic crimes inherited from the previous period. Such groups may involve employees throughout the entire enterprise or perhaps only those in sensitive positions. Because they involve accounting manipulations, the crimes are committed in an atmosphere that considerably reduces the risk of discovery.

On the other hand, development of control does not keep pace with the increase of economic crime. It is safe to assume, in fact, that, in some cases, the leaders of these groups are sufficiently influential to oppose successfully the improvement of control. Furthermore, such opposition is supported by those managers who, although unconnected with economic crimes, aim at reporting higher profits by lowering quality. (Kalecki 1962k, pp. 73-77; 1964aa, pp. 89-90.)

In his political views, Kalecki always (i.e., since before World War II) considered himself a socialist. He was a most unorthodox one, supporting socialism because he felt that it *might* be a better system. He did not expect the socialist system to fulfill all dreams, merely to bring some improvement. Obviously, he did not view socialism as practiced in Eastern Europe as ideal; in fact, he was profoundly disturbed by the variances between the practice and the ideal.[2] As an economist he looked upon the socialist system as being superior to the capitalist one particularly because the planners could manipulate the setting of prices and wages, thus reducing the dangers of fluctuations and unemployment, and because he felt that the system would be more likely to provide a fairer distribution of income.

Kalecki did not believe that the waste and mistakes so often encountered in centrally planned socialist economies were necessarily reflective of the system. Instead, he placed the blame on the people responsible for decisions, seeming to imply that mistakes will be unavoidable as long as crucial decisions are made by irresponsible people who lack a comprehension of economic interdependencies and whose deliberations are not subject to wider discussion and debate, i.e., social control. He also implied that blunders would recur as long as expert opinions were disregarded and decisions were made primarily on the basis of political reasons or some ignoramus' notion of how the economy should be run.

Throughout his career, Kalecki was a stern critic of capitalism, but he was not committed to destroying it. His formulation of the General Theory points to many inconsistencies of the system and also shows how the system could be made to work better. During World War II, Kalecki seemed to believe that a more just and healthy order could arise from the turmoil. Although his suggested reform of capitalism was clearly outlined in his "Three Ways to Full Employment," as a supreme realist he knew the limitations of reform. Clearly foreseeing the opposition to a full employment policy, he formulated the political business cycle. After the war, probably as a result of his experience during the McCarthyist period and his strong pacifist leanings, his criticism of American capitalism intensified, especially his attack on maintenance of prosperity by military spending. In many respects his harsh attacks on the U. S. were hypercritical and prejudiced. His disillusionment with life in general during his later years was caused not only by the developments in socialist countries, but also by what he regarded as dehumanizing factors in the capitalist world. The war in Vietnam was the most obvious of such factors; indeed, it was on those grounds that he refused an extremely tempting invitation from Stanford University.

It appears that Kalecki retained, to the end of his life, a keen interest in radical reform of the capitalist system. This was evidenced by his attempt to provide some kind of advice to "popular front" governments, starting with Blum and ending with Kalecki's attempt to help the Italian left, which he considered "promising" but economically "undereducated." This was quite obvious in his stand at the 1965 Ancona seminar on conditions of planning under a reformed capitalist system. This position toward reform of capitalism is also reflected in his last published contributions. (Cf. Kalecki and Kowalik 1971b, pp. 190-96; Kalecki 1971a, pp. 1-9.)

As his career drew to a close, Kalecki's disappointment with existing social systems was obvious. Professor John Kenneth Galbraith's astute comment in a letter to Kalecki does not seem to be far off the mark:

> It seems scarcely possible that thirty years and more have elapsed since first we met at Cambridge. I suppose both of us are wiser now than we were then. But I wonder if, in social matters, it isn't sometimes better to be less than completely wise. The optimism that goes with unwisdom has been a great spur to effort in your case and in lesser measure also in mine. Over the years, I imagine that we have both discovered that the social spectrum of problems associated with both socialism and Keynesian liberalism is wider than we thought. Certainly that has been true in my case. If I had been aware of how much the system I espoused in 1937 would leave unsolved and how many new problems it would create, I would have committed myself to any inaction which might, with the collaboration one always gets in inaction, have left things even worse.
>
> So I suggest it is with socialism. Nor can I think that the world belongs indefinitely to the dull organization men. (Galbraith to Kalecki, June 25, 1969.)

The Student of Life

Kalecki was a born political economist in the sense that his research had "always been connected with practical needs and his theoretical models were always meant to help solve particular problems of economic policy." (Lange 1964, p. 61.) Thus in the 1930s he was concerned with the questions of effective demand and the whys and wherefores of business cycles. During World War II his interest shifted to the allocation of scarce resources to the war effort, fairer distribution of the war burden, a more equitable distribution of income after the war, and the problem of maintaining full employment in the postwar period. On his return to Poland he became concerned with solving the problems of low living standards, excessive investment rates, and bottlenecks arising in various sectors of the economy. From this emerged his theory of growth in a socialist economy. His familiarity with both capitalist and socialist systems gave Kalecki a deep insight into the problems and solutions for emerging nations.

For many years Kalecki conducted statistical analyses of the Polish economy. He used statistical evidence extensively during the years he spent at the Oxford Institute of Statistics, the International Labour Office, and the United Nations. Upon his return to Poland, in his few years as advisor to the government he was able to command a substantial staff that helped him in gathering pertinent statistical evidence. Later, when he no longer had access to this source for understanding the actual economic situation, he was able to recreate the picture of the whole situation simply by using only the officially released data.

> The great strength of Kalecki as an abstract thinker was his close knowledge of life. Those who are familiar only with his basic studies, look upon him as a great master of deductive reasoning; a logician of a mathematical cast of mind (to say nothing of those who look upon him as a formalist without any real contact with life). However, anyone who has worked with him or has read him more attentively is bound to realize that he possessed an almost ideal blend of inductive and deductive powers. Even in his most general mathematical formulae one could feel the presence of real life. (Lipinski 1970c.)

Kalecki believed that there are far too many urgent economic problems affecting the welfare of society, awaiting solution, to concentrate on refinements of theories that are not immediately relevant. Such theories are being created, he said, which "may raise problems of great interest but are not very conducive to understanding what actually happened, is happening or should be happening." (Kalecki 1970e, p. 311.) For example, he stressed that growth models are often built on the assumption of laissez faire and do not assign the crucial and empirically relevant role to the government sector, to the state's widespread intervention, and to the interaction between the state and private sectors. The institutional framework of a social system exerts a strong impact on its economic dynamics. A theory of growth must be relevant to that system. Although he felt that many of today's economists, no matter what the social system under which they live, are more interested in discovering cures for nonexistent ills than in finding cures for our actual diseases—that economists have often strayed into the realm of fantasy—Kalecki did not imply that they should switch to pure empiricism. He meant only that, in order to understand reality, simplified models should be constructed, safeguarding all the while the attributes of reality, and that the models should be developed so as to approach reality as much as possible in the further elaboration. (*ZG* Nov. 29, 1964.)

A tinge of skepticism was an integral part of Kalecki's very great realism. In the midst of World War II when many others (including himself at times) saw that the holocaust could give rise to a more just social system, he also perceived the negative factors: the many-faceted opposition of the ruling class to maintaining full employment and to extensive social services. In dealing with centrally planned socialist economies, he exhibited particular distaste for slogans without backing of real resources. He denounced "heroic" and unrealistic plans. He was often branded as a pessimist, but his caution looked merely like level-headed realism when the results of overoptimistic plans came in.

In his later years, however, Kalecki became increasingly disenchanted with economics, just as he found disappointment in social systems. Although his life's work had been spent in attempting to prove the contrary, he reverted increasingly to the theme that economics was an inexact science. He viewed economics as generally resembling theoretical physics in that both are "quantifiable disciplines which, on the basis of general premises derived from the knowledge of real phenomena, develop a deductive system which is then confronted with the external world." (Kalecki 1964z, p. 62.) By way of illustration, he offered his interpretation of Say's Law of the Market:

> This law asserts, speaking roughly, that all incomes, wages or profits are fully spent on the purchase of goods and services. This is self-evident as far as expenditure on consumption is concerned while accumulation is treated as being always spent on investment. This doctrine obviously rules out the possibility of general overproduction, total demand being always equal to total supply. The law has certain affinities with the laws of the preservation of matter and energy. The difference, however, is that it is definitely wrong. It implies that the value of national income is constant. If, for instance, less is spent on consumption then pro tanto more is spent on investment. But it was always clear that this is not the case since the value of national income is subject to abrupt changes. . . . Any divergence from Say's law was interpreted as a divergence of the actual rate of interest from the equilibrium rate. It took a long time to realize that the idea of a rate of equilibrium was totally misconceived since the actual rate of interest had nothing to do with it. To discard the law of the preservation of

purchasing power meant admitting the possibility of general overproduction. In particular investment may be lower than the accumulation corresponding to full utilization of productive resources since its volume is determined by altogether different factors. This leads to piling up of unsold goods. A situation of this kind cannot, obviously, continue for long and is soon followed by a state of underutilization of resources. . . .

How could the belief in the preservation of purchasing power be maintained for so long? In my view for two basic reasons: the class interests of the capitalists and the apparent corroboration of the law by the experience of the individual. A doctrine which ruled out general overproduction made the capitalist system appear capable of a full utilization of productive resources and dismissed cyclical fluctuations as insignificant frictions. These apologetics were facilitated by the application to the economy as a whole of the experience of housekeeping where clearly a lesser consumption means higher saving. But whereas the income of the individual is given, the national income is determined in a capitalist system by consumption and investment decisions, a fall in one of these components by no means leading automatically to a rise in the other. Thus individual experience does not correspond to the course of the economy as a whole. (Kalecki 1964z, pp. 62-63.)

In addition to all these factors, he continued, economics can have little claim on exactitude because of the impossibility of conducting experiments.

Let us once again take the example of Say's law. Having rejected the assumption that investment is determined by accumulation, we are still left with the problem of what are its actual determinants. This problem has not yet been satisfactorily solved. Various hypotheses concerning the factors determining investment decisions may be advanced. But a conclusive corroboration of one of them is hardly achievable by means of analysis of statistical data: no hypothesis is fully confirmed because of disturbances which cannot be eliminated as in a physics experiment. (Kalecki 1964z p. 64.)

Kalecki then proceeded to show similar pitfalls in the study of the economics of socialist countries, especially in the theory of growth under socialism, which he believed was its most important problem.

This theory is based on the principle that the object of the socialist economy is to raise the standard of living. But this does not suffice to construct a theory of growth. An increase in the relative share of investment in the national income leads to an improvement of the standard of living in the long run, but it affects consumption in the near future adversely. . . . In the theory of growth we take as given the government's comparative valuation of consumption in the near future and in the long run which underlies such decisions. We have

> also to assume ceilings on the rate of growth in single branches of economy arising out of such technical and organizational factors as limited natural resources, the time required to introduce new techniques and to train experienced personnel, etc. The theory of growth built on these foundations is a purely deductive discipline. But these deductions do not determine fully the course of economic development since the "external" factors just mentioned play a very important part. Thus in the sphere of pure economics the theory of growth is basically an exact science but this does not exhaust all the issues involved in the problem of economic development. On the other hand, those factors which do not enter into it, being assumed as given, are and will be intrinsically disputable. . . . Moreover, in our discussions we often fail, putting it mildly, to meet the highest standards of precision in formulation and argument. There also appears a tendency to present as axioms assertions which in fact require proof and which, on closer examination, do not always turn out to be tenable. (Kalecki 1964z, pp. 64-65.)

In modern times we have witnessed a serious attempt by many economists to render economics more precise through the use of mathematics. Generally, mathematical economists can be divided into two groups: (1) those for whom the economic issue is of utmost importance and who use mathematics to present and explain a set of circumstances; and (2) those for whom the elegance of the mathematical model governs their attitude and who would be equally willing to draw up a refined model on the basis of totally unrealistic assumptions as on those closely related to pertinent and real problems. Undeniably, Kalecki belonged to the first category. He found it unthinkable that an economist, confronted by the multifariousness of current problems, could be satisfied with spinning empty theories even if buttressed by the most elegant mathematical models. He would often advise such devotees to give up economics and concentrate on pure mathematics. He had an ambivalent attitude toward computer technology in planning—what is often referred to as planometrics: (1) he believed that use of computers could help solve many of the specific problems that confronted planners in particular areas; (2) he considered that application of planometrics to solve general lines of development could have disastrous effects.

Even in the first case, he warned incessantly about the necessity of elaborating theoretical models for applying planometrics to specific problems. He pointed to the need for revamping the statistical and information systems, adapting them to requirements of computer technology. He stressed that even before this could be successfully accomplished, certain planning methods developed so far, often intuitive and imprecise, could be used to great advantage if they were consistently applied. (Kalecki 1962f, pp. 6-7.) (Presumably, he had in mind such planning techniques as realistic balancing of resources and uses, and analysis of investment and foreign trade efficiency.)

In the second case, Kalecki was apprehensive about deriving the general development rate and pattern from an "optimized" economic plan. I have inferred from his writings and conversations that he was apprehensive that computomania might replace common sense. He feared that the planner might fail to state explicitly the limiting conditions of adequate share of consumption in the short run when growth of national income would be set as the optimand for the economy. He realized that, given certain assumptions, one could show through mathematical analysis that a high share of productive investment in national income allows for a high rate of growth. This so raises the level of national income in the ensuing years of the long-term plan that consumption throughout the period would be shown to be higher than with a lower share of investment in national income. Computer technology applied to national economic planning has many other pitfalls: It curtails the scope of give and take between economists (planners) and politicians. It impoverishes the process of learning-by-doing during plan construction. It also enshrouds the plan in spurious precision and develops a satisfaction with results which may be derived from wholly untenable assumptions. Kalecki had a distinct preference for the method of successive approximations inasmuch as it was more intelligible, more flexible, and permitted a closer examination of the efficiency of investment in various sectors.[3]

The computer would be only as good as the primordial decisions made by the leadership. I believe that Kalecki feared that an unscrupulous leadership, whose actions were uncontrolled by social pressures from below, would be able to use planometrics and computer technology as oracles whose verdict was not to be questioned, to achieve ends at cross purposes with the aims and desires of the population.

All those who have read or studied Kalecki agree about the concentration of content in a highly laconic style. He wrote like a mathematician. Perhaps it was the very taciturnity of Kalecki's mode of expression, the restraint in the language, and the utmost concentration of thought that made his writings so difficult to understand and rather unpopular among his fellow economists.[4]

In Kalecki's writings one finds few references to the literature on the subject. In a sense, his contribution is value-added, rather than gross.[5] Clearly, such an approach has both advantages and drawbacks. On the one hand, the argument is uncluttered and the original idea is fresh and unencumbered. On the other, it fails to place the argument within the stream of thought. Actually, there are two questions that may be posed: (1) Did Kalecki "know" the pertinent literature on the subject? (2) To what extent would his contributions have been enhanced had they included the usual scholarly appurtenances? It seems that, early in his career, Kalecki was not particularly familiar with "Western" economics. However, after his prewar visit to Cambridge, he gradually acquired the usual economist's stock in trade. His understanding and reformulation seem to imply that he had arrived at many of the propositions independently and by a different route, before he learned that they were part of the mainstream of economics. Since he was also a highly skilled technician, he could easily adapt himself to different techniques of presentation. It is difficult to give an unequivocal answer to the second question. I feel that, with Kalecki's bent of mind and predisposition, his work would not have benefited if he had attempted a gross contribution. One major exception comes to mind. A more careful scrutiny of development of the growth theory in the West might have enhanced Kalecki's contribution to the theory of growth of a socialist economy. But, of course, in this also, I doubt that the fundamental ideas would have been different.

At the jubilee honoring him and Lange, Kalecki spoke of the difficulties an advisor meets in any political system. Yet, no matter what the hardships and obstacles, he claimed that an economist should not be satisfied with explaining phenomena, but should attempt to change the course of economic policy. Speaking of his own experience he noted that the only palpable result of his advice was in the case of Israel, where the government proceeded to do the exact opposite of what he had recommended.

Kalecki spoke of the contretemps of economic advisors in capitalist and developing nations, where the good and disinterested advice often meets an impenetrable wall of prejudice and class or personal interests. But, he commented, such advice does not fare much better in socialist economies, where such prejudice and interests were supposedly eradicated. He did, however, offer one glimmer of hope. Advisors should write extensive reports of their findings, for even if they are not listened to in their own lifetime, conscientious and professional advice leaves some trace in one form or another, which in the near or distant future will somehow affect economic policy. For politicians always listen to economic experts—those of the past generation(s), that is.[6]

Personality Traits

Because of his dignified silence about his priority of publication at the time Keynes's *General Theory* appeared, and in general his distaste for "promoting" or "advertising" his ideas, Kalecki has always been regarded as a very modest man. He believed that a man's worth will sooner or later be recognized by others, and that real dignity lay in waiting for that recognition, rather than in demeaning oneself to prod it along. That for him the recognition came later rather than sooner, however, made him quite bitter and generally disenchanted. He was totally free of false modesty, but knew his worth and was resentful when it was not acknowledged by others.[7]

A picture of Kalecki the worker has been drawn by his former students and co-workers:

> One should not presume that he ever treated any of his posts as a sinecure. He only undertook those tasks to which he could devote sufficient attention. He worked very hard and with pedantic precision. He imposed his work style on his co-workers. He did not really impose, rather he infected them with it. He was very exacting towards his co-workers, but he had every moral right to be so, for he was always far more exacting towards himself. (Dobrska and Szeworski 1970.)

Behind a somewhat austere exterior, Kalecki was a kind and understanding person. While in personal dealings he was extremely careful not to offend, in matters of economics he was merciless and would never surrender.[8] He cared only for the logic of the argument, thereby antagonizing those who did not know him well and were offended by his polemics. In this respect he had much in common with Keynes. Both men would not stand fools lightly and were often rude to their antagonists. In arguing with Kalecki one could get the impression that he was doing all the talking and that he did not listen. However, he never really missed anything that was said and always thought carefully about other people's ideas, even if he appeared to ignore them when they were first presented. Kalecki's ready wit could be extremely destructive. All this earned him numerous adversaries in academic circles and among politicians both East and West.

Another of Kalecki's characteristics was his scorn for the "top pupil"—his own expression. This is the man who studies according to instructions, memorizes his lessons well, knows how to flatter his teachers, and so gets "top marks." But he is also the man who lacks true depth or understanding, originality, or creativity. Kalecki believed that some people go through life as "top pupils." They may be quite successful in terms of income and status, but are not really worthy of admiration or even of serious consideration. Obviously, Kalecki was as far from being a "top pupil" as a man could be; and his disdain for this type caused him much hardship throughout his life.

Kalecki possessed a natural sense of humor which he often used as a double-edged instrument to ridicule opponents and as a tool of self-criticism. His jokes of thirty years ago are still making the rounds in after-dinner conversations at Cambridge and Oxford. One of these sayings, so frequently repeated in the British academic circles (particularly among economists) that its origin is often lost, is the one concerning "real English gentlemen." He said that, on his arrival in England, he was anxious to meet the famous species. But he found only two English gentlemen: Piero Sraffa, an Italian, and Maurice Dobb, a communist.

Another characteristic of Kalecki's personality was his stubbornness. His closest friends and admirers often complained that he was a "difficult man." Perhaps the clearest and most incisive explanation of a difficult man was that offered by Sraffa when he heard the term applied to Kalecki: A difficult man is one who does not want to do what he is told to do.

Kalecki never formally aspired to form a school of economics or to surround himself with disciples, but he was anxious to influence and mold the thinking of talented economists. He was not liberal with people who did not share his views, especially those who had started out as his followers. He was the *spiritus movens* of dedicated research groups in the Economics Department of the Polish Academy of Sciences and the Center for Underdeveloped Economics. His seminar on the theory of growth in a socialist economy, conducted from 1962 to 1968 at the Central School for Planning and Statistics (SGPiS,Warsaw), was popular and intellectually stimulating. Because he inspired and infused the spirit of good work in many research workers at the Planning Commission, his brief interlude there must have left an indelible mark.

Kalecki's work has also been a major influence in the West, particularly in England, where most "Kaleckians" are to be found. Although he is generally less well known in the U.S.A., almost unknowingly a good many American economists have imbibed Kaleckian economics. Galbraith reminded Kalecki of this in a letter to acknowledge his seventieth birthday:

> I wonder if you realize how much those of us the world around have owed to the intellectual capital you have provided over these past decades. I am struck to this day by the number of people at Harvard who mention your ideas without associating themselves with your name. Or even, on occasion, use the name Kalecki as an abstraction. And I think there is something particularly satisfying about the way in which you have done this without concessions to salesmanship or banality. Over the years, I have tried consciously to propagate my ideas. You never have. (Galbraith to Kalecki, June 25, 1969.)

PART ONE

MODERN CAPITALISM

The Prewar Period (1899-1939)

MICHAL KALECKI WAS BORN IN LODZ, POLAND, on June 22, 1899. Because little solid information is available on the early part of his life, the bare essentials presented here must be based on personal recollections of people who knew him.[1]

In 1917, Kalecki graduated from high school. Six years before, his father had lost the small spinning mill he had been operating and had begun earning his living as a bookkeeper. While going to high school (in fact, beginning at age fourteen), Kalecki supported himself with odd jobs—no easy task at that time in Russian-occupied Poland. He continued earning his keep throughout his engineering studies. From 1917 to 1918 he studied at the Warsaw Polytechnic, but his studies were interrupted by military service. Not until 1921 did he resume his formal education, this time at the Gdansk Polytechnic.

He was a promising student. In 1918 he had written what was apparently an original mathematical paper: a generalization of Pascal's theorem concerning a sexagon inscribed into a curve of second degree (conic)—which Kalecki generalized for a polygon of $2n$ sides.

In 1924, just before Kalecki was to graduate from the Gdansk Polytechnic, his father lost his job. Because the odd jobs with which young Kalecki had been supporting himself were not sufficient to help the family, he left the Polytechnic for good and sought employment. This, the first of the serious hardships and privations that were to face him, although seemingly a blow to his career, was a distinct gain for economics. He was just twenty-five, had not finished his formal education, and times were difficult in newly reunited Poland. If hardship is supposed to refine the soul and enhance understanding, this period provided excellent training ground. Unfortunately these years were to be followed by many more of adversity.

Although Kalecki had become acquainted with certain works in economics while he was at the Polytechnic, none of them were in the mainstream of economic theory. (Among the first known to have caught his attention was the work of Tugan-Baranovsky, which was then being widely read and discussed among students in Russian schools.) During the next four or five years, however, he was gaining experience in economics. His first job in this relation consisted of gathering data on enterprises applying for credit.

Later he became an economic journalist, attempting first to establish a trade paper *Koniunktura wlokiennicza*. It folded after the first issue, but Kalecki's journalistic career continued. He wrote for *Polska gospodarcza* and *Przeglad gospodarczy*, producing articles that were concerned mainly with market analyses for particular goods. The articles were painstakingly researched and documented, undoubtedly a factor that led to his subsequent employment at the Research Institute of Business Cycles and Prices.

It was toward the end of 1929 that Kalecki applied for a job at this Institute. Professor Edward Lipinski, director of the Institute at that time, described the encounter: "Are you an economist?—No. I studied at the Polytechnic.—What have you written?—Articles.—Please leave them and return in three days. After three days Kalecki was hired." (Lipinski 1970a, p. 3.)

Only at this Institute did Kalecki's lifelong career as an economist begin to take shape. Concomitantly, his personal life also took on new meaning, for on June 18, 1930, just a few days before his thirty-first birthday, Kalecki married Ada Szternfeld in Warsaw. The union proved to be lasting as well as salubrious for Kalecki and his work: Ada was not only a caring companion, but she was also a participant in his achievements. She translated some of his texts into English, and Kalecki himself often stressed how well trained she was as a statistician. As a hostess, her hospitality is proverbial among Kalecki's friends and colleagues, and as a wife now widow, her continuing dedication to the "Kalecki message" is boundless. To paraphrase Lady Churchill, one might say that Ada's life with Kalecki must have been always interesting, even if sometimes difficult.

With a new wife and a new job, Kalecki plunged into his first ambitious project at the Institute, a study of Polish national income undertaken in collaboration with the very talented statistician, Ludwig Landau. This team effort resulted in two works, still recognized as the foundation for studying economic development of Poland during the interwar years: one providing an estimate of national income for 1929 and the other presenting 1933 income and setting out a basis for research in periodical changes of income (1934h and 1935a). In a tribute paid to Landau on the twentieth anniversary of his death at the hands of the Gestapo, Kalecki described their prewar collaboration in these terms:

> In his work on the structure of Polish population in 1927, Landau aimed at analyzing the class structure of Polish society, hence at dismembering such general classifications as "industrialist" and "farmer". He differentiated capitalists from the *petite bourgeoisie* and wealthy farmers from the small scale owners. This required extremely arduous estimates, already of the 1921 census, and later further estimates for the 1927 extrapolations. Later these results became the basis for our joint study on national income. It is in this work that Landau's many-sidedness became noticeable. We worked together on the first volume based on estimates of relatively easily obtainable data. But the second volume about wages, requiring arduous evaluation of basic data was contributed by Landau alone. Yet without this second volume, without knowing the amount of wages, we could not have achieved our ultimate goal—namely distribution of national income among classes. It might be worth recalling that our work was probably the only attempt in the capitalist world to establish a detailed distribution of national income according to classes. Just as Landau did it for the structure of the population, we apportioned the income of capitalists and the *petite bourgeoisie.* Similarly in agriculture we distinguished between the income of wealthy and poor farmers. After World War II we were accused of having obscured rural class differences because we did not differentiate between medium and poor peasants. But these were rather exaggerated demands, especially in view of the fact that such estimates were not made during the twenty-odd years of the existence of People's Poland. (Kalecki 1964l.)

During this same early period at the Institute, Kalecki continued to write innumerable articles for the two periodicals that had previously published his work. He also contributed no less than a dozen articles of a socio-political-economic nature to the short-lived *Przeglad socjalistyczny,* under the pseudonym of Henryk Braun. This periodical, formed by a group of socialist intellectuals, began publication late in 1931 and folded in 1932. Kalecki's articles dealt primarily with the international political and economic situation. One of them, discussing wage reduction during a depression (1932j) was a foretaste of his development of new economics.

While collaborating with Landau, Kalecki also pursued his own theoretical studies. This led to the Institute's publication of what was one of the most controversial and revolutionary economic studies of the twentieth century, even though it was not recognized as such at the time: Kalecki's outline of a business cycle theory, *Proba teorii koniunktury* (1933f). It contained the essentials of the

"Keynesian Revolution," but among its Polish readers, perhaps too ill-informed to recognize its impact or too orthodox to acknowledge it, the study created little stir. He presented the theory's basic outlines to the more sophisticated audience of the International Econometrics Association in October, 1933, and in article form in 1935 in *Econometrica* and *Revue d'Economie Politique.* Jan Tinbergen, Ragnar Frisch, and Herald Holme commented on it in the same issue of *Econometrica.* But there was still no sign that the world at large had recognized the impact of what the obscure Polish economist had to say.

A Rockefeller Foundation Fellowship enabled Kalecki and his wife, Ada, to travel in 1936 to Sweden, where the first rumblings of a similar line of thought were heard. He made contact with Gunnar Myrdal and other Swedish economists. Apparently, he had begun to dictate a more comprehensive version of his initial work to Ada when news of the publication of Keynes's *General Theory* reached Stockholm. Upon reading it he realized that, essentially, it was similar to what he had in mind for the expanded version. Later he admitted that it was an eerie feeling, reading his own thoughts almost word for word expressed by someone else. Even the jokes were the same. As Professor Joan Robinson later attested, the fact that two men, miles apart in space, political outlook, and social circumstances had come to the same conclusions "was a great comfort." (Joan Robinson 1964, p. 337.)

Kalecki then journeyed to England. At first he was active at the London School of Economics, where the Keynesian Revolution was being heatedly debated. Kalecki also visited Cambridge and made contact with the Keynesians. His lifelong friendship and intellectual exchange with Joan Robinson, Richard Kahn, and Piero Sraffa date from that period. In 1937 he met Keynes. But as Joan Robinson later related, oil and vinegar would not mix. (Joan Robinson 1971b, p. 1.) Aside from their common conclusions, they shared little. Keynes was not particularly taken with this provincial. He only marveled at how quickly Kalecki understood his (Keynes's) revolutionary theory. In fact, Kalecki had informed Keynes's entourage about his own prior publication in 1933. Yet this was never related to Keynes nor made public before Keynes's death.

From the very beginning, Kalecki was acknowledged as a particularly keen and gifted interpreter of Keynes. Although he could not possibly be satisfied with the role of Keynes's disciple, "he never made any reference in public to his priority of publication (apart from one footnote in his first English book which could mean nothing to a reader who was not already *au fait*).[2] Only just before his death, long after others had publicly made the claim for him, did he allude to it briefly in the Introduction to *Selected Essays on the Dynamics of the Capitalist Economy*": (Joan Robinson 1971b, p. 1.) "The first part includes three papers published in 1933, 1934 and 1935 in Polish before Keynes' *General Theory* appeared, and containing, I believe, its essentials. . . ."[3]

Shortly before his death, Professor Kalecki admitted to me that, with the benefit of hindsight, he would not have acted differently. He considered that it was up to Keynes's disciples to have brought the matter of Kalecki's priority of publication to Keynes's attention. He did not regret not having done it himself. In fact he acknowledged that Keynes's worldwide reputation and academic and intellectual position probably contributed significantly to the propagation and acceptance of the Keynesian Revolution. Without the backing of Keynes's prestigious name, the new ideas might have lingered in limbo for another two decades or more. ". . . as Michal Kalecki is the first to admit, the Keynesian Revolution in Western academic economics is rightly so called. For without Keynes' wide sweep, his brilliant polemic, and, above all, his position within the orthodox citadel, in which he was brought up, the walls of obscurantism would have taken much longer to break." (Joan Robinson 1964, p. 339.) But being human, Kalecki undoubtedly resented being relegated to the ranks of Keynes's interpreters. Any creative work is a part of its author, and we all seek some form of recognition for what we do.[4]

That the economic fraternity had not recognized from the start that the system he had created was in essence the Keynesian Revolution contributed to Kalecki's bitterness. Characteristically, in Joseph A. Schumpeter's *History of Economic Analysis,* published in 1954, Kalecki is hardly mentioned.[5] Neither, for that matter, does Sir Roy Harrod refer to Kalecki in his biography of Keynes. The first intimation in print of Kalecki's independent discovery seems to have been made by Professor Austin Robinson in a commemorative article to Keynes, published in 1947 in the *Economic Journal.* Austin Robinson did not acknowledge priority of publication. He suggested that "it is not necessary, if one would advance Keynes' claims to greatness, to argue that we might not have reached the same destination by other routes or at a later date; to name only one other, Michal Kalecki was independently approaching the same goal."

(E.A.G. Robinson 1964, p. 58.) Fuller recognition came in 1951. In a review of Harrod's biography of Keynes, Professor Lawrence R. Klein acknowledged that, not only did Kalecki create a system "that contains everything of importance in the Keynesian system," but that Kalecki's system was in many respects superior to Keynes's. (Klein 1951a, pp. 447-48.) The record was finally and fully set straight by one of Keynes's most distinguished collaborators, Joan Robinson, who attested that:

> Michal Kalecki's claim to priority of publication is indisputable. With proper scholarly dignity (which, however, is unfortunately rather rare among scholars) he never mentioned this fact. And, indeed, except for the authors concerned, it is not particularly interesting to know who first got into print. The interesting thing is that two thinkers, from completely different political and intellectual starting points, should come to the same conclusion. For us in Cambridge it was a great comfort. Surrounded by blank misunderstanding, there were moments when we almost began to wonder if it was we who were mad or the others. In the serious sciences, original work is *discovery*—finding connections that were always there, waiting to be seen. That this could happen in economics was a reassurance that what we had discovered was really there. (Joan Robinson 1964, p. 337.)

Early in 1937, Kalecki found himself in a peculiar predicament which became familiar to him throughout his career. His two closest colleagues at the Institute of Business Cycles and Prices in Warsaw, Marek Breit and Ludwig Landau, were discharged at the end of 1936 in response to pressures from the government. Whatever the actual reason, or combination of reasons, (Cf. Kalecki, Kowalik, and Secomski 1969a, p. 342.) the dismissal of these two competent and talented co-workers was an overt act of prejudice and political repression. Kalecki resigned in protest and decided to remain abroad longer. But the fellowship funds were running out, and again only temporary, low-paying jobs came his way.

In 1938 he returned to Cambridge after a several-month sojourn in Paris studying Blum's economic policies. The modest employment he found in Cambridge permitted him to remain in this highly charged intellectual ambiance until the outbreak of World War II. These were fruitful years for the development of Kaleckian economics. He amplified his system with the theory of income distribution. The first of the three books which trace the development of the Kaleckian system, *Essays in the Theory of Economic Fluctuations,* was published in 1939.

I

THE KALECKI-KEYNES REVOLUTION

Independent Discovery of General Theory

•

MICHAL KALECKI EARNED AN IMPORTANT PLACE in the history of economic analysis and political economy by anticipating the Keynesian Revolution, from which modern macroeconomic theory evolved, and his model is, in many respects, superior and shows essential originality. Keynes's monumental and epoch-making *General Theory of Employment, Interest and Money* was published in 1936. In 1933, outside of the mainstream of traditional economic theory, an unknown Polish economist, without any contact with Keynes, discovered all the basic components which entered also into Keynes's analytical system, and put them to good use. In addition to making other contributions, such as integrating the theory of aggregate output determination, value, and distribution, Kalecki's system was more successful in integrating the dynamic element with the static analysis apparatus which is somewhat confused in Keynes's *General Theory*.

This coincidental discovery was not immediately acknowledged by the economics profession. One of the first to do so publicly was Professor L. R. Klein, who pointed out that, "after having re-examined Kalecki's theory of the business cycle, I have decided that he actually created a system that contains everything of importance in the Keynesian system, in addition to other contributions." Indeed, Kalecki has a theory of employment that is the equal of, and, in some respects, is superior to that of Keynes. "Kalecki's theory attracted attention for reasons largely unrelated to its revolutionary statement of the theory of employment, and he certainly lacked Keynes's reputation or ability to draw world-wide attention; hence his achievement is relatively unnoticed." (Klein 1951a, p. 447). The cold, analytical business cycle theory that Kalecki presented to the Econometrics Association in 1933 "attracted little attention compared with Keynes' splash, but eventually the theorists would have seen through the matter and given Kalecki's pre-*General Theory* model its full due." (Klein 1966, p. 224.) Some of the reasons for the superiority of Kalecki's theory are "that it is explicitly dynamic; it takes income distribution as well as level into account; and it makes the important distinction between investment orders and investment outlays. The dynamics of Kalecki's model attracted interest immediately." (Klein 1951a, p. 448.)

Professor Joan Robinson, one of Keynes's leading disciples, has often underlined Kalecki's contributions. She pointed out that "Keynes himself was not very much interested in the theory of value and distribution. Michal Kalecki produced a more coherent version of the *General Theory,* which brought imperfect competition into the analysis and emphasized the influence of investment on the share of profits. Kalecki's version was in some ways more truly a *general* theory than Keynes'." (Joan Robinson 1972, p. 4. Cf. Baran and Sweezy 1966, p. 56; Kregel 1971, p. 96 and *passim.*)

Kalecki's model was also more advanced and bolder than the Swedish (Scandinavian) forerunners of Keynes. "Generally speaking, Ohlin and, possibly, Frisch were more reserved and timid than Keynes on policy recommendations to fight the depression, but they were consistently pointing in the right direction and undoubtedly would have become bolder and more forceful as the magnitude of the world-wide problem became more apparent and persistent. They had substantial pieces of the Keynesian system in their grasp but not a well-articulated complete system that was capable of mathematization. In this respect, Kalecki was far ahead of the Keynesian precursors."[1]

Our task here is not to detract from Keynes's historical achievement, but to establish the precedence and originality of Kalecki's contribution. Kalecki and Keynes were not rival inventors; they were rather coincidental discoverers. Indeed, in some respects the contributions of the two men were complementary and not competitive.

On the Keynesian Revolution

To grasp fully the breakthrough of the Keynesian Revolution, it is necessary to set the stage against the backdrop of the orthodox doctrine against which the revolt took place.[2] It is in this light that the protagonists' silhouettes loom large indeed. Prior to the Kalecki-Keynes breakthrough, the classical theory that dominated economic thought and policy viewed the capitalist economy as a natural, self-propelled, and self-regulating mechanism ("supply creates its own demand"),[3] where a tendency to establish full employment prevails. Such an economy tends to maintain full employment, and unemployment may be considered merely as an accidental, temporary displacement and deviation from full utilization of economic resources—a rather unimportant frictional occurrence which may largely be disregarded. The flexibility of wages and prices ensures the mechanism. Unemployment may be cured by reducing money wages, since employment will rise with a decline of real wages. Unemployed workers, competing for employment, will be willing to lower the price for their labor. The wage reduction, by making labor relatively cheaper, should induce substitution of labor for other factors, thereby increasing employment. Rigid prices and institutional factors, such as trade unions, may obstruct the equilibrating process by artificially maintaining wages. *Ceteris paribus,* should wages be appropriately reduced, the unemployed, willing to accept a cut in wages, would find employment. Wages would fall more rapidly than prices. Profit margins would be improved.

But wages have both cost and income effects. The reduction of money wages, *inter alia,* reduces money income and effective demand. Wages enter as a cost component in profit calculations and thus influence entrepreneurial decisions. However, wages also enter as a component of income earned by employees and thus influence spending and effective demand for output.

Among the most deleterious notions in a large body of traditional, orthodox economics (in this case in both classical and neoclassical theory) is the one claiming that lapses from full employment result from rigidities which prevent the unimpeded working of the endogenous market mechanism in the capitalist economy, above all the hindrances to the flexibility of wages. If the cause of unemployment can be traced to wage rigidity, the recommended prescription is to lower wage rates as a way of overcoming unemployment and to remove obstructions inhibiting the downward movement of wages.

Full employment is not automatically assured, and removal of wage stickiness is no remedy. Wage flexibility does not necessarily correct unemployment, but leads merely to contraction, and unemployment can persist in macroeconomic equilibrium. Kalecki summarized the results of his inquiry into the theory and practice of money and real wages through the 1930s as follows:

> We attempted to show that the reduction of wages in a closed system does not lead to an increase in production; that in conditions of perfect competition the level of production remains unchanged while prices decline in the same proportion as wages; however, under existing conditions of monopoly or imperfect competition a reduction of money wages tends to cause a decline in real wages associated with a decrease in employment. Moreover, it appears that in such a system there is in general no reason—in spite of the widespread belief—for the decline in production to be accompanied by an increase in real wages or vice versa. The analysis of the problem in an open system shows that even in such a case the reduction of wages does not necessarily lead to an increase in employment, and the prospects of raising the aggregate real income of the working class are even dimmer. In particular, under the system of high and rising tariffs it is very likely that a reduction of wages will have an adverse effect upon employment also in an open economy.
>
> The slogan "Rigid wages as a source of unemployment" . . . proves in the light of the above analysis entirely unfounded. And equally hopeless is the case of the supporters of this slogan who preach that collective bargaining by making wages "rigid" causes unemployment and poverty of the working class. (Kalecki 1936b; rpt. in 1966h, pp. 58-59.)

Even after the publication of the *General Theory,* Professor A. C. Pigou argued that unemployment is impossible if flexible wages are admitted into the theoretical system. He stated authoritatively: "Until recently no economist doubted that an all-round reduction in the rate of money wages might be expected to increase, and an all-round enhancement to diminish, the volume of employment." (A. C. Pigou, *EJ* [Sept. 1937], p. 405.) Wage-rate flexibility was the essential adjustment mechanism by which the automatic Say's Law was supposed to operate.

Subject to various qualifications, on the assumption of unlimited wage and price flexibility, Say's Law maintains that effective demand will be sufficient to support full-employment capacity output automatically; i.e., irrespective of the quantity of money supplied and without the support of expansionary fiscal policy ("functional finance").

In his standard comment on Professor Pigou's "The Classical Stationary State," Kalecki said:

> Professor Pigou attempts to show in his article that full employment in a stationary state would be established automatically provided wage-earners would act competitively, i.e., provided wage rates would continue to fall as long as any unemployment is in existence. The gist of the argument is roughly as follows:

In a stationary state equilibrium net investment and thus net saving must be equal to zero. Thus in order that full employment should prevail in such an equilibrium saving out of full employment real income must be equal to nought. If saving out of full employment income is positive, zero investment will entail a level of real income so much below full employment that the saving out of this income *is* nought.

Such may be the situation in the initial position but the existence of unemployment causes—according to the assumption of unrestricted competition between the workers—a continuous fall in money wages, and consequently in prices. Now Professor Pigou makes the assumption that when incomes fall the banking system maintains the stock of money constant. As a result the fall in money wages and prices causes a fall in the rate of interest; for with the rate of interest unchanged the stock of money would have to fall more or less proportionately to the money volume of transactions. Professor Pigou assumes that this fall in the rate of interest reduces somewhat saving out of a given income, and thus tends to increase employment, but he admits that even if the rate of interest (net of all risks) approaches closely to zero it may still not be enough to create full employment. He centres his argument on another factor which takes care of this task.

As mentioned above, on Professor Pigou's assumption the stock of money is constant, and thus its real value increases in the course of the wage fall. Thus, argues Professor Pigou, the real value of existing possessions increases. The richer people are, however, the less they are willing to save out of a given real income. Thus if the increase in the real value of the stock of money reaches a certain limit, people will save nothing out of real incomes corresponding to full employment. At that point full employment long-run equilibrium will be reached. The following reservations must be made with regard to this argument. The increase in the real value of the stock of money does not mean a rise in the total real value of possessions if all the money (cash and deposits) is "backed" by credits to persons and firms, i.e., if all the assets of the banking system consist of such credits. For in this case, to the gain of money holders there corresponds an equal loss of the bank debtors. The total real value of possessions increases only to the extent to which money is backed by gold. In other words, the total real value of possessions increases as a result of the wage-fall only by the increase in the real value of gold. If in the initial position the stock of gold is small as compared with the national wealth, it will take an enormous fall in wage rates and prices to reach the point when saving out of the full employment income is zero. The adjustment required would increase catastrophically the real value of debts, and would consequently lead to wholesale bankruptcy and a "confidence crisis." The "adjustment" would probably never be carried to the end: if the workers persisted in their game of unrestricted competition, the Government would introduce a wage stop under the pressure of employers.[4]

The classicists considered the rate of interest as another device for equilibrating saving and investment. Since the alternative to consumption is saving (income not consumed), a decline in consumers' expenditures increases saving. With a larger volume of saving, the savers compete to earn the highest terms. Unable to find borrowers at the prevailing rate, the savers lower their price. At the lower rewards, some savers are discouraged and choose to consume. At the same time investors are encouraged to invest more and to employ a larger volume of saving since, at the lower terms for borrowing, the previously unprofitable investment ventures may become profitable. Thus employment, in producing both consumption and investment goods, is expanded.

However, an *ex ante* increase of nonspending on consumption (saving) does not guarantee additional investments. Equally, an *ex ante* rise in saving is not a prerequisite for additional investment. The decision to invest is often made for different motives from the decision to save. While the former is, *inter alia,* governed by the businessman's anticipation of profit, the latter in its simplest form is mainly a function of income. There is no mechanism to ensure that investment will increase so as to fill the gap for the deficiency of effective demand. Moreover, a decline of consumption expenditures reduces derived demand for additional equipment required for the production of goods. As a result of a decrease of consumption, the businessman's revenue drops. Part of the product produced will remain unsold, and, thus, inventories of goods will pile up. Losses permeate the system. Output will be cut down, and businessmen will reduce their labor force. With a growing unemployment, income declines. With a fall in income, savings are reduced. Should the volume of investment remain stationary, income will decline to the point where, at the lower income, the reduced savings will equal investment. The equilibrating mechanism takes place through the variation of income rather than through the rate of interest.[5]

The Keynesian Revolution refers primarily to the impact of the theory of determination and fluctuations of the level of aggregate output and employment, underscoring the dependence and impact of the level and structure of effective demand on the level of economic activity and on the degree of utilization of labor and productive capacity, emphasizing that fluctuations in the volume of investment will cause and be accompanied by corresponding fluctuations in economic activity, expenditures, output, incomes, and employment. The policy, implicit in the theory, assigns a crucial role to deliberate government policy as an instrument for regulating or influencing effective demand; in case of deficiency of demand, the government fills the gap between total income generated and private expenditures on consumption, capital formation, and net exports by means of a compensatory fiscal and monetary policy and government expenditures to increase (or to reduce, in case of deficiency of productive capacities) the volume of expenditures.[6]

Kalecki's Version of the Revolution

I shall present in chapters three through six Kalecki's rigorous formulation of his version of the *General Theory.*[7] What follows draws largely on the nontechnical versions of his pre-*General Theory* argument,[8] which appeared in Polish between 1933 and 1935.[9]

The most conspicuous sign of a depression is widespread unemployment. Such unemployment is certainly not owing to a shortage of productive capacity. In fact, the situation is rather quite opposite: existing capacity is not fully utilized, with unemployment corresponding to idle capacity. To what causes should this situation be attributed? The individual businessman's argument for not using unemployed labor to man the idle machinery is that this is not a profitable proposition; even prime (variable) costs would exceed revenue. The following remedy is then prescribed: wage reduction as a means for overcoming depression. The argument suffers from the "fallacy of composition": what is advantageous for a single businessman is not necessarily favorable for the economy as a whole. If one businessman cuts wages he is able, *ceteris paribus,* to expand output; but once all businessmen follow suit, the result is very different and the problem remains unsolved.

Assume that general cuts in wages and taxes have taken place. Owing to "improved" price-wage relations, businessmen fully utilize capacity and full employment prevails. Has the slump been overcome and has the problem of effective demand been solved? Not at all, for output produced still has to be sold. Production has increased considerably, with an even larger increase in the share accruing to profit (and depreciation). In order for output at this higher level to be sold in its entirety, the part nonconsumed by labor must be immediately purchased by entrepreneurs; i.e., the profit-earners (capitalists) must spend immediately all their additional profits on investment or consumption. It is unlikely, however, that this precondition for an equilibrium at this new higher level will be fulfilled. Capitalists' consumption changes but little in the course of the business cycle. Investment decisions will be delayed until businessmen are convinced of the sustained higher profitability. The immediate result will be an accumulation of monetary reserves by firms and banks. But the output which is the equivalent of increased profits will remain unsold, and stocks will pile up. The mounting stocks of unsold output suggest renewed price reductions. A further price cut will cancel out the benefits derived by businessmen from cost reduction. The pre-existing unemployment and idle capacity will reappear.

In reality, even the wage cuts will not be followed by this temporary increase in production. Improvement of profitability not only produces delayed reaction on the part of investors, but it is not immediately followed by increased employment and use of capacities. Immediately after the cut of wages and before the firms manage to expand output up to capacity, a fall in prices makes its appearance. Since the businessmen do not instantaneously make use of the enlarged funds resulting from a shift from wages to profit for expenditure on investment or for enlarging their consumption, the revenue of industry is reduced *pro tanto.* Whatever businessmen have gained in wage cuts they are soon likely to lose through falling prices. If for no other reason, wage cuts are no remedy because the gains of capitalists are not immediately spent on investment or consumption. The prescription of wage-cutting as a way out of a slump is often supplemented by a remedy against falling prices. Thus cartels (monopolization) are advocated to stop the "cutthroat" competition. But this is only partly effective because not all industry is cartelized. Assuming that cartelization were to apply everywhere, wages were duly cut, but the reduced effective demand of workers could not have any effect on prices because cartels would maintain stable prices, would the change in price-wage relations be instrumental in overcoming the slump? It is unlikely, for it still would not mean that cartels would be more prompt to invest profits derived from wage cuts than purely competitive businesses. Therefore, here also revenue of industry would diminish as much as costs. Since prices remain unchanged in the cartelized industry, the quantity of goods sold would decline in the same proportion as the revenue has fallen. While in a competitive economy wage-cutting cannot be a solution for overcoming the slump, in a fully cartelized system, such a "solution" would lead (due to price rigidity) to a reduction of output and intensification of unemployment. In a system where there is both competitive and cartelized industry, the outcome would be something intermediate; i.e., a reduction of output would take place, but the effect would be weaker than in the case of a fully cartelized economy.

If a wage cut is ineffective in combating the slump, partly because the gains in profits are not applied immediately by businessmen for procurement of investment goods, Kalecki proceeded to prove that the opposite is the case: the rise in investment unaccompanied by wage cuts brings about a business upswing.

Assume that some invention has stimulated investment activity. Capitalists will finance additional investment by creating purchasing power. Demand for bank credits increases (abstracting from the intricacies of the financial process). Those funds are expended for products of the capital goods industry. Prices of these goods rise, activating idle capacities, which are then manned by hitherto unemployed labor. This expansion in employment is a source of additional demand for consumer goods and, therefore, results, in turn, in higher employment in respective industries. Finally, the additional funds spent on investment come back directly and through the workers' expenditures on consumption (it is assumed that workers spend what they earn) into the "pockets" of capitalists. In turn, the additional profits find their way into banks whose reserves are restored and which are ready to extend credit to finance future inventions. Whereas in the case of wage reduction one of the problems was whether profits ensuing from cost cuts are invested, in this case profits are invested even before they are effectuated and are realized only because they are invested. Uninvested profits cannot be retained because they are cancelled out by the ensuing fall in output and prices.

The creation of purchasing power for financing additional investment brings about expansion in the output from the low level reached in the slump and hence creates profits equal to this investment. Increase in output will result in an increased demand for money for "transaction" purposes and requires expansion of credits by the central bank. If the bank responds to it by raising the rate of interest to a level at which aggregate investment would fall by the amount equal to the additional investment brought about by the new invention, no rise in investment will take place, and expansionary forces will not be set into motion. Hence the precondition for unobstructed upswing is that the rate of interest should not rise to such an extent as to inhibit investment. The question arises: What would happen if the original source of the business upswing had exhausted itself and thus the inducement to invest vanished? Is such a contraction inevitable? Kalecki says no, for, in the meantime, the higher profitability pervading the economic system will have resulted in an increase in investment. Thus investment stimulated by increased profitability will step in when the effect of the new invention terminates.

This brings into focus Kalecki's basic proposition that workers spend what they earn and capitalists earn what they spend. As Kalecki warned, this proposition is likely to appear paradoxical to many readers. Here we digress only briefly for a rudimentary statement of certain basic relationships that underlie Kalecki's model. This important subject is treated at length in chapter four.

Kalecki first considers determination of profits under the simplifying assumption that workers do not save, (Kalecki 1933f; 1939b), government economic activity (public sector) is tentatively abstracted, and the system is closed (with respect to foreign trade). In such a system the national income is simply composed of profits and wages, and expenditures consist of capitalists' investment and consumption plus workers' consumption. Since the workers are assumed to spend what they earn, it follows directly that Profits = Investment = Capitalists' Consumption. This identity equation is of fundamental importance as it enables us to focus on the fluctuation in production. Profit (national output, effective demand) changes whenever one (or combination) of its components changes. (In expanded form, Kalecki shows that aggregate profits are equal to consumption by capitalists plus investment, plus export surplus, plus budget deficit, and that profit *changes* whenever its components change and the effect on other components and national income are taken into account.)

If we consider the investment, capitalists' consumption, and workers' consumption components in a certain period, the question that arises is: In which of these three constituents of national income will spontaneous changes most likely take place? Given the assumption that workers spend what they earn, their expenditure cannot exceed or be smaller than what they get. However, capitalists may reduce their consumption or investment expenditure below their current profits by repaying credits or accumulating financial assets. If so, the above equation clearly indicates that the income accruing to the capitalists as a whole will rise or fall precisely by as much as their spending was increased or reduced. The total output is bound to reach the level at which the profits derived from it by the capitalists are equal to their expenditure on consumption and investment. For, if the workers spend on consumption what they earn in wages, the nonlabor share of national income, being here the share accruing to capitalists, is just equal to the size of their expenditures on consumption and investment goods. Thus the capitalists, as a whole, determine by their spending decisions their profits and, as a result, national income. The point is that capitalists may decide to invest or consume in a given period more than in the preceding one, but they cannot decide to earn more profits. Fluctuations in output and profits depend on the fluctuations in profit-earners' investment and consumption expenditures.

Increased profit-earners' consumption has an influence similar to that of the manufacture of capital goods: output of goods consumed by the capitalists grows, which tends to expand employment, and this, in turn, increases the demand for goods consumed by workers which again increases production. "*The aggregate production and the profit per unit of output will ultimately rise to such an extent as to assure an increment in real profits equal to that of production of investment goods and capitalists' consumption. . . .*" The conclusion that, as profit-earners' consumption increases, their profits grow as well, seems to conflict with the commonly held view that the more consumed, the less saved. Such an approach, sound enough with regard to one entrepreneur, does not apply to them as a group. If some profit-earners make outlays on consumer or capital goods, their money passes to others in the form of profits. "Capitalists as a class gain exactly as much as they invest or consume, and if—in a closed system—they ceased to construct and consume they could not make any money at all." Thus, to the extent of their investment and personal consumption, entrepreneurs, as a group, determine their own profits. "In a way they are 'masters of their fate'; but how they 'master' it is determined by objective factors, so that fluctuations of profits appear after all unavoidable. Capitalists' consumption is a function of the gross accumulation. The gross accumulation which is equal to the production of investment goods is determined by investment orders which in turn were undertaken in a past period on the basis of the profitability in that period, i.e. on the basis of the gross accumulation and the volume of capital equipment in that period." (Kalecki 1966h, pp. 13-14.)

After this brief digression the question is whether, without investment stimulated by such "external" factors as innovations, the slump would endure indefinitely. Kalecki asked: Is it not inherent in the slump to generate forces that terminate it by bringing about a rise in investment activity?

Assume that the economy stabilized at the trough of the cycle and investment activity does not even cover replacement requirements. Assume further that productive capacity is composed of 2,000 factories with 100 factories becoming "used up" each year, but only 60 new factories are built. Hence productive capital shrinks annually by 40 factories. This is a factor initiating an upswing after a rather prolonged period. For with a diminishing productive capacity, the same demand meets an increasingly diminished number of better utilized factories, accompanied by an increase in prices in relation to wages, for otherwise the exploitation of hitherto idle capacities would not be profitable.

But as soon as the profitability of existing productive capacities rises, investment grows, financed by additional purchasing power. There will result an increase in output of investment goods and employment in respective branches of industry, increased demand on the part of newly employed workers for consumer goods, and therefore increased employment in consumer goods industries. This general increase of output is accompanied by a higher price-wage ratio and further rise in profitability. *Ceteris paribus,* this is a cumulative, self-propagating process. But as soon as investment activity exceeds requirements, as soon as annually more than the 100 obsolete factories are rebuilt, factors restricting the upswing come into play. Just as previously the shrinkage of capacity became an upturn factor, its expansion restrains the boom, eventually stopping its ascent and finally causing a downswing.

The process of collapse of the boom will be the opposite of that starting the upswing. Assume that, at the peak of the cycle annually, 140 factories were built to replace the 100 retired ones. As demand will be met by an increasing number of factories, the rate of utilization will drop and the ratio of price to cost will fall. The decline in profitability will provoke a curtailment in investment, a contraction of production, and an increase in unemployment.

Obviously, investment has a favorable effect on the economic situation when it is being executed and generates purchasing power. But every completed investment adds to the stock of capital. It is the productive character of investment that contributes to the retardation of expansion and finally brings it to an end. Here is one of the remarkable paradoxes of the capitalist economy: The expansion of the economy and growth of national wealth bear the seeds of depression, where the additional wealth proves to be only potential, for it lies idle until the next upswing.

Another paradox lies in the answer to the often raised question: Why should more capacities be built when the existing ones are underutilized? Kalecki replied that, in order to employ the existing capacity, it is necessary to enlarge it. The reason for this is simple enough. Take the case of two towns connected by two railway lines, both of which are greatly underutilized. What should be done at the onset of a depression? Obviously, a third railway line should be built, because then the first two could be utilized for transporting labor and materials required for construction of the third line. What happens when the third line is put into service? Of course, build a fourth, and so on. Kalecki stressed the paradox only to drive the point home. He suggested that clearly some other form of investment in the region should be chosen.

As previously seen, an invention is a stimulus for entrepreneurs to undertake new investment. The additional purchasing power so generated and propagated sets into motion an upswing of activity. There is a close analogy between this case and the opportunity for government countercyclical intervention. For, in order to bring the economy out of the slump, one can replace the enterprises' investments by government investments financed by additional purchasing power.

Assume that the government issues treasury bills and sells them to the banks. For example, the government spends the proceeds on building a railroad. As before, employment in the investment goods sector expands. Subsequently, owing to enlarged workers' incomes and spending, employment in consumer goods industries also expands. Directly or through the medium of workers' spending, the money spent by the government flows in as profit and is deposited at the banks. The latter are then able to discount further bills to finance the continuation of railroad construction. On the side of the bank's assets, the government's debt to the bank accrues in the form of discount bills. On the side of the bank's liabilities, there is an increase in deposits equal to the size of additional profits. Through the banks the government borrows funds from businessmen to finance the investment. Here also increased profitability of industry will lure investment and strengthen expansion, which will continue even when the government gradually tapers off its investment activity.

The pattern of public investment undertaken is not essential for the effect of the demand created by government intervention. It is of fundamental importance that the investment should be financed by creating additional purchasing power. The generation of spending power for the sake of financing the budget deficit, whatever its reason, is similar in its consequences. The difference is mainly that, initially, the additional purchasing power flows into different industries. Assume, for example, that the proceeds from discounting treasury bills is spent entirely on unemployment compensation. Then the initial stimulus will be in the consumer goods industries, and will hit the capital goods industries when the former are induced to invest in view of their increased profitability. This upswing will continue even when budget deficits are made up by the influx of tax revenue from the enlarged income.

Given a certain time-lag, private investment steps in and takes over from public investment. The "artificial" boom manufactured by the government intervention is replaced by a "natural" one. This in turn is sooner or later hampered by the capital accumulation (when executed investment orders have exceeded the replacement requirements, the stock of capital starts to expand). To recall, this initially restrains the rate at which investment activity is expanding and at later stages brings about a decline in investment orders.

The argument is often heard that neither public investment nor deficit spending can generate an upswing, for they are conducted at the cost of shrinking credits for private investment, and that "productive" expenditures are exchanged for "unproductive" ones. But such an argument assumes that no additional purchasing power will be created, and that only hitherto spent funds will be shuffled around. This would be the case if, in the process of discounting treasury bills, the interest rate were increased, discouraging the hitherto private investment. The assumption is, of course, that interest rates would not be raised. If the banks reacted so drastically to all increased demand for investment credit, the volume of investment could generally not be increased, which would hamper an upswing caused by inventions as well. Investments would then no longer be the opening through which flows additional purchasing power, which is undoubtedly the *spiritus movens* of the upswing. (Kalecki 1935e, pp. 1320-23.)

A precondition for successful government countercyclical intervention is the requirement of meeting the increased demand for credits (as a result of stimulation by expansionary fiscal policy) by the banking system without material increases in the rate of interest. The question arises: If the interest rate could be lowered (availability of finance improved), what is the likely potency of such a measure in stimulating investment and thus an upswing?

The ability to finance investment over and above retained savings constitutes a necessary, but not a sufficient, condition for undertaking investment.[10] In addition to the existence of a favorable financial apparatus, a condition for undertaking investment is clearly the willingness of the businessman to take advantage of the opportunities provided by the apparatus. The entrepreneur may spend his gold holdings or other "valuable assets," he may use received foreign credits, he may borrow from other businessmen, or he may borrow from the bank. But the question is whether, in addition, the financial apparatus ("inflationary apparatus") can induce the entrepreneur to take advantage of the services it offers. The answer to the question is affirmative, but subject to very serious qualifications. The bank can increase the demand for credit by reducing the rate of interest. Reduction of the interest rate induces investment because it raises the profitability of future enterprises by reducing the interest charges. Indeed, reduction of the rate of interest is a typical means of intervention of the banking apparatus to promote prosperity. But the action is, in any case, largely ineffective. The interest rate is not by and large *the* determinant of investment decisions. A much more weighty factor is the expectations of gross profitability of the enterprise, formed on the basis of profitability of already existing enterprises. During the slump when the profitability falls considerably below its average level and the existing capacities are greatly underutilized, a fall in the interest rate may only exert a weak influence as an inducement to invest. At any rate, a protracted time lapse is required for its influence to produce palpable results. The disappointing effect of this method of intervention is owing to the fact that it acts through the person of the entrepreneur by attempting to influence his volition. Unfailing means of intervention would be those that would ensure that the scope of investment activity would, in fact, be expanded. This brings into focus the state's undertaking of investments as a means for alleviating the slump or accelerating recovery. The state may certainly employ the various forms of "credit inflation" to promote prosperity.

To accelerate recovery, Kalecki advocated government intervention via inflationary financing of public works. Large-scale public works would help to reduce the idleness of productive capacity, raise profitability, and after a certain perhaps protracted time-lag, would induce investment activity and spur prosperity.[11]

Fluctuations in the rate of investment activity are the decisive factor conditioning the pattern of the trade cycle. During expansion, growth of investment affects directly and indirectly expansion of employment, while during contraction the fall in investment activity considerably below the renovation requirements leads to the spread of unemployment and marked underutilization of capacity. If not for the violent swings in investment activity there would be no unfailing business fluctuations; at least they would not assume such a scope and would not be so pervasive as they have been. (Kalecki 1932e, p. 1411.)

In retrospect, Kalecki interpreted the application of new economics to the contemporary scene and expressed his bitterness about the unethical use of the tools. He postulated that "the main problem of a developed capitalist economy is the adequacy of effective demand. Such an economy possesses a capital equipment which more or less matches the existing labour force, and therefore it could generate a rather high *per capita* income provided that its resources are fully used. This, however, is by no means necessarily the case." Kalecki noted that the view that unemployment is only an accidental, short-lived deviation from full utilization of resources was basically revised during the Great Depression. The problem of underemployment of resources is, in a sense, "inherent in a developed capitalist economy and . . . potentially, at least, it may emerge at any time." This is evident when the position of full employment is examined. A part of the full employment output will be consumed by labor and a part by profit-earners, but a remaining part is not consumed and corresponds to savings out of profits (for simplicity, savings out of wages are disregarded). "Now, if investment is so high as to absorb this surplus, full employment will be maintained. If, however, investment falls short of savings of capitalists then part of the product will remain unsold, and thus goods will accumulate on stock." Then output will be contracted until such a level of national income is reached at which saving is equal to the prevailing investment. The decline in national income and employment will entail a fall in consumption and saving. (Kalecki 1968b, pp. 9-10.)

The role of investment in establishing a certain level of national product is not associated with the final destination or the uses to which the investment will eventually be put. Its income-generating effect is what matters at the time when it is carried out. Whether the investment will prove to be useful or useless in the future is inconsequential from the standpoint of the equilibrating process of current (short-run) macroeconomic equilibrium. What matters is its role from the standpoint of the equilibrating process: that it generates the same effective demand when it is executed. It follows that, from the standpoint of creating effective demand, it is inconsequential, ruling out offsetting effects, whether private investments are replaced by government expenditures, financed by loans—to mention here only one policy alternative—as long as no reduction of any purchasing power by taxation is involved. By the means of what Kalecki calls "financial tricks" (fiscal weapons, functional finance) the government expenditures, financed by loan or budget deficits, can solve the insufficiency of effective demand; and, if they are appropriately large, they can ensure full employment. If the aim is to restore full employment, as far as the generation of effective demand is concerned, the direction of government expenditures is largely immaterial (perhaps given some appropriate assumption about the propensity to consume). When investment falls short of saving, or of that level which is necessary to maintain effective demand, it is the basis of government policies in modern capitalism that the gap is governed by governmental expenditures (or taxes are reduced so as to increase disposable income and expenditures on consumption, and measures are taken to induce investment).

Is it absolutely necessary to finance government expenditure by budget deficit in order to generate adequate effective demand? Kalecki's answer is no. Suppose that initially full employment is achieved by budget deficit, but subsequently the savings out of profits generated by this deficit are taxed away. As a result "profits are reduced to the levels that existed before the increase in government expenditure but nothing changes in the sphere of production." Government outlays financed by profit tax may also ensure full employment. This differs from deficit financing in the impact on profits after tax and its consequences; "in the case of budget deficit financing profits are increased by the amount of additional government expenditure which leads to an increase in capitalists' consumption and in private investment. When government expenditure is financed by taxation of profits they remain unaltered and capitalists' consumption as well as private investment do not tend to rise." (Kalecki 1968b, pp. 10-11.)

While the direction of government expenditure to sustain full employment is largely immaterial, the most rational use would be to direct expenditures so as to foster the development of the economy and to increase the living standards of the broad masses of the population. It is reprehensible, absurd, and perverse that, from all the alternatives for filling the gap in effective demand, the manufacture of armaments emerges as the acceptable way of keeping the economy going; and that people are assured a relatively high standard of living through the manufacture of means of destruction.

> But, absurd though it is, even such a method of maintaining full employment assures modern capitalism of a fair degree of political stability, because although the levels of mass consumption are not as high as they could be, they are still much higher than those that would prevail under conditions of unemployment. Moreover, if full employment is consistently maintained, and if the relative share of labour in national income remains constant, there will be also some continuous increase in the real wage because of the rising productivity of labour: if the labour forces are continuously employed, if there is a rise in productivity and if the relative share of labour in the national income is unaltered it is perfectly clear that the real wage is bound to rise. (Kalecki 1968b, p. 13.)

General Theory: Old and New

The revolutionary character and impact of the *General Theory* have been the subject of extensive and searching inquiry. I would not presume to add to the controversy. I merely propose that the available evidence seems to suggest to me a fundamental breakthrough in economic theory and policy. This is not to say that the view is universally held. Clearly, "we are all Keynesians by now" has a different meaning to economists of different persuasions. Neither am I certain that I grasp the full impact and implications of the Keynesian Revolution. A participant in the revolution recalls that "some of Keynes' contemporaries and seniors dislike the expression 'Keynesian Revolution.' There was nothing, they say, so very new in the *General Theory.*" And she adds in a footnote: "They are in a very weak position to say that to the present writer, who learned the pre-Keynesian orthodoxy at their feet." By all means, "everything can be found in Marshall, even the *General Theory.* But we know what Marshall's pupils who had gone into the Treasury believed, from the famous White Paper of 1929 which was an example of neo-classical theory in action. . . ." (Joan Robinson 1962a, p. 73.)

The impact that the *General Theory* made on some economists is vividly depicted by Paul Samuelson:

> I have always considered it a priceless advantage to have been born as an economist prior to 1936 and to have received a thorough grounding in classical economics. It is quite impossible for modern students to realize the full effect of what has been advisably called "The Keynesian Revolution" upon those of us brought up in the orthodox tradition. What beginners today often regard as trite and obvious was to us puzzling, novel, and heretical. . . .
>
> The *General Theory* caught most economists under the age of thirty-five with the unexpected virulence of a disease first attacking and decimating an isolated tribe of south sea islanders. Economists beyond fifty turned out to be quite immune to the ailment. With time, most economists in-between began to run the fever, often without knowing or admitting their condition. (Samuelson 1964, pp. 315-16.)

From the time of its publication to this day, the *General Theory* has found its critics. But even the critics will agree that, for better or worse, the *General Theory* "was the outstanding success of the 1930s and that it dominated analytic work for a decade after its publication, to say the least."[12] For instance, over the years Professor Pigou, who was among those "from whose hands the classical theory has received its most mature embodiment" (Keynes 1936, p. 32), came to retract with some reservation his earlier criticism of the *General Theory.*[13] In an exemplary and virtually unique admission of error, Pigou stated that in his original review article of the *General Theory* he "failed to grasp its significance and did not assign to Keynes the credit due for it." In setting out and developing his fundamental analysis "Keynes made a very important, original and valuable addition to the armoury of economic analysis. Any economist afterwards elaborating or refining on that conception is, so far, a follower of Keynes. All economists, whether followers or not, owe to the stimulus to thought which his book gave, even to the controversies that it aroused, a very great debt." (Pigou 1951, pp. 64-66.)

This is not the place to review the influence of Keynesism on modern economic thinking. There is much controversy among "modern Keynesians" about interpretations, misunderstandings, etc. Recently, Joan Robinson has pointed out that Professor Leijonhufvud "suggests that we who worked with Keynes were saved from the misunderstandings rife in America because we had the benefit of oral teaching which was not made clear in the book. No doubt there is something in that, but I think that there are more important explanations. First, Kalecki brought to England his own version of the General Theory, which tightened up some loose threads in Keynes' version and brought it into relation with imperfect competition, supplying a missing link in Keynes' theory of prices. To judge by this survey, Kalecki had very little influence on American doctrines." (Joan Robinson 1969c, p. 582.)

II

KALECKI AND KEYNES

THE TWO ARCHITECTS OF THE KEYNESIAN REVOLUTION came from two radically diverse social, cultural, and economic strata. They differed in almost as many aspects as can distinguish men: background, social position, education, experience, political outlook, and not the least in predisposition and temperament. However, certain similarities linked these two men who, in a world crisis, miles apart, under divergent circumstances, unbeknown to each other, came to fairly similar conclusions. I shall try to summarize here what separated and what joined them. An exposition of Kalecki's views and positive programs will be found in the subsequent chapters. Here I am merely contrasting the sociopolitical outlook and background of the two men, and their analytical differences.

PERSONALITIES AND OUTLOOK

1. Keynes was born into the privileged upper class of the stable and secure British Empire of the latter part of the nineteenth century.[1] He was brought up in the intellectual atmosphere of Cambridge, where his father, John Neville Keynes, taught logic and political economy. His early youth was spent in the enlightened reformist environment of his parents and their friends. By contrast, Kalecki was born into hostile surroundings. As I have pointed out, the family's financial position was not particularly secure. He was born a Jew in a country where there was overt anti-Semitism. He was born a Pole while the country was partitioned among three foreign powers. His early childhood was spent under Russian tsarist occupation. From the very beginning—whereas Keynes's life was well ordered and in accord with the elements, so to speak—Kalecki had to battle an inimical world. Whereas Keynes had observed the havoc wrought by business downturns, the suffering and misery of the unemployed, and the sheer waste of idle resources, Kalecki knew the misery at first hand when his father lost his sustenance, and young Michal had to interrupt his studies permanently and look for

a livelihood — by no means an easy task. If suffering helps to understand this queer world of ours, Kalecki was well equipped for understanding it.

2. Keynes enjoyed what was probably the best education that the British Empire could provide. After seven years at St. Faith's in Cambridge, he was enrolled at Eton. The next step was King's College, Cambridge. At the university he first specialized in mathematics, although his field of interest was very broad. Only later in his studies did he become attracted to economics and imbibed the Cambridge school under Alfred Marshall and A. C. Pigou. Kalecki's formal education was in engineering, where he got a solid grounding in mathematics. In economics he was self-taught. He had read Tugan-Baranovsky, Marx, and Rosa Luxemburg. In contrast with Keynes, who was well steeped in certain aspects of classical and neoclassical economics (but was quite ahistorical in his outlook as a scholar), Kalecki observed the phenomena of modern capitalism with a fresh mind unencumbered by traditional modes of thought. In a way, the new economics came much easier to Kalecki who started from Marx's reproduction schemes. A large part of the *General Theory* is concerned with shedding the shackles of past heresies. Apparently, for many years, Keynes was constantly grappling with the constraining effect of inculcated fallacies. In developing the theory of effective demand, Kalecki did not have to wrestle with this devil—it simply did not exist for him.

3. After graduating from the university, Keynes worked in the civil service. Shortly thereafter he became University Lecturer in Economics and later Fellow of King's College, and subsequently its most gifted bursar. During World War I, he held a responsible position in financial administration. Later he participated in an advisory capacity in the Treaty of Versailles. He moved from the theoretical-teaching plain to the observation of economic phenomena from political-administrative pinnacles. Kalecki's career as an economist had a very humble start. One of the first temporary jobs he found was in credit inquiry. Later he undertook painstaking statistical studies of commodity markets and a large-scale study of Polish national income. His career as an economic theoretician was begun by close observation of life. In this sense also the new economics came easier to him than to Keynes. Yet both men had a genius for the realities of life. They had an uncanny insight into how things actually worked and a keen theoretical mind to extract the essence and the tendencies. This common faculty probably enabled them to

come to similar conclusions and to discover what had always been there, but unperceived by others.

4. By the mid-1930s, Keynes had gained worldwide recognition as an economist for his controversial *The Economic Consequences of the Peace, A Treatise on Money,* and many original and thoughtful articles in *Economic Journal* and elsewhere. Even before the *General Theory* he was a leading economist of the Cambridge school. An important work by Keynes was certain to create a stir among his *confrères,* whether they embraced or rejected the new ideas. On the other hand, Kalecki was a relatively obscure newcomer to the economic fraternity. His work was published in Polish, hence for a limited readership to start with. Even in his own country he was either not well understood or not given much credence. As Professor Edward Lipinski acknowledged: "I only understood fully Kalecki's discovery when Keynes's similar theory became the basis for effective stimulation of the market." (Lipinski 1970c.) In 1933, Kalecki expounded his theory to a meeting of the International Econometric Society. But it did not even ripple the placid waters of existing theory. In a word, Kalecki lacked status, authority, and influence.

5. In addition to being recognized as a leading economist, Keynes was at the forefront of the intellectual and artistic movements of his time. The breadth, variety, and enormous spectrum of his interests is truly breathtaking. By contrast, Kalecki revolved in a much narrower circle. He was not the worldly man that Keynes was. His overriding passion in life was social justice, full employment, and an adequate and growing living standard for all. Both men were acute and sharp observers and commentators of the political and social scene of our age.

6. Aside from the fact that they both possessed superbly clear and sharp minds, a link between Keynes and Kalecki was their profound concern for humanity. True the concern manifested itself differently; it was more or less intense, and the remedies sought varied.[2] Kalecki was always by far more radical. Keynes was certainly not a radical, as a perusal of his essays in politics shows beyond a doubt. (Cf. Keynes 1963b, pp. 297-345.) He wanted to preserve capitalism and realized that, in order to do that, it needed reforming. The basic idea is conservative—that of preserving the existing order of free private enterprise. The approach is liberal—that of the socially conscious observer of the evils of his time whose aim is only to reform the existing order so as to make it function better, more

equitably, more humanely. "In general, we can say that Marx analyzed the reasons why the capitalist system did not and could not function properly, while Keynes analyzed the reasons why the capitalist system did not but could function properly. Keynes wanted to apologize and preserve, while Marx wanted to criticize and destroy."[3]

7. By nature, upbringing, and environment, Keynes was a reformer. His entourage was that of social reformers who conceived their tasks within "a framework of stable and unquestioned values." In due course public opinion would be enlightened and poverty alleviated. After World War I the stability and prosperity of the British Empire were shaken. Keynes matured during a period when, on the one hand, many Englishmen of a conservative bent could not grasp the extent of necessary adaptation if old values were to be safeguarded; and, on the other, there were those without a sense of these values. "To many of the former, Keynes may have seemed a mischievous radical; many of the latter, while welcoming him for his modernity, failed, to a large extent, to understand the purport of his message, lacking his presuppositions." (Harrod 1951, pp. 2, 4.)

Writing as early as 1926, Keynes questioned the myth that there is a self-regulating mechanism channeling private interests into social optimum: "The world is *not* so governed from above that private and social interests always coincide. It is *not* so managed here below that in practice they coincide. It is *not* a correct deduction from the Principles of Economics that enlightened self-interest always operates in the public interest. Nor is it true that self-interest generally *is* enlightened." (Keynes 1963b, p. 312.) Keynes was troubled by waste, plain stupidity and mismanagement of resources, and needless poverty. But he concentrated attention on expansion of output and not so much on the problem of resource allocation and who got the output. (Klein 1966, pp. 186-87; Joan Robinson 1951, pp. 3-7.) "For my part, I believe that there is social and psychological justification for significant inequalities of incomes and wealth, but not for such large disparities as exist to-day." (Keynes 1936, p. 374.)

Both Kalecki and Keynes had a distinct preference for inflation over unemployment and deflation. But they differed in their relative emphasis on how to deploy economic resources to enhance and maintain full employment, and on what full employment is for and who are its beneficiaries; i.e., on the problem of level, content, and distribution of aggregate output. As Keynes said, his *General Theory* "is moderately conservative in its implications." (Keynes 1936, p. 377.) In politics, Keynes was a "pragmatic" English liberal.

Did Kalecki criticize capitalism to destroy or to reform and preserve? This question cannot be answered unambiguously. First of all, Kalecki had no dogmatic commitment to destroy the system. He always associated criticism with finding remedies. Even if one should answer that Kalecki was a reformer, it bears underlining that reform had a different meaning for Kalecki and Keynes. For Kalecki it would entail more fundamental changes in the features of the capitalist economy and society. Above all he was dedicated to a more equitable distribution of national wealth.

Kalecki's political position underwent some shifts under the influence of contemporary developments: (a) In his original articles on the business cycle, Kalecki pointed out very forcefully the absurdities and waste of the capitalist system. He showed how the creation of effective demand by investment could be the very reason for the ensuing slump simply because these investments are useful. He pondered over the paradox of a system where useless investments would be more beneficial. (b) During World War II, Kalecki seems to have been caught by the prevailing expectations that a more just world would emerge from the holocaust. His writings indicate that he inclined toward reform of the capitalist system. His masterful "Three Ways to Full Employment" is still a valid and timely reform blueprint. But he was skeptical and predicted the emergence of the political business cycle. (c) Kalecki was thoroughly disillusioned by the experience of postwar capitalism. He denounced and repudiated creation of effective demand and an increased living standard by military production. His disappointment was made evident in his refusal to write a second edition of his full-employment essay. Would Keynes have approved the modern methods of creating effective demand? No one really knows.

8. Another link between Keynes and Kalecki was the lack of understanding with which their theories met at first. Outside of the small group of his students and close collaborators—the so-called Circus—at first few economists understood where Keynes was heading. Later he gained a number of followers on both sides of the Atlantic. But it is only after World War II that Keynesian economics came into its own and became a respectable subject in economics curricula. Disheartened, Keynes drew a parallel between his theory and that of Newton, which no one under the age of forty understood at the time.

Notwithstanding Keynes's "moderately conservative" attitude, his scheme for bolstering up the capitalist economy was vigorously opposed by those who stood to gain most by its preservation in a more viable form. This opposition stemmed (and still does) from an ill-conceived concept of the viability of the capitalist order without Keynesian-type government intervention. Also, there is a distorted view of the personal interest of the individual capitalist and of that of the system as a whole. (Cf. Klein 1966, p. 184.) Paradoxically, the Keynesian toolbox is often abused on the grounds that it is rampant socialism, or at least is paving the way for a socialist order. Such critics seem to ignore that laissez faire capitalism cannot survive, and without the use of Keynesian prescriptions the two existing alternatives are either socialism or fascism. Without considering the opposite humanistic values of these alternative social systems, they both involve a far larger dose of government intervention in the economic system than that foreseen by the Keynesian-type reform. "The authoritarian state systems of to-day seem to solve the problem of unemployment at the expense of efficiency and of freedom. It is certain that the world will not much longer tolerate the unemployment which is associated . . . with present-day capitalistic individualism. But it may be possible by a right analysis of the problem to cure the disease whilst preserving efficiency and freedom. . . ." (Keynes 1936, p. 381.)

Kalecki was just as misunderstood. Professor Lipinski reports that, among his colleagues, few comprehended the purport of Kalecki's essay. A striking example is that from his two closest collaborators, Ludwig Landau, the statistician, and Marek Breit, the economist, it was the former who grasped immediately the essence of new economics, whereas the latter had to break down numerous barriers of orthodox economic theory to assimilate Kalecki's revolutionary concepts. (Lipinski 1970c.) Kalecki met with similar misunderstanding from the militant left. Instead of using the paradoxes of the capitalist economy that he outlined to bolster up their own criticism of capitalism, they attacked him on the grounds that he attempted to save capitalism, which they claimed was an impossible task. They viewed deficit spending as aggravating the situation. These Marxists did not differ much from the traditional school. On a theoretical plane, Kalecki's Marxist critics misunderstood his method. A socialist writer, Antoni Panski, affirmed that Kalecki's theory of the business cycle can be considered of Marxist origin. He pointed out that the criticism attached inordinate importance to the form of exposition (mathematical formulation) and not to the substance of the argument. Panski argued that the critics failed to see the "clear genetic relationships between the substantive context of Kalecki's theory and Marx's schemes." (Panski 1937, p. 745.)

The Intellectual Family Trees of Kalecki and Keynes

Except for Malthus and others,[4] in the main pre-Keynesian academic economics skirted the vexing question of finding adequate markets for full employment output that can be produced and used to justify the assumption of full employment, by what Marshall called the familiar economic axiom;[5] i.e., Say's Law of the Market. (Cf. Keynes 1936, p. 19.)

It is a truism that no scientist or researcher works in a vacuum, and that his discovery is not totally new. Our thoughts are molded and influenced by those who came before us. The discovery consists of many elements, ideas, or interdependencies known before, but really unseen, waiting to be perceived in a new configuration and light. The merit of the discoverer lies in integrating new and old ideas, supplying the missing links in creating an analytical system, and in perceiving new implications. So it was with Keynes and Kalecki. Although they arrived basically at the same conclusion, the many differences in their approach, perception, and inferences can be traced principally to the fact that they were descended from widely disparate genealogical trees of knowledge. Clearly, comparisons are hazardous. There is a large element of incomparability between economists, for both similarities and differences may be emphasized and a body of evidence can be cited to support each contention. Original minds have common traits with respect to certain ideas and diverge considerably on others. Granted that construction of a family tree is not an easy task, one can detect Keynes's intellectual linkage to Malthus and Kalecki's affinity with Rosa Luxemburg.[6]

The *General Theory* is best understood as the culmination of the intellectual development of the Cambridge school of economics, steeped in the classical tradition. Keynes revolted against all those theories familiar to him that did not explain the question of effective demand. He was fascinated by Malthus, downgraded Ricardo, and was distinctly biased against and "could never make head or tail of Marx."[7] Keynes believed that "the idea that we can safely neglect the aggregate demand function is fundamental to the Ricardian economics, which underlie what we have been taught for more than a century. Malthus, indeed, had vehemently opposed Ricardo's doctrine that it was impossible for effective demand to be deficient; but vainly." Since Malthus was not able to explain satisfactorily "how and why effective demand could be deficient or excessive, he failed to furnish an alternative construction; and Ricardo conquered England as completely as the Holy Inquisition conquered Spain. . . . The great puzzle of Effective Demand with which Malthus had wrestled vanished from economic literature. . . . It could only live furtively, below the surface, in the underworlds of Karl Marx, Silvio Gesell or Major Douglas." (Keynes 1936, p. 32.)

It seems that in his essay on Malthus, Keynes went much too far in commenting on passages of the famous Malthus-Ricardo correspondence.[8] He appears never to have grasped the problem with which Ricardo was wrestling: "One cannot rise from a perusal of this correspondence without a feeling that the almost total obliteration of Malthus's line of approach, and the complete domination of Ricardo's for a period of a hundred years has been a disaster to the progress of economics." Keynes continued, "If only Malthus, instead of Ricardo, had been the parent stem from which nineteenth-century economics proceeded, what a much wiser and richer place the world would be to-day!"[9]

Schumpeter was obviously right that, in the controversy between Malthus and Ricardo, "generous enthusiasm carried Keynes beyond all bounds of reason. There he punctuated his report with applause for Malthus and derogatory comments on Ricardo's 'blindness' and became blind himself to obvious weaknesses in the former's and to all the strong points in the latter's argument."[10]

Keynes praised the anti-Marxian student of Proudhon, Sylvio Gesell, as an "unduly neglected prophet" and suggested that future generations "will learn more from the spirit of Gesell than from that of Marx." (Keynes 1936, pp. 353-55. Cf. Dillard 1942, pp. 63-76.) It is appalling that Keynes placed Marx in the company of Major Douglas, or that he even mentioned both names in the same breath. (Keynes 1936, p. 32.) How revealing is Keynes's attitude in this context: He treated *Das Kapital* as an obsolete economics textbook, "not only scientifically erroneous but without interest and application for the modern world." (Keynes 1963b, p. 300.)

To a large extent, Keynes's great achievement was negative in the sense that he undermined orthodox economics and policy. He revolted against the tyranny of Say's Law of the Market from within the citadel of orthodoxy. (Sweezy 1964, pp. 301, 305.) At least he shook up orthodox economics and provoked re-examination and reassessment. In this respect, Keynes's achievement is incommensurately greater than that of Kalecki.[11] In fact, the Keynesian Revolution "explodes once and for all the myth of a harmony between private and public interests which was the cornerstone of nineteenth century liberalism." (Sweezy 1964, p. 301.)

Both Kalecki and Keynes supplied the theory of effective demand,[12] which had been dimly perceived by some of their predecessors, but never developed into a General Theory. In a certain sense, Kalecki's version is richer in that it is in the Ricardian tradition. It emphasizes the distribution of total produce between wages and profits. Also it takes into account the level (and variations) of output (income and employment).

What did Marx and his followers have to offer on the question of effective demand? A leading Cambridge economist testified, "I began to read *Capital*, just as one reads any book, to see what was in it; I found a great deal that neither its followers nor its opponents had prepared me to expect. Piero Sraffa teased me, saying that I treated Marx as a little-known forerunner of Kalecki. There is a certain sense in which this is not a joke." (Joan Robinson 1966b, pp. vi-vii.) Kalecki believed:

> That Marx was deeply conscious of the impact of effective demand upon the dynamics of the capitalist system follows clearly from this passage of the third volume of the *Capital*: "The conditions of direct exploitation and those of the realisation of surplus-value are not identical. They are separated not only by time and space but logically as well. The former are limited merely by the productive capacity of the society, the latter by the proportions of various branches of production and by consumer power of the society."
>
> However, he did not systematically scrutinize the process described by his reproduction schemes from the point of view of the contradictions inherent in capitalism as a result of the problem of effective demand.
>
> It is one of his most prominent followers, Rosa Luxemburg, who expressed very definite and even extreme views on the subject: she rejected altogether the possibility of long-run expanded reproduction if no "external markets" are in existence. By "external markets" she understood those outside the world capitalist system consisting not only of underdeveloped countries but also of the non-capitalist sectors of developed capitalist economies, for instance, peasant agriculture as well as government purchases. (Kalecki 1968e, pp. 78-79.)

The economic writings of Rosa Luxemburg—one of Marx's most brilliant, original, and unorthodox followers,[13] "rarest of all rare phenomena—a Marxist critical of Karl Marx" (Stark 1968, p. 11)—were neglected by both Marxists and non-Marxists alike. She was considered "the queen of underconsumptionists." (Sweezy 1942, p. 171.) Marxist economists generally neglected the underconsumption element in Marx's theory. They treated Luxemburg as a heretic.[14] Although Kalecki rehabilitated Luxemburg's views, she is still treated as *persona non grata* by many orthodox Marxists. Her attitude to *Capital* is revealing; "We must not look to the last two volumes of *Capital* to provide us with a final and completed solution of all economic problems. In some cases these problems are merely formulated, together with an indication here and there as to the direction in which one must work to arrive at a solution. In accordance with Marx's whole attitude, his *Capital* is not a Bible containing final and unalterable truths, but rather an inexhaustible source of stimulation for further study, further scientific investigations and further struggles for truth." (Luxemburg 1936, p. 371, quoted after Dobb 1967, p. 264.)

Kalecki himself related his argument to Marx and Rosa Luxemburg in the first English edition of his studies on modern capitalism. After presenting certain macroeconomic relationships by means of equations, Kalecki stated:

> It may be interesting to notice that the above equations are contained in the famous Marxian scheme of "extended reproduction." Marx even considers the questions of how to provide "means" for increased expenditure on investment. It must be added, however, that the problems discussed here are treated by Marx from a rather special point of view. He is interested in finding out, with the help of exchange equations, the pace of investment in investment and consumption goods industries respectively, which is necessary in order to secure a steady expansion of output. (The rates of profit in both divisions of industry are assumed to be equal throughout and on this basis the process of expansion is constructed so as to make investment in each, at the end of every "production-exchange cycle," equal to its saving so that there is no "shift of capital" from consumption to investment goods industries or conversely.) He does not pay attention to the problem of what happens if investment is inadequate to secure the moving equilibrium, and therefore does not approach the idea of the key position of investment in the determination of the level of total output and employment.
>
> Exactly the reverse attitude is represented by one of his eminent pupils, Rosa Luxemburg. In her *Akkumulation des Kapitals* she stressed the point that, if capitalists are saving, their profits can be

> "realized" only if a corresponding amount is spent by them on investment. She, however, considered impossible the persistence of net investment (at least in the long run) in a closed capitalist economy; thus, according to her, it is only the existence of exports to the non-capitalist countries which allows for the expansion of a capitalist system. The theory cannot be accepted as a whole, but the necessity of covering the "gap of saving" by home investment or exports was outlined by her perhaps more clearly than anywhere else before the publication of Mr. Keynes's *General Theory.* (Kalecki 1939a, pp. 45-46)

Rosa Luxemburg saw the possibility of finding a market for surplus goods only outside the world capitalist system. (Kalecki 1967o, pp. 241-49.) Again, the "external markets" are not only composed of underdeveloped countries but also include the noncapitalist sectors of developed capitalist economies, such as the peasant agriculture and the purchases by the government sector. Only the "exports" from the capitalist system were considered by Luxemburg as the *spiritus movens* of development. Thus here is the pessimistic view of the future of the capitalist economy: By undermining the noncapitalist mode of production and gradually pervading the whole world, capitalism eliminates simultaneously the possibility of its further development. To the quantitative exaggeration of the role of "external markets," Luxemburg contributed a fundamental error, which she perpetuated in her analysis of impact of these markets on the development of capitalism. In the main core of her argument she considered erroneously that the market for the surplus is created to the extent of total exports to the noncapitalist sector and not only to the extent of surplus of export over import. Indeed, as Kalecki has shown, "capturing of new foreign markets is frequently mentioned as a way out of depression. But it is usually not added that what is essential in this context is an increase in the export surplus rather than in absolute exports. . . . In order to stimulate the upswing by means of foreign trade, the balance of trade component of profits must increase, i.e., new surplus of exports over imports must be achieved." (Kalecki 1933c, p. 27. Trans. and rpt. in 1966h, p. 16.) Imports absorb purchasing power similarly to domestically produced goods, and to the extent that exports are accompanied by imports they do not contribute to the expansion of markets for national output. Kalecki showed that Luxemburg unduly stressed the impossibility of the development of a capitalist economy and disregarded expansion owing to certain aspects of technical progress which, however, do not ensure a satisfactory long-run utilization of productive capacity. But despite her slips, the significance of "external markets" for development of capitalist economies cannot be dismissed.

Kalecki argued that one of the most interesting elements of Luxemburg's theory relevant to present-day capitalism is the treatment of government purchases, especially of armaments, as a form of "external markets"—markets that play a crucial role in the functioning of modern capitalism. Nor did she envision the possibility of averting crises by the income effect that such expenditures generate. Moreover, as in the case of other "external markets," she consistently committed the error of treating the total government expenditures as a factor of realizing surplus production; i.e., independently of the means of financing. Government expenditures (armaments), to the extent that they are financed by budgetary deficits or by taxation of capitalists, contribute to solving the problem of effective demand because their effect—in contrast to financing government expenditures by indirect or direct taxation burdening workers who largely spend what they earn—contributes to solving the cardinal problem of effective demand as their effect is not offset by the decline of investment and consumption expenditures.[15]

Luxemburg correctly saw armaments orders as "external markets" which can absorb a part of accumulation. But she failed to exclude from this type of "external market" the case in which armaments are financed by taxations of wage and salary earners' incomes. Significantly, Luxemburg did not treat the "external markets" created by government activity as a problem of paramount importance. She predicted the general crisis of capitalism caused by the exhaustion of noncapitalist markets, but she did not envisage the possibility of counteracting the crisis by "external markets" of government purchases ("armament markets"). At present the "external markets" of this particular form are of much greater importance for expanded reproduction than at the time (1913) when the author of *Accumulation of Capital* propounded her theory.

Luxemburg treated expanded reproduction in the long run without the existence of "external markets" to be not only far from obvious but outright impossible. But as Kalecki commented, she argued this contention naively, showing the irrelevance of the question of effective demand for the development of the capitalist economy. One of the flaws in her reasoning was that identification of investment decisions lies not with individual investors, but somehow with the capitalist class, taking the investment decision as a whole. Kalecki wondered why the capitalist class, frustrated by the knowledge of the absence of final markets for the surplus of goods corresponding to accumulation, should see reason in undertaking such investment.

Kalecki realized that, despite errors in her argument, Luxemburg's skepticism about the possibility of long-term expanded reproduction was valuable since the self-propelled development of the capitalist economy cannot be taken for granted. Kalecki noted that, even though following a different line of reasoning, he also arrived at the conclusion that expanded reproduction is by no means a "natural" phenomenon, and that he attempted to find the source of expanded reproduction in properties of technical progress ("technical dynamism"). Thus Kalecki maintained that development of capitalism does not depend entirely on "external markets," but the latter factor is still significant.

In elucidating the problem of effective demand, Kalecki considered juxtaposition of Luxemburg's and Tugan-Baranovsky's views of great interest. He attempted to show where, in fact, both of them committed major errors in their arguments and where they contributed to the understanding of the processes of the "queer and perverse world in which we are living."

Michael Tugan-Baranovsky expounded the thesis that the capitalist system has unlimited possibilities of development.[16] "Tugan was perhaps the most influential and original of the economic thinkers produced by the so-called 'revisionist' movement which began to make headway in all branches of European socialism after the death of Engels in 1895. The propriety of calling Tugan a revisionist might be questioned, since he never claimed to be a Marxist of any kind. . . ."[17]

In the arguments about the market for national output advanced in terms of the Marxian reproduction scheme, the stands taken by Rosa Luxemburg and Tugan-Baranovsky were diametrically opposed. Tugan-Baranovsky denied altogether that the problem of effective demand may obstruct the development of the capitalist mode of production. The latter depends entirely on the growth in productive capacity. (Cf. Clark 1898, p. 15.) On the other hand, Luxemburg considered expanded reproduction in a closed capitalist system impossible. She attributed its entire development to the possibility of realization in external markets.

According to Tugan-Baranovsky there could be no overproduction or deficiency of effective demand, irrespective of the level of consumption, as long as correct proportionality of production is maintained. He traced crises to "disproportionality." If the correct proportions are satisfied in the use made of the national product, the question of effective demand does not arise. Tugan-Baranovsky made skillful use of the Marxian schemes of reproduction. He argued that, at any level of consumption by wage earners and capitalists, the national product can be sold, provided that investment is of sufficient size. These are the appropriate proportions which must be fulfilled in order that the aggregate output produced should be bought. *Ipso facto,* distortion of such "proportional production" leads to crises in the course of which the deviations are corrected and correct proportions established.

Kalecki pointed out that the fundamental notion of Tugan-Baranovsky rests on an error in attributing that that which may happen is actually taking place. Tugan-Baranovsky failed to show why capitalists in the long run are to invest to the degree necessary for full utilization of capacity. (Kalecki 1967o.)

In the main, Tugan-Baranovsky identified the *possible* use of the national product created by the full utilization of resources with the *actual* fact. Although his approach was erroneous, it does not necessarily follow that his theory was wrong, but merely that it is totally unfounded. Kalecki then asked whether the problem of the markets does not really create an impediment to expanded reproduction of a capitalist system. He realized that, in order to give a complete answer, one must first construct a satisfactory theory of determinants of investment decisions covering all pertinent aspects of the dynamics of a capitalist economy (long-run trend and cyclical fluctuations) and not only those relevant to cyclical fluctuations (the problems of investment decisions involving the elements associated with a long-run trend are considerably more difficult than in cyclical fluctuations in a trendless economy). Kalecki considered the work along these lines as one of the central problems of the economic theory of capitalism. As we shall see later, he also made a contribution toward solving this intricate problem, although he considered his work in this field to have been only of a pioneering nature.

But let us return to Kalecki's critique of the core of Tugan-Baranovsky's theory. By an elaborate argument, Kalecki demonstrated that long-run development is not inherent in the capitalist economy but requires certain supporting factors (but not necessarily Luxemburg's "external markets") to sustain it. (See ch. 6.)

Kalecki showed that development of a capitalist economy which is not obstructed by the problem of effective demand, even if possible, is unstable. But a process of unstable equilibrium ceases to exist if it is not supported by some stabilizing factor. In this context, it may be said that growth (expanded reproduction) will occur if there are factors present that will disturb the stationary state and transform the stationary system into one subject to an ascending trend. Among such factors, Kalecki singled out technical innovations in the broadest sense as the first and foremost promoter of development, opening before businessmen new perspectives.

This is not to say that such a possibility of growth (expanded reproduction) without support from "external markets" is tantamount to the elimination of the impact of deficiency of effective demand. The rate of growth generated by innovations is by no means necessarily sufficient to ensure the full utilization of productive capacity or even to maintain the rate of utilization of this capacity at a constant level.

In any case, criticism of Tugan-Baranovsky's theory suggested to Kalecki that (1) as a consequence of the problem of effective demand, expanded reproduction is far from obvious and clearly an "unnatural" state of the capitalist economy; and (2) nevertheless, such reproduction does not necessarily depend on "external markets." There is still something to be learned from Rosa Luxemburg, both as far as her positive contribution and the errors she committed are concerned. The same is, of course, true of Tugan-Baranovsky.

Tugan-Baranovsky emphasized the "antagonistic" character of the capitalist economy, in which the production of consumer goods is not an ultimate aim and the demand for them is not a moving force of its development. The aim of production is not the satisfaction of the needs of the broad masses of population but the pursuit of profits by businessmen. Consequently, it is not at all absurd to base development of the economy on an expansion of "coal and steel," which serves for the production of more "coal and steel." The output of "coal and steel" is as justified as that of consumer goods if it earns profits. Kalecki argued that consumption is the ultimate aim and proof of a "harmonious" but not of an "antagonistic" system. Kalecki maintained that it is this part of Tugan-Baranovsky's argument that is his lasting contribution to the analysis of the functioning of a capitalist economy in its various phases of development.

Kalecki observed that the theories of Tugan-Baranovsky and Rosa Luxemburg find something like a point of intersection in postwar capitalism (with particular reference to the U.S.A.), where a decisive function is performed by the "armaments market"—a market created by the government for the production of means of destruction. (Kalecki 1967o.)

Kalecki on Keynes and Their Analytical Differences

As we have seen, Kalecki and Keynes came from widely disparate backgrounds and descended from different family trees in economics. The first similarity between them was that they were both deeply troubled by the misery and plight of the Great Depression. Times of great stress have a way of influencing and precipitating theoretical solutions to urgent problems. Of course, the second similarity is that they both arrived independently at basically similar solutions. Yet within this affinity there were many and multifarious differences. For one, Keynes was really concerned with the 1920s as well as with the 1930s, hence with stagnation and depression.

Perhaps one of the most interesting and fruitful sources of outlining the common features and differences between Keynes and Kalecki is the little-known Kalecki 1936 review of the *General Theory*. A note of warning: it is a short piece in a Polish periodical, addressed to an audience for whom these solutions were novel. This summary touches only the highlights of the review and omits the exposition of new economics.[18] I have followed very closely Kalecki's text. In order to share with the reader Kalecki's personal opinion of the *General Theory,* I have not interrupted the text by commentary. Interpretation of some of the points raised will follow.

Kalecki's Review of Keynes's General Theory

"Keynes' latest book, the *General Theory of Employment, Interest and Money,* which constitutes undoubtedly a turning point in the history of economics," can be generally subdivided into two essential parts: (Kalecki 1936c, pp. 18-26.) (1) determination of short-run equilibrium, restricted by given productive capacity and a given level of investment (per unit of time); and (2) determination of the size of investment.

It seems that the first question was solved quite satisfactorily in Keynes's theory, even though a certain lack of explicitness and rigor of exposition might arouse doubts. In this article, Kalecki attempted to present his own interpretation of this part of Keynes's theory, arriving at his essential conclusions through a somewhat different road.

The question is entirely different concerning the second essential problem, namely, the analysis of factors determining the level of investment. Here it is not the exposition, but the analytical construct that suffers from serious shortcomings, so that the question remains, at least partly, unsolved.

Before embarking on the exposition of Keynes's argument, Kalecki made some observations regarding Keynes's analytical apparatus. Kalecki introduced important modifications in the presentation of the argument. His exposition of the determination of short-term equilibrium is of interest (including the introduction of the theory of imperfect competition into the argument and the restatement of short-term equilibrium), but it is the second part of the review that is of primary importance here.

Kalecki noted that, throughout his work, Keynes dealt with a closed system, disregarding, therefore, the influence of foreign trade. Among the important assumptions that Kalecki made in his own exposition is that workers do not save (nor do they live above their means). Kalecki believed that taking workers' saving into consideration obscured certain characteristic features of the capitalist economy in general and, in particular, rendered Keynes's theory less incisive.

Kalecki noted that Keynes employed so-called wage units, i.e., wages per man-hour of labor as his *numeraire,* with the simplifying assumption that wages for all types of labor remain in constant ratio to each other. Kalecki observed that such a manner of measuring the value of goods has a more profound significance since Keynes argued that the wage movement elicits a proportionate price movement. By his choice of units of measurement and by expressing everything in wage units, Keynes eliminated one of the most important factors in the overall price movement.

The basic issue in Keynes's theory is his assumption of a reserve of unemployed. If a fall in nominal wages, provoked by unemployment, results in a proportionate fall in prices, there is no tendency to absorb unemployment.

Kalecki concluded that, in Keynes's theory, investment is of decisive importance for short-run equilibrium, therefore, for the size of employment and national income per unit of time. It is the size of investment that determines how much manpower will be absorbed by the existing productive apparatus.[19] Therefore, the answer to why we have high or low employment and production must be looked for in factors that decide about the size of investment. It is to this analysis that Keynes devoted the second part of his theory.

According to Kalecki, at this point it should be emphasized that it is not saving that decides about investment, but on the contrary, investment creates the saving. There is always, with any level interest rate, equilibrium between demand for and supply of capital since investment generates its equivalent in saving.[20] Therefore, the rate of interest cannot be determined by the demand and supply of capital. According to Keynes this rate is determined by other factors, namely, the supply and demand for money. If there is a certain quantity of money in circulation and national income increases, demand for money would rise and the rate of interest would rise to such an extent that it would force use of the same quantity of money despite increased turnover. This is at least one aspect of Keynes's monetary theory in a nutshell.

So far it has been assumed that a wage unit is a constant magnitude. What changes will occur in the short-run equilibrium situation described above as a result of, for example, a fall in this unit owing to a reduction of nominal wages? Briefly, assuming that the size of investment expressed in wage units will not be subject to change, therefore nothing will change in the overall short-run equilibrium. Employment and production will remain unchanged, and only prices will fall proportionately to the wage unit.

However, is it possible that investment, expressed in wage units, will not be subject to change if, for example, nominal wages fall? Keynes asserted that this is the case, but his arguments are not overly convincing. The most important counterargument that can be advanced is that a reduction in wages increases profitability and could induce an increase in the size of investment. However, Keynes underestimated the influence of *current* profitability on investments and, therefore, did not at all consider this most essential question. But, despite these shortcomings, Keynes's argument that the size of nominal wages does not influence, at least directly, short-run equilibrium seems correct.

To show its probability it is sufficient to assume that, in their investment activity, the entrepreneurs do not *immediately* act when profitability increases as a result of a fall in wages. For if they do not immediately increase investment, short-run equilibrium will remain unchanged for the time being, and prices will fall proportionately to wages. Hence the improvement of profitability will prove illusory and the basis for increasing investment will disappear—if after lowering wages the businessmen do not increase investments immediately, they will not do so later either. Thus the movement of nominal wages would be really a factor that does not influence short-run equilibrium.[21]

A basic concept of the Keynesian theory of investment is the marginal efficiency of a particular type of capital. Keynes defined it as being equal to the rate of discount which would make present value of the series of annuities given by the returns (the difference between receipts and appropriately defined expenditures) expected from the project throughout its lifetime. Obviously, the expected rate of profit of a unit of capital goods will be higher, the higher the prospective yield (the value obtained by capitalizing the series of expected annual yields) and the lower the price (cost) of the capital goods. In Keynes's system the size of investment is determined by the equality between the expected rate of profit and the interest rate. If, at a given point in time, the expected rate of profit is greater than the rate of interest, there is inducement to invest and the rate of investment activity will expand. But as a result of increased demand for investment goods, their prices will rise and the expected rate of profit will decline. Finally, investment will be pushed to a level where the prices of investment goods equate the expected rate of profit with the current rate of interest and there is no longer any investment project of which the marginal efficiency of capital (MEC) exceeds the current rate of interest.

The MEC concept has two serious shortcomings: First it says nothing about the investment *decisions* of the entrepreneur who calculates in *existing* market prices of investment goods in the state of "disequilibrium." It only indicates that, if the expected rate of profit, calculated on the basis of that price level, will not equal the rate of interest, a change of the level of investment will take place, transforming the existing situation into one where the expected rate of profit *equals* the rate of interest. Using the terminology of Swedish economists, one could say that Keynes's theory determines only the *ex post* level of investment and says nothing of *ex ante* investment.

Furthermore, let us assume that initially the expected rate of profit was higher than the rate of interest, and that an increase of investment has taken place which has increased the prices of investment goods so that the expected rate of profit, computed at these new prices, and the *initially* anticipated revenue is equal to the interest rate. It should be noted that the increase of investment not only raises the prices of investment goods, but that, according to Keynes, it is followed by a general rise in activity, increasing prices and production in all branches. Since, as Keynes remarked, the current situation is strongly overweighed in forming expectations about the future, the expectations will become more optimistic and again a difference between MEC and the rate of interest will appear. Thus equilibrium is not reached and the increase of investment continues (here occurs the Wicksellian cumulative effect).

Keynes's concept—which tells us how large investment will be when a given "disequilibrium" is transformed into "equilibrium"—also meets here with serious difficulties. It is quite apparent that the increase of investment is not at all a process that leads the system into "equilibrium."

It is difficult to accept Keynes's solution of the investment problem as satisfactory. The cause of this lack of success is the essentially static approach to the problem which by its very nature is dynamic. Keynes accepted the state of expectations of returns as datum and deduced therefrom a certain given level of investment, neglecting the influence that, in turn, the investments will have on expectations. Here is a clue for reaching a realistic theory of investment. Its starting point should be the solution of the problem of *ex ante* investment decisions. Let us assume that, at a certain point in time, we have a given state of expectations of future income; determined prices of investment goods; and, finally, a given rate of interest. How large then would be the intended investment of businessmen for a given period? Let us assume that this problem has been solved (which appears to be impossible without introducing some special assumptions about businessmen's psychology, or assumptions about the imperfections of the money market). A further development of the investment theory would be as follows: Investment decisions, corresponding to the initial state, would not generally be equal to the existing level of investment. Therefore, in the following period the size of investment would generally be different and, with it, the short-run equilibrium position would change. Thus we have to deal with a different state of expectations from that in the initial period, different prices of investment goods, and a different rate of interest, from which a new level of investment decisions would result.

Notwithstanding the criticism of Keynes's theory on the grounds that it neglects the dynamic aspects, the first part of Keynes's theory retains its intrinsic value. In the dynamic process investments are continually changing, but to each level of investment there will correspond a level of employment and production, determined according to the first part of Keynes's theory. Keynes did not explain precisely the causes that influence the changes of investment, but he has analyzed exhaustively the close relationship between these changes and the general movement of employment, production, and income. (Kalecki 1936c, pp. 18-26.)

Some Aspects of the Investment Problem

Before summarizing some of the differences in the analytical apparatus and wider implications of Kalecki's and Keynes's versions of the theory, it needs to be emphasized here for the sake of continuity that the former version is considerably superior to the latter in the treatment of the intricacies of the investment process and its effect on the dynamics of economic activity as a whole. The subject is clearly complex and will be discussed at greater length in the following chapters. Here very limited coverage will be accorded and only *some aspects* stressing the contrasting features will be touched upon.

In Keynes's treatment the inducement-to-invest function depends on the relation between the expected rate of profit on newly produced capital goods (which he called MEC)—which probably means marginal efficiency of investment[22]—identified as identical with Irving Fisher's "rate of return over cost"; (Keynes 1936, p. 140) and the cost of securing funds ("the complex of rates of interest on loans of various maturities," but to simplify the argument he abstracted from complexes of rates of interest). Thus the inducement-to-invest function depends partly on the MEC and partly on the rate of interest. (Keynes 1936, pp. 135-254.)

Keynes argued that the actual rate of current investment will be pushed to the point on the investment-demand schedule where the marginal efficiency of capital in general (to recall, defined in terms of the *expectation of prospective* yields of investment, allowing for risk and the *current* supply price of the capital asset) is equal to the market rate of interest that must be paid to secure financing. As there exists at any time a variety of investment projects which can be arranged in descending order of their expected rate of return over cost (excluding interest, but allowing for risk), the actual rate of investment will be pushed at any time to the point where the spread between the prospective yield and rate of interest is reduced to naught. *Ceteris paribus,* a fall in the rate of interest relative to the given MEC will raise the rate of investment. The MEC for any given type of capital asset during any period of time will fall as the investment in it is increased (movement along the MEC curve), "partly because the prospective yield will fall as the supply of that type of capital is increased, and partly because, as a rule, pressure on the facilities for producing that type of capital will cause its supply price to increase." Keynes believed that the second factor is usually of greater significance in producing equilibrium in the short run. However, the first factor becomes more important as the period is extended. A schedule can be constructed for each type of capital "showing by how much investment in it will have to increase within the period, in order that its marginal efficiency should fall to any given figure." By aggregating these schedules for the different types of investment "so as to provide a schedule relating the rate of aggregate investment to the corresponding marginal efficiency of capital in general which that rate of investment will establish. We shall call this the investment-demand schedule; or, alternatively, the schedule of the marginal efficiency of capital." (Keynes 1936, p. 136.)

Kalecki asked the fitting question: If there are investment opportunities offering a positive prospective rate of return in excess of the cost of financing, why would not each entrepreneur undertake an indefinitely large volume of investment and exploit the opportunities of reaping extra profits? He differed from Keynes in the reply. (Cf. Joan Robinson 1964, p. 338.) Kalecki disputed Keynes's contention on the reasons why the rate of return on new investment became depressed (downward movement on the MEC curve as the MEC is pushed lower and lower by the rising short-run costs of continued investment) and thus further investment ceases when MEC is pushed down to the prevailing rate of interest. Subsequently, Kalecki was explicit on this subject in another context: "Keynes' idea is that investment is pushed up to the point where prices of investment goods equate the marginal efficiency of capital with the rate of interest (allowing for risk). As the marginal efficiency of capital depends considerably on the current level of income because this affects to a great extent the expectation of future yields, the higher the level of current income the higher the level of investment decisions. The most important objection against this theory is that it presupposes a rising supply curve in production of investment goods which is unrealistic, at least for a considerable range of output." (Kalecki 1949b, p. 61.)

But even if investment costs do rise sufficiently, the increase occurs as a consequence of investment plans actually carried out, i.e., *ex ante* investment converted into *ex post.* The propensity to invest (MEC) relates to the planned (intended) investment, and the MEC is defined in terms of the *expectation* of yields and the *current* supply price of the capital asset. (Keynes 1936, p. 136.) Kalecki provided an answer.[23] Here Kalecki's basic distinction between investment decisions (orders) and realization (deliveries of actual capital goods), as well as his other contributions to the analysis of the investment process, is pathbreaking, as outlined in subsequent chapters.

Moreover, Kalecki brought into the argument the fact that there are distinct limits to the financing of investment at a given rate of interest; i.e., the problem of availability of finance. The outside finance that a firm can secure is largely determined by the amount of capital owned by the firm. Kalecki viewed the limitation of the size of the firm by the availability of entrepreneurial capital as going to the very heart of the capitalist system, which cannot be ignored in the theory of investment decisions. One of the important determinants of such decisions is the accumulation of firms' capital out of current profits (generated by investment in the past). Profit influences the investment-demand function not only by providing a motive to do so, but also by providing the means to be able to perform such an act.

Thus, with a given expected rate of return, greater availability of credit (improved terms of borrowing) may raise the rate of investment decisions. If it does and the new investment orders are placed, during the gestation period extra purchasing power is generated and propagated both owing to the primary effect of investment outlays and the multiplier effect.

Business improves and actual profits rise. This colors the expectations about the future rate of profit and leads to a rise in investment plans and an expansion of investment activity, with its income-generating favorable effects on the economic situation. But there are bounds to the process which cannot go on ad infinitum. A reversal is bound to set in, unless it is averted by definite measures. For, to recall, investment, considered as an income-generating expenditure, is a source of expansion, and its increase improves the economic situation and stimulates a further increase in investment. But, on the other hand, the productive property of investment contributes to the slackening of expansion, brings it to an end, and finally to a slump. As investment decisions are embodied in capital goods, they add to the stock of productive capital and tend to discourage further investment when current profit per unit of capital declines. And investment plans are largely forged by present profit experience. While leaving for subsequent discussion Kalecki's theorizing about the mechanism of the business cycle and the question of investment decisions versus realization, we need only note here that, at any rate, decisions to invest cannot be satisfactorily treated as if they were independent of the actual volume of investment and the stock of capital.

It will be recalled that in Keynes's model the amount of current investment depends on the inducement to invest, which, in turn, depends on the relation between the schedule of the MEC and the ruling rate of interest. The schedule of MEC governs the terms on which loanable funds are demanded for the purpose of new investment, whereas the rate of interest governs the terms on which funds are currently supplied. Thus theory is required for the determinants of the rate of interest.

Keynes considered the analysis of the propensity to consume, the definition of MEC, and the theory of the rate of interest as the three main gaps he had to fill in the orthodox theory. He attacked the classical theory of interest as being indeterminable, and even the most sympathetic interpreters suggested that the same criticism applied to Keynes's theory of interest in its simpler form. (Cf. Hansen 1953, pp. 140 ff.) The place of interest rates in the economic process, and defense and criticism of Keynes have been the subject of controversy. The novelty and relation to other theories of interest and the very role of the liquidity preference theory itself in Keynes's system, as well as its peculiar features, have been subject to searching scrutiny.[24] For instance, Shackle argues that the liquidity theory itself, though intimately necessary to the *General Theory*, can be considered in isolation and stands as Keynes's most inalienable piece of original economic thought. (Shackle 1967, p. 145.)

Following in Keynes's footsteps many authors have treated the schedule as a pillar of Keynes's system (in addition to the MEC and consumption function). It should be noted that Klein argued that the liquidity preference is more incidental than central to the core of Keynes's theoretical argument—it is not an essential element of the modern Keynesian system of income determination. (Klein 1966, pp. 42-43 and *passim*.) However, it is not our purpose here to survey the controversy but merely to point to the controversial nature of the role of liquidity preference in Keynes's system.

It is remarkable that, in his original formulation, Kalecki did not treat liquidity preference and the interest rate. But shortly after the publication of his original model, Kalecki introduced a theory of interest, suggesting that the velocity of circulation of cash balances in fact closely depends on the short-term rate of interest.[25] In traditional economics the rate of interest was customarily considered to be the factor equilibrating demand and supply for capital. According to Kalecki this rate cannot be so determined because investment automatically generates an equal amount of saving, i.e., in Kalecki's conception, as we know, investment plans once executed automatically provide the savings required to finance them.

If investment "finances itself," irrespective of the level of the rate of interest, the rate of interest itself is determined by the interplay of other factors. Kalecki proposed that the short-term rate of interest is determined by the value of transactions and the supply of money by the banking system. In turn, the long-term rate is determined by anticipations of the short-term rate based on experience and on estimates of the risk involved in the possible capital loss of holding long-term assets. Velocity of circulation is not a constant, but depends on the movements of the interest rate. A short-term rate of interest is closely connected with the marginal convenience of holding cash. With a given turnover of cash balances, the smaller the volume of cash balances possessed, the greater the convenience derived from holding the marginal unit of cash for transaction purposes. But after the volume of cash holdings drops below a certain level, its further reduction involves a very strongly rising marginal inconvenience. If, however, cash is abundant with a given turnover, the marginal convenience declines to zero and remains at this level if the supply of cash increases further.

Thus, subject to qualification, the marginal convenience of holding cash is an increasing function of the velocity of circulation. If the short-term rate of interest exceeds this marginal convenience, the opportunity cost provides stimuli for lending extra cash; if the interest rate is lower, it becomes beneficial to withdraw from short-term assets and get cash. Thus equilibrium is reached when the short-term rate of interest equals the marginal convenience of holding cash. This theory set forth by Kalecki "is an alternative way of looking at the Keynesian theory of liquidity preference. Both theories are alike in assuming that velocity is not a constant and is affected by interest-rate movements."[26]

One more point has to be noted in this context: While Keynes's contribution to the analysis of the propensity to invest is controversial, it is ungenerous to maintain that he merely adopted the Fisher-Wicksell concept, for he crystallized the distinction and relation between the rate of profit and the rate of interest. With great force he illuminated the role of expectations and noted that the schedule of MEC "is of fundamental importance because it is mainly through this factor (much more than through the rate of interest) that the expectation of the future influences the present." (Keynes 1936, p. 145.) The accent is on an uncertain future in an irrational world, even though the dynamic considerations do not enter into an explicit statement of the major structure of his analytical model.

But here again the basic restrictions of Keynes's ingenious construct in the exposition of the MEC cannot be overlooked: "Keynes did not attempt to supply a theory of the rate of profit in the long run. His argument was concerned purely with a short-period situation." (Joan Robinson 1971a, p. 30.) The actual rate of return on the already existing stock of capital has no meaning in the short period considered by Keynes's "discussion of 'the state of long-term expectations' which is devoted to the Stock Exchange rather than to the accumulation of means of production. Where he allowed his mind to play upon long-term problems, his conceptions are still more obscure." (Joan Robinson 1971a, p. 32.)

Points of Difference

1. Kalecki's short-period theory is more overtly "dynamic" (short-period dynamics in the trade-cycle-theory sense) than Keynes's. Essentially, Keynes's *General Theory* not only dealt with a static model, but his argument was concerned explicitly with the fundamentally short-run situation (Marshallian short period),[27] and thus purely short-term determinants in changes in output and employment. Kalecki's model was broader as he tackled the problem in the long run. But this endeavor was not successfully completed. He was never really satisfied with his long-period analysis and kept searching for novel solutions.

2. Joan Robinson wrote in a review of Harrod's well-known book *Towards a Dynamic Economics:* "No one will disagree with Mr. Harrod that modern economic theory lacks, and badly needs, a sys-

tem of analysis dealing with a dynamic society. Keynes' *General Theory of Employment* broke through the husk of static analysis, but, apart from some *obiter dicta,* scarcely developed any theory of long-run development. Mr. Kalecki's pioneering work has been very little followed up (Mr. Harrod makes no reference to him); many others have shot at a venture into the mists, but we have no systematic body of long-run dynamic theory to supplement the short-period analysis of the General Theory and to swallow up, as a special case, the long-run static theory in which the present generation of academic economists was educated."[28]

Indeed, one of the key and often neglected determinants of investment decisions is the stock of capital. "Keynes' own treatment of the capital stock was exceedingly superficial."[29]

Kalecki's investment function as initially formulated "is one that is still in use [in econometric research] and not refuted by data available today. It is also very popular to include the stock of capital in the investment function." (Klein 1964, p. 190.) Kalecki's ideas of investment are highly original and truly seminal. For instance, the investment function, as propounded in Kalecki's early model, "is a close foreshadowing of many modern developments in econometrics." (Klein 1964, p. 190.)

3. "The analysis of the Propensity to Consume, the definition of the Marginal Efficiency of Capital and the theory of the Rate of Interest are the three main gaps in our existing knowledge which it will be necessary to fill. When this has been accomplished, we shall find that the Theory of Prices falls into its proper place as a matter which is subsidiary to our general theory." (Keynes 1936, pp. 31-32.) Keynes seems to have had little genuine interest in the problem of value and distribution, whereas Kalecki integrated price theory with distribution theory and the theory of output and employment as a whole. Kalecki's version of the theory places the main stress on the distribution of national product between wages and profit and thus on the determinants of national income and its distribution (factors determining the distribution of income).

Keynes accepted the traditional (neoclassical, perfect competition) theory of value and (neoclassical, marginal productivity) distribution, in contrast to Kalecki, who strongly believed that only by dropping the untenable assumption of perfect competition and penetrating the real world of imperfect competition and oligopoly could one derive any reasonable conclusions about economic behavior. For Kalecki the perfect competition tenet constitutes "a most unrealistic assumption not only for the present phase of capitalism but even for the so called competitive capitalist economy of past centuries: surely the competition was always in general very imperfect. Perfect competition when its actual status of a handy model is forgotten becomes a dangerous myth." (Kalecki 1971a, p. 3.) What Professor Shackle called "the Sraffian Manifesto of 1926, demanding the revision of value theory," (Shackle 1967, p. 12) and the struggle of Joan Robinson and others to dispense with perfect competition (essentially in the microtheory sphere) made little imprint on Keynes's approach. By contrast, Kalecki builds his macrodynamic model on the base of a micromodel, incorporating forces of market imperfection. In other words, Kalecki simultaneously provides a macro and micromodel, whereas Keynes stays essentially on a macroscale. Keynes concentrates his attack on the macroeconomic failure of the system, but essentially he does not challenge the framework of the established corps of value and distribution theory. Kalecki's version avoids the pitfalls of dichotomy and fragmentation of economic theory into micro and macro compartments. By integrating micro and macro, Kalecki's model provides a critical starting point for understanding the simultaneous occurrence of unemployment and inflation phenomena. Thus, Kalecki's model describes a wider range of economic phenomena and describes these phenomena more realistically.

As we shall see in a subsequent chapter, Kalecki provided an ingenious explanation of how prices are determined. He offered a theory of distribution outside of the mainstream of neoclassical economics and showed that distributional factors, such as semimonopolistic and monopolistic forces (nicknamed the "degree of monopoly"), are the key for dividing the output between wage- and profit-earners in short-period conditions. Thus they are essentially pertinent to the question of effective demand and fluctuations in aggregate output and utilization of resources.

One point needs emphasis here. Kalecki showed that, under conditions of imperfect competition, a decline in real wages (prices are rigid and are reduced to a lesser extent than nominal wages) is associated with a fall in employment.[30]

The following point made by Joan Robinson cannot be overstressed: "The analysis of imperfect competition was being developed side by side with the *General Theory* but they were not brought to bear on each other. Already in 1935 Kalecki had seen the connection when he showed that, if prices are sticky, a cut in money-wage rates actually reduces employment. This theme is further elaborated in the last essay in this volume, which points the way to an important element in the extension of the analysis into long-run problems that is going on today."[31]

4. Keynes restricted the argument in *General Theory* to a closed system.[32] To have general validity the system must be open with respect to international trade and finance. (Cf. Harris, ed. 1947, pt. 5; Meade 1951; Joan Robinson 1951, pt. 4.) Already in 1929, Kalecki analyzed the balance of payments as a promoter of prosperity. He took into account the rate of export surplus as a promoter of prosperity and the balance-of-payments difficulties that tend to accompany an upswing as a factor limiting expansion. This was attested to by Joan Robinson, who, herself, made important contributions to the extension of Keynes's model: "Keynes' *General Theory* was worked out in terms of a closed system. It was left to me to sketch its extension into the theory of foreign trade in slump conditions. Here also Kalecki's work claims priority." (Joan Robinson 1966c, p. xi.)

Expansionary policy in an open system is impeded by its likely adverse repercussions on the balance of payments. An upswing is usually followed by a rising demand for goods which were not produced in that country at all, or not in sufficient quantities. A contributing factor is the rise in domestic prices (relative to those of trading partners) in the course of the upswing. There is, however, no mechanism ensuring that growth of production will be accompanied by appropriate growth of export.[33] In fact, certain forces are in operation blocking correction of the balance-of-payments disequilibrium.

When expansion has gained momentum, balance-of-payments trouble may prevent continuation of the upswing, and restraint of the pressures of demand may be required prior to reaching a full employment level on account of balance of payments, integrity of exchange value, and currency considerations. The implication is that the upswing stimulated by deficit spending has a limit.

Kalecki argued that the widespread theory about the direct link between the budget deficit and the deterioration in the foreign-trade-exchange position is unfounded. But there is an indirect connection. For if the budget deficit is covered by the creation of spending power, it engenders an increase in output and, by this route, contributes to a rise in imports and to the deterioration in the foreign exchange position. But if the budget were financed by credits without any creation of spending power (e.g., at the expense of credits to private business), then no increase in output would follow and thus foreign exchange would not deteriorate. The point is that the budget deficit has a negative effect on foreign exchange only when it has a positive effect on output. However, there is an important qualification to this rule. If the belief is widely held that there is a direct link between the budget deficit and the foreign exchange situation, the appearance or rise of the budget deficit encourages the hoarding of gold and foreign exchange. This may upset the foreign exchange position of the currency even to a much greater extent than the effect of the budget deficit engendering expansion of output.

Kalecki discussed the relative efficiency of some of the alternative measures of coping with the balance-of-payments problem thus arising. He maintained that the tensions in the balance of payments which accompany expansion, produced by the deficit from the start, in the case of an expansion brought about by securing a surplus in foreign trade, arise "only at the point when investment has reached a level several times greater than this surplus, i.e. at an advanced stage of the boom." But prior to this a marked improvement in economic performance that does not entail balance-of-payments perturbations will lead to an influx of foreign capital. If this inflow persists there may be no balance-of-payments tensions and prosperity advances as well. There are advantages in an upswing stimulated by measures to secure a surplus in foreign trade. "It is worth mentioning that the 'natural' upswing based on the automatic increase in investment activity does not enjoy these advantages, and if there is no influx of foreign capital, it will be confronted with the same balance-of-payments difficulties as the upswing based on . . . [budget deficit]." (Kalecki 1966h, pp. 24-25.)

5. One of the great achievements of the Keynesian Revolution was a refutation of the supposition that "any individual act of abstaining from consumption necessarily leads to, and amounts to the same thing as, causing the labour and commodities thus released from supplying consumption to be invested in the production of capital wealth." (Keynes 1936, p. 19.)

Both Kalecki and Keynes showed that there is no automatic mechanism for ensuring the full employment level by an endogenous, effective economic process. In essence, both men showed vividly that a part of income that is not spent does not exist, unless there is private investment or government expenditures. To put it in familiar terms, if at the level of income generated, desired saving exceeds desired investment, deficiency of effective demand plagues the system, contraction of output and employment will follow, and the economy will settle at the level of income short of full employment. The government's task is to transform "excess savings" into spending (or to transform saving into investment). The saving and investment problem is an essential element in both Keynes's and Kalecki's approaches.

Keynes's approach to the process of determination of national income (i.e., rejection of the orthodox saving-investment theory of interest in which savings flow automatically into investment irrespective of the level of income and, in its place, substitution of a saving-investment theory of determination of the level of output, where income is the cardinal variable in the saving-investment process and the interest rate is of major importance in the liquidity preference function) has by now permeated economics textbooks and become commonplace.[34]

But whatever the relative merits of Kalecki's and Keynes's approaches, they should not be evaluated independently of the confusion about the equality of saving and investment when the "Keynesian Gospel" was spreading. (Cf. Samuelson 1972, pp. 650-61; Hansen 1953, ch. 2; Harris, ed. 1947, pt. 9; Lerner 1964, pp. 203-34; Joan Robinson 1969b.)

6. In some respects, Kalecki's version of the theory was narrower and more compact, but no less precise analysis of the *modus operandi* of the aggregate output and its fluctuation theory. Notably, Kalecki did not approach the theory of effective demand by the theory of the multiplier, "which makes his version in a way less rich than Keynes', though no less forceful. On the other hand, he went straight to a theory of the trade cycle, on which Keynes was very weak." Kalecki's discerning treatment of "the capital-stock adjustment mechanism is now recognized as the basis for all modern trade cycle models."[35]

The theory of the multiplier was a major contribution to economics by a brilliant and original student of Keynes, now Professor Lord Kahn. By formulating the multiplier theory, Kahn supplied "the missing link between what Keynes was saying in policy and what he wanted to say in theory." (Klein 1966, pp. 36, 103.) One of the chief protagonists of the Keynesian Revolution was Kahn, "whose share in the historic achievement cannot have fallen very far short of co-authorship." (Schumpeter 1954, p. 1172. Cf. Harrod 1951, ch. 11; Shackle 1967, chs. 10-12.) In addition, Keynes was ably assisted by an outstanding group of students and young colleagues who later came into prominence on their own as some of the ablest economists of our time.

Keynes made ingenious use of Kahn's discovery and integrated the multiplier into the theory of aggregate output determination. Kalecki's works of the early 1930s indicated that he had a good grasp of the multiplier. But he never formalized it.

7. Even this limited coverage would be remiss if it did not underline Keynes's most notable contribution in forging tools of analysis—his celebrated concept of propensity to consume, establishing functional relations between income and consumption. "The psychology of the community is such that when aggregate real income is increased aggregate consumption is increased, but not by so much as income." (Keynes 1936, p. 27.) This concept was praised by Hansen as the greatest invention in analytical economics, comparable to the Cournot-Marshall invention of the demand curve. However, Schumpeter vehemently argued against dignifying "pseudo-psychology" with the title "psychological law." (Schumpeter 1954, pp. 1059-60.) On this point, Kalecki's treatment is much superior because his analysis is based on class distribution, rather than on psychological factors.

As previously noted, Kalecki assumed that workers spend what they earn and that capitalists are the savers. The implied assumption of unit marginal propensity to consume for wage-earners is markedly at variance with facts (but the assumption that marginal propensity to consume of profit-earners is smaller than that of wage-earners holds). In this way, Kalecki simplified his model extremely, but not without benefits for attacking the problem. At any rate, Kalecki's theoretical construct can be easily adopted to account for the fact that wage-earners make some contribution to savings. (Klein 1964, p. 190.)

In Kalecki's analysis of the mechanism of income determination (discussed in the next chapters), national income is pushed up to a point at which the share of profits as determined by distribution factors, such as the degree of monopoly, corresponds to the level of investment. The function of distribution factors is to determine income on the basis of profits which, in turn, are governed by investment plus consumption out of profits. Variations in income distribution take place through a change in the national output (income) and not through the change in the amount of profit. Since the share of profits in a short period is governed by the degree of monopoly, if the latter rises, so does the relative share of profits in national income. However, the amount of profits will remain unaltered for it continues to be determined by investment—a function of past investment decisions—but wages and output will decline. The level of national output will fall to the point at which the higher share of profits renders the same absolute amount of profits.

Kalecki-Keynes and Econometrics

The Keynesian analysis provided a framework for and stimulated quantitative economic research. (Cf. Kuznets 1972, p. 31; Burns 1946; Heller 1966.) Understandably, this extraordinary and flourishing invasion met with mixed reception. The "literary economists" often resisted the infusion of a foreign body into the professional ranks. But, clearly, both the causes and consequences of "mathematization of economics" go much deeper. Among the great problems of our times are those of explaining the course of national production and employment and of indicating ways of influencing them. Indeed, we badly need solutions for "problems of society as a whole; problems not solved by traditional theory, since it started from hypotheses eliminating them beforehand. This is why a man like Keynes tackled them; this is also why various econometrists, moved by the same desire, came to apply macro-economic concepts." (Tinbergen 1947, p. 220.)

Both Kalecki and Keynes displayed a genius for identifying the most substantive economic problems requiring immediate solution and for perceiving the working of the economic process and distilling the essential theoretical content. Again they differed widely on the approach to and use of analytical tools in tackling the problems. In particular emphasis should be put here on both the common traits and the differences in attitude to and uses of mathematical formulations in forging their argument and to econometrics in testing and extending the theory. Keynes was very harsh, if not altogether hostile, in his attitude toward mathematical economics and econometrics. (Cf. Keynes 1963a, pp. 125-238; 1939a, pp. 558-68; Tinbergen 1940, pp. 141-54; Keynes 1940a, pp. 154-56.) It was often considered as one of his primary failings. For example, "Keynes failed to make the *General Theory* clear and . . . it was never fully understood until mathematically inclined economists formulated it in unambiguous, precise models." Keynes's review of Tinbergen's famous study for the League of Nations "was one of his sorriest professional performances. Many econometricians have remarked on Keynes's review with the comment that he simply did not understand the methods he was criticizing and failed to see at what Tinbergen was aiming, a type of comment Keynes frequently used to characterize his own critics."[36]

Although he expressed a more "moderate attitude" toward mathematical economics in the *General Theory,* Keynes felt that it was "a great fault of symbolic pseudo-mathematical methods of formalising a system of economic analysis, . . . that they expressly assume strict independence between the factors involved and lose all their cogency and authority if this hypothesis is disallowed. . . . Too large a proportion of recent 'mathematical' economics are mere concoctions, as imprecise as the initial assumptions they rest on, which allow the author to lose sight of the complexities and interdependencies of the real world in a maze of pretentious and unhelpful symbols." (Keynes 1936, pp. 297-98.)

Keynes is deservedly famous for many predictions. There is undoubtedly an element of truth in his apprehension of the great invasion of quantitative economics. Joan Robinson recently expressed the view that Keynes would not have been impressed by the claimed evidence for the merit of quantitative economics and probably would not have changed his indictment. But this is only one aspect of the "second crisis" in economic theory which Professor Robinson has argued so vividly and provocatively. Clearly, there are "good" and "bad" mathematical economics and econometrics. Whether Gresham's type law of "good displacing the bad" applies here is another question. After all, econometrics is but a tool. Like all tools it can be used to advantage or disadvantage. It all depends on the intent of the user.

Those who participated in giving birth to (or propagating) "mathematization" of economics are increasingly concerned about the state of the discipline and its practitioners. "The achievements of economic theory in the last two decades are both impressive and in many ways beautiful. But it cannot be denied that there is something scandalous in the spectacle of so many people refining the analysis of economic states which they give no reason to suppose will ever, or have ever, come about. . . . It is an unsatisfactory and slightly dishonest state of affairs." (Hahn 1970, pp. 1-2.) Professor Wassily Leontief alarmed many of his colleagues by his Presidential Address to the American Economic Association:

> Much is being made of the widespread, nearly mandatory use by modern economic theorists of mathematics. . . . Uncritical enthusiasm for mathematical formulation tends to conceal the ephemeral substantive content of the argument behind the formidable front of algebraic signs. . . . By the time it comes to interpretation of the substantive *conclusions*, the assumptions on which the model has been based are easily forgotten. But it is precisely the empirical validity of these *assumptions* on which the usefulness of the entire exercise depends.
>
> What is really needed, in most cases, is a very difficult and seldom very neat assessment and verification of these assumptions in terms of observed facts. "If you do not like my set of assumptions, give me another and I will gladly make you another model; have your pick." . . .
>
> Continued preoccupation with imaginary, hypothetical, rather than with observable reality has gradually led to a distortion of the informal valuation scale used in our academic community to assess and to rank the scientific performance of its members. Empirical analysis, according to this scale, gets a lower rating than formal mathematical reasoning. (Leontief 1971, pp. 1-3.)

All this is very relevant and extremely disturbing. But the simple and unadorned fact is that this enlightened criticism does not apply (nor was it intended to) to the brand of mathematical economics practiced by Kalecki. In fact the aspiring young mathematical economists of our time would be well advised to model their research on Kalecki's example. Kalecki is here in good company.[37]

Keynes was not only apprehensive of mathematical economics and econometrics, but, as we know, he held that there is no clue in Marx to the economic riddle and was contemptuous of Marx's methodology. This might be a good place to touch briefly on Kalecki's views on the econometric model and historical materialism. Clearly our purpose here is not to comment on Marx's vision and his analysis,[38] nor to pass judgment on such a controversial subject as historical materialism (economic interpretation of history),[39] but to note that Kalecki held the view that econometrics and historical materialism are not irreconcilable.

True, the econometric model-building approach and the materialistic (economic) interpretation of history are two different approaches to the development of society: "The former is based on functional relations between the econometric variables in the period considered as well as between these variables and the same variables in the past periods. The relations are assumed to be given and not subject to change. In this way a definite dynamic process is established which, however, corresponds to the actual developments only in the case where the basic assumption of the invariability of functional relationships referred to above is fulfilled." (Kalecki 1964e, p. 233.)

On the other hand, historical materialism views society's process of development as one of productive forces and relations (the base), which in turn influence all other social phenomena (e.g., government, culture, science, and technology), with a feedback effect. Kalecki also viewed the Marxian reproduction schemes as "nothing else but simple econometric models. In fact in a special case where no changes in natural resources, productive relations and the superstructure affect the development of productive forces the system will follow the path determined by an econometric model because the condition of relationships between the economic variables not being subject to change is then fulfilled. In a more general case these functional relationships alter under the impact of events in three other spheres of the system and the economic development is then a much more complicated process than that presented by an econometric model as it reflects the evolution of the society in all the aspects." (Kalecki 1964e, p. 233.)

Kalecki proceeded with his provocative argument and examined in depth the problem of the relation between econometrics and historical materialism. He concluded that, "there emerges . . . a new way of presenting the evolution of society. The phocal [*sic*] point of it is in a sense the economic development whose course is determined by a 'generalised econometric model' which involves changing relationships between the economic variables present and past. . . . These changes result from the impact of the evolution in the spheres of natural resources, productive relations and the superstructure which is in turn profoundly affected by the course of economic development." (Kalecki 1964e, p. 238.)

Take the instance of the highly relevant phenomenon of certain basic issues coming gradually to a forefront, culminating in an explosion. Conflicts between modes of production and superstructure develop. The existing productive relations may obstruct the economic development (which may even result in stagnation or retrogression) and the superstructure (form and composition of government and so on) may even be incompatible with the so far achieved stage of production relations. Consequently, an explosion takes place, with both the underlying production relations and the superstructure undergoing a violent transformation. And although the explosive process is possible, it is by no means the only possible outcome. The situation may lead to a reform, and in such case, the transformations of productive relations and of the superstructure are substantially less essential and propagate over a longer period. Whether in the case of explosive processes or reforms, the process of economic development will be affected, but in different ways: "Sometimes the reform caused by poor performance of the system may even not change basically the productive relations or the form and composition of the government. It may consist merely of implementation of government policies which, however, have an important bearing upon the economic dynamics of the system. To quote an example of a recent period: The Great Depression of the thirties shook capitalism to its foundations. What resulted from it, however, was merely a technique of government antislump intervention which barely scratched the surface of the capitalist system but nevertheless affected significantly the pattern of the business cycle." (Kalecki 1964e, p. 238.)

To return to the crux of the argument: The contributions made by Keynes's *General Theory* from the standpoint of the econometrician were admirably explored by Jan Tinbergen. (Tinbergen 1947, pp. 219-31.) What is the significance of Kalecki's contribution from the standpoint of mathematical economics and econometrics? Here we have the benefit of evaluation by another leading econometrician, Lawrence R. Klein. It should be noted that, as a crude work for organizing thinking and illustrating basic ideas, Klein distinguished between a pedagogical model (an informative and succinct way of expressing a theory which has important teaching attributes, but obscures reality "intolerably") and a working model. (Cf. Klein 1966, ch. 8.) Klein's paper has to be consulted in order to appreciate fully its rich content. Here I can only quote excerpts:

> In macroeconomic model building there are two distinct branches of the subject. One deals with matters of principle and shows the logical mathematical structure of a self contained system that brings out the essence of economic dynamics, by focusing attention on very specific aspects of behavior. From very few main principles of behavior, systems that are not wholly realistic or practical are built to exhibit movement like that of the actual dynamic economy. These are *pedagogical* models that are intended to emphasize some main points of economic dynamics. This exercise belongs largely to *mathematical economics.*
>
> In the other branch of the subject much larger, more detailed, and more cumbersome models are prepared that are designed to be fitted to data of the economy and trace out actual movements of economic variables over time. These are part of econometrics. They are pieced together by combining several *a priori* hypotheses from the pedagogi-

> cal models of mathematical economics and adding equations to bring out the institutional nature of the economy being studied. . . .
>
> The econometric models that I have constructed as practical tools for analyzing or predicting the economies of the United States, Canada, United Kingdom, and Japan have been based on combinations from the theoretical models of Marx, Kalecki, Keynes, Lange, Hicks, Kaldor, Metzler, Goodwin and others. It is fitting at this time to reexamine the position of the Kalecki model in this hierarchy and its relevance to model building of the present day.
>
> The Marxian schemes of reproduction and accumulation and the Keynesian models of effective demand are the forerunners of the present theoretical model building. It is often not adequately appreciated how the Kalecki model, constructed in the Marxian spirit, actually preshadowed all the essential ingredients of the Keynesian system that have made the latter system so popular among the present generation of Western economists. It is usually thought that the recent rapid development of macroeconomic model building in the econometric branch of the subject is an outgrowth of the neo Keynesian development. Actually most models in existence today could be decomposed into ideas first found in the models of Kalecki, Kaldor, Metzler, and Goodwin. The latter three could have been developed as natural extensions of the Kalecki theory. The mathematical interpretations of Keynes by Lange and Hicks undoubtedly reinforced the development and certainly enhanced it, but the basic ingredients of the Keynesian development were already available in Kalecki's model. . . . While it should not be said that all the basic ingredients of modern econometric systems stemmed from Kalecki's model, it can be said that all the components of Kalecki's model are finding their way into strategic places in modern econometric models. His theories of the early 1930's are seen to be intellectual *tours de force* in the light of modern developments. (Klein 1964, pp. 188-89, 191.)

Kalecki emerges not only as the anticipator of modern theory of effective demand and its fluctuations, but his seminal and highly original work has special qualities that enrich and generalize Keynes's truly great *General Theory.* In their own way both men of genius contributed to this scientific discovery and historical achievement. They resembled each other not only in their devotion to the same problem. Both of these incisive minds had the gift of perceiving not only how a problem could be solved, but how the problem itself should be shaped, or formulated, so as to lead most directly to a solution which would be demonstrated to those who knew little of the technique of the subject. Kalecki especially had a genius for effective and powerful simplification.

Kalecki's original macrodynamic model has become, as Klein attested, a fountainhead of later developments in econometric research and generally has withstood the rigorous test of time. Whatever one's feelings or prejudices about mathematical economics and econometrics, it needs to be emphasized that Kalecki never produced models in order to produce more models, and, in turn, to produce more models. To him a model was always a vehicle with which to study economic reality and to solve substantive and urgent economic and social problems; to be put to effective use depending on the philosophical, social, and political outlook of the scholar.

Nothing said here is intended to underrate Keynes's genius, greatness, and incalculable contribution; it is intended merely to call attention to Kalecki's contribution and to this remarkable coincidence of science. We are dealing with intellectual giants and the manifestations of their greatness and failures. They clearly cannot be compared and graded like schoolboys. What matters is not only the creation of a new system of analysis and its influence on a body of economic analysis, but the impact of economic theory on policy and society. There seems to be undue optimism in the note on which Keynes completed his *magnum opus:*

> . . . the ideas of economists and political philosophers, both when they are right and when they are wrong, are more powerful than is commonly understood. Indeed the world is ruled by little else. Practical men, who believe themselves to be quite exempt from any intellectual influences, are usually the slaves of some defunct economist. Madmen in authority, who hear voices in the air, are distilling their frenzy from some academic scribbler of a few years back. I am sure that the power of vested interests is vastly exaggerated compared with the gradual encroachment of ideas. Not, indeed, immediately, but after a certain interval; for in the field of economic and political philosophy there are not many who are influenced by new theories after they are twenty-five or thirty years of age, so that the ideas which civil servants and politicians and even agitators apply to current events are not likely to be the newest. But, soon or late, it is ideas, not vested interests, which are dangerous for good or evil. (Keynes 1936, pp. 383-84.)

In final analysis here lies the strength and limitation of the Keynesian Revolution in longer perspective.

The protagonists of the Keynesian Revolution differed in the conclusions they derived about the applicability of their theoretical models. Kalecki's vision was much more pessimistic and, in retrospect, proved to be more realistic. Within a decade of his original essay he propounded the theory of the political business cycle—a contribution that may yet rank in its importance with his contribution to the Keynesian Revolution.

Both men built solid foundations for generalization of the General Theory and had an impact on the course of development of theory. What the final effect will be (joint ventures or in terms of separate versions if identifiable) only the future can tell. Kalecki and Keynes also differed in the emphasis they placed on how to reach and maintain full employment and in their attitudes to the interpretation of the Keynesian Revolution. Here again it is preferable not to make any sweeping statements but to wait for the verdict of the future. However, it appears to me that Kalecki was nearer the mark.

III

THE THEORY OF INCOME DISTRIBUTION

> The general discontent with the complacency of text-book economics found its main expression in Keynes' *General Theory*, and the theory of employment was, of course, far more important, both for analysis and for policy, than anything concerned with the theory of individual prices. Keynes himself was not much interested in price theory, but the two streams of thought were combined by Michal Kalecki. (Joan Robinson 1960, p. 241.)

•

KALECKI'S THEORY OF DISTRIBUTION of the national product between wages and profits derives genealogically from the Ricardian tradition.[1] His theory is not merely a deviation or departure from the neoclassical marginal productivity theory (or what Frank Hahn called the neoclassical production function approach to the theory of distribution, employing a model of perfect competition in permanent equilibrium). (Hahn 1972, ch. 1.) He simply never started from it. Kalecki proceeded from a different approach in building his analytical construct, and marginal productivity did not enter into his argument.[2] He did not simply relax the restrictive assumption of universal rule of perfect competition; the model of perfect competition is foreign to his method of attacking economic problems. He argued that only by dropping the untenable assumption of perfect competition and penetrating the real world of industrial and market structures (imperfect competition and oligopoly) could any plausible propositions about determinants of macrodistribution be advanced.[3] Kalecki's theory of distribution "is important both because his theory is important in its own right and because it focuses attention on an aspect of distribution theory which had hitherto been neglected because of the preoccupation of earlier writers with the production function and perfect competition."[4]

While his argument is derived from the precepts of imperfect competition, Kalecki's contribution seems to lie in integrating micro and macro theories; in building a macrodistribution theory on firmer foundations of a more plausible theory of the firm; in bringing the strength of the forces of market imperfection, or "degree of monopoly" (a term he later regretted), in touch not only with the mode of behavior and pricing policy of the firm and process of price formation in an industry, but in incorporating forces of market imperfection in his model of the economy as a whole; and in demonstrating that the intensity of the degree of monopoly is pertinent to the determination of distributive shares and thus closely tied in with the theory of effective demand and his conception about the typical state of underutilization of productive resources in a modern capitalist economy. "It was Michal Kalecki rather than I," wrote Joan Robinson, one of the inventors of the theory of imperfect competition, in the Preface to the second edition of her classic *The Economics of Imperfect Competition* "who brought imperfect competition into touch with the theory of employment." But clearly Kalecki was here influenced by the work of Joan Robinson and Abba P. Lerner. (Joan Robinson 1969a, viii. Cf. Lerner 1934, pp. 157-75.)

Originally, Kalecki undertook his investigation of the distribution of national income prompted by a desire to provide an explanatory hypothesis for the relative constancy of distributive shares in the long run—enunciated as Bowley's Law.[5] Subsequent scrutiny of economic statistics has shown that the law was at variance with facts. The record seems to indicate slight signs of upward wage-share movements, without, however, sufficient basis to predict the probable course of labor's share in the future. If the constancy is really illusory, some economists argue that there is much ado about nothing. They then argue that, since Bowley's Law is invalid, Kalecki's theory of income distribution flounders. (Cf. Pen 1971, *passim*; Bronfenbrenner 1971, pp. 407 ff.)

Whatever may be said about great constants in economics,[6] Kalecki's theory does not need to be propped up by the validity of Bowley's Law. Even if economic statistics would record approximate constancy of distributive shares in the long run, it would be a special case where the net effect of configuration of determinants produces such a result. But Kalecki did not claim overall stability of labor's share in modern capitalist economies. Indeed, if Bowley's Law were to be universally valid, Kalecki's theory could be criticized for not providing a hypothesis to explain why changes in one determinant (or combination of determinants) should always be nearly counterbalanced by changes in another (or others).

Essentially, there are two theories in Kalecki: (1) The short-run theory of distribution connected with the controversial notion of the "degree of monopoly," and (2) the theory that workers spend what they earn, and capitalists earn what they spend. From the latter proposition is derived the conception that the rate of profit on capital is governed by the rate of investment and the propensity of profit-earners to save. "Kaldor has called this the Keynesian theory of distribution, since it is adumbrated in the *Treatise,* but, like the *General Theory* itself, it has a separate source in Kalecki." (Joan Robinson 1964, p. 341.) The chapter that follows is concerned largely with point 2, and chapter 5 deals with the short- and long-run theory.

Distribution as the "Principal Problem"

In Ricardo's view the "principal problem" in political economy was the division of the national product among social classes.[7] In an often quoted passage from a letter of October 9, 1820, to his friend Thomas Malthus, Ricardo stressed the difference in their individual approaches to this problem. Malthus conceived political economy as an inquiry into the nature and causes of wealth (income), whereas Ricardo regarded it rather as an inquiry into the laws that govern the distribution of income among the classes that participate in its creation. "No law can be laid down respecting quantity, but a tolerably correct one can be laid down respecting proportions." For Ricardo "the former enquiry is vain and delusive and the latter only true object of science." (Ricardo VII, p. 278.)

Since Ricardo, there have been sporadic revivals in investigating the causes and consequences of partition of national product between wages and profits.[8] In the neoclassical school of thought, the problem of distribution is treated just as one aspect of the theory of determination of relative prices.[9] The earnings of any productive factor depend on the factor price and the quantity employed. "If we wish to build up a theory of distribution, we thus need a theory of factor prices and quantities. Such a theory is a special case of the theory of price." (Lipsey 1966, p. 407; cf. Stigler 1946; Ferguson 1969.) But clearly, the group of writers commonly compressed under the classification of "neoclassical" is a heterogeneous one, marked by a variety of approaches, which can be brought under a common umbrella only at the expense of great oversimplification.[10]

Most major exponents of marginal productivity theory disregarded Ricardo's "principal problem" (cf. Hunt and Schwartz, eds. 1972, pts. 1-3; Joan Robinson 1962a, chs. 2-3), or, at best, gave it only marginal attention. The Ricardian treatment of the macrodistribution problem was touched upon briefly by such neoclassical giants as Wicksell (who attempted to integrate the Austrian capital theory with the Walrasian general-equilibrium theory) and Bohm-Bawerk (cf. Davidson 1959, pp. 42 ff.; Kaldor 1960, pp. 219-20), and has been the subject now and then of ingenious, if inconclusive, abstract formulations largely to the effect that anything may happen. (Cf. Hutchison 1952, p. 424. Solow 1968a, 449-75; 1958, pp. 618-31.)

For Ricardo, value and relative prices were rather a facet of the distribution problem. Neoclassical economics shifted the inquiry from the laws governing the determination of the relative class shares in functional income distribution to the determination of relative prices—a primary concentration on the question of how products and factors of production get priced by the supply and demand mechanism in the market, where pricing takes place. Demand for factors of production is derived indirectly from the demand of the final user for the product (or in Walras's interpretation, though it is true that factors "are bought and sold in their special markets, nevertheless the prices of these services are determined in the market for products.").[11] To investigate the demand for factors of production (income distribution), the inquiry turns to the general pricing mechanism for commodities, to the technical laws governing production and to constraints imposed by nature, to the state of technology and factor endowments, to cost conditions (technical and economic efficiency), to the maximizing behavior of units of economic activity, and to markets. "We can understand the economic question of distribution primarily by focusing on the markets where factors of production get priced." (Samuelson 1970, p. 513; Fellner and Haley, eds. 1951; Johnson 1972b.) With fixed supplies of all means of production, whether a factor will be employed, and in what quantities, depends on its contribution to production and on the revenue gained from sales of marginal physical products obtained by employing additional units of the factor. In the absence of increasing returns to scale, every factor will be hired until the marginal benefit from its hire exceeds (or is equal to) the cost that the firm must incur to secure the marginal unit of the factor. Any variable factor in supply will earn a reward which, if competitive conditions are satisfied, must correspond to its contribution to production as measured by marginal products. Under competition, the marginal physical product can be sold by the price taker at the ruling market price, without reducing the price. With each economic agent maximizing his gain, the forces of unimpeded competition will bring about throughout the system an equality of factor prices and marginal products. Competition is to ensure that the entire aggregate product is distributed among the factors by each getting its remuneration equal to its exact marginal product.[12] When the marginal products of a factor in alternative uses are all equal to their market remuneration rate, resources are considered employed efficiently, and any reshuffle, *ceteris paribus,* would lead to a less efficient allocation of resources.

Under simplifying assumptions, the argument is extended to the system as a whole to show how the marginal productivity theory distributes the aggregate product among productive inputs.[13] The neoclassical macrodistribution theory has been based on two principal notions derived from the theory of pricing of factors of production (microdistribution): (Marchal and Ducros, eds. 1968, pp. 476-510; Bronfenbrenner 1971, ch. 16.) (1) the aggregate production function and (2) the elasticity of substitution or specific assumptions about the values of the elasticities of substitution.[14] As Bronfenbrenner pointed out in his survey of the characteristics of and objections to the Cobb-Douglas type function, "the Cobb-Douglas verification of marginal-productivity theory, or what we should today call their evidence for neo-classical macro-distribution theory, has seemed, since 1928 'too good to be true.' Objections have accordingly crowded thick and fast." (Marchal and Ducros, eds. 1968, p. 483.)

While Bronfenbrenner's account should be studied, it should be noted, *en passant,* that critics have emphasized, *inter alia,* that the marginal productivity theory was originally developed with reference to microeconomics. In the most fundamental sense it is a microeconomic theory that was adopted and extended to grapple with the macroeconomic problems by the means of the analytical tool of production function. Thus that a specific form of production function was chosen for the analysis was obviously a consideration of fundamental importance. As Robert Solow admitted, presentation of the marginal productivity theory "in macro-economic terms is an act of empirical desperation."[15]

The "Sraffian" critics argue that it is precisely the extension of the microeconomic conceptual framework to the sphere of macroeconomics that makes the neoclassical theory vulnerable; they focus attention on the necessary conditions for the validity of the neoclassical theory and what the fulfillment of these conditions entails. The dissenters argue that the neoclassical theory has been thoroughly exploded and maintain that failure to meet these conditions has disastrous consequences for the neoclassical theory.[16] A review of the discussion and controversy about the foundations of neoclassical economics and marginal productivity is on the fringe of this discussion, but we would be remiss not to mention it. Anyway, most of the storm came after Kalecki's original contribution. The neoclassical theorists were not answering Kalecki, but ignoring him.

However, a recent statement by Frank Hahn, who is not unsympathetic to the neoclassical mode of analysis, may be noted in this context. He contends that the neoclassical theory of distribution "has nothing simple to offer in answer to the question why is the share of wages, or profits, what it is?" The question arises when distribution of income among social classes is considered. Neoclassical theory, formulated in terms of inputs and outputs, does not take into account social class as an explanatory variable. "This lack of contact between the economic theory and sociological reality may well be the most damaging criticism of the neo-classical construction." (Hahn 1972, p. 2.)

Dissatisfaction with the solution of the distribution problem by the marginal productivity theory, or rejection of the whole approach, gave rise to many vocal dissenting views that adopted a mode of analysis that rejects or radically departs from a conventional theory or builds a theory on different premises.[17] Bronfenbrenner, who underrates Kalecki's contribution in this field, remarked that, since the unveiling of the Cobb-Douglas production function, the "initial analytical dissent"—against what Bronfenbrenner called the Good Old Macro-distribution Theory, alias the Conventional Wisdom—"is the monopoly theory of the distinguished Polish socialist economist Michal Kalecki. . . . This theory dominated British macro-distribution thinking for nearly a generation."[18]

The "good old theory" was unsatisfactory in the 1930s, and the critics argue that the contributions of the neoclassical persuasion that were inoculated afterwards have been shown "not to hold water." At any rate the neoclassical theory has nothing coherent to say when perfect competition is abandoned, or when there are increasing returns, or both. Kalecki did have something important to say. He offered a new starting point. In a sense it was the neoclassicists who dissented from Kalecki.

The Determinants of Macrodistribution

Microfoundations

Kalecki's argument is developed from micro to macro. One of the essential features of Kalecki's macrodistribution theory is his novel approach to the microeconomic behavior of the firm and his assumptions about the shape of cost curves, the firm's price policy, relevant rates of output, and capacity underutilization. Thus Kalecki's model represents a more useful microeconomic account of the theory of output and distribution as a whole. Macroeconomic models require a microeconomic foundation. While it is not at all reprehensible to concentrate on building macroeconomic models without paying much attention to the underlying microrelations, the efforts of those who attempt to provide such an underpinning are particularly commendable. (See Machlup 1963, p. 140.)

In building his macrodistribution theory, Kalecki proceeded from an unorthodox concept of the theory of the firm. He assumed surplus capacity to be a typical phenomenon in manufacturing and perfect competition rather the exception in the economic system as a whole. He then focused attention on the firm's price-*making* opportunities and constraints and the policy decisions that the entrepreneurs actually have to make about prices and other forms of nonprice competition under various types of imperfect markets.[19] Kalecki's special assumptions about microeconomic behavior are:

1. Supply is elastic. Firms with a given plant and equipment operate normally *below* the point of practical capacity.[20]

2. Contrary to the "customary assumption" in the theory of the firm that cost curves are (or tend to be) U-shaped, Kalecki's assumption, in Sraffa's footsteps (Sraffa 1926, pp. 535-50), underlying cost-price relations, is that the unit prime (variable) cost is independent of the degree of utilization of plant and equipment (ratio of actual to capacity output), and that the limit of practical capacity of the plant (beyond which cost curves marginal cost [*MC*] sharply slope upward) is not "normally" reached. Since underutilization of capacity is a typical condition in the greater part of the manufacturing industries, short-period prime costs per unit of output (costs that can be avoided if that output were not produced) are more or less stable over the "relevant range of output," up to the point (neighborhood) of practical capacity.[21] Kalecki qualified this statement by acknowledging that, in fact, unit prime costs tend to fall somewhat in many

instances as output increases (short-period increasing returns), but he considered this complication of no major importance. The assumption of constancy of unit prime costs is considered only as a first approximation of reality. Kalecki based it on the following hypotheses, which reflected empirical observations: (a) The short-run *MC* curve is usually almost horizontal over the relevant range of production (i.e., *MC* is approximately equal to average prime cost)[22] which the entrepreneur identifies with unit prime cost in the short period.[23] (b) The main components of *MC* are (nonoverhead) wages (w) and cost of materials (cm). The change in cost resulting from producing an additional unit with a given and not fully used plant, is made up of the sum of short-period cost of overhead (o) and wages (notably, salaries are included in overheads) and raw materials ($MC=w+cm+o$). (c) The cost of overhead for manual labor and materials usually accounts for only a very small proportion of the total cost of these cost components, within normal variations in the scale of output, and thus can be treated as negligible (near 0) in relation to the cost of labor and materials and, consequently, can be discarded. As far as this is the case, the principal components of *MC* are cost of materials and labor, (i.e., nonoverhead labor), always within the relevant range and below the point of the practical capacity of the plant ($MC=w+cm$).

Keynes opposed the assumption of approximate constancy of marginal costs.[24] He argued that the identification of marginal cost with the marginal wage cost (wage plus materials) is dangerous in that it ignores the "marginal user cost." This is an alternative way of accounting for the fact that prices are greater than marginal costs. Keynes maintained that the marginal user cost is likely to increase when output is expanding, even long before the point of full capacity is reached; that generally the marginal total cost could be expected to increase more than the marginal wage cost; and that the short-run-period cost curve would turn upward accordingly. If the rate of production is very substantially below capacity, so that even the most efficient plant and labor are greatly underemployed, the marginal real cost is likely to fall with the expansion of production within a certain range or, at worst, to remain independent of the rate of production. But Keynes asserted "a point must surely come, *long before* plant and labour are fully employed, when less efficient plant and labour have to be brought into commission or the less efficient organization is employed beyond the optimum degree of intensiveness." Even conceding that the course of short-run *MC* is downward in its early reaches, Keynes maintained that Kahn's assumption that it "eventually turn upwards is, on general common-sense grounds, surely beyond reasonable question, and that this happens moreover, on a part of the curve which is highly relevant for practical purposes." (Keynes 1939b, pp. 44-45; cf. 1936, app. to ch. 6.)

3. In view of the uncertainties faced in the process of price formation, Kalecki explicitly states: "it will not be assumed that the firm attempts to maximize its profits in any precise sort of manner."[25] However, he sharply differentiated his theory from the so-called full-cost theory,[26] on the grounds that the degree of monopoly (reflected in the markup on prime costs) *may*, but need not necessarily, increase due to a rise in overheads in relation to prime costs; and that the price-setting process is influenced by the prices of rival firms—about which later.

At the expense of oversimplification of Kalecki's austere argument of the influence of the degree of monopoly upon price formation (Kalecki 1943k, p. 9), each firm in an industry fixes the price for its product by "marking up" its average unit prime cost in order to cover overheads and to achieve profits, i.e., prices are formed by adding a proportionate markup onto the prime cost.

The definitional framework can be shown as follows:

p price per unit of output $(u+s)$

Unit cost consists of:

$$\left.\begin{array}{ll} m & \text{raw materials costs per unit of output} \\ w & \text{wage costs per unit of output} \end{array}\right\} u \quad \text{unit prime costs}$$

$$\left.\begin{array}{ll} o & \text{overhead per unit of output} \\ r & \text{profit per unit of output} \end{array}\right\} s \quad \text{unit gross profit}$$

The markup over prime costs is measured as the excess of price per unit of output over unit prime costs to the unit prime costs $(p-u)/u$. Clearly, the markup is equal to gross profit margin to cover overhead and achieve profits in relation to prime costs $(o+r)/u$. Alternatively, the markup may be conceived in the form of a coefficient k, by which the unit cost is multiplied in order to obtain the price $(p=ku)$, where k is larger than unity. The relationship between the markup and the coefficient which brings u into equality with p is simply $(p-u)/u=k-1$.

Introduction of Behavioral Relationships

The crucial proposition is that the markup depends on the process of industrial concentration, on the vigor and weaknesses in competition, on market imperfections, on the industrial setting, on the morphology of markets, on the degree of freedom and constraints in price-setting, and on income distribution. Thus the markup is governed by a firm's price-fixing policy in relation (or as a reaction) to price formation in an industry. Its determination will contribute to the distribution of national income, which, in its turn, affects spending propensities and the degree of utilization of resources. True, the margin is a "catch-all" term, grouping the numerous factors that affect its size.[27] It is *determined* by and *reflects* what Kalecki called semimonopolistic and monopolistic influences resulting from imperfect competition or oligopoly (for short, the degree of monopoly).[28] The widely held view that Kalecki's theory is "tautological" is a *non sequitur.*[29] True, Kalecki starts, as we have seen, with a definitional equation (identity) and manipulates the equation so as to provide a theoretical explanation which, of course, can be proven right, wrong, plausible or logically inconsistent, or can be refuted by economic statistics—but this is a different matter. However, once attention shifts to the major factors underlying changes in the degree of monopoly, a behavioral relationship is introduced. Here exits tautology, so to speak, and we enter the field of theorizing where the aim is to explain observable reality. The hypothesis can be supported or disproved by facts. It is common knowledge that hypotheses about reality in general, and in the social sciences in particular, greatly oversimplify and distort reality. The explanatory value of hypotheses depends on the question raised and propositions advanced that help to illuminate facts and processes. Kalecki offered a hypothesis about the major causes of change in the degree of monopoly, or rather a framework for the study of chief determinants affecting distribution of national income. True, it might be difficult to quantify the many influences that play on the degree of monopoly. One could argue that Kalecki did not provide quite a satisfactory measure. The problem is not only how much is still to be done and how far Kalecki advanced toward a solution, but whether he took a significant step in the right direction. He never claimed that he solved all the problems of this thorny issue. His several reformulations are prima facie evidence that he considered it merely as a first serious attempt to tackle the formidable problem. In this context, it has been suggested to extend Kalecki's theory by incorporating various entry barrier classifications and measures of industrial concentration.[30]

It is noteworthy that the markup is not defined *as* the degree of monopoly, but depends on and is a *symptom* of the degree of monopoly. It reflects the changes in the state of market imperfection and oligopoly. It is not an *ex post* quantity, but is governed by the pricing policy. (Kalecki 1965l, pp. 12-13) Thirty years after the publication of his original article, reflecting on the reception his distribution theory received, Kalecki somewhat regretted the use of the term "degree of monopoly," which he blamed for facilitating the dismissal of the theory as being tautological. He argued that he demonstrated in *Theory of Economic Dynamics* (pp. 11-19) "that in any case no problem of *tautology* is involved." (Kalecki 1968j, p. 265.)

With surplus capacity and constant prime costs over the relevant range of output, the firm fixes the price of the product, taking into consideration mainly its prime costs per unit of output and the prices of other sellers in industries that are producing similar products (and only to a much lesser degree is price-fixing influenced by prices and expected reactions outside the product group or an industry). Prices are fixed by allowing for the "mobility of customers" (market imperfections) and the influence of their own prices and expected reactions on those of their rivals (oligopoly). The firm must be satisfied that the price fixed is more advantageous than a higher or lower one. As Kalecki put it, the price-fixing firm "must make sure that the price does not become too high in relation to prices of other firms, for this would drastically reduce sales, and that the price does not become too low in relation to its average prime cost, for this would drastically reduce the profit margin." (Kalecki 1965l, p. 12.) This is now recognized as being the right approach, though, *admittedly,* Kalecki is oversimplifying.

When each firm in an industry sets the price of its products in relation to unit prime cost, the price maker exercises care that the ratio of the price set by the firm to the weighted averaged prices of all rival firms constituting the industry (P_a) (weighted by the respective outputs of various firms constituting an industry, including the firm in question) does not become excessively high. In reconsidering prices, when wage rates or material costs increase, p can be increased proportionately only if P_a rises proportionately as well. However, if P_a increases less than u, p will also be raised less than u.

In other words, in setting p, the firm must satisfy the condition that the markup is not out of step with competition, as it depends on the relation of the ensuing p to P_a.

The markup over the prime costs is an increasing function of P_a/p: the lower p in relation to P_a, the higher the markup that will be fixed; or alternatively, the markup equals $f(P_a/p)$, where f is the increasing function.[31] Only in a special case could f be the same for various firms in an industry. The function will reflect the influences on the price-fixing policy of the firm (markup) resulting from imperfect competition or oligopoly. (Kalecki 1965l, pp. 11-16.) The stronger the degree of monopoly, the higher is $f(P_a/p)$ corresponding to a given relation P_a/p. Prices fixed by individual firms will be, in general, different for various firms in an industry because of dispersion of prime costs,[32] and because of differences in f. Save for basic raw materials produced frequently in conditions approaching perfect competition (largely demand determined prices), for most of the products prices are generally nonuniform.[33] Kalecki notes that the argument applies strictly to imperfect competition only or to differentiated (imperfect) oligopoly, but not to homogeneous (nondifferentiated) oligopoly or monopoly. (Kalecki 1971a, pp. 4-5. Cf. Sylos-Labini 1969, pp. 12-14.)

To continue with Kalecki's argument, the markups are "determined" by the degree of monopoly; the ratio of average price to average prime cost is equal to the ratio of aggregate proceeds of an industry to aggregate prime costs of an industry, and, thus, the relationship between unit price and unit prime costs is "determined" by the degree of monopoly. Subject to the assumption of elastic supply, the "ratio of average price to average prime cost is equal to the ratio of aggregate proceeds of industry to aggregate prime costs of industry" and "the ratio of proceeds to prime costs is stable, increases or diminishes *depending on what happens to the degree of monopoly*." (Kalecki 1965l, p. 16. Emphasis supplied.)

Starting from this variant of the model of the firm and after discussing the influence of monopoly on price formation in an industry, the next step in the development of the argument is to link the ratio of proceeds to prime costs in an industry with the relative share of wages in the contribution to output by that industry. Then the following step in Kalecki's derivation is to proceed from a single industry to the manufacturing industry as a whole (to account for industrial composition of value added) and to generalize the theorizing to embrace the determinants of the relative share of wages in the economy as a whole (private sector only). Thus we can proceed through successive stages of aggregation to a general macrodistribution theorem. Briefly, revenue from the sales of an industry's output (or average price times average quantity) (T)[34] is composed of prime costs (U), which, in turn, are made up of labor prime costs (aggregate wage bill of an industry) (W); and basic raw material costs (aggregate raw material bill of an industry) (M); and gross profits (S), consisting of overhead (O) and profit (R). Hence: $T = W + M + O + R$. Gross profit (overhead plus profit) equals the excess of an industry's sales revenue over its prime costs: $T - (W + M)$.

With the sales value of an industry's output equal to $K(W + M)$, or alternatively $\{W + M\}\{1 + [(p - u)/u]\}$, the excess of sales revenue over prime costs is equal to $(K - 1)(W + M)$; or the amount of gross profit is equal to the product of the amount of prime costs times the markup coefficient (noteworthy, the markup is on both wage and material elements of prime costs). To obtain the relative share of wages in net output (and to avoid multiple counting in determining the national product), the gross value of output is reduced, as usual, to the net by deducting the cost of raw material inputs. Thus the value added by an industry, measured by the sales value of that industry's output, less the cost of material procured ($T - M$),[35] is equal to the sum of wages and gross profits ($T - M = W + O + R$). Thus the value added—the denominator in the ratio of the relative share of wages in net output—can be represented as: $Y_1 = W + (K - 1)(W + M)$. Clearly, the relative share of wages in the value added of that industry is: $W/Y_1 = W/[W + (K - 1)(W + M)]$. By dividing the numerator and denominator by W, we get: $W/Y_1 = 1/[1 + (K - 1)(1 + M/W)]$. The above formula shows that the relative share of wages (other than overhead) in the net output (or value added) is "determined" by the degree of monopoly and by the ratio of the raw materials bill to the wage bill. The degree of monopoly (reflected in the markup) "determines" the distribution of the net output between wages on the one hand and profits (plus overheads) on the other, if, in addition, the relation of the cost of materials to the wage bill is given. The share of net output accruing to (nonoverhead) labor is a diminishing function of the degree of intensity of monopoly and the proportion of the prime costs spent on materials. If, however, a change in the degree of monopoly tends to compress the ratio of proceeds to prime costs (markup on prime costs), it tends to increase, *ceteris paribus*, the relative share of net output going to wage earners. But apart from the forces that play on the markup, grouped together as the degree of monopoly,[36] the relative share of wages in the product depends on the share of material costs in prime costs (on the ratio of material costs to wage costs). The wage share falls when the cost of materials increases in relation to that of the cost of labor. Conversely, only in the absence of other variations, is the degree of monopoly *the* central "determinant" of the distribution of product of industry between wages and profit.[37] As this is not usually the case, attention focuses on the principal determinants. Obviously, propositions about reality are always great oversimplifications. Further research and theorizing usually expand the number of determinants. Kalecki's theory is a great oversimplification of reality, but its strength lies in clearing the path to identification of the crucial forces.[38] Clearly, the degree of monopoly is not the only determinant of class shares in national income. Despite its classification as a monopoly theory of distribution, Kalecki's distribution theory is broader than this term implies.

To proceed with the determinants of global distribution, a similar equation to that derived for a single industry can be written for the manufacturing sector as a whole. But here the markup and the ratio of the material bill to the wage bill are also conditioned by the composition of industrial structure. Substituting K' and M'/W' for K and M/W, respectively, the equation of the relative share of wages in value added for the manufacturing industry as a whole (W') can be written as: $W'=1/\{1+[K'-1][(M'/W')+1]\}$, where the ratios K' and M'/W' are adjusted in such a way as to allow for the effect of changes in the importance (weights) of particular industries in manufacturing taken as a whole. Here W' is defined as a "standardized" wage share over time which measures changes in the wage share after allowing for structural changes. Kalecki also used W' as a measure of the actual aggregate wage share at any moment of time where K' and M'/W' represent weighted averages of the individual K's and W/M. The parameter K' is determined by the degree of monopoly in the manufacturing industries. (Prices of materials are determined by the prices of primary products, wage costs at the lower stages of production, and by the degree of monopoly at those stages.) Roughly, the ratio of unit material costs to unit wage costs is determined by the ratio of prices of primary products to unit wage costs and by the degree of monopoly in manufacturing industries.

A digression on Kalecki's distinction between cost determined and demand determined prices is in order. As contrasted with short-run changes in prices of finished products, which are mainly cost determined, short-run variations in the prices of primary products are considered largely to reflect variations in demand (demand determined). According to Kalecki, the distinction between these two types of price formations arises out of divergent conditions of supply in short periods. The output of finished goods is elastic due to a prevalence of surplus capacity. A rise in demand is met chiefly by an increase in the rate of production, and the price changes that do occur are caused chiefly by changes in costs of production. While, in general, prices of finished goods are mainly determined by changes in the cost of production, they are affected, of course, by any demand determined variations in the prices of raw materials; but it is through the medium of costs that the impulses are transmitted. The supply of raw materials is usually inelastic in the short run. Increasing the supply of agricultural products takes considerable time. In a more restricted sense, the same statement applies to mining. In supply constrained activities, in the short run, a rise in demand causes disinvestment in inventories and a consequent rise in price (the initial price movement is frequently accompanied by secondary speculative demand, making it even more difficult in the short period for output to catch up with increased demand). The demand determined prices of raw materials (inclusive of primary foodstuffs) tend to decline considerably during slumps and to rise considerably during upswings in economic activity. Even with invariable wage rates, the prices of raw materials tend to fall in a depression owing to a fall in "real" demand. Thus the ratio of prices of raw materials to unit wage costs is a function of the rate of aggregate economic activity and effective demand for raw materials in relation to their inelastic supply in the short run.

Thus the relative share of wages in the value added of manufacturing is determined by the degree of monopoly, the ratio of raw material prices to unit wage costs and the industrial composition of the value added. Extending the analysis to sectors, such as construction, transportation, and services, where the pattern of price formation roughly resembles that in manufacturing, the theorem is derived that, for this group as a whole, the "relative share of wages in the aggregate value added will decrease with an increase in the degree of monopoly or an increase in the ratio of prices of primary products to unit wage costs." (Kalecki 1965l, p. 30.) This condition is subject to the provision that the outcome will be affected by changes in the sectoral composition of the value added of the composite. Then, this theorem is generalized to comprise the whole economic system (excluding the public sector).[39]

Kalecki concludes that, broadly speaking, the principal determinants of the relative share of wages in gross, domestically produced national income—national income gross of depreciation, exclusive of incomes of government employees and derived from foreign investments—are:

1. the degree of monopoly,
2. the ratio of prices of raw materials to unit wage costs, and
3. the structural composition of the value of the gross income of the private sector.[40] There is no a priori reason why changes in (1) and (2), *ceteris paribus,* should exactly counteract each other, or that, on balance, variations in (1) always nearly counterbalance variations in (2), in combination with or independently of variations in (3).

Various forms of the determinants of the wage-share equation may be applied, and were originally employed so by Kalecki, to explain the alleged magic stability of the proportion of the national product accruing to labor. But this is only one application of the equation used to explain that which appeared to Kalecki, on the basis of a generalization of economic facts, to be the approximate stability of functional shares in advanced capitalist economies. If the facts fit, the magic constant may be explained as a balance between two offsetting tendencies, or that one kind of variation always serves exactly to compensate for another. But, actually, a hypothesis is needed to show why this is so and what forces are operating behind the scene. Kalecki attempted to provide an explanatory hypothesis of the determinants of changes in macrodistribution in the long and short run. But he did not specify the quantitative dimensions and did not argue that (1) and (2) must necessarily offset each other. Contrariwise, he emphasized that no a priori statement is possible as to the long-run trend of the relative share of wages in income, but it is possible to be more specific about variations in the relative share in the course of a business cycle.

Determinants of Long- and Short-run Changes in Distribution

As we have seen, apart from the industrial and sectoral composition of value added, the relative share of labor in national income depends on the markups and the relation between unit wage costs and prices of basic materials. The markups are determined by the play of factors nicknamed the degree of monopoly. This shifts attention to the causes of variations in the degree of monopoly in the first place, and, indeed, to the more general question of the forces behind the long- and short-run variations in the distributive shares.

Among the chief causal factors of changes in the degree of monopoly in a modern capitalist economy, the first and foremost force is attributed to the process of industrial concentration leading to the formation of corporate giants accounting for a substantial share of an industry's output. (Cf. Bain 1965; Zimmerman 1951; Mann 1966, pp. 296-307.) In such an industrial structure the seller knows that the price he fixes influences appreciably price formation in the industry, and that the other sellers will be pushed in the same direction because their price formation depends on the average price. Therefore, the price maker can set his price at a level higher than that which would prevail in the absence of protection stemming from a highly concentrated industry, imperfect competition, and forms of oligopoly. (Cf. Joan Robinson 1960, pp. 222-38; Sylos-Labini 1969, pp. 1-15; Bain 1956.) A similar game is played by other big firms. If unchecked and not offset by other factors,[41] the degree of monopoly tends to increase substantially as time goes by.[42] Many branches of industry become oligopolistic, and oligopolies may be transformed into cartels. Also the progressive concentration in industry is likely to enhance the degree of oligopoly.

The propensity of the degree of monopoly to rise is reinforced by tacit agreement which may take many forms: *inter alia,* price leadership when the price-fixing is exercised by one large firm ("The Leader"), while other sellers "loyally" follow the behavior of the leader and adapt themselves accordingly. (Cf. Kaldor 1960, pt. 3; Kaplan, Dirlam, and Lanzilotti 1958; Silberston 1970.) Tacit agreements may result in more or less formal cartel arrangements. In such cases full-scale monopolization is restrained merely by fear of new entrants and checked by fear of public discontent. In practice, industries do exist which are dominated by one firm or a cartel; but in a modern capitalist economy, manufacturing industry operates predominantly under conditions of imperfect competition and oligopoly (with a more typical situation where sellers prefer survival and offensive neutrality to profit maximization and outward cutthroat tactics for supremacy). Even "pure monopolies" must reckon with potential outsiders. This makes their pattern of behavior broadly similar to that of oligopolies. (Kalecki 1943k, pp. 20-22; 1965l, p. 17.)

Kalecki singles out the development of marketing and high pressure salesmanship as the second crucial factor underlying the rise in the degree of monopoly. Under competition there is no need to spend on persuading the buyer to buy more as the producer is a price taker and quantity adjuster. He need not reduce price or incur sales promotion expenses in order to sell more. At a certain stage of development of the capitalist economy, the expansion of advertisement may, in many cases, create an "artificial" market imperfection. Price competition is replaced by such things as nonprice competition, contrived product differentiation, and proliferation of services, to shape and perhaps distort the consumer demand (to deceive the consumer).[43] Sales promotion campaigns create or maintain consumer demand, protect the seller, lead to high prices and profits to the detriment of the public, and account for the bulk of wastefulness of market imperfections. In addition to the above determinants of change in the degree of monopoly, Kalecki considers two other factors: the impact of changes in the level of overheads in relation to prime costs and the influence of the trade union's power.

The degree of monopoly may rise as a consequence of a rise of overheads in relation to prime costs. A substantial rise in the level of overheads in relation to prime costs entails constriction of profits, unless the ratio of proceeds to prime costs is allowed to rise. This situation may give rise to various forms of collusion among the rival sellers to guard profits, thus giving rise to a propensity to increase prices in relation to unit prime costs. (Cf. Kalecki 1942m, p. 123.)

The potency of the drive to avoid a "squeeze of profits" manifests itself especially during periods of depressed economic activity. However, the production of profits is by no means an automatic force, but merely a tendency which may even not materialize. According to Kalecki, the basic tendency operates as follows: Aggregate proceeds tend to decline in the same proportion as prime costs if the degree of monopoly remains unaltered. Simultaneously, aggregate overheads, by their very nature (largely independent of the rate of production within a certain range), fall less during a depression than do prime costs. This situation provides the setting for tacit conspiracy not to lower prices in the same proportion as prime costs. While in some instances the process of cutthroat competition may develop in the slump, there appears to be a basic tendency for the degree of monopoly to rise in a slump, a tendency which seems to be reversed in prosperous times—more about which later. Admittedly, all this merely shows a channel through which overheads may influence price formation, but their influence upon prices is much less definite than that of prime costs. "The degree of monopoly *may*, but need not necessarily increase as a result of a rise in overheads in relation to prime costs." (Kalecki 1965l, p. 18.)

The cost-price relations previously discussed were based on short-period considerations (a firm with a given capital equipment). The f function reflecting the degree of monopoly may, but by no means has to, change in the long run. In the absence of such alterations the long-period variations in prices will reflect only the long-period changes in prime costs per unit of output. Technological advance will tend to lower the unit prime cost. However, Kalecki maintained, the *relations* between prices and unit prime costs can be affected by changes in capital goods and production techniques *only to the extent to which they affect the degree of monopoly.* This is subject to the assumption of elastic supply, stable unit prime costs up to the limit of practical capacity,[44] and investment decisions.

The existence of powerful trade unions restrains the markups, i.e., it causes the values $f(P_a/p)$ to be lower than they otherwise would be. If wage increases are granted, but the function f is not changed, prices will also be raised, which, in turn, would provoke a new round of pressures for wage increases. High markups cannot be maintained without "wage (cost) push" pressures, and the process tends to go on with price levels steadily rising. This process adversely affects the competitive position of a firm or an industry (bargaining usually proceeds by industries) and induces adoption of a policy of lower (more reasonable or tolerable) profit margins. Thus the degree of monopoly is restrained to a certain extent by the pressures of organized labor. The power of trade unions manifests itself in the scale of wage increases demanded, compared to those obtained.[45] A rise in bargaining power represented by a spectacular wage rise results in a downward shift in the function $f(P_a/p)$ and the markups are depressed. The change in the degree of monopoly produces a redistribution of national income from profits to wages. But this redistribution effect is much smaller than it could be if prices were stable. The rise in wages is, to a great extent, shifted to consumers. "Normal" wage increases will usually leave the function f unaffected while, otherwise, markups may tend to get higher because of the rise in labor productivity. "High mark-ups in existence will encourage strong trade unions to bargain for higher wages since they know that firms can 'afford' to pay them." (Kalecki 1971a, p. 6.)

The argument here presented draws on Kalecki's last article on the modern capitalist economy, published posthumously. The conclusions may seem somewhat startling to certain economists.[46] We are told that trade unions indeed may affect the distribution of income, but in a much more sophisticated fashion than expounded by the traditional doctrine. A rise (decline) in trade-union bargaining power leads to a rise (fall) in employment. Redistribution of income in favor of labor's share is feasible only if surplus capacity exists. While the real volume of capitalists' spending remains unaltered, total employment and output change "unconventionally," as noted in chapter four.

Kalecki argued that a wage increase, showing a rise in trade-union power, tends to expand employment, contrary to the precepts of classical doctrine. Conversely, wage reduction resulting from a weakening of trade-union bargaining power tends to reduce employment. The weakness of trade unions in a slump is exhibited in their allowing wage cuts, which, instead of relieving unemployment, contribute to the situation. Trade unions may affect income distribution, but in a considerably more sophisticated way than is envisaged by the crude doctrine that, when wage rates are increased, profits decline *pro tanto.* This proposition proves to be completely unfounded. Such shifts that take place are (1) linked with widespread presence of imperfect competition and oligopoly and (2) are contained within fairly narrow limits. But the daily bargaining regime is an important co-determinant of distributive shares.

Kalecki noted that it is possible to devise other methods than wage-bargaining which are likely to affect the distribution process more directly. For instance, measures may be taken for containing increases in the cost of living. This may be achieved by price controls which are difficult to administer. Alternatively, prices of wage goods may be subsidized by means of a direct taxation of profits. If these measures cannot be carried out by the legislators who represent the trade unions, supporting strike movements could be organized by the trade unions. Moreover:

> . . . redistribution of income from profits to wages . . . is feasible only if excess capacity is in existence. Otherwise it is impossible to increase wages in relation to prices of wage goods because prices are determined by demand, and functions f become defunct. . . .
>
> Price control of wage goods will lead under the circumstances to scarcities of goods and haphazard distribution. Also subsidizing prices

> of wage goods (financed by direct taxation of profits) can reduce prices only in the longer run by stimulating investment in wage good industries.
>
> It should be noted, however, that even contemporary capitalism, where deep depressions are avoided as a result of Government intervention, is in general still fairly remote from such a state of full utilisation of resources. This is best shown by the fact that prices of finished goods are fixed on a cost basis rather than determined by demand. (Kalecki 1971a, p. 9.)

Generalizing on the probable effect of the degree of monopoly on long-run variations in the distribution of national income between "workers and capitalists," Kalecki concluded, in *Theory of Economic Dynamics,* that the degree of monopoly displays a "general tendency to increase in the long run and thus to depress the relative share of wages in income, although . . . this tendency is much stronger in some periods than others. (Kalecki 1965l, p. 30.)

It is venturesome to generalize about probable relations of raw material prices to wage costs which are a function of long-term shifts in the demand-supply situation of raw materials (or to generalize about trends in exploitation of raw material producers and benefits accruing to the working class in advanced capitalist countries partly derived from exploitation of labor in materials-producing [mostly underdeveloped] countries), as well as to predict changes in industrial and sectoral composition of production. Kalecki seems to prefer to remain uncommitted and to leave the question of likely movements of industrial structure and terms of trade open. It would be interesting to extend his theory by incorporating some hypothesis as to the probable trends in these areas. (Cf. Rothschild 1961, pp. 178-79; ed. 1971. Cf. Sichel, ed. 1967.) In final analysis, "no *a priori* statement is therefore possible as to the long-run trend of the relative share of wages in income." (Kalecki 1965l, p. 31.)

Kalecki was much less reluctant to commit himself more specifically about variations in the relative share of wages in income during the course of a business cycle. Contrary to Harrod's argument that the degree of monopoly increases in the boom and falls in the slump, Kalecki maintained that the degree of monopoly changes in the opposite direction to variations in output. Kalecki found, as stated above, that "there is a tendency for the degree of monopoly to rise in the slump, a tendency which is reversed in the boom."[47]

According to Harrod's Law of Diminishing Elasticity of Demand, the degree of monopoly increases as activity increases because the ordinary consumer finds it increasingly less necessary to search for bargains when times are prosperous. However, the same force of habit, which in times of prosperity tends to make the consumer an imperfect buyer, renders him more cautious and demanding when a reduced income compels him to economize, thus increasing the elasticity of demand. In turn, the shopkeeper, being under the consumer's pressures, also searches for bargains and tries to reduce his costs. Therefore, once the slump has set in, demand becomes much more elastic, imperfection of competition is reduced, and the degree of monopoly tends to diminish, whereas the opposite tendencies are manifested in the course of the upswing. (Harrod 1936, pp. 86-97; 1972, pp. 392-401.)

Harrod was criticized on the grounds that powerful factors, which he disregarded, influence the degree of monopoly in the opposite direction. The degree of monopoly is affected not only by "the imperfection of the market for a commodity, but also [by] the number of separate units of control engaged in selling it, and, since the fear of loss is more powerful than the hope of gain, the tendency towards restrictive combinations is stronger in a slump than in a boom. This is a factor tending to amplify the swings of activity, and works against the operation of Mr. Harrod's Law." (Joan Robinson 1951, pp. 59-61.) Formation of cartels to save profits, price-fixing agreements, and other devices to reduce competition and raise barriers to entry are fostered by the low level of activity. This increases the degree of monopoly and, very likely, more than counteracts the impact of Harrod's Law. On the contrary, when activity revives, the cartels are dissolved because of improving prospects for independent action and the emergence of outsiders. But even more important, despite the decline of raw material prices and wages, some prices of finished products display a relative rigidity in the slump. This stickiness of prices is due partly to the fact that firms avoid price cuts because they fear the reaction of their competitors. (Kalecki 1939a, pp. 35-36.) Subsequently, Kalecki modified his position by stating that the "tendency for the degree of monopoly to rise in the slump, a tendency which is reversed in the boom" is a basic tendency, but "in some instances the opposite process of cut-throat competition may develop in a depression." (Kalecki 1965l, p. 18.)

The possible influence of changes in structural composition of output cannot usually be abstracted from, as they tend to reduce the relative share of wages during a slump. In fact, these changes are ruled by a greater reduction in production of investment goods than in the manufacturing industry as a whole. The relative share of wages in the income-of-investment-goods sector is higher than in the rest of the manufacturing industry. Consequently, the relative decline of output of investment goods during a slump tends to reduce the relative distributive share of labor in the net output of manufacturing as a whole. During a depression there is a tendency for a relative shift in the distribution of national income away from "wage-paying" industries, and within the "wage-paying" industries from activities with a higher relative share to those with a lower wage share in output.[48] The data examined by Kalecki indicated no pronounced changes in the relative share of wages in national income during the course of the business cycle. (Kalecki 1965l, p. 31.) As a result of accumulated evidence, the concept of the relationship between monopolistic tendencies and the trade cycle has altered. Cartels do not generally disappear in the boom; depressed economic situations can give rise to tensions within cartels. Although post World War II experience seems to bear out that the profit share in national income tends to increase in the depression and decrease in the boom, this was not the case in the 1930s.

This is not the case with the relative share of wages plus salaries combined. As salaries are largely independent of volume of output (within a certain range), they are likely to fall less during the slump and rise less during the boom than wages taken alone. The fluctuation of the "real" wage and salary bill is likely to be less pronounced during the course of the cycle than the fluctuation of the real gross income. Admittedly, the application of the theory of income distribution to the analysis of long-term variations in the distributive share of wages and salaries combined would encounter difficulties in view of the growing share of salaries in the sum of overheads and profits owing to increasing concentration in industry.[49]

When Kalecki's theory is applied to the conditions of price formation during the course of a business cycle, the problem of its applicability during the boom arises. However, we should note that Kalecki started the argument in the slump. Instead of developing it, the modern representatives of the neoclassical school went off on another, seemingly improper, track.

In fact, during expansion, plants may be operated at the limit of practical capacity and a further rise in demand may entail price increases above the level indicated by the price-fixing considerations (the pricing formula) noted previously. Thus, when demand increases in relation to available capacity, the price charged by the firm may be increased so as to bring into equilibrium rising demand with limited supply in spite of the fact that unit prime costs and the degree of monopoly remain unchanged. However, the price maker, fearing adverse effects of rising prices, may prefer to maintain the level of the price (markup) for some time, while the firm allows orders to pile up and delays delivery.[50] Kalecki maintained, as we know, that availability of surplus capacity is a typical phenomenon. In view of the possibility of expanding capacity whenever bottlenecks occur (cf. Kalecki 1943k, pp. 15-21, 1965l, p. 20; Hahn 1972, p. 41), this situation is not likely to be a normal occurrence even close to the top of the boom. The situation seems to be "restricted to war or post-war developments, where shortages of raw materials or equipment limit severely the supply in relation to demand. It is this type of increase in prices which is the basic reason for the inflationary developments prevailing in such periods." (Kalecki 1965l, p. 20.)

Kalecki offered a theory of distribution that was independent of the neoclassical tradition. The state, merit, and failures of the neoclassical theory are subject to controversy and debate that question the very premises of the theory. This is not the place to add to the controversy or to try to resolve it. Whatever else may be said on the subject, in a certain sense, it is sufficient to note that the neoclassical theory has nothing coherent to say when perfect competition is abandoned or when there are increasing returns or both. Kalecki did have something important to say and came forward with a promising alternative theory of distribution, even if it lacked a comprehensively formulated theory of market behavior and was, in some respects, deficient in dealing with the formidable problem of investment decision.

Here we may recall and paraphrase Pigou's observation about Keynes's *General Theory:* Kalecki has devised a new way of tackling a seldom climbed mountain. Although we may regret that this did not lead him to the very top, we must credit him for the pointers and advances he made toward reaching the destination.

The content of Kalecki's distribution theory is, in some respects, negative: He tried to show that income distribution has nothing to do with marginal productivity and with the production function. It depends entirely on the forces of the market, i.e., on market power, or monopoly. In practice, this takes many shapes. Therefore, Kalecki can only give a general framework and terminology for this complex of factors of power over the market.

To build a realistic theory of distribution, Kalecki offered an explanation of how prices in fact are formed by markup on prime costs. This use of markup to cover overheads is very important then, and, although it involves monopoly power, it is not synonymous with it.

In a personal communication to me (dated February 18, 1971), Professor Abba P. Lerner observed that, among Kalecki's contributions to economics that he has found particularly useful, was "the use of the concept of the 'degree of monopoly' in explaining the distribution of income between capital and labor . . . . His use of the degree of monopoly I once rather played down as being too tautological, but recently I have come to find it extremely useful."

The influence of Kalecki's theory of distribution has been growing in recent years,[51] propagated particularly through the writings of Professors Joan Robinson and Nicholas Kaldor:

> Kalecki transformed the highly academic theory of imperfect competition into a realistic account of the formation of prices by a mark-up on prime cost. The contention that profits per unit of output depend upon the 'degree of monopoly' is reconciled with the view that profits per annum depend upon capitalists' outlay by the argument that a higher level of prices, with a given volume of money demand, must lead to a lower level of utilization of plant and lower employment, so that the *share* of profit is increased only by reducing the amount of wages paid out. This has always been well-known to any businessman, but it was not formerly brought into the canon of economic theory. (Joan Robinson, 1971b, p. 2.)

Thus the theory of profits, which in economic literature is called Keynesian, really derived from Kalecki.

IV

INVESTMENT, PROFITS, AND NATIONAL INCOME

AT LEAST IN ITS SIMPLIFIED VERSION,[1] Kalecki's theory of profits is based on the principle that wage-earners do not save, but spend what they get, and that capitalists get what they spend.[2] In other words, capitalists' profits are governed by their propensity to invest and consume and not the other way around. Profits are determined by investment (with a time-lag), not investment by profits. Kalecki clarifies the role of factors determining the distribution of income in the theory of profits: Given that profits are determined by the profit-earners' (capitalists') propensity to consume and investments undertaken by them in the past, it is labor's earnings (and consequently what workers spend) that are determined by such factors underlying the distribution of income as, for instance, the degree of monopoly.

In this way profit-earners' consumption and investment depend on entrepreneurial behavior and jointly with the determinants of distribution (degree of monopoly) determine the wage-earners' income and expenditure, and, consequently, the level of aggregate output, employment, capacity utilization, and its fluctuations. Subject to the assumption of elastic supply, the aggregate output will be pushed up to the point where profits out of it, as determined by the determinants of distribution, are equal to the sum of investment and profit-earners' consumption. The function of distribution determinants is to determine output or income on the basis of profits, which are, in turn, governed by investment. If the output of wage goods reaches capacity level, any increase in capitalists' outlays merely entails higher level of prices of these goods. Thus real wages decline, reflecting the fact that an enlarged wage fund chases an unaltered supply of consumer goods.

In view of the fact that, in a specific short period profits are determined by the capitalists' decisions about their consumption and investment in the past, the factors affecting the distribution of income influence the real wage bill rather than real profits. For example, if the degree of monopoly grows, with a concurrent increase in the ratio of profits to wages, real profits are not altered "but the real wage bill falls, first, because of the fall in real wage rates, and secondly, because of the consequent reduction in demand for wage goods, and thus of output and employment in the wage-good industries." (Kalecki 1943k, p. 50.) Even though percentage gross margins increase, the national output drops by so much that "as a result, the real total profits remain the same. However great the margin of profit on a unit of output, the capitalists cannot make more in total profits than they consume and invest (inclusive of accumulation of unsold goods)." (Kalecki 1943k, p. 50.)

The Fundamental Profits Equation

Kalecki starts his investigation of the determinants of profits by concentrating deliberately on a closed, laissez faire type economy. He abstracts initially from the influence of the balance of foreign trade on profits by assuming a closed system and from complications arising out of government expenditure and taxation operations by postulating a balanced state budget. Kalecki assumes a two-class society: workers (including salary-earners as well) and nonworkers (property owners or capitalists) where wages and salaries and profits account for the entire national income. As we know there are fundamental differences in propensities to save (consume) of each class. The propensity to save out of profits markedly surpasses that out of wages. In the limiting case of zero workers' savings, the argument can be based on the equality between profits and gross investment plus capitalists' consumption. Workers' savings complicate the argument considerably, but they do not introduce particular problems of principle. To simplify his exposition, Kalecki assumed away these savings: Workers spend what they earn and do not save out of their earnings. Hence attention is concentrated on fundamental issues, and the aggregate saving is identified with capitalists' savings.

Kalecki's argument is couched in terms of the customary conceptual framework of national income accounting, and first certain definitional relationships are established. By definition: Gross national product (Y) is equal to the sum of gross private investment (I) and personal consumption (C). Gross investment consists of newly produced, fixed capital goods plus changes in inventories. The value of gross national product is distributed between two social classes, workers and capitalists, and virtually nothing is paid in taxes (personal income=disposable income). Thus: $Y=C+I$. The income of labor consists of wages and salaries (V), while income accruing to capitalists is in the form of gross profits (P), consisting of depreciation and maintenance allowances and undistributed (retained) profits, dividends, drawings from unincorporated firms, rent, and interest. Thus $Y=V+P$. Gross profits equal gross investments plus capitalists' consumption; i.e., Kalecki establishes the equation between gross profits on the one hand, and profit-earners' outlays on consumption and private investment on the other.

Kalecki then poses the fundamental question: What is the proper meaning of this definitional equation? Does it signify that, in a certain period, profits "determine capitalists' consumption and investment or the reverse of this"? The answer depends on which of these items is directly subject to the capitalists' decisions; for they "may decide to consume and to invest more in a given period than in the preceding one, but they cannot decide to earn more. It is, therefore, their investment and consumption decisions which determine profits, and not vice versa.[3] If the period under consideration is short, the capitalists' investment and consumption are determined by decisions made earlier, partly shaped by certain factors operating in the preceding periods. The time-lag between investment decisions and investments is emphasized, since clearly the execution of investment orders takes considerable time. Also, realistically, it is only with a certain delay that capitalists' consumption expenditures respond to changes in the factors that affect them.[4] Undeniably, there is an appreciable time-lag between income and corresponding consumption of capitalists, contrasted with the close relationship between income and consumption of wage-earners.

The interpretation of the above identity equation would have little meaning in a stationary situation where capitalists would decide repeatedly to consume and to invest in a given period what they had earned in the preceding period, with profits in a given period invariably equal to those in the preceding one. In fact, profits are not stationary, but fluctuate, and it is their variability that is the dominant phenomenon to be explained. Despite the fact that profits in the preceding periods are not the key determinants of capitalists' spending propensities, typically capitalists refrain from consuming and investing in a given period exactly what they have earned in the preceding one.

Then two important qualifications are introduced:

1. Investment in fixed capital is not the sole important component of investment. The past investment decisions may not completely determine the volume of investment in a given period, i.e., *ex ante* investment may diverge from *ex post,* owing to unexpected changes in inventories. However, Kalecki maintains that the importance of unexpected accumulation and reduction of inventories "seems to have been frequently exaggerated." (Kalecki 1965l, p. 46.) This is not to say that abstracting from changes in inventories would be an acceptable assumption—indeed, it is one of the most drastic simplifications of reality. (Cf. Kalecki 1968j, p. 264.)

2. Investment and consumption have to be expressed in constant prices, yet investment and consumption decisions are supposed to be made in real terms. Given the time-lag between the decisions and their final implementation, it is likely that, in the meantime, terms of purchase may change. To overcome these difficulties, Kalecki assumes that profit and spending variables considered are calculated in constant prices; i.e., both sides of the equation are deflated by appropriate price indexes.

Thus incorporating the qualifications, Kalecki concludes that "the real gross profits in a given short period are determined by decisions of capitalists with respect to their consumption and investment shaped in the past, subject to correction for unexpected changes in the volume of stocks."[5]

Aspects of Saving and Investment

Before examining the relation between profit, investment, and capitalists' consumption, let us digress very briefly to the saving and investment equality. Since gross profits are equal to gross investment plus capitalists' consumption, by deducting capitalists' consumption from both sides, we obtain the equality: capitalists' gross savings = gross investment. The validity of the saving-investment equality is not confined to the special case considered.[6] Kalecki stressed that the equality between saving and investment is independent of the level of the interest rate, which in the classical economic theory was considered as the factor equilibrating saving and investment (in contrast to the Keynesian approach in which the equilibrating mechanism is through a variation of income). Here Kalecki and Keynes had the same idea, but Kalecki made it more dependent on stratification of classes. To reiterate, in Kalecki's version saving is treated as specifically accruing to profit-earners, generated by variations in investment activity. Fluctuations in output and profits depend on fluctuations in investment and capitalists' consumption. Capitalists' expenditures on consumption are "relatively inelastic" and only to some extent vary as a result of changes in profits. Thus, given the capitalists' propensity to consume, profit is determined by the rate of investment, and changes in profits are largely generated by changes in the rate of investment (with appropriate lag).

In the 1930s, Kalecki argued that, if at some time the entrepreneurs' optimism rises, their investment activity and thus employment in that sector will expand. The resulting increase in income and consumption of labor will, in turn, be accompanied by an expansion of output of the wage-goods sector. The aggregate output "will expand to the point where profits will be higher by an amount equal to the value of additional investment—if it is assumed that capitalists' consumption remains unchanged." But if entrepreneurs' consumption spending expands also, owing to enlarged incomes, the rise in profits will be correspondingly augmented. In any case output (income) will be "finally pushed up to the point where the increase in profits will be equal to the increase in expenditures on investment and capitalists' consumption." What would be the sources for financing expansion of investment if capitalists do not simultaneously reduce their consumption and release some spending power for investment activity? "It may sound paradoxical, but according to the above, investment is 'financed by itself.' " (Kalecki 1966h, p. 46).

Kalecki envisaged that investment, once implemented, automatically furnishes the savings required to finance it. In a simplified model, profits in a given time are the direct outcome of profit-earners' investment and consumption in that period. And if investment expands by a certain amount, savings out of profits are *pro tanto* larger. In more concrete terms it means that, if some entrepreneurs increase investment financed by their own liquid assets, the profits of other entrepreneurs will "rise *pro tanto* and thus the liquid reserves invested will pass into the possession of the latter." If extra investment is financed by bank credit, the spending of such funds "will cause equal amounts of saved profits to accumulate as bank deposits. The investing capitalists will thus find it possible to float bonds to the same extent and thus to repay the bank credits." (Kalecki 1965l, p. 50).

As long as there is idle capacity and unemployed labor, it is investment that determines the level of saving and not saving that imposes a limit on the size of capital accumulation. The overall rate of saving is determined by investment outlays and not vice versa.

Simplified Profits Equation

The next step is to examine the relationship between profit and its determinants. This entails an inquiry into the basic relations among profit, investment, and consumption. In this chapter we are concerned only with certain consequences of investment decisions. What is behind such decisions is discussed in the chapters on the theory of cyclical fluctuations.

Turning to the examination of how capitalists' consumption in a given year C_t is determined, Kalecki postulated that it roughly consists of the "constant part *A*" and a part proportionate to P_{t-v}, disposable profits (net of direct taxes) in real terms, with appropriate time-lag. The parameter *A* is a slowly changing function of time which, for the sake of simplicity, is treated as a constant in the short period, but is subject to long-run shifts. The magnitude of *A* depends on habits acquired during the past economic and social development process and is considered as a "semiautonomous" variable, since no attempt is made to relate it to any other variables entering into the argument. We obtain the relation between capitalists' consumption and profits: $C_t = bP_{t-v} + A$, where v denotes the time-lag between reaction of capitalists' consumption spending to the change in their current income and the coefficient b stands for the capitalists' marginal propensity to consume (*MPC*), indicating what part of the increment of profit will be directed to consumption. It is postulated that b is positive and smaller than one, since capitalists tend to consume only a part of the incremental income. In fact, Kalecki maintained that b is rather likely to be a small fraction and considerably less than unity.

The capitalists' propensity-to-consume equation is considered only as a first approximation which disregards a number of significant determinants.[7] There must be some connection between capitalists' income and their consumption out of it; it is very important to consider, *inter alia,* that capitalists' propensity to consume "depends to great extent on the actual level of capital values; in particular on that of stock exchange prices. For if he feels wealthier, the capitalist may assume less thrifty habits, even though his current real income has not altered. Or one can imagine him being influenced not by the *level* of actual capital valuations but by the *change* in these valuations within the period considered. For he may be supposed to consider as income not only his current revenue but also the windfall gain or loss due to changes in the valuation of his assets." (Kalecki 1939a, pp. 56-57.) While only a two-class society is considered, Kalecki noted complications arising out of different propensities to consume of various groups within each class. Thus it is not only the variations in the amount of income, but also the considerable shifts in the distribution of income among groups which determine changes in consumption. (Kalecki 1939a, pp. 59-60.)

Now, gross profits are equal to the sum of investment and capitalists' consumption ($P=I+C$) and I, with whose determinants we are at present not concerned, is equal to the difference between P and C. Making use of the relation between capitalists' consumption and profits, we substitute the propensity-to-consume behavioral equation for the term C, and obtain the profits determinants equation under the hitherto stipulated simplifying assumptions where profits at time t are determined by current investment and profits at the time $t-v$; i.e., $P_t=I_t+bP_{t-v}+A$, Kalecki then derives[8] what may be called a simplified profit-determination equation, which reads (Kalecki 1933f, trans. 1966h, pp. 3-4, *passim*): $P_t=(I_{t-w}+A)/(1-b)$, where $1>b>0$ and $A>0$. (Kalecki 1965l, pp. 53-54; cf. 1939a, pp. 42-74.)

The equation is based on: (1) the equality between profits and investment plus capitalists' consumption, and (2) the postulated relation between capitalists' consumption and profits at some earlier period (where A is the stable part of capitalists' consumption and b is the coefficient of consumption out of an increment of profit—*MPC* of profit-earners).

The importance of this equation is in that "it reduces the number of determinants of profits from two to one as a result of taking into consideration the dependence of capitalists' consumption on past profits as given by the [capitalists' propensity to consume] equation." (Kalecki 1965l, p. 54.) Profits are determined entirely by investment, subject to a certain time-lag. Furthermore, investment depends on investment decisions, determined by certain factors operating in the previous period. Thus profits are a direct outcome of former investment decisions and are sensitive to the variability of investment in time. The time-lag is not only caused by the length of the gestation period, but, *inter alia,* reflects delayed entrepreneurial reactions. (Kalecki 1965l, pp. 109-16.)

Kalecki's analysis led him again to conclude that capitalists' savings "lead" profits. He noted that this result may seem paradoxical, for good common sense would suggest the reverse sequence—viz., that savings are determined by profits. But he was emphatic that this is not so. Capitalists' consumption in a certain period is, *grosso modo,* the consequence of their decisions based on past profits. Since, typically, profits change intermittently, actual savings do not match intended disposal of income. "Indeed, actual savings which are equal to investment *will* 'lead' profits," as shown by the profit determinants equation. Kalecki shows how this can happen in a case where, for some time, both investment (and, therefore, saving) and profits are steady. Suppose a sudden rise in investment occurs. "Savings will increase immediately together with investment, and profits will rise by the same amount. However, capitalists' consumption will rise only after some time as a result of this primary increase in profits. Thus profits will still be increasing after the rise in investment and savings has already come to a stop." (Kalecki 1965l, p. 55; cf. pp. 57-58.)

Generalized Profits Equation

Let us now consider the implications of the profits determinants equation for the more realistic situation in which the system is not closed, government operations are not disregarded, and workers do save. How important is the influence of the budget deficit, foreign trade, and workers' savings on profit? Gross national product is composed of gross private investment, consumption, government expenditures on goods and services (including public investment), and the excess of exports over imports. The major claimants against income produced are the capitalists, workers, and government in the form of taxes. Thus gross national product earned equals gross profits after taxes, plus wages net of taxes, plus all taxes siphoned off by the government. By standard procedure of national income accounting it can be shown now that: Gross profits after taxes equals gross investment, plus budget deficit, plus export surplus, plus capitalists' consumption, minus workers' savings. Clearly, this equation differs from the simplified case.[9] Here, instead of simply investment, we have the sum of private investment, export surplus, and budget deficit (denoted by I'), minus workers' savings (S); i.e., $P=I'-S+C$.[10]

Allowing for the complication, the profit equation established for the simplified case can be modified and generalized to read: $P_t=(I'_{t-w}-S_{t-w}+A)/(1-b)$, where I' differs from I by the amount of export surplus and budget deficit. Before, such an equation was derived from the postulated income-consumption behavior of profit receivers and from the assumption that I amounts to the excess of profits over profit-earners' consumption. But if workers do save, profits, plus workers' savings, less capitalists' consumption is equal to the nonconsumed part of national product. But aggregate savings are equal to the sum of private investment, export surplus, and budget deficit in the general formulation (the expanded version) that takes into account complications arising from introducing export surplus and budget deficit. Then, the relevant difference between profits and capitalists' consumption becomes $I'-S$. It is the latter expression that replaced I in the simplified profit determination formula. If $I'=I$ and S is negligible or statistically indeterminable, the simplified equation may be used instead of the expanded version (or I is modified accordingly to allow for export surplus, plus budget deficit). (Kalecki 1965l, pp. 57-58.) But, in general, profits are governed by private investment decisions, by export surplus, by budget deficit, and by the different propensities of each class to save.

Ceteris paribus, the increase in the export surplus component of the expanded profit equation will increase profits *pro tanto.* (Cf. Kalecki 1966h, pp. 16-19.) The same applies to the budget deficit. The existence of the export surplus (budget deficit) permits profits to increase above the level which would be determined by the rate of private investment and capitalists' propensity to consume. In this sense domestic capitalists who succeed in increasing their export surplus to foreign countries are able to reap extra profits at the expense of their foreign rivals. "It is from this point of view that the fight for foreign markets may be viewed." (Kalecki, 1965l, p. 51; cf. 1956d, pp. 3-13.)

Budget deficit generates saving just as investment does, and it is available to be lent to the government. In a certain sense, the budget deficit can be treated as "an artificial export surplus." In case of an export surplus, a country's proceeds from exports exceed those from imports. The budget deficit denotes that the private sector gets more from the government than is expropriated from it in the form of taxes. Whereas the counterpart of the export surplus is an increase in external lending, the counterpart of the budget deficit is an increase of government's liability to the private sector.

The important thing is that both export surplus and budget deficit generate profits in a similar way. To recall, the argument—inspired by Rosa Luxemburg's work—once again points to the significance of the problem of effective demand and of "external markets"—both foreign markets *stricto sensu* as a source of external profits and those created by the government deficit (including armaments markets)—for the realization of production and the expansion of the economy. "Without such markets profits are conditioned by the ability of capitalists to consume or to undertake capital investment. It is the export surplus and the budget deficit which enable the capitalists to make profits over and above their own purchases of goods and services." Kalecki maintains that the fight for the control of existing foreign markets and the expansionism which gives new opportunities for export of capital associated with export of commodities, can be treated as a drive for export surplus, "the classical source of 'external' profits. Armaments and wars, usually financed by budget deficits, are also a source of this kind of profits." (Kalecki 1965l, p. 52; cf. Kalecki 1939a, pp. 44-45.)

Determination of National Income

Kalecki proceeded from examination of the determinants of the relative wage share in national income to the determinants of profits and then to the determination of national income. Again, the last inquiry concentrates on the most essential issues, by examining first the special case (a simplified model) where the country's international trade and the state budget are in balance and only capitalists save. The task is to establish the basic relation between national income and investment. Kalecki used here the aforementioned profits determinants equation. The difference between aggregate Y and P represents the nonprofit spendable earnings or the return paid to labor.[11] But for some purposes it is better to concentrate on the share of wages and salaries.

While the share of wages alone during the course of the business cycle may not record significant fluctuations, this is not the case if both wages and salaries are treated together. For salaries, to a large extent, are independent of variations in the rate of output, at least within a certain range. With constant money-wage ratio, salaries tend to rise less during the boom than wages and to decline relatively less during the slump. The real wage and salary bill (V) is likely to display less pronounced fluctuations during the course of the business cycle than real national income. Kalecki derives the following relationship (in real terms): $V = \alpha Y + B$, where coefficient α is positive and less than unity, and B is a positive constant in the short run, but subject to long-run variations. The coefficient α denotes that part of the relative share of wages and salaries in Y that is independent of the level of Y; the other part B/Y indicates the impact of the stable part (fixed cost element) in salaries. By dividing both sides of this equation by Y, we get the following formula for the relative share of wages and salaries in national income (V/Y): $V/Y = \alpha + (B/Y)$. It follows that V/Y increases when real national income falls—a relationship of considerable importance for explaining the business cycle.

In the simplified case where national income is composed of wages plus salaries and profits, substituting $(Y-P)/Y$ for V/Y, we get: $(Y-P)/Y = \alpha + (B/Y)$, and solving for Y, we obtain: $Y = (P+B)/(1-\alpha)$. The gross national product or income in time t is: $Y_t = (P_t + B)/(1-\alpha)$. Together with the profits determinants equation, the last given equation serves for the determination of national income Y_t, in terms of I_{t-w}. Subject to simplifying assumptions, it is evident that the gross national income is fully determined by investment with a time-lag. As the first equation *reflects* the determinants of distribution of national income "we can also say: the gross income, Y_t, is pushed up to a point at which profits out of it, as determined by the 'distribution factors,' correspond to the level of investment I_{t-w}." The function of the factors determining the distribution of income (including the degree of monopoly) is therefore "to determine income or product on the basis of profits which are in turn determined by investment." (Kalecki 1965l, p. 61.)

Given the postulated scaffolding, real profits are determined by capitalists' investment decisions and their propensity to consume. It is labor's income that is determined by the "distributional factors." Labor's share is the inverse of the degree of monopoly. In this manner profit-earners' expenditures on investment and consumption jointly with the determinants of distribution determine labor's consumption and thus aggregate production and employment. The aggregate output "will be pushed up to the point where profits carved out of it in accordance with the 'distribution factors' are equal to the sum of capitalists' consumption and investment." (Kalecki 1965l, p. 47.)

As a result of the rise in the degree of monopoly, the relative share of profits in income increases only by lowering the relative share of labor. The real wage depends on the degree of monopoly. The distribution determinants will affect not the real profits which will remain the same, but rather the real wages and salaries, effective demand, national income, employment, and the level of utilization of capacity. A rise in the degree of monopoly entails rise in the P/Y ratio, but real total profits do not change, since they continue to be determined by past investment decisions. With an unchanged amount of investment there is the same total amount of profits (savings). (Cf. Kalecki 1943k, p. 50.) While profits remain unyielding, the real wages and salaries and the real national product will decline partly because of a fall in effective demand for wage goods, with a consequent fall in output and employment in the sector producing consumption goods for workers.[12] Thus forces will set in to contract aggregate output and income which will adjust itself just so much that the higher percentage share of profits in output renders an unchanged absolute amount of profits. Here the salient point is that shifts in the distribution of income take place not by way of a change (increase) in profits, but through a mechanism of variations (decline) in national output (income). The clue is that with a given level of output and income, an increase in the "degree of monopoly" and thus a shift from wages to profits will produce a rise in underutilization of productive capacity.

Reverting to the equations for the determination of national income, the rise in the degree of monopoly will be reflected in the reduction of the coefficient α (rise in the denominator). Hence, only a reduced volume of national income (Y_t) will be compatible with a given level of maintainable investment (I_{t-w}). Clearly, a rise in investment will increase national income by a multiplied amount owing to the well-known induced effects. *Ceteris paribus,* the greater the *MPC,* the higher is the number by which the increase in investment must be multiplied to yield the resulting cumulative increment in income; and the larger the "saving leakage" (*MPS*), the smaller is the value of the multiplier. Of course, the final effect of change of investment depends on the postulated functional relation between the spendable income and consumption of each class.

Here the sharp differences between the marginal propensities of wage-earners and nonwage-earners are of primary importance.

Again, profits are determined by investment with a time-lag. An increase (change) in investment by ΔI_{t-w} produces with a time-lag an increase (change) in profits in time (t) ΔP_t so that: $\Delta P_t = \Delta I_{t-w}/(1-b)$. Clearly, the ratio of an increment (change) of income of capitalists to the corresponding increment (change) of investment (with a time-lag) is equal to $1/(1-b)$, or the size of the multiplier is equal here to the reciprocal of the *MPS* out of profits.

But ΔY_t increases more than ΔP_t, owing to the combined effect of the rise of investment on capitalists' and labor's consumption. The entire increment in national income corresponding to and caused by the increment of investment consists of an increase in income in the form of profits ΔP_t and that amount which is paid out (accrued) to labor in the form of wages and salaries ($\Delta Y_t = \Delta P_t + \Delta V_t$). With assumed zero savings out of V, labor's income equals consumption out of wages and salaries. $V_t = Y_t - P_t$ and $\Delta Y_t - \Delta V_t = \Delta P_t$. Since ΔP_t equals ΔI_{t-w} times the reciprocal of *MPS* out of profits, by substitution (referring to the right-hand side of the change in investment-profits relation equation), we get: $\Delta Y_t = [\Delta I_{t-w}/(1-b)] + \Delta V_t$. By simple algebraic manipulation, and substituting the coefficient α (denoting that part of change in income which accrues to wages and salaries) for $\Delta V_t/\Delta Y_t$, we obtain $\Delta Y_t = \Delta I_{t-w}/[(1-\alpha)(1-b)]$, where both $(1-\alpha)$ and $(1-b)$ are smaller than one,[13] so that ΔI_{t-w} produces an amplified effect on income: $\Delta Y_t/\Delta I_{t-w} = 1/[(1-\alpha)(1-b)]$. *Ceteris paribus,* with a given rise in investment, the higher the coefficient b (marginal propensity to consume out of incremental profit), the larger is the resulting increase in ΔP_t; the smaller *MPS,* the greater is ΔP_t. The higher the value of α, the lower is the share of profits in income, and vice versa. The lower the value of α, the larger is the value of b and the larger the *MPS.* With a given b, the profit share would be higher (and labor's share lower), the higher the $\Delta I_{t-w}/Y_t$ ratio is.

Investment calls the tune and changes income by a factor larger than one. A change in investment entails an equivalent primary change in profits (national income), but it sets into motion a chain reaction; i.e., national income changes more in relation to investment owing to the effect that a change in investment produces on consumption out of profits [factor: $1/(1-b)$] and on wage- and salary-earners' income and consumption [factor: $1/(1-\alpha)$].[14]

The above discussion concentrated on the relation between the absolute changes of *I*, *P*, and *Y*. The proportionate changes or discrepancy in fluctuations of key variables in the course of the business cycle are of considerable interest. To repeat, in the equations for the determination of national income, both *A* and *B* denote positive constants. Thus *P* changes proportionately less in the course of the business cycle than *I*, and the same holds for variations in *Y* and relations to *P*. This means that the relative changes of *I* in the course of the business cycle are greater than the fluctuations of *Y*, and, *a fortiori*, greater than those of *C*. (Since *Y* is the sum of *I* and *C*, and if one component varies proportionately more than *Y*, *ipso facto*, the relative variations of the other must be smaller—i.e., the relative variations of *C* must be smaller than those of *I*.) Thus *I* declines in the relation to *C* during the slump and rises during the upswing of economic activity. Given the foregoing assumptions, the level of economic activity is determined by the highly volatile and variable adjustment.

If *I* fluctuates more than *Y* in the course of a business cycle, it need not necessarily be a long-term trend, since the two factors chiefly responsible for the disproportionate cyclical variations of *I* and *Y* may be absent or substantially modified in the long-run process of growth. Indeed, the variations in the cyclical fluctuations of rates of *I* and *Y* are primarily due to: (1) consumption out of profits fluctuates less than profits; and (2) the relative proportionate changes of the wage and salary component are smaller than those of national income. But the constants on which the argument rests are likely to vary considerably in the long run. Item (1) need not necessarily hold, as the relatively stable part of the capitalists' consumption (assumed constant *A*)—indeed, a slowly changing magnitude conditioned by economic and social developments in the past—may rise in the long run proportionately with profits. Similarly with item (2), since the approximate constancy of *B*—the stable part of wages and salaries, which reflects the fixed cost element in salaries—may not be satisfied in the long run. In fact, *B* may, but by no means must, rise in the long run *pari passu* with income. Therefore, *Y* and *I* need not record in the long run the variations in the rates of change that they do show in the course of a business cycle, where certain economic variables are always subject to far greater fluctuations than others.

It cannot be stressed enough that the argument advanced on the determination of national income clearly rests on the assumption that the condition of elastic supply prevails. (Indeed, the equation for the determination of national income reflects Kalecki's approach to the theory of the firm and the special price-cost relationship postulated). However, such repercussions of an increase in investment (or capitalists' consumption) are clearly possible only if there exist idle capacities in the consumer-goods-producing industries. If the capacity output of consumer goods is already produced, a rise in investment will not increase the flow of output of consumer goods, but will merely entail a rise in the prices of these goods. This is an inflationary situation: The result is that real wages will fall compared to the levels which would have been achieved if there existed surplus capacities to produce wage goods.[15]

During contraction the multiplier works backward, magnifying the initial fall in investment (employment) owing to repercussions of such a decline on reduction of workers' and capitalists' income and consumption. Kalecki noted that, in order to bring into sharper focus the nature of the process generated by a decline in investment activity in the capitalist economy, it would be instructive to contrast it with the effects of curtailment in investment in a socialist economy. The labor released from the investment goods sector, owing to curtailment of investment activity, should be absorbed by the sector producing consumer goods, thus increasing the flow of output from this sector. (Cf. Kalecki 1968e, pp. 73-79.) The increased supply of consumer goods "would be absorbed by means of a reduction in their prices. Since profits of the socialist industries would be equal to investment, prices would have to be reduced to the point where the decline in profits would be equal to the fall in the value of investment." (Kalecki 1965l, p. 62.)

Kalecki envisaged that the socialist system would solve the problem of effective demand, full employment, and distribution by determining appropriate relations between prices and costs (wages). Output and employment of human resources and productive capacity would not be limited by insufficiency of effective demand. The socialist economy would resort to a flexibility of prices in relation to wages, in order to maintain the full-employment equilibrium, instead of relying on the output and employment contraction mechanism which serves to achieve "under-employment equilibrium" in the capitalist economy. In fact, there is only limited price flexibility in the modern capitalist economy. To recall, the oligopolistic and monopolistic factors involved in price formation significantly affect distribution (i.e., relation between prices and wage costs) in the course of the business cycle and even in the long-run process of growth. In a socialist economy, prices of consumer goods would be fixed by planning authorities in relation to wage costs in such a way as to achieve full utilization of productive capacity and "tolerable distribution," both in the short and in the long run. In practice, however, there appear to be formidable difficulties and institutional obstacles to even "moderately frequent and significant" price changes. In the existing socialist economies, there seems to be a deeply rooted propensity to effect changes by varying output, which in itself is not objectionable, if it were not for the institutionally created, inordinately protracted time-lags. There is a proverbial reluctance to rely on the controlled "price mechanism." It is probably true that the planners are less reluctant to revert to downward price adjustments—and once they do, they advertise them loudly—than to upward changes. Various camouflage devices are used to disguise price increases or to limit the increase of real wages or households' incomes. It may be noted here parenthetically that the planners have sometimes resorted to deliberate creation of unemployment, while underutilization of resources is commonplace. But what is being done is in sharp contradiction to what could be done. Whatever the rationale of policies (and shifts in policies) pursued—more about which later—it is instructive to reflect on the following passage:

> Full employment would be maintained through the reduction of prices in relation to costs. In the capitalist system, however, the price-cost relationship, as reflected in . . . [the equation for determination of national income], is maintained and profits fall by the same amount as investment plus capitalists' consumption through the reduction in output and employment. It is indeed paradoxical that, while the apologists of capitalism usually consider the 'price mechanism' to be the great advantage of the capitalist system, price flexibility proves to be a characteristic feature of the socialist economy.[16]

V

THEORY OF CYCLICAL FLUCTUATIONS AND LONG-RUN CHANGES

A General View

"THE OBJECTIVE OF ECONOMIC DYNAMICS is to describe and explain the fluctuations in economic magnitudes," including the pervasive cyclical fluctuations and long-run changes in the development of the capitalist economy. (Tinbergen and Polak 1950, p. 3.)

The theory of economic fluctuations seeks to explain certain swinging motions in the rate of economic activity, as reflected in the movement of economic variables, and to provide a systematic insight into the type of movement that the economic mechanism can perform (damped or fading out with ever decreasing amplitude of fluctuations; unstable or explosive with ceaselessly increasing amplitude; and oscillations that are of nonexplosive and nondying variety). The fundamental questions to be answered are what causes the recurrence of fluctuations, in what ways are the swinging movements generated (from within the economic system or externally precipitated), and how is their motion kept alive; i.e., how does one position grow out of the preceding one, how does the cyclical mechanism work and how is it maintained or constrained.[1] Clearly, these questions entail not only a study of interrelations between economic quantities at a given point of time, but the relations between economic variables at different points of time.[2] The latter case is essentially different from a static system (e.g., as represented by the Walrasian system of equations, in which all the values of the variables are determined by the data relating to the same point of time) wherein the economy is considered as devoid of dynamic elements, such as a lagged response.[3] Static analysis does not admit self-generating or endogenous movements created by the structure of the internal economic mechanism itself. Dynamic theory is required to explain movements when one situation develops out of the foregoing one, and certain variables depend on lagged values of the others, i.e., when it is necessary to introduce certain equations which embrace simultaneously several relations among variables whose magnitudes relate to different moments of time.[4]

A crucial difference between economic statics and dynamics is that dynamic theory can never be indifferent to the inquiry into the time a certain movement (process of adaptation to change) takes. "Economic dynamics must measure time also; it must incorporate time in its analysis as one of the variables. As a consequence, economic dynamics is nearer to reality and, by being less abstract, is sometimes simpler." (Tinbergen and Polak 1950, p. 103.)

Thus in business cycle analysis it is of particular interest to investigate reactions to certain economic conditions: how a given change at a given moment acts on other phenomena with a certain time-lag. In dynamic theory time appears in a most essential way; the system is evolving; present events are the result of preceding developments, which contribute, in turn, to the further development of the system. It is thus that a dynamic process arises. (Cf. Kalecki 1943k, pp. 80 ff.; Hickman, ed. 1972.)

The empirical record indicates that fluctuations in economic variables—as manifested in fluctuations in production, income, employment, rate of utilization of productive capacity, and other indicators of the changing rate of aggregate economic activity—occurred around a path of ascending, long-run growth trends.[5] Long-term factors determining the economic development of the capitalist economy certainly affect the course of a growing economy and the course of the business cycle as such. Clearly, the term *business cycle* does not imply approximate regularity in the pattern and timing of the recurrent swings in the rate of economic activity. The term *fluctuations* is the more appropriate designation of the phenomenon. Indeed, no two cycles are exactly the same. Some economists, like Irving Fisher, thought that there are just a number of ups and downs. Not surprisingly there is no unanimity among economists about the proximate causes of the oscillatory phenomena. The prevalent view seems to be that the fluctuations stem primarily, if not exclusively, from fluctuations in effective demand. (Cf. Hansen 1964, ch. 14; Duesenberry 1958, ch. 11; Matthews 1959, ch. 4; Hamberg 1951; Haberler 1958; and Lundberg 1968.) Yet, though they are not closely related, observed oscillations have much in common and there is room for emphasizing their common characteristics or differences. Not only do the views on the nature and remedies for the "old" business fluctuations sharply differ, but with changing postwar capitalism we face a new emerging pattern of "political business cycles." Contemporary capitalism where sharp depressions are avoided as a result of the intervention of the new actor in the cycle drama—the government—is generally still fairly remote from the full utilization of its resources. Although the relative severity and character of economic fluctuations have markedly changed, the cycle did not become obsolete. Varied configurations of old and new forces produce fluctuations in the economic time series.

Skeleton of Kalecki's Theory

The "pre-Keynesian capitalism" used to achieve a more or less full utilization of its productive potential only at the peak of the boom, and frequently not even then. Nor did these full-employment booms fill a major part of the full cycle. A good part of capital stock lay idle in the slump. Fluctuations in the utilization of available manpower paralleled those in the utilization of capacity. "The reserve of capital equipment and the reserve army of unemployed are typical features of capitalist economy at least throughout a considerable part of the cycle." (Kalecki 1965l, p. 131.)

The number of models of economic fluctuations available is "embarrassingly large." (Tinbergen 1967, p. 43.) Both literary (largely nonmathematical) and mathematically formulated theories have been constructed in an attempt to explain the cyclical pattern of the development of the capitalist economy.

Kalecki's pioneering and distinct theory of cyclical fluctuations belongs to the family of maintained (periodic swinging motions which neither peter out nor explode), macrodynamic,[6] mathematical (econometric) models of the economic system.[7] Obviously, it is the economic content of the analytical construct and not its mathematical properties that are of fundamental economic significance. Indeed, it is of the utmost importance "to distinguish between the *mathematical form* of the [economic] mechanism, i.e., of the equations [system of relations existing between variables] defining it, and the *economic sense* of these equations. The mathematical form determines the nature of the possible movements, the economic sense being of no importance here. Thus, two different economic systems obeying, however, the same types of equations may show exactly the same movements. But, it is evident that for all other questions the economic significance of the equations is of first importance and no theory can be accepted whose economic significance is not clear." (Tinbergen 1935, p. 242.)

In the Polish essay (1933f), whose essential part was translated into English (1966h, pp. 3-15), in the paper he read at the Econometric Society in Leyden in 1933 (1935h), and in the less mathematical French version (1935d), Kalecki dealt with a number of basic issues which were at the center of economic discussions during the subsequent twenty years. Those studies also reflect the most essential features of his theory of the business cycle. Kalecki modified, reformulated, and improved the model many times, seeking to bring it closer to reality. The basic contours of the early version of the analytical construct and some of the changes introduced in later versions will occupy the rest of this chapter. In the next section I attempt only to sketch the development of the argument.

"A happy feature of Kalecki's system is the fact that he places capital goods production in the center. A very remarkable feature is that the very small number of variables included is sufficient to get a closed system." (Tinbergen 1935, pp. 269-70.) The fundamental and interesting dynamic characteristics of Kalecki's model, namely the separation of investment decision from actual investment and the determinants of investment decision function, will be examined at greater length later.

In a closed economy without government demand, the level of economic activity is determined by investment. Fluctuations in investment engender the corresponding fluctuations in aggregate economic activity. It is the volatile fluctuations in investment that generally dominate the ups and downs in economic activity. The accent is on the acute variability of investment, which varies relatively more than consumption (falls in relation to consumption during the slump and rises during the boom). That is, aggregate output (income, expenditure) and consumption show smaller relative fluctuations than investment activity. Kalecki approached the problem essentially by establishing two basic relations based on: (1) the impact of effective demand generated by investment upon profit and national income; and (2) the determinants of investment decision. If fluctuations in investment cause fluctuations in economic activity what determines investment? This is the thorny question that preoccupied Kalecki most of his life. The most controversial of the assumptions underlying business cycle models "are those concerning the determinants of investment decisions. The rate of investment decisions is assumed in some theories to be determined by the rate of change in income (or output) and in some by the level of income. Indeed the problem of determinants of investment belongs probably to the least explored subjects of modern economics." (Kalecki 1949b, p. 57. Cf. Meyer and Kuh 1957; Klein 1951b.) Some two decades later, Kalecki reflected that the first relation "does not involve now particularly intricate questions. The second, to my mind, remains the central *pièce de résistance* of economics." (Kalecki 1968j, p. 263.)

Briefly, in his original presentation, the decision to invest is considered an increasing function of national income (real profit accruing to profit-earners) and a decreasing one of the volume of stock of capital of some time ago. The gist of the theory presented in *Studies in Economic Dynamics* (1943) consists of the dependence of investment decisions in fixed capital goods per unit of time; on the stream of current profit (savings); and on the rate of change in factors determining the profitability of investment, particularly the rate of change in the level of national income. Also considered is the change in the stock of fixed capital that adversely affects the profitability of investment. Further refinements are introduced in *Theory of Economic Dynamics* (1954, 1965). But broadly speaking, investment is determined, again with a certain time-lag, by the level and the rate of change of economic activity. Thus investment in a given period is determined by the level and the rate of change in the level of investment at some earlier period. In the last version, "Trend and Business Cycles Reconsidered" (1968j), Kalecki introduced certain novel features, particularly regarding some effects of innovations which affect the dynamic process as a whole.

Abstracting here from several distinct features of Kalecki's construct, the preliminary mechanism of business fluctuations can be explained in terms of the mutual interaction of the two principal determinants that induce investment: (1) the stimulating effect of higher income on investment; and (2) the depressing effect of growth of productive capacity in view of the distinctive relation between investment and the stock of capital (investment decisions once converted into the form of actual investments enlarge the stock of productive capital), and vice versa. "We see that the question, 'What causes periodical crises?' could be answered shortly: the fact that investment is not only produced but also producing." Investment viewed in its income-generating capacity "is the source of prosperity, and every increase of it improves business and stimulates a further rise of investment." Simultaneously, however, additional capital equipment adds to productive capacity and as soon as it is put into operation it competes with the stock of equipment of older vintage. "The tragedy of investment is that it causes crisis because it is useful. Doubtless many people will consider this theory paradoxical. But is is not the theory which is paradoxical, but its subject—the capitalist economy." (Kalecki 1939a, pp. 148-49.)

Development of the Argument

In view of the rather cool initial reception that Kalecki's theory received, it is worth noting that, in his illuminating survey and suggestions for the development of a quantitative business cycle theory, in 1935, Jan Tinbergen called attention to the importance of "some business cycle theories that form macrodynamic closed systems and are formulated mathematically. The first publication of this sort was a paper in Polish by Kalecki in *Proba teorii koniunktury,* Warszawa, 1933. A few months later appeared Frisch's 'Propagation Problems and Impulse Problems.' "[8] Tinbergen briefly summarized Kalecki's model and concluded that his system entails certain difficulties of great practical importance, but that "there are important features in the theory and that the exact form in which it is presented creates the possibility of a clear and fruitful discussion."[9] Ragnar Frisch, although critical of certain aspects (the imposed condition that the solution should be undamped—about which later) praised Kalecki for presenting at Leyden "a highly interesting macrodynamic study of the economic system." (Frisch and Holme 1935, p. 225.)

The highly technical and often austere manner in which Kalecki presented his paper to the Econometric Society, at a time when literary economics flourished, was undoubtedly a factor in the coldness of its reception and lack of interest from the profession in general, as noted in a preceding chapter. Indeed, much was left unsaid. Perhaps a few more equations would have helped. Kalecki's approach was unfamiliar to most of his readers at the time. Some economists still maintain that Kalecki is totally unintelligible, and that it is virtually impossible to follow his cycle theory. Yet his mathematical model contained all the essential elements of the revolutionary Keynesian system and "made it dynamic in the bargain." This fact, as was previously noted, was recognized by leading participants in the Keynesian Revolution later on. Indeed, it is also remarkable that, in reconsidering Kalecki's macrodynamic model some three decades later, another leading econometrician of our times, a distinguished student of the Keynesian Revolution, Lawrence R. Klein, acknowledged Kalecki's great contribution in the early 1930s in the light of modern developments. Klein considered that all the essential components of Kalecki's model have found (or are finding) their way into strategic places in modern econometric model-building. In many respects, Kalecki's contribution was the foundation of all modern cycle theory.

However, the mathematical formulation offers only a partial explanation of the initially cool reception of Kalecki's theory. I do not suggest that generally business cycle theorists or their students were frightened by mathematics in those days. Kalecki's model was not much more difficult to understand than, say Robertson's or Ohlin's, or even the three-dimensional diagrams of Hayek, surrounded as they were by obtuse language. Here a factor of major importance was rather that, at the time, business cycle theory was largely an English monopoly, with a bit of competition from Stockholm. The general academic approach was still that economic fluctuations *ought* not to occur; that they result from some institutional imperfection, probably in the banking system, which quite literally should be outlawed. In such a climate the academic interests centered on the monetary theories of cycles and on the behavior of the banking system. It took, as we know, the Keynesian Revolution to lead economists to more fundamental business cycle models like Kalecki's. (Cf. Higgins 1950, pp. 255-74; Hickman, ed. 1972, vol. 2, pp. 601 ff.)

In the somewhat less mathematical French version of the theory of business cycles, the general principle of the theory of effective demand was again the central feature. The exposition was recast and some points were elaborated (e.g., the money market). It was perhaps unfortunate that the General Theory was advanced through the medium of the cycle, and the fact that the paper was in French did not help either. Be that as it may, in this context it is important to note that the French version contained a reference to the original theory of Aftalion and set out its differences from Kalecki's own analytical construct. (Cf. Aftalion 1913; 1927, pp. 165-70.) In the opening paragraph, Kalecki referred to the fact that he was dealing with a problem similar to that with which Aftalion was preoccupied. Interestingly, at the end of the article, Kalecki remarked in a footnote that Aftalion—though in a different way—also arrived at the conclusion that production of capital goods fluctuates more markedly than that of consumer goods. But Aftalion's ingenious observations are based on the thesis of permanent exploitation of capacity—a thesis which shows that growth of production is always connected with expansion of capacity, whereas in Kalecki's exposition the variations of utilization of capacity play a crucial role. (Kalecki 1935d, p. 305.) One wonders whether Kalecki was aware of Aftalion's contribution when he framed his theory. This does not seem likely. Probably, Aftalion's work was called to his attention by the editor of the journal or some French economist who might have read the article prior to its publication.

After some years in England, Kalecki published *Essays in the Theory of Economic Fluctuations* (1939a). The sixth essay of the volume, entitled "A Theory of the Business Cycle," was an altered version of the article published under the same title in *Review of Economic Studies* (1937b).[10] By that time the essay had become, at least in some circles, "a classic of contemporary business cycle theory." (Lange 1941, p. 283.) As compared with previous expositions, in general the book expounds to a much greater extent on what Kalecki called the Keynesian theory of the multiplier. But, as noted before, elements of the multiplier theory could be traced to his early Polish paper. The contact with the Keynesians undoubtedly made an imprint on his thinking and was acknowledged in the foreword to the volume (p. 7).

The exposition of Kalecki's argument is probably clearest and simplest in *Essays in the Theory of Economic Fluctuations.*[11] It is not surprising that Cambridge students are always referred to this book rather than to its successors. But, whereas the earlier model is superior in its expository powers and its focus on fundamentals, the later developments are closer to reality.

The two new versions of the model (1943 and 1954) aimed at generalizing the earlier model in a number of ways and relating Kalecki's theory to some of the models that had been constructed by others in the meantime. (Cf. Kalecki 1949b, pp. 57-64; Allen 1965, pp. 259-62; Lange 1961b.) A number of important modifications, elaborations, and refinements, particularly regarding the factors determining investment decisions and influencing the investment process, were introduced both in *Studies in Economic Dynamics* and *Theory of Economic Dynamics.*

Studies in Economic Dynamics was prepared for publication in 1942 while Kalecki worked on the problems of the war economy for the Oxford Institute of Statistics. Whereas in the earlier work Kalecki dealt with an economy without a secular trend, part 2 of this slim volume contains two chapters on the pure business cycle and trend, respectively.[12] Kalecki concentrated on the influence of factors from which he had abstracted hitherto in order to obtain a pure business cycle in a trendless economy (see also Kalecki 1939a, p. 117). For instance, in the investment determinants function additional determinants were introduced, depending on the preceding history and evolution of the developing system. Thus the economy ceased to be trendless. Furthermore, this current trend, being the result of foregoing development, contributes in turn to the future long-run development of the economic system. It is in this way, as Kalecki showed, that the dynamic process arises. The shift in approach is evident from the foreword to *Studies in Economic Dynamics,* where he pointed out that in that work he focused more attention on "the long-run aspect of the problems considered." (Kalecki 1943k, p. 7). The opening paragraph of the part of *Studies* dealing with business cycle and trend offers the following justifications for this new version of the theory: (1) the problem is approached from a new angle and new factors are introduced in the explanation of the cycle mechanism; (2) the new treatment allows for some of the previously used simplifying assumptions to be discarded and for obtaining new results; and (3) "I do not now consider only the problem of the 'pure' business cycle, but deal in the last essay with the trend superimposed on the cycle." (Kalecki 1943k, p. 59.)

In a review of the book, Tibor Scitovsky wrote about Kalecki's theory as "the most convincing explanation of the business cycle." Indeed, Scitovsky considered that the essay on long-run economic development "breaks new ground in being the first theoretical analysis of a dynamic long-run trend, its determinants and its relationship to the pure business cycle." He appropriately concluded that "in general, one may say that the book whets rather than assuages the reader's appetite. It contains more ideas than can be adequately discussed within the compass of its ninety pages. But to the intelligent reader this should be a stimulus rather than a source of dissatisfaction." (Scitovsky 1946, p. 452.)

The results are again generalized in the *Theory of Economic Dynamics,* in which the relationships that were the basis of the business cycle theory, developed in *Theory of Economic Fluctuations* and elaborated thereafter, are treated as a special case of the theory now advanced. Kalecki showed that his theory covered as special cases some of the existing theories of investment decision. He presented a searching criticism of the acceleration principle. In the Foreword to *Economic Dynamics*, Kalecki wrote that it was "essentially a new book." He admitted that although "the basic ideas are not much changed, the presentation and even the argument have been substantially altered." (Kalecki, 1965l, p. 5.) Kalecki added that, in some instances, particularly in the chapter on the business cycle and shocks and on the process of economic development, new material has been introduced and new statistical material has been added. A. W. Phillips, himself a distinguished contributor to the mathematical models of business cycles, wrote about *Theory of Economic Dynamics:* "... whatever the limitations, Mr. Kalecki's contributions have been of the greatest importance in the development of dynamic theories and methods of analysis and this new presentation of his ideas will repay careful study."[13]

Again in 1962h, Kalecki first developed a business cycle equation of a fairly general character devised to cover: (1) his own theory as formulated in *Theory of Economic Dynamics;* (2) the business cycle theory based on the acceleration principle; and (3) Harrod's theory as presented in "Notes on Trade Cycle Theory," (*Economic Journal,* 1951). Then modifications of the basic relations for expanding economy are introduced. That is, the business cycle equation is generalized and dynamized so as to apply to economic systems subject to a tendency of long-run economic development. Next, Kalecki argued that the Harrodian rate of growth is ephemeral in the sense that any deviation from the path determined by it renders the system nonexpanding; i.e., generating cyclical fluctuations but not subject to growth trends.[14] He maintained that the business cycle equation arrived at offers two solutions for the rate of balanced growth: one, zero, so that the system is not subject to a long-run trend and another rendering a positive but unstable rate of growth.[15] Thus the system is incapable of long-run growth (proceeding along an ascending trend line) and merely fluctuates around a static position (horizontal line). Finally, Kalecki introduced the impact of development factors, such as innovations upon the investment in the business cycle equation. The system then yields two positive solutions for the rate of growth for which the lower is stable. Consequently, the system is subject to a uniform trend (steady growth), depending on the intensity of innovations. Cyclical fluctuations do occur around the trend line in accordance with the business cycle equation. Development factors like innovations enable the capitalist system to break the impasse of a stationary state and to expand at a rate depending on the intensity of such factors. Also such factors play a decisive role in determining the utilization of existing capacity. But the approach was not fully satisfactory in tackling the intricate question of the interrelationship of growth and cycles. (Cf. Goodwin 1955, p. 203.)

Kalecki was aware of the great difficulties of integrating growth and cyclical processes. He nevertheless tried to avoid splitting the argument into the pure business cycle and trend compartments and sought to advance theory toward a more unified approach. He wrote in his last major paper on this subject:

> I myself approached this problem in my *Theory of Economic Dynamics* and my "Observations on the Theory of Growth" in a manner which now I do not consider entirely satisfactory: I started from developing a theory of the "pure business cycle" in a stationary economy, and at a later stage I modified the respective equations to get the trend into the picture. By this separation of short-period and long-run influences I missed certain repercussions of technical progress which affect the dynamic process as a whole. I shall now try to avoid splitting my argument into these two stages just as much as applying the approach of moving equilibrium to the problem of growth. (Kalecki 1968j, p. 263.)

One more point needs to be noted here: R. G. D. Allen, and particularly Oskar Lange, expressed the view that the new version of the model represented in *Economic Dynamics* "has not the elegance which was characteristic of the original construct. . . . Kalecki's original model is doubtless far from realistic. However, it represents clearly and simply the active forces present in the process of economic development." (Lange 1961b, p. 285. Cf. Allen 1965, p. 261.) While I fully share Allen's and Lange's evaluation about "some very characteristic features and a convenient simplicity" of the early model, (Allen 1965, p. 261.) I believe that the later attempts to bring the model closer to reality were major forward strides.

The Simple Model

In studies of business cycle it is important to identify the intrinsic dynamic properties of the model which give rise to cyclical behavior. Here we concentrate on the internal economic mechanism which generates by its very own structure fluctuations from within, rather than on distinguishing between the mechanism and exterior influences (outside disturbances) as between undisturbed and disturbed oscillatory movements.[16] This kind of analysis pertains not only to a set of magnitudes at a given point of time whose interrelations are examined, "but we consider the magnitudes of certain variables in different points of time, and introduce certain equations which embrace at the same time several of these magnitudes belonging to different instants. This is the essential characteristic of a dynamic theory." (Frisch 1933, 1965, pp. 155-56; cf. Lundberg, 1937.)

Kalecki introduced fundamental and interesting dynamic features into his system, notably: (1) the time delay between investment decisions (orders) and realization,[17] and (2) the determinants of investment decision relations.[18] Indeed, among the most distinctive and remarkable features of Kalecki's model is the clear separation he makes between the decision to invest and the actual implementation; the difference in timing between the initiation of investment, investment production, income generating expenditures spread out throughout the period of production, and commissioning capital goods; the magnified effective demand and the actual delivery of finished investment goods enlarging the stock of existing productive capital.[19] Investment decisions, once they have been embodied in the form of actual investment, entail growth in the stock of productive capital (the capital-creating effect of investment). Once investments are so absorbed, they discourage further investments. Investment *decisions* in a given period, determined by certain factors operating in that period, are followed by actual investments with a time-lag; i.e., time elapses between the moment when decisions to invest are made and when decisions are completely executed. The length of time necessary for the realization of these decisions depends on technical and organizational conditions prevailing at the time of execution of these decisions. Clearly, the rate of investment in the period must not be confused with the rate of investment decisions of that period; the actual investment in time (*t*) is the result of past investment decisions. There exists this relation between the rate and investment decisions and deliveries of finished capital goods: The rate of the latter follows the former with a time-lag which is equal to the average period of construction (gestation).[20] The time-lag helps us to understand the cumulative nature of expansionary and contractionary processes.

In the later works the time-lag was still largely owing to the average period of construction but also reflected such factors as delayed entrepreneurial reaction. Consequently, we have the lagged relation where investment at time $(t+1)$ is equal to the rate of investment decision at time t $(I_{t+1}=D_t)$. The equation expresses the lapse of time between the conversion of the decision to invest into the actual investment.[21] Because of the time delay the variables in the equation need to be dated. The size of investment decisions in period t predetermines the size of completed investments in the following period $(t+1)$, i.e., decisions to invest logically take place in advance of their realization. Kalecki recognized that investment decisions embodied in investment orders are not strictly irrevocable, which further complicates the matter. Cancellation of investment orders, in spite of the considerable loss entailed, do take place, but probably not on a sufficient scale to invalidate the results. Thus this factor disturbs the relationship between investment decisions and implemented investments.

As noted, the basis of the business cycle theory originally presented is the proposition that the rate of investment decisions is an increasing function of national income (profits, or nonconsumed part of profits) and a decreasing one of the stock of capital some time ago.[22] Present decisions to invest are partly determined by present national income (aggregate effective demand) and partly by the existing stock of capital (K_t). Current national income at time t does not depend on the investment decisions taken at that time (D_t), but on investment decisions taken previously at time $t-1$. Whether national income will rise, fall, or remain stationary, depends on whether current investment decisions will surpass past investment decisions, fall short of past decisions, or neither increase nor decrease.

Thus the system behaves as if a certain delay were involved in the functional relationship between investment and income. That is, national income is lagging behind investment, and investment behind investment decisions, past investment decisions determine the present national income, which influences current investment decisions, which, in turn, determine the future national income.[23]

The level of real national income delimits approximately its distribution among wage-earners and profit-earners, particularly the profits accruing to the capitalist sector. The prospective rate of profit, and, therefore, investment, is determined, *grosso modo,* by the level of national income and stock of capital, with an appropriate time-lag. Therefore, these two factors are treated tentatively as the determinants of investment decisions. With a given stock of capital, the rate of profit that can be obtained under current conditions from a new investment is the greater, the larger the level of national income (effective demand). But the rate of current profit that can be obtained at present from carrying out a new investment does not represent sufficient basis for estimating the prospective rate of profit, for expected future developments must be taken into consideration. But since there is great uncertainty about what the future may bring forth, and yet the entrepreneur must make decisions in an uncertain world, the present state influences predominantly long-term expectations. Entrepreneurs often act as if they expected the existing situation essentially to continue in the future. Clearly, they tend to be optimistic when business prospers, and pessimistic when it does not. Generally, the prospective rate of profit is a function of the actual rate of profit. Thus, with a given volume of capital, the prospective rate of profit is greater the greater the national income. For a given volume of capital profits will rise with growth of effective demand; i.e., the rate of profit will rise. Contrariwise with the growth of the stock of capital for a given aggregate demand, profits yielded per unit of capital will decline. The larger the profit and the smaller the stock of existing capital equipment, the larger will be the prospective rate of profit on new investment. An increase in the volume of capital equipment, if profits are constant, is tantamount to a fall in the rate of profit.[24]

For the rate of investment decision (D), as an increasing function of the prospective rate of profit, Kalecki establishes the relation $D=g_eY$, or $D=g(Y,K)$, in which g is an increasing function and the index e denotes that it is determined only with a given stock of capital. The curve depicting the function g resembles an S-shape,[25] since when activity is improving, the state of business, as we know, colors the entrepreneurs' predictions about their future. The glowing optimism tends to be reflected in considerable increases in the rate of investment decisions. But after a certain point, disappointments and doubts begin. Optimism in the sustained strength of prosperity abates. The rate of investment decisions tends to slow down. Waves of economic optimism are followed by waves of pessimism. This situation leads to cutbacks in economic activity. In the slump the process is more or less reversed.[26] Thus we see that a higher investment in this period than in the preceding one means a higher level of current profit, and as current profit weighs heavily on forming businessmen's expectations about future profits, it means a higher anticipated rate of profit, with the ensuing augmented investment demand manifested in more orders placed and, therefore, in an increased rate of investment in the following period. But this is only a part of the story as investment exerts other influences; it is a "double-edged" instrument. The "dialectics" of the investment process envisaged by Kalecki cannot be overstressed. (Cf. Domar 1957; Harrod 1966.)

Considered from the standpoint of its income generating activity, during the gestation period investment raises effective demand, stimulates consumption, and prompts further increase in investment decisions. A rise in profits within the period under consideration renders additional projects attractive; propels the forces of prosperity; and, through the multiplication process, enlarges effective demand. While, undoubtedly, investment has a favorable effect on economic activity at the time it is executed, simultaneously every completed investment constitutes an addition to the existing stock of capital. Such growth of capacity affects adversely the rate of investment decisions; i.e., without it the rate of investment orders would be higher. Thus the accumulation (decumulation) of capital tends to restrict (extend) the boundaries of investment plans.

As the reader will observe, in Kalecki's model considerable importance is attached to the influence exerted on the dynamic process by changes in the capacity of capital equipment. The rate of change of capital per unit of time is equal to the difference between deliveries of newly produced capital equipment and the volume of retired capital equipment (replacement). Thus investment decisions cause lagged relations in two directions: If investment is rising this entails an increase both in income and in capital; the higher investment will raise (directly and indirectly) demand and encourage higher investment decisions, but the rising stock of capital will tend to reduce them and vice versa. It is the interplay of these two opposing forces that creates the cyclical movement. Sooner or later one will overtake the other, and a turning point will be reached. In such a way the system will self-generate four phases of the cyclical movement: Boom will give rise to recession, recession to depression, depression to recovery, and recovery to boom. (Cf. Kalecki 1966h, pp. 10-13.) The expansion of the productive apparatus hampers the upward cumulative movement, bringing it to an end and to the eventual slump. Expansion is converted into contraction, which assumes a cumulative character by a process inverse to that of cumulative expansionary movement. Investments exert a retarding effect when positive or an accelerating effect when negative. This means that, in a trendless economy, negative investments extricate the economy from the slump,[27] just as the accretion of capital stock is responsible for the turning point in the boom.[28] The growth of national wealth contains the seeds of retardation of the growth rate of economic activity. During a considerable part of the cycle, the additional wealth proves to be merely potential in character, as the accumulated capital is substantially underutilized. It becomes productive only in the successive upsurge. Disinvestment, or decapitalization of national wealth, spurs prosperity, breeds forces that put an end to the shrinkage of capital, and stimulates an increase in investment. The shrinkage of capital stimulates the upswing, and, again, the expansion of capital contains the seeds of depression. (Kalecki 1966h, pp. 29-31.)

Mixed Exogenous-Endogenous Cycle

In a field as prolific as business cycle theory, various classifications were offered of the essential elements of major streams in modern analysis and opposing theories. As noted, one of the fundamental questions that the cycle theorists are trying to answer is: By what principle are the economic oscillations maintained alive? One of the pioneering mathematical theories of maintained economic fluctuations was developed by Kalecki. Since then the explanation of the maintained cycle has preoccupied some of the ablest economists of our time. (Cf. Gordon and Klein, eds. 1965, pp. 3-5.) In this context the distinction between exogenous and endogenous movements (models) is essential. (Cf. Samuelson 1965, p. 335 and *passim*.)

Exogenous theories of the cycle see the origin of the fluctuations in some sort of disturbances or shocks which impinge on the economic system and which engender oscillations in economic activity. In other words, the system does not determine the values of all the variables and parameters contained in the equation defining its structure and behavior. Some of the variables are determined by forces acting from "outside-in" (with essentially one-way causation direction). Their values are externally given and their frequency of occurrence is quite random.

The celebrated and extreme example of exogenous factors is Jevons's sun spot theory. (Cf. Schumpeter 1954, pp. 1132-33, 742-45.) The less extreme exogenous variables include such development factors as innovations, autonomous investments, population movements, international economic relations (foreign demand), government policy, international tensions, and wars.[29]

By contrast, purely endogenous theories find the explanation for fluctuations in the forces operating within the economy itself; i.e., the *modus operandi* and the movements generated are explained by the inherent internal structure of the system.[30]

A purely exogenous theory views the swinging motion that the economic mechanism performs as nothing but a purely arbitrary, random, or unsystematic succession of external causes or disturbances which lead to cyclical movements. The exogenous movements are those during which certain externals to the system, non-economic data, vary, while in the case of endogenous movements, the exogenous variables are supposed to be constant. (Tinbergen 1951a, pp. 77 ff.)

Mathematical or econometric theories of business cycles tend to focus attention on systematic oscillations which spring from the internal structure of the economic mechanism and attempt to explain how the fluctuating process is produced from the response of the economic mechanism to changes in exogenous variables; i.e., how the economic mechanism responds and adapts itself to the random succession of changes in data. With very few exceptions, all serious explanations are neither purely exogenous nor purely endogenous. (Cf. Samuelson 1965, pp. 340 ff.)

Change in exogenous variables would give rise to corresponding swings of the economic system if the economic mechanism would react immediately and adapt itself instantaneously to the outside impulses (if lagged responses could be realistically ruled out). The mixed endogenous-exogenous explanation of cyclical movements focuses attention on the lagged functional relation variable and lagged adaptational adjustment of the economic mechanism. A system exhibiting a lagged response to the current endogenous variables is not only affected by the values of exogenous variables, disturbances, and parameters, but by the values of endogenous variables determined by the history of the economic mechanism. In this sense, the values of current endogenous variables depend on, or are predetermined by, exogenous disturbances and lagged endogenous variables. (Christ 1966, p. 179 and *passim*. Cf. Klein 1962, p. 60.) The cycle may be regarded as the interplay of the externally originating factors with the internal economic structure (the interaction of the exogenous and endogenous factors) and the economic mechanism possessing the capacity to perform cyclical movements in response to such disturbances. (Frisch 1933, 1965, pp. 155 ff.) Except in very special cases, values of coefficients, in essentially linear models, as that presented by Kalecki (1935h), are incapable of providing a satisfactory theory of maintained economic fluctuations. If the coefficients are such that the system generates damped fluctuations, theory must rely on the support of external impulses or shocks.[31] In order to constrain the explosive fluctuations, an externally imposed ceiling is usually added beyond which output cannot be expanded. (Cf. Hicks 1950; Kalecki 1965l, pp. 126-27 and *passim;* Matthews 1959, pp. 16 ff.)

In the previously mentioned mathematical model of the business cycle advanced by Frisch, there is an inherent tendency for the endogenous system to produce damped cycles, the amplitude of which will continuously decline, so that exogenous shocks, introduced from time to time, reinvigorate the oscillatory movement. Thus Frisch distinguishes between the impulses of shocks operating on the economy and originating from outside and the inner structure of the swinging system. He indicates the shapes of six-year movements that will follow when such shocks occur. Frisch showed that the length of economic oscillations and the tendency toward damping are determined by the intrinsic structural properties of the swinging pendulum (the internal propagation mechanism). Whereas the character and intensity (the amplitude) of fluctuations determine impulses from outside, the economic mechanism initiates more or less regular cyclical movements in economic activity and maintains the oscillations of an otherwise stable system. The character of the swings is determined by the economic system. The pattern of the motion is determined by the inner structure of the system, but the existence of the motions is determined by outside impulses.[32] Frisch acknowledged that Knut Wicksell was probably the first to distinguish clearly between the two types of problems in the theory of business cycle: the propagation problem and the impulse problem. Wicksell explicitly formulated the proposition that the source of energy maintaining the economic oscillations is erratic shocks. He conceived the economic system as being pushed along irregularly and jerkingly by impulses such as innovations that may cause, however, more or less regular wavelike swings. Wicksell illustrated his ideas by a simple but profound example: "If you hit a wooden rocking-horse with a club, the movement of the horse will be very different to that of the club."[33]

In view of the ideas expressed above, Kalecki qualified his analysis in *Theory of Economic Fluctuations,* by stating that: "Clearly it is an arbitrary and even unlikely assumption that the moving point comes back to its initial position E" after a full cycle (p. 148; fig. 15, p. 145). In reality instead of a closed curve in which the terminal position coincides with the point of departure, the trajectory may well be spiral (the fluctuations produced by the cyclical mechanism have a tendency to subside; i.e, the spiral converges toward the point of long-term equilibrium or the rising curve ceaselessly increasing the amplitude of fluctuations). Concentrating on the first case, Kalecki recognized that "an important point about any trade cycle theory is whether the cycle may be damped down or not." The course of the business cycle "may be such that the amplitude diminishes from cycle to cycle so that the system gradually approaches a state of equilibrium." (Kalecki, 1943r, p. 73.) However, as Frisch has shown, this is prevented by the existence of "erratic shocks." (Kalecki, 1939a, p. 148.) A combination of a damping mechanism with erratic shocks produces nondying fluctuations. To sum up, the cycle theory faces a fundamental difficulty in demonstrating that the oscillations are of a nondying and a nonexploding variety. The difficulty may be escaped by departing from a purely endogenous model and treating the actual process as a result of the operation of the self-generating mechanism and external impulses. For if external influences are ruled out, admittance of damping entails eventual termination of the cyclical movement. Once the cycle comes to an end, the basic question to be answered is how the cyclical swing can again be set into motion. Here we exit from the purely endogenous model and seek assistance of exogenous movements, cycle-generators and maintainers, or account for the maintenance of oscillations by nonlinearities.

In his early work, Kalecki concentrated on a system with constant amplitude of fluctuations (zero damping). Indeed, the original Kalecki model used the available statistics and smoothed the coefficients in such a way as to render the main cyclical solution of undamped character on the shaky grounds that, in reality, fluctuations do not disappear and are pervasive. In his address at Leyden, Kalecki said that the case in which the amplitude of fluctuations remains constant is of particular importance "as it appears to be nearest to actual conditions. Indeed, in reality we do not observe any *regular* progression or degression in the intensity of cyclical fluctuations." (Kalecki 1935h, p. 336.)

Frisch subjected this view to sharp criticism. He protested against the imposition of the condition that the solution shall be undamped; and he argued for "any damping which the empirically determined constant will entail, and then explain the maintenance of the swings by erratic shocks." (Frisch and Holme 1935, p. 225.)

Kalecki admitted that his original model was unrealistically constrained and agreed with Frisch's and Holme's objections to his assumption of a constant amplitude. It is hardly sufficient to maintain that an assumption is correct just because it corresponds to real life. The scholar must explain "why the real life is like that, otherwise the particular predilection it shows for a constant amplitude might appear metaphysical." Kalecki attempted to provide "in a summary way, a hypothetical explanation of that state of affairs without pretending to have found a definite solution of that very complex problem." (Kalecki 1936a, pp. 359-60.)

In subsequent presentations, Kalecki attempted to remedy the instability and shortcomings of earlier presentations.[34] The actual cases examined by Kalecki turn out to be, in general, damped cycles which theoretically tend to reach the state of stable equilibrium. In fact such a state is not reached owing to external shocks. Thus the state of equilibrium is avoided, and the swinging motion is kept alive. Kalecki abandoned his preoccupation with a system possessing zero damping and relied on shocks as the source of energy.[35]

It is noteworthy that Tinbergen was rather sceptical about the potency of the supposed influence of the capital effect factor, in particular the way revival is generated in Kalecki's initial model.[36] Indeed, save for periods such as the Great Depression, the business cycle may as well not pass at all through the negative values of investment (or such periods may be of short duration whose effect is not appreciable) (Kalecki, 1939a, p. 148). But this does not invalidate Kalecki's fundamental cyclical mechanism. While his earlier writings were clearly influenced by the severity of the experience in the early 1930s, in the subsequent development of the argument, Kalecki generalized the theory and made allowances for the relative weakness of impact of the capital destruction effect. Moreover, he allowed for the special importance of fluctuations in inventories during the course of economic fluctuations—a factor of particular importance in the United States. Later Kalecki incorporated those factors in his analytical construct. He introduced a certain "corrective" and focused increasing attention on the trend component. Investment fluctuates along the long-run trend line. The influence of long-term development factors cannot be meaningfully abstracted from in the analysis of the dynamic economic process. Kalecki sought to advance theoretical development in the field toward integration of growth and cyclical processes. The main lines of development are evident in the successive recastings of the argument.

Development Factors and Business Cycle

In the discussion of the mechanism of the automatic business cycle it was noted that the position at the trough of the slump is symmetrical with that at the peak of the boom. Kalecki addressed himself to this important question.[37] He observed that, indeed, the capital shrinkage effect on investment decisions during the slump is considerably weaker than that of capital accumulation in the boom, because often the "decapitalized equipment" is idle in the slump in any case. Slumps might be protracted, at least if a nongrowing economic system is considered. The business cycle mechanism implies that there is always recovery from the slump. Save for the Great Depression, which is representative of neither earlier nor successive depressions, (cf. Duesenberry 1958, p. 4), the decumulation of capital was not common. But even if present, the "destruction of capital" may prove to be insufficient as a factor causing recovery. How then will the system extricate itself from the slump?

To make allowance for this phenomenon, a certain corrective is introduced into the process: *a trend factor which shifts investment upward as the cycle continues.* The "exogenous or autonomous" factors determine additional requirements for investment, independent of income and capital stock, and ensure that the investment function shifts its position upward with time. Indeed, the situation is different if the system is no longer considered as static except for cyclical fluctuations, and the economy is subject to long-run development.

The equations used in the study of the business cycle remain valid but are dynamized so as to apply to an economy subject to growth. Certain parameters assumed heretofore constant for the sake of analysis of pure business cycles (oscillations without net accumulation of capital) are treated now subject to long-run changes. The emphasis shifts on the effect of *long-run changes* of certain parametric constants. In such an economy, the business cycle is superimposed on the smooth long-run trend. In a growing system, investment fluctuates around the long-run trend line and not around the zero level, which, in a trendless economy, means that investment fluctuates around the depreciation level. (Kalecki 1965l, p. 123.) Clearly, the situation changes if some of the assumptions are relaxed, and attention focuses on the factors influencing the change. Graphically, at a point corresponding to the trough of the slump, the level of economic activity is actually expanding at the rate of long-run growth while capital stock grows at a slower rate, thus the rate of profit is rising. (Kalecki 1965l, p. 147.)

Kalecki contended that it was never demonstrated that fluctuations initiated by the instability of the growth do take their course around a rising trend line and not around a horizontal line. He argued that the Harrodian rate of growth "is ephemeral in the sense that any deviation from the path determined by it renders the system stationary—i.e., subject to cyclical fluctuations, but no trend. In fact, it appears that to any theory of the business cycle of a fairly broad category there corresponds an unstable rate of growth which is devoid of practical significance." (Kalecki 1962h, p. 134.) Kalecki differed strikingly from Harrod on what constitutes the basic conflict of the capitalist economy. Harrod believed that the antinomy leads to fluctuations around a rising trend line, but Kalecki took the stand that "the antinomy of the capitalist economy is in fact more far reaching: the system cannot break the *impasse* of fluctuations around a static position unless economic growth is generated by the impact of semi-exogenous factors such as the effect of innovations upon investment. It is only in such a case that cyclical fluctuations do occur around the ascending trend line." (Kalecki 1962h, p. 134.)

Before discussing the probable forces behind economic development of the capitalist economy, it is instructive to contrast an economy subject to cyclical fluctuations, but having no trend, and a dynamic system subject to long-run growth. The former is a familiar one. Briefly, let us abstract from the effect of such "exogenous" factors as innovation and resort once again to the simplifying assumptions, including those that both foreign trade and the government budget are balanced and that workers spend what they earn. Assume that gross savings equal depreciation and investments are made out of the retained earnings of business. Thus the economy can be maintained in a static state and the disturbances will engender only cyclical movements. For, if gross investment in fixed capital is at the depreciation level, it generates aggregate gross savings which are equal to it. As these savings accrue fully to the business community, they will tend to be reinvested. Thus the capital will be kept intact. Given the assumption that the stock of capital will neither expand nor contract, profits and output will remain stationary since they are determined by the level of investment which, in itself, is constant.[38] As long as the stipulated conditions are met, the system remains static, with the exception of cyclical fluctuations around the zero level.

The dynamic factors determining the economic development of the capitalist economy prevent the economic system from settling to a static position and engender a long-run, upward development trend. This is an original and provocative, though incomplete, theory of long-run development trend. An interesting discussion of steady and retarded growth is included. The material is condensed on a few pages, but it is much worth consulting. Only some aspects will be touched upon here.

Kalecki demonstrated how the dynamic development factors transform the "static" system into one subject to growth trend. His central proposition reappears, and the economic function of innovation as the development factor is explained. Invention (technical progress) which occurs in the course of a given process makes certain new investment undertakings more attractive, causing the emergence of new investment decisions. The innovation effect gives further stimulus to investment, and so on. For new inventions influence investment by making the profitability of a certain type of investment higher than it would have been in the absence of innovations (shifts in investment function). *Ceteris paribus,* innovation entails investment over and above the level which would otherwise obtain. The flow of inventions has an impact on investment similar to the continuous increase in profits in the endogenous theory of determinants of investment decisions; or, to express it another way, the emergence of innovations has a similar effect in the sphere of investment activity to that of a rise in aggregate current profits.[39] Clearly, innovation activity is not confined to the development of new technology,[40] but induces related activity, such as the introduction of new products, which require capital formation for their production; the conquest of new sources of supply of raw materials, which entails new investments in productive facilities; and transportation.

Thus innovation becomes another factor—conjointly with change in the rate of profit and the rate of change of stock of capital—in the determination of investment function. Innovation tends to raise the long-run level of investment and to engender a long-run ascending trend.

While innovations are singled out as of paramount importance as promoters of economic development (cf. Schumpeter 1964), such factors as rentiers' savings (current gross savings outside of business firms) tend to depress, rather than to stimulate investment, and detract from long-run upward movement. The existence of rentiers' savings tends to generate a negative long-run investment in a manner somewhat similar to the way in which innovations tend to increase a long-run level of investment. (Cf. Kalecki 1965l, p. 159.) If the positive effect of innovations is combined with the retarding effect of rentiers' savings, it is clearly the net result that determines the long-run development.

Therefore, some of the development factors tend to add to a long-run level of investment (over and above the level which would otherwise obtain by the "normal"or endogenous determinants of the investment function) and thus make for a long-run upward trend, while evidently others tend to depress investment and therefore retard a long-run development path; i.e., without the existence of the negative factors the long-run development would be higher and the net result of the interplay would depend on the direction and intensity of growth (decline) determinants.

Innovations are not conceived as an exogenous factor in a strict sense, but as a semiexogenous factor "since they are inherent in the normal functioning of the capitalist system. There is no doubt, however, that the influence of changes in profits, national income, the stock of capital equipment, etc., upon the stream of inventions is very complex and subject to long time-lags." (Kalecki 1962h, p. 147. Cf. Goodwin 1955, *passim.*)

The discussion of the development factors contains a brief section on the role of growth in population as a stimulus to economic development. If the population (labor force) is stagnant, output can increase only by growth of productivity (due primarily to technical progress embodied in capital goods) or drawing on the unemployed or underemployed reservoir of manpower. Population growth extends the opportunities of possible long-term expansion or reduces constraints imposed on the long-run expansion of production. In the absence of other growth propellers, growth of population constitutes a necessary condition for a long-run expansion of output in an economy without a labor reserve. The question Kalecki asked was whether the rise in population also provides sufficient stimulus to long-run development which contributes to the effective exploitation of such opportunities. His answer was that, although the problem is complex and beset by uncertainties, population growth does not play an important role in inducing development. Take first a static system and superimpose on it a rise in population. Initially, output remains stable; but in the long run, there will be a rise in unemployment, with the reserve army of unemployed forcing the money wages down. The problem is thus whether a long-run fall in money wages induces the long-run growth of a capitalist economy. To explore this question, Kalecki reverted in part to the analysis of the monetary phenomenon accompanying investment and drew a distinction between short-term and long-term interest rates and the relations between them. A long-run fall in money wages brings about a fall in prices, with a stable output and fall in the money value of transactions. The short-term rate of interest is determined by the value of transactions and the supply of money by the banking system. The long-term rate of interest is supposed to be determined by the anticipation of the short-term rate, based on experience and estimates of risk involved in the possible capital loss resulting from holding long-term securities. If the fall in the money value of transactions is accompanied by less than proportionate reduction of the supply of money by banks, this will tend to reduce a long-run decline in the short-term rate of interest, which results in a decline in the long-run rate. (Kalecki 1965l, pp. 73-88; cf. 1939a, pp. 107-15.) Now, such a fall would be equivalent in its effect on investment to a long-run rise in profits and produce an ascending trend movement. However, a rise in output in such a movement cannot be sufficiently large to prevent a long-run rise in unemployment, because in such a case the very cause of the trend would vanish. In fact, Kalecki doubted that such a mechanism would be operative in augmenting production. For one thing, the link between the fall in turnover and the fall in the short-term interest rate is quite loose in the long run. If such a decline in the turnover persists, the banking system may adapt itself to the secular fall by an appropriate policy so as to sustain the short-term rate of interest.

There is still another likely effect of the fall in the long-run money wages if it is accompanied by a weakening of trade union bargaining power—an important co-determinant of the distribution of national income. The lessening of the forces of competition tends to raise the degree of monopoly, and leads to a shift from wages to profits. Changes in distribution of income take place, not via a change in profits, but through a change in income (output). The amount of profit remains constant, for it continues to be determined by investment which depends on past investment decisions. It is real wages and national product that will fall; i.e., output (income) will contract to the level at which the higher relative share of profits in reduced national income yields the same absolute amount of profits. Thus a fall in money wages, if associated with a rise in the degree of monopoly, tends to raise the relative share of profits in national income, but production tends to expand at a slower pace than investment and profits. This would hardly be a stimulus to the long-run expansion of output. Rather, *ceteris paribus*, it tends to retard output. Also, if the weakening of trade unions in the slump manifests itself in permitting wage cuts, this contributes to the aggravation of unemployment, rather than to relieving it, as discussed in chapter 3.

Kalecki criticized the view that growth of population stimulates economic development through growth in demand. (Cf. Matthews 1959, pp. 233 ff.) He contended that, for this purpose, the point is not so much an increase in population, but an increase in purchasing power. The need or willingness to buy is necessary, but does not constitute a sufficient condition for the presence of effective demand. What matters in this context is not population growth, but growth in income of the lower income groups. "An increase in the number of paupers does not broaden the market." (Kalecki 1965l, p. 161.)

Thus development factors, such as innovations, enable the capitalist economy to break the impasse of the stationary state and to grow at a rate dependent on the intensity of such growth determinants. But cyclical fluctuations take their course around the resulting upward trend line. Whenever the peak of the boom is reached a contraction follows, reflecting the inability of the system to expand in the long run at a higher rate than the trend line.

Kalecki concentrated on the process of adjustment and showed that the transition from a system subject to cyclical fluctuations but no trend to one of long-run growth is reflected first in a disturbance in the cyclical swings. It is through this change in the pattern of fluctuations that the readjustment takes place. Indeed, the boom is not analogous to the slump. The former is more pronounced than the latter. Consequently, a new long-run position with a higher investment is reached. (Cf. Kalecki 1965l, pp. 151-52.)

An interesting discussion of a uniform trend (steady growth) and retarded growth follows, setting the stage for discussion of views on maturity and stagnation of the capitalist economy.[41] In the case of steady growth, both current investment and the stock of capital expand at the same constant rate. (Kalecki 1968l, pp. 29-39; 1969b.) The system grows in size without a change in focal proportions; investment, profits, output, and capital all expand at a uniform rate in the long run. (Kalecki 1965l, p. 147.) The rate of output and output-capital ratio remain invariant in the long run. But it cannot be overstressed that steady growth depends on a steady intensity of development factors (increasing proportionately with the stock of capital). Strengthening or weakening the effect of these factors will accelerate or retard economic development. The discussion leads to the examination of the conditions under which steady growth can be achieved and to the contrasting of this situation with those in which the conditions are not fulfilled. The analytical construct is employed to convey Kalecki's pessimistic view regarding the probable configuration of development forces. Thus it accents growth retardation.

Ceteris paribus, if the intensity of innovations is constant, the effect on investment generates a stable uniform growth of the economy—a growth that is impossible when Harrodian "induced" investment *only* is taken into account. Indeed, when the intensity of innovation is equal to naught, the growth rate is also equal to naught, and the economic system is stationary. A slowdown in the intensity of innovations in the later stages of development of a capitalist economy entails a retardation of capital accumulation and rate of output expansion as well as a fall in the rate of utilization of productive capacity. As Kalecki put it, "Capital will accumulate at a diminishing rate or, in other words, the ratio of net investment to capital will be falling. The same will be true of gross investment. From the assumption that profits and output vary in the long run proportionately with investment it follows that both the rate of profits and the ratio of output to capital will be declining. Thus, retarded growth has far-reaching repercussions upon the capitalist economy: the slowing down of the rate of progress is associated with a falling rate of profit and a reduction of the degree of utilization of capital equipment."[42]

Again, if the retardation of the innovation stream is also accompanied by a rise in the degree of monopoly, and not counteracted by other forces, a shift from wages to profits occurs and the relative share of profits in national income increases. This means that aggregate output will expand at a slower pace than investment and profit.

Therefore, output will decline even more in relation to capital than in the case of retarded growth, where investment, profits, and output were assumed to vary proportionately but all of them were rising at a slower pace than the stock of capital. The relative shift from wages to profits will not arrest the fall in the rate of profit, but will aggravate the problem of underutilization of capacity. *Ceteris paribus*, a rise in the degree of monopoly will be another reason for the deceleration of long-run expansion of output.

If the intensity of innovation is relatively retarded, the long-run underutilization of productive capacity is considerable; but if innovation exceeds a certain level, the tendency for a secular boom pushes the utilization of productive capacity to its highest feasible rate.[43] Indeed, Kalecki suggested that the retardation in intensity of innovations provides an explanation for the phenomenon of long-run excess productive capacity which, in varying degrees, makes its frequent appearance in developed capitalist economies.

As we know, in his important and rather technical "Trend and Business Cycles Reconsidered" (1968j), Kalecki reproved the contemporary theory of growth of capitalist economy for tending to consider the problem of trend and business cycles in terms of a moving equilibrium rather than adopting an approach similar to business cycle theorizing. He offered an integrated approach.

In contrast to demand-dominated models, in truly Keynesian persuasion, in the neoclassical growth models which occupy a central place in the voluminous body of recent literature on the theory of economic growth, the rate of growth is determined by supply considerations. (Hahn and Matthews 1964; cf. Domar 1957.) (Or at least the demand side has usually been given little prominence.) Contrariwise, the theories of the business cycle have been chiefly concerned with causes of fluctuations in *effective demand* (theory of income determination). The supply considerations have often been underrated. (Cf. Matthews 1959, p. 3; Duesenberry 1958, ch. 11.)

In his last public lecture given at Cambridge University, Kalecki reflected on the tendency in contemporary Western economics to build a "non-institutional" *general* growth theory, fairly remote from the realities of contemporary capitalist, socialist, and "mixed" economies. He felt that many writers relate, at least by implication, to some sort of idealized laissez faire capitalism. The problem considered and the results obtained are easily translatable into categories of a socialist economy. Indeed, they fit better there than in contemporary capitalism, but still not quite well, as they often concentrate on points that are not of overriding importance. "There thus arises a situation which is not infrequent in the history of economic thought: theories are being created which may raise problems of great interest but are not very conducive to understanding what actually happened, is happening or should be happening." (Kalecki 1970e, p. 311.)

There is no better way of concluding this chapter than by quoting from Kalecki's last reflection on the particular problem that concerns us here:

> To my mind the central problem of the *laisser-faire* capitalist system to which apply the theories referred to above is that of effective demand. . . . It is also this problem that in the fifties was still generally in the centre of interest of Western economists. . . .
>
> But from the time the discussion of economic dynamics has concentrated on problems of *growth* the factor of effective demand was generally disregarded. Either it was simply *assumed* that in the long run the problem of effective demand does not matter because apart from the business cycle it need not be taken into consideration; or more specifically the problem was approached in two alternative fashions: (a) The growth is at an equilibrium (Harrodian) rate, so that the increase in investment is just sufficient to generate effective demand matching the new productive capacities which the level of investment creates. (b) Whatever the rate of growth the productive resources are fully utilized because of long-run price flexibility: prices are pushed in the long run in relation to wages up to the point where the real income of labour and thus its consumption is adequate to cause the absorption of full employment national product.
>
> I do not believe however in justifying the neglect of the problem of finding markets for the national product at full utilization of resources either in (a) or in (b) fashion. It is generally known that the trend represented by the (a) case in unstable: any small fortuitous decline in the rate of growth involves a reduction of investment, and in consequence of the national income, in relation to the stock of equipment, which affects investment adversely and induces a further fall in the rate of growth. The belief that such disturbance creates merely a downswing followed by an upswing in relation to the growth proceeding at an equilibrium rate i.e. that it yields a trend *cum* business cycle is mathematically indefensible: the underlying equations are uncapable [*sic*] of producing a solution corresponding to a combination of an experimental curve with a sine line. Nor do I subscribe to the long-run price flexibility underlying theories of the (b) type. The monopolistic and semi-monopolistic factors involved in fixing prices—deeply rooted in the capitalist system of all times—cannot be characterized as temporary short period price rigidities but affect the relation of prices and wage costs both in the course of the business cycle and in the long run. (Kalecki 1970e, pp. 311-12.)

In "Trend and Business Cycles Reconsidered," Kalecki emphasized that he failed to see why the business cycle approach should be abolished in studying the process of economic development. He now approached the growth rate at a given time as a phenomenon deeply rooted in past economic, social, and technological developments of the system (where the current state is the result of the preceding developments and contributes, in turn, to the future long-run development of the economy): "In fact, the long-run trend is but a slowly changing component of a chain of short-period situations; it has no independent entity." (Kalecki 1968j, p. 263.) The two basic relations in the approach to business cycles: (1) the impact of effective demand generated by investment on profits and national income and (2) the determination of investment function by the level and the rate of change in income or expenditures "should be formulated in such a way as to yield the trend *cum* business cycle phenomenon." (Kalecki 1968j, p. 263.)

Admittedly, such a task is incomparably more exacting than the pure business cycle model. But the results of such inquiry are closer to the reality of the process of development. The approach of "mechanistic" theories is based often on such indefensible assumptions as a constant long-run rate of utilization of capacity. However, the difficulty in approach Kalecki suggested was "no excuse for dropping this approach, which seems to me the only key to the realistic analysis of the dynamics of the capitalist economy." (Kalecki 1968j, p. 262.) In his last lecture (at Cambridge) he returned to the point that the question of long-run growth in a laissez faire economy should be approached in exactly the same way as that of the cyclical fluctuations and reflected on the broader implications of the argument he advanced:

> The "pure" business cycle is a special case of the general phenomenon of trend *cum* business cycle where the rate of growth is equal to zero i.e. where the economy is stationary. In the argument on which the theories of the business cycle were based certain quantities were assumed constant—this was partly linked with inadequate accounting for technical progress—which in an expanding economy must certainly grow. Thus it is necessary to deal with this limitation—which ties down the theory of the business cycle to a stationary economy—and arrive at a movement of the system comprising both the trend and cyclical fluctuations. Or to put it somewhat differently: the central problem of the dynamics of the *laisser-faire* capitalist system is to show what makes the system expand if the solutions on the lines (a) and (b) are discarded as inadequate. Indeed the mere fact that capital

> accumulation creating new production potentialities is *feasible* does not prove yet that the investment will be adequately used. (Kalecki 1970e, pp. 312-13.)

And he concluded this argument with the following poignant statement:

> There may arise a question at this point whether this problem is still of interest in the world of to-day in which the *laisser-faire* capitalist system is dead because of widespread government intervention. I still believe that the inquiry into dynamics of a *laisser-faire* system is of importance both in connexion with economic history, even fairly recent one, and because the present state of capitalist economies is an offshoot of a somewhat chaotic interplay between the *laisser-faire* tendencies and of a government action.
>
> In any case these complicated phenomena cannot be adequately portrayed by models of *laisser-faire* economies referred to above in which the problems of effective demand and of utilization of resources are neglected. There *is* probably some interconnexion between government intervention and these models but rather psychological in character: the high level of employment creates a climate favourable to their construction being unperturbed by the problem of effective demand. (Kalecki 1970e, p. 313.)

VI

THEORY OF CYCLICAL FLUCTUATIONS AND LONG-RUN CHANGES

Details

•

Closer to Reality

As put forth by Kalecki, oversimplified economic models are "the beginning and not the end of economic dynamics." To "approach the dynamic process in all its complexity is certainly a hopeless task." In the successive refinements, Kalecki aimed at bringing the model closer to reality. The modifications regarding the intricate factors influencing the rate of investment decision were of particular importance. Allowance was made for the problem of changes in inventories during the course of the business fluctuations. Kalecki distinguished between net investment in finished fixed capital goods (I')—the excess of deliveries over the replacement requirements[1]—and change in inventories of materials, work in process, and finished goods (I'') (cf. Abramovitz 1948; Metzler 1965, pp. 100-29) $I_t = I'_t + I''_t$.

Broadly, investment in fixed capital goods per unit of time is determined, subject to an appropriate time-lag, by (a) the nonconsumed part of capitalists' profits (the stream of current internal savings of firms); (b) the rate of increase in profits (income); (c) the rate of increase in the stock of fixed capital; and (d) trend components taken initially as parametric constants, but capable of variations over time in a developing economy. The first two determinants are positive; the third is negative. Investment decisions in inventories per unit of time are determined by the rate of change in output (income). Investments in fixed capital (I'_{t+1}) are equal to the investment decisions made in the period t. As alluded to, the time-lag is largely owing to the gestation (or construction period) of investment goods, but also includes such factors as "the delay with which investment decisions are taken under the influence of inducements" (lagged entrepreneurial reactions). (Kalecki 1943k, p. 66.)

While Kalecki operated with time-lags of varied durations (*r*, *w*, theta [see fig. 1]), for convenience I have disregarded the differences

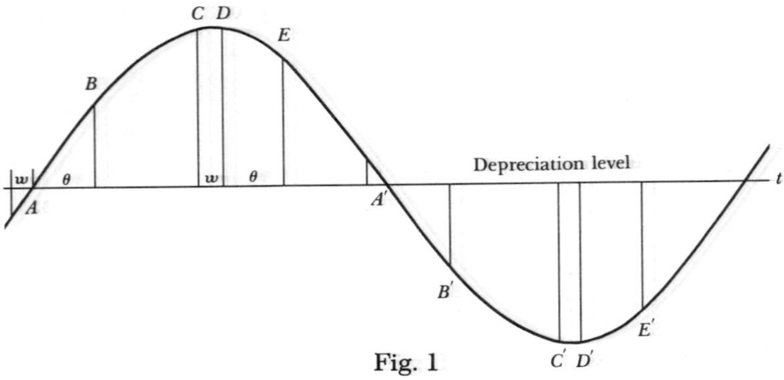

Fig. 1

and adopted one unit of time-lag ($t-1$ or $t+1$). Capital investment decisions are now a function of the level of economic activity *and* of the rate of change. Such decisions are an inverse function of the rate of change in the stock of capital and not only the level of the capital stock as in the earlier model. (A rise in the rate of change in the stock of capital now exerts a retarding influence on the rate of investment decisions and conversely its fall exerts an accelerating influence.) The amount of savings (availability of capital) is associated with the level of economic activity (national income—aggregate demand), while the rate of increase in profit (influx of new savings) is related to the rate of change in the level of income. As before, workers do not save; savings are looked on specifically as accruing to profit-earners as a result of investment activity. From the assumption that both foreign trade and the government budget are balanced, it follows that savings at any period of time are equal to investment. That is, aggregate savings (which are capitalists' savings here since workers do not save and rentiers' savings are tentatively abstracted from—an assumption to be relaxed later) are equal to the sum of investment in fixed capital goods plus increased stocks of inventories.

Indeed, in some business cycle theories, the rate of investment decision is assumed to be determined by the level of national output income and in others by the rate of change in this level. Noteworthy in 1949, Kalecki argued that the level of income is frequently considered in analysis of fluctuation of income to be a direct determinant of investment decisions, as in Keynes's *General Theory,* if properly interpreted. Kalecki offered an interpretation and raised certain important objections against the marginal efficiency of capital theory as previously discussed. Often enough, income is considered in business cycle models as a direct determinant of investment decisions, for the higher the level of income, the higher the difference between the prospective rate of profit and the rate of interest which induces investment.

Kalecki acknowledged that this argument, which appears plausible prima facie, is questionable as soon as one is aware that one's concern here is with investment per unit of time. High profitability in a given period which stimulates investment cannot be expected to continue doing so in the following period, for all investment plans will already have been made under the stimulus of the initial period profitability. "As a matter of fact it appears that it is the new high level of income that makes for greater investment decisions. In this way, however, we really are back to the acceleration principle (although interpreted in a different way) for it is the *rate of change* in income that thus becomes the determinant of investment." In interpreting the inter-relation between the income level and investment decisions, one must take into account the fact that, with the high level of the former, "there is correlated a high level of savings and that the stream of new savings stimulates investment because it makes possible to undertake investment without increasing indebtedness." (Kalecki 1949b, p. 61.)

An interesting discussion of Kalecki's earlier construct represents the theory developed in 1939a as a special case of that presented in 1943k. Then Kalecki arrives at a regression equation, representing the investment decisions as a function of current savings (level of income) and the rate of change in income. The regression equation was fairly close to that presented in 1943k. As stated previously, the argument was elaborated more fully in 1965l, on which the core of this section will be based, and further refinements were introduced in successive writings.

While the argument will be presented at greater length in what follows, the broad approach to the problem of the determinants of fixed capital investment decisions taken in the *Theory of Economic Dynamics* may be presented as follows: Consider the rate of investment decisions in a short (unit) period. Suppose that, at the beginning of the unit period considered, entrepreneurs "have pushed their investment plans up to a point where they cease to be profitable either because of the limited market for the firm's products or because of 'increasing risk' and limitation of the capital market. New investment decisions will thus be made only if in the period considered, changes in the economic situation take place which extend the boundaries set to investment plans by those factors." (Kalecki 1965l, p. 96. Cf. 1943k, 61 ff; 1939a, pp. 95-115.)

Kalecki distinguished two broad categories in such changes in a given period: (1) the profit factor influences the rate of investment decisions not only by providing a motive for it, but also (2) by providing funds for financing it, and reducing restrictions on the size of investment by the firm. Investment decisions are closely related to gross accumulation of capital by firms out of current profit. There will be a tendency to plow back savings into investment. Moreover, investment may be financed by outside funds on the strength of accumulation of internal entrepreneurial capital. The size of the firm is circumscribed by the size of the entrepreneurial capital, both through its influence on the capacity to borrow outside funds and its effect on the degree of risk. According to the principle of "increasing risk," the larger the investment financed by a businessman, from his own capital, the greater is the marginal risk. Thus internal accumulation of capital by firms expands the boundaries set on investment plans by the factor of increasing risk and the limitation of the capital market. The amount that the firms apply to their own retained profits to finance investment influences the amount that the firm can borrow from outside sources.

The changes in profit generate changes in investment, which produce changes in stock of fixed capital, which conjointly determine changes in the rate of profit. An increase in profit from the beginning to the end of the period considered renders certain projects profitable which previously were considered unattractive and permits extension of the boundaries of investment plans in the course of the period. Innovations that take place during the course of a given period make certain new investment projects more attractive. The influence of this factor is similar to that arising from total profit between the courses of given periods which makes the investment project generally more attractive than it was at the start of the period. Just as the rise in profits within the period considered renders additional investments more attractive, accumulation of real capital tends to lower the rate of profit and to restrict the boundaries of investment plans.

The factors considered above are taken into account by postulating the decisions of investments in new fixed capital to be an increasing function of gross accumulation of capital by firms and the assumption that the latter is, in turn, positively correlated with aggregate gross savings as it is concluded that the rate of investment decisions is an increasing function of gross savings.[2] Factor 2, discussed above, is taken into consideration as postulating that the amount of investment in fixed capital decisions per unit of time considered is an increasing function of the change in profit during the period considered (dP/dt) and a decreasing function of the change in the stock of fixed capital equipment during that period (dK/dt). Thus D_t is an increasing function of dP/dt and a decreasing function of dK/dt, where the changes in profits and the stock of capital denote the changes from the beginning to the end of the period considered. Assume the above functional relations to be linear with a, b, and c, the corresponding coefficients of linear dependence, and let e stand for the constant parameter, and we get $D = aS + b(dP/dt) - c(dK/dt) + e$. Taking into account the separation between investment decisions and actual investment and the assumed time-lag, i.e., according to the relation $I'_{t+1} = D_t$, we obtain by substitution $I'_{t+1} = aS_t + b(dP_t/dt) - c(dK_t/dt) + e$. If, simplifying, it is assumed that the trend component equals zero, the system is not subject to long-run growth. Thus the rate of investment decisions is an increasing function of gross savings and of the rate of change in aggregate profits (demand) and a decreasing function of the rate of change in the stock of capital. As noted linear relations are assumed.

The investment demand function advanced by Kalecki covers, as special cases, some of the "competing" theories of business cycle. Only one case will be noted in this context, viz. the famous theory of investment decision based on the acceleration principle. The latter rests on the essentially technical notion that there is a certain normal correspondence between the required stock of real capital and the level of real national output or income. Expansion of the stock of capital will take place only if output (income) is growing. Thus the principle relates the level of net investment (rate of change of stock of capital) to the rate of increase in national income. A boom may come to an end not because demand has declined, but because it has leveled off. Kalecki subjected the economic interpretation of the accelerator principle to sharp and searching criticism. Suppose that the coefficients a and c of Kalecki's investment decision function are equal to naught, then the equation is reduced to the form $D=b(dP/dt)+e$. Moreover, if e is equal to depreciation, then net investment is determined by the rate of change in real profits. This very roughly corresponds to the acceleration principle. Although the latter is stated in the form of relation between net investment and the rate of change in output, and the theoretical derivation is different (cf. Kalecki 1965l, p. 100; Armstrong 1952), Kalecki criticized the basis of the acceleration principle approach chiefly on two grounds: It is fallacious to deduce the necessity of expanding capacity in order to expand output. The increase of output during the course of the business cycle is based largely on changes in the rate of utilization of productive capacity. Large idle capacity exists, at least throughout a good part of the cycle. During the course of the cycle, the volume of capital stock fluctuates relatively little, so that fluctuations in output reflect chiefly the amplitude of fluctuations of the existing stock of capital. Also, the principle does not accord with the facts, unless an unrealistically long time-lag between a decision to invest and its realization is postulated.[3] Moreover, the principle does not take into account the other determinants of investment decisions—the strength of reinvestment of current savings factor and the effect of the accumulation of real capital.

Using a longer mathematical argument and introducing some simplification,[4] Kalecki obtained the fundamental equation for the determinants of the rate of I': $I'_{t+1}=[a/(1+c)]S_t+b'(dP_t/dt)+e'$. Kalecki reduced the determinants of I'_{t+1} to past savings S_t and to the past rate of change in profits dP_t/dt. The retarding effect of an increase in the stock of capital goods is reflected in the denominator of the coefficient $a/(1+c)$. The equation expressed the lagged relation between investment in fixed capital goods on the one hand and savings, the rate of profits, and the rate of change in the stock of capital goods on the other. Clearly, the pattern of the process depends on the values of the coefficients of this equation. The coefficient a represents the strength of influence of current savings on investment decision, i.e., the degree to which savings are being reinvested. The extent of increase of investment decision as a result of a rise in total current savings would be conditioned by a number of factors. It is difficult even to say, a priori, whether a will be larger or smaller than unity. Tentative conclusions on the basis of examination of data for the United States in the 1930s suggested that a is near unity (0.95). This means that the overwhelming share of savings of the capitalist sector is reinvested. A relatively small change in aggregate savings can have important repercussions on investment and demand. In support of the idea that the value of a is smaller than unity seems to be the fact that internally generated savings—generally relevant for investment decisions—are considerably less than the increment of aggregate savings in the economy. The factor in itself would tend to make $a < 1$. Moreover, reinvestment of savings may encounter difficulties because of limited opportunities and risks. But a rise in internal business savings provides the means for self-financing and enables the investor to absorb outside funds of investment undertakings that are considered profitable. It is difficult to assign relative weights to the relative strength of conflicting factors. The coefficient c is positive and likely to be a fairly small fraction.[5]

The treatment of the role of saving in Kalecki's equation does not seem altogether clear. It does not appear that saving in this context is used in its Keynesian sense (where it is identical with investment), nor can saving mean here just the act of not consuming. For it is consumption, and not nonconsumption, that stimulates investment activity. It appears that Kalecki had in mind here something much more subtle, namely, what Klein included as a strong factor in his econometric investment function, i.e., liquidity. Here by saving, Kalecki probably meant accumulated liquid assets, particularly those in the hands of enterprises. The effect of past investments on current investment decisions comes into the equation indirectly and positively through the change in profits; and directly and negatively through the increase in capital stock.

Clearly, the coefficient $a/(1+c)$ is dependent on the values of coefficients in the initial equation: We know that the $a/(1+c) < a$, for $c > 0$, and the adverse effect of expanding capital stock is reflected in the denominator. Kalecki postulated that $a/(1+c)$ falls short of unity for the following reasons: (1) The assumption is essential to demonstrate that the dynamic process yields cyclical movements. (If this coefficient is larger than unity there would be in fact no business cycle at all inherent in the business cycle equation.) (2) On the basis of statistical research which Kalecki himself conducted, he reached the conclusion that U.S. data for the period 1929-40 yields for $a/(1+c)$ value considerably less than unity (the coefficient of S was estimated to equal 0.634). Thus the results, even if only no more than "statistical illustrations," conform tentatively to the assumption that $a/(1+c) < S$. (Cf. Kalecki 1965l, pp. 109-16.) (3) Since c is a fairly small fraction, that $a/(1+c) < 1$ means that a cannot be considerably larger than 1, but, clearly, can be smaller than or equal to 1. If a does not exceed 1, the condition $a/(1+c)<1$ is certain to be fulfilled. The $a/(1+c)$ is the only coefficient about which Kalecki made definite assumptions. Kalecki attested that nothing could be said on a priori grounds about its likely values. The value of coefficient b' is of decisive importance in determining the character of cyclical fluctuations. Kalecki proceeded by a method of elimination. He postulated several alternative cases assuming different values of the coefficient.

Let us turn briefly to the noncapital goods component of investment. Investment in inventories is related to the rate of change in aggregate output,[6] with a certain time-lag. It is assumed that the rate of change in the volume of inventories is roughly proportionate to the rate of change in output. But investment in inventories frequently follows only with considerable delay the rate of change in output. Again, for convenience, let the adjustment lag equal 1. (Kalecki 1949b, p. 57.) The inventory equation expresses the relation between investment in inventories and the rate of change in output, $I''_{t+1}=l(dY_t/dt)$, where l stands for the coefficient of proportionality, as one of the important factors of investment decisions in the accumulation of the firms' capital out of current profits. Kalecki noted that the question may be raised whether the availability of entrepreneurial capital does not play an equally significant role in I'', as in I'. The answer is that the contention that investment in inventories depends not only on the rate of change in output, but also on the influx of new savings does not seem generally to hold for inventories which are part of working capital and any expansion in stocks related to increases in output and sales may be financed by short-term credit.[7]

Adding the equation for I' and for I'', we get the equation determining aggregate investment function activity, where S_t depends on the level of economic activity, whereas dP_t/dt and dY_t/dt depend on the rate of change in this level:[8] $I_{t+1}=[a/(1+c)]S_t+b'(dP_t/dt)+l(dY_t/dt)+e'$. The following equation for the analysis of dynamic economic process and in particular the phenomenon of business cycle follows from the equation determining aggregate investment and the equality of savings and investment: $I_{t+1}=[a/(1+c)]I_t+b'(dP_t/dt)+l(dY_t/dt)+e'$.

Drawing on his analysis of relations between investment, profits, and national income[9] (and tentatively abstracting from long-run growth),[10] and by employing a more elaborate argument, Kalecki derives the business cycle formula. Profits are generated by investment with a certain time-lag being involved. Investment is determined by investment decisions still further back in time, i.e., profits are determined by past investment decisions. Both the rate of change in profits and the rate of change in investment (with appropriate time-lags) can be expressed in terms of the rate of change in investment. By substituting the expressions of dP_t/dt and dY_t/dt in the investment equation, we get a relation expressing *that investment at time* t+*1 is a function of investment at time* t *and of the rate of change in investment at some earlier time* t−*1*.[11] After some simplification,[12] the equation employed for the analysis of the automatic trade cycle reads: $I_{t+1}-U=[a/(1+c)][I_t-U]+u(dI_{t-1}/dt)$, where U again denotes depreciation, and u is employed for the sake of convenience (as shown in the preceding note). Since depreciation is conceived to fluctuate slightly during the course of the business cycle, U is considered as the average level of depreciation, and thus treated as a constant and not dated. $I_{t-1}-U$ represents the deviation of investment from (constant) depreciation. To simplify further the deviation, $I-U$ is designated by i. Thence the fundamental equation used as a basis for investigating the mechanism of business fluctuations becomes:[13] $i_{t+1}=[a/(1+c)]i_t+u(di_{t-1}/dt)$. And, as before, the explicit assumption that $(a/1+c)$ is smaller than unity is a necessary condition fcr the existence of the business cycle and the postulated values of the coefficients are of decisive importance in determining the character of cyclical movements.

The Mechanism of Business Cycles

To show that the factors expressed in the "business cycle equation" create an automatic business cycle, Kalecki employed a hypothetical time curve of investment, as shown in figure 1. According to the automatic business cycle equation, i_t fluctuates around the zero level, which means here that investment fluctuates around the depreciation level in a "trendless" economy. The original position is represented by point A, where investment is equal to depreciation; thus $i_t=0$. Further, suppose that the rate of change of net investment is positive. Before A was reached, "disinvestment" took place, but investment was increasing to the level of depreciation. Clearly, at A, i_{t+1} is positive (exceeds the depreciation level) for the first component on the right of the business cycle equation equals zero and the second component is positive. The query is whether, beyond point A (after the investment curve intersects i_t from below), i will continue to increase; i.e., whether successive periods will be larger than i_t and the rate of change of i will be positive. As before, the relative value of the first component on the right side of the equation depends on the assumption made about the likely size of the coefficients $a/(1+c)$. If it is smaller than 1, it will necessarily be smaller than i_{t+1}, and if it is greater than 1, the product of the multiplier $[a/(1+c)]i_t$ must be greater than i_t and thus i_{t+1} must be larger than i_t. In other words, the first term on the right-hand side is smaller, equal to, or larger than i_t for the very reason that the coefficient $a/(1+c)$ was assumed smaller, equal to, or larger than unity; and this, in turn, tends to reduce, make stationary, or raise i_{t+1} relative to the level of i_t.

But the second component $u(di_{t-1}/dt)>0$, for i was increasing before it reached the level of i_t (point A), and this tends to raise i_{t+1} above i_t. Thus there are two distinctive alternatives here: (1) the coefficients $a/(1+c)$ and u are of such order of magnitude that the rate of increase of investment is finally terminated, and investment temporarily ceases to change at point C; or (2) the upward movement continues until economic activity is prevented by the technical and organizational production barriers and ceilings, i.e., the rise in investment in the boom is halted by scarcities in existing capacities, by labor shortages, or other barriers. When such constraints are imposed on the system's expansion, production orders will accumulate rapidly while deliveries will lag behind requirements, interrupting production flows. This will restrain the rise or even cause the accumulation of inventories. Construction activity and output of capital goods may be similarly constrained by bottlenecks in the investment sector or in activities that supply inputs to that sector. As a result, Kalecki observed a proposition that later became of crucial importance in his development of the theory of growth under socialism—namely, the period of execution of investment orders becomes inordinately extended, efficiency of investment falls, and the expansion of investment in plant and equipment will have to taper off. Here the ceiling is not brought about by assumption of such coefficients of $1/(1+c)$ and u as to produce an automatic stop to the expansion of investment in the boom, but rather by technical and organizational constraints. Thus an essentially endogenous movement may run into "ceilings," and expansion may be halted by the upper limit on available resources before the turning point is reached. It is noteworthy that, after expansion of investment runs into a halt and the level of national income is maintained for some time at this ceiling, the automatic mechanism starts to operate again, investment starts falling, and the contraction continues in the same fashion as in the automatic business cycle.[14]

A rise in the actual rate of investment cannot go on indefinitely. Returning to the first alternative, after investment has ceased to grow at *C*, it cannot be stabilized at this level, but must fall from *D* to *E*. If the highest level of *i* is identified by i_{top}, then for point *D*, the rate of change is zero; i.e., $i_t = i_{top} = di_{t-1}/dt = 0$. For i_{t+1} at point *E*, the second component $u(di_{t-1}/dt)$ is equal to naught, and the first component $[a/(1+c)]i_{top}$ is smaller than i_{top}, because its coefficient $a/(1+c)$ falls short of unity. Therefore, i_{t+1} is smaller than i_{top}, and investment falls from the top level to that of point *E*. Thereafter, investment will decline $i_{t+1} - i_t < 0$, because (1) as before, $a/(1+c) < 1$, and this reduces the component $[a/(1+c)]i_t$ below the level i_t, and (2) the component $u(di_{t-1}/dt)$ will be negative. So *i* will finally fall to zero at point *A′*, where the rate of investment equals the level of depreciation necessary to maintain the stock of capital "intact." Subsequently, the cumulative pattern of the movement will be repeated through a process inverse to that of expansion, and a slump comes on. In particular the level of investment shrinks to such a degree that it does not cover the necessary replacement requirements. After the point *A′*, depreciation exceeds investment and the fall of investment will continue until it finally terminates at *C′*, where the rate of change of investment is zero. But this will not mean that a stationary level of investment is maintained and that fluctuations of investment are brought to a halt. Indeed, investment will *increase* from *D′* to *E′*. It will keep rising to the depreciation level and will again eventually reach the level of depreciation from below.

Kalecki showed that the cyclical mechanism is based on the interaction of two factors. The basic argument is familiar from his earlier version of the automatic business cycle model: After investment returns to its initial point of departure (i.e., after the full cycle is completed), point *A* (where $I = U$) is not a position of equilibrium, but the upward movement of investment continues.[15] Significantly, point *A* would be a position of "static" equilibrium only if two conditions were satisfied: (1) investment was equal to depreciation, and (2) investment was stationary, i.e., had not changed its level in the recent past. The first condition is satisfied, but the second condition is not met (the investment curve crosses the level of depreciation from below) and the upward push (above the depreciation level) continues. Similarly, when investment reaches the depreciation level from above at point A', investment does not come to a halt here, but the depreciation level is crossed at A' moving downward. Again at A' condition 2 is not fulfilled.

The rise in investment activity and consequent growth in profits and in national product before point A is reached causes investment to expand. While they are being implemented, the investment projects encourage further investment to be planned.

But equilibrium will not be reached at point C or C'. When the expansion of investment reaches its highest level, investment cannot be maintained in this position but starts to fall, and thus a slump is started. Expansion turns into contraction and the downward movement occurs because the coefficient $a/(1+c)$ falls short of unity. Investment projects, once they are embodied in plant and equipment and emerge as increment to the stock of productive capital, tend to discourage further investment. Clearly, it is possible also that the factor of incomplete reinvestment of saving (if $a<1$) is of importance for the explanation of the turning point. If the accumulation of capital could be overlooked (i.e, if the coefficient c could be supposed to be negligible), and if there were complete reinvestment of entrepreneurs' savings (if the coefficient a would equal unity), the system would remain stationary at its highest level so far achieved. But, in fact, the addition to the stock of capital causes a reduction of investment. Accumulation of capital with a constant level of national income lowers the rate of profit and also lowers investment decisions. Since the capital stock effect on investment is not negligible and a gap may exist between aggregate savings and their reinvestment, investment falls and a downswing is initiated; i.e, investment starts to contract as a result of an increase in capital stock and possibly because of an incomplete reinvestment of savings, whose factors make $a/(1+c)<1$. (Kalecki 1966h, pp. 10-15.)

Again the explanation of the behavior and why the boom eventually brakes essentially lies in the interaction of two major determinants of investment function: the stimulating effect of expanding activity and the hampering effect of its usefulness. To focus attention on the forces generating a downswing in the capitalist economy, Kalecki contrasted it with the capacity of the socialist economy to deal effectively with the effects of a reduction of investment. The changes in national income would not be linked to those of investment, but would follow those in capacity to produce. If investment remained stationary while the stock of capital enlarged, effective demand would have to be "adjusted" by appropriate price reduction or wage increase. By such measures the demand for consumption goods will rise in accordance with the expansion of the stock of productive capital. The manpower released from production of investment goods will be redirected to the expansion of production of consumer goods, and the increased supply can be duly absorbed by setting an appropriate price-cost (accumulation) ratio.

At the peak the rate of profit falls because the stock of capital expands. At the trough of the slump it is rising while capital stock is contracting. If less than full reinvestment of savings occurs, this will be an additional factor supporting the recovery of investment from the trough of the slump. The condition $a < 1$ signifies here that decisions to invest tend to fall in the slump less than savings do, abstracting from the effect of the rate of change in profits and in capital stocks. At maximum investment, profits and national income—whose changes are linked to those of investment—cease to grow. But increase in capacity is not matched by rise in effective demand, thus investment falls and causes, in turn, a fall in profits and output.

Trails of Cyclical Fluctuations

The type of the resulting fluctuations may be stable, explosive, or damped pending on the value of the coefficient $a/(1+c)$ and u and the postulated time-lags. Given a certain set of these values, the resulting theoretical construct is a linear endogenous or self-generating model with a constant amplitude of fluctuations. This assumption, as we know, figured prominently in his 1933 attempt. But the business cycle equation can be "manipulated"—a standard device used by Kalecki and others in their approach to economic problems. By increasing the value of the coefficient u, while the other coefficient $a/(1+c)$ and time-lags are held constant, the amplitude of fluctuations continuously rises with time, and *ceteris paribus*, by a reduction in u, the amplitude is continuously decreasing.

The problem of the explosive-type cycle is "disposed of" by demonstrating that cumulative overshoot is constrained by certain limiting factors. The rising amplitude of fluctuations will sooner or later be transformed into an automatically operating mechanism of business cycle. Indeed, Kalecki showed a possibility of cyclical swings which do not hit the ceiling. He attempted to explain the actual pattern of fluctuations when the ceiling is not reached in the boom. He believed that this is a frequently encountered pattern in practice.

If the system is characterized by potentially explosive-type movements, it is apparent that the cumulative expansion of investment during the boom phase must eventually hit the ceiling imposed by the limits of productive resources, which were discussed previously. After the rise of investment comes to a halt and the level of activity is maintained for some time at the supply-determined limit, the self-generating mechanism of the cycle starts to operate again: investment falls, and contraction follows, giving way, sooner or later, to expansion; investment strikes the ceiling again, and the recurrent movement goes on. The trough of the slump is sustained at the same level for the contraction path is fully determined, according to the business cycle equation by the level i at the peak of the boom, the assumed values of coefficients $a/(1+c)$ and u, and the postulated time-lags.

In this context, the important question is once again: If the system exhibits continuously diminishing amplitude of fluctuations, does it necessarily follow that the cycle will peter out or disintegrate? The answer is familiar by now, but certain new elements were introduced by Kalecki. He enlisted the support of exogenous stochastic disturbances to explain the maintenance of fluctuations,[16] with the damped swings subjected to random shocks. Kalecki incorporated into his model "the experiments in cyclical fluctuations generated by shocks, which were first carried out by Slutsky, and in specific application to economic cycles by Frisch."[17] The relations among investment, profits, and income on which the business cycle equation is based are *stochastic.*[18]

Integrating the damping mechanism with shock approaches (Kalecki 1965l, pp. 137-42), the "business cycle and shock" equation reads: $i_{t+1}=[a/(1+c)]i_t+u(di_{t-1}/dt)+e$, where e stands for random disturbance. The effect of erratic shocks counteracts the damping immanent in the basic cycle-generating mechanism. "Some sort of semi-regular cyclical movement is generated, the amplitude of which is determined by the magnitude and pattern of shocks, e, and by the parameters of equation."[19] While Kalecki considered the result obtained of considerable importance (Kalecki 1965l, pp. 129, 142), he was concerned with the difficulties in the involved application of the above theory. (Cf. Kalecki 1965l, pp. 137-40.) Investigations made by Kalecki (based on U.S. data for the 1930s) suggested that if damping is strong (or not weak) the ensuing fluctuations will be of very irregular character and their amplitude will be of the order of the magnitude of the shocks.

Because there are no reasonable grounds to suppose that the interrelationships among investments, profits, and income should necessarily be of such order of magnitude as to give rise to a weak damping (or prevent strong damping), this might appear to be an impasse. Kalecki sought to provide a theory free of this difficulty. He suggested a way out. He argued that the difficulties were mainly owing to the type of shocks considered and if more realistic assumptions were made about the pattern of the shocks (cf. Kalecki 1965l, pp. 137-41), a more or less regular trade cycle with a relatively large amplitude would be produced even if the damping were strong.[20] The amplitude of fluctuations is either proportionate to the magnitude of random shocks or is determined by the supply determined ceiling of productive potential of the economy. The magnitude of erratic shocks is related to the size of the economy.

Worthy of notice is the section on the business cycle and utilization of resources. Briefly, fluctuations in investment activity, as we know, entail corresponding fluctuations in aggregate economic activity, and output and consumption vary proportionally less than the volatile investment. The size of the stock of fixed capital tends to fluctuate relatively little during the course of the trade cycle, so that the *fluctuations in the rate of production reflect primarily the substantial variations in the rate of utilization of existing capacities.* The degree of utilization of capital stock depends above all on the extent to which it is possible to find profitable outlets for the output of existing productive facilities and the typical underutilization of resources is related to fluctuations in demand. In later analysis, Kalecki introduced and made great use of the coefficient reflecting changes in the rate of utilization of existing capacity. He concentrated on factors that improve or hamper full utilization of productive capacity in an economy not suffering from a deficiency of effective demand, as we shall see in the chapter on the theory of growth under socialism.

VII

WAYS AND MEANS TO FULL EMPLOYMENT

In the state of underemployment, output is not limited by the availability of resources, but primarily by the deficiency of effective demand. The major problem is one of finding markets for the output that could or would be produced at full utilization of resources. Under such conditions it is essential to study the factors that prevent the economy from achieving and maintaining full employment and to explore and evaluate the efficacy of alternate, or a combination of, ways to create and sustain a state of full employment. Kalecki distinguished three major ways of generating effective demand in a modern capitalist economy and reflected upon their adequacy and relative efficiency in effecting and supporting full employment.[1] He concentrated on the relative merits of (1) deficit spending, (2) stimulating private investment, and (3) redistributing income from higher to lower income groups. Kalecki's contention was that, in the main, 2 is not sufficient and not satisfactory, but both 1 and 3, subject to an appropriate monetary policy and supporting measures (or neutralizing adverse circumstances), provide adequate (but not necessarily equally satisfactory) means for permanent maintenance of full employment. Kalecki underscored that much will depend on the working arrangements for resource allocation. But he did not spend too much time on this subject (nor have many others for that matter).

It is, however, of utmost importance that the questions of the purpose of full employment, both of the level and content of output and employment, are keenly perceived by Kalecki. While recognizing that these are two different and distinct analytical questions, Kalecki demonstrated concern for both of them from the very beginning. Once the catastrophe of the 1930s was overcome, his emphasis increasingly shifted to the ways to full employment and what it should be for—a kind of full employment normative question.

To be sure, the welfare of economic subjects is considerably affected by the composition of the national output (produced directly and indirectly); by how it was brought about; by the manner of economic decision-making; and for whom the bells toll (or the economic machine works). If one clearly conceives what is wanted (given the preferences or policy aims, however determined—by itself a weighty issue), using resources to the best advantage to achieve the aim is the right approach. With given resources the chosen aim(s) of economic activity can be realized to a varied degree, efficiently, or wastefully, at higher or lower material and human costs. At the same cost, a higher or lower degree of the realization of aim(s) can be achieved, depending on the "degree of efficiency" in the use of resources. But the efficiency is not an end in itself; it is what the efficiency is for that really matters.

While the customary warning about confusing the ends in view and the tools for achieving them (with the everpresent danger of subordination of ends to means) is in order,[2] a certain similarity in the approach among writers of various convictions cannot be ignored. Not surprisingly, in discussions on the objectives of economic policy the aim of full employment is variously interpreted. What constitutes the desirable state of employment or rather the extent to which unemployment is to be tolerated as a price for achieving this or that objective are highly controversial matters, clearly colored by normative judgments. Full employment does not always rank high or assume overriding priority (objective of first order). Indeed it may be subordinated to this or that "ultimate" objective (forced mechanization, irrespective of the state of labor supply, fascination with the index of labor productivity, etc., as is sometimes the case in developing nations or paradoxically in so-called socialist countries).

Aside from the substantial differences regarding the aim of full employment, it appears that the sharpest division is regarding the ways to full employment. In a sense, those who assign high priority to the objective of full employment tend to favor consumer-welfare oriented policies, with some redistribution in favor of labor or lower income groups. They do not assign priority to stimulation of the private sector and market-type arrangements. A perfectly competitive system, satisfying optimum conditions for maximizing welfare, is not necessarily the *optimum optimorum.* The contention that restoring perfect competition will solve all our major problems is flatly rejected. Not only is this alternative deprived of priority, but the lack of competition is no longer viewed as the cause of the problem. At the other end of the broad spectrum, there are those who advocate anticyclical measures primarily by means of stimulating the private sector and relying on automatic stabilizers. Probably the most acrimonious bone of contention is the ends to which government expenditures are put, while serving as a means to raise effective demand. In a purely economic sense there is nothing ideological or political about techniques, although certainly their application is not politically neutral. Like atomic energy, marginal analysis, budget deficit, or Kahn's multiplier can be used by capitalist, fascist, or socialist states of various make-up within their particular "ism" to promote peaceful uses, to enhance consumer welfare, to redistribute income to this or that group (labor, capital, bureaucracy, military, etc.), or for waste and destruction. The Keynesian Revolution provided an armory of tools that can be put to various uses: deplorable or commendable, more or less efficient or wasteful, constructive or destructive; for social progress or regress; and in general uses that are supported or opposed by a majority of the population. In a certain sense, employment for its own sake is not a rational objective. It is a political one. The basic question of what employment (efficiency) is for, depends on one's political philosophy.

Deficit spending can solve the problem of generating effective demand and, if it is sufficiently large, it can ensure full employment. From the standpoint of generating effective demand various ways may produce the same results, but this is not to say that they are equivalent if account is taken of their economic, social, and political content. That is, various ways have similar favorable effect on effective demand, but in addition they may lead to better or worse allocation of resources, income distribution, structure of the economy and society; and may produce different side effects. The role of investment in establishing a certain level of national income is not associated with its final destination: whether investment will prove socially useful, useless, or destructive, it generates the same effective demand when it is executed. From the standpoint of creating full employment, the proverbial digging of holes in the ground and filling them again (or the piling up of military hardware) produces the same results as building schools, hospitals, roads, etc., and the induced income is fairly independent of the object of primary expenditure. This statement has to be reiterated in view of the persisting misunderstanding that the originators of the Keynesian Revolution were indifferent to the degree of usefulness of the projects. Of course they realized that there are useful and wasteful ways of creating full employment and preferred the useful to the wasteful. But the problem during the Great Depression was to show the beneficial pump-priming effects of useless projects and to fight disastrous fiscal orthodoxy, which propounded that "nothing could be done."

Obviously, the first question was to establish the legitimacy of deficit spending and then to concentrate on alternative ways of realizing the potential that the economy has, whether it needs help to get there, and if so what, and how the funds were to be spent most effectively and in the best social interest.[3] The second question involves alternative ways of achieving full employment most economically in terms of allocation of resources. This is clearly colored by preferences or prejudices as to composition of output, the choice between more consumption and what kind of consumption or for whom (structure of private and public consumption and its distribution), and investment and what kind of investment (capital formation in profit-oriented private sector, infrastructure, welfare-oriented investment not offering sufficient private gain, investment in human capital, etc.). It is also marked by prejudgments and predilection for government direct intervention or stimuli to private enterprise, institutional arrangements for resource allocation (planning versus market or planning and market), etc. The point is whether full employment is to be achieved subject to *grosso modo* maintenance of existing order, distribution of income, economic power groups; or whether it is to be accompanied by a fundamental overhaul of the system. Another crucial aspect of the same problem is the willingness to tolerate various side effects or repercussions of the measures. For example, the closer we come to achieving full employment, the more difficult it becomes to maintain a high level of effective demand without palpable inflation (balance of payments difficulties). To put this in more fashionable form, it really depends on one's objective function and various constraints that one may tolerate or wish to impose on the function.

It is probably true that the range of socially and politically acceptable ways of steering the economy and affecting its pattern of development undergoes cyclical fluctuations, i.e., it widens during a slump and narrows down with recovery. The preconceived ideas about the range of ways and incompatibility of measures with some more fundamental desiderata (e.g., complete freedom) are usually shaken by an economic disaster (or the threat of political suicide as a price for not coping with deteriorating economic performance). Then the restrictions imposed on the means used (such "side conditions" as no incomes policy or price controls, no this or that direct control, no nationalization, etc.) are relaxed or abandoned. When the economic situation improves, the opposite tendency is pronounced. Also, overreliance on a particular instrument may be accompanied by the growing disadvantage of using it and certain restrictions may be imposed on its use. (Cf. Tinbergen 1967, *passim.*)

Mindful of political and ideological objections to putting his envisaged full-employment program into practice—about which presently—Kalecki concentrated first on the fundamental theoretical problems of full employment. Later he exposed the practical problems of opposition and resistance with equal force, perception, and lucidity. Even his exploration of alternative ways and relative emphasis on points of detail were probably colored by what he considered to be the realistic range of choices within the confines and constraints of the economic and political realities as he saw them. Moreover, his wartime work on fundamental postwar economic problems, on the various methods of regulating employment, and on the limitations of anticyclical policy (as contrasted with a policy of full employment) was conducted under the auspices of the OIS, where he was employed. Probably a certain toning down was needed to avoid stirring up political controversies adverse to the advancement of the very cause of full employment. Hence we do not have here a Santa Claus theoretical viewing of abstract alternatives, and the degree of freedom is circumscribed already at the initial stage by pragmatic considerations.

Kalecki saw that the process of establishing full employment could be used as a vehicle to effect basic changes in the capitalist system in the direction of what he considered a more just distribution of national income and towards advancing the standard of living of the masses. He saw the opportunity, but he was mindful of the grave problems that this would entail. In Kalecki's interpretation a policy of full employment not only means "to push employment up to the level where unemployment, other than frictional, is abolished," but it is a "programme for lasting full employment which must be based either on a long-run budget deficit policy or on the redistribution of incomes"; and the opportunity of state intervention to achieve and maintain full employment is taken as effecting major changes in the character and *modus operandi* of the economic system. (Kalecki 1944h, p. 135.) Thus in Kalecki's version the Keynesian Revolution is distinctly put into service as an engine of economic and social change and progress, where mere mitigation of business fluctuations and maintenance of economic activity around an underemployed equilibrium cease to be the goal of economic policy, and a new pattern of employment and direction of government spending and intervention becomes a crucial test of successful performance of the economy. Thus, the aim is not to reproduce "extensively" the existing capitalist system on a larger scale, unhampered by lack of markets, but to effect intensive-type qualitative changes in the very pattern of economic processes. Surely such an approach is bound to encounter strong opposition from many quarters, including on the one hand those who would wish to preserve the present order (subject to relatively minor modifications), and, on the other, those who would prefer to demolish the existing system, in order to set up an entirely different order.

Kalecki's approach appears to be that of a radical reformer of the more fundamental features of the capitalist mode of production, distribution, and social organization.

A Note on Full Employment Proposals

The work on full employment in the postwar period was developed by Kalecki during his employ at the OIS, although, as noted, the building blocks are already outlined in his prewar studies. A fuller account of the work done under the auspices of the OIS, embodied in a series of articles mostly published in the OIS *Bulletin,* will be presented below, in part 2, "The War Economy." In 1944, the OIS published a book entitled *The Economics of Full Employment.*[4] It came out almost simultaneously with Sir (later Lord) William Beveridge's *Full Employment in a Free Society.* However, it seems that the former was a more fundamental and systematic study than the Beveridge book, which enjoyed much greater notoriety. Indeed, in the preface to his own book, Beveridge acknowledged this fact. The Oxford book contains a rather short chapter by Kalecki, which says very concisely much, if not nearly all, that needs to be said about the theory of maintaining full employment in a free capitalist economy.

Beveridge's book is an outgrowth of his report to the government on the subject of full employment. (See preface to Beveridge 1944;

Hancock and Gowing 1949, pp. 540 ff.; and Harrod 1951, pp. 533-35.) It is closely related to Beveridge's great enterprise in the field of social security, from its very beginning in Britain in 1908 to the quite generous scheme elaborated during the war for a general reform of the complex of social insurance schemes.

In 1944 there appeared almost simultaneously a Government White Paper on Employment Policy and Beveridge's Report on Full Employment. In contrasting the two,[5] Beveridge suggested that whereas the program he independently proposed was one of full employment, that endorsed by the government was only one of countercyclical policy.[6] Whereas the White Paper considered private ownership of the means of production as axiomatic, Beveridge considered it only as one form of ownership to be tested by the results it brought forth. The White Paper was particularly concerned with instilling monetary stability and budgetary equilibrium as a means of gaining businessmen's confidence, rather than with reassuring the population in general that all those willing and able to work would find jobs. Instead of planning for full employment, the White Paper enunciated a policy of fighting unemployment. (Beveridge 1944, pp. 273-74.)

Such as it was, the White Paper was already a tremendous step forward, for it called on the government to remedy slumps in economic activity, in contrast with the previously accepted doctrine of the advantages of periodic depressions.[7] The White Paper contained the valuable statement that countries faced with difficulties in their balance of payments would not be permitted recourse to a deflationary pressure on domestic employment, and that this would not involve autarky if sensible arrangements to govern international trade and finance were made. Briefly the suggestion was that stabilization of effective demand could be achieved by: (1) maintaining the balance of payments in equilibrium; (2) trying to stabilize private investment and, if unsuccessful, by planning public investments so as to mitigate the vacillations of private investment; and (3) if the above efforts were not fully successful, by preventing fluctuations in private consumption by a scheme of varying contributions to social insurance and flexible taxation. Kalecki subjected the three methods to searching and incisive criticism:

1. Exports and imports do not necessarily have to be kept in permanent equilibrium in order to stabilize employment. The influence of a deterioration of the balance of foreign trade on employment can be mitigated either by a rise of public investment or stim-

ulation of consumption. If anything, it would be rather the exchange position that might force Britain either to cut down imports or increase exports.

2. Among the various methods for mitigating the fluctuations of private investment is that of reducing the rate of interest in a recession and increasing it when economic activity comes into its own. Even the White Paper recognized the shortcomings of this method. Furthermore, it is difficult to manipulate the long-term rate. The White Paper also suggested appealing to businessmen to maintain a fairly stable rate of investment activity, which would be advantageous for the *whole* business community. The results of such an appeal are questionable—to say the least. By far the most effective method of counteracting fluctuations in private investment is by appropriate public investment.

3. It was expected that the above methods would not be entirely sufficient. Then measures to control "derived" fluctuations of consumption were proposed. One of them was to institute a scheme whereby contributions to social insurance would fall as unemployment grew, thereby increasing purchasing power and reducing prices by cutting down costs in terms of lower employers' contributions; and vice versa as unemployment was dwindling. The scheme could be reinforced by a corresponding system of taxation. Kalecki's primary objection to this part of the proposal was on the grounds of the quantitative effect. He suggested that this intervention would be insufficient to prevent a fall in total consumption, let alone to stabilize national expenditure as a whole—which should be its aim. After all, it is the "stabilisation of effective demand which is the proper way to eliminate fluctuations in private investment, and not *ad hoc* inducements in the form of manipulating the rate of interest and the rate of taxation on profits." (Kalecki 1944h, pp. 131-34.)

Even if the anticyclical policy advocated by the White Paper were successful, it still did not mean that a state of full employment would be reached. For one, although the White Paper supported annual budget deficits, it maintained the principle of balanced budget for longer periods, and did not propose deficit spending to eliminate all but frictional unemployment. For another, the White Paper remained mum on any forms of income redistribution. And, Kalecki claimed, these were the two main pillars of any consistent full employment program (with considerable preference for the second). (Kalecki 1944h, pp. 134-35.)

The program presented by Beveridge was far more along the lines of Kalecki's vision, with the *differentia specifica* that Beveridge did not accord the first place to income redistribution.[8] Beveridge's work is very general in character. He did not provide sufficiently comprehensive measures to ensure achievement of the objectives. (Kahn 1972, pp. 97 ff.) This is not meant to detract from the service Beveridge performed for the cause of promoting a full-employment policy. One point is of considerable interest: The Beveridge Report stirred up great controversies. Its radical features created considerable disquietude in many quarters. The government found itself not only divided, but in great difficulties, because on the one hand, in order to win the support of the more radical members of trade unions, a vision of brighter and more egalitarian postwar conditions was needed, and, on the other, there was tremendous opposition to using the war period as an engine of social change. The stand taken by Keynes himself is most revealing. He appears to have had some preference for the more conservative interpretations.[9]

Government Spending

Kalecki considered that probably the best way of maintaining full employment should rely on the following principles: "(i) The Government spends so much on public investment and subsidizing consumption of the poorer sections of the population that this secures full employment in combination with that private investment which is necessary to increase the productive capacity of equipment proportionately to the rise in the 'full employment national income.' (ii) Public investment is carried on at the rate actually required for satisfying the needs of the community, while all Government spending above this level is devoted to subsidizing mass consumption." (Kalecki 1945a, p. 89.) This regime may involve a rising national debt.[10]

Kalecki maintained that a policy which attempts to achieve full employment exclusively or primarily by stimulating private investment cannot be regarded as satisfactory nor is it likely to be successful for reasons to be discussed later. It should be noted here that the effects of the stimulation of private investment depend on the difficult-to-predict and changeable moods and reactions of entrepreneurs. It is quite possible that, when businessmen entertain a very pessimistic mood, they even may fail to respond to considerable stimuli. This clearly happens, for instance, when there is lack of confidence in political leadership or there is insecurity owing to a worsening international political situation. (Kalecki 1944g, p. 53.) The question then is: What is the position, if, in an attempt to solve the problem of full employment, instead of relying on encouraging private investment, the government directly creates effective demand through public investment or through subsidizing mass consumption?

The contention is that government spending on public investment and subsidies to mass consumption, either in the form of deficit spending or financed by an increase in income tax, is always theoretically capable of generating sufficient effective demand for achieving and maintaining full employment. Thus, from the standpoint of generating effective demand, private investment may be replaced by government expenditures and the problem is of eliminating or minimizing compensatory adverse effects of public spending on private spending. To satisfy this requirement, the government undertakes public investment which does not compete with private capital formation (the usual examples are public works, highway construction, building of educational institutions, hospitals, and presumably such other undertakings that would stimulate desirable private investment, but would not be undertaken by private enterprise itself). This is a political limit, but not necessarily a desirable one.

If the government undertakes construction of objects that do fall into the typical sphere of activity of private enterprise and "competes" with private investment, this tends to reduce the expected rate of profit on the latter and its volume. But direct government investments are clearly beneficial in activities where businessmen find it unprofitable to channel capital, but where social benefits outweigh private costs (e.g., slum clearance). Kalecki maintained that reduction of profit taxes in a slump, as a device for eliminating as far as possible swings in private investment, is promising, but he thought that a more reliable approach to offset the swings would be an appropriate and well-planned timing of public investment. However, the method is not devoid of limitations, owing, *inter alia,* to (1) the unpostponability and urgency of certain types of public investment projects in a given period which makes it very difficult to subordinate their time structure to the needs of stabilization policy; and (2) administrative and political difficulties in view of the insufficient power of direction of the central government over local administrations which are the main agents of public investment. (Kalecki 1944h, p. 133.)

Alternatively, government spending may generate effective demand by subsidizing mass consumption by tax reduction, or its counterpart, appropriate transfer payments (granting family allowances, old-age pensions, etc.). Direct taxes may be lowered in order to increase spending power. The burden of indirect taxes may be reduced, or the government may choose to pay subsidies to reduce prices of necessities. This expenditure (or fall in government revenue) can be financed by borrowing, so that income is not reduced by taxation. Financing by loans does not involve offsetting or curtailing private investment (provided that the rate of interest is kept constant by an appropriate monetary policy) and does not encroach on nonsubsidized consumption expenditures, thus creating additional effective demand.

There are strong distributional relations and implications in terms of the maintenance of debt. Kalecki was concerned with tax policies and financing in view of the effects of various kinds of taxes on employment, national income, and its distribution.[11] He emphasized, for instance, that some policies, even if effective on the grounds of efficiency, seem to him "in the wrong way from the social point of view," because the method of increase of employment "boils down to the stimulation of capitalists' consumption." (Kalecki 1946a, p. 82.)

The basic rule should be that both public and private investments should not be carried beyond the point where they cease to be useful. (Cf. Samuelson 1966, vol. 2, pp. 1272-73.) If the effective demand created by public investment is insufficient to ensure full employment, the gap should be closed by increasing consumption, rather than by piling up wasteful public or private capital goods. (Kalecki 1944g, p. 53.) The problem is similar to that of maintaining full employment by stimulating private investment. Public investments cannot be carried out beyond the point when they become useless: "Two bridges over a short stretch of a river may be useful, but to construct a third, fourth, and fifth merely to provide employment is absurd." When public investment becomes useless, "the excess of Government expenditure necessary to maintain full employment over this reasonable level of public investment must be devoted to consumption." (Kalecki 1945a, p. 89.)

The next question posed by Kalecki was: If effective demand adequate to secure and maintain full employment is generated by deficit spending and such deficit is a permanent feature, what are the implications of the continuously expanding national debt and of the alleged burden of interest on increasing principal? Will not the increasing burden set an upper limit to the size of deficit spending as a "fiscal trick" to promote full employment? How can the burden be best tackled?

Indeed, the case for the balanced budget and ideological attachment to budget balancing have a long history. There were also notable dissenters from budget-balancing. Among them, Thomas Malthus argued that the public debt is not the evil that it is generally assumed to be.[12] The strong pro-balanced-budget position of one of the leading classical economists, Adam Smith, was conditioned very largely by his view of the adverse effects of the national debt—a product of his antimercantilist passion rather than pro-laissez faire stand. Smith rightly saw the mercantilist state as wasteful, diverting resources from capital formation and creation of national product toward riotous consumption by special privileged groups. Governments would borrow from industry and commerce and thus absorb the funds which otherwise could be productively reinvested. Moreover, once the state started to borrow, its political power would be increased because it would be no longer constrained by exaction of unpopular taxes from the subjects and would continue on the road of irresponsibility. Borrowing encourages war-mongering and extravagant expenditures. But if taxes had to be raised to meet the cost, wars would be generally more speedily concluded and less willingly undertaken. Ricardo, writing at the end of the Napoleonic Wars, shared Smith's aversion to the growing debt described by him as "one of the most terrible scourges which was ever invented to afflict a nation." (Ricardo 1951, vol. 4, p. 197.) Marked changes occurred in the intensity of repugnancy for growing debt in the writings of leading classical and neoclassical economists over time, with a general tendency for greater toleration of the national debt.

The Keynesian Revolution changed completely the approach to the economic role of government and taxation.[13] Taxation is no longer looked on as a method of financing government expenditures, but as one of the ways of government intervention for actively influencing, mobilizing, and allocating real resources with the aim of ensuring general economic and monetary stability.[14] While the subject is complex, it should be noted that, when resources are underemployed, "functional finance" (to use a term coined by Abba Lerner) is used not to divert real resources from private capital formation and make them available for governmental goods and services (or "to be wasted by government"), but in a certain sense government deficit performs the compensatory function of "honorary private investment"—to borrow Sir Denis Robertson's phrase. (Robertson 1939, p. 354.)

During the war period, Kalecki attacked the then widespread, and still not uncommon, misconception that it is impossible to have a budget deficit in peacetime whenever it is necessary to promote and sustain full employment, if this leads to a long-term rise in the burden of the debt. He showed the implications of such a debt, and that it is feasible to devise special taxes for financing the interest on public debt which will prevent the rise of debt from adversely affecting output and employment. Application of the regime of budget deficit as a way of achieving full employment does not involve insuperable difficulties. If to maintain such a state, budget deficit is required, the scare of the rising national debt is unfounded.[15] This is a very old story. Regretfully, the argumentation is not only of historical importance. Kalecki is here in good company.

Let us note here only one aspect. As long as the rate of increase of interest on the national debt is not higher than the rate of increase of national income, no rise in the burden of the debt will take place. In an expanding economy the interest on public debt need not necessarily increase out of proportion with the tax receipts at existing tax rates if the expansion of output is sufficiently large in view of the increase in employment and technical advancement. And even if the interest charge should increase more quickly than the national income, the problem may be solved by devising a system of taxation to service the debt, based on financing a part of interest on public debt by an annual capital tax, levied on firms and individuals, which will not entail disturbances in output and employment.[16] A rise in national debt will increase the amount of capital tax to be collected, but will simultaneously increase the interest-yielding assets (inclusive of government securities) in private holdings, which would not have come into existence if the budget had been annually balanced. The current income after capital tax of some property owners will be lower and of some higher than if the interest of the national debt had not grown. However, their aggregate income will remain unchanged and their aggregate consumption is not likely to alter appreciably. Moreover, the profitability of investment is not affected by incidence of capital levy since it is paid on any type of wealth in possession. The same capital tax is paid on the principal, irrespective of whether it is in the form of cash, government securities, or invested in real capital goods. If investment is financed by borrowing, its profitability is not affected by the capital tax which is not imposed, since no increase in the wealth of the investing businessman takes place, more about which presently. Thus, Kalecki argued, a rise in the national debt, if the interest on it is financed by annual capital tax, is in the main "neutral" as far as forces governing private investment and capitalists' consumption are concerned.[17]

Kalecki paused on the problems involved in the administration of the capital tax and attempted to resolve some of the difficulties. But wherever administrative problems are considered insurmountable, he explored the alternative device of a modified income tax—the incidence of which on the national economy as a whole would be more or less similar to that of a capital tax. The trouble with such an income tax scheme is that, as opposed to capital tax, it reduces the net (after tax) rate of profit, and thus it has a disincentive effect on the propensity to invest. To counteract this adverse effect, Kalecki proposed a modification which would levy income tax on gross income prior to deduction of depreciation. In addition both replacement investment and that for expansion were to be deducted from the taxable amount and should such a sum exceed taxable income the excess could be carried forward to subsequent accounting periods. Such a tax does not affect the anticipated rate of profit on new investment.

In more general terms, in a prewar discussion on the theory of taxation, debating the relative merits of commodity taxes, income taxes, and capital taxes as far as their effects on employment and national income (and its distribution) are concerned, Kalecki argued that, in case of capital taxation, "the course of events does not follow the same path as in the case of income taxation." The rise in capital taxation rates does not reduce net profitability of investment (which covers risk) or increase interest rates. If someone borrows funds to build a factory, he hardly increases his own capital by such an action nor does he pay a higher capital tax. And if he finances it by his own funds, he pays the "same tax as he would if he abstained from investment. Thus the net profitability of investment is unaffected by capital taxation. Unlike income tax, the capital tax is not a cost of production in the long run either." Similarly, everybody is prepared to lend at the prevailing interest rate; for the capital tax is not affected by whether he lends or not. Hence the propensity to invest is not lessened by an increase of the rate of capital tax if expected returns are unaffected. But, because under the new taxation the gross profits of an enterprise have increased, these expectations are improved. The motive to invest is now stronger than before the introduction of the additional taxes. Thus investment expands and entails a new rise of gross profit and of employment. "Curiously enough, capital taxation not only makes the gross profit rise by the total amount of this taxation," but also profit after taxes increases significantly. Contrariwise, in the case of income taxation, entrepreneurs' consumption and investment remain unchanged and gross profit is increased by the amount of the taxation. Kalecki claimed that "capital taxation is perhaps the best way to stimulate business and reduce unemployment. It has all the merits of financing the State expenditure by borrowing, but is distinguished from borrowing by the advantage of the State not becoming indebted." (Kalecki 1937c, pp. 449-50.)

PRIVATE INVESTMENT IN A FULL-EMPLOYMENT SCHEME

Investment constitutes the accretion of the stock of real capital, the enlargement of the existing productive capacity per unit of time where $I = dK/dt$. Generally, investment has a dual effect: (1) Capital formation adds to future capacity to produce output. If resources are fully employed, resources used to produce capital goods must be diverted from the production of current consumption goods. (2) Investment expenditures have an income effect, being a source of effective demand for current output. Changes in production techniques affect new investment and not the existing stock of capital. A sensible policy for full employment faces the formidable question of appropriate rate and structure of capital accumulation. Kalecki touched upon this intricate problem when examining the possible alternative policies of securing full employment and elaborated on the many points in other writings. (Kalecki 1944g, pp. 46-53; 1945a, pp. 83-92; 1950, pp. 62-64.)

In principle the government varies spending on public investment and/or subsidies to mass consumption without altering the tax rates,[18] up to a point where the effective demand, created directly by this expenditure and indirectly by subsequent induced rising incomes (multiplier effect), establishes full employment. (Cf. Kalecki 1939a, pp. 42-74.) Granted that the government maintains employment at this level, the questions arise: (1) will private investment continue to exhibit cyclical fluctuations? and (2) what should be the "equilibrium" level of private investment?

The regime of full employment should have a stabilizing effect on private capital formation because volatile cyclical fluctuations of investment activity are appreciably conditioned by violent fluctuations in such important determinants of investment decisions as profits. (A fall in investment generates a magnified decline in national income and profits, and this, in turn, leads to subsequent decline in investment.) A well designed and implemented macroeconomic policy should have a moderating effect on reducing risks of investment and thus stabilizing this highly variable and capricious component of national income, reducing risks, and appreciably moderating fluctuations.

Nevertheless, the regime of full employment will not eliminate fluctuations in output and profits altogether. Fluctuations in private investment will still occur for all sorts of reasons. For one, accidental fluctuations in the rate of private investment may occur as a result of discontinuous (exogenous) technical progress or spurts in investment activity influenced by other dynamic factors ("autonomous investment"). To neutralize or dampen such accidental fluctuations, a well-designed policy of appropriate timing of public investment is required; but this, as noted, is not devoid of administrative and political difficulties.

But if a policy of maintaining full employment were consistently enforced so that cyclical fluctuations in national income would be eliminated as far as possible, the fluctuations in private investment would be considerably smaller than under laissez faire, and the *regular* investment cycle would largely disappear. As far as this is achieved and the full-employment regime is maintained for some time, considerably smaller compensatory variations in public investment should be necessary to offset the fluctuations in the rate of private investment. However, it is important to note that, under full employment, output and profit exhibit long-term changes due to alterations in the size of the labor force and rise in productivity.[19]

The second question—what should be the "equilibrium" *level* in a regime of full employment?—involves the intricate concept of productive capacity. (Kalecki 1968j, pp. 273-75.) For the purposes at hand the degree of utilization of productive capacity means the ratio of actual output to the maximum capacity. The rate of utilization must be neither too small nor excessive. In the first case there will be idle capacities (waste of resources), and in the second the reserves of equipment will be insufficient to ensure elasticity for adjustment. Let the initial position describe a situation where a "desirable" rate of capacity utilization is achieved. In the next period there is a desire to maintain this rate of utilization. However, in this next period full-employment output will be higher owing to an increase of the labor force and of labor productivity (owing to technical progress). To preserve the rate of plant utilization, capacity must grow proportionately to the expansion of the labor force and productivity. Here is a clue to what the level of private investment should be. "*Private investment must be at a level adequate to expand the capacity of equipment* pari passu *with the increase in working population and productivity of labour, i.e., proportionately to full employment output.*"[20]

Let us now turn to the discussion of "two levels of investment." Private capital formation is required to ensure that the private investment is at a level adequate to expand productive capacity proportionately to the long-run rise in full-employment output, but no more, and it is folly to push it beyond that level for reasons of insufficiency of effective demand. If saving is "too high" in relation to private investment, the gap cannot be filled by the stimulation of private investment. For if investment is above the level at which productive capacity increases *pari passu* with the expansion of full-employment output that results from growth of population and productivity, it creates overcapacity and this tends to depress long-term investment. Thus measures to stimulate private investment above a certain level will eventually prove self-defeating.

But again, if investment is successfully stimulated to expand, there is no a priori reason for such a level of investment to be of the same order of magnitude as that required to create sufficient effective demand to achieve full employment. Thus, Kalecki's argument centers on the consideration of two levels of the rate of private investment and the important distinction is made between I_f—the level of gross private investment which creates effective demand sufficient to maintain full-employment output, and I_c—which is just sufficient to expand stock of capital proportionately to the rate of change in the work force and productivity. If productive capacity increases proportionately to the stock of capital, I_c expands productive capacity *pari passu* with full-employment national output. If in this case full employment is sustained, the rate of utilization of capacity is independent of time. However, if technical progress is of the capital-absorbing variety (entails a rise in capital in relation to productive capacity), the increase in capacity (with I_C) will be insufficient to obtain full-employment output; and, obviously, the assumption that productive capacity increases proportionately to the stock of capital does not hold. Therefore, if investment is at a rate of I_C while full employment is maintained, the rate of utilization of capacity must increase because productive capacity expands at a slower rate than the stock of capital. This must finally lead to a situation where productive capacity is insufficient to employ available manpower. The long-run unemployment that arises is not caused by insufficiency of effective demand, but by a lack of productive capacity.[21] If this state of affairs is to be avoided, a stimulus to profit-seeking investors is required, not to create effective demand sufficient for maintaining full employment, but to prevent the deficiency of productive capacity which would otherwise hinder the system.

A sensitive policy aimed at satisfying real needs involves full employment as a by-product. Kalecki maintained that a government spending policy could be so conceived as to allow it to overcome the fundamental problem of the capitalist economy: the insufficiency of effective demand. But if the prevailing technical progress should be of such a variety as to entail expansion of productive capacity at a slower pace than that of the accumulation of capital, even though government intervention can ensure private enterprise markets and solve the problem of effective demand, it is "still necessary to grant cumulative subsidies to private enterprise in order to induce it to expand its productive capacity to keep pace with the increase in population and productivity of labour." (Kalecki 1945a, p. 91.)

If private enterprise is unable to meet the task of creating the required rate of new capacity, Kalecki conceived that the logical solution to the problem is for the function of private enterprise in this respect to be taken over partly by the government, by means of state-owned enterprises. This would be also particularly advantageous in those activities which are unprofitable to private interests. For example, in slum clearance the authorities could gradually ban certain obsolete buildings, thus raising the level of necessary investment to preserve housing capacity. Then, instead of stimulating private construction, state housing could be built. (Kalecki 1944g, pp. 48-49; 1945a, p. 92.)

Kalecki believed in the potency of subsidies for modernizing equipment in the form of granting cheap credits for modernization projects, submitted to government agencies for approval. He also thought that the creation of modern state-owned enterprises might force the private firms to modernize, but whether such firms would be more "efficient" and whether they were likely to exert the effect Kalecki anticipated is a controversial question.[22] Nonetheless he emphatically declared that "such activities should not be governed merely by the wish to achieve full employment through investment in the 'private sector.' It is only to the extent that the acceleration of technical change has a social priority over public investment (in the strict sense) and subsidies to consumption that such schemes should be put into operation." (Kalecki 1944g, p. 52.)

Once the state steps in to substitute for private investment activity, forces for cumulative expansion of the government sector will set in. This will magnify the political opposition against what Kalecki considered to be the most rational way of achieving full employment. The very notion of deficit spending and particularly the direction of such spending is clearly not entirely a technical economic problem.

If, as in the case examined by Kalecki, the level of private investment is pushed up to the point at which it ensures effective demand sufficient to obtain full employment and if this level is in excess of that necessary to expand productive capacity proportionately to full-employment output ($I_f > I_c$), there will be a continuous rise in surplus capacity and some investment will prove to be abortive. The decline in the rate of utilization of capacity will be reflected in a falling rate of profit, which will, in turn, adversely affect investment decisions. If deficiency of private investment is not here compensated by government deficits, macroeconomic policy must be aimed at averting the decline in the rate of private investment in order to prevent setting into motion the forces of contraction where a fall in investment gives rise to a magnified fall in national income (through the working of the multiplier). Thus the government would have to revert to more of the stimulative medicine to spur private investment. After a certain time the need for further stimuli will reappear to offset the influence of the falling rate of profit.[23] Kalecki demonstrated that, under assumed conditions, to maintain full employment by stimulating private investment alone, it might be necessary to apply the stimulative measures not only once, but to stimulate in a *cumulative* way; i.e., the rate of interest must fall *continuously,* [24] and quite rapidly or the profit tax must be *continuously* reduced or subsidies to stimulate investment must *constantly* rise (Kalecki 1945a, pp. 83-87; 1944g, pp. 46-51), i.e., a lopsided policy of cumulative stimulation in favor of business is followed (as, indeed the record of postwar American policy, and especially of the Nixon administration, shows).

On the whole stimulation of private investment is necessary, but it is neither a satisfactory nor a sufficient way of securing full employment. As such private investment may very well fall short of this level, employment has to be pushed up to the level where unemployment, other than frictional, is eliminated by using public loan spending as a significant device to achieve such an end. Cyclical fluctuations in private investment should be eliminated as far as possible by a sensible policy of stabilization of effective demand. This is a proper way of ironing out fluctuations in private investment, rather than by *ad hoc* stimuli in the form of manipulations of the rate of interest and the rate of taxation of profits or subsidies to firms undertaking investment.

The analytical distinction drawn by Kalecki between the two levels of investment is of major importance (even if his formula for the desirable level of capital accumulation is not satisfactory).[25] But labor productivity is not a function of technical progress per se, and changes in techniques affect largely new investments and labor productivity is influenced by technical progress embodied in the means of production. "The rate of increase in productivity of labour is not something given by Nature." The quantum of resources devoted to technical research and the rate of retirement of equipment can be varied. To choose "the most desirable rate at which to increase the productivity of labour is itself a problem," since at any time a speed-up in the growth rate of productivity entails higher investment and lower consumption. "Once the principle of full employment is accepted, the old concept of 'abstinence' comes into its own again, and the allocation of resources between consumption in the present and accumulation for the future becomes one of the central problems of economic policy." (Joan Robinson 1951, p. 101.)

As we have seen many aspects of income distribution were already discussed in chapter three. Some of them will reappear again in subsequent chapters. Here I shall deal with the problem only briefly.

Kalecki suggested that the relative advantages of basing a full-employment policy on the income tax method, rather than on budget-deficit policy tools, "can be seen in the fact that it not only secures full employment, but at the same time it renders the distribution of incomes (after taxation) more egalitarian. But precisely for this reason, 'full employment through taxation' is likely to encounter a much stronger opposition than a 'Budget deficit policy.' " (Kalecki 1944g, p. 55.) He argued elsewhere that, if "it has been decided to achieve full employment by increasing consumption, this may be done in a more direct way, and it is not the consumption of the rich that should be increased." (Kalecki 1945a, p. 87.) But this is a kind of theoretical problem that could not be considered *ad abstractum* of political difficulties of implementation, such as the strong opposition from the powerful vested interests for whom it is a "wrong" kind of policy as it encroaches on their power, which lies in the concentration of wealth. (Kalecki 1939a, p. 92.) Kalecki maintained that, because of this resistance, policy makers cannot simply choose between using the tax weapon as against budget deficit. Rather, they should use the former as much as realistically possible, and fill the remaining gap by the latter.

If macroeconomic policy is used as a deliberate weapon for redistribution of incomes, aggregate consumption spending will tend to increase because the lower income groups have a higher propensity to consume (as there are "poor" and "rich" of different income and wealth gradation, the shift to the poorer within each of the broad categories tends to increase overall propensity to consume).[26] Thus redistribution of income is capable of generating effective demand and achieving full employment, particularly if the effect of such measures on private investment is taken into account. Often the increase in income tax by itself is an insufficient measure and an accompanying action may be required to neutralize or offset depressing effects on private investment. With reference to redistribution of income by taxation, for instance, changes in the structure of taxes and transfer payments, such as a progressive rise of tax rates of higher income groups and simultaneous reduction of indirect taxes on necessities or seminecessities to the same extent, or an increase in transfer payments to the poor, have the effect of increasing the propensity to consume. But the rise in income tax may have depressing effects on investment, imposing therefore specific limits on taxation. Moreover, uncertainty about taxation may depress private investment, as investment is a risky undertaking under most circumstances, and this added factor may have a destabilizing effect.

An income tax on a sufficiently high scale provides a workable solution to the full-employment question, provided that an appropriate part of it is modified or replaced by a capital tax. (Kalecki 1946a, p. 83; 1944g, p. 54.)

In retrospect it is commonplace to acknowledge that a high-level (near-full) employment has become a canon of economic policy in the postwar world. As Joan Robinson put it: "The war was a sharp lesson in Keynesism." But she adds: "Then the economists took over Keynes and erected the new orthodoxy. . . . Now that we all agree that government expenditure can maintain employment we should argue about what the expenditure should be for." (Joan Robinson, 1972, p. 6.)

When severe unemployment occurs, the task of employment policy is relatively simple. With the expansion of the economy and employment, new problems crop up. The policy of maintaining high employment levels becomes a more complex proposition. But, above all, once the objective or necessity of high employment level becomes indispensable, the larger and more fundamental complex and controversial issue is how and by what means to achieve it, and whom it is to benefit. Then Keynesian policy has to be generalized and extended on the policy level.

Granted the limitations of his pioneering work, the questions that Kalecki posed both in the field of *General Theory* and in that of employment and policy are very topical indeed. After Keynes, a good number of "Keynesians" came in, refusing to take any notice of Kalecki's suggestions. Their alternatives have proved to be largely not viable. Undeniably much valuable work has been done in the field of employment theory and policy. But whatever the other merits of such works, they failed by and large to answer the questions that Kalecki dealt with, on the plane of both theory and policy of the modern capitalist economy.

VIII

FULL EMPLOYMENT, INFLATION, AND BALANCE OF PAYMENTS

THE FIRST PART OF THIS CHAPTER records Kalecki's view of the essence of inflation. This view is not only an integral part of Kalecki's work, by itself a necessary part of this study, but also points to an explanation of the intricate phenomenon, even though the present course of the debate has shifted. Of particular interest is Kalecki's prefatory treatment of the characteristic measure and structure of inflation and the attention he focused on both macro and micro aspects of the phenomenon. Indeed, it is doubtful whether effective anti-inflationary policy can be designed without a realistic view of how prices are formed in a modern capitalist economy.

This chapter also contains a short account of Kalecki's prewar work on full employment in an open economy, showing how balance-of-payments problems may prevent an economy from achieving full employment. In a sense the analysis here, granted that it was written at an early stage of Kalecki's development as an economist, is not only of historical interest and characteristic of Kalecki's approach, showing both the benefits of and the constraints on full employment, but also of value because balance-of-payments problems have proven very insidious. In a certain sense Kalecki's analysis shows, as we have come to realize, that inflation and balance of payments are the two major constraining factors of full employment.

Again we need to keep in mind that Kalecki was writing at a particular time, and combating the fallacies then prevalent. Often different ones are believed now. Full treatment would require an exposition of what he was dealing with and conveying the atmosphere of the times.[1] I do not undertake this ambitious task here, but merely attempt to record Kalecki's views and the argumentation he advanced in fighting orthodoxy. Obviously, in the depth of the Great Depression, Kalecki was concerned primarily with the causes and consequences of the deficiency of effective demand. He treated the problem of inflation as a contrasting phenomenon in the exposition of the theory of employment.

Kalecki's work on inflation came about as a result of the actual problems of a war economy working at full capacity, which will be discussed in greater detail in part 2 of this study. In discussing what inflation is he proposed to show that government-advocated stabilization of wages as a remedy to inflation would not be workable, and that the preferable alternative would be comprehensive rationing.

Another example of the topicality of his work on inflation deals with the immediate postwar period. During his tenure at the United Nations (1946-55), among the important reports he supervised and took a large hand in preparing are the two major reports on inflationary and deflationary phenomena and analyses in the *World Economic Reports.*

Understandably, the problem of inflation was not particularly real to those who set themselves the task of remedying the depression of the 1930s. In the postwar period, with near-full employment, the problem of inflation has become increasingly more significant: "Now, in the fourth decade of the Keynesian era, we have graduated from a state of innocence of the inflationary dangers from full employment policies to a state of obsession with them." (Lerner 1967, p. 1.)

In recent years a new phenomenon has baffled economists at large: the co-existence of unemployment and inflation.[2] The famous Phillips curve that attempted to quantify the trade off between unemployment and wage-price increases has been viewed as a dramatic way of describing (but not explaining) the "cruel dilemma" and the necessity of policy makers to choose between two evils. So viewed, the problem is of finding ways of improving the trade off, or how to shift the curve downward, so that a lower rate of price advance is associated with a tolerable level of unemployment.[3] After a dramatic career, the Phillips curve has been subjected to scrutiny and criticism, and many economists doubt its validity.[4] However, this is not the place to review this controversy.

Budget Deficit and Inflation

An increase in deficit spending creates additional effective demand; and, in *some* cases, this tends to be inflationary. Inflation is not infrequently identified with the existence of a large budget deficit, but a budget deficit does not necessarily involve inflation.[5] Under conditions of considerably underutilized plant capacity, unemployed labor, and sufficient raw material imports, even a big increase in effective demand, however brought about, may not have any appreciable influence on the movement of the general price level. The primary effect is an increase in output and employment. (Cf. Kalecki 1944g, pp. 39-58.) The question of how to employ economic resources and for what uses is far more important than that of public debt. On the other hand, a balanced budget is not a safeguard against inflation.

The most clear-cut and relatively unobstructed example of full employment and inflation is the case of mobilization of resources for the war effort (away from consumption), where the most vexing and perplexing question is how to get resources for the war and the problem of war finance is often presented as: "how to avoid inflation?" Only some aspects of the problem which transcend a *sui generis* war economy will be discussed in this chapter, such as have a more general implication for the postwar period and for economies where the influence of bottlenecks in production and structural maladjustments is not a temporary, but more or less recurring and widespread, phenomenon.[6]

The problem of inflation arises in a wartime (or war-type) economy as the volume of employment and earnings is appreciably increased (or maintained), whereas the production of consumer goods declines considerably, partly because labor must be diverted from civilian to armaments production and partly because of difficulties in importing foodstuffs. Conditions of rising prices exist owing to the increase in effective demand for goods and services over and above the country's productive capacity and ability to furnish the growing and competing needs of a high-pressure economy resisting structural changes. This is only a once-and-for-all rise if money wages do not go up.

Unless non-wage-earners' consumption is curtailed (to the full extent of the decline of output available for domestic consumption, or even more), by the increased propensity to save, taxation, and rationing, the volume of goods bought by the workers for their hourly wage must decline. With unimpeded price movements, prices rise in relation to wages so as to equilibrate the demand for and supply of consumer goods, i.e., the real wage will fall. In an endeavor to restore the previous level of real wages, the workers demand higher money wages, leading to the vicious inflationary spiral—a wage increase to a new plateau, followed by a price increase, and so on—"*not* it will be noted *as the cause, but only as a symptom of inflation,*" (emphasis supplied; Kalecki 1941e, p. 44; cf. Samuelson 1966, vol. 2, pp. 1336-53; Solow 1968b, pp. 3-4) in the sense of deficiency of produce relative to the volume of spending power.[7] The root of the trouble lies in the fall of the relative ratio of production of consumer goods.

Take the case of income tax on higher income groups, increased to such an extent that sizable budget deficit disappears. However, the rich taxpayers do not reduce their consumption, but merely reduce their savings. Ignoring the effect of income tax on investment in fixed capital goods, which in wartime is anyhow severely restricted by direct controls, (Kalecki 1940g, p. 4) nothing really happens except that the amounts in question are extracted by taxation instead of being borrowed. The underlying conditions of demand for and supply of commodities remain unaffected: if inflation already existed, it would not be prevented by the prudent old-fashioned policy of budget-balancing. In reality the increase in income tax reduces disposable income and is likely to compress consumption to a certain extent. However, the extreme case of its having merely a savings-reduction effect cannot be excluded. It is difficult, if not impossible, to secure a sufficiently large cut in consumption by taxation. Those endowed with considerable wealth can always maintain their consumption standards in the face of increasing taxation.

Since identification of a large budget deficit with the intensity of inflation is tenuous, an attempt is sometimes made to determine inflation as the amount by which the deficit is "excessive" in relation to available savings. The fundamental difficulty with such an explanation is that, in fact, a budget deficit always provides automatically just sufficient savings to finance itself. That is, *ceteris paribus,* an increase in government expenditure always causes such an increase in incomes and alterations in their distribution as to create just enough of an increase in savings to finance it. (Kalecki 1944g, p. 41; 1965l, pp. 45-52.) This is a very general point about saving and investment. The very basis of the Kalecki-Keynes theory, the budget deficit theory of inflation, belabors the distinction between so-called genuine and nongenuine savings. As far as deficit is financed by long-term debt it is considered to be covered by genuine savings as contrasted with the financing by floating debt. Specifically, if treasury bills are sold to banks and a corresponding amount of deposits accumulates, the budget deficit is described as financed by credit creation not by genuine savings. It is this particular manner of government borrowing that is said to generate inflation. Clearly the accumulation of bank deposits corresponding to the accumulation of treasury bills in banks signifies an increase of the claims held by the public against the government. In such a form, it is just as genuine a saving as the accumulation of long-term securities held by the public in the sense that both signify an increase in assets belonging to individual and institutional financial investors. However, savings are held in the form of deposits either because a larger amount is required as money for transaction purposes, or because this form of storing financial resources is considered, for various reasons, preferable to the holding of bonds. In the first case, increasing deposits on current accounts are "tied-up" in settlement transactions and are not generally available for financing consumption. Storing money chiefly on deposit accounts does not differ fundamentally from holding assets in the form of long-term securities.

The contention that deposits are more "liquid assets" and are more easily spent on consumption than long-term securities is relevant only when actual dissaving occurs. As long as consumption is below current income, the form of accumulated savings is largely irrelevant. But even if actual dissaving takes place, the hindrances suggested in connection with disposing of bonds as contrasted with reduction of bank deposits is rather exaggerated. Thus the method of financing the budget cannot be regarded as the essence of inflation. (Kalecki 1941p, pp. 159-61.)

More generally, in a regime of full employment, there is a danger of inflation if effective demand increases to such an extent that a general scarcity of labor and/or capacity arises (or rather this is true whatever caused it). Up to a certain point the short-run supply curves are horizontal or mildly increasing for most goods. In cases when effective demand increases appreciably beyond this point, the steeply upward sloping section of the short-run supply curve becomes the relevant range. Consequently, a general *price increase* out of proportion with average prime costs will result. In this way the progressively vicious inflationary spiral of prices and wages—the ever-rising level of money wages and the cost of living—if not checked, will be on its course. This is a serious danger of inflation, if the government pushes the deficit spending beyond the mark, however difficult to ascertain, indicated by full utilization of labor and capacities.

A prerequisite to full employment without the danger of inflation is a balance between existing stock of capital and available manpower (but not to balance the budget). The plant and equipment must be adequate to employ available labor and still allow for reserve capacities and need of flexibility. If the capacities are insufficient to ensure full employment in the short run, this may easily lead to inflationary pressures in a large number of sectors of the economy because the *structure* of existing stock of capital does not necessarily correspond to the structure of demand. But even if the structure of capital stock *is* matched with that of full employment demand in the initial position, the deficiency of required reserves will be a source of trouble when shifts in the pattern of demand develop subsequently. (Kalecki 1944g, pp. 40-44.)

The Vicious Spiral

Rising prices are attributed to the excess of income generated over available supplies. Inflation is sometimes defined as a state in which a rising effective demand for goods is not met by a corresponding increase in supply. In its crudest form this notion incorrectly identifies any rise in the general level of prices (a depreciation of the monetary unit) with inflation.[8] In Kalecki's opinion this is a confusion, as there are many factors pushing the price level to a higher plateau, without being inflationary in the proper sense of the term. A rise in the price level owing to currency devaluation, or a rise in wage rates followed by a rise in prices in an economy with appreciably underemployed resources will not, *ceteris paribus*, initiate the type of self-generating spiral (cumulative) process for which the term *inflation* is generally reserved.

If the above definition of inflation is understood in the sense that an expanding effective demand for goods *cannot* be matched by a corresponding expanded supply owing to capacity, labor, or raw material shortages, it is nearer the mark. But even such a modified version is exceedingly general. For one, it hardly indicates how to measure the extent of inflation and its speed. Since prices may and do usually increase not only because of the scarcity of inputs, but also because of the subsequent rise in wages, the increase in prices cannot be considered a measure of inflation. These difficulties may be overcome, if it is understood that the vicious spiral arises from the fact that, after a decline in real wages, money wages cannot "catch up" with prices and regain the level of the real wages previously held. This is conditioned primarily by the inelasticity of supply of consumer goods in a war-type economy for one reason or another.

The problem appears to be to distinguish between the concept of *primary inflation,* i.e., the rise of prices relative to money wages, and the *vicious spiral* that sets in when money wages rise.

Under conditions of mobilizing resources for the war, the problem is of increased pressures of money incomes on a diminishing supply of civilian consumer goods and, if unchecked, the scarcity prices of consumer goods must rise even if the costs of labor and raw materials inputs remain unchanged. Unless excess purchasing power is taxed away, cut, or frozen by rationing, or sterilized by encouraging savings, the increased effective demand is confronted with a constant (or reduced) supply, and it is the price increase which brings them into equilibrium.

Prices rise in relation to wages so as to equilibrate the demand for and supply of consumer goods and services. Workers endeavor to preserve their living standard, i.e., to restore the previous level of real wages. A fall in the purchasing power of money occasions higher wage demand. The money wages are increased to compensate labor for a drift in prices. The increase in wages occasions further price hikes, and so on the "chase" continues. But the distribution effect of price increases cannot be overlooked. The rate of increase of money wages is never uniform throughout the system. The process of adjustment is of varied duration in various sectors of the economy. The pattern, setting, speed, and extent of diffusion depends on the degree of organization and strength of a particular sector of the labor force.

Under the circumstances, the increase in nominal wage rates cannot restore the previous level of real wages, and merely gives rise to a new wave of price increases. The real source of inflationary pressures is the increase of the aggregate employment (wage fund) unaccompanied by a commensurate rise in the supply of consumer goods. Hence, if the consumption of non-wage-earners is not reduced accordingly, the average real pay for an hour's work (i.e., in terms of consumer goods) must decline. This is to be identified as the real source of the "vicious spiral." But not every fall in real wages leads to a vicious spiral. If such a fall results from a deterioration of the terms of trade, it may always be compensated by a sufficient rise in money wages. (Kalecki 1941p, pp. 161-64.)

More generally, there is a danger of continuing increase in prices in a state of full employment resulting from the disproportionate growth of demand and supply of consumer goods. Under such conditions, the power of trade unions is very strongly enhanced,[9] and the conditions are conducive to a spontaneous tendency for money wage rates to increase, which leads to a subsequent rise in prices and the standard of living, which leads to a secondary rise in wages, followed by a rise in prices, etc.

The root of the problem is excess effective demand when the wage fund is overexpanded in relation to wage goods available. The situation can be redressed on the demand side by clamping down on disposable income and on the supply side by redirecting resources to the consumer goods sector, modifying the structure of production by foreign trade and/or increased productivity in the consumer goods sector. Failing to take such (or combination of) measures on a sufficient scale to eradicate excess demand cannot remedy the situation, as it does not remove the actual cause of the vicious spiral. However, such measures may be necessary, but not sufficient for sterilizing inflationary forces, for structural factors play a significant role in the process. (Kalecki 1944g, p. 44; 1943k, pp. 17-20.)

Characteristics, Measure, and Structure of Inflation

In Kalecki's view the characteristic of inflation is the rapidity of rise of prices of consumer goods in relation to the relevant prime costs. Under normal conditions, when certain productive inputs required to produce consumer goods are in ample supply (say, absence of shipping bottlenecks and general availability of imported raw materials), there will be more or less close correspondence between the product price on the one hand and prime costs on the other. Under such circumstances, the supply curves are, on the whole, horizontal or slightly rising over the relevant range of output; and therefore expansion of employment need not be accompanied by marked decline in real wages. (Cf. Keynes 1939b, pp. 34-51.) It is during inflation that the steeply rising part of the supply curve becomes relevant. Prices leap significantly above the level corresponding to the "normal" relation between prices and prime costs.

If this discrepancy is *X* per cent of the price, then *X* per cent of total sales revenue of the goods in question constitutes inflationary profits. The sum of all such profits, wherever they emerge, may be taken as the measure of inflation. According to Kalecki, the advantage of such an approach is not only that of measuring the total inflationary phenomenon, but also of identifying in what *sectors* (activities) of the economy it really manifests itself. Generally the effects of inflation on the economy will vary depending on *where and how rapidly it develops.*[10] This is of particular significance in designing remedies to combat inflation. It follows directly that *to fight inflation in general, it is necessary to deal with "inflations" in partial markets* (in markets for specific groups of goods).

Price increases out of proportion with costs are not the only symptom of an inflationary situation. Another indication is the dangerous inroad into stocks. Depletion of private stocks indicates that there was a discrepancy between actual consumption and the supply of consumer goods as determined by imports, domestic production, and the government's policy of increasing or reducing its inventories. As long as consumption is not diminished or supply, as ruled by the above three factors, is not increased, the disinvestment of private stocks will continue at the same rate.

Depletion of inventories may delay for a certain time the actual inflationary pressures. Should demand for a certain product rise, while the factors required for its production are in inelastic supply, the price of the product may not rise if the shortage in production is temporarily made up out of inventories. Depletion of stocks provides a breathing space but is limited by the size of the stocks and cannot continue forever. After running down stocks to a critically low level, the inflationary pressures to raise prices must set in. Thus it is reasonable to consider the intensity of the reduction of stocks of consumer goods as latent inflation, which may be measured by the rate at which stocks are being exhausted. In this case, again, although the total magnitude of latent inflation can be identified by adding the value of particular items, it is the specific commodities or groups of commodities that have special significance for locating in which economic sectors (activities) the latent inflation develops. Here again the only effective remedy against a complete running down of stocks will be exactly the same device as against inflation proper: rationing of expenditures on goods in deficient supply.

Hidden inflation may, and often does, go hand in hand with inflation proper: disinvestments of inventories are accompanied by inflationary price increases and emergence of windfall profits, which might be dangerous if left free. What is the consequence if inventories of some articles are exhausted, rationing is not introduced to cut down demand to equality with available supplies, but rigid price controls are instituted to prevent prices from rising and the emergence of surplus profits? Then the effect is a very haphazard distribution, difficulty in buying goods owing to shortages, and queues which are a symptom of *sui generis* inflation. While it is not a state of inflation proper as prices are kept from rising (but excess demand relative to supply is not eliminated), the bidding for commodities goes on. A state of repressed inflation develops.[11]

While repressed inflation is not measurable, it shares the common characteristic with inflation proper, in that it produces an inequitable distribution of goods in short supply, discriminating against those who have not the time, the servants, nor the influence for time-consuming hunting for goods and against those who are *personae non gratae* with shopkeepers. Inappropriate distribution arrangement of available supplies make the shortages more noticeable and less tolerable. Inflation cannot be considered overcome by mere control of prices. With artificially maintained fiat prices (legal price ceilings), supply and demand do not match and more radical, equitable, and efficient ways are required to deal with the problems. (Kalecki 1941p, pp. 159-61; 1940i, p. 7.)

The crucial question is: What are the consequences if money wage rates are stabilized? The answer was particularly important in wartime in view of the widespread advocacy of the policy of wage stabilization as a remedy in the fight against inflation. The following may be expected: Prices would rise to the point at which real wage rates are cut sufficiently to equate the demand for consumer goods with the available supply. But under the conditions of a wage freeze (i.e., wages are kept artificially stable) no subsequent rise of prices follows. (Cf. Poole 1971, pp. 429-43.) Real wages are cut without setting into motion the vicious inflationary spiral. However, real wages will not be stabilized at the lower level they initially reach. Any further dwindling in the supply of consumer goods will automatically produce a further fall in real wages. True, if the deficiency in the domestic production and imports of consumer goods is initially somewhat compensated by destocking, the rise in prices and decline in real wages is likely to moderate. Yet after using up stocks, prices must rise to a level which equilibrates demand with reduced production and imports.

Both open inflation and stabilization of money wages have a common distributional effect: The impact on different sectors of society is unequal and the burden of sacrifice is maldistributed. The lower income groups are particularly hit as it is the curtailment of their consumption that serves to equilibrate demand with a falling supply of goods for civilian consumption. The result is not only serious inequities among economic groups and economic discrimination against workers (particularly against those wage-earners at the lower levels of the economic scale), and fixed income groups, but this hardship tends also to have adverse effects on labor productivity both in the war sector and in the consumer-goods-producing sector.

Economic incentives have a significant role to play under most arrangements, including that of a war economy. The problem is of spurring maximum possible effort both in the war and civilian sectors. The policy of wage stability might endanger war production and reduce even further production of consumer goods, effecting an additional rise in prices and decline in real wages. Even in wartime, patriotism by no means supersedes the power of money as an incentive. An increase in earnings is in many cases necessary to facilitate a rapid transfer of labor to the war effort and to secure maximum exertion and efficiency in production. (Cf. Steindl 1942, pp. 269-74.)

Kalecki vehemently objected to the policy of wage stabilization advocated by the Government White Paper on Price Stabilization and Industrial Policy as a remedy against inflation. He propounded comprehensive rationing as a preferable alternative.[12] It was also argued that inflation may be stopped directly by complete price control. However, price control without rationing suffers from an inequitable distribution of scarce goods. Inflation cannot be overcome by mere control of prices. The results of price-fixing measures are either that: (1) prices continue to rise illegally; or (2) excess demand is reflected in a haphazard distribution, a shortage of goods, queues, shopping aggravation, waste of time, deterioration of quality and services, and customers' rising tempers and anxieties. Open inflation may be eliminated or reduced, but inflation in altered form (repressed inflation) still exists. Under such conditions, goods are distributed according to the buyers' shopping power. The primary victims are those who have no time or servants to make the best of the state of very random distribution; inordinate burdens and hardships are placed on those who work hard and suffer from low incomes—a state of affairs bound to demoralize and lessen the incentive to produce. (Kalecki 1941e; cf. 1971a, pp. 8-9.)

Aspects of Inflation

The United Nations study of inflationary and deflationary developments in 1946-48 is prefaced by a brief theoretical note on aspects of inflationary and deflationary processes. While much of it is sensible, by now the analysis is familiar. We report briefly to convey the flavor of the arguments advanced.[13] The report's comprehensive analysis of inflationary and deflationary developments is subdivided into the following categories: (1) noncontrolled or partially controlled economies which had no effective comprehensive rationing and price control system for goods in short supply in 1946-48 (French inflation is taken as a typical case of open inflation and a detailed analysis of developments in Italy, Poland, India, and Latin America is provided); (2) countries with a comprehensive system of rationing and price controls, adequate to prevent price increases for scarce essential items (detailed analysis of the United Kingdom, the Scandinavian countries, the Netherlands, Czechoslovakia, and Australia); and (3) countries which decontrolled during 1946-48 (U.S.A., Canada, Belgium), with separate treatment of the U.S.S.R. and China, where hyperinflation persisted in the course of 1946-48. While clearly those comprehensive studies are invaluable, their analysis is beyond our undertaking.

Using the customary framework of national income accounting, and drawing on his analysis in the early 1930s, Kalecki showed that a country's gross national expenditures on goods and services in a given period consist of: (1) personal consumption of goods and services; (2) gross private capital formation; (3) export surplus (excess of imports over exports is treated as a negative export surplus; the export or import surplus applies to all goods and services and is thus identical with the balance of international payments on current accounts); and (4) government expenditures on goods and services. As is well known, all these components of expenditures generate in the period in which they take place an equal flow of private incomes or government revenues. Adjusted for government revenue, transfer payments, and interest on public debt, gross private income (after tax, but including depreciation) in any given period is equal to the sum of 1, 2, and 3 and budget deficit (budget surplus is treated as a negative budget deficit.)

With a given propensity to consume, the last three items (private investment, export surplus, and budget deficit) are of key significance in the analysis of the inflationary and deflationary phenomenon, for they generate private incomes which are not derived from current output of goods available for current personal consumption. Clearly, in contradistinction to the income originated from production of consumer supplies, the other three items do not have a counterpart in *currently* produced output of consumer goods (investment makes it possible to increase the future stream of consumer goods by adding to the stock of capital, but during the period that investment takes place, it adds only to effective demand and not to consumer supplies). For the sake of brevity, the sum of these three items may be treated as net nonconsumption payments—NNCP (equal to private saving)—in the sense that they are not derived from current production of consumer goods, and they are net payments as government expenditures are taken net of taxes.

A rise in net nonconsumption payments (accumulation) increases, and a fall lowers, the pressure of effective demand upon the consumer supplies. If the initial situation is taken in which NNCP are just sufficient to generate an effective demand adequate to support full employment, and thereafter a reduction in the payments occurs, it leads to the unemployment equilibrium of demand and supply for consumer goods, brought about by a primary and induced decline in output, income, and employment.

Consider first the case in which the real gross private national income is given and increase in NNCP (say a rise in investment or defense spending) leads to inflation and results in redistribution of income from wages to profits. In a full employment situation, a rise in NNCP entails a shift in resources from consumption to nonconsumption uses, and supply of consumption goods falls without a fall in spending power. In the absence of price controls, this will lead to a rise in prices of consumption goods. Such a rise in prices generates new money incomes and thereby augments demand for consumer goods. The increase in prices tends to a relative shift from wages to profits in the distribution of private incomes. Since the propensity to consume of profit-earners is lower than that of wage-earners, a point is reached in the rise in prices where the relative shift to profits is sufficiently large to equilibrate the demand for consumer goods with the reduced supply made available.[14]

Alternatively, the equilibrium is described as the point where profits have risen sufficiently in relation to private income so as to raise the ratio of current private saving to income, up to the increased level of the ratio of NNCP to income. Thus inflation engenders a redistribution of income from wages to profits, whereas deflation from a full-employment level, entails a contraction in output, income, and employment.

An inflationary or deflationary process may also be engendered by a shift in the propensity to consume. For example, a major factor in immediate postwar world-wide inflationary pressures was the influence of demand for consumption goods pent up during the war, which in many instances was supported by accumulated holdings of liquid assets (in some cases the factor of greatest importance was the fall in per capita consumer supplies). (United Nations 1949b, ch. 2.)

Ceteris paribus, a rise in the propensity to consume in a state of full employment leads to a rise in prices and relative redistribution of income in favor of profits. Such a shift will equilibrate the increased demand for consumer goods with the given volume of supply. A rise in the propensity to save will not materialize in a change in the proportion of income actually saved if the ratio of NNCP to income remains unaltered. Instead it will engender inflationary pressures which will redistribute private income to such an extent as to keep the ratio of overall private saving to income at the given level of the ratio of NNCP to income. *Ceteris paribus,* a fall in the propensity to consume at the full-employment level will lead to a contraction of output and employment, which will reduce the supply of consumer goods to the level of effective demand.

Consider now the case in which inflation is associated, not with changed distribution of a given real private income from wages to profits, but with the fall in the very level of income. If the supply of consumer goods falls while the ratio of NNCP remains constant, real private income (i.e., money private income deflated by the price index of consumer goods and services) will decline via a rise in prices, *pro tanto,* as the supply of consumer goods. If, however, not only the NNCP/private income ratio, but propensity to consume were constant, there would be no redistribution of income from lower to higher income groups (but there might be horizontal shifts in the distribution of income within given income groups which do not affect overall propensity to consume) as a consequence of price advance. Such a result is termed the primary inflationary effect of the fall in real private income.

A secondary inflationary effect results from the fact that the propensity to consume is not constant, irrespective of the level of income; but the lower the real private income, the higher the share which tends to be consumed out of it. When real income falls, with an unchanged NNCP/income ratio, this factor will lead to an additional price advance. For unlike the primary price increase, this secondary increase will entail a relative redistribution from wages to profits.

The reasons for a fall in real private income and consumption, with a constant NNCP/income ratio may include a fall in the productivity of the consumer goods sector or a fall in agricultural output; a rise in indirect taxes for the financing of increased government spending, or a rise in foreign trade prices in relation to income, while the ratio of import or export surplus to income remains constant. In the last case it is useful to distinguish (1) an equal change in export and import prices, and (2) a change in terms of trade. If a net importing country is faced with (1), this will tend to lower the real value of the import surplus. If, as a consequence, imports of consumer goods are cut the total supply available for domestic consumption will decline. Assuming that the ratio NNCP/income remains constant, real private income will fall *pari passu.* Clearly if a deterioration of terms of trade (2) also occurs, there will be an additional decline in consumption and real private income. The effect of deterioration in terms of trade results even if the country's exports equal imports.

In case higher indirect (commodity) taxes for financing increased government outlays are imposed, a fall in real private income follows through the increase in market prices (brought out by such a rise in indirect taxes), while the NNCP/income ratio will remain unaltered, for the budget will remain balanced. If direct taxes on higher income groups are levied to finance any rise in government outlays in a full employment situation, they will tend to reduce not only consumption outlays, but also the savings of the taxpayers affected. To forestall inflation, the new taxes should exceed expenditure sufficiently to offset this effect. If direct taxes are levied directly on wage-earners, they will lower their real income in the same way as would price hikes. Similarly, a rise in prices of wage goods, or any other method of reducing labor's real income will likely provoke demands for higher money wages, which may produce an inflationary spiral.

Clearly the burden of inflation is unequally distributed. For one, not all workers are in a position to secure the same rate of increase of money wages in the course of the inflationary spiral. Apart from differentials among the ranks of organized labor, the pay of unorganized or weakly organized employees tends to fall behind. This fall is more intense. Of course, the real value of fixed income groups declines continuously during the course of inflation. Thus any rise in taxation to finance enlarged government spending which does not reduce the NNCP/income ratio tends to produce inflation, similarly to a fall in productivity (decline in supply of consumer goods).

Apart from the question of aggregate supply of consumer goods and services, it is important to note that the *structure* of supply must be considered in connection with analysis of the inflationary phenomenon. Of particular interest in this respect is a fall in food supply in relation to aggregate consumer supplies (decline in per capita food supplies in relation to per capita consumer supplies). The importance of food in an inflationary situation is of special interest for (1) food constitutes the key item in the budget of lower income groups; thus a rise in prices of foodstuffs tends to exert a stronger effect on real wages than price hikes of non-food consumer goods; and (2) the more essential the article in short supply, the greater the probable fall in the propensity to save of those affected; for food is in the most essential position in consumption, the effect of its scarcity on the share of income saved will be particularly significant; (3) to the extent that small and medium farmers benefit from the rise in food prices, apart from redistribution of income to higher income groups, there will occur a relative shift from non-farm-labor income to farmers, which further contributes to the fall in real wages.

The effect of the food supply factor is particularly pronounced when the reduction in the ratio of food to aggregate consumption supply is associated with a fall in aggregate (per capita) consumption. According to Engel's Law, with given income distribution and with constant price relations, the percentage importance of food expenditure declines as income increases, and a higher proportion of income is likely to be spent on food when income falls. Thus demand for foodstuffs in relation to aggregate demand will rise, while supply of food in relation to aggregate supply falls. "Inflation is not necessarily incompatible with unemployment." When inflation occurs because of a rise in effective demand under conditions of capacity output, it will lead to overemployment only if labor is the bottleneck limiting the expansion of production. If there are bottlenecks in capacity or raw materials, then inflation may coexist with unemployment, for these bottlenecks will make it impossible to utilize all employable manpower. Inflation may also stem from a fall in productivity or in agricultural output in case aggregate effective demand is insufficient to sustain full employment.[15]

Whether the pressures stem from excess aggregate demand or are produced by shortages of specified goods, open inflation may be contained or prevented by a system of direct controls. The essence of such an arrangement is the distribution of supplies of essential consumer goods by rationing. This and price control shall be examined in the part of this book on the war economy.

Hyperinflation and Quantity Theory

After some time, if it is not contained, an inflationary spiral may develop into hyperinflation. Once the process of inflation has gathered momentum, the consciousness of the steady advance of prices develops a general expectation of the continuation of the inflationary spiral of prices. Expectation of continuous increases in prices may lead to a general reluctance to hold money, save for a minimum required for transaction purposes. The anticipation of rapid advance in prices stimulates hoarding of commodities and thus reduces the supplies available for consumption. Consequently, all proceeds tend to be spent promptly on consumption, investment, or the hoarding of goods. As hyperinflation progresses, people tend to spend more money and part with it faster, i.e., the velocity of circulation of money rises. (Cf. United Nations 1949a, pp. 13-14, 48-49.) The two basic characteristic features of hyperinflation are: (1) a very rapid rise in prices, and (2) a general reluctance to hold money and a propensity to convert money into goods quickly. These two features are closely interrelated.

In a provocative lecture given at the University of Cambridge in 1955, Kalecki explored a "model of hyperinflation," which can only be called to the reader's attention here. He argued at the beginning: "The theory of hyperinflation is of interest even though the phenomenon is rather exceptional, because this phenomenon is striking and because, even though hyperinflation does not last too long, it leaves considerable traces in the economy in the years to come, one of the consequences being the wiping out of the wealth and income of the rentier. However, the discussion of hyperinflation has an added theoretical interest because this happens to be the one case where the quantity theory of money finds its full application." (Kalecki 1962g, pp. 275-76.)

In the absence of hyperinflation, the increase in quantity of money (M) results directly in greater liquidity and lower velocity of circulation (V), rather than producing an increase in the price level (P). True, the ensuing decline in the rate of interest (i), with given profit prospects, tends to increase investment, the multiplier gets to work on increased consumption, output rises, and prices advance. However, this effect may be very small. Normally, the decline in the short-term rate of interest is only partly and moderately reflected in the long-term rate of interest in the short or intermediate periods. This limits the stimulative effect on private investment. Under this condition the effect of increase of M on P will be very indirect in character, but not so under conditions of hyperinflation. (Kalecki 1965l, pp. 73-82.)

Under hyperinflation every fresh increase in the quantity of money in circulation is bound to engender a direct rise in the price level. In view of the universal preference for goods and away from money, the additional money created is converted into goods within a certain spending period—the length of which is itself a function of the rate of acceleration of price advances. Kalecki argued that the greater the rate of increase of prices per unit of time, the larger the real value of the increase in the money in circulation per unit of time which takes place through the channels of financing budget deficit and the expansion of bank credit to business (the real value of these two items is denoted by D) and the velocity of circulation V. If it is supposed that D is maintained at a stable level by macroeconomic policy, the rate of advance in prices is proportionate to the velocity of the circulation of money. (Kalecki 1962g, p. 276; cf. 1965l, pp. 32-38, 73-76.) But V is itself a function of the anticipated rate of increase in prices. Clearly, as long as these anticipations about the rate of change do not alter, the rate of increase of prices will continue at a uniform speed. However, in a longer period, the "steady state" of an advance of prices can persist only if there is no divergence between the *ex ante* and *ex post* rate of increase in prices. But if this is not the case, if, for example, the latter is higher than the former, with some time-lag, there will be an upward revision in the *ex ante* rate of increase in prices and in the velocity of circulation, because it is determined by the anticipated increase in prices (Kalecki 1962g, p. 276). In turn, this will produce a further speed-up in the rate of price advance and the spiral will tend to continue, propelled by an increasing *V*, but not without a ceiling. Indeed, this "phenomenon of accelerated hyperinflation is nothing else but the galloping inflation which is based on the increasing velocity of circulation." (Kalecki 1962g, p. 278.) But the phenomenon does not go on *ad infinitum*, and the galloping will be stopped because there exists *some limit* to the velocity of circulation, however high such a level may be. The crux of the matter is that the galloping prices might not continue under their own steam until the theoretical point is reached (Kalecki 1962g, pp. 278-79); indeed, it may never be reached if it is deliberately stopped by stabilization schemes earlier, and the question is why a stop was put to the hyperinflation momentum in the meantime. The clue is provided by the impact of hyperinflation on income distribution.

In a state of hyperinflation, changes in money wages will not affect prices, provided that the real value of the budget deficit, plus banking credit to private business, remains unchanged. Thus if the increase in money wages is sufficiently rapid, a rise in real wages is feasible which enhances the consumption of the working class at the expense of the hoarding of goods. (Kalecki 1962g, p. 280.) But in reality such increase in real wages may not be achieved, as the increase in money wages may lag behind price advances. Kalecki thought that the mere time-lag owing to negotiations may be of decisive significance and even automatic adjustments will be insufficient owing to an institutionalized method of payment of wages at certain intervals (unless presumably such increases will be more or less anticipated). He argued that, in point of fact, under hyperinflation real wages are usually falling (cf. UN 1948, pp. 48-49), and the fact that their level is much less than normal can be seen from the distribution of national product. Under hyperinflation the real budget deficit is very high, and so usually is investment in fixed capital. In addition there is a considerable volume of hoarding of goods. It is clear that much less than normal is left for consumption, and this reduction reflects mainly the reduced real income of the working class. (Kalecki 1962g, p. 280.)

The main burden of the reduction will be reflected chiefly in the curtailed real income of wage earners (presumably of the group that can protect itself and resist the cut least). Another consequence of the hyperinflationary process is that it leads to impoverishment of rentiers. The counterpart of this phenomenon is "the enormous profits of entrepreneurs in general and big business in particular."

(Kalecki 1962g, p. 280.) Kalecki believed that hyperinflation may be used as an income redistribution device, thus explaining the support that big business gives the continuation of the hyperinflationary momentum once started. But in order to grasp the likely turn of events, one should perceive that big business's interest in hyperinflation "begins to vanish at the point where the techniques of fixing wages are so perfected as to enable the workers to increase the real wages. Since at the advanced stage of hyperinflation when this occurs the rentiers are already so impoverished that they cannot be squeezed any more, hyperinflation ceases to be a profitable proposition. It is at this point that usually emerge stabilization schemes which put a stop to hyperinflation." (Kalecki 1962g, p. 281.)

The warnings that a steadily ascending inflationary spiral, if permitted to develop, is bound to result in hyperinflation seem frequently to be exaggerated. There are probably some stabilizing factors at work, with the economic system more or less capable of adapting itself to a steady decline in the purchasing power of money. Of course, recently the costs of inflation and the costs to contain it were significant and serious. (Cf. Okun, ed. 1972, pp. 12-20.) In the post-World War II period the experience of Germany's great inflation after World War I was not forgotten. (Cf. Joan Robinson 1951, pp. 69-77.) It seems interesting that, in countries that experienced a very great and rapid fall in the value of money, the mystique of inflation dies hard, and governments are more sensitive to control the beast at the expense of other economic desiderata.

Balance of Payments

As mentioned, in a number of prewar articles, Kalecki examined the function of foreign trade in the cyclical development of the capitalist economy. He paid particular attention to the role of export surplus as a stimulus of prosperity and to the extent that the progressing upswing tends to affect balance of trade adversely and limits the expansion via deterioration of the balance of payments if this expansion is not accompanied by an influx of foreign capital. This deterioration in the balance of payments may impose a limit on the promotion of prosperity prior to achieving full-employment potential. Generally, all attempts to stimulate an upswing lead to deterioration of the balance of payments. The formidable difficulties encountered in overcoming such imbalances restrain and hamper continuation of expansion. Clearly, a new dimension is added to the discussion of expansionary macroeconomic policy when the system becomes open with respect to foreign trade.

The repercussions of the upswing on the international payments position are not affected by the manner of bringing about the upswing; i.e., whether by "natural" forces or "artificially" stimulated by government intervention. Whatever the reasons for expansion in output, it will be followed by increased demand for imports. This results chiefly from an increased demand for goods which were not produced in that country at all, or not in sufficient quantities. When expansion has gained momentum, balance-of-trade trouble may prevent continuation of the upswing. Absence of such complementary factors as raw materials precludes further expansion of production. (Kalecki 1935f, p. 1385; 1935g, p. 703.)

Another factor that adversely affects the balance of payment is the rise in domestic prices that occurs during the course of the upswing. This rise in prices entails deterioration in the relative competitive position of products of domestic industry as compared with foreign producers. As a result, imports tend to rise and exports to fall. However, the impact of price advances on the balance of trade is generally of smaller importance than the impact of higher demand for imports. In fact, as a result of existing high tariffs protection, the rise of domestic prices—as long as it does not exceed a certain limit—prevents foreign competition. Much more serious are the domestic price increases in case of exports. But even here this will not take place in view of fairly widely practiced price discrimination (dumping by cartels) in international trade (charging different prices in different markets, characterized by different demand elasticities). (Kalecki 1935f, p. 1385.)

Clearly an upswing in a given country may have international repercussions and be accompanied by a rise in demand in the world market. Kalecki admitted that the balance of payments may not deteriorate because of the increased demand for the country's exports, but he abstracted from such repercussions. (Cf. Kalecki 1933d, p. 11.)

Whereas in an open system expansionary policy is made difficult by repercussions on its balance of payments, it has the advantage over a closed system that a slump in it is mitigated by improvement in the balance of payments. If a slump occurs only in one country, or does not permeate a large part of the world, then the fall in prices in the country hurt by a depression enhances its export capacity and simultaneously checks the demand for imports. But in an interdependent world economy, the influence of this factor is reduced or even nonoperative. (Kalecki 1932e.)

In its broader implications the upswing stimulated by deficit spending has a limit: Aggregate output cannot be allowed to expand to the level where required imports would exceed the maximum imports that could be secured by lowering the value of currency. Again, it is likely that an upswing engendered by deficit spending will fail to lead to full utilization of productive capacity because of the deficiency of complementary factors of production (particularly raw materials). The greater the dependence of the economy on imports and the greater the difficulties for this economy to expand its export through devaluation, the quicker does the upswing caused by deficit spending reach its maximum level. With progressive currency deterioration the real domestic income reaches its highest level at an earlier point than output produced. This is so because a declining amount of real income is yielded by a unit of aggregate output, and a share of this output is exchanged for imports at worsening terms of trade.

In a world of unrestricted international trade, the exports of a country which relatively depreciated its currency would flood foreign markets that were previously inaccessible. With existing high tariffs, devaluation is not likely to produce such results, for a moderate depreciation of currency may not be sufficient for exports to overtake the tariff barriers and a more drastic one is likely to provoke retaliatory measures in the countries affected. (Kalecki 1933c, trans. and rpt. in 1966h, pp. 16-25.)

Kalecki stressed elsewhere that the German case of a lopsided boom is a sad experiment. By winding up prosperity, Hitler's Germany expanded the internal market and overcame the deficiency of effective demand. But soon it faced a different crisis—ensuring the supply of needed materials. This is the limitation on the expansion of the internal market. But the really sad part was that expansion of national output and acceleration of the pace of armaments was accomplished by reducing the two other items of national output—consumption and investment. Despite higher output and employment, workers' income and consumption rose much slower and incommensurately with the expansion of the national product.[16]

IX

THE POLITICAL BUSINESS CYCLE

WHATEVER THE RATIONALE OF THE ARGUMENTS of the *economics* of full employment, the *political* problems involved in achieving and maintaining full employment are formidable. This chapter focuses primarily on the interaction between politics and economics in contemporary capitalist economies. The setting for the regime is parliamentary democracy (or its U. S. counterpart). In such a regime the government is sensitive to the electoral process. The elections are subject to business, organized labor, and other group pressures. The thrust of Kalecki's theory was in terms of whose interests the government is, or is forced, to consider when making and implementing policy decisions.[1] More specifically I shall deal with the ruling powers' reception, rejection, wariness, or half-hearted acceptance of Keynesian policies and techniques.[2] Indeed, "full employment seems to be such a desirable economic policy that we may well be led to wonder why there must be any opposition to it." (Klein 1966, p. 179.) Kalecki prophetically pointed out during World War II that it was not sufficient to know how to cure slumps and maintain full employment. The point was to be able to sell the idea politically. Indeed, as Joan Robinson noted, "with most problems nowadays the economic answers are only political questions." (1960, p. 275.)

FROM ECONOMICS TO POLITICS OF FULL EMPLOYMENT

In 1943, Kalecki envisaged business opposition to government intervention whose aim would be to maintain full employment.[3] He foresaw the probability of the emergence of a *political* business cycle,[4] since theoretically economists and politicians had learned how to avert business cycle fluctuations.[5] Kalecki acknowledged that a good majority of economists were already agreed that a government spending program could ensure full employment in a capitalist system, as long as there exists sufficient capacity to employ the existing labor force and as long as the required foreign raw materials can be gotten in exchange for exports. But this was not even the case a few years before 1943. The opposition was mainly from economic advisors to banking and industry. Hence, Kalecki inferred that there was a political background in the opposition. This did not mean that those in opposition did not "believe in their economics, poor though these are. But obstinate ignorance is usually a manifestation of underlying political motives." (Kalecki 1943g, pp. 322 and 324.)

Essentially, Kalecki felt that business cycles (in milder form than hitherto) would continue not because we did not know how to prevent them, but because the inherent fear of government interference, of laxity in workers' discipline, and of inflationary pressures would result in some sort of stop-go activity. These short-lived and relatively moderate cycles would proceed from a situation where the government would stimulate business activity, then withdraw at the early signs of an upswing under the clamor of an "unsound" financial situation (and even undertake deflationary policies near the peak) only to re-enter as a stimulating agent when unemployment would again rise beyond an "acceptable level," thus vacillating between combating unemployment and inflation.

Such stop-go alternations between overacting too late and/or inordinately concentrating on curing a particular economic ill that has already reached serious and intolerable proportions (for instance, an open economy's balance-of-payment disequilibrium) are a direct consequence of having done too little, or having moved at a snail's pace before. This does not follow only from the well-known difficulties in diagnosing and applying the right dose of Keynesian prescriptions, but is largely dictated by political (and often electoral) considerations. For example, basing its platform on growing popular discontent with the wage-price spiral, a party in opposition is elected to clamp down on the creeping inflation. The new government then takes deflationary measures. As the effects of such policy become apparent in growing unemployment, discontent rises; defeat in future elections threatens; and a sharp reversal in policy takes place. In a sense, the pressures of future elections make the politicians more responsive to the particular economic ills of the moment (whether inflation or unemployment), but make them over-react in one direction, often at the expense of upsetting the applecart in the other. Obviously, political circumstances, electoral systems, traditions, configuration of pressure groups, and so forth differ considerably from country to country.

Clearly, such stop-go policy could be broadly contrasted with one where full employment would be maintained with moderate price advances and without considerable fluctuations, thus reducing the cost of shifts in policy and loss of potential output, avoiding human suffering, and probably increasing the system's productivity.

Kalecki based his gloomy predictions of the political business cycle on the experience of the New Deal in the United States, the Blum experiment in France, and the pre-Hitler German experiment. Several years thereafter (in 1946) in the United States the Full Employment Act was passed by Congress. Without specifying practical policies, it placed direct and continuing responsibility on the federal government deliberately to promote maximum employment, production, and purchasing power, if spontaneous market forces failed to provide them. (Cf. Dillard 1964, pp. 328-29; Hansen 1964b; Galbraith 1965; Samuelson 1972, pp. 603-39, 717-21.) The several toning-down stages that it had to go through and the main objections thereto largely corroborated Kalecki's predictions.[6] Kalecki contended that business opposition to government full-employment policies will give way in particularly deflationary situations, and will disappear when the government intervention relies on armaments expenditures. In the latter case his position was buttressed by observations on the business upswing in Nazi Germany, the economic recovery of the United States during World War II, about a decade later by the upswing generated by the Korean War, three decades later, by that stimulated by the war in Vietnam, and the flourishing of the military-industrial complex. In a thoughtful and significant analysis of the influence of war on the American economy, Lawrence R. Klein concluded that although war is not a *sine qua non* for stable growth in the United States and that this can be induced by peaceful means, during peace the American economy "limps along at less than full employment" and "rises to full employment levels of activity only during a major war." (Klein 1971b, p. 512.)

Largely the problems faced by present-day capitalism in both Western Europe and the United States confirm Kalecki's predictions during the war: If the United States, the United Kingdom, and other Western democracies have lived through a period of political business cycles, do these economies as presently constituted have to live through such cycles again? It is difficult to give an unqualified answer to this question. This is true because economics is a field of study in which it is difficult, or even impossible, to establish categorical proof of most propositions. A very provisional investigation and conversations with economists having first-hand knowledge of government and business (particularly in Britain) seem to bear out that Kalecki was on the right track. Even if his original and prophetic statement should be somewhat modified and restated, it represents a seminal contribution and is an avant-garde approach to the subject of political business cycles.

A Sketch of the Political Aspects of Full Employment

Toward the end of World War II, Kalecki came to the conclusion that one could not expect a government in a capitalist economy to maintain full employment simply because the economic tool box for doing so had been developed.[7] He based his contention on the New Deal experience in the United States where he viewed the collapse of the boom in the second half of 1937 as owing to a severe curtailment of the budget deficit in response to pressures to balance the budget. In the sharp slump that followed, the government reverted to its previous spending policy. In fact before World War II—in all countries except Nazi Germany—business strongly protested against government intervention for increasing effective demand. (Kalecki 1938c, p. 39.)

Such opposition by business groups is somewhat paradoxical. Profits rise with a fuller utilization of productive capacities. Additional government spending does not rely on increased taxation. Periods of depressed economic activity make businessmen hanker for a boom, yet they are not eager for the "synthetic boom" that the government can provide. Kalecki presented three reasons for industrial leaders' opposition to full employment promoted by government spending: "(1) the dislike of Government interference in the problem of employment as such; (2) the dislike of the direction of Government spending (public investment and subsidising consumption); (3) dislike of the social and political changes resulting from the *maintenance* of full employment." (Kalecki 1943g, p. 324.)

It is worth noting that most of the objections of businessmen that Kalecki foresaw in 1943 came to light in 1945-46 in the United States when the Full Employment Act was being debated. In this context, I shall limit comparisons or divergencies strictly to specific, more outstanding points.[8]

1. Kalecki maintained that business opposes government interference per se mainly because it is afraid of losing power.[9] Under laissez faire, business has a measure of control over the government in that private investment (and the level of employment) depends on the state of confidence. The government is diffident about any moves that might weaken the state of confidence. But once it has learned how to manipulate employment, the government no longer relies as heavily on the preservation of confidence of businessmen and may undertake almost with impunity actions of which businessmen disapprove. "Hence budget deficits necessary to carry out Government intervention must be regarded as perilous. The social function of doctrine of 'sound finance' is to make the level of employment dependent on the 'state of confidence.' " (Kalecki 1943g, p. 325.)

In the United States extended government economic power is feared as gradually encroaching on "free" private enterprise. In fact, the businessman wants government out of the picture because he feels that his profits will grow faster if he is unfettered by government intervention. But whenever government action strengthens the profit-making ability (protectionist tariffs, regulation of trade unions, and so forth), the businessman does not clamor that "free" private enterprise is being trampled underfoot. The businessman intrinsically fears the omnipresence of a government that would become a job-maker. The government would then be the agent responsible for the overall level of activity, with consequent ominous loss of power for business. (Alexander 1948, pp. 192-97.)

In this context, the myth of the balanced budget is of special importance in the United States, particularly in view of the "ideological attachment in the country to budget balancing" (Stein 1969, p. 54), where, for instance, at the end of the 1950s, deficit financing "stirred up a strong political movement by fiscal conservatives to reverse the spending and deficit trend." (Hansen 1964b, pp. 11-12.) Cyclical fluctuations are aggravated by moods of pessimism and optimism, which allegedly stem from the state of the budget. The concern about preserving the state of confidence is used as a major argument by the proponents of the "sound" economic policy of balanced (annual) budgets heresy. Allegedly, a balanced budget has marked positive effects on the state of confidence, on the private investor, on the stock market, on government credit and currency, and so forth. An unbalanced budget is regarded as a manifestation of national financial instability. Expansion of government spending during recessions is supposed to have a retarding effect on private investment (reducing marginal efficiency of investment), a depressing influence on security prices, promoting a decline in the value of bank assets, etc. Government borrowing to finance deficits entails competition from government for available funds. In order to restore confidence, the government is not so much troubled by the existence of the deficit (various accounting manipulations could be resorted to to disguise it) as by the measures that it has to take to demonstrate that it checks the growth of deficit.

Those opposed to deficit spending are particularly prone to raise the banner of the balanced budget—the myth of sound financing. This is usually done by appealing to public sentiment and indignation about mismanagement.[10] The appeal to the principle of sound financing has persisted to this day. The opponents to government interference promote the myth of the "free" private enterprise system's being able to maintain an adequate level of employment without government intervention. They refer openly to unemployment as the price for economic freedom.[11] Freedom and liberty are somewhat intangibly wrapped up with minimum government intervention in economic affairs. Klein reports that, in an informal talk, Kalecki countered this argument "very elegantly with the remark that the regimentation of unemployment and poverty is infinitely more severe than the regimentation of economic planning." (Klein 1966, p. 179.)

Finally, the libertarian position is buttressed by the more sophisticated argument that government countercyclical action is neither effective nor sufficient. (Cf. Alexander 1948, pp. 183-89.) For example, the diagnoses of the efficacy of fiscal policies in the 1930s differ considerably: some knowledgeable observers claim that the reason why recovery was choked off in 1938 was a desperate effort by the administration to balance the budget. In this spirit taxes were increased in depressed conditions and budget expenditures were cut, arresting the forces to complete recovery. Taxes were still looked upon as a necessary means of financing government expenditures, rather than of attaining economic and monetary stability. (Hansen 1963, pp. 320-23.) Recent interpretations of the efficacy of fiscal policy in the 1930s suggest that, in fact, the policy was not employed vigorously, consistently, or with proper timing. Moreover, whatever constructive impact the fiscal policy might have had was largely lost by restrictive monetary policies and by institutional failures. (*Economic* . . . 1963, pp. 66-77.)

2. Here again one should underline that Kalecki's predictions of the political business cycle and hostility of business to government intervention were constructed on the assumption of peace (absence of cold war and massive arms buildup). His analysis of the objects of government spending that follows totally disregards government expenditures on military objects. Under such conditions he foresaw eventually increasing government encroachment on the areas traditionally restricted to private activity. At first the government would enter areas that do not compete with private activities, such as the infrastructure, health, education, and so forth. The businessman would not object too strenuously to such investments that would not impair the returns on private investments. But in view of the restricted scope of such public investment, the businessman fears that government would gradually take over (nationalize) transport, public utilities, and even some (probably nonprofitable) industries (as was the case in Great Britain). Hence the businessman suspects and apprehends the emergence of the state as a potential competitor in his own field of activity. (Kalecki 1943g, p. 325.) This position is compressed in capsule form in the following statement of a former United States Democratic senator who for many years championed sound finance: "At home we can get along without Federal usurpation of individual, local, and State responsibilities, and we can get along without Federal Competition in business whether it be hotels, furs, rum, clothing, fertilizer, or other things." (Byrd 1970, p. 156. Cf. Stans 1970, pp. 156-60.)

To a certain extent businessmen might take a kinder view of government action to subsidize consumption by means of family allowances, price subsidies for necessities and children's clothing, and so forth; thus government would not encroach on their private preserves. Yet, according to Kalecki, such moves will be opposed perhaps even more vehemently than direct government intervention in economic activity, in view of the prevailing ethic that one's bread be earned in sweat—that is unless one was lucky enough to have inherited or come by chance across private means.[12] Some of the cruder objections against a full-employment stabilization program are: (a) unemployment causes adversity, and suffering is good for the worker's soul and his outlook on life; and (b) with good job opportunities, the institution of the family will be weakened as an increasing number of members of the household will engage in activities outside the home.

3. Indeed, businessmen would object strenuously to a regime of permanent full employment on the grounds that it would relax the fear of the stick. In fact without the "reserve army of unemployed," the managers would have a hard time preserving discipline.[13] Unemployment is required to compel the worker to perform diligently. While there are probably grains of truth in it, this narrow-minded approach to efficiency is repugnant. Efficiency has little meaning without considering the question: "Efficiency for what?" The enormous real cost in terms of human suffering, misery, and pain cannot be disregarded. Both in capitalist and socialist economies today the problem is how to make the worker work without resorting to the stick. With full employment, the boss's ascendency would diminish and the self-assurance and demands of workers would grow. There would be an increasing wave of strikes. Even though under full employment profits would be on the rise, Kalecki believed that the business community would be prepared to take a cut in profits for "discipline in the factories" and political stability. Actually, it boils down to the question of class interest. (Kalecki 1943g, p. 326.) But the structure of the economy and income stratification have changed since the Full Employment Act, and this situation, in turn, affects various interest groups.

During the 1960s and 1970s it became increasingly difficult to judge whether any "tolerable" degree of unemployment could possibly restore the fear of the sack as a real stimulus to productivity. Furthermore, the extent of unemployment required to induce such a fear might be totally inadvisable (and even dangerous) from other points of view. It appears that partly for structural reasons, the politically "tolerable" unemployment (say, 6 per cent in the United States and 3 per cent in Great Britain) is insufficient to discipline those who hold relatively secure jobs. Nor is the slack in effective demand experienced powerful enough to arrest the price-wage advances, though it is possible that the rate of advance would have been higher with larger aggregate demand.

In his observations of the post-World War II position of American business, Sidney J. Alexander fully backed Kalecki's analysis. He went as far as to claim that, actually, businessmen did not want full employment because of the expected difficulties in controlling labor and because of their desire to contravene labor's increasing power to gain a larger portion of the product. Generally, businessmen identified full employment policies with the New Deal which they alleged was hostile to business and only had labor's interests at heart. This often obscured for American businessmen the beneficial implications of full-employment policies for business. (Alexander 1948, pp. 189-92. Cf. Sutton *et al.* 1956; Harris 1964, pt. 2; Stein 1969, ch. 5.)

Implied here is a fourth reason which first and foremost underlies business opposition to full-employment policies: the intrinsic apprehension of resulting redistribution of income. The fact that such a redistribution might be long in coming (perhaps too long for the lower income groups) does not matter. Its ultimate threat is sufficient.[14]

Kalecki recognized that, in the postwar period, the question would no longer be: Will business want government to step in in a recession? But rather: What will be the extent of such intervention and will it simply be a slump-mitigating activity or an instrument for maintaining full employment?

The next question, then, as it is now, was: Is stimulation of private investment sufficient to bring the economy out of a recession into sustained full employment? (Cf. Kalecki 1945a, pp. 83-92; 1939a, pp. 45-46.) In a way such a move would assuage businessmen's fears of encroaching government interference and power. But no matter how attractive and stimulating the financial tricks used, business will not be persuaded to undertake such investment, unless it has confidence in the economic situation.

Kalecki foresaw that such stimulation of private investment would be insufficient for recovery. He analyzed two alternative methods: (1) The rate of interest and/or profit tax are substantially reduced in a recession and increased during the upswing. The duration and amplitude of the business cycle will be substantially subdued, but full employment will not be reached even in the boom, although it will not be subject to serious variations. (2) The rate of interest and/or profits tax are pared down in a recession, but not raised again during the upswing, and/or subsidies are offered to private investors (for example, by allowing deductions from taxable income for the full purchase price or a percentage of it in the form of accelerated depreciation). Here the upswing will be of longer duration, yet not permanent. A single reduction in the rate of interest or a one-shot cut in profit tax does not eliminate the cycle-generating forces. In the subsequent slump, it is necessary to repeat the measures, i.e., the rate of interest or profit tax must be continuously pared down or the investment subsidies must continuously rise. "Thus in not too remote a time the rate of interest would have to be negative and corporate income tax would have to be replaced by an income subsidy." (Kalecki 1943g, p. 329.) Besides one may never be sure of businessmen's reactions, which are greatly influenced by their expectations about the future, colored by the current state of business. During a sharp downswing investment is largely inelastic to the fall of the interest rate (even assuming that monetary policy can lower the interest rate). Tax stimuli might prove to be insufficient partly because the shift of the investment schedule, owing to very pessimistic anticipation of the future, is much sharper than any movement along the curve. If the recession is severe enough, the financial tricks might have little or no influence on the rate of investment. Thus even the more conservative economic advisors realize that recovery requires a measure of public investment in conjunction with financial measures.

Kalecki conceded that even those who believe in stimulating private investment as a slump-mitigating device acknowledge that it is not entirely reliable and should be accompanied by public investment. Business interests would not be altogether averse to public investment financed by borrowing as a slump-mitigating device. "They seem, however, still to be consistently opposed to creating employment by subsidising consumption and to *maintaining* full employment." (Kalecki 1943g, p. 329.)

On the basis of these arguments Kalecki predicted the "pattern of the political business cycle":

> In the slump, either under the pressure of the masses, or even without it, public investment financed by borrowing will be undertaken to prevent large scale unemployment. But if attempts are made to apply this method in order to maintain the high level of employment reached in the subsequent boom a strong opposition of "business leaders" is likely to be encountered. As has already been argued, lasting full employment is not at all to their liking. The workers would "get out of hand" and the "captains of industry" would be anxious to "teach them a lesson." Moreover, the increase in the up-swing is to the disadvantage of small and big *rentiers* and makes them "boom tired."
>
> In this situation a powerful block is likely to be formed between big business and the *rentier* interests, and they would probably find more than one economist to declare that the situation was manifestly unsound. The pressure of all these forces, and in particular of big business—as a rule influential in Government departments—would most probably induce the Government to return to the orthodox policy of cutting down the budget deficit. A slump would follow in which Gov-

ernment spending policy would come again into its own. (Kalecki 1943g, pp. 329-30.)

As a footnote to that theory, it is interesting that, having observed at close range the barrage of opposition evinced by American businessmen against the relatively mild, toned-down, and innocuous Full Employment Act of 1946, Professor Alexander came to a similar conclusion. Namely, he foresaw that, as soon as massive unemployment is threatened, any government, no matter what its prejudices, will resort to deficit-spending.[15] However, no government will explicitly avow the policy of deficit-spending. At the same time, business opposition to deficit-spending will be lulled at times of depression only to resurge in the upswing. (Cf. Alexander 1948, pp. 197-98.)

In closing this presentation of Kalecki's original exposition of the political business cycle, I should be remiss to neglect his 1943 prescription for reforming the capitalist order and preventing the occurrence of these cycles. Perhaps this prescription was not republished thirty years later because Kalecki had become overly bitter and skeptical about the hopes he had voiced then. Parenthetically, he appears to have suffered from, for lack of a better expression, what we might call the Einstein syndrome: Having shown (together with Keynes) to the capitalist world how it could save (and reform) itself by relieving (and in some sense doing away with) periodic depressions, Kalecki saw that world turning insane; for instead of raising the standard of living to a higher level than that achieved so far by public investment, resources were being wasted in armaments production and periodic small-scale wars that turned into large-scale disasters.

In Kalecki's view, at the end of World War II a sane approach would have been for governments to attempt to eradicate business cycles. The point was for the government to undertake such public investments that were actually needed. The remainder of government spending required to keep up full employment should be used to subsidize consumption. Writing immediately after World War II, Joan Robinson was confident that, if government was to see to full employment, it was also bound to ensure that the uses were "useful," i.e., that they met the needs of the community and not those of profit-seeking firms. In this sense, government policy would bear on the direction of employment. In a democracy the decisions should be arrived at by juxtaposing conflicts of interests. (Joan Robinson

1951, pp. 108-109; 1972, pp. 1-10.) Kalecki underlined that the goal of government economic activity should be raising the standard of living. Institutional reforms would have to accompany such changes. Interestingly, he rejected at that time the suggestion that full-employment capitalism could have fascist leanings. (Kalecki 1943g, pp. 330-31.)

At this juncture perhaps a short digression on fascism and economic policy is in order. Businessmen's opposition to government spending in a fascist regime (e.g., Nazi Germany) is obviated by control of the state machinery and by a coincidence of interests between the government and powerful business groups. In a democracy there is always the uncertainty of the attitudes of the next government. But under fascism there is no next government. Here also the abhorrence of public investments to benefit the poorer segments of society is overcome by concentrating state investment on armaments production. Economic discipline which is supposed to be wielded by a sufficiently high level of unemployment is enforced by various political threats, the most powerful of which is the concentration camp. (Kalecki 1943g, pp. 326-27.)

In 1935, Kalecki looked at the business upswing in Nazi Germany and deduced that a higher rate of utilization of capacities does not necessarily mean that the population's standard of living grows commensurately. In fact, the gains of the business upswing, which *should have* stimulated a rise in consumption, were used primarily to finance armaments build-up. The investment in military activities competed severely with civilian investments. The situation was aggravated by balance-of-payments difficulties. Imports were primarily directed towards arms manufacture. Prices of consumer goods produced by imported inputs rose sharply due to shortages, thus bearing down on real wages. In fact, whereas about 60 per cent of the decline of industrial production was made up during 1932-33, only 28 per cent of the decline of consumption was redeemed. (Kalecki 1935b, pp. 1574-76.)

The question whether fascism is a threat today is no longer so topical. Undoubtedly, there has been some rise of fascist-like movements in many Western countries. The fascism of our time cannot claim that it would eradicate unemployment, simply because government intervention in economic life has become a reality, with a resulting relatively high level of employment in most of these countries. In general its appeal is to protection of the self-interest of various groups (capitalists; privileged, highly skilled workers; the military; and so forth), racism, and chauvinism. Its economic platform is usually a denunciation of government intervention and a strong appeal for a return to laissez faire.[16]

On Political Economy of Prosperity

Kalecki was not only one of the original architects of the general theory of employment, but a fountainhead of political economy of full employment par excellence. He was a great pragmatist and realist who took political realities into account. He predicted the opposition to full-employment policies and the likely course of events. His political business cycle is a brilliant and perceptive piece. One should remember that it was written in 1943, and one could not expect the "prophet" to be right in the smallest detail or to foresee all the ramifications. But this compact work abounded with ideas. The concept of the political business cycle was strikingly in advance of its time. Though it has not been borne out in all respects, the most remarkable thing is the degree to which Kalecki did foresee the future.

I venture to say that Kalecki's prediction of the political business cycle is likely to rank in importance to his role as protagonist and "generalizer" of the general theory of employment. Indeed, the propagation of the general theory and its policy implication made "depression economics" no longer so topical. The same applies to Kalecki's theory of "automatic business cycles." In our day and age, and in the foreseeable future, it is the pattern of the political business cycle that, together with the distribution of income and the determination of what growth and employment are for, is the crucial issue awaiting solution.[17]

In concluding his 1943 paper, Kalecki stressed that "a progressive" should strive for lasting full employment and government subsidy of consumption. Slumps should not be mitigated but eliminated. Public investment should only be undertaken to the extent that it is needed, and the balance of government spending required to maintain full employment should go toward subsidizing consumption. "The opposers of such Government spending say that the Government will then have nothing to show for their money. The reply is that the counterpart of this spending will be the higher standard of living of the masses. Is not this the purpose of all economic activity?" New social and political institutions would have to be developed by such a system which would reflect the increased power of the working class. "If capitalism can adjust itself to full employment a fundamental reform will have been incorporated in it. If not, it will show itself an outmoded system which must be scrapped." Kalecki then mused whether the struggle for full employment might not lead to fascism. His answer was negative. "The fight of the progressive forces for full employment is at the same time a way of *preventing* the recurrence of fascism." (Kalecki 1943g, pp. 330-31.)

In the 1960s, Kalecki's original article on the political business cycle was republished in both Polish and English. However, Kalecki omitted the above conclusion. In a preface to a Polish collection of essays including a translation of that article, published about twenty years after the original, he reflected on how well it withstood the test of time. "It appears that current events correspond *grosso modo* to these forecasts. On the other hand, my article deals with full employment on the basis of arms build-up in a fascist regime. However, experience has shown that fascism is not an indispensable system for armaments to play an important role in counteracting mass unemployment." (Kalecki 1962m, pp. 7-8.)

The Great Depression has changed the character of the capitalist economy. The Keynesian Revolution supplied the remedies which could cure the mortal ills of the ailing patient. The fact that the patient is still not well after more than thirty years is not a reflection so much on the potency of antidotes as on their misuse and often disuse. This is not to say that, if there were no political considerations, the existing framework of fiscal and monetary policy could practically eliminate the amplitude of fluctuations. For one, because of built-in lags and rigidities, it is indeed quite possible for intervention to help in keeping oscillations alive. Moreover, it is necessary to take into account the quite separate fact that political interventions have a timing of their own which may produce fluctuations.

There are obvious limitations to fiscal and monetary policy interventions. The problem is not only of the level of full employment, but of its content, of the ways and means to achieve it, of minimizing adverse effects of such policies, and of a veritable host of other problems. Clearly, men do not live by economic growth, employment, or even economics alone. But to the extent that they do, prosperity becomes a weighty issue. Indeed, "although prosperity is a small component of any broad social appraisal, it is an essential vitamin for the body politic, and is sorely missed in its absence."

And prosperity becomes "the number one political issue when we don't have it." (Okun 1972, p. 25.)

All the signs of collapse were apparent in the 1930s, but the capitalist system survived. Its postwar dynamism and employment performance have been remarkable. Indeed, the very nature of the policies applied in "postwar Keynesian capitalism" has affected the structure of the economy and the stratification of income. The interest of the various strata of the population and the configuration of pressure groups have been somewhat affected. For example, in the U.S.A. we witness the "unholy alliance" of the big armaments producers and the labor unions representing workers in military production in their joint clamor and pressure for expanded armaments production. Moreover, as Kalecki pointed out, there was a cleft in the position of the U. S. business interests on the economic consequences of the war in Vietnam. The old established eastern business interests had little to gain from that venture, which became pointedly apparent by 1966. However, the western interests (including the largest armaments producers, Texas oil, and others) benefited from the war and supported it. (Kalecki 1967m.)

Kalecki warned against dogmatic prejudices and understatement of the real achievements of postwar capitalist economies where profound changes have taken place. Undoubtedly, the standard of living has risen considerably above that which would have been achieved under laissez faire. All these real advances cannot be ignored. The point is, however, that resources could have been utilized to fuller potential and that the standard of living could have been higher if more sustained non-military-type, full-employment policies had been pursued. There has been widespread acceptance of government intervention to prevent intolerable recessions, but as soon as economic activity picked up momentum, renewed pressures for a return to "sound finance" were exerted, contributing to the manifestation of the political business cycle. There is still continuing and forceful opposition to maintenance of full employment by means of reshuffling resources in favor of subsidizing consumption, particularly to measures that tend to redistribute income from the upper to the lower income groups. The tendency is still to stimulate the private sector rather than consumption. As Nixon's New Economic Policy showed, the measures continue to be lopsided in favor of business—which is not only a blunder, but a crime, as Samuelson noted. (*Newsweek*, Aug. 30, 1971.) The view that the country's economic might, far from depending on the war effort, could be considerably increased by reducing military expenditures and applying resources to civilian uses, is becoming increasingly popular in the United States—at least among many academic economists.

All that has been said before does not purport to imply that managing high-level prosperity is an easy task. Continuous high employment is accompanied by a continuous fall in the value of money. Many economists believe that we are facing the cruel choice between the two evils of unemployment or inflation. But prices and wages tend to rise even if the economy is intolerably below full-employment and -capacity output. Recent experience seems to indicate that the unemployment-inflation dilemma is vastly exaggerated. Realistically, such a choice would not give palpable results because of the tolerable level of unemployment (which varies from country to country) that the government cannot transgress. Indeed, the very meaning of the Phillips curve and of the unemployment-inflation trade off has been questioned.

Although it requires some qualifications, the following proposition may be advanced: Entrepreneurs use the spectre of inflation as a device to check increases in wages, in order to arrest the decline of (or to increase) the share of profit in national income. Under the regime of full employment, there is no mechanism, such as the reserve army of workers, to check wages from rising; in a certain sense it might be argued that the fear of inflation is used as a substitute for such a mechanism.

Kalecki felt deeply that we are still intolerably far from reasonably full employment and capacity output. He was particularly concerned about changing full-employment composition of output (demand). The question that really preoccupied him was how to deploy economic resources to enhance the real progress which would be equitably shared among the various strata of society. Perhaps one of the most important ethical messages that comes through from Kalecki's study of modern capitalism is his condemnation of arms pile-up as a means of cutting down on unemployment. "The economy is kept going by armament expenditures and people are assured of their livelihood through the manufacture of the means of destruction. To an outsider, this looks fairly absurd, because the surplus could have been used to increase either investment or consumption. In fact, however, it is wasted or worse." (Kalecki 1966o, pp. 971-73; trans. 1968b, p. 12.

PART TWO
THE WAR ECONOMY

The War Years

FROM 1940 TO 1945, Kalecki was employed by the Oxford Institute of Statistics (OIS), a part of Oxford University. In fact, at various times, rather irregularly, Kalecki lectured at the university. During the war years the institute was host to a number of able economists and statisticians from Eastern Europe, Germany, and Austria who, either because of their political persuasion or religious antecedents, were forced to flee their homeland. Kalecki's colleagues at the OIS included Frank (F. A.) Burchardt, Thomas (later Lord) Balogh, Joseph Steindl, Jozef Goldmann, Kurt Mandelbaum (later changed to Martin), and E. I. Schumacher. Among the young and able Britishers were G. D. N. (David) Worswick, and J. L. (Leonard) Nicholson. During most of the war years the head of the institute was A. L. Bowley. Later Lord Beveridge became associated with the institute.

Kalecki was active at the OIS, participating in much of the research conducted there. He was a prolific contributor of succinct pieces to the *Oxford University, Institute of Statistics, Bulletin* (*OISB*)—the official organ. Although, according to some of his colleagues, he was intellectually the *spiritus movens* of the institute, he never attained any of the official positions achieved by some of his fellow émigrés. His prickly and intransigent disposition and controversial personality were no doubt partly responsible for this lack of advancement. Throughout this period the main concern of the OIS was the rational management of the war economy. Scores of articles were published dealing with the novel problems faced by an economy where the bulk of resources was to be diverted to armaments and the military; rampant inflation was a threat; exorbitant profits were reaped by the manufacturers of increasingly scarce products (whether raw materials or consumer goods); wages were rising in view of the increasing scarcity of skilled manpower; consumption had to give way to the war effort; and some sort of *modus vivendi* had to be established between restrictive measures and the incentive to produce.

The problems arising from a war economy taxed the faculties of the best economists in Britain, and the various solutions were obviously tinged by the political philosophy of their proponents. Not surprisingly, Kalecki found himself again facing and trying to solve the same problems that were confronting Keynes. Kalecki's assessment of the incidence of inflation during the war and how it might be dealt with most effectively (general rationing) was more profound and radical, however, than that of Keynes. Keynes tended to identify rationing with Bolshevism and the regimentation of a totalitarian state. He did not seem to appreciate, as did Kalecki, that a scheme of rationing could be devised that would afford the consumer a considerable choice among alternatives.

Kalecki was among the very first in Britain to urge adoption of rationing as a means of solving the onerous problems of the war economy. Because some observers hold the distorted view that Kalecki was a "planner" who disregarded welfare implications, it should be emphasized that the general rationing scheme he proposed (sometimes referred to as expenditure rationing) was elaborated as a "welfare" measure. His proposal was designed to allow the consumer the widest possible choice under restrictive conditions; it would divert real resources from consumption to the war effort while keeping down inflationary pressures and reducing inequalities of distribution. By contrast, physical rationing, which the British adopted for some goods, was a very restrictive and cumbersome process. Point rationing, adapted from the Germans and widely applied in Britain, allowed greater room for flexibility, but still less than Kalecki's general rationing scheme. Nevertheless, once the point scheme was generally adopted, Kalecki strove to refine and improve its specific applications.

In view of the practical and sensible suggestions emanating from Kalecki and his colleagues in the OIS, two pertinent questions come to mind: (1) Why did not government officials make greater use of these findings? and (2) Why is not more credit given to the institute's work in the postwar publications describing the British war economy?

1. Although neither Kalecki nor the institute was in any way connected with the British government during the war, the development of his ideas about rationing probably did have at least some practical influence. It is difficult for an outsider to determine the extent of that impact, however, for the reason that, even today, those who were affiliated with the government during the war

years cannot seem to agree with those who previously worked for the institute in arriving at any real assessment of the institute's contributions. The government economists, willingly or unwillingly, had a vested interest in underrating the contributions of their colleagues who were on the fringe of public affairs.[1] Although universities and similar institutions were hospitable to refugees from Nazi tyranny, the government was not enthusiastic about making use of advice emanating from that "hotbed of refugees"—the OIS. Furthermore, the economists who had been drafted into government work frequently resented those who remained in academia, who were able to resolve the daily problems of war economy without having to refer their work for approval to government bureaucrats (often knowing or understanding little of the problem).

2. The infrequent mention of the institute in postwar publications can perhaps be traced to the disparity in reporting policies during the war years. Whereas the institute's work was given full coverage in the OIS *Bulletin* of those days, the deliberations of government economists remained secret. After the war, the writers of official histories of war finance and economy obviously found their "newest" material in the government papers to which they then had access. Unfortunately, few of the writers made any apparent effort to relate the government work to the previously published reports of the OIS, despite the many mutual concerns of the two groups of economists.

As a consequence of this void in historical reporting, Kalecki's work of the war period is far less known than it deserves to be. Such work had an important bearing on his postwar activities and especially warrants exposition because, as is well known, the problems of a war economy project into peacetime. Much can be learned from further study of war economics and finance in general, and from Kalecki's work on inflation, taxation, rationing, and price control in particular; not only does such study shed light on the contemporary capitalist economy—increasingly facing problems of supply constraint—but it is also extremely relevant, despite organizational and institutional differences, to understanding the operation of the socialist economy of the forced industrialization period—what Oskar Lange so aptly termed the *sui generis* war economy.

As was recounted in the first part of this book, in connection with the development of Kalecki's theoretical thought on modern capitalism, he produced three major studies during these early war years: *Studies in Economic Dynamics* and his article elucidating the political business cycle, both published in 1943, and an essay on *Economics of Full Employment*, published in 1944.

The first book was a slim volume in which Kalecki elaborated on his theoretical study of modern capitalism. Both this book and his article on the political business cycle were regarded by him as studies conducted independently of the institute, for he worked on them "after office hours." These off-duty hours also produced a rewarding friendship for Kalecki, which, in turn, contributed to *Studies in Economic Dynamics.* The book acknowledged, for many developments incorporated in the study, Kalecki's indebtedness to Erwin Rothbarth, a German refugee, with whom Kalecki spent many hours discussing and debating their mutual interests following their first meeting in England.[2] Rothbarth was intensely interested in Kalecki's business cycle theory and planned to extend it but was prevented by his untimely death at the front. They had remained in close contact up to that time.

The 1944 publication on the economics of full employment was a compilation of studies by OIS members that appeared almost simultaneously with Sir (later Lord) William Beveridge's study on the same subject. The institute publication was much more methodical and substantial, although it received far less publicity than did the Beveridge book. Among the very interesting essays, which were said to be largely inspired and influenced by Kalecki, was a relatively brief essay bearing Kalecki's own name, in which he said almost everything that needs to be said about reform of the capitalist economy.

In 1945, Kalecki resigned from the OIS. He resented being bypassed in promotions and he had little faith in British recognition of émigrés, doubting that a position in keeping with his merits could be found in British academia. Perhaps he was too pessimistic and did not allow sufficient time for things to fall into shape after the war. On the other hand, although many of his colleagues remained at the OIS and found respectable niches at Oxford and elsewhere, there is some question that Kalecki would have been equally successful.[3]

X

THE CRUCIAL PROBLEMS OF A WAR ECONOMY

Orthodox Solutions

WHEN WORLD WAR II STRUCK, the economic situation in the developed capitalist countries was the antipode of that when prewar depression engulfed the capitalist economy. There was a turnabout from peacetime underutilized productive capacity, vast unemployment, and deficiency of effective demand. Wartime was the opposite of a depressed economy. It called for policies of "over-full employment." Reflecting on the imminence of new problems in England after the outbreak of hostilities, John Maynard Keynes pointed out how difficult it was to remodel one's thinking to face the consequences of war. In prewar Britain the size of the "civilian's cake" depended on the quantity and quality of the work done. But war changed the situation with a fixed size of the cake for private uses. If people worked harder, Britain could fight better; but they were to consume even less. This only slowly penetrated the general consciousness: " . . . we have become so accustomed to the problem of unemployment and of excess resources that it requires some elasticity of mind to adapt our behaviour to the problem of full employment and of resources which are no longer adequate to supply our needs. In war we move back from the Age of Plenty to the Age of Scarcity." (Keynes 1940b, p. 17. Cf. Harrod 1951, ch. 12; Klein 1966, ch. 6.)

FROM PLENTY TO SCARCITY

The fundamental problem of the war economy is to mobilize effectively resources for the war effort and to adjust civilian expenditures to the supply which can be made available. Purchasing power has to be curtailed in order to prevent a violent upward movement of prices—bound to occur with the limited productive resources. Steeply rising government expenditures and constraints on the supply side (with regard to labor, raw materials, and capacity), make the problem of effective curtailment of consumption particularly acute as the war goes on. (Kalecki 1940c, p. 7. Cf. *Studies* . . . 1947, *passim;* Joan Robinson 1951; Scitovsky, Shaw, and Tarshis 1951, ch. 2; Galbraith 1952b.)

The strategy of resource mobilization aims at a maximal increase of production with available resources. The smaller the expansion of output, the larger must be, *ceteris paribus,* the inroads into civilian consumption and capital formation (disinvestment). Obviously, diverting resources to the war sector is easier if there has been considerable idle capacity before the war. The mobilization of resources for the war involves usually a massive and rapid absorption of potentially productive manpower into the labor force. It includes the previously unemployed; increase in work hours; activation of housewives, young men and women, retired people, and "people of leisure"; and release of labor from peacetime occupations. The problem is that incentives should be provided to support the transformation and to spur each worker, wherever employed, to give his very best.

Obviously, incentives are required for labor in both the war and the civilian sectors; for, given the economic interdependencies, no matter how blurred and fluid the distinction might be, higher productivity and saving of labor in the civilian sector generally allow for a release of resources for war production. In order to stimulate *everyone's* full potential effort, better performance should be rewarded, no matter what the moral or psychological suasion.[1] But spending has to be restricted and leakages of real resources from the war to the civilian sectors prevented. As such, a war economy does not allow for improved performance to be rewarded by increasing current consumption. On the contrary real consumption has to be reduced for labor as a group. Hence the danger that the producer will perform suboptimally. During the war, a minimum requirement for voluntary compliance was probably the reassurance that the war burden was distributed fairly and everyone did his share.

Even without a rise in nominal wage rates, the aggregate wage bill will drift upward appreciably owing to the marked increase in employment and in overtime payments. Total earnings are pushed up by competitive bidding, especially by contractors working for the government on the cost-plus basis—a method that encourages such malpractices.[2] Moreover, there is also a conflict of interests within the government machinery charged with the task of mobilizing resources for the war effort. To discharge their responsibilities some agencies press for wage (price) increases as a means for diverting resources to the war sector. There is more spending power generated and fewer consumer goods on which it can be spent. But measures that constrain growth of purchasing power at the income-generating end tend to restrict growth of production. (Kalecki 1940h, pp. 2-6; 1940e, pp. 10-13; 1943f, p. 11.)

Given that resources must be mobilized for full war effort and supplies for civilian consumption must be cut down, the real danger seems to lie not in expanding earned incomes, but in pressures of increased consumers' spending. Inflation may be relieved by restraining income earners from spending their income. But the point is not to destroy production incentives. There are alternative measures of restricting civilian spending and of shifting the functional relationship between income and consumption. The adopted solution is not a matter of indifference. The economic problem is to devise the best method of reconciling the requisites of the war with production incentives and efficiency and to maximize consumers' welfare under the constraint of the war economy. Among important "side conditions" is a choice of such an arrangement for resource allocation that would minimize the deleterious effects, or better still, maximize the benefits after the hostilities are over.

When it has been resolved how much and by what mechanism the resources would be mobilized for the war effort and how much could be made available for private consumption, there is still the thorny issue of deciding on the most prudent and equitable way of distributing the consumption fund among consumers. Of course, the various decisions are interdependent if for no other reason than that the consumer and producer often coincide. Maldistribution must be avoided in view of both equity and efficiency. At the very least, what is considered acceptable maldistribution of the available consumer supply among the civilian population should be maintained.

In this connection, one might mention the social reformers (both Kalecki and Keynes belonged to this group even though their vision of social reform differed considerably) who were bent on seizing the opportunity of the radical reshaping of working arrangements during the war for social reform in the postwar period. The idea was to redesign the economic mechanism in order to redress the inequities in income distribution. The situation seemed propitious. Dictates of industrial peace enhanced the importance of labor's cooperation, and pressures were exerted by trade unions to diminish the inequalities of income distribution. In the end, however, results were most disappointing.

Siege and Market

In wartime financial and price policies are employed as indirect instruments of shifting real resources to the war effort. Finance is only one, and not necessarily the most important or swiftest means used in transferring resources. A war economy is usually associated with many controls, but there is controversy about the required type and scope of controls. (Cf. Bowen and Worswick 1940, pp. 77-104.)

In order to present opposing views as objectively as possible, the position of those who argued that the pricing system should be used to the fullest extent at the time of war, when the efficient operation of the economic mechanism is imperative, shall be reviewed briefly, without delving into the finer lines of division that separate some proponents from others.[3] According to this school direct controls should be avoided and the market should be relied upon to divert resources from private to government use. Resources would be mobilized by applying the conventional tools of taxation and interest policy, as such measures tend to interfere least with the operation of the market mechanism. If only the government would courageously extract enough spending power by sufficiently high taxation and arrange its borrowing on a "noninflationary basis," (cf. Keynes 1940b, pp. 57-74; Harrod 1951, pp. 490-91), direct controls could be avoided and the market mechanism could be relied upon to divert efficiently the required real resources to the public sector. In the civilian goods sector, the market price advances to the equilibrium level rationing the reduced supply among eager demanders whose demand prices are high enough to choke off excess demand. It is only due to "fear of inflation" and for *"noneconomic"* reasons that market prices are not permitted to reach their scarcity level. In the war sector, an unfettered market, under the stimulus of profit, should perform the reallocative function.

Inflation as a means of reaching equilibrium is the worst possible solution to the problem. The market performs best when dealing with "small" or "marginal" variations. The process of adjustment may be protracted, and the market is inadequate to perform a structural break and is usually too slow and not forceful enough for any major war reallocation requirements. (cf. Scitovsky, Shaw, and Tarshis 1951, p. 139; Galbraith 1952b). War production imposes heavy demands for speedy restructuring of production, reallocation of inputs, and conversion of plant and equipment to war uses. Efficiency must often be sacrificed for the sake of expediency. The job must be done fast. The alternative of not doing it promptly is too risky and the dangers of leakage of resources to "nonessential" uses too great. The requirements are: "mobilization of resources," "action," "shift," and "change." At the time of siege only the crudest alternative choices rather than "refined marginal adjustments" are taken into account. This is not to say that efficiency in the service of the war effort and of the producer and consumer should be disregarded.

If prices are allowed to be pushed up to the level where personal disposable incomes will match the supply of civilian goods (i.e., if prices are permitted to rise until they equate the reduced supply with the enlarged consumers' income), the reduced supply will be rationed by the higher prices. High prices ration goods according to the purchasing power of the buyer. The lower income groups are immediately eliminated from market distribution, as they do not have the necessary "number of votes" to claim the goods.

If the aggregate consumption fund is fixed, each consumer can increase his share only at the expense of other consumers. With rationing by price and purse, those with higher incomes and wealth can claim the very scarce supply. Those who can command the means to pay the high scarcity prices do not have to curtail their consumption. The drop in consumption befalls the lower income groups and those with fixed incomes. Moreover, compression of consumption standards of various income levels clearly depends on its initial levels. Further decline of the consumption of some groups on, or below, the poverty line is bound to provoke decline of productivity.

Rampant inflation is of some advantage to the entrepreneurs, but a burden on the lower income groups. The capitalist class is favored when prices are allowed to rise to the point equating supply and demand. Higher taxes can extract a considerable share of the windfall profits from sharply increased prices in relation to costs. Irrespective of how high and harsh the taxation, there are usually sufficient loopholes for the taxpayer to escape at least part of the heavy burden. *Ceteris paribus,* the higher the burden, the greater the risk of tax evasion. The profiteers are lured to spend on luxuries. There is imminent danger of resources leaking from essential to nonessential consumption, adding fuel to the inflationary pressures and aggravating the inequities of sacrifice. Another share of the gain may be borrowed from the capitalists and repaid to them with interest after the war. Hence the capitalist class alone, instead of all income-earners alike, would be the principal owners of the increased national debt with consequent inequitable distribution of sacrifice, special privileges, and social injustice. (Keynes 1940b, pp. 21 ff.)

Thus one of the principal objections against the inflationary solution of financing the war is on the grounds of equity. The major problem is that the disparity of incomes operating through the market gives rise to inequitable distribution of goods and services and undesirable sharing of the burden of war. During the war the manufacturing and distribution of consumer goods is usually very profitable. The problem is of constricting civilian claims on resources and suspending the allocative function of the market to divert resources to the most profitable uses. This usually requires a fair amount of planning, controls, and outright allocation. When diversion of resources from civilian to war uses becomes a cardinal task, it is not only necessary to prevent an increase of output of consumer goods *pari passu* with effective demand, but, indeed, to distribute the burden of the real fall in the standard of living as equitably as possible. When the problem is to compress civilian production to redirect resources swiftly and expediently among alternative uses, direct limitations on the mobility of resources and direct controls (including direct allocation of strategic materials, restrictions of private investment, direct labor allocation, key production determined by the state, level of costs fixed by fiat, etc.) are introduced.

This is not to say that, under these circumstances, the production and distribution mechanism should not salvage as much as possible of the market-type arrangements and instruments of influence and should not work through the supply-and-demand apparatus. Reflecting on the economic mechanism adopted in Britain during the war, Lionel Robbins commented, ". . . with the outbreak of war and the consequential development of severe scarcities, we abandoned free prices and went over to rationing on a large scale. Nor, in my judgment, was this policy without complete justification, both in the needs of the situation and in the tradition of classical political economy. From the time of David Hume onwards, economists have held that conditions of siege justified the imposition of rationing; and, in the recent six years' siege some of us devoted much time to devising new methods of carrying out the classical prescription." (Robbins 1947, p. 5.) The British advocate of the market par excellence concurred that, in conditions of siege, the initial distribution of purchasing power operating through the price system would result in inequitable distribution of goods and services. But, he argued, it is not the price system as a mechanism for distributing given goods among possessors of given incomes that is deficient, but the initial distribution of income and property. Referring to Britain's World War II experience, Robbins concluded that the accumulated experience "vindicates completely the doctrine of the textbooks, namely, that with *given* goods and *given* distribution of income and capital" there is no allocation device better than "the market mechanism for getting the goods, roughly speaking, into the right hands." (Robbins 1947, *passim.*) Robbins correctly emphasized the distribution of income and wealth. This is a key issue confronting any community. When dealing with the strategy of resource mobilization, production drives and incentives for output growth, and productivity, the distribution problem must receive its due attention.

Taxation as an Instrument to Fight Inflation

Broadly speaking there are three ways of adjusting consumers' expenditures to available supplies: (1) open inflation, (2) taxation, and (3) rationing. The inadvisability and inequities of open inflation were previously discussed. In the next chapter the advantages and disadvantages of various rationing schemes will be reviewed. The common drawback of all taxation measures is that their consequences are not appreciably different from outright inflation. For example, flat-rate income taxation affects the real consumption of various income classes in about the same way as an increase in prices. Those who prefer taxation as an alternate scheme to outright inflation assume, probably unrealistically, that, when taxed, workers and salary-earners will not press for higher wages ("pretax earnings illusion"), while they usually demand higher nominal earnings when the cost of living climbs. While increased taxation will probably tend to curtail somewhat the expenditures of higher income groups, the extent of the curtailment is most uncertain, because those income groups are likely to reduce the amount of current voluntary savings and, in many cases, even to dissave. Moreover, the war economy is affected by the direction of the higher income groups' cuts in expenditures. Retrenchment of expenditures on such items as education, entertainment, or housing, might not be helpful, since the basic actual problem is to put a brake on consumption of foodstuffs, clothing, fuel, and other articles in short supply. The shifting of a greater burden of taxation on the rich cannot be expected to contribute appreciably to the prevention of inflation. (Kalecki 1941d, p. 2.)

Taxation is not only a weapon to curtail consumption; it is primarily a source of government revenue and may be aimed at reducing the future government debt. If this function is emphasized, increased taxation of the rich comes to the fore. Another source of revenue for this purpose may be an annual capital tax. (Kalecki 1942a, pp. 129-32.) Indirect taxation is only one instrument of taxation in the battle for current revenue and attempts to restrain inflation. Indirect taxes levied on goods and services (and thus only indirectly on the people) are a handy device to expand the fiscal sector buoyantly. It is a more expedient device for psychological and other reasons and has many advantages from the standpoint of the treasury. But indirect taxes, for instance, might not be increased appreciably without falling heavily on seminecessities which may be socially inexpedient.

To note only here, in Britain during the war indirect taxation was greatly increased. With every increase it was held by many that, beyond that limit, incentives for war production would be stifled. The vexing question was whether and at what point the limits of indirect taxation were reached and what was the burden of its incidence. Indirect taxes were levied on all but the minimum essential goods, and the rates increased sharply over the war years. Indirect taxation rose more gradually than direct taxation, but toward the end of the war indirect taxation remained the only device whose expansion was still considered justified for practical and psychological reasons. From a fiscal standpoint, one of the key features of indirect taxation during the war was its remarkable and consistent buoyancy. The Revenue's best payers were taxes on tobacco and alcohol. But the increased rates on tobacco and alcohol imposed further burdens on the low and medium income groups. (Sabine 1970, pp. 285-96.) According to Kalecki there may be two reasons for imposing an indirect tax:

1. Like any other tax, it reduces the budget deficit, and therefore lightens the future burden of the national debt. But the revenue aspect is not of primary importance. The increase in the size of the national debt does not burden the economy as a whole because the payment of interest on it is only an internal transfer. The transfer should not involve any disturbances in output and employment. This may be achieved, to note *en passant,* by financing the interest on the national debt by an annual capital tax or a modified income tax. (Kalecki 1943b, pp. 76-80.) Since this does not influence significantly the total volume of investment and consumption, it is more or less neutral with regard to output and employment. Hence war finance is not preoccupied with keeping down the budget deficit and with curtailing the increase in the national debt. At any rate, under emergency conditions, the considerations of the future burden of the national debt are of secondary importance.

2. Indirect tax depresses consumption of either the article taxed or of other goods and services or savings. Therefore, it is supposed to counteract the danger of inflation. In the case of indirect tax on beer and tobacco—products consumed by various strata of the population—the likely effect is as follows: The propensity of the lower income groups to save is low, and their savings are rather "inelastic" (e.g., insurance). Their choice is either to cut consumption of beer and tobacco or such nonfood expenditures as clothing, household goods, and entertainment, rather than to draw on savings. (Kalecki 1943h, pp. 260-65; 1942f; Durant and Goldmann 1945, pp. 1-7.) The better-off can encroach on their savings and, in this way, prevent reduction of consumption. Therefore, even if outlays on beer and tobacco constituted the same percentage shares of expenditures of lower and higher income groups, the consumption of the poorer strata would probably be reduced more than that of the well-to-do. But the higher the income (above a certain limit) the lower the share spent on beer and tobacco. The taxes on tobacco and beer are regressive, as they take a larger fraction of income from the poor than from the rich.

It is precisely for these reasons that consumption cuts by rising prices, i.e., by inflation, are harmful. Similarly, inflation cannot be fought successfully by taxation of seminecessities, which has related consequences. *Indirect taxation is nothing else but a government-controlled inflation.* Also the repercussions of indirect taxation on the vicious spiral of prices and wages are similar. Price rises caused by indirect taxation differ from those caused by open inflation, because the first is designed by the government and thus affects merely certain goods. But beer and tobacco are articles of mass consumption quite comparable as necessities with certain types of foodstuffs. Indirect taxation does not in fact differ substantially from laissez faire inflation in its incidence upon consumers. There was only one formal advantage of taxation of tobacco and beer: Tobacco was heavily underweighted in the cost of living index of the Ministry of Labour, and beer was not represented in it at all. But if the index should violate the realities of economic life intolerably it would lose its significance.[4]

Neither direct nor indirect taxation is a satisfactory instrument to cope with inflation, which must be attacked by reducing consumption in a fairly equitable way. (Kalecki 1942a, pp. 129-32.) In a community of unequal incomes and wealth, the fundamental problems of a war economy cannot be tackled successfully by financial measures alone. However important the contribution of the financial front may be to the war effort and to the struggle against inflation, complementary measures and controls must be instituted to grapple with the realities of the problems of allocating scarce resources under especially demanding conditions when equality of sacrifice is of prime importance and incentives cannot be suspended. If the state is not content with the existing (the *status quo ante bellum*) distribution of income, it could redistribute income by taxing the rich and transferring to the less privileged members of society. (Bowen and Worswick 1940, pp. 77-104.) However, taxation or any other indirect methods cannot achieve the same results as direct rationing of expenditures. Usually even very high taxation cannot eliminate or radically reduce the inequalities of spending power. Taxation is needed to curtail demand and to keep the spendable income down. The excess spending power is dangerous if allowed to chase the relatively smaller-than-in-peacetime supply of consumer goods. But the point is not only of restricting the supply of civilian goods and matching purchasing power, but of ensuring a fairer distribution of goods among the population. Under the circumstances, rationing becomes the key device to reduce demand to equality with constricted supply and to allocate available goods according to the prevailing standards of equity and requirements of efficiency. In this sense, taxation is merely a useful device to support rationing. (Kalecki 1943a, p. 97; 1941e, pp. 43-48.)

A Note on British Wartime Taxation

When the war broke out the level of taxation in Britain rose at a very slow pace. Only from 1941 onward (i.e., from Sir Kingsley Wood's first "real" war budget—to be discussed later) was taxation put on a war basis. (Sabine 1970, p. 285.) Taxes were raised considerably. New taxation was introduced in each wartime budget, but the last. (Kalecki 1944a, pp. 101-104.) The standard rate of income tax reached a high level, and for the first time in the country's history the mass of wage-earners was subjected to the income tax. Direct taxation on income—"whose level was regarded as ruinous by all concerned whether the standard rate was 4/6 or 10/"—extended drastically the taxing base, so that total revenue jumped from £855 million in 1938 to £3,480 million in 1945. Here the key changes were techniques of payment, with few major innovations in other directions, save for the idea of postwar credits. Successive chancellors of the exchequer refused to touch capital gains or to alter significantly estate duties.[5]

Indirect taxes on goods and services played an important role as a source of budget revenue. Here the major innovation was the widening of coverage through a general purchase tax instituted in 1940. The effect of the tax was an increase in prices and rationing by the purse. While it was a new feature among British fiscal measures, given the existence of import and excise duties, the purchase tax did not represent a change in the principle of taxation, but rather a significant extension. (Moggridge 1971, pp. 424-25; Sabine 1970, pp. 285 ff.)

To a large extent wartime conditions were responsible for the revolutionary change in the aims of fiscal policy, accompanied by a remarkable stability in fiscal techniques. The chancellor of the exchequer declared that the success of a wartime budget must be judged not principally by the amount of revenues it raises, but by the way it serves to concentrate the country's resources for the war. (*The Times*, Apr. 15, 1942.) Taxes were used as means of reducing the excessive spending power, but not of closing the "inflationary gap." Heavy taxation was allegedly avoided during World War II, so as not to interfere with incentives for production drive and efficiency. (Hancock and Gowing 1949, pp. 501 ff.) Yet the break with the past was not complete, and a considerable dose of fiscal orthodoxy remained. There was great resistance to trying "Keynesian Voluntarism." (Cf. Sayers 1956, pp. 31 ff.; Hancock and Gowing 1949, ch. 6; Sabine 1970, pp. 160 ff.)

Production Incentive and Profits Tax

Following the outbreak of hostilities there was widespread apprehension that the war would give rise to windfall profits. An obsession with profiteering developed. The Excess Profits Tax (EPT) was instituted to dispel public fears. It was a political device, mainly introduced for its psychological effect—a measure considered necessary to secure the earnest cooperation of the Labour party in ensuring industrial peace and in obtaining a relaxation of trade union restrictions and pressures for higher wages. Public fear that business was reaping surplus profits was seen as nurturing demands for higher wages. (Hancock and Gowing 1949, p. 157.) However, excess profits are really the essence of inflation. They result from "abnormal" rise in prices owing to inelastic supply; i.e., due to shortages of labor, materials, or capacity. (Kalecki 1940i, p. 15.) It is these escalating prices that give rise to demands for increasing wages. Central control of wages was considered politically unpopular and difficult to implement. There was only a "gentlemen's agreement" between the government and trade unions to contain wage demands within moderate limits.

At the outbreak of war a 60 per cent EPT was imposed, subsequently increased in May 1940 to 100 per cent. It was claimed that the EPT encouraged waste and extravagance. Due to the pressures for a reduction of the EPT, in January 1941 the War Cabinet agreed to maintain the 100 per cent tax, but to incorporate some inducement to exceed the standard level of profits by promising to reimburse 20 per cent of the EPT in the postwar period. Moreover, if the firm did not reach its standard profit in some years, the deficiency was to be reimbursed out of previous EPT payments. By all accounts these inducements to make profits above the standard level were rather weak.[6]

Labor and trade unions resisted proposals to decrease the EPT to restore the profit incentive, without readjustment in production organization allowing adequate representation and safeguard to labor. With the then prevailing rates of income tax, a very drastic cut of the EPT would have been required (even a 50 per cent EPT might have been excessive) to act as an incentive. Furthermore, 100 per cent EPT need not necessarily restrict the income of those actually in charge of production. It only ensured that higher money incomes were not distributed to shareholders who, in that capacity, did not make a contribution to the increased war production. (Balogh 1941, pp. 311-14.)

The EPT was repeatedly attacked by conservative critics and their friends in and outside of Parliament for the alleged damage it did to the war effort. They argued that profit is the motive of private enterprise and that incentive arrangements should be used in the service of the war. The EPT might check, if not halt altogether, badly needed entrepreneurship and initiative. The EPT was said to deprive the entrepreneurs of the profit incentive and therefore to prevent the full mobilization of available resources. (Sabine 1970, *passim.*)

In this context attention focused on the connection between the impact of the EPT on production and the level of profit per unit of output (profit margin). (Kalecki 1942h, pp. 114-17.) Kalecki scrutinized the repercussions of the EPT on production and showed that it is possible to restore the production incentive under a regime of EPT. Because the strength of the incentive depends on the level of the margin, Kalecki proceeded to develop a profit margin formula which would reconcile the incentive for an optimum use of available resources with 100 per cent EPT. He applied the principle of low profit margins to the important case of profit margins in government contracts. (Kalecki 1942e, pp. 40-43.) Two cases were representative:

1. Assume that a fixed price government contract is awarded to a firm that has considerable opportunities of undertaking improvements in its production organization. If prices are set so that, by applying existing production techniques the firm can earn a total profit which exceeds or equals the standard profit, the incentives for reorganization are absent because any additional profit would be entirely siphoned off by the EPT (problems of tax evasion, distorted information, audit, and control aside).

2. In the coal industry there are considerable cost differentials from pit to pit and from region to region. One problem is how to obtain output from high-cost producers without increasing intolerably prices and profits of low-cost producers and destroying incentives for husbandry of resources. Apparently, the colliers were exploiting their worst seams because, given the then existing costs and prices, they were thus assured of standard profits, and could leave

the best seams for future mining. (Cf. Hancock and Gowing 1949, pp. 466-79, 506-11.) The question was how to raise coal output which had fallen below the level that could have been attained with available manpower. If the better seams were used, working conditions would also be improved.

In neither case was the EPT the only adverse factor. In fact, what was often taken as the adverse effect of the EPT on production was, in some cases, owing to the labor situation and, in others, to bottlenecks. If there were no shortage of appropriate labor, operating on war contracts would certainly increase production, since employing additional trained workers does not require any special effort. But it is altogether different when production has to be reorganized in order to produce larger output with the same manpower or unskilled workers have to be trained. To stimulate such undertakings requires much more powerful incentives. Thus a proposed moderate reduction of the rate of EPT would not markedly improve the situation as the incentives to increase production with the same labor force would still be too weak.

Clearly, if profit margins per unit of output are fixed so low that the producer cannot reach his standard profits unless he makes a reasonable effort to expand the rate of production, the EPT ceases to be a brake on production. The firm would be compelled to use its production capacity efficiently because otherwise it would get substantially less than its standard profit. The EPT would be beside the mark here because excess profits would not accrue; i.e., the EPT would be managed so that it would yield as little revenue as possible. It would resemble the prohibitive customs duty. (Kalecki 1942h, pp. 115-16.)

Kalecki argued that, in the critical case of industries working on government contracts, the repercussions of 100 per cent EPT depended closely on the type of contract.[7] First take the case of "costs plus percentage profit margin" contracts.[8] Clearly, by siphoning off the excess of profits over the so-called standard level, the 100 per cent EPT did not discourage production, as profits are here proportionate to costs and thus are no indicator of efficiency of production. Abolition of the EPT would not induce maximization of output by improving methods of production organization. Contrariwise, the entrepreneurs would merely intensify their efforts to increase costs.

Obviously, when a contract stipulates "cost plus fixed profit margin per unit of output" the total profit is proportionate to expansion of output, but the strength of the incentive for output expansion depends on the level of the margin. If the margin is very high—even without EPT—there is little palpable incentive to reorganize production. But with 100 per cent EPT, the entrepreneur would hardly strive to increase output. However, should the profit margins be fixed sufficiently low so that only at a high level of resource utilization the standard profit could be reached, even the 100 per cent EPT would not have the attributed adverse effect, as the entrepreneur would have to make a bold push to augment his profit within the range not subject to EPT.

In the case of a fixed price contract, the entrepreneur is prompted to expand output and to reduce costs. However, if the profit margin is high, the entrepreneur may not strive hard to reorganize production. This is a likely action particularly when cost reduction would augment profit only for that contract but "spoil the business" for the next contract which would be geared to reduced costs. As in the case of "cost plus percentage profit margin" contracts, with a sufficiently low profit margin, even 100 per cent EPT would not discourage the entrepreneur from improvements in production techniques. Generally, the contract price should not be so high as to enable the producer to reach his standard profit without special effort. (Kalecki 1942e, pp. 41-42,) Some of the major problems here are the difficulty of determining or estimating future costs, the self-interest of producers to provide for "safety" margins, the lack of knowledge on the part of the outside party (government) of the internal costs, wide opportunities for cost manipulation, and a host of other problems. (Worswick 1945, pp. 79-90.)

In essence the problem was one of reconciling incentives for the best use of available resources with 100 per cent EPT. Kalecki's proposal was, roughly, that the producer should get a "standard profit" upon reaching a "target output" (fixed on the assumption of reasonable efficiency management) and proportionately less if the output was below the target rate. In the simplest case of a homogeneous output firm on contract from one government agency, assume that the contract stipulates the following conditions: (1) actual costs of production are covered, but such items as excessive repair and maintenance charges or unreasonably high managers' salaries or salary-type payments are excluded; and (2) the profit margin (P) is fixed at the level of the ratio of standard profits (S) as calculated for the purposes of EPT, and the target output (M), so that the "simple" formula of the profit margin reads $P=S/M$.

If the firm reaches the target output it earns standard profits under EPT, but no more. If the actual rate of output falls short of target output, it gets proportionately less. In no case, under this arrangement, is the firm subject to EPT. The management ought to strive to reach the target output so as to earn the standard profit. Since under this scheme the firm will be unable to benefit from 20 per cent repayment of EPT after the war, the level of standard profit may be fixed a little more liberally, especially where the prewar profits were depressed, as was often the case in small firms.

But, admittedly, it is the complex concept of the target output that needs further elucidation since it is difficult to provide a precise definition of productive capacity. (Cf. Kalecki 1968j, p. 275.) With a given work force, target output is defined here as that output that could be produced if each man worked the optimum time and if the organization of production (inclusive of the arrangements for wage and wage-type payments) were reasonably satisfactory. One problem is to allow for the uncontrollable "external" factors like the hitches in the supply of raw materials. But an experienced technician should be able to come up with a reasonable estimate.

Another complication is understaffing of a factory that could absorb more labor than it actually employs at the time of calculation. If the target output is fixed on the basis of the existing work force, the firm is not interested in employing more labor, even if it were available. But it may be impractical to fix the target output on the basis of attainable productive capacity of the plant and equipment, simply because the firm may be unable to secure additional employees. The difficulty could be remedied by estimating the target output on the basis of the full employment of the factory, but after deducting that number of vacancies communicated by the firm to the appropriate agencies which the latter are unable to fill. With such a provision, the firm should have a palpable incentive to make use of available labor, but it is not penalized if it cannot hire additional employees.

Kalecki allowed for the complications arising from the prevalence of multi-product firms with contracts placed by a variety of government agencies. Before considering a more general case, the formula of profit margin may be rewritten as $P=(S/m)(m/M)$, where m stands for the actual output and m/M for the degree of utilization denoted by u, thus obtaining $P=(S/m)u$. If $u=1$, the firm earns the total standard profit; if u is smaller than 1, it earns proportionately less.

Consider the case of a firm that produces a heterogeneous output and for a number of government agencies. Number the respective contracts as subscripts 1, 2, 3, . . . *n*. In applying the formula devised by Kalecki to this case, the first question is: what part of standard profit should be charged to a particular contract? A similar problem arises in allocating overheads. These are usually distributed proportionately to the respective prime costs (if they should be distributed at all). Whatever the method used for allocating overheads to a particular contract, the same procedure may be used for allocating standard profits. A series of coefficients $a_1, a_2, \ldots a_n$ is obtained, the sum of which equals 1 and the standard profit chargeable to each contract is $a_1S, a_2S, \ldots a_nS$, respectively. Thus the more complex formula for the profit margins for particular contracts when production is heterogeneous may be constructed as follows: $P_1=(a_1S/m_1)u$, $P_2=(a_2S/m_2)u, \ldots P_n=(a_nS/m_n)u$, where $m_1, m_2, \ldots m_n$ denote the respective rates of actual outputs, and u stands for the general degree of utilization of a factory (adjusted appropriately for the difficulty arising from understaffing). The amount of profit per annum obtained on various contracts equals, of course, profit margin times the respective rates of actual output, i.e., according to the above formula $a_1Su, a_2Su \ldots a_nSu$, and the total profit equals $a_1Su+a_2Su, \ldots +a_nSu$. Since $a_1+a_2, \ldots +a_n$ equals 1, the total amount of profit equals Su.[9]

Kalecki emphasized that an effective application of the system required not only a high degree of coordination and cooperation between the supply ministries and the Treasury, but also a keen insight into the internal conditions prevailing at the factories. (Kalecki 1942e, pp. 42-43. Cf. Steindl 1941b, pp. 272-78; Worswick 1945, and 1943, pp. 80-85.) A similar scheme can be devised for fixed price contracts. The price of goods must be fixed at such a level that the target output ensures the producer his standard profits, with reasonable efficiency. If the management fails to obtain the target output, the unit costs are higher than those which served for determining the contract price. Thus the firm that produces less than targeted is penalized in this case more harshly than in case of a cost plus fixed profit margin contract. To alleviate the situation some excess profit might be exempted from the tax, if the producer exceeds the target output (which is likely to induce pressures to set a low target output).

The application of the principles of low profit margins is not confined to government contracts where profit margins or prices are fixed for each firm individually. The problems of incentives under EPT for marketable commodities whose prices are not differentiated according to producers are similar to those of coal mining. Not unlike the colliers' propensity to leave the best seams for future exploitation, the industrial firms will be prompted to use their equipment of the oldest vintage if they can thus secure their standard profit. Moreover, there will be no incentive for them to reduce costs, if the extra profit is extracted. While in coal mining the main bottleneck is labor and in other industries shortage of raw materials may halt expansion of output, there still remains the problem of economizing labor, which could be released for the war sector or could be diverted in the industries manufacturing standard "utility goods."

If the price is fixed at such a level that a medium-cost producer obtains his standard profit when performing with reasonable efficiency, it could be expected that: (1) The medium-cost producers will tend to achieve reasonable efficiency. (2) The lowest-cost producers may still slacken off efforts and fail to exploit their potential. This group usually includes large-scale producers who may perhaps be restricted or "guided" by direct controls. (3) Some high-cost producers may be unable to cover even their variable costs. If output of low- and medium-cost producers cannot be economically expanded, the required output of the high-cost producers should be subsidized.[10]

Kalecki maintained that pegging prices at a level where the average producer is pressed to perform with reasonable efficiency is preferable to having prices above that level. The problems of fixing an appropriate level of profit margins point to the importance of price control. Price control was usually considered from the standpoint of the fight against inflation. But price control could also perform the task of restoring the production incentive under EPT. This aspect could not be overlooked. (Kalecki 1942h, pp. 114-17.)

Finance at the Early Stages of the War

The first wartime budget delivered in September 1939 "at best represented only a tentative step in the right direction." The chancellor of the exchequer, Sir John Simon, argued against really heavy taxation. At that phase of the war great scope was to be left to incentives. Only as total war would develop, the latter might be circumscribed more severely. The standard rate of income tax was increased from 5/6 to 7/6; "reduced rate" relief was raised; the EPT was set at 60 per cent as previously discussed; indirect taxes on beer, spirits, tobacco, and sugar were increased; and estate duties and surtax rates were raised. (Sabine 1970, pp. 153-59.) The large and growing gap between expenditures and tax proceeds was to be filled by voluntary savings. Keynes's plan for compulsory savings (to be discussed later) was turned down. There were drives to encourage small savings.

In the spring of 1940 the government was finding out how unrealistic it was to finance war expenditures by old precepts. Taxation was high, but tax revenue covered less than half of war outlays. It was held that the most powerful instrument for mopping up purchasing power was taxation, as it finally removes purchasing power without complications for future years. The disadvantages of taxation accumulate as the burden of taxation increases and the waste of evasive effort and policing become costlier. If for no other reasons, government in a major war cannot rely on taxation alone. (Hancock and Gowing 1949, pp. 171-72.)

Simon's interim budget of April 1940 was criticized for lacking the courage to face the war challenge. (See *Manchester Guardian*, Apr. 23, 1940, and Apr. 24, 1940.) The government did not undertake sufficiently drastic reduction of civilian consumption, thus diverting the released purchasing power into war production. The budget should have abandoned the pretense that the taxation of higher income groups had reached a tolerance ceiling. Stiffer taxation was required. The new fiscal measures struck relatively hardest at the lower income groups. Stiffer taxation should have been combined with curtailed consumption and greater equality of sacrifice. Voluntary loans did not suffice. The country was prepared for stiffer taxation provided that government waste could be avoided and that no additional burdens were imposed on the poor. The government was accused of timidity and of distrusting the country's capacity to sacrifice and bear hardships. (Sabine 1970, pp. 161-68.)

The reason for another interim (July 1940) budget—the first budget of the coalition government—was the sharply increasing cost of the war. The rate of war expenditures rose rapidly from a weekly average of £33 million in April 1940 to £52 million in June 1940. The urgent problem of inflation was mounting as the wage bills and employment drifted upward and the supply of goods for civilian consumption downward. The problem was to find an appropriate mechanism for restricting spending. Financing the war by imposing stiffer taxation on the wealthy or appeals for increased voluntary savings were considered insufficient. People with moderate or low incomes were to bear their share. (Sabine 1970, p. 170.)

In Sir Kingsley Wood's July 1940 budget, the standard income tax rate (for the entire year) was raised to 8/6, and the reduced rate (normally one-half the standard) was pegged at 5/-. The rate of the surtax was increased. Taxes were raised on beer and tobacco—the highest revenue-yielding commodities. A revised scheme of purchase tax was adopted so as to limit immediate consumption and to provide a new source of fiscal revenue. To placate labor, children's clothing was exempted from the tax, and two sharply differentiated rates of tax were adopted—the lower for essential goods and the higher for luxuries.

While the new tax burden was severe on the taxpayer, taxes were estimated to cover only some 35 per cent of expected (and what proved to be considerably understated) additional war expenditures. More generally the budget produced inadequate and unimaginative measures. (Sabine 1970, pp. 174-80.) The budget speech was hardly delivered when it became obvious to the Treasury officials that more drastic measures were required. Proposals for novel taxes abounded, but it was difficult to impose additional burdens.

The 1941 Budget

Commenting on the 1941 budget, Kalecki pointed out that it was based entirely on an increase in income tax.[11] The standard rate was increased from 8/6 to 10/-, and the "reduced rate" from 5/- to 6/6 on the pound, with the highest surtax rate 19/6. Simultaneously, allowances and relief for salary- and wage-earners were substantially cut. These measures were to reduce the size of the inflationary gap and to yield £250 million in revenue. The tax burden fell severely on the lower income groups. It was expected to bring in two million new taxpayers at the lower end of the scale. True the revenue from reduced allowances and relief (estimated to yield £125 million) was to be made available to the taxpayers after the war (in such a manner as Parliament would determine). But, Kalecki argued that the deferred advantage was likely to be heavily discounted by the taxpayers. (Kalecki 1941a, pp. 112-13.) Indeed, this seems to have been the effect. In practice people were not enthusiastic about "promissory notes."

Kalecki criticized the budget for lacking realism. The chancellor assumed that, without the new tax and the planned domestic government expenditure, the inflationary gap would be of the order of £500 million, of which half was to be counteracted by a new tax and the other half by an increase in personal savings. The chancellor calculated the size of the inflationary gap as the difference between future domestic government expenditures and the tax yields expected at previous tax rates, plus the existing level of savings. Scrutiny of the savings item showed that this was the total sum available for government borrowing from domestic sources. It included the sizable amount released by running down inventories or provided by inflationary savings, i.e., savings out of profits owing to rises in prices disproportionate to costs. (Kalecki 1941a, pp. 112-13.) The postulated future increase in noninflationary savings was too optimistic, especially in conjunction with the probable effect of the increased burden of taxation. A more sober view of the situation was that the budget would fail to prevent inflation, that the running down of stocks of consumer goods would be intensified, and that it would be followed by sharp increases in prices relative to costs.

As the record showed, the spreading of the income tax to wage-earners created severe difficulties. It tended to hinder the war effort by taxing overtime pay severely, and to a lesser degree, it diminished the financial incentives for married women to join the industrial work force. Formidable difficulties were also encountered in the collection of income tax, originally designed for taxing the upper and middle income brackets and not the wage-earners. The *P.A.Y.E.* income tax system was introduced. This meant that deductions were made at the source and paid by the employer to Revenue, rather than by the taxpayer directly after one or two years of earning his income. This system was a major improvement of the tax collection system. Without it, it would have been impossible to include the majority of wage- and salary-earners in the scheme. It might have been preferable to increase the exemption and release thereby a larger part of wage-earners from income tax altogether. A budget that imposed a heavy burden on low and medium income groups could not be considered a viable safeguard against inflation. As we shall see the fight against inflation would be best served by an extensive and flexible rationing system. (Kalecki 1941a, pp. 112-13; 1942a, pp. 129-32.)

The 1941 budget deliberately rejected inflation as a solution of the Treasury's difficulties. This was not only because the adverse distributional effects of inflation were recognized, but because the government had to assuage the great public anxiety about profiteering and inequality of sacrifice. Allowing prices to rise to reach a runaway equilibrium level had become impractical as wages were, to some extent, linked to the cost of living index and tended to follow an upward movement of prices. If a rise in the official cost of living index occasions higher wage demands, there is a "natural" tendency for governments to manipulate the velocity and composition of the index. There were a number of wage agreements with the cost of living clauses written in. But they covered only a minority of workers. Of course when prices rose, unions bargained for their members to catch up, but this is not exactly the same thing. Rampant inflation was rejected largely because it was recognized that the nature of wage-bargaining and dictates of industrial peace precluded the use of inflationary finance to compress consumption. Moreover, to the extent that the government procured goods and services, it was vitally interested in price stability. To prevent a vicious spiral, the 1941 budget resorted to cost of living subsidies.[12] The latter were to reduce the dangers of cost-push inflation. But artificially low prices would encourage consumption, and this had to be avoided in the case of goods in short supply.

Although prices of controlled goods, especially of those entering into the cost of living index, had been kept nearly stable since April 1941, there was a violent rise of prices in the uncontrolled sector, both in food and household goods. This was accompanied by a dangerous depletion of stocks of "unessential" goods, including household goods, whose supply would become essential when bombing was resumed. While the official cost of living index was kept "reasonably steady," the actual cost of living climbed steadily as the war progressed.[13] Despite the chancellor's statement that during 1941 "we have definitely held our own against the onset of inflation," in the uncontrolled sectors a typical inflationary development had set in. (Cited after Kalecki 1942a.) Kalecki noted that the cost of living subsidies were a useful instrument to keep down prices of some consumer goods despite certain increases in the costs of their inputs. But when prices of consumer goods are pushed up due to demand pull, the situation is different. Here subsidies *cannot produce goods.* If supply is short, demand prices are pulled up to adjust demand to supply, and a subsidy cannot remedy the situation. (Kalecki 1941a, p. 113.)

THE 1942 AND 1943 BUDGETS

In 1942 the dangers of inflation in one form or another were much graver than those depicted in Sir Kingsley Wood's 1942 budget speech (Cf. Sabine 1970, pp. 202-23; Sayers 1956, pp. 92ff.), the more so as prudence required that supplies of consumer goods be cut further. Again the chancellor failed to propose a satisfactory remedy against inflation. The important parts of the 1942 budget were merely amendments preceding the budget proposal: increase in the allowance to gainfully employed married women, exemption of men in armed services from the tobacco tax, and exemption of utility clothing from the purchase tax.

Although direct taxation played but a small part in the 1942 budget, the subject figured prominently in the budget speech. The chancellor of the exchequer argued that, owing to sharp previous intensification of direct taxation, it was clearly unwise to contemplate any immediate extension. He tried to show also that any further taxation of the rich was out of the question. (Kalecki 1942a, pp. 129-32.) Contrary to the chancellor's assertions, an estimate by J. L. Nicholson indicated that "taxing of the rich" remained an important source of revenue.[14] If, as the chancellor asserted, there was little scope for extending direct taxation, he had "to fall back upon the old faithfuls of Customs and Excise." (Sabine 1970, pp. 207, 295 ff.)

Both the 1942 and 1943 budgets relied heavily on indirect taxation for an increase in revenue. The leading roles were played by substantial increases in the handy taxes on beer and tobacco. As in the two 1940 budgets, the primary motive appears to have been the raising of revenue. But the declared objective and subsidiary aim was to enable the Treasury and other departments to keep demand and supply in better balance through fiscal measures. It was envisaged that the stringent increases in the taxes on tobacco, beer, and entertainment would provoke an appreciable fall in consumption.[15] But the anticipated cut in consumption did not materialize. Despite sharply increased prices, consumption was only slightly less than before.[16] Virtually throughout 1941-42 there was an often acute shortage of tobacco, which provoked independent rationing by shopkeepers. The increase in prices of tobacco in 1942-43 cut out the weaker buyers and reduced the pressure of demand, thus enabling the higher income groups to increase their consumption.

At that point, Kalecki asked what taxes should have been introduced by the 1942 and 1943 budgets? None at all? Perhaps that would have been the most reasonable course to follow. At that juncture the fight against inflation was being waged not by the Treasury, but by the Ministry of Food and the Board of Trade. "For they have at their disposal the most effective weapon: the ration book." (Kalecki 1943a, p. 97.)

In a fairly controlled economy, like that of Britain during the latter part of the war, taxation is generally not very potent as a means of cutting consumption. Only when some sectors of the economy remain free and the supply of goods and services in these sectors declines while incomes are still on the increase, does direct taxation provide a useful device in the fight against inflation along with rationing and price control. Such, however, was not the situation on the eve of the 1944 budget.

THE 1944 BUDGET

As compared with the preceding one, the 1944 budget envisaged a small increase in expenditures. The transfer of manpower from the civilian to the war sector was practically completed. There was little danger of drastic cuts in imports that would depress rations and increase pressures on the uncontrolled sector. There were signs of war weariness. The reserves for sacrifice were near exhaustion, and revenue raising difficulties became quite formidable. Hence the 1944 budget was the first of the wartime budgets that did not introduce any new taxation. But on closer scrutiny, measures equivalent to new taxation were involved. An actual or potential cut in subsidies is equal to or more harmful than an increase in indirect taxes, because it entails a rise in the price of necessities. (Kalecki 1944a, pp. 101-104.)

In his 1944 budget speech the new chancellor of the exchequer, Sir John Anderson, expressed disquietude over the sharply growing subsidies: a cost of living figure of 25 to 30 per cent above prewar level could no longer be regarded as inviolable. His predecessor, Sir Kingsley Wood, stressed that a steady wage level was part and parcel of the stabilization policy: if wages rose the policy might have to be abandoned. By January 1944 the Ministry of Labour's index of money wages had risen 40 per cent above the prewar index. The new chancellor argued that the purpose of stabilization would be countervailed if the government were to continue pouring out subsidies to keep the cost of living artificially down without regard for the movements of wages and costs. The cost of living must be allowed to float in cases where increases in wages had raised the actual cost of necessities (e.g., coal). Under the circumstances, the chancellor affirmed that he guaranteed the increase over the prewar level of the order of from 30 to 35 per cent, and proposed a revision of the subsidies policy.

Several Parliament speakers and the leftist press doubted the wisdom of letting the cost of living rise. (Sabine 1970, pp. 244-68.) Kalecki questioned the underlying statistics provided by the chancellor of the exchequer. In March 1944 the Ministry of Labour's cost of living index was 28 per cent above the 1938 level. But in 1943 the index of retail prices of all consumer goods and services, after eliminating the influence of both subsidies and indirect taxes, was 43 per cent above the 1938 level. Using additional data released by the government, Kalecki calculated that the index of market retail prices (i.e., prices actually paid by consumers) was 51 per cent above the prewar index. This was an "artificial" price level, in the sense that it was influenced both by subsidies and by indirect taxes. The same prices after subtracting taxes and adding subsidies gave the previously mentioned figure of 43 per cent for the increase in the "natural" price level over the prewar level. Hence the natural price level was far above the artificial price level. Indirect taxes, in fact, heavily outweighed subsidies. The chancellor's measure of the price level was the cost of living index and not the figures depicting the overall increase in prices to consumers—the index of retail market prices. The cost of living index was substantially below that of retail prices because subsidized necessities were heavily overweighted and goods subject to indirect taxation heavily underweighted in the Ministry of Labour's cost of living index.[17] By introducing the necessary corrections, Kalecki and Nicholson suggested that the cost of living index had risen by 48 per cent (or more) over the prewar level. On this basis, accepting the rise in money wage rates at about 40 per cent from the prewar level, a certain decline in real wages had taken place. (Kalecki 1944a, pp. 101-104; Nicholson 1945, pp. 230-44.)

Aside from the question of validity of the underlying statistics, to what extent would workers' consumption be affected by the government sponsored increases in retail prices? First, wages of a large number of workers would rise immediately, because of existing agreements linking wages to the cost of living. A pattern would be set and other workers were likely to press for corresponding increases. It would be difficult to reject such claims if a large share of the labor force had already obtained a raise. The rise in wages would provoke further price increases. Even assuming that the policy were successful in compressing real wages by scaling down subsidies without appreciable effect on money wages, what would be the meaning of such an undertaking? Anderson quite correctly conceived that this would permit the abolition of war controls earlier, without producing a sharp inflationary rise in prices thereafter. Both the Right and the Left were already uneasy about the nature of postwar controls, and some wished to synchronize an armistice with a return to an uncontrolled economy. Kalecki emphasized that, after abolition of controls, inflationary pressures would be reduced only to the extent to which prices had risen in relation to wages before decontrol. Such a method amounts merely to preventing price increases after dismantling controls by making prices rise in the same proportion as before. Similar to indirect taxation, it consists of replacing rampant inflation with government planned inflation.[18]

Taxation and Measuring the Cost of the War

The question "who pays for the war?" was often answered by counterposing statistics of direct taxes paid by various strata of the population. But this was a rather biased way of showing that the poor did not contribute to financing the war at all, if they were not subject to income tax. Any serious attempt at ascertaining the financial war burden of various income groups should obviously take into account indirect taxation. The latter is known to fall most heavily on low income groups. Its yield during wartime was much greater than the amount spent on subsidies. True, these calculations are handicapped by the lack of reliable statistical information on relative consumption of alcohol and tobacco by the poor and the rich. The sources of information on the composition of consumption of various income groups are household budgets, where the items of alcohol and tobacco are known to be understated.

There is a more general objection against measuring the cost of the war by tax payments, even if indirect taxation is in some way accounted for. The payment for the war is by no means limited to the payment of taxes. Take the case of cargo-sinking by the enemy. The financial loss is covered by insurance, but the premium cost is added to the price of the imports. The resulting higher prices paid for consumer goods certainly represent a payment for the war. Another important case is the disproportionate-to-costs rise in prices due to demand pull. Assume that the windfall profits arising in this way are taxed away. Though technically paid by producers or merchants, these taxes, in fact, are borne by the consumer.

Such inconsistencies and misconceptions may be avoided with a broader notion of paying for the war. The distribution of the war burden can be ascertained in the following way: Assume that one can estimate roughly the change in real income of certain income groups had employment risen in peacetime as it actually did during the war. Potential real income of each group—i.e., the real income which might reasonably have been expected at the existing level of economic activity in normal peacetime conditions—is higher by x per cent than in the year preceding the war. Then the reduction of the actual real income is calculated. Denoting this by y, the potential real income is $100+x$ (assuming the year preceding the war is equal to 100), and the actual real income is $100-y$. The difference between those two items may then be taken as the measure of the financial sacrifice imposed by the war on the income group in question. (Kalecki 1942b, pp. 10-11; Nicholson 1945 and 1944b, pp. 153-61.)

This method of distributing the war burden developed by Kalecki was applied by Nicholson to estimate the changes between 1938 and 1944 in the net incomes of wage-earners and the financial war burden endured by each group. Nicholson showed that, in Great Britain, the war burden on wage-earners, relative to that on non-wage-earners remained fairly constant, at about 2 : 5 throughout the war period. If effects of limitations of consumers' freedom of choice were allowed for, both sets of estimates would be raised, with an increased burden of wage-earners relative to non-wage-earners. The financial burden of the war reached its peak in 1942-43. (Nicholson 1945; 1944b.)

How to Pay for the War

As shown, the vexing problem of the war economy was how to reconcile the demands of the war sector with the claims of civilian consumption. While earnings were to be increased, consumption had to be diminished. The increased war effort required that those who received higher incomes consume, at least on the whole, less than before (or less than the equivalent of their increased productivity). The question was: What was the best method for the government to get hold of the required real resources which the public was not willing to release at the current price level?

In an ingenious scheme, Keynes offered an answer to this perplexing question. (Keynes 1940b.) Keynes argued that nothing is of the least use to financing the war which does not diminish consumption out of current income. If one aims at preventing a certain share of consumers' spending power from being spent, the sensible thing is to start at the income-generating end, withholding by compulsory saving or by taxing that proportion which is not to be spent on consumption. "A world of trouble and an ocean of waste will be avoided, and the consumer will enjoy far more satisfaction. . . . The abolition of consumer's choice in favour of universal rationing is a typical product of the onslaught, sometimes called bolshevism, on differences between one man and another by which existence is enriched." (Keynes 1940b, p. 53.)

Keynes suggested that the correct approach was to withdraw from expenditures a proportion of earnings by a high and progressive rate of income tax, a share of which would be refunded after the war was over. He rejected the adventitious aid of the mechanism of inflation which favors the wealthier classes that emerge after the war enriched by the amount of increased national debt which inflation enables them to subscribe; and which "allows wage-earners to spend but deprives them of the fruit of spending." He believed that the inflationary gap could be further appreciably reduced by voluntary saving without any significant degree of inflation; he was convinced that, on the scale on which it was necessary, outright taxation was impractical. He advanced that the entire cost of the war could not be financed without putting some burden on the wage-earners (subject to special reliefs), and that there was no avoiding a postponement of expenditures on the part of this group. Keynes hoped that workers would work harder during wartime, motivated by the *ultimate* enjoyment of their earnings. This led to the admirable Keynesian invention of the "compulsory saving" scheme, or as it came to be called later, probably to woo greater acceptance, "the deferred pay plan." With his great perception and lucidity, Keynes argued that those who exerted greater effort faced really two alternatives: viz., wage-earners could forgo the equivalent consumption altogether, or they could defer it. This suggested a way out: an appropriate share of current earnings must take the form of deferred pay (compulsory savings)—the retention of the rights to the fruit of labor, even though the wage-earner is forced to postpone enjoyment to the future.

The principal provision of Keynes's plan was to ascertain a share of each wage-earner's earnings to be withdrawn. The rights to deferred consumption after the war, "another name for the national debt," would be widely and equitably distributed among all those who were forgoing current consumption, instead of being concentrated, as they were during World War I, in the hands of the capitalist class.[19] The latter method was socially unjust and led to inequitable distribution of sacrifice.[20] That part of earnings to be deferred under the scheme would be placed to the credit of its owner as a blocked deposit (in the friendly society or the approved saving institution selected by him, or failing such a choice, at the Post Office Savings Bank, carrying interest at 2½ cent). Obviously, the deposits were not intended to be used until the end of the war, when they would be released in a series of installments at dates fixed by the government (but discretionary releases to meet special emergencies were envisaged to allow compulsory savings to perform some of the functions of voluntary savings). Keynes wisely argued that the appropriate time for the ultimate release of the deposits would have arrived at the beginning of the first postwar slump. The deferred scheme would be "twice blessed": It would help as much in combating postwar recession and unemployment as it would help to decrease consumer demand during the war, preventing inflation.

Keynes admitted the existence of alternatives to his scheme which were not less drastic and, if they were put into practice, not less effective; for example, a wage tax of the order of 20 per cent, or a retail sales tax of 50 per cent, or stiffer income tax whose incidence would be exactly the same as that of the compulsory saving scheme proposed. He emphasized that the choice between these stiff alternatives must be decided on grounds of public psychology, social justice, and administrative expediency.

Originally, Keynes merely attempted to advance an alternative solution to high income taxes imposed on wage-earners. He rightly feared that such measures would excite serious political difficulties and higher wage demands.[21] Keynes's proposal was put forward as a solution of an urgent problem of the war economy; "but the more he reflected upon it the more he fell in love with it as an engine of social reform." (Harrod 1951, p. 492. Cf. Sayers 1956, p. 81.) Indeed,

Keynes himself commented that in the first version of the proposal published in the *Times* he "was mainly concerned with the questions of financial technique and did not secure the full gain in social justice for which this technique opened the way." In the revised version he attempted "to snatch from the exigency of war positive social improvements." (Keynes 1940b, p. 111.) War should be an occasion for diminishing rather than increasing the existing inequalities of wealth. The exigencies of war finance require the upsetting of established arrangements and simultaneously create the opportunity for a positive social improvement. "The new plan is required to satisfy ideals of social justice much higher than we have been attaining without it." (Keynes 1940b, p. 31.)

The 1941 budget embodied a very novel feature—a part of the increased income tax was designated as a "withholding tax"—a tax to be repaid after the end of the war. This was in part a minor adoption of Keynes's proposal. While Keynes's plan made a great impression, there was widespread opposition to it. (Cf. Sayers 1956, pp. 81 ff.) Whereas for Keynes his deferment-of-income scheme was to be, as Sir Roy Harrod argued, "the centre piece of war finance," in effect the "post-war credit scheme was an interesting experience, but only played a minor part in the whole situation. The large diffusion of property which he hoped to bring about painlessly has not taken place." (Harrod 1951, p. 494.)

In his comments on Keynes's scheme, Kalecki voiced two principal objections:

1. In many cases compulsory savings would tend to be offset by a decline in voluntary savings, or even by actual dissaving. Moreover, compulsory savings might be made by curtailing outlays on housing or giving up entertainment and other services which practically release no resources in terms of scarce raw materials and little in terms of labor. Thus the scheme might fail to release the critically needed real resources for the war effort. If one's forced savings are realized by saving less voluntarily, say, reducing one's dwelling space or giving up cinema attendance, there is little contribution, indeed to mobilization of resources for the war.

2. The scheme devised by Keynes did not attempt to establish a certain maximum for the consumption of the rich before imposing the forced postponement of consumption on the poor. Moreover, it is clearly the upper income classes who may evade the reduction of consumption by dissaving. (Kalecki 1940c, pp. 7-9.)

Kalecki concluded that Keynes's scheme " . . . does not differ essentially from income taxation. For the working class the consolation offered by prospective post-war enjoyment of compulsory savings is of a rather shadowy character. As to the well-to-do, on whom in the last version of Mr. Keynes' scheme falls the chief burden of compulsory saving, it is even less efficient than income tax in cutting their consumption: seeing compulsory savings accumulating on blocked account they are more likely to save less on a voluntary basis or to dissave than they would if taxed to the same extent." (Kalecki 1941d, p. 2.)

Indeed, the wartime experience appears to have confirmed the gloomy prediction, even though the full-scale application of Keynes's scheme was never put into practice. People received "little pieces of paper" informing them that they were entitled to a certain amount of the postwar credits, but no one seemed aroused by these promissory notes, which did not even provide palpable inducement for working overtime. (Joan Robinson 1951, p. 95.) When consumption levels are depressed below recent levels (or the rate of increase is substantially below that expected), people are not likely to place a high value on the benefits of future consumption. Probably when the size of the private consumption fund is fixed so that consumption per capita is reduced (or customary consumption levels of various groups curtailed or endangered), people will try to concentrate their efforts on how to get the largest possible share at the expense of others.

Keynes was right when he pointed out that, when the decision is made regarding how much can be made available for private consumption, "we have still to settle the thorniest question of all, how to distribute it most wisely." (Keynes 1940b, p. 2.) The problem is how to adopt best the mechanism of distribution to the regime and constrictions of the war economy.

XI

GENERAL RATIONING

A Scheme for Curtailment of Consumption

THE MOST DIRECT METHOD OF CONTROLLING EXPENDITURES and of achieving more equitable distribution of commodities among consumers than by taxation or open inflation is outright *specific* rationing of a wide range of consumer goods. (Kalecki 1941d, p. 3.) The government can deliberately reduce or dry up the opportunities for private spending as a way of adjusting consumers' spending to available supplies. At a stroke direct allocation cuts down the claims against products (shifts downward the demand curve) to equality with supplies and allows for more egalitarian distribution. Allocation by ration tickets becomes not only a device for sterilizing excess demand, but also for ensuring distribution of products in short supply along preordained patterns, however determined. Of course, such a method of allocation, where everybody can count on getting his fair quota of the limited supply (which may, or may not, be on a completely egalitarian basis), is only one of the variants of the distributional arrangement. Distribution according to some weighted scale of priorities or various discriminatory or differentiated treatments is possible. (Cf. Robbins 1947, pp. 5 ff.; Hancock and Gowing 1949, *passim.*)

As Kalecki noted, the specific rationing scheme is not devoid of serious and familiar drawbacks. To be effective, such a scheme must be fairly comprehensive, embracing an enormous number of goods, resulting in considerable regimentation and inconvenience for shoppers, and creating serious problems of control of implementation. (Kalecki 1941d, p. 3. Cf. Keynes 1940b, pp. 51-57.) Of course, rationing of the entire range of commodities by description is quite impractical. In case of certain nonstandardized articles, it becomes quite unmanageable or inapplicable. As a result, resources are needlessly wasted and consumers' satisfaction is diminished.

One of the principal difficulties of specific rationing is coping satisfactorily with the problem of transferability of ration coupons from poorer people who do not consume *in toto* their allotted rations, to those who can afford to consume more. Those who cannot afford to use all their coupons may be persuaded to sell the balance or to use them to buy goods for other persons and resell them at prices higher than those fixed for rationed goods. A black market develops. The distribution of goods allocated, but not consumed by the low income groups tends to be haphazard, inequitable, and inefficient. Furthermore, in anticipation of the introduction of rationing for particular goods, the retailers tend to deplete sharply their stocks and to sell promptly at higher prices. Here lies the danger that, unless permanently controlled (with all the inherent difficulties of such policing), stocks will reach critically low levels. (Kalecki 1941d, p. 3; 1941a, pp. 112-13.)

What was needed was a scheme to adapt the rationing mechanism to the exigencies and limitations of a war economy and to allow maximum freedom of choice, compatible with full war effort.

THE EXPENDITURE RATIONING SCHEME

The point was to find a better arrangement for curtailing consumers' spending that would overcome the nuisances of specific rationing of individual groups of consumer goods. The arrangement would have to limit consumers' total expenditures in shops by less cumbrous means and with less inconvenience to the buyer and the seller and thus reduce the constricting effects of rationing on the consumers' freedom of choice and promote a better shopkeepers' service. And finally an arrangement that would be free of the two major disadvantages of Keynes's ingenious solution, as outlined at the end of the preceding chapter, would have to obtain.

Such an arrangement could be found *grosso modo* in rationing retail expenditures in the aggregate. This was the essence of the very clever and subtle device invented by Kalecki, allowing an improved range of economic choice under trying conditions.[1] Kalecki's scheme is based on a simple principle. A total maximum limit of expenditure in retail shops is fixed at, say, 25/- a week per adult and 15/- per child under fourteen. Coupons are issued to this effect. Any sale by a retailer without coupons, subject to the exceptions noted below, is prohibited and considered a punishable offense.

The general principle of the scheme is the rationing of expenditures on goods in retail shops. There is little to be gained from the rationing of services, for it would release little of consequence in the way of raw materials and labor. In fact, some services, like education and entertainment, were not scarce. If a need arose, other services could be controlled much more expediently by direct methods (e.g., dwelling space assigned by billeting, gas and electricity by direct rationing, traveling by reducing the number of trains and abolishing first class, etc.). In addition to services, certain goods, such as medicine, newspapers and books, etc., could be bought without coupons. Special allowances would have to be made for people who lost their furniture and household goods in bombing, for newly married couples, etc. If restaurant meals were not rationed, restaurant customers would be a privileged group. But the restaurants' meal coupons should be only a certain definite proportion of their price, owing to the charge for service.[2]

In elaborating his scheme, Kalecki paid particular attention to the problems of administration and of lessening difficulties and hardships. The most intricate problem was to prevent sales of goods without coupons. In contrast to a flat-rate issue of coupons (which could be arranged on the same line as the then existing rationing of specific goods), the adoption of an income percentage maximum provision complicates to a great extent the administration of the scheme. Kalecki advocated establishment of a retailers' controlling office to which retailers would have to return all coupons received to obtain retailers' coupons which they must, in turn, surrender to wholesalers when obtaining goods from them. The returned retailers' coupons must cover their entire turnover as ascertained for payment of purchase tax to the authorities.

If an egalitarian method of rationing is adopted, i.e., if all are issued coupons entitling them to the same amount of spending, the low income groups will not fully use their coupons and might be induced to sell or otherwise transfer the residue of coupons to the better-off. To prevent this, two different courses of action may be taken: (1) Although the transfer of coupons is prohibited under severe penalty, it is unlikely that the penalty would be a sufficient deterrent since very harsh penalties must be ruled out. (2) For all practical purposes expenditures can be reduced to the difference between the actual amount spent in shops prior to the rationing scheme and that which would ensure the full use of their coupons by everyone. (Kalecki 1941d, pp. 2-5.)

Every rationing scheme is riddled by the problem of low income groups being unable to purchase the full ration. Hence rationing fails the desired criterion of equitable distribution, and the more so since the poor, being unable to spend some of their coupons, are likely to use them for the benefit of the better-off. In designing the rationing scheme, Kalecki offered two alternatives for distributing "expenditure coupons": (1) coupons are distributed at a flat rate as previously noted; and (2) as a device to reduce the transferability of coupons, apart from the maximum amount of total spending limit, a maximum percentage of income to be spent in shops is fixed at a level equal approximately to the upper limit of the actual percentage spent in shops by the poorer population.

The administrative problem is to issue coupons for the amount corresponding to the lower of these two maximums. If the income percentage maximum were 80 per cent, then a family consisting of a couple with a child under fourteen, having an income of 60/- per week, would get coupons only for 48/-, although on the basis of the standard maximum of 25/- per adult and 15/- per child, it would be entitled to an expenditure ration of 65/-. The second alternative complicates appreciably the administrative task and makes no attempt at exploiting rationing to correct striking inequities at the outset and to increase the consumption of the poorest segments of the population. (Kalecki 1940c, 8-9; 1941h, pp. 103-105.)

In a further elaboration of the general rationing scheme, Kalecki suggested that the government distribute the spending coupons at an egalitarian rate, but simultaneously promulgate that it is prepared to repurchase unused coupons at the values to which they relate. Consequently, anyone who cannot afford to use a certain part of his coupons could sell half of the unused coupons to the government and, in such a way, secure the wherewithal for making use of the other half of the coupons. As a result allowances are granted automatically to the lower income groups, while sale of coupons on the black market is discouraged. Such a scheme is more costly to implement, but every coupon purchased by the government ensures that consumption of rationed articles will be below the expected level. Kalecki pointed out that putting into effect such a measure would create a fairly comprehensive, democratic, and elastic system of distributing commodities in short supply, though it would probably be advantageous to include in the rationing scheme additional categories of nonfood articles and services. (Kalecki 1941e.)

This improved arrangement is, in many respects, superior to the original formulation of the scheme, viz:

1. The illegal transfer of coupons from the poorer to the richer segments of the population is largely counteracted. Kalecki believed that a poor man would rather sell his coupons to the government on the above terms than on the black market even at a higher price. This would be the case if the differential were small, but a large difference between the legal and illegal price tends to corrupt. The scheme discourages the rich from procuring coupons illegally, as they would have to pay more than the coupons' face value and, consequently, pay for the purchase of any particular article more than twice its price.

2. The poorer segments of the population receive automatic allowances.

3. The above are secured without any administrative machinery, such as census of incomes, filling fairly detailed forms by each income earner to establish income percentage maximum; audits whether a higher income was declared in order to benefit from more coupons, etc.

4. Admittedly, the "coupon repurchase" scheme would be more costly for the government, but combined with the reduction of aggregate expenditures in shops, it would be still more advantageous from the standpoint of reducing consumption than if all coupon recipients used them fully. (Kalecki 1941g, p. 104; 1941d, pp. 4-5.)

Kalecki concluded by pointing to the definite advantages of the general rationing scheme: (1) Above all it safeguards against inflation and can be expediently adapted to the most stringent supply shortages. (2) Rationing of expenditures is a more comprehensive and more convenient device than specific rationing of a corresponding range of consumer articles—"instead of struggling with an avalanche of coupons, for boots, clothing, electric torches, pots and pans, etc. etc.," the consumer and retailer have to cope with only one set of coupons. (3) Whereas for particular reasons, like ensuring nutrition standards, some goods must be rationed specifically, the general rationing scheme offers the consumer the widest possible freedom of choice among the remainder. (4) The administrative complication of the issue of coupons according to income graduation was introduced only to cope with the problem of coupon transferability. To the degree that this device could not be used in case of the specific rationing of goods, it was another advantage of the scheme. However, the device might be dropped if the administrative difficulties should outweigh the advantages derived from reducing transferability.

Such a scheme, like others, would have to be introduced before stocks reached critically low levels for two reasons: (1) to secure a higher uniform ration for a longer period (the not too promising alternative is unnecessarily high and inequitably distributed consumption until inventories are exhausted followed by a very low ration thereafter), and (2) because run down stocks are always accompanied by serious dislocations and disturbances in the distribution process. (Kalecki 1941a, pp. 112-13.)

Although Kalecki criticized income tax (or Keynes's scheme) and specific rationing of commodities as methods for curtailing general expenditure, he emphasized that "they not only do not interfere with this [Kalecki's] scheme, but actually supplement it." (Kalecki 1941d, p. 6.) He argued that the savings derived from this scheme should be at least partially siphoned off not by borrowing, but by taxation. For this reason the income tax rate should be increased. In some cases, this was likely to involve expenditure and so reduce the possibilities of evasion from the rationing-of-spending scheme. (Kalecki 1941d, p. 6.)

The general rationing scheme also involves the specific rationing of some essential goods because the scheme only reduces, but does not abolish entirely the inequality of spending. Hence, Kalecki considered it advantageous to "differentiate the scheme" by introducing food and non-food coupons—to be discussed at greater length in the section on nonegalitarian rationing.

Toward Comprehensive Rationing

In wartime Britain rationing was introduced gradually and hesitantly.[3] At first only a few foodstuffs in particularly short supply were rationed. In time more and more foodstuffs were brought within the ingenious points scheme.[4] The points scheme was relatively flexible. The points were adjusted upward and downward depending on the shifts in the supply and demand of such goods. The scheme did not favor larger stores and required far less regimentation of retailers and consumers than specific rationing.[5]

As the supply situation deteriorated during the winter and spring of 1940-41, the extension of rationing, especially of foodstuffs and clothing, became a major problem. The extension of rationing in 1941 was rather under the pressures of events than a part of a comprehensive plan to prevent a divergence between demand and supply. (Kalecki 1942a.) In August 1941 Kalecki noted that, since the publication of the final version of his scheme at the beginning of the year, his plan for rationing expenditures in shops "has been superseded to a certain extent by a substantial expansion of specific rationing which has taken place in the meantime."[6] To superimpose rationing of expenditures on the then-existing, rather elaborate specific rationing of food and clothing would have been cumbersome. A system of great complexity would have been created.

Under the circumstances, Kalecki proposed that the rationing of expenditures be used for closing loopholes in the existing rationing arrangements. Among the most important of these gaps were nonrationed foodstuffs, which constituted two-thirds of the aggregate expenditures on food, drink, and tobacco. (In practice beer and tobacco were excluded from rationing for reasons of tax revenue and morale.) Kalecki advocated as a minimum program the rationing of joint retail expenditures on these items. In addition, the cloth rationing scheme should have been amended and stringent rationing of coal, gas, and electricity started at once. While making rationing fairly comprehensive, such measures would still leave a considerable number of nonfood commodities outside the rationing system whose further extension could be considered in the future. (Kalecki 1941n. Cf. Hancock and Gowing 1949, pp. 492-93.)

The restriction of the total expenditures on food then unrationed (including drink and tobacco) had two principal advantages over a further extension of specific rationing: (1) Further extension of specific rationing would be very complicated and cumbersome. It was not possible to expand substantially traditional specific rationing, for its limitations would soon become apparent. (2) More importantly, commodities rationed thus far were universally consumed, which was not the case for many goods that remained unrationed. Aside from the striking examples of alcohol and tobacco, consumption of many foodstuffs depends on individual tastes and habits. Therefore, securing freedom of choice of the consumption of these remaining commodities was of fundamental importance.[7]

Because wholesale and retail prices differ, rationing by value is more cumbersome than allotments by weight or points. But in the case of foodstuffs, drink, and tobacco, such impediments may be easily overcome, for here most prices are generally uniform all over the country. Thus it would be possible to enforce the following rule: When the retailer procures these goods from the distributor or producer, he must surrender coupons for the amount representing their retail value.[8] The value of the expenditure ration on foodstuffs, not allotted specifically,[9] would have to be fixed at such a level that: (1) disinvestment in inventories would cease; (2) prices in general would stop from advancing, they would actually decline where price increases had been very acute;[10] and (3) acute shortages, queues, and other irksome aspects of haphazard distribution would be avoided.

In addition, Kalecki suggested that: (1) the point rationing of clothing and footwear be supplemented by forbidding the production or import of commodities over a certain price limit, which would render allotments by points nearly corresponding to rationing by value; (2) a stringent, combined point rationing of coal, gas, and electricity be introduced without delay; and (3) restaurant meals be incorporated in food rationing, but the total value of coupons surrendered be equal not to the price of the meal—which includes a markup for cooking and services—but to the retail value of the ingredients. (Kalecki 1941e.)

The chief drawback of the point rationing of clothing and footwear in operation was that it placed no limit on the value of commodities bought. This induced the better-off people to buy cloth of very high quality, thus absorbing labor for producing such goods at the cost of the war effort, and also higher imports wherever high quality production required more expensive materials. The simplest way of coping with this problem was to prohibit the manufacture or import of cloth or clothing over a certain price limit. According to Kalecki the measures he advocated would create a fairly comprehensive and equitable distribution system of goods in short supply.[11]

Clearly, Kalecki's scheme was likely to give rise to objections of various kinds. He anticipated some of them:

1. Why should the expenditure on consumption be curtailed by the vexing device of comprehensive rationing? Could not income tax, or Keynes's deferred income scheme, do the job in a less troublesome way? Again the answer is that an increased burden of income tax or the imposition of "blocked forced savings" may produce chiefly a cut in voluntary savings or even dissaving. Such reduced spending might be channeled in the wrong direction. It is quite impossible to achieve by taxation or any other indirect ways the same results as by direct rationing of food expenditures.

2. What will be the effects of possible wage increases on the scheme of comprehensive rationing? It is the vicious spiral that really pushes wages up. When prices rise, the workers who have to pay

for the consumer goods do not care how the cost of living has climbed. As soon as the price level is controlled by comprehensive rationing, there is less agitation for higher wages. Wages will mainly rise to make moderate adjustments. Wage increases would then affect the demand for actually scarce goods only to the extent that they enable the lower income groups to take fuller advantage of the rations to which they will be entitled. Clearly, this might involve some curtailment in general rationing. Nevertheless, if the arrangement of granting allowances by buying up unused coupons is accepted, such adjustments could only be small.

Under comprehensive rationing a rise in wages is largely divorced from demand for commodities in critically short supply. The impact of a rise in wages on prices via costs is only a special case of a more general problem; for instance, a rise in costs of imported raw materials creates exactly the same predicament. It is in such cases that price controls and subsidies (which will be discussed later) may play their proper role. While the policy of price control and subsidies cannot win the battle against inflation arising out of the deficient supply of goods, it may be used effectively to prevent price inflation coming not from the demand, but from the cost side.

3. Comprehensive rationing may affect labor performance, reducing the incentives to work harder and better, because earnings over a certain limit cannot be spent. Although savings are neither a palpable nor powerful incentive, they are undeniably a reward for greater effort. Moreover, a certain range of commodities, and particularly of services, remains beyond rationing. But, above all, the incentive system can be strengthened by differential rationing. For instance, it was officially recognized that heavy work has to be compensated by higher food rations. There is a wide scope for introducing a more refined differentiation (e.g., based on working time). It would be advisable to introduce nonfood coupon premiums for extra work or improved performance.[12] Lastly, comprehensive rationing of foodstuffs would remove these obstacles to work resulting from haphazard distribution, acute shortages, and waste of time and aggravation in queues. (Kalecki 1941e.)

Nonegalitarian Rationing

Nonegalitarian rationing should be introduced for mainly three reasons: (1) the nature of the work may necessitate that some workers get more than an average ration of a particular commodity; 2) egalitarian rationing may in fact discriminate against low income groups because (a) the consumption of the product in question constitutes an appreciably higher share of total spending of the poor than of those of moderate or high income,[13] and (b) the better-off have a greater opportunity of compensation by consuming more expensive substitutes; and (3) unequal distribution of stocks at introduction, thus opportunity to rearrange distribution of available produce not only according to the power of the purse, but also according to the initial distribution of stocks.[14]

The rationing of bread may become necessary as a result of the shortage of shipping facilities (in practice, although rationed after the war, bread was left unrationed during the war for morale and other reasons).[15] Usually, manual workers require more bread as an energy food, and egalitarian rations would cause greater hardship for the poor than for the better-off. A prudent rationing of bread should provide higher quotas for the manual workers. If the higher bread ration were only given to the wage-earner, workers' large families would still be at a disadvantage. To mitigate the situation, relatively high rations should be allowed for children in general. Rations should be differentiated among various members of the work force; for productivity considerations for example, heavy workers, like miners, should get higher rations than other manual laborers.

An important consideration is the likely repercussion of a cut in bread consumption on the consumption of other foodstuffs. While consumption of a substitute like potatoes would probably increase, such a development would create no difficulty as the supply of potatoes is abundant and could easily be augmented. (In fact, the proposal of substantial admixture of potato flour in bread in order to economize on wheat was really equivalent to the rationing of wheat bread). Measures to cut consumption of bread were likely to intensify demand pressures for other goods, and rationing would have to be extended to goods which were more or less close substitutes for bread.

Kalecki argued that the burden of low income groups could be relieved if the prices of goods included in the point scheme were cut. Such action would enable persons who could not afford to utilize their ration to purchase more. However, if the supply of food points were constant, rations would have to be curtailed. In wartime bread consumption was considerably higher than in peacetime, as the population thus compensated for the deficiency in protein foods. A lower bread ration could be imposed without great hardships if some portion of the shipping space economized thereby could be appropriated for increased imports of cheese or dehydrated meats.

Even ruling out increased imports of cheese and meat, the bread situation could be eased somewhat by differential rationing of meat. In fact, Kalecki argued that a particular form of differential meat rationing was already in effect. Restaurant meals were not rationed, and most workers had canteens at their work places. Actually, people who had their meals in restaurants and canteens benefited from a differential ration of meat (apart from a moderate price). Such a situation was hardly equitable. Canteens might be considered a substitute for differential rationing in favor of manual workers, but even here the rationing was of haphazard character, since not all workers (e.g., miners and agricultural laborers) were able to use these facilities. The situation could be rectified by making it mandatory for all to surrender meat coupons in restaurants and canteens and to use the meat saved for increasing uniformly the rations of manual workers; i.e., shifting a certain amount of meat consumption from the better-off to the workers. Differential rationing of meat would be useful in saving shipping space, even if bread would remain unrationed (i.e., higher meat rations for workers would probably reduce considerably bread consumption). On the other hand, those generally eating out were unlikely to compensate the reduction in their consumption of meat by appreciably increasing consumption of bread. They might rather direct their spending to other goods which, in turn, might require some further expansion of the scope of rationing. (Kalecki 1942c, pp. 215-17.)

Retail distribution of fuel was one of the most intricate and controversial problems and a key bottleneck in nonfood consumer goods' distribution.[16] As the war progressed it was increasingly clear that the measures adopted to cope with the shortages of coal were insufficient to balance demand and supply. Stocks were likely to fall to intolerably low levels.[17] Without substantial increase in coal production, it became obvious—as Kalecki argued— that rationing was the missing link in the system of distribution.[18]

One of the big problems was to design a scheme for the distribution of fuel that would provide sufficient fuel for people in large houses without particularly favoring them in comparison to people in small houses. The fuel requirement of a family is not necessarily proportionate to the number of members of the household, as it depends to a certain extent on the number of habitable rooms. Generally, the better-off households have a relatively higher per capita dwelling space. Those families are likely to be in possession of larger stocks of clothing and may thus, with less hardship, abstain from the purchase of new clothing. In fact, a satisfactory solution to fuel rationing could be devised by combining it with the scheme of footwear and clothing rationing.

William Beveridge had suggested that older people and invalids should be able to use clothing coupons for fuel purposes. Following Beveridge, F. A. Burchardt proposed that this scheme be extended, and that fuel and clothing coupons be interchangeable. (Beveridge n.d.; Burchardt 1942, pp. 193-97.) The poor would be permitted to use "surplus" fuel coupons to purchase clothes; the rich, clothing coupons for buying fuel. Such a combined rationing by points would avoid differential rationing of each category taken separately and permit construction of a scheme which would cut down the import of materials and would not interfere with coal consumption. Kalecki elaborated on the proposed scheme of mutual substitution, concentrating on the problem of fixing the point relation between clothing and coal. (Kalecki 1942i, p. 326.)

Let a denote the number of clothing coupons representing a moderate reduction of the then prevailing level; x, the unknown number of coupons to be increased for coal. Thence, $a+x$ denotes the total number of interchangeable coupons for clothing and coal. Assume further that the amount of fuel per coupon is represented by y. A poor man will be unable to reduce his consumption of clothing, therefore, his fuel consumption will be xy. Let b denote the level at which xy is fixed, so that $xy=b$. A very rich man may choose not to spend any coupons on clothing and apply all his coupons to fuel. His purchases would amount to $(a+x)y$. With the constraint that a rich man's purchases of fuel should not exceed that of the poor by more than m per cent, the second equation is: $(a+x)y=b[1+(m/100)]$. Solving the simultaneous equations, we obtain: $x=a(100/m)$ and $y=(b/a)(m/100)$. If, for instance, $m=50$ per cent, then $x=2a$ and $y=(1/2)(b/a)$. The value b of the fuel purchases per head of a poor household must be fixed so as to balance the total demand for and available supply of fuel for civilian use. In addition this scheme resolves the difficulties of households with many children which usually need more clothes and less fuel, enabling them to use the coupons to their advantage: more on clothes and less on fuels.

The number of clothing-fuel coupons that should be allowed to children should depend primarily on two principal considerations: (1) large households require less fuel per capita if they heat only one or two rooms; and (2) children require more clothes and footwear, which is accounted for in the scheme devised by Kalecki. Some allowances for differences in climatic conditions of various regions could be made by varying the number of clothing-fuel coupons geographically. Also, in the clothing-fuel scheme the hardships due to diversity of climatic conditions would be lessened somewhat by the opportunity of purchasing less clothing and more fuel. (Kalecki 1942c, p. 217; 1942i, pp. 325-28.)

While the rationing scheme of total retail spending is rather comprehensive, it does not fully solve the critical food problem. An individual pattern of preferred expenditure depends, *inter alia,* on the initial distribution of power to demand and initial distribution of stocks of various commodities. An individual whose total spending in shops is limited, say, to 25/- per week exercises choice about the composition of his purchases: (Worswick 1942, pp. 33 ff.) he may spend nearly all of it on food, especially if he is fortunate to possess a fairly large stock of durables, or semidurables. If the choices are overwhelmingly in favor of foodstuffs, food consumption may not decline; food stocks may be depleted; and the critical depletion and food prices may rise. Such a development may be counteracted, not only by retaining the specific rationing of foodstuffs in addition to the general rationing of retail expenditures, but also by the rationing scheme that is differentiated by the introduction of food and nonfood coupons.

But what should be the level of the food expenditure ration? Given the marked deficiency in food imports and without a considerable increase in domestic food production, stocks of foodstuffs must decline. This critical development may be prevented by curtailing the total spending on food. A rough estimate suggested that 12/6 per week per adult and 8/- per child was the level of food expenditure ration required to keep the demand in balance with the then current value of food imports. (Kalecki 1941h, p. 104.) However, even if the aggregate food spending were brought into balance with the value of food import, the food problem would not be entirely resolved. The resulting composition of food spending might be such as to require disproportionately high demand in terms of the critical shipping space, one of the major bottlenecks. Nevertheless, specific rationing of crucial products would probably suffice in general to allow for the shortage of shipping space constraint.

While food rationing expanded, the extraordinarily intricate problem of retail distribution of nonfood articles during prevailing shortages remained to be tackled. In fact, nonfood rationing did not expand after the introduction of the point system for clothing and footwear (except for the incorporation of towels, tea towels, and curtains in the clothing scheme). The most urgent bottlenecks in nonfood consumption were (1) household goods, and (2) long-distance traveling.

1. Rationing of household goods had to be supplemented by licensing. Rationing could take account only of the calculated requirements arising out of replacement demand for durables in existing households. But adequate supplies had to be provided for the newly married and for victims of bombing. The distribution of household goods would have to be based on (a) a small personal point or value ration, corresponding to the wear-and-tear requirements; and (b) licensing in special cases. While it would be fairly easy to operate such a scheme for new production (which overwhelmingly consisted of utility lines), its extension to merchandise in stock would encounter considerable difficulties as the merchandise was not standardized and coupon control would be hardly effective. One way out was simply to leave the existing inventories outside the rationing scheme (indeed, a procedure followed for expediency reasons by the Board of Trade which licensed only newly manufactured utility furniture). Kalecki objected to this solution, primarily because (a) it was unfair, as everybody with sufficiently large means could buy from the existing stocks at high prices; and (b) the inclusion of existing stocks, at least partly in the rationing and licensing scheme would allow for greater reduction in current consumption or for storing up emergency reserves of household goods to be distributed among victims of future bombings.

Kalecki suggested that a government agency earmark household articles suitable for mass consumption in shops, pay a reasonable price to the dealers for them, and fix for them prices comparable to those of utility goods[19] (which are likely to be lower than those paid to the dealers). The goods so procured would be made available for the rationing and licensing scheme (reducing the requirements on current production) or stored for emergency purposes. The proceeds from the sale of these goods would be transferred to the account of the government agency that would control the shops by taking periodic inventories of specific merchandise.

2. Traveling is not easily controlled by rationing. The demand for traveling services fluctuates widely. The natural system for equitable curtailment of travel is comprehensive licensing, but the administration of such a scheme is cumbersome. In fact, travel rationing was not as important as the following might suggest. Travel was generally considered extremely uncomfortable in view of the bombing, blackouts, and the like. The traveling population consisted primarily of soldiers and workers visiting families and girlfriends. Any stringent rationing on traveling might have discriminated against those working (or serving) at great distances from their family circle. Train services had been progressively reduced after the outbreak of the war. By fall of 1941, trains became so overcrowded that it was more reasonable to reduce the number of passengers before introducing further cuts on the frequency of services. While rationing of travel was being considered by the government, objections were raised on the grounds that the administrative barriers would be virtually insuperable and the savings would be small, as the bulk of long-distance traveling was done by servicemen. A campaign was launched asking the population to abstain from "unnecessary" travel, and some minor restrictions were introduced (withdrawal of restaurant and sleeping cars, restrictions on luggage, and prohibition of servicemen from traveling on public holidays, and later, in 1943, cheap day-fare tickets were abolished). Probably the measures contained somewhat the traveling urge, but they were impotent in preventing the number of passenger journeys from soaring. (Hancock and Gowing 1949, pp. 480-90.)

The bottleneck in traveling was mainly attacked by reducing the number of trains and suspending some bus lines. Attempts were made to cut out as much dispensable traffic as possible. Passenger trains became overcrowded, services less frequent, and travelers either had to put up with the discomfort or cut down on traveling. But the discouragement (including higher fares) was not effective enough, and the burden fell inequitably on passengers. As the situation became more strained, the methods used for economy of transport became unsatisfactory.

Kalecki proposed a combined licensing-rationing scheme. He stressed that the scheme would not be easy to implement, but seemed practicable. The licensing part of the scheme provided that

(a) workmen's tickets would not be affected by rationing; (b) holders of season tickets could renew them, and those who did not possess such tickets at the time of the institution of the scheme and who required them for transportation to and from work could obtain them; (c) people who traveled regularly in connection with their duties, but not frequently enough to warrant purchase of a normal season ticket, would get cheaper season tickets of a special type; and (d) for irregular traveling on duty, emergency tickets would be provided. With the exception of soldiers, the rest of traveling would be rationed by distance. The scheme should provide for a relatively high personal ration, since the demand for some traveling services was high, while a large share of the population traveled little. In some cases, even a relatively high ration might involve serious hardships. Thus the scheme would permit the substitution of other non-food and perhaps also some food coupons for traveling, (but not in reverse order) at established rates of substitution. Such an arrangement would make the traveling scheme more elastic, while, simultaneously, more traveling would entail a sacrifice in other spheres of rationed consumption. Traveling could be reduced both by cutting the basic travel ration and by increasing the rate of exchange of the other coupons to be surrendered for a given number of traveling coupons. Owing to the uneven demand for traveling, transferability of coupons had to be prevented. Admittedly, the proposal involved substantial administrative work, but with further straining of transportation services, something along these lines would become unavoidable. (Kalecki 1942i, pp. 325-28.)

Rationing and Price Control

While it can be argued that price control without rationing is not effective in combating wartime inflation, the contention that rationing makes price control superfluous is questionable. The problem can be examined by proceeding from the simple case of allocation by rationing of a single article of consumption and then turning to the more complex one of the point rationing scheme. (Kalecki 1944e, pp. 29-32.)

A given commodity is rationed in order to prevent its price from rising while distribution is maintained at a level corresponding to the available current supplies. If the ration is too high in relation to the available supply, the price will tend to advance. Yet, in some cases, prices may go up after introduction of rationing, even if the ration has been made equal to the available supply (e.g., when rationing is instituted when there is a "demand push" tendency for inflationary price advances). Assuming that rations have been properly matched with available supply and that rationing brings into balance the quantities demanded and supplied, prices may nevertheless go up for a *different reason.* To a certain extent institution of rationing reduces the sensitiveness of buyers to price differences between alternate sources of supply. Rationing may cause the market to become considerably more imperfect; competition becomes less intense, the consumer less choosy, and the price may rise although the imbalance between demand and supply has been removed. Kalecki argued that, to cope with such a situation, price control is required.

If there are good reasons for supporting rationing with price control in order to maintain the price level, price control is even more necessary if price reduction is the goal. For example, this would be the case when rationing is introduced after the price of a given product has risen appreciably in proportion to its prime costs under the pressure of demand. Under such circumstances rationing alone cannot be expected to do the trick.

Rationing is usually combined with a system of allocation of supplies to firms in certain fixed proportions. The firms cannot strive at increasing sales by competing between themselves. But even if rations have been fixed somewhat below the level of available supply, it is very uncertain whether price would decline. The reason is, as noted, that rationing tends to increase market imperfections and prevents the forces of competition from pushing the price down. In order to reduce the inflated price to the level which shows a "normal" ratio to prime cost, rationing must be supported by price control. However, if prices are reduced considerably below the level they had previously reached, the quantity demanded might rise, stimulated by those who, at higher prices, abstained from fully using their coupons. This may necessitate some reduction in the ration. In general the ration must be somewhat below current supply at the price which prevailed at the time of putting the rationing scheme into effect.

The same conclusions arrived at in the simple case of rationing of a single commodity are applicable to the point system of rationing. The ration in terms of points must match the current supplies in terms of points. Rationing should be accompanied by price control, if prices are to be kept at the level prevailing when rationing was instituted. Price control is mandatory if the aim is to reduce prices below that level. The problem now is complicated by dealing with an aggregate of commodities. Given that demand and supply are equilibrated by rationing for all commodities in terms of points, it does not follow that such a "partial" equilibrium exists for each commodity in question, taken separately. In case of disequilibrium for a particular product, demand and supply may be adjusted and brought into equilibrium either by the automatic movement of uncontrolled prices or by variations in point values, i.e., the number of points that must be surrendered to buy a unit of a given commodity.

If the equilibrating adjustments are left to the price mechanism, it is by no means certain that the price index of the commodity group considered would remain stable. Examine, for instance the case of only two commodities *A* and *B* in the point scheme. Assume that the total number of points in the ration is divided equally between these two commodities and so is their value in terms of money. Suppose now that demand shifts from *A* to *B*, while the supply of either commodity is fixed. In addition, assume that *A* has closer substitutes among the commodities outside the group than *B*. Under such conditions, the relative price rise of *B* will be higher than the relative price decline of *A*, and the price index of the group will record an increase. Contrariwise, when demand shifts from *B* to *A*, there will be a fall in the price index of the group. However, the presence of a factor which raises the price index of the group when relative demand shifts from one commodity to another cannot be ignored. So far it was assumed that price changes have to be such that the volume of sales of either item would remain invariable. In fact, that will be the case only of the item in greater demand if its supply cannot be augmented. On the other hand, the price of the less demanded item may not decline at all, or at least not sufficiently to prevent a fall in the volume of its sales. The decrease in demand may cause a curtailment in supply or an increase in inventories. It would be preferable to stabilize the price index of the group by exercising price control and *varying* the relative point values until equilibrium of supply and demand is attained for all goods. It would be advisable to supplement this measure by changes in the relations of the controlled prices, especially when a considerable number of consumers do not use fully the coupons to which they are entitled and thus are not subject to the influence of alterations in relative point values.[20]

Price control *by itself* offers no answer to inflation. When the state fixes prices by fiat or promulgates legal restrictions on price increases, it might be relieving a spectacular symptom, but it is not curing the disease, if at the decreed price supply and demand do not match. It is always useful and in most cases necessary to supplement rationing by price control. Kalecki argued that this conclusion is of some practical importance for the postwar transitional period. As long as some goods are very scarce, both rationing and price control must be maintained. Even after the acute and prolonged shortages are eradicated, and rationing becomes obsolete, price control does not cease to be a relic of a war economy. Price control "may be usefully applied for pressing down prices which are 'high' owing to a considerable degree of market imperfection or the existence of industrial monopolies." (Kalecki, 1944e, p. 32.)

PART THREE

GROWTH, PLANNING, AND CONSUMPTION

Postwar (1945-1967)

DURING THE DECADE preceding his final return to Poland in 1955, Kalecki served the French and Polish governments and the International Labour Office for brief periods and then moved to New York for an extended stay as a leading economist for the United Nations.

His first assignment after leaving the OIS was in Paris, where he remained long enough to prepare a report for the French government on comprehensive rationing and control of the postwar economy. In March of that same year, 1945, the Kaleckis moved to Montreal for a stay of some fifteen months while Kalecki conducted research on problems of full employment and postwar economic reconstruction at the ILO. The Canadian period must have been a relatively happy time for the Kaleckis, for they always spoke with fondness of Montreal and its people. He was often invited to lead seminar discussions at McGill and the University of Montreal.

In July of 1946, Kalecki accepted an invitation of the Polish government to become economic advisor to the Central Planning Office and the Ministry of Finance, a post he held until October of that year. Upon this first return to Poland following the war, the Kaleckis were deeply distressed by the devastation of the country and the decimation of its population. Families on both sides and most friends had been killed by the Nazis, and the effect on Kalecki was indelible. Even two decades later, when speaking of Nazi atrocities, his usually restrained language gave way to profound feelings. He spoke of the war period as "the most ghastly years of contemporary humanity—a time when the bestiality of civilized cannibals had reached its apogee." (Kalecki 1964cc, p. 116.) By the end of 1946, Kalecki left Warsaw for New York, where he would remain for the next eight years.

With the consent of the Polish government, Kalecki had accepted a post in the Economic Department of the United Nations Secretariat. From his arrival until 1954, he served as deputy director of the department's Division of Economic Stability and Development. More specifically, he was head of the Economic Stability Section of the division and, in that capacity, exerted a direct influence on the studies prepared during the period he was guiding the section. The most important of these studies were:

1. *Survey of Inflationary and Deflationary Tendencies* (Sept. 1947)
2. *Post-War Shortages of Food and Coal* (July 1948)
3. *Inflationary and Deflationary Tendencies*, 1946-48 (July 1949)
4. *World Economic Report 1948* (1949), chapter 2
5. *World Economic Report 1949-50* (1951), pt. 1
6. *World Economic Report 1950-51* (1952), pt. 1
7. *World Economic Report 1951-52* (1953), pt. 1
8. *World Economic Report 1952-53* (1954), pt. 1[1]

Also during this period, Kalecki prepared a number of internal documents for the UN's Economic and Social Council (Ecosoc) and its various committees and commissions.

Once again, his lack of diplomacy and distaste for compromise made life very difficult. He was often in opposition to the UN authorities. Finally he resigned in protest against discrimination on grounds of alleged political beliefs. Even so, he remained in a loose relationship with the UN following his departure from New York. He was chairman of the Polish delegation to the 1963 UN conference in Geneva on applications of science and technology to development, and his reputation was instrumental in obtaining some UN support for the advanced course in economic planning held in Warsaw for economists from underdeveloped countries.

Despite the frustrations and difficulties he encountered towards the end of his UN service, and although the tragic McCarthy witch hunt affected personally many of his friends and colleagues and distressed him profoundly, Kalecki's years at the UN were not totally unhappy ones. The Kaleckis enjoyed living in cosmopolitan New York, and they traveled throughout the United States, appreciating particularly its natural beauty. For a while at least, Kalecki also was greatly diverted by the many "stupidities" of economists "in residence," and he seemed to enjoy confronting and confounding various diplomats and officials. He was pleased by the visits of foreign economists who stopped off at the UN, often for the sole purpose of meeting and debating with him. Additionally, his section at one time was composed of an interesting and well-integrated group of people, considered to be something of an elite at the UN.

These fringe benefits were not enough to keep Kalecki happy in his UN work, however, and early in 1955 he returned to Poland to stay. The remaining years of his life were spent first as an active participant in the economic affairs of the country (from 1956 to 1959), next as a teacher and research worker (from 1960 to 1967), and finally (from 1968 to 1970, his last three years) as a despairing realist who had lost his last illusions. This final period will be discussed at the close of the book.

Kalecki arrived in Poland believing that, despite the problems and distortions of the recent past, the socialist system was potentially an advantageous one, which could be made to work better in the interest of the broad masses. Within a short time he had plunged into work designed to reinforce this belief. The Central Qualifications Commission in 1956 nominated him professor—his first academic title—and in February of 1957 he became one of the deputy chairmen of the Economic Council (Oskar Lange, chairman)—an advisory body, consisting mostly of academics, to the Council of Ministers. The same year he was nominated chairman of the Commission for the Perspective Plan (a part of the Planning Commission), where he remained until 1960.

The mood of the country was propitious for reform. Within a year of Kalecki's return, the rumbles of the Polish October were heard. Workers were dissatisfied with the low standard of living, and the intellectuals were decrying the political and cultural repression. The Poznan riots, essentially a strike-type revolt by the working class against all sorts of material and moral deprivations, were an impulse for shedding the shackles of Stalinism and for reform leading to a better, more humane, enlightened, and democratic future. The slogan "Polish road to socialism" was coined, meaning that not all countries had to follow in the footsteps of the U.S.S.R. Each country could adapt its way of reaching socialism according to its own cultural, natural, and economic endowments and heritage.

In the political sphere, the year 1956 also marked the return to power of Wladyslaw Gomulka. Although an old-time Communist, Gomulka was strongly nationalistic and had been kept under house arrest during the Stalinist period. His ascension to power brought bright hopes of an end to police terror, an enlargement of horizons for cultural activity, an improvement of the living standard and more rationality in economic life, a return to private farming, some reconciliation with the Church, and greater relaxation in international affairs.

The economic sphere likewise was in ferment. The New Course, which had been initiated in 1954-55 to combat the increasing, serious dislocations, was essentially a partial restructuring and a slowing down of economic activity. The Polish economists, even before the advent of the Poznan riots and the return of Gomulka, were revolting against the traditional system. A milestone was reached when the Second Congress of Economists was held in June 1956. Economics professors, many of whom had been among the most conformist supporters of the regime, now denounced the basic foundations of the Six-Year Plan (1950-55) and the bottlenecks and dislocations it brought on. They especially decried the centralized economic system, attributing the country's problems to such "villains" as centralization, lack of freedom, cramped initiative, formalism, dogmatism, and apologetics of socialism. Against these impassioned denunciations and the calls for liberty, initiative, and improvisation in economic thinking, Kalecki's matter-of-fact and restrained statement on economic dynamics in a socialist economy, notwithstanding its enormous influence on his fellow economists, made little public impact. It contained the most essential aspects of his later developed theory of economic growth in a socialist economy, which stressed the contest between investment and consumption—probably one of the most crucial issues of the Polish economy.

For about two years after the 1956 congress, there was much relatively free discussion among Polish economists. Many preached reform of the system of functioning, some of them even going so far as to liken the socialist economic system to laissez faire capitalism. Kalecki staunchly defended central planning as something quite different from countercyclical intervention of modern capitalism (which some advocated).

His work points the way to understanding the interdependence between growth strategy and functioning system. He warned against too much faith in an incentive system for managing the economy as some sort of panacea for accelerating economic growth and raising welfare.[2]

In 1957-58 Kalecki and his staff at the Commission of the Perspective Plan worked out what is probably the most exemplary long-term (1961-75) so-called perspective plan ever devised for a socialist economy. The plan was a practical embodiment of his theory of growth under socialism. It showed how the rate of growth of national income in Poland could be determined throughout a fifteen-year period in which consumption would be expected to rise and the barriers of foreign trade, investment organization, raw materials, and labor would be alleviated. This plan was sharply attacked at a party meeting in October 1958 which was followed by various meetings in academia where the party's reproaches were echoed. The Polish leaders strongly upheld economic voluntarism. Super-optimism was the keynote of the period; any mention of barriers and ceilings was regarded as defeatist. At the end of 1958 it was already clear that Kalecki's perspective plan and the key targets for the first Five-Year Plan segment (1961-65) would not be adopted. A more optimistic perspective plan would be prepared. However, even the man in charge of this second—and unrealistic—plan paid post-mortem tribute to Kalecki's contributions in perspective planning: "At the forefront is Kalecki's decisive role in formulating the first perspective plan of Polish economic development for 1961-75. Kalecki's four-year work in this field can also be equated with the formation of perspective planning and its methods and with improvement of both endogenous and exogenous coordination principles. While he headed the Central Commission for the Perspective Plan he contributed to educating and inspiring a considerable cadre of researchers and policy-oriented personnel interested in perspective planning." (Secomski 1971, p. 190.)

By 1959 the policy makers had forsaken rationality altogether and had reverted to "hurrah planning." Constraints on the growth rate were disregarded under the spell of optimism engendered by the good performance in 1956-57. Although Kalecki remained with the Commission of the Perspective Plan for another year beyond 1959, all concerned knew that it was a *pro forma* function. The end of 1958 had marked the beginning of the erosion of his influence.

In fact, the role of economic advisors in general flourished only briefly in Poland, mainly during the years 1956-57. Thereafter, the influence of professional economists of independent thought was steadily on the decline as sycophants climbed over them to positions of greater voice in the nation's affairs. In the political arena, Gomulka had begun to distrust the spontaneous movement that had elevated him to power, and his regime slowly became increasingly totalitarian. As post-Gomulka revelations indicate, he would not tolerate disagreement, and only "yes-men" could effect any palpable influence on the course of events. *Par contre* those who stubbornly defended truth, efficiency, and social interest, irrespective of the interests of the party machinery, increasingly fell into disgrace. Although the Economic Council had served well during its first two years, at least as a means of dialogue between academics and policy makers, it led only a moribund existence from 1959 until its formal demise in 1963.

After 1960, Kalecki in effect retired from public life, retaining only two advisory posts with the government. He continued as scientific advisor to the chairman of the Planning Commission, from which he resigned in 1964 following Gomulka's brutal attack at the Fourth Party Congress on Kalecki's proposals for the 1966-70 plan, and as chairman of the Polish delegation to the Economic Commission of the Council of Mututal Economic Assistance (CMEA), which he did not relinquish until 1968. For the next several years he devoted himself almost exclusively to teaching and research—scholarly activities that had engaged his attention even before he left his government posts.

Beginning in 1955, Kalecki had assumed leadership of a research group in the Economics Department of the Polish Academy of Sciences to investigate modern capitalism. These investigations resulted in a four-issue series entitled *Studia z zakresu koniunktury wspolczesnego kapitalizmu* (Studies of Business Cycles in Modern Capitalism), published between 1957 and 1960. The main topics included business cycles in the U.S.A. and Western Europe in 1950-55; structural transformation of capitalist economies; the 1956-58 recessions; and the role of capital export from developed to developing economies.

Since 1959, Kalecki, along with Professors Lange and Bobrowski, had also conducted a seminar on socioeconomic problems of the third world, involving participation by a large number of research workers and staff members of the Academy of Sciences, Warsaw University, and Warsaw's Central School for Planning and Statistics (SGPiS). He was also the moving spirit of the Center for Underdeveloped Economies, formed during this period to focus the attention of specialists from Poland and elsewhere on problems of the third world. Although Kalecki retired from the Academy in 1961 to devote himself to teaching at SGPiS, where he held classes and seminars on modern capitalism and the theory of growth in a socialist economy, his interest in third-world problems continued unabated. When an English-language course for planners of the third world was initiated in 1963 in Warsaw under auspices of the United Nations, he became a leading figure in the endeavor.

This concern about the development of the third world had occupied Kalecki's attention for many years, tracing back to a lecture in Mexico in 1953, when he outlined his theoretical concept of underdevelopment and the financing of development. He later reviewed, reformulated, and elaborated on this basic theme, and the ideas thrashed out at the center often provided the impetus for his formulations. The needs of the UN planning course also constituted a motivating factor, leading him to attempt to clarify the fundamental differences between growth under different social systems. Additionally, part of the work at the Center for Underdeveloped Economies consisted of adapting Kalecki's ideas of long-term planning to the specific conditions of a mixed economy.

Kalecki apparently enjoyed his teaching responsibilities during this period, judging by the anecdote recalled by one of his associates. He was a liberal grader. When asked why, he replied that, in comparison with their instructors, no matter how little they knew, the students were rather knowledgeable.

Throughout these years of retirement from public life, Kalecki continued an active research career. He elaborated in two successive editions his theory of growth in a socialist economy, and he published several articles on developing economies. In two important contributions to the *Economic Journal* (1962 and 1968), he advanced his theory of modern capitalism.

This period also saw the fruition of a long-time interest in pure mathematics. He had been fifty-nine when his first publication in this field appeared, a study (1958g) on the borderline between the theory of numbers and probability, reflecting his particular fascination with the theory of numbers. In 1964, when Kalecki was sixty-five, a subsequent publication appeared, dealing entirely with the theory of numbers. From then on, he devoted increasingly more time to pure mathematics, particularly the properties of prime numbers, and contributed rather regularly to scholarly mathematical periodicals (1965e, 1965m, 1967i, 1967k, 1968g, 1969c, 1969d, and 1971c). Mrs. Kalecki recalls that his interest in mathematics was born of his disappointment in the uncertainties of economics. He was probably reacting also to his disillusionment with the lack of influence exerted by economics on the practical policies of both capitalist and socialist countries. At least in mathematics one knew where one stood. In a way it was a form of escapism from the hard realities of economic life.

Kalecki's work in pure mathematics has been evaluated recently by two Polish mathematicians (Schinzel 1970, pp. 1021-22; Oderfeld and Schinzel, n.d.), who appraise his contributions as pertaining to theorems of a central character, and give him a lasting place in the history of mathematics. They were particularly impressed that the first attempts at pure mathematics had been made successfully by a man in his sixties, for it is well known that modern mathematics is a science in which the first serious results are customarily achieved at a relatively young age. Kalecki's case is particularly uncommon because, in this field, he was an amateur—in the most valid sense of the term.

Although wielding no influence with the policy makers, Kalecki continued to be supremely interested in Poland's economic affairs. His analyses of the 1961-65 and 1966-70 five-year plans are full of perception and understanding of the vast and complex relationships among various sectors, departments, and areas of the economy. He criticized the plans for being unrealistic and for assuming excessive growth of investment and de facto insufficient growth of consumption—and he was upbraided at the highest level for his incessant predictions of gloom. Had Gomulka listened to Kalecki, would his own fate have been different?

The Polish leadership "compensated" Kalecki for his removal from influence on economic policy by giving him academic honors. In 1957 he had been elected corresponding member of the Academy of Sciences; in 1966 he was made a full member. In 1964 he and Lange were honored at a Jubilee Celebration of their sixty-fifth and sixtieth birthdays, respectively. Commemorative books, including contributions from leading economists from many lands, were issued. Also in 1964, Kalecki was granted honorary doctorates in economics at Warsaw University and at the Higher School of Economics at Wroclaw.

Poland even attempted to use Kalecki as a "product for export," but he never really succumbed to the implied flattery. This was one of the reasons for his resignation from the UN course for third-world planners. He did serve as advisor to the Indian government in 1959-60 and later was sent to Cuba in a similar capacity, but he was not satisfied in either case that he had exerted any perceptible influence. In addition, he attended a few international meetings. As examples, he read a paper on long-term planning at the plenary session of an international conference in Geneva in 1963; addressed the reunion of Latin American Schools of Economics in Mexico in June 1965; and offered a background paper for the May 1968 symposium on the influence of Karl Marx on contemporary thought, organized by UNESCO.

Despite his country's efforts to honor him, Kalecki could neither be "impressed" nor "bought off" by merit badges. Like many other economists, he would have traded them gladly for a voice in policy-making.

XII

GROWTH AND PLANNING

Background

•

In the West, Kalecki is mainly known for his contributions to macrodynamics. His work on growth in centrally planned economies is also a major contribution. In many ways it was developed in a manner similar to the theory of modern capitalist economy. It was also born in response to a need to improve the lot of the common man and from close observation of economic realities. Undeniably, by the mid-1950s the population of the U.S.S.R. and Eastern Europe had endured fearful deprivation in the cause of building "socialism" (in the first case for more than three decades, and in the second for almost ten years). These sacrifices were all the more objectionable because, in some cases at least, they were avoidable.

The mismanagement of the economy gave rise to serious disproportions, retardation of the long-term rate of economic growth, marked fluctuations in economic activity, and incalculable adverse effects on social consciousness, quality of life, and human performance. Moreover, to Kalecki and others the system was irrational, for they considered socialism as a system "which makes possible a full and rational utilization of the economic surplus for the benefit of the present and future consumption of the working population." (Kalecki 1965f, p. 60.)

In looking at the system that evolved in the U.S.S.R. and Eastern Europe, some of the basic questions are: does the process of rapid economic development really require such a low and stagnant (and sometimes declining) standard of living? How could the development of the economy be planned so as to find a reasonable compromise of the consumption-accumulation dilemma when such a dilemma arises? How to achieve a steadily increasing rate of growth together with a maximum possible increasing consumption standard? What was the purpose and who were the beneficiaries of economic growth? How efficient was the utilization of resources, even when they were more or less fully utilized? The advances Kalecki made in paving the way to answering these questions will be found in the following chapters.

Kalecki's immediate inspiration for the theory of growth in a socialist economy was his analysis of the current economic situation of the U.S.S.R. and Eastern Europe during the years he headed the Economic Stability Section at the United Nations. A faint *esquisse* of the idea can be detected in the analysis in *World Economic Report*, 1952-53 and 1953-54.[1] Upon his return to Poland, Kalecki had already formulated the initial outline of the theory of growth in a socialist economy. An excellent opportunity of developing and refining the theory further in closer contact with practice presented itself during the years of his close involvement with the Planning Commission. In his own section, while preparing the perspective plan, he could put into practice what he preached in theory, given certain constraints. At the same time the theory benefited at further stages of refinement from closer contact with the inexorable exigencies of practice.

Kalecki viewed the theory of growth of the socialist economy as the most important part of the economics of socialism. This theory is based on the tenet that the aim of the socialist economy is to raise living standards. But this is insufficient to construct a growth theory. A rise in the relative proportion of investment in national income tends to improve consumption in the long run, but it affects it adversely in the immediate future. A compromise decision to this dilemma is based on a political decision.

> In the theory of growth we take as given the government's comparative valuation of consumption in the near future and in the long run which underlies such decisions. We have also to assume ceilings on the rise of growth in single branches of the economy arising out of such technical and organizational factors as limited natural resources, the time required to introduce new techniques and to train experienced personnel, etc. The theory of growth built on these foundations is a purely deductive discipline. But these deductions do not determine fully the course of economic development since the "external" factors just mentioned play a very important part. Thus in the sphere of pure economics the theory of growth is basically an exact science but this does not exhaust all the issues involved in the problem of economic development. On the other hand, those factors which do not enter into it, being assumed as given, are and will be intrinsically disputable. (Kalecki 1964z, p. 65.)

He noted that not only do sharp differences exist in the sphere where they are inevitable, but also unfortunately in the growth theory proper, which is basically an exact science. This is owing partly to being on the threshold of developing an extremely complex discipline and to the fact that even its most essential issues have not been mastered. Also in the argumentation "we often fail, putting it mildly, to meet the highest standards of precision in the formulation and argument." (Kalecki 1964z, p. 65.) Discussants tend "to present as axioms assertions which in fact require a proof and which, on closer examination, do not always turn out to be tenable." (Kalecki 1964z, p. 65.)

Let us now digress briefly to an examination of the growth strategy adopted by Stalin at the threshold of the 1930s, later transplanted to Eastern Europe, and its results, in order to provide a background for Kalecki's theoretical exposition and practical advice.

On Soviet Growth Strategy and Planning

Among the canons of the Soviet growth strategy was the postulate of industrialization (or of a specific pattern of industrialization) as an end in itself. The division of national product (into accumulation and consumption and their main constituents) and the structure of nonconsumable goods (capital formation) were subjected to this task.

Soviet development was not only distinguished by its insistence on industrialization; among its distinctive features, the priority of producer goods industry (heavy industry) was a hallmark. The tenet was not development of industry in general, but development of specific branches—those producing producer goods, rather than those producing consumer goods. The rule was that, to ensure steady growth, the rate of increase of producer goods must always outpace that of consumer goods. (Cf. Kalecki 1967o, 1968e.)

Forced industrialization required a massive, swift, and expedient redirection of resources. This goal was considered to be best accomplished through centralized disposal and direct intervention, rather than through inducement and use of economic instruments. Centralization of economic activity was evolved as a strategic device for mobilizing and concentrating resources on selected crucial targets, preventing their dispersion on other uses, and imposing the value scale of the system's directors on producers and consumers, at least for consequential decisions. Planning was equated with daily operational management and intervention. Administrative measures, commands, and direct distribution of resources were characteristic of the system. This was accompanied by overdevelopment of the bureaucratic apparatus.

The Soviet industrialization strategy adopted an "unorthodox development sequence" by concentrating on the preferential growth and lead of the capital goods industries. (Cf. Erlich 1960; Spulber, ed. 1965; Feiwel 1972.) Stalin uttered the "law of balanced [proportionate] development of the national economy." The remark has been given various interpretations which can probably be reduced to the single statement that, as a result of nationalization of the means of production, the planners are at liberty to predetermine the proportions which should be maintained. However, what the correct proportions are, the degree of determinateness, and, above all, the criteria to be used for determining and assessing them, are not spelled out.

According to the Nestor of Soviet economists, Academician Strumilin, "the law can be reduced to the rule that in conditions of expanded reproduction the growth rate of output of means of production must necessarily, according to the plan, outpace the increase in the production of consumer goods." (Strumilin 1959, p. 243.) The precept can also be restated as a condition to ensure steady (accelerated) growth of the economic system as a whole; that the growth of gross capital formation must always outpace that of gross national product, i.e., the relative share of investment goods in total output must continuously increase, or that capital formation must increase more rapidly than consumption.[2]

To understand the real urgency of the problems facing countries that have served as guinea pigs for a misguided growth strategy, one should examine the consequences of such policies. The manifested "disproportions" and the "New Course" have to be kept in mind as a background for the development of Kalecki's growth theory of a socialist economy.

Disproportions and New Course

Poland, like other countries that came under the Soviet sphere of influence after World War II, mechanically copied the methods of building socialism accepted in the Soviet Union. (Lange 1956.) Soviet economic structure could not be transplanted without grave repercussions to the smaller East European countries, where, in the past, economic development took place under divergent political, economic, social, and environmental circumstances. They were lopsidedly endowed with natural and human resources. The industrialization policy featured maximum reduction of dependence on foreign markets and largely disregarded gains from trade. In particular this had adverse effects on diffusion of advanced technology and thus on the productivity of the system. Imports were viewed mainly as supplementing domestic production or as a reserve in carrying out the strategic tasks of the industrialization program. Exports were considered as a means of financing indispensable imports.

In Poland the Six-Year Plan's (1950-55) goal was to build the country's own base for capital formation relying primarily on its own heavy industry. Production of consumer goods became a subordinate target. The priority of heavy industry was also adopted as the basic principle of Polish industrialization of that period. The stepped-up investment activity of 1952-53 was not merely a continuation of the investment push embarked on in the first year of the Six-Year Plan. Considerably higher rates of expansion of heavy industry were imposed and a sizable part of production apparatus was switched to military production contributing to marked retardation of the long-term growth rates and to serious fluctuations in the rate of economic activity. Lange wrote in 1956 that "those disproportions have grown to such an extent that the national economy is on the verge of collapse." (Lange 1956.) These were the ubiquitous disproportions between development of agriculture and industry; between branches of industry, broadly heavy versus light or consumer-oriented industry; between capital formation (newly created processing capacity) and the supply of raw materials (material base); between investment activity and the capacity of the construction industry and industries supporting investment activity; between sheer quantitative growth of industrial output (extensive growth) and output quality, improvements in production techniques and the cost of production; and between investment in new factories and obsolete and dilapidated equipment in many underprivileged industrial establishments.

The disproportions became most disturbingly apparent in serious difficulties in foreign trade, in lack of sufficient material reserves, and in shortages on the consumer market. But the most serious was the failure to raise living standards, i.e., in Lange's words "in the field which constitutes the social justification of socialist construction." (Lange 1956.)

During the Six-Year Plan period the upsurge of employment and gains in average incomes, owing to the vast industrial transfer from agriculture to industry and construction, produced a moderate average annual increase in the total consumption fund. Real wages per employee declined. However, total employment was growing faster than the decline in real wages. The reported total consumption fund increased. The increased labor participation rate of the members of households previously supported by a single breadwinner somewhat mitigated the situation. Improvement or maintenance of living standards depended to a very large extent on the composition of the household. Freezing or retardation of growth in the standard of living is detrimental to productivity and efficiency of the entire production and distribution process, thereby reducing or destroying the effect aimed at by the very high investment effort. This policy had incalculable adverse effects on productivity owing to lack of technical progress transplanted from abroad or to internally generated and faulty economic organization, etc., resulting in a loss of potential dynamic efficiency.

The paralyzing effects of disproportions and dislocations were by no means confined to Poland. Retardation of growth rates of the national product in many countries of Eastern Europe was probably the most crucial outward demonstration of the need for remedial action. The death of Stalin was only one and probably not the key factor in the adoption of the New Course in economic policy (about 1953). This is not to say that the extent and timing of the shift in economic policy that occurred in Eastern Europe at that time were not influenced by the political situation and social pressures. But I would venture the opinion that the pivotal factor in altering the course was the marked deceleration of growth rates in 1953-54 that could be discerned virtually throughout the area. The timing and intensity of the retardation in growth performance varied significantly among the countries of the bloc, and the attribution of the proximate causes of the phenomenon differed somewhat. The remedial measures adopted were, in turn, conditioned by the relative severity of the disproportions and decline in growth rates, the relative stage of development, the dependence on foreign trade, and a host of other factors. The New Course was more strongly emphasized in some countries than in others. (Cf. Feiwel 1971a.)

The New Course brought into focus some of the problems that, to a varied degree, remained focal, unsettled or half settled, and kept recurring in subsequent years. The New Course was the first installment in a series of shifts in policy of resource allocation that has continued into the 1970s. It also brought to the fore some of the issues with which Kalecki dealt in his theory of growth in a socialist economy—the subject of the next chapter.

XIII

THEORY OF GROWTH[1]

The Framework

IN APPROACHING KALECKI'S WORK on growth in socialist economies, there are two aspects that should be noted: (1) the economic content of Kalecki's argument and its relevance to the pressing problems of the real world; and (2) the techniques he used in formulating and presenting it. From the standpoint of the first the work is pioneering and germinating with ideas. While the fundamentals of the problem are underlined, all its complexities are not treated. Much remains still to be done. Kalecki's accent and emphasis were dictated by the rationale of policies pursued and the exigencies of the day. This somewhat limited the range of subjects, but his basic ideas can be extended and adapted. Looking at the second aspect, one should remember that the purpose of the work was not an exercise in tool-making or in mathematical elegance and sophistication of presentation whatever the advantages of such an approach. While there are some skillful innovations in the use of techniques, it is not here that the contribution lies, and it should not be judged by that standard. Unquestionably, more sophisticated mathematical techniques would have rendered the argument more precise. The important part is the use Kalecki makes of the techniques to help solve the essentials of central problems.

Obviously, there is an overriding preponderance of the first aspect over the second. This again clearly shows Kalecki's approach as an economist. He consciously sacrificed mathematical elegance and precision for economic reality. His focus was on the practical significance of theorizing. Obviously, the benefits are not without costs. But by bringing out the essentials of the problem, he provided an analysis that may serve as a point of departure for applying more elaborate and complicated methods and for enriching the scope of the subject. Whether the underlying realism of Kalecki's theory would not be lost in the process is another question.

If one wishes to stress the technical properties of Kalecki's theory, it should be remembered that it was developed in the second half of the 1950s and early 1960s. At that time it was one of the most original presentations of the vintage approach in world literature. Another important aspect: Kalecki's growth theory educated both professional economists and policy makers in Eastern Europe, and it made economics a science in that part of the world.

In a nutshell, Kalecki uses two equations as a framework for analyzing growth processes and strategies. What follows is a brief introductory statement of the technical framework employed. Kalecki explores at length—but does not confine his analysis to—the relationship among three aggregate variables: (1) the growth rate of national income, denoted by Kalecki as r_t; (2) the capital-output ratio (referred to below as the coefficient of capital intensity), k_t, or in its simplified version denoted as m_t by Kalecki; and (3) the relative share of accumulation in national income (or the saving rate), denoted by Kalecki as i_t.

The capacity of the system to generate growth and the limits to potential expansion are ultimately governed by the dynamic forces of technical progress, including organizational changes and the rate of increase of the labor supplied. Technical progress is usually, although not exclusively, injected into the economic process via investment which, in turn, creates the potential capacity to produce. Taking advantage of the capacity depends on the availability of labor. In case of a labor shortage, the potential cannot be translated into actual.

The capital-output ratio is a variable "planner's action parameter," so that it would be possible to equate the potential growth of output with that allowed for by supply of labor and technical change (including the substitution effect on the growth rate of labor productivity). The growth rate of output can be manipulated via changes in the coefficient of capital intensity which entail a change in the relative share of investment in national income.

If labor supply is unlimited then capacity is necessary to produce more and to employ the employable labor. In this case the potential growth rate of output—i.e., the growth rate of capacity—can always be equal to the actual one, and the capital-output ratio plays no role in equilibrating the two rates. It only plays a role in determining the level of labor productivity. For convenience purposes, in discussing this case, Kalecki assumes initially that the capital-output ratio is a parametric constant.

When the supply of labor is limited, the growth rate allowed for by supply of labor consists of three elements: (1) the rate of growth of labor; (2) the rate of growth of labor productivity at a given capital-output ratio (pure technological effect in Kalecki's sense); and (3) relative increase in labor productivity due to substitution effect (a change in the capital-output ratio). Clearly, in the long run, when the substitution effect plays no role, the growth rate of output is determined by the first two items. But in the relatively "short run," the substitution effect may play an important role as a planner's policy variable. In Kalecki's exposition of his growth theory the emphasis is on the role played by this effect in determining the growth rate of output, the investment rate, and the pattern of consumption. The "natural" rate of growth of the labor force β and the rate of technical change α, are both assumed "exogenous." We may argue, therefore, that, in a sense, Kalecki's theory is one of transitional processes where the implications of a change in capital intensity are studied, rather than of long-run growth where the implications of a change in α and β are the principal subject of inquiry. Kalecki did not consider explicitly the factors influencing α and β.[2] This poses the fundamental question of the determinants of the generators of long-term economic growth.

Before introducing the basic growth relationships formulated by Kalecki, it would be helpful first to consider briefly his treatment of the technical input-output relations which enter into the economic decision-making process as data, given by the state of know-how or some other noneconomic constraints. The planner faces the important task of choice among different eligible and efficient techniques of producing an increment of national output. The technical variants to choose from are subject to change as a result of technical advance.

Production Curve and Technical Progress

Production Curve

Given national income (with respect to size and structure) can be produced by different combinations of capital and labor inputs, and any planned increment in the rate of output can be obtained by investment variants representing different techniques of production; i.e., by locus of various combinations of increments of capital stock (investment) and labor inputs which make it possible to produce the same output.

> Let us assume that this increment has a given structure—in other words, it consists of given quantities of various final products (i.e. products that do not go through further manufacturing processes within the period considered). Usually, each of these products, or rather group of similar products, can be produced by several different methods of production based on technical knowledge existing at a given time. It follows that to produce a given increment in the national income there exists an immense number of variants, each of them consisting of a combination of variants for producing particular types of commodity. Let us denote by s the number of types of commodity, by N_1 the number of variants for the first group of products, by N_2 of those for the second type . . . and by N_s of those for the s-th type. The total number of combinations for all types of commodity will then be $N_1.N_2.N_3. \ldots N_s$ which for a large s will be a very large number, even if we only have two alternatives for each type of commodity.
>
> When production is considered in all its stages, each variant is characterized by specific outlays of investment and labour. Out of all the possible variants for producing given increment in the national income, we may discard those which are 'worse' than some others, with respect to both investment and labour inputs—i.e. which require higher outlays of both factors (or an equal outlay of one and a higher outlay of the other), i.e. variants which are absolutely inferior. We shall then be left with only those variants where greater investment is associated with less labour and vice versa. (Kalecki 1969b, pp. 54-55.)

If on the axis of abscissas we plot investment outlays and on the ordinates labor outlays indispensable to produce a unit increment in the rate of national output of a given composition, each combination will correspond to a point in the plane. Such combinations, for which in comparison with some other combination, one of the coordinates is larger and the other not smaller, are discarded. The points corresponding to the combinations remaining after this elimination are on a downward sloping curve, identified as the production curve. Thus each efficient variant is shown by a different point on the production curve, in Kalecki's terminology, corresponding to an aggregate production function, and using the isoquant technique as a device to present the production relationships graphically.[3]

It is convenient if the production curve refers to a unit increment of national income, for then the denominator of the input-output ratio is simply 1. The investment outlays (valued at constant prices) per unit increment of national output are equal to the investment-output (incremental capital-output) ratio m ($m=I$). Labor outlays (valued at constant wages) per unit increment of national income are equal to the labor-output ratio. Moving up the vertical axis, labor intensity increases (labor-output index rises) and, *ipso facto,* the output-labor ratio, i.e., the commonly designated index of labor productivity, falls (constant increment in output is divided by increasing L) and vice versa, as shown in figure 2.

In the case of two inputs, in the discussion of the production techniques the focus is on the opportunities provided by the various combinations of investment and labor to obtain an increment in the rate of production, at the "blueprint stage," with a given product composition. Thus in the construction of the production curve the accent is on *ex ante* substitution possibilities. But in planning, the determination of the increment of output and its structure and the choice of future techniques (variants of capital intensity of investment) are interdependent problems. It is restrictive to suppose that product composition can be determined prior to the choice of future techniques, unless it can be postulated that the freedom of choice of future production techniques is, to a large extent, unrestrained by the nonversatility of inputs, rigidities, etc., or that such problems can be overcome by indirect production. The more realistic case seems to be when the choice of *ex ante* techniques is largely predetermined by the productive apparatus.

Kalecki assumes that, within certain limits, shifts between output of investment goods and that of consumption goods may be made without disturbing significantly the composition of the production program. But still the problem remains that, for purposes of selection of techniques within the investment sector, the possibility of the substitution maneuver is circumscribed by the adopted production program and output composition in the investment sector. If the assumption of a given composition of output is relaxed, such changes entail a shift in the production curve. Kalecki suggests that, to solve this kind of problem in practice, a method of successive approximations would have to be applied.

A dynamic economy is characterized by change, and, in a similar vein, the assumption of output valued at constant prices is not without its problems. If the production curves in successive periods are defined in terms of price relations of the initial period, clearly they may not reflect technical and value relations in the period under consideration. Production curves shift whenever changes in the underlying price relations take place. Thus planning convenience requires stable price weights, but this involves well-known difficulties, e.g., as in the case of a new product mix for which prices did not exist in the base period.[4]

Concrete construction of a production curve and its use in planning and efficiency analysis is not without difficulty. Kalecki proceeds to show how a concrete construction can be visualized in practice and the problems resolved by successive approximations.

One of the reasons for the complexity of the phenomena of economic growth is that the economy is an interdependent whole, consisting of many sectors and activities. This difficulty is first avoided by introducing some simplified assumption which enables the analyst to treat the economy as an entity. Only after the core of the argument is presented is a two-sector model introduced.[5] Various parts of so-called aggregate productive investments are allocated in different cases to the investment sector itself; i.e., to the sector that produces productive equipment and to the noninvestment goods sector. Kalecki deals with changes in the structure of investment and their impact on growth. He warns that when a decision on growth acceleration is made, one must ascertain that the ceiling to the difference between the rate of growth of investment and that of national income must not be exceeded in the course of this process.

Technical Progress

Production possibilities at time t reflect the body of accumulated technical and organizational knowledge existing at that time. But technical (organizational) progress does not stop at time t; it goes on. To take one manifestation,[6] as techniques change, new variants come into existence and some or all "old" become technically inefficient. Thus, as a result of technical progress, the same effect (output) is produced with smaller quantity of at least one input, while no compensatory variation of another input is required to produce the same output. Of course, technical progress may be manifested in many ways affecting, for instance, the quality of inputs and outputs, broadly defined, with positive or adverse effects on the quality of life and environment.

Moving along the production curve to the right increases the coefficient of capital intensity m of the increment in the rate of national income (increases the recoupment period parameter), while the manpower in newly commissioned factories is reduced; i.e., labor intensity in those new capacities is reduced and labor productivity, *ipso facto,* increased. A manifestation of technical progress may be identified as a continuous downward shift of the production curve. The technical advance allows for an increase of productivity without increasing the capital intensity of production (investment). That is, the motive power for growth of output (productivity) is not a change of techniques by substitution of capital for labor, but is owing to the "exogenous force" of a change in technology. Although treated as an exogenous variable, advance in the technique of the economy is not unrelated to investment in human capital and science, "advantages" of backwardness, openness of the economy, structure of foreign trade, and the working arrangements (including those for diffusion of techniques). An "extra" increase of labor productivity can be achieved by moving to the right along the production curve. But this by itself is not a sufficient criterion for affecting such a maneuver. On the cost side this "additional" increase of productivity requires an increase of capital intensity. The benefit side depends on the type of technical progress. But this is not all.

Graphically, the new ways of combining inputs (without affecting output) is reflected in a downward shift of production curves (a new configuration of isoquants) which takes the successive positions $t+1$, $t+2$, etc., as progress in the state of technical knowledge goes on in the course of time. It is not only the direction of the shift of position of the production curve that is of interest, but also whether technical progress modifies the shape or curvature of the shifting production curve (movement along the production curve). What is the impact of the shift of production curve (owing to technical progress) on the set of configurations of labor and capital combinations required to produce a given increment of output?—relates to the types of technical progress.

Types of Technical Progress

The growth rate of labor productivity α is a general function of (1) technical dynamism (time, t) and (2) the capital-output ratio (m); $\alpha=f(m,t)$.[7] Graphically a rise in labor productivity is a result of a shift of the production curve—pure technical progress effect; and of a movement along the production curve—pure factor substitution effect. The rate of growth of labor productivity generated by technical progress may not be the same for all values of the capital-output coefficient m. "From the fact that to a given m there corresponds . . . a definite rate of increase of productivity, it does not necessarily follow that this rate is the same for all values of the capital-output ratio m." (Kalecki 1969b, p. 57.) Such a case is possible, as shown in figure 2, but by no means inevitable. Conceivably, the growth rate of labor productivity is greater the higher the value of m, as in figure 3, or vice versa, as in figure 4. While this is not the only policy instrument available, the relationship between m and its effect on the growth rate of productivity has significant implication for the choices to be made by the planner. The attraction for the planner to raise the coefficient of capital intensity depends on the consequences of such action as measured by the rise of α. Higher (lower) m is more likely to be selected if α is positively (negatively) associated with the capital intensity m. Accordingly, technical prog-

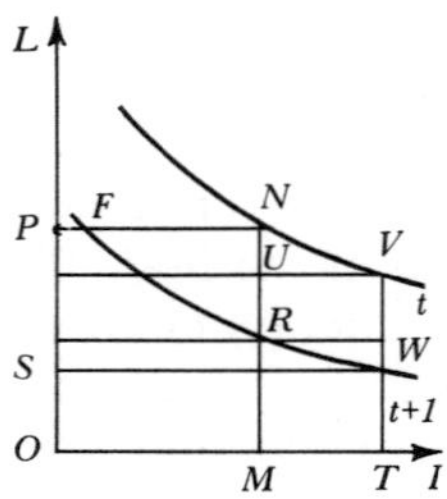

Fig. 2

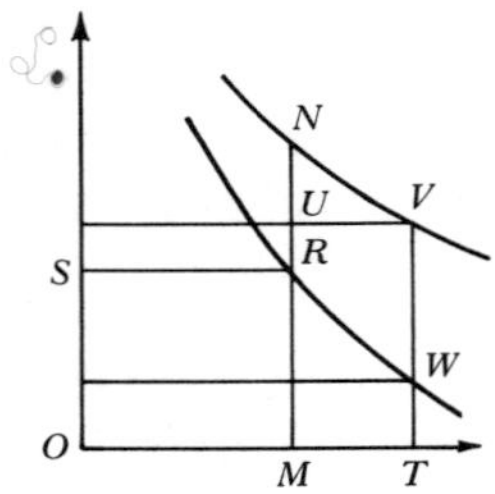

Fig. 3

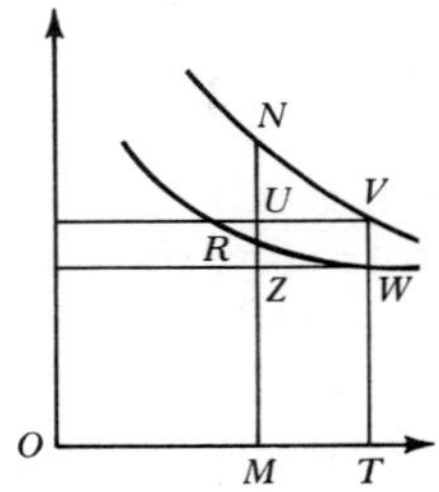

Fig. 4

ress is classified neutral if raising the capital intensity of investment entails a once-and-for-all increase in productivity in new plants, but does not raise the growth rate of this productivity (with shifts toward abscissas all ordinates decrease in the same proportion: $MN/MR = TV/TW$, as shown in fig. 2). If the relative rate of increase of productivity is greater the higher the capital intensity, the type of technical progress is classified as encouraging capital intensity (the ordinates fall more rapidly for larger abscissas: $TV/TW > MN/MR$, as shown in fig. 3).[8] If increase in the capital intensity of investment, while bringing about a rise in the level of productivity in new plants, leads simultaneously to a fall in the relative rate of increase in productivity, technical progress is described as discouraging capital intensity (the fall of ordinates will be greater for lower abscissas: $TV/TW < MN/MR$, as shown in fig. 4).[9]

The prevailing type of technical progress does not prejudge the path of economic development to be followed in practice, nor does it prejudge the actual course of changes in capital intensity. As we have seen, capital intensity could be increased with neutral technical progress, if at the same time there is a movement to the right on the production curve. With technical progress encouraging capital intensity, *m* may remain unchanged. Only in the latter case would it be easier, *ceteris paribus,* to decide to increase capital intensity, for such an increase not only raises the *level* of productivity in new factories, but also its *rate of growth.*

This does not necessarily imply that *m* is bound to rise, or that the planner should decide on such action. Even if *m* is maintained at the same level, certain regular increase in the growth rate of productivity will be obtained in new plants. But such a policy maneuver to accelerate the growth rate of productivity by superimposing substitution (extra growth over and above that owed to technical progress) is much more attractive when technical progress is of the type that encourages capital intensity (as compared with a neutral type), because the gain in dynamics of productivity is then reinforced by the advantages of a higher growth rate in productivity, associated with a higher *m.*

It is an interesting coincidence that "Kalecki's classification of technical progress, although different in its formulation, corresponds exactly to Harrod's classification."[10] Kalecki's classification of technical progress seems to reflect the behavior of a growth-oriented planner in the process of selecting production techniques at a macro level. Indeed, the planner should be expected to select more (less) capital-intensive techniques if such choice corresponds to a higher (lower) growth rate of productivity. Harrod's classification is based on the observation that private investors in capitalist economies will tend to choose more (less) capital-intensive techniques if, at a given rate of interest, marginal productivity of capital increases (decreases) over time. (Cf. Harrod 1937, p. 329; Joan Robinson 1962b, pp. 88 ff.) These two classifications seem to be entirely different in concept. They refer to different institutional frameworks, with different classificatory variables. The equivalence cannot be easily seen. Kalecki's classification should be particularly convenient in the theory of long-run growth since α, Kalecki's classificatory variable, is the prime growth determinant. The usefulness of Kalecki's classification is, for instance, evident in the recent challenge to the widely held view in growth literature that it is only the neutral form of technical progress that is consistent with balanced growth. (Cf. Chilosi and Gomulka 1973; 1969b, pp. 37-38.)

Capital stock at a given time consists of investments carried out in the course of the preceding n years, for the old plant constructed earlier has already been retired. Kalecki assumes that n, the number of vintages of capital or its life span is a given constant. At the end of a year t, a brand new vintage is introduced and the oldest one is taken out of use. The net output gain $\Delta Y_t = Y_{t+1} - Y_t$ is equal to the difference $[(1/m_t)I_t] - a_t Y_t + u_t Y_t$. ΔY denotes the absolute increment of national output of unchanged composition during a given year (per unit of time t), computed as the difference between the level of national income at constant prices at the beginning of the following period (Y_{t+1}) and the beginning of a given period (Y_t). It is assumed that during the year considered (period t), both the volume and composition of national output remains constant, and the change occurs at the juncture of the two consecutive years. Thus ΔY is the difference between the level of national income of the given year and that of the following year. One component of ΔY is the increment in national income resulting from new productive capacities created by gross investment I_t. The brand new vintage plant is represented by the investment outlays yielding at the beginning of the following year the output stream. Here investment is a prerequisite for the growth of national income; and the productive effect of investment is the amount by which national output is increased as a result of that investment, $(1/m_t)I_t$. The incremental capital-output ratio (investment outlay per unit increment in national income) to be chosen for the new vintage is denoted by m_t. Investment serves as one of the *means* for increasing national income, but does not constitute the end of its creation. The aim underlying production is consumption in the broad sense (private and collective consumption and so-called nonproductive investments).

The second component of ΔY is negative and has the opposite effect to that of increase in national income resulting from capacity-creating investments. This is the effect of some productive capacities coming out of use, for capital stock is subject to continuous obsolescence and depreciation as a result of wear and tear. This results in scrapping the equipment of oldest vintage, thus in curtailment of productive capacity. The effect of this factor is the second component, as national income declines at the beginning of the successive year by aY, where a stands for this capacity-reducing coefficient, or the parameter of amortization. Actually, a_t=*output of the oldest vintage*/Y_t.

The third component of the increment of national income is the output effect of improvements in the utilization of the existing stock of capital which do not require significant outlays—they are a non-investment source of change in output. Greater output may be obtained by more effective utilization of existing capacities owing to a number of factors. For example, within the year t, the economy might absorb some innovations, primarily of an organizational or managerial kind, resulting in improvement in working arrangements for resource allocations, plan implementation and functioning of the economy, improvement in work organization and incentive arrangements, quality of labor, or alleviation of system-made impediments to full utilization of capacity. This source of growth also reflects primarily noninvestment measures for alleviating disproportions of the various degrees of plan fulfillment, widening of bottlenecks, improving inter-enterprise and inter-branch flows, economy in the use of materials, eliminating waste, decreasing work stoppages, and overcoming other obstacles to full utilization of productive capacity. Owing to such measures, national income increases at the beginning of the following year by the amount of uY, where u is the coefficient of improvement independent of investment. Thus as a result of absorption of this type of innovation by plants, or capital vintages of the age 1 year, 2 years, . . . , $n-1$ years, output increases at a given percentage rate per annum u_t of the aggregate output Y_t. Although there is a limit to the gains in output obtainable from a given stock of capital, a period of relatively long duration can be envisaged during which utilization of capacity is improving by a certain fraction u per annum (and if such progress continues, u is constant over time). Thence, $\Delta Y_t=[(1/m_t)I_t]-a_tY_t+u_tY_t$.

Since in the analysis of a dynamic economy the preoccupation is with the variation of rates at which various economic quantities are growing over time, by dividing both sides of the equation by Y_t, we get proportionate or percentage changes, where $\Delta Y_t/Y_t$ measures the proportional rate of growth of gross aggregate volume of production: $\Delta Y_t/Y_t=[(1/m_t)(I_t/Y_t)]-a_t+u_t$. Clearly, $\Delta Y_t/Y_t$ is the rate of growth of gross national income, denoted by r, and if i stands for the relative share of productive accumulation (investment) in gross national income, I/Y, and for convenience purposes the reference to time t is not given, we have Kalecki's first growth equation:

$r=(1/m)i-a+u$. If both parameters a and u are assumed constant over time, the equation is thus a relationship among the three variables r, m, and i. Only with given and appropriate assumptions as to the behavior of the noninvestment improvement coefficient and the rate of retirement of plants, the three principal variables are the growth rate of gross national output, the capital intensity of investment, and the relative share of gross capital formation in gross national output (the saving rate). So far this does not tell us which of these variables (or parametric constants) should be selected as policy instruments. Nor does it provide the basic framework for analysis of essential growth relationships as formulated by Kalecki.

The rate of growth r_t is a "potential" rate as allowed by productive capacity; it may not be "actually" attainable if there is not enough manpower to operate the new plans. For r in equation 1 is admissible only if it does not exceed the rate of growth of output warranted by the state of supply of labor in year t. *Ceteris paribus,* under full employment both rates must just be the same. The labor required to exploit fully new capacities that are commissioned is a function of the level of the coefficient of capital intensity m_t chosen for those plants. Thus the labor requirement to attain capacity output in brand new vintage is equal to: $[(1/y_t)(1/m_t)]I_t$, where $y_t=y(m_t, t)$ stands for "incremental" labor productivity at time t, provided the capital-output coefficient m_t is adopted by the planner. Under the conditions this is the "demand for labor," and if it cannot be satisfied by "labor supply," it would lead only to the creation of an underutilized productive capacity potential.

Under full employment, there are three components on the labor supply side. First there are additions to the labor force, owing to the natural rate of increase of population. If the rate of increase of the labor force from that source is proportionate to the natural rate of growth of population and is equal to β, the number of workers made available because of this increase is equal to $\beta_t L_t$, where L_t denotes labor at time t. Apart from the new additions to the labor force, there is labor released by scrapping of the capacity of oldest vintage. Let this labor be represented by $b_t L_t$, where b_t=employment in plants of oldest vintage/total employment L_t. Finally, in Kalecki's theory there is also the employment effect of the disembodied technical progress, for, as a result of all kinds of noninvestment improvements, the employment required to operate pre-existing capacities, of the age 1 year, 2 years, . . ., $n-1$ years, falls by, say, s_t per cent per annum (assuming that the effect is on reduction of employment in old plants, the surplus is released). This augments the supply of labor for employment in new plants correspondingly. (Kalecki 1969b, pp. 22-25, 63-64.)

Adding together the three components of supply, and if supply equals demand for labor as it should under maintained lasting full employment, then $(\beta_t+b_t+s_t)L_t=[(1/y_t)(1/m_t)]I_t$. For, simplifying, at time t, the total increment in the supply available for employment in the new plant, times the incremental labor productivity in this new vintage (compatible with the capital-output ratio m_t) gives rise to an increment of output generated by this new capacity of ΔY per annum. This is, of course, equal to the "productive effect of investment" representing the brand new vintage, $(1/m_t)I_t$. Thus $(\beta_t+b_t+s_t)L_t y_t=(1/m_t)I_t=\Delta Y$, and by dividing both sides by y_t we obtain the previous equation. But $(1/m_t)I_t$ can be rewritten as $(i_t/m_t)Y_t$. By substitution we get $(\beta_t+b_t+s_t)L_t=[(1/y_t)(i_t/m_t)]Y_t$. Solving with respect to Y_t/L_t (average labor productivity), we obtain $Y_t/L_t=(m_t/i_t)(\beta_t+b_t+s_t)(m_t,t)$. This is the relationship between average and incremental labor productivities. If, as Kalecki assumes for purposes of exposition, β_t, b_t, and s_t independent of time, it follows that $r_t=\alpha+\beta+(q_t+1)(\dot{m}_t/m_t)-(\dot{i}_t/i_t)=\alpha+\beta+$ substitution effect, where $q=(m/y)(\partial y_t/\partial m)$, "the elasticity of labor productivity with respect to capital-output ratio." This is the second growth equation.

To emphasize the relations between the two equations, let us concentrate briefly on cases where m is a fixed capital-output ratio, in order to contrast later with the situation where m is a variable policy instrument.

Kalecki constructed a full employment "uniform growth" state—a variant of the mythical "Golden Age" or "steady state"—as a point of departure for analysis. In a balanced growth path, the rate of growth of national income r is independent of time; all the parameters m, a, and u are also constant over time; and labor productivity in the new plants in successive years increases at a constant rate of α per annum. And so increases the overall productivity of the system. Also full employment prevails in the economy, and for full employment to be maintained the growth rate of employment must be equal to the "natural" growth rate of labor force β. Since constancy over time of r and α are postulated as a characteristic of the "uniform growth" state, the constancy of β must also be postulated. Investment (consumption) rises at the same rate as national income

r, and i is constant over time. Thus under "uniform growth," growth equation 2 is reduced to the form: $r=\alpha+\beta$.

It is clear from equation 2 that the substitution effect, in Kalecki's sense, does not exist under "uniform growth," and, therefore, the growth rate of output is determined solely by α and β. Once r is known, the ratio i/m can be found from equation 1, "given the parameters m, k, u and a, the rate of growth r determines the constant share of productive accumulation, i, in the national income, which is necessary in order to sustain it, on the basis of the [first growth] equation."[11] Thus here equation 1 serves to determine the level of i.[12] It cannot be overemphasized that, as long as the constancy of m and other parameters holds, and the condition of full employment holds, the rate of growth is determined by the increase in productivity resulting from technical progress and by the natural increase in the labor force. If the rate of growth were planned at a higher level than $\alpha+\beta$, and investment corresponding to this rate (in accordance with equation 1) was implemented, this would entail a labor shortage, and capacity would be partly underutilized. "Acceleration of growth over and above the rate r is impossible, since it would come up against the barrier of a manpower shortage. There would, therefore, be no sense in raising the relative share of productive accumulation in the national income in order to accelerate the rate of growth. In these circumstances it would lead only to the creation of idle productive capacity." (Kalecki 1969b, p. 27.)

Of course, as soon as the rigid assumptions about the constancy of parameters are relaxed and a labor plethora, or limited reserve, postulated, the problem of choice emerges. In general, when m_t and i_t are changing over time, $r_t=\alpha+\beta+$substitution effect. The level of i depends on the choice of the capital-output ratio. It affects only the level of output through the level of labor productivity. If the planner raises m, the level of output increases, but the level of consumption may or may not increase, depending on whether a positive output effect of higher m (equation 1) is larger or smaller than the adverse effect on consumption owing to a higher investment rate i (an increase in m affects i, both directly and indirectly, through an increase in r), as indicated in the illustration.

There is a question of optimal level of capital-output ratio at which the level of consumption is at a maximum. As we know, the investment rate corresponding to that capital-output ratio is referred to in growth literature as the Golden Rule of Accumulation.[13] But Kalecki did not concentrate his analysis on that rule. One rea-

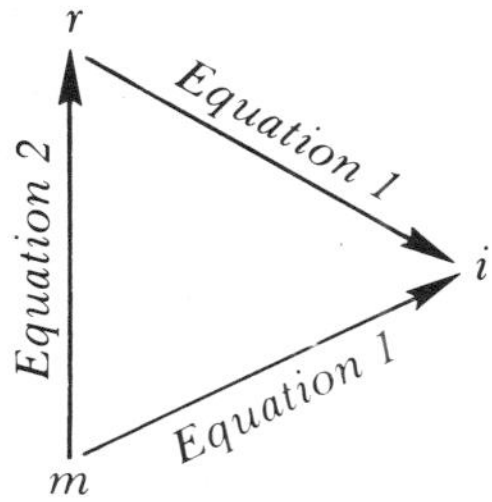

son was because he was more concerned with the choice of the investment rate under nonbalanced growth. This problem is discussed further in the sections dealing with the planner's decision curve and with growth acceleration.

Under conditions of full employment, the increase of the growth rate may be achieved by accelerating the rate of increase of productivity by one or the other or combinations of the following means: (1) In the transitory or "intermediate" growth process, by raising the capital-output ratio if technical progress is of neutral type, by more intensive exploitation of the existing stock of capital (shortening the time of exploitation of capital goods reflected in the rise of parameter of amortization), and by improvements independent of investment activity. (2) In the "long-run," by raising the capital-output ratio if technical progress is of the capital-using type, and by the possibility of raising the rate of increase of productivity α at a *given* capital-output ratio. Before discussing some of the uses to which Kalecki put his apparatus under varied initial conditions, let us introduce elements of political choice into the decision-making process in a planned economy.

Planner's Decision Curve

Accumulation and Consumption Conflict

The decision about the level of the targeted rate of capital accumulation involves a compromise between its adverse short-run and favorable long-run effects. Kalecki warns that immediate (short-run) effects of growth acceleration strategies must be taken into account.

A rise in the relative share of accumulation in national income leads to an increase in the flow of production and thus to an improvement in the standard of living in the long run, but it impinges on consumption in the near future. Simply, as a result of an increase in the relative share of accumulation in national income, there is an equal fall in the relative share of consumption. The slogan of "sacrificing the present for the future" is a popular one: In order to achieve a higher level of consumption in the long run, it is necessary to restrain consumption in the short run. This deterioration in the consumption level is the price paid by the population for raising the growth rate of national income in the short run and the level of the increase in the long run. In the long run consumption may rise—at least it is favorably affected by the cumulative effect of a higher rate of growth of national output. While *the short-run effects of the increase of accumulation are manifestly clear*; *not always a higher share of accumulation renders a higher standard of living in the long run*. This seems to be one of the main propositions of the policy implications of Kalecki's theory of growth.

Therefore, the policy maker has to strike a compromise solution to the accumulation-consumption dilemma (in a limited sense, between the present and future consumption conflict) based on political premises ("exogenously given" political decisions of the planner). The nature of such a choice from the political and social standpoint, the consequences of such decisions, what the planner should and should not do, the specification of the terms of choice for the planner, the factors that must be taken into account when making a decision on the rate of accumulation and "short-run" growth rate of output—these appear over and over again in Kalecki's book. He emphasizes that a study of the logic and consequences of such choices is of particular importance for a socialist economy where the increase in the future consumption standard requires imposition of real hardship on most of the population in the short run. Thus, usually, the planner really can only increase moderately the growth rate of national income over the level determined by the "natural" rate in order not to deteriorate the consumption standards in the immediate future.

Kalecki views the situation somewhat differently in a mixed economy, for the consumption of the rich and the well-to-do can be restrained in the short period without causing extremely great hardship. The problem is one of feasibility and advisability of changing the growth rate—the planner's problem par excellence. While it cannot be assumed that there is always a possibility of changing the growth rate, the problem here is of criteria for such a decision, and the rationale of such a choice. In this respect, Kalecki attempts to lay a foundation for the future positive theory of such choices in the socialist economy (centrally planned economy)—and as such it is an important accomplishment. Let us briefly follow Kalecki in his analysis of the effects of higher or lower growth rate on the time pattern of consumption.

Consider first the determination of the growth rate of national income in a situation characterized by the existence of an unlimited supply of labor (thereafter Kalecki considers the more realistic case of limited labor reserves which are eventually exhausted). Suppose that housewives would be willing to enter the labor market if proper jobs were easily available; some surplus labor in agriculture; and so on. That is, the rate of expansion of employment can be raised above the level determined by the natural rate. Thus there is a possibility of raising r over and above the level of $\alpha+\beta$ by drawing on labor reserves. True this would only lift the limitation imposed on raising the growth rate by the manpower situation and, in time, when the surplus labor has been absorbed, the growth rate will reset to the initial level determined by the natural rate. But the effect of the higher rate of growth during the time when the labor surplus is being absorbed in the production process would be to yield a net increase in the level of national output.

Initially, we abstract from the problem of eventual emergence of labor bottlenecks in order to concentrate on factors other than labor limiting the growth rate. In order to simplify the problem, and to take one factor at the time, we also initially assume a closed system. This allows us to concentrate on the cost in terms of the adverse effects on the level of consumption in the immediate future as the crucial limiting factor in the choice of a growth rate.

The decision to raise the growth rate to the level $\alpha+\beta'$ where $\beta'>\beta$ clearly entails a rise in the accumulation rate and, as noted, a decline in the rate of consumption. What matters is that this constitutes a barrier, and increasing the growth rate via such action is unrestricted by the labor supply situation. Because in the near future the expansion of national income will be small, the absolute level of consumption in the period directly following the speed-up maneuver is likely to decline. In the long run the situation will be reversed.

The specification of consequences of the planner's decision with regard to the growth of the accumulation rate (choice of saving rate) on consumption can be presented in the following way: Suppose that the planner considers two variants only. Without changing the rate of accumulation, national income would grow at a steady rate r. If Y_o is the base level of national income, income at time t, Y_t, would amount to $Y_o(1+r)^t$. With constant proportion of income allocated to consumption throughout the period, the absolute level of consumption at time t is clearly given by the equation $C_t = Y_o[(1-i_o)(1+r)]^t$. The second variant is presented to test consequences of growth speed up. Clearly the choice must not be confined to two variants but to testing the consequences of alternative intensities of accumulation. In order to raise the growth rate to r', the accumulation rate must be increased correspondingly to i, and *ipso facto*, the consumption share falls to $1-i$. Now, at time t the consumption level C_t' would be $Y_o[(1-i)(1+r')]^t$. To portray the choice problem

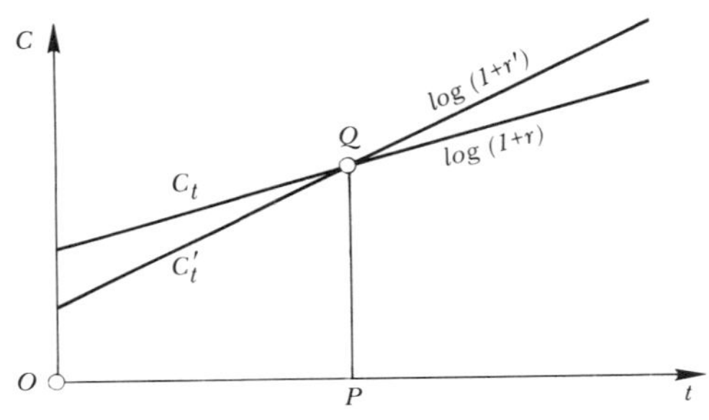

Fig. 5

graphically, it is useful to operate with the logarithms of consumption. In figure 5 time is plotted along abscissas and the ordinates are given on a logarithmic scale. The logarithms of the two linear equations correspond to the straight lines C_t and C_t', whose slopes are r and r', respectively.

In evaluating the consequences of strategy, one of the crucial issues is the time horizon one takes into account and the relative weights assigned to the trade off between immediate and more distant consumption. Since by raising the growth rate the level of consumption may be less favorable over a given period and will be more favorable thereafter, the relative advantages of the exercise become greater, the longer the time span one is considering.

With reference to the two variants considered, if we compare the two consumption paths, it is apparent that throughout period *OP*—up to the point of intersection at *Q* (i.e., until the time when consumption burdened with acceleration reaches the value of consumption had the steady course been pursued)—the advantage of the first variant is clear. The area between the lines shows the difference it makes to consumption over time which variant is pursued. It is assumed that m, i_O, and i are such that this distance is positive. (If it is not, there will be no conflict—to be discussed later.) The distance is clearly largest at the outset (the difference between the intercepts *M* and *R* on the ordinate). Thereafter the distance progressively decreases, until point *Q*, indicating that the loss to consumption is progressively smaller, and it becomes naught at *P*. Thereafter variant 2 yields better results in terms of consumption levels, and the longer the period of waiting, the more progressively advantageous is the second variant. And because with more remote benefits in the future greater relative gains can be shown, some planners are prompted to operate with an inordinately long time horizon. Therefore, the calculus of gains and losses should be restricted to a specific length of time horizon.[14] This again shows the accumulation-consumption antinomy and the weight of the political decision in this field. And as the decisions usually reflect the planner's intertemporal preferences and are influenced by factors of a political nature, with the population's preferences not taken sufficiently into account (for various reasons, and rightly or wrongly violated), it is of major importance at least that the decision-maker should realize the consequences of alternative actions.

Thus one of the key problems of the development strategy is the choice of the time horizon for maximization of consumption. While the intertemporal choice is customarily presented as a resolution of the conflict between present and future consumption, the problem is complicated by the fact that the future can be interpreted as a time interval of various lengths. The choice is not only between the present and future generation(s), but of intertemporal allocation in the life span of the present generation. The resolution of the conflict between immediate burdens and more or less distant benefits for the present generation is the crucial choice—where the overall size of consumption during that period is not the only concern, but where the time distribution is the key issue.

Maximization of consumption during the life span of one generation, or during a somewhat limited version of this time horizon, seems to be an inequitable and unrealistic prescription, whether such a policy leads to significant inroads into consumption during a longer span of life of that generation or whether it produces such consumption paths that the fruits are to be enjoyed only in the relatively distant future. The implications of such a policy were brilliantly driven home by Kalecki:

> Nearly two years ago I was shown a working paper setting the share of investment in national income with the aim of maximizing total consumption for the long-range plan period. Through mathematical analysis the method offered not too attractive results: it showed that for a twenty-year period productive investments should constitute about 80 per cent of national income. This is not even as bizarre as it might appear; a high share of productive investments in national income allows for its high rate of growth and this so raises its level in the following years of the long-range plan, that consumption not only in those years, but even for the entire period of the plan is higher than with a lower share of investment in national income. But that which is comprehensible is not always reasonable: even if one would not be concerned with the suffering of the unfortunate population in the first years of the long-term plan, one would have to take into account that, with the assumed standard of living, this population would soon perish, and thus would be unable to fulfill the plan. (Kalecki 1962a, p. 706.)

Returning to the presentation of Kalecki's positive theory of the planner's decision-making process with regard to selecting the rate of growth (saving rate), suppose that, at a certain time t, the planner compares benefits from raising the growth rate from what is considered an admissible level r by some small increment and changing r to $r+\Delta r$, with the disadvantages that this would entail; namely, the necessity of increasing the rate of accumulation by Δi. Immediate consumption then has to be cut by the fraction $\Delta i/(1-i)$. If, as a result of such a calculus the gain in the growth rate would outweigh the loss due to the increment in the saving rate, the planner will continue to increase until such point is reached where there are no further net advantages in increasing the saving rate (and, of course, in going beyond such point the disadvantages would outweigh the advantages). More precisely, Kalecki introduces the critical sensitivity (or viewed from another vantage, the consumers' frustration) coefficient w which is an increasing function of i. That is, the higher the value of the coefficient w the stronger are the objections, or likely consumers' resistance, against curtailment of consumption in the immediate future. Clearly the value of w is critical to the outcome of the equilibrating process: "If our problem is that of deciding how far the rate of growth is to be raised above the level $r_O=\alpha+\beta$, we may postulate that . . . [w] will be the higher, the greater becomes the difference between i and i_O. Indeed, the further we move away from the initial situation, the more important become the objections against further reducing the relative share of consumption in the national income." (Kalecki 1969b, pp. 31-32.)

Ceteris paribus, there is cost $w\Delta i/(1-i)$ in raising the growth rate by Δr. As long as gain exceeds cost $\Delta r-[w(i)\Delta i/(1-i)]>0$, this difference is positive. Thus it is beneficial to increase i, but it is necessary to stop at the point of equality. Dividing both sides by Δi, this "equilibrium condition" reads $\Delta r/\Delta i=w(i)/(1-i)$. And according to Kalecki, "This is the condition which determines the 'correct' i. The ratio $\Delta r/\Delta i$ is simply the yield in terms of an increase in the rate of growth of national income, Δr, of raising the rate of accumulation by Δi." (Kalecki 1969b, p. 33.)

The left-hand side of the above equation is determined by technical conditions (production possibilities) of the economy [the reciprocal of the capital-output ratio m; with a and u constant, $\Delta r=\Delta i(1/m)$]. And with the given $w(i)$ function—which depends on the planner's intertemporal preferences—together with the "underlying facts of economic life," under specified conditions the loss in short-run consumption must be compared with the advantages that can be derived from an increase in capital formation. This provides the basis for political decisions on growth "with an economic content."

The above consideration poses the basic question about the nature of the decision curve. Before embarking on this thorny subject, we ought to present the situation diagrammatically. To present the process of the planner's decision-making, Kalecki makes use of a two-part diagram, as shown in figure 6. In both parts the accumulation rate i is plotted on the horizontal axis. Whereas in the upper part the growth rate r is plotted on the vertical axis, in the lower part $\Delta r/\Delta i$ is plotted on this axis. Since m and u are assumed constant, the growth rate r is a linear function of accumulation rate i (as follows from the growth equation), and is represented by a straight line CN. The line intersects the vertical axis at point C situated at a distance $OC=(a-u)<0$ below the origin (or above the origin if the difference is positive). Thus the straight line CN (and, of course, its

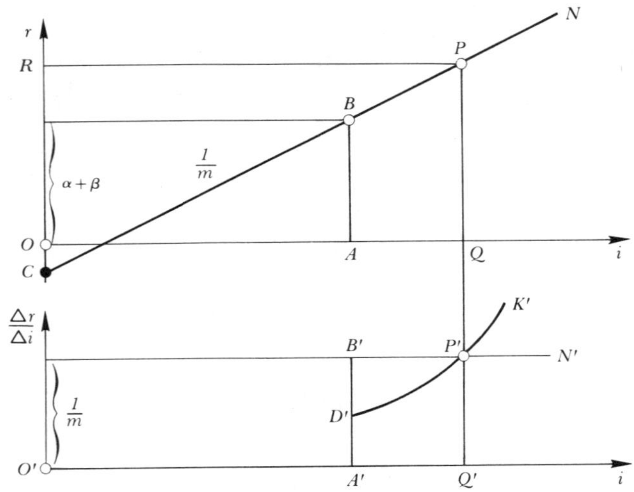

Fig. 6

segment BN) represents the functional relationship between r and i, given the assumption that a, u, and m are all constant. The slope of $CN(BN)$ is equal to $1/m$. But, clearly, if the value of m is allowed to change, the slope of the line changes accordingly. To the upward-sloping straight line BN (with constant slope$=1/m$) in the upper part there corresponds a horizontal straight line $B'N'$ (depicting the linear relationship between *changes* in the ratio r/i and i) in the lower part. Clearly $B'N'$ is horizontal to and equidistant from the i axis. The accumulation rate i_0, compatible with the natural growth rate $\alpha+\beta=AB$, amounts to OA. To raise the growth rate to the level PQ, the accumulation rate must be increased (disregarding the effect on the amortization coefficient a) to OQ.

Instead of intertemporal preferences of the savers as reflected in the function relating interest rate and saving propensities, we have here the planner's preference function incorporating "his" comparative evaluation of the trade off between consumption in the immediate and more distant future. The $w(i)/(1-i)$ function is introduced to locate the equilibrium point. The function appears to perform a similar role to that of the interest rate in the neoclassical growth model. Thus in Kalecki's formulation the interest rate does not appear explicitly in the analysis of the dynamics of the socialist economy.[15] The incremental effect from additional capital formation in terms of national output is related to the planner's decision curve $D'K'$, reflecting the planner's intertemporal preferences and the constraints imposed by the reaction or resistance of the population, represented by the function $w(i)/(1-i)$. The decision curve is upward-sloping. This is because, with an increase in i, w increases, and the relative share of consumption falls. "We shall find r by projecting the point P′ onto the straight line BN in the upper part of the diagram; this gives us the point P whose ordinate OR is equal to r. We shall call the curve D′K′ the 'government decision curve,' since it shows what value of $\Delta r/\Delta i$ will satisfy the government for a given i. Hence, together with the value of $\Delta r/\Delta i$ which is determined by the conditions of production (in our case by the value of the capital-output ratio k), it forms the basis for the decision as to the rate of productive accumulation i and the rate of growth r." (Kalecki 1969b, p. 34.)

For values of i smaller than the optimum value i^*, the benefits outweigh costs, and it is decided to speed up growth at the expense of inroads into consumption for "marginal productivity of capital" is greater than the "appropriately weighted burden of increasing the saving rate." But, *ceteris paribus*, the level of capital accumulation and the targeted growth rate should not exceed $O'Q'$ (OQ) and PQ, respectively, since such a decision will entail smaller advantages in terms of an increase in the growth rate of national income than the disadvantages ensuing from raising the saving rate. If the locus of decision, for whatever reason, was to the right of P', it would be prudent to redress the situation by moving in the opposite direction (by abrupt change or gradually) by *reducing* i as long as $\{[\Delta r/\Delta i]-[w(i)/(1-i)]\}<0$.

It should be added that the "equilibrium point" clearly depends on the planner's knowledge of the $w(i)$ function. The planner may misjudge the intensity of population's resistance, the information system may generate and channel wrong information, etc.,—an example of which may be the Polish December, 1970.

This raises the fundamental question of the interaction between the central planner and the population. It would be useful to extend the framework of analysis of various cases assuming concordance and various degrees of divergence between planner's and population's intertemporal preferences, with alternative institutional and political arrangements of mutual influence and resolution of conflicts.

The foregoing considered an *abrupt* decrease of consumption from its initial level as a result of increasing the rate of investment. In such a case the decision curve would have a rather steep upward slope, so that the planner could not decide on a growth rate much in excess of $r_0=\alpha+\beta$, because any substantial increase in i would make intolerable inroads into current consumption. Kalecki extended the analysis by examining the more realistic case where this difficulty is obviated if the relative accumulation rate is increased *gradually*. This can be accomplished by increasing consumption *pari passu* with employment during a sufficiently long transitional period. It should be underlined that the objections against raising the relative share of accumulation in national income will be stronger the longer is the transitional period. Realistically, the maneuver of increasing the rate of accumulation, with real wages being constant, can take place only in a relatively short period. Thereafter, real wages again begin to rise at a rate α, with a faster rate of employment than in the initial position. Somewhat differently, real wages can be increased over a longer period at a rate lower than α.

In Kalecki's formulation the planner's decision curve is an analytical device that aims to portray the actual decision-making process. Actually, what is known is not a locus of points a priori (it is assumed that the planner has performed such a process of testing and selection), but only the *ex post revealed* point by the decision actually taken. The curve is needed to show how the process of decision-making works and to locate the equilibrium point. In Kalecki's words:

> It is not out of place here to add a few observations on the nature of the "government decision curve." Its general features follow directly from our argument—namely that it is upward-sloping and that the lower is the rate of increase in productivity the higher are its ordinates corresponding to given levels of the rate of productive accumulation i. But is it possible to draw this curve in a precise fashion? Are its ordinates determined quantitatively similarly to those of the line CN which represents the relationship between the rate of growth r and the rate of productive accumulation i? The answer is definitely in the negative. Our curve serves only to illustrate the attitude of the government towards "sacrificing the present for the future." . . .
>
> The main advantages of using the "government decision curve" in our analysis will be seen in the discussion of cases where the relationship between the rate of growth r and the rate of productive accumulation i differs from that represented by the line BN (e.g. in the discus-

sion of the problem of the effect of difficulties in balancing foreign trade or that of labor shortage). Indeed, the concept of the "decision curve" will then enable us to show the effects of the changes in the relationship between r and i on the choice of the rate of growth of national income, given the attitude of the government towards "sacrificing the present for the future." (Kalecki 1969b, pp. 36-37.)

In this context, Kalecki's analysis is not dynamic, for he considers only one planning period instead of a sequence of planning periods (continuous or discrete). The method is that of comparative statics. The comparison is made between benefits and costs in immediate planning periods, and the aim is to find the difference between the rate of accumulation in that period and the present one.

Factors Alleviating Conflict.

The conflict argument rests on assumed values of parameters, on bias of technical change over time, and on the level of technical change. If technical change is of a "strong" capital-using variety, such conflict may not arise, for then the consumption gain as a result of a higher growth rate more than offsets the adverse effect in consumption resulting from a higher share of investment in output. A similar phenomenon may appear if the rate of technical change is *increasing over time with a given capital-output ratio.* Here again a positive effect on consumption of a higher growth rate of output may outweigh a depressing effect of a higher share of investment in national income.

A difference, however, is to be noted: In the first case the process of adjustment takes place via an increase in the capital-output ratio m, as such an increase is a necessary condition to ensure a higher growth rate, whereas in the second the planner may even *reduce* m, since the increasing α occurs for all capital-output ratios in an admissible range. If such conditions are fulfilled the conflict between present and future consumption is less likely to occur as the increase in the accumulation rate i may be positively associated with the growth rate of consumption. But in general the outcome depends on (1) the value of initial m, (2) how strong the bias of the capital-using technical progress is, and/or (3) the magnitude of the increase in the rate of technical change over time.

In the analysis of the phenomenon the assumption of the closed system must be relaxed and the possibility of financing by external accumulation (by credits, aid, and indirect production) taken into account. Also if the values of the parameters would be such that there would be no (or only meager) increases in the standard of living in the immediate future, the population may resist such strategies, no matter how high future benefits might be.

Alternatively, the problem of whether or not the conflict arises may be considered by assuming an increase of the rate of employment by increasing the labor participation rate. *Ceteris paribus,* such a possibility is in its output effect and total consumption effect similar to that of increasing α. However, there is a difference with respect to the pattern of change of the real wage rate. An increase in the growth rate of output requires an increase in the accumulation rate. At the rate of growth of employment higher than that of the population, the growth rate of the wage rate must be lower than that of consumption per capita. There may arise, therefore a "political and psychological" conflict between the latter and the former (if α is increased and the participation rate is constant, this conflict will not arise).

There are a number of factors at work generating or aggravating such conflicts in a planned economy. To take only one case here, even if α grows or labor surplus prevails, a "conflict-generating" factor would appear at the inception of the period of increase of the accumulation rate. So far we have abstracted from the period of gestation and fruition of investment. As output does not emerge immediately after a decision to invest has been made and construction begun, it takes times before the effect is translated into increase of consumption and the conflict is bound to appear within the gestation period.

Moreover, there are many factors at work extending and protracting the gestation period and of "learning by doing" in the new capacities. In this respect conflict can be reduced by a properly working foreign trade sector, etc. But here system-made impediments in practice cannot be disregarded in the analysis of the problem. It appears that the above observations do not detract from the essential conflict between accumulation and consumption as Kalecki saw it for a period of medium-term plan.

XIV

THEORY OF GROWTH

Acceleration and Barriers

Speed-up via Raising Capital Intensity

THE OPTIONS AVAILABLE TO THE PLANNER to speed up the growth pace of productivity (national income) are discussed by Kalecki under varied assumptions regarding the states of labor availability. First the case of inexhaustible labor reserves is examined in order to disregard initially all problems related to the barrier of labor shortage, so as to concentrate on other growth-limiting factors. Then consideration is given to the more realistic case of a limited reserve of labor to draw upon as a possibility of raising r, but still with parameters m, a, and u remaining constant. Kalecki then proceeds to examine a situation in which no such surplus exists (in the initial situation there is no underemployment or unemployment). As we know the rate of increase of the labor force is taken as being governed by an autonomous pattern. In order to speed up r it is necessary to overcome impending labor shortage and to raise the growth rate of productivity. For r is determined by the natural rate of growth of the labor force and the growth pace of productivity ($r=\alpha+\beta+$substitution effect). If the planner cannot raise the first, the acceleration maneuver must produce a rise in the value of productivity. This focuses attention on the feasible and efficient ways of achieving such a speed up.

First let us pause on the feasibility and consequences of the planner's maneuver to change the values of m and a parameters under conditions of full employment. Let us observe the behavior of the system during the process of adjustment to a higher (reforged) m and after the process is ended. Let us first take the case of neutral technical progress as illustrated in figure 2. If at time t, capital intensity is raised from OM to OT, this entails a certain proportional increase in productivity in new plants put into operation. Regarding the aggregate stock of capital, the rejuvenation adjustment proceeds gradually. Each year some equipment of old vintage, incorporating "old techniques" (corresponding to *OM*) is retired, while some new equipment, incorporating "new techniques" (corresponding to *OT*) is installed. The longer the process, the larger the share of reforged equipment in the aggregate stock. After a period of n years—equal to the life span of equipment—the process of elimination of "old" and replacement by "new" techniques is completed. The entire stock of capital features equipment of *OT* capital intensity and productivity rises correspondingly. But the increase in productivity achieved once for new equipment requires a period of n years to permeate the entire capital stock. During such a period the average labor productivity rises at a higher pace than that resulting from technical progress. *Ceteris paribus,* the latter rate remains unaltered unless m has been readjusted to a higher level. Labor engaged in the new plants (manpower released from the discarded plants and the new additions to the labor force) produces a higher output than if recasting to higher m had not been initiated. Therefore, the increment in the rate of national production brought about by new investment is increased while the diminution of national output owing to the "death" of old equipment remains constant. The difference between the increase of the growth rate of productivity and the "normal" growth rate of productivity is largest at the beginning of the reforging period. Successively the share of equipment with higher m becomes larger and larger; new plants contribute relatively less and less to the rise of capital intensity (productivity); and the difference between "new" investments and the "old" vintage structure of capital stock becomes less and less pronounced. Finally—after the readjustment to a higher m has been completed and the decline of national product owing to the discarding of old equipment is also increased accordingly—the growth pace of the increase in productivity stabilizes. That is, the growth pace of productivity abates and eventually returns to the normal level, solely determined by technical progress, given the size of m (the substitution induced effect of growth of productivity has been exhausted and the initial growth rate of productivity due to the technical progress effect is once again restored as the overall productivity of the system grows at the same rate as productivity of plants of the latest vintage). Clearly, the entire stock of capital features the same capital intensity and productivity as the generation of investment carrying "*OT* techniques." The rate of growth of national income *r*, returns to its normal level, determined by the level of growth of productivity (function of technical progress) and the natural rate of growth of the labor force.

Whereas in the case of neutral technical progress, the growth pace of productivity, after reforging, returns to its initial level, determined solely by technical progress, such a process follows a different course if technical progress is not neutral. In case of encouraging capital intensity, the adoption of a higher *m* results not only, as we know, in a once-and-for-all rise in productivity in new plants, but also in a speed-up of the growth pace of this productivity. Thus when the process of reforging the system to a higher *m* is completed, after some time (*n* years), the rate of growth of productivity does not set. Its initial level α has been changed and stabilized at some *higher* level $\alpha'(\alpha' > \alpha)$. During the process of reforging, the retardation of the rate at which capital stock is adjusted to a higher *m* is, at least in part, compensated by the increasing impact on the rise in productivity in the new plants at the rate α which exceeds that of *a*. On the contrary, if technical progress is of the discouraging type, after the process of readjustment to higher *m* comes to an end, the growth pace of productivity again does not return to its initial level, but is now stabilized at a *lower* level $\alpha'(\alpha' < \alpha)$.

Assume that the process of rejuvenating the capital stock is achieved by intensifying the scrapping of the existing productive apparatus. The shorter the life span of equipment (modernization of production techniques) and the younger the age composition of the capital stock, the higher is the average output-labor ratio, for this average is then closer to the level of productivity of new plants. After the rejuvenation of the vintage structure has been completed the rate of increase of productivity will reset to the initial level α. The situation is similar to that of the reforging process in the case of neutral technical progress. For once the readjustment process is completed, the growth rate of productivity falls back to the initial "normal" level. Kalecki proceeds to show that after equipment existing at the outset of the rejuvenation process has been scrapped, the system returns to a steady growth of productivity α and that of national income $r_0 = \alpha + \beta$, with the parameter of amortization *a* treated as independent of *m*. (Kalecki 1969b, pp. 63-64.)

If under conditions of full employment the growth rate of national income can be accelerated, at least for the period of reforging, (and such a speed-up may be achieved by raising the coefficient of capital intensity *m*, so as to raise productivity in new plants), the problem is whether and to what extent it is desirable to raise capital intensity in the aggregate productive apparatus. For clearly the fact that it is feasible in this way to modify *r*, does not necessarily mean that it is always advisable to do so, nor that it is necessarily the best way of doing so.

Again the analysis of the modification of the growth momentum is organized according to the possibilities offered by the state of the labor supply. The problems of speed-up under conditions of full employment are briefly examined here. The rationale behind changing (raising or reducing) the capital intensity under conditions of unlimited labor supply are discussed subsequently.

To recall, if technical progress is of a neutral kind, the growth rate of labor productivity (with a constant level of *m*) is not a function of the coefficient of capital intensity and cannot be permanently changed (upward or downward) by a change in the capital coefficient *m*. On the contrary, in the case of biased technical progress, the rate of change of labor productivity is a function of the level of coefficient *m*, and a maneuver to modify the level of capital intensity brings about, *ceteris paribus,* permanent changes in the growth rate of labor productivity in aggregate production. But temporary modifications of the dynamics of productivity can be brought about—irrespective of the type of technical progress—by changing the value of the capital coefficient.

Let us assume that the planner increased labor productivity by raising the capital-output ratio, with a neutral-type technical progress to begin with. The planner raises the capital coefficient from its initial level m_0 to the level *m*, and productivity in newly commissioned capacities is raised $(1+p)$ times. For the aggregate stock of capital in existence, the reforging process takes *n* years. During the reforging period the average productivity increases at a higher rate than in the initial situation; i.e., at a rate exceeding α. As we have seen, this extra growth of productivity gradually loses its momentum, and finally the extra growth rate fades out, and the process of reforging capital is completed. Then the system returns to the original rate of growth of productivity, determined by technological progress. Over the n years of the reforging period, national income will grow by $(1+r_o)^n(1+p)$.[1] The average annual growth rate over the reforging period will be $r_a=(1+r_o)\sqrt[n]{(1+p)}-1$, where r_a is determined by r_o, p and n, and $p>0$. On the average, national income will expand in the proportion $(1+r_o)\sqrt[n]{(1+p)}$ each year. From the pattern of growth of productivity, it follows that the average rate of growth of productivity (national income, given constant rate of increase of employment) is higher than the initial rate before the reforging maneuver was started, r_o, but lower than the rate at the outset of the period when the "extra" productivity was at its highest, and thereafter gradually declined.

Kalecki presents the process of acceleration of the growth of national income by diagram and analyzes it in detail. Omitting the steps here, the problem is that, as the planner increases capital intensity from its initial level m_o to a higher level, this results in a growth of productivity in new plants in the proportion $1+p$, and the rate of growth of national income in the first year of reforging is increased from r_o to r. But this is accompanied by a rise in the rate of accumulation, and, *ipso facto,* reduction of the rate of consumption (relative share of consumption in national income). During the period of reforging the rate of growth of national income slackens, and the rate of accumulation falls. But whereas, at the termination of the process of reforging, the growth rate of national income resets to the initial rate r_o, the rate of accumulation is higher than in the initial position i_o, as, *ceteris paribus,* the investment rate must rise in proportion to the rise in capital intensity. Thus a rise of the investment rate, required to sustain the growth rate of national income equal to the initial one, is a permanent effect of reforging capital to a higher capital intensity. "The rate of growth falls back to its initial level, but the rise in the capital-output ratio is irreversible and burdens the economy 'for good' with a higher rate of productive accumulation." (Kalecki 1969b, p. 68.)

Once again this brings into focus the question of aims of the economy. The whole purpose of the capital intensity raising maneuver (reforging process) is just to raise "now" the growth rate of national income. Such a speed-up maneuver is always beneficial (abstracting from barriers) in terms of increasing the rate of production. But if the aim of the socialist economy is to raise the standard of living, the paramount criterion is the effect of the strategy on the level and time pattern of consumption. The point is that the maneuver of raising m clearly affects the level (rate) of consumption at the end of the reforging period, and thus the average rate of growth of consumption during this period. When the rate of growth resets to its initial level, to sustain such a growth rate ultimately a higher rate of investment is required than the initial one, and, *ipso facto,* it entails a permanent drop in the rate of consumption. This is to say that, at the end of the reforging period, after a lapse of n years, national income will be $(1+r_o)^n(1+p)$ larger than at the outset, over n years the increase in consumption will be smaller, or the proportion of consumption to national income falls from the initial level of $1-i_o$ to $1-i_n$ when the recasting process comes to the end. Thus consumption increases in the proportion $[(1+r_o)^n(1+p)][(1-i_n)/(1-i_o)]$, and the aggregate "extra" growth brought about by the reforging up to the higher capital intensity will be $[1+p][(1-i_n)/(1-i_o)]$. In this expression the first factor is clearly larger than 1 (the rise in the capital-output ratio results in a rise in productivity in the new plants) and the second smaller than 1 (the terminal rate of accumulation is higher than the initial, and so the numerator—the terminal rate of consumption—must be smaller than the denominator—the initial rate of consumption). Thus it is by no means certain that the product will exceed unity. This suggests that fulfillment of certain criteria is necessary to undertake such a maneuver. *Ceteris paribus,* raising the capital intensity is beneficial only if the following condition is fulfilled:[2/3] $[1+p][(1-i_n)/(1-i_o)]>1$. This leads to the rule that the raising of the capital-output ratio is legitimate only if the following condition is fulfilled:

$$(1+p)\frac{1-i_n}{1-i_o}=[1+p]\left[1-\frac{(r_o+a-u)\,(m-m_o)}{1-i_o}\right]>1.$$

"If the response of the productivity of labour to the rise in capital intensity is weak, the condition . . . is not fulfilled—i.e., there is no increase in consumption." (Kalecki 1969b, p. 69.)

The growth acceleration maneuver by raising the capital-output ratio entails raising the national output somewhat, but it *might* not succeed in increasing consumption at all. With low efficiency of mechanization, the effect of substitution of capital for labor is meager (increase in productivity is small and $1+p$ may only slightly exceed unity) for a small temporary rise in output requires a relatively large increase in capital intensity—in investment. The share of consumption falls, i.e., $(1-i_n)<(1-i_o)$ and thus $(1-i_n)/(1-i_o)$ is smaller than unity. Hence, contrary to the widely held views in the official circles in Eastern Europe, raising the capital-output ratio cannot be considered a universal remedy (save for certain cases of technical progress) and the maneuver of increasing the rate of growth by raising the capital intensity does not always lead to higher consumption in the long run. Indeed, such a maneuver may entail a deterioration in the long run.

This raises another important question for economic policy, particularly relevant to the strategy pursued in Eastern Europe. So far the discussion focused mainly on the rationale of raising m. The results obtained beg the question as to the movement in the opposite direction, if, for whatever reason, a wrong decision was made regarding m (if capital intensity was overshot). Indeed, Kalecki argues that growth acceleration, retardation, or maintenance are distinct alternatives to be considered. In the case under consideration, he states explicitly that, if the condition stated above is not fulfilled, "it is definitely advantageous to 'recast' aggregate equipment in order to *reduce* its capital intensity; this causes consumption to grow at a rate higher than r_0 in both the short and the long run." (Kalecki 1969b, p. 74.) Here a reduction of capital-output ratio clearly brings about reduction in the growth rate of aggregate production, for, *ceteris paribus*, productivity will be $(1+p)$ times smaller than it would have been, had the reduction of m not occurred. Such a reduction will not only have a beneficial effect on consumption in the short run (as, *ipso facto*, the investment rate will be reduced), but the terminal rate of accumulation will be lower (and the consumption rate higher). The growth rate falls in proportion to the decline in m. *Ceteris paribus*, the fall in the accumulation rate to that compatible with a lower growth rate of national income is a permanent effect of reforging capital to a lower m. Consumption might be, but is not necessarily, adversely affected in the long run. The future level of consumption will depend on the size of the national income and the share of consumption in that income, and thus on the relative strength of the two opposite pulls: (1) the depressing (or stimulating) effect of factors' substitution on change in national income; and (2) the favorable (or depressing) effect of an altered rate of accumulation. It is possible, but not inevitable, that a reversal of an excessive rise of capital intensity will entail only a relatively small decline in productivity (i.e., $1+p$ will hardly surpass unity), but the consumption rate will increase more than proportionately $[(1-i_n)/(1-i_o)$ is considerably larger than 1]. This will result in gains in both short- and long-run consumption. Evidently, the speed-up by higher capital intensity always raises p and thus Y, and deceleration has the opposite effect. But the same cannot be said of consumption. (Cf. Kalecki 1963c.) Under certain conditions a deliberate deceleration of the growth momentum via lowering m is as "legitimate" as increasing growth by raising m. The underlying idea is skepticism about the folklore of sophisticated technology and the slogan of maximization of productivity as applicable to all cases and advantageous in all circumstances.

Over the n years of the reforging period, the average annual growth rate of consumption (c) is clearly lower than the average annual growth rate of national income (r_a), which is lower than the growth pace of national income at the outset of the reforging period (r). The average growth rate of consumption is: $c=(1+r_o)^n\sqrt{(1+p)^n}\sqrt{[(1-i_n)/(1-i_o)]}-1=(1+r_a)^n\sqrt{[(1-i_n)/(1-i_o)]}-1$. Through the reforging period, consumption rises on the average at a slower rate than national income at the outset of the reforging maneuver. "This fact has much relevance for the decision as to how far it is desirable to accelerate the growth of national income by means of raising the capital-output ratio. For at the expense of increasing the rate of accumulation by $i-i_o$ . . . at the outset of 'recasting' period we obtain an average rate of growth of consumption during this period c . . . which is lower than r . . . but (according to our assumption about the purpose of 'recasting') higher than r_o—i.e. and 'additional' increase in consumption over n years at an average rate of $c-r_o$." (Kalecki 1969b, p. 70.) This argument rests on the assumption about the very aim of the recasting maneuver and the consequences of such action must be taken into account in the "cost-benefit" calculations of such decisions.

The advisability of raising capital intensity is the extent to which such a modification is desirable, presented diagrammatically by the means of the decision curve. In figure 7 the curve BV portrays the functional relationship between the productive accumulation rate (i) and the growth rate of national income (r) at the outset of the reforging period n. Curve BZ depicts the functional relationship between the same productive accumulation rate and the average annual growth rate of consumption during the n years period of reforging. The slope of the straight line connecting the point on the BV curve with point F is equal to the value of output-capital ratio or the reciprocal of the capital-output ratio. The slope of the curve BZ increases at a decreasing rate up to point S, where the curve reaches

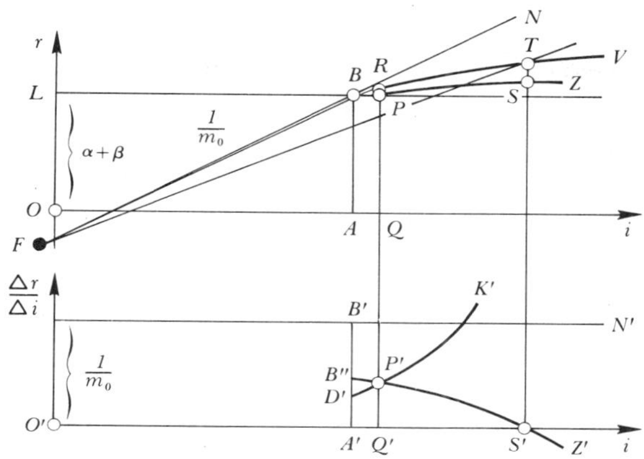

Fig. 7

a maximum and declines thereafter. The "extra" relative increase in consumption during the reforging period is:

$$(1+p)\frac{1-i_n}{1-i_o}=[1+p]\left[1-\frac{(r_o+a-u)\ (m-m_o)}{1-i_o}\right]$$

In testing the consequences of growth acceleration by higher capital intensity, the larger the modification of the capital coefficient, the larger, of course, the difference $m-m_o$. If the coefficient m is sufficiently large, the second factor in the right-hand side of the equation may even approach 0 and c must be negative (the curve *BZ* intersects the horizontal axis and, therefore, reaches a maximum at some point *S*). In no case must the planner allow the capital-output ratio to exceed the level which corresponds to a maximum at point *S*.

On the lower part of figure 7, i is plotted on the horizontal axis as in the upper part, while the vertical axis represents the yield in terms of increase in the rate of growth of national income by raising the rate of productive accumulation by incremental units, whereas in the upper part the vertical axis denotes the rate of growth. Curve *B″Z′* depicts $\Delta c/\Delta i$ for the curve *BZ* (the slope of its tangent for a given accumulation rate). The curve *B″Z′* lies below the straight line *B′N′*, for slopes of all tangents to the curve *BZ* are smaller than the slope of the horizontal line BN. The $B''Z'$ cuts the horizontal axis at the point S' corresponding to the maximum point S. $D'K'$ is the decision curve of the planner. The point P' at the intersection of curves $B''Z'$ and $D'K'$ portrays the productive accumulation rate at the outset of the reforging process. The projection of P' into the curve BV gives a growth rate of national income at the outset of this process $r=OR$. Similarly, projecting the point P' into the curve BZ in the upper part of the diagram gives the average growth rate of consumption. And the slope of the straight line connecting point R on curve BV with point F gives the capital-output ratio that should be adopted by the planner.[4]

Only if the weighty problem of the pattern of consumption during the reforging process is ignored, the optimum choice is the case corresponding to the maximum point S *on the curve* BZ (the capital intensity corresponding to the straight line FT). Such choice permits the planner to achieve the highest possible value of the average growth rate of consumption over the n years period. This amounts to achieving the highest level of consumption which may be obtained, given the state of labor supply $\alpha+\beta$ and the process of reforging comes to an end. "Many authors, especially in the West, concentrated their attention on this solution which was even nicknamed the 'golden rule.' However, it follows from our argument that this solution is purely theoretical in character because the key problem in the choice of capital intensity is the standard of living in *the course* of 'recasting.' The ascending 'decision curve' which allows for this factor leads . . . to the adoption of a much lower capital intensity and a lower average rate of growth of consumption during the period of 'recasting.'" (Kalecki 1969b, p. 74.)

Gradual Versus Abrupt Growth Acceleration

The above considerations beg the question of a more satisfactory approach to the problem perhaps by reducing the sharpness of the inroads into current consumption by gradually achieving the increased rate of accumulation required at the outset of the period of reforging. Suppose that this is being done, during some transitional period the fruits from the normal increase in productivity owing to technical progress α are used up exclusively for accumulation, i.e., for a gradual raising of capital intensity in the new plants which is made possible by the expansion of national income promoted by the growth of productivity. Thus the growth speed-up is based on a gradual increase in the capital intensity of investment and thus of labor productivity in the new plants. To the degree that the normal increase in productivity at a rate α is absorbed by accumulation, the "extra" increase in productivity can be used to increase both consumption and accumulation in the same proportions. Consequently, real wages do not remain unchanged throughout the transition period, but grow, *pari passu,* with the extra rise in productivity. This increase in real wages is a counterpart of the increase in consumption during the transition period which ensues from the speed-up in the expansion of the labor force. *Ceteris paribus,* the length of the transition period varies inversely with the size of α; i.e., the transition period will be shorter, the higher the normal rate of growth of productivity owing to technical progress. During the reforging process consumption will benefit from what is made available for it from the yields of α.

Thus the emerging pattern is that during the course of the transition period the growth rate of national income increases, but then flags over the n years of the reforging period; and at the termination of the period, the growth rate recedes to its initial level. Throughout the transition period the relative share of accumulation in national income rises more rapidly than the income itself. During the period of reforging, the process is reversed; the relative share of accumulation in national income falls, but does not reset to its initial level, for the rate of growth of national income outpaces that of accumulation.

The question posed by Kalecki is: Is it possible, and if so how, to prevent the retardation of growth of national income in the period of reforging and to maintain the rate reached at the end of the transition period? So far the argument has rested on the assumption of a once-and-for-all increase in capital intensity; i.e., after the increase in the transition period m remains permanently at the same level. As we have seen, this results from the fact that a rise of m to a higher level leads to a growth speed-up, but the maintenance of this coefficient at a constant level is accompanied by a fall in the growth rate back to its initial level. From this, one would tend to conclude that the planner may prevent the decline in the growth rate and maintain that rate at the level reached in the transitional period by relying on a continuing rise of capital intensity. Prima facie the planner may counteract the tendency of the growth rate to fall by an adequate increase of capital intensity of investments.

Manifestly in order to maintain a constant growth rate of national income, supported by a rising capital-output ratio, the planner would have to raise steadily the share of productive accumulation in national income. Although it is theoretically possible to maintain a constant growth rate in this way, it does not follow that such a policy is feasible or sensible. Obviously, it is utterly unreasonable to continue such a process ad infinitum, for a continuous increase in the rate of accumulation would ultimately require the channeling of the entire national income to accumulation which, of course, is absurd. However, much earlier than that aggregate consumption would begin to decline, and per capita consumption will be depressed still earlier. Evidently, the planner can pursue a policy of maintaining the growth rate at a level higher than that determined by the natural rate of growth of population and technical progress, but for a limited time only. For sooner or later the planner will be compelled to stop the incessant rise in capital intensity which will entail a gradual retardation in the growth momentum of national income until it resets to its "natural" rate r_O.

In choosing techniques the planner should not neglect the methods of production embodying techniques of other capital intensity than that corresponding to the Golden Rule of Accumulation. Albeit certain capital intensity, corresponding to the Golden Rule, permits the maximum consumption per capita in the long run, it is not a sufficient condition for the adoption of such techniques. Benefits resulting from long-term consumption are a necessary condition for reforging capital to a higher m, but not a sufficient one. Such gains must be weighted against encroachment into consumption in the immediate future owing to the immediate rise in the accumulation rate. Then significant gains in future consumption have to be discounted, for they might not warrant increases in capital intensity. Such a consideration should lead the planner to select techniques which embody capital intensity below that dictated by the Golden Rule. Kalecki's admonition to the planner is: "If, however, there must sooner or later be a return to the rate of growth $\alpha+\beta$, this process must not be continued beyond the point of optimum capital intensity corresponding to the 'golden rule.' Moreover, there may be, and probably will be an even earlier decision to stabilize the capital intensity in order to achieve the gain in consumption sooner." (Kalecki 1969b, p. 77.)

Consideration of this strategy constitutes a significant departure from the analysis of relatively "transitory" effects and brings into focus aspects of "long-run" growth. Consider the same problem of growth acceleration by raising the capital-output ratio with capital-using technical progress. In this case the *differentia specifica* is that, when reforging, the aggregate productive capacity for a higher capital intensity raises not only the average productivity of the system, but also the rate of its increase. Beyond the readjustment process of aggregate capital, the system exhibits not only a higher level of average productivity, but also a higher future rate of increase in productivity exceeding that in the initial position. Clearly, the same pattern of change takes place during the process of reforging. The behavior of the system is determined by the more rapid rise in productivity in the new plants; and the effect of this factor is greater, the further the process of reforging.

At the outset of the process of reforging, the impact of new plants on the behavior of the system as a whole is negligible. The fact that productivity in plants commissioned in the first year exceeds that of the preceding year by α', rather than by α, affects the growth of aggregate productivity only slightly. The fact that the *level* of productivity in new plants is increased in the proportion $1+p$ after the start of reforging is quantitatively much more significant. However, at the end of the reforging period, "the rate of increase in *average* productivity is α' rather than α. The rising importance of the higher *rate of increase* in labour productivity in new plant neutralizes to some extent the tendency of growth due to the increased *level* of productivity of this plant to decline over the course of the period of 'recasting'. . . ." (Kalecki 1969b, pp. 77-78.)

Thus after the end of the phase of reforging to a higher capital intensity, the rate of increase in average productivity does not, as in the case of neutral technical progress, fall back to the initial level, but to the level of α'—exceeding the initial level. The corresponding growth rate of national income falls from the level r to the level $r_0+\alpha'-\alpha$, which exceeds the initial rate r_0.

Once again, Kalecki poses the pertinent question (but now with reference to technical progress of the type encouraging capital intensity): What gains in the form of accelerated long-run growth of consumption could be reaped at the cost of reducing the rate of consumption at the outset of the reforging period? For a rate of growth at the end of the reforging period higher than at the outset, a corresponding proportion of national income allocated to accumulation must be larger and the consumption rate is bound to be depressed correspondingly. In order to proceed with the "cost-benefit" analysis, Kalecki adopts the techniques employed in the case of neutral technical progress. He simplifies the analysis to make it comparable with the case of the neutral type by supposing that, beyond the readjustment of the system to a higher m, the growth rate of the labor force is reduced by a steady decline of the time worked to the level $\beta' = \beta + \alpha - \alpha'$. Subject to qualification, this may be considered roughly equivalent to the return to the initial rate r_o in the case of the neutral type. (Thus the accumulation rate declines to the level compatible with r_o, and the relative consumption rate rises correspondingly.) The growth rate of consumption can be related to the share of accumulation in national income at the outset of the reforging period, and the decision curve argument can be applied to the problem of choice of capital intensity as before. The average rate of growth of consumption is the same as before.

Now the question is: Is not the result exactly the same as in the case of the neutral type technical progress previously discussed? Kalecki emphasizes that the answer is definitely negative. The growth rate of productivity in new plants α' is higher than α. That has an impact throughout the process of reforging and tends to neutralize somewhat the tendency for the rate of growth of national income to fall under the impetus of a declining accumulation rate. The point is that here the response of the rate of expansion of productivity is stronger and r_a greater than in the case of neutral technical progress. Therefore, the average growth rate of consumption is also larger, and the difference is sharper, the greater the difference of $\alpha' - \alpha$. As always, an increase in the rate of accumulation entails inroads into consumption in the short run, and the larger and more abrupt the increase, the greater is the immediate adverse effect on consumption. But in the case under consideration, in the long run, gains in consumption are bound to be reaped from increases in capital intensity. But in such a case to raise m continuously cannot be interpreted as a precept for the planners. Given the opportunities provided by technology, Kalecki's planner is bound to weigh more favorably the maneuver of increasing capital intensity in the case of technical progress encouraging capital intensity than in the case of neutral technical progress, and he would be discouraged from taking such a decision in the case of technical progress discouraging capital intensity.

This is only one consideration in the decision regarding capital intensity. Another problem is how the planner evaluates the willingness of the population to take on the burden. The extent to which the population is prepared to "sacrifice the present for the future" sets the limits, *inter alia,* on the extent to which the planner can increase the accumulation rate and raise capital intensity. True, in the case of technical progress promoting capital intensity, the same sacrifice in terms of inroads into short-run consumption is repaid by greater rewards in the form of long-term gains in consumption than in case of technical progress of the neutral type. However, such a reward in future consumption, even if large, might not be sufficient to compensate losses in the present and near future in view of the population's intertemporal preferences.

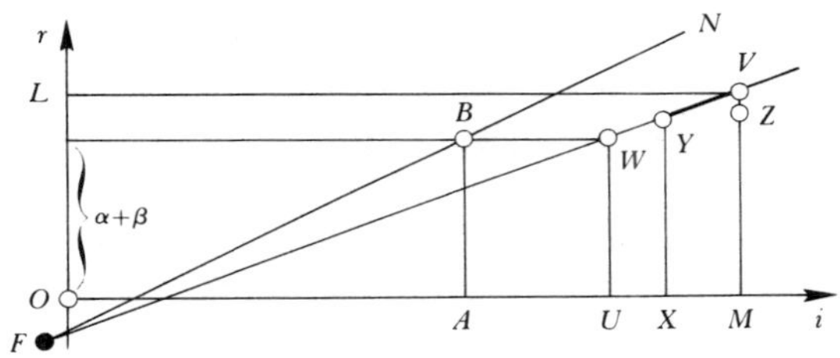

Fig. 8

Again the argument is presented graphically, as shown in figures 8 and 9. In figure 8 the rate of productive accumulation i is plotted on the abscissa, the growth rate of national income r on the ordinate. The initial situation growth rate r_O is AB, the accumulation rate i_O, and the slope of the line FN is $1/m_O$. Let us contrast briefly the case under consideration with neutral technical progress. In the latter case, owing to the rise in productivity in the new plants in the proportion $1+p$, the growth rate of national income in the first year of reforging rises to the level represented by the ordinate of the point $V(MV=OL)$. Also the abscissa increases accordingly from OA to OM. Subject to qualification, during the process of reforging, the point corresponding to the growth rate and accumulation rate moves from V to W. The latter depicts the position of the point when the reforging process comes to an end. W describes the initial

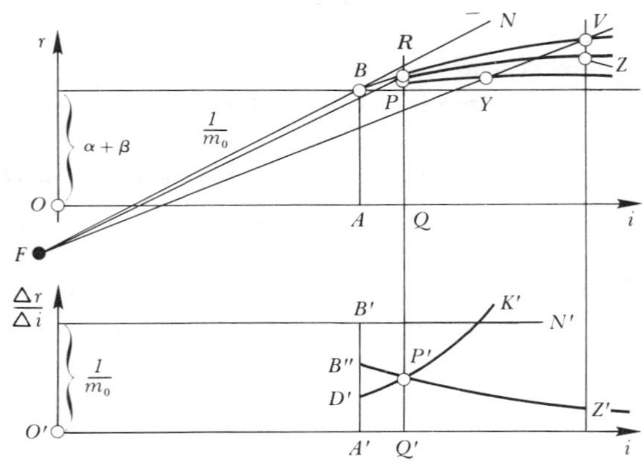

Fig. 9

growth rate $r_O = AB$, but the abscissa OU is characterized by a higher rate of accumulation than in the initial position ($OU > OA$) as a result of increase in capital intensity. In the case of technical progress encouraging capital intensity, point V moves to Y, which is higher (it corresponds to a higher level of growth rate of national income and accumulation rate) than W in the case of neutral type technical progress. Y, the growth rate of national income at the end of the process of reforging, is equal to $r_O + \alpha' - \alpha$, whereas W is equal to r_O.

In figure 9 the curve BV is drawn for the growth rate at the outset of the reforging process, and such a curve is the locus of the moving point V in figure 8. The curve BY portrays the growth rate at the termination of the reforging period, representing the locus of the moving point Y. It should be noted that, with this type of technical progress, BY is upward-sloping, for the growth rate of productivity α is quickened the greater the coefficient of capital intensity. On the supposition that, beyond the period of reforging, the current rate of growth is reduced to its initial level, the curve BZ portrays the average pace of increase of consumption. BZ is the locus of the point Z, and its position is above the curve BZ in the case of technical progress of the neutral type. Thus the accumulation rate i, is determined by the point of intersection P'—of the planner's decision curve $D'K'$ and the curve $B''Z'$, representing $\Delta c / \Delta i$ for the curve BZ in the upper part of the diagram—located further from the abscissa than with neutral technical progress. The average growth rate of consumption and capital intensity (represented by the reciprocal of the slope to line *FR*) are higher than those obtained with neutral technical progress. This is to demonstrate that Kalecki's planner, confronted with technical progress encouraging capital intensity will, *ceteris paribus*, choose a higher capital intensity of investment, for, in this way, a larger increment in consumption can be secured. Kalecki adds that, with technical progress encouraging capital intensity, it is impossible to demonstrate that the curve *BZ* reaches a maximum point, for the average growth rate of consumption tends to rise together with α' which, in turn, is greater the larger the value of the capital-output ratio. Therefore, with this type of technical progress the problem of the Golden Rule of Accumulation does not arise. There can be no critical limit to capital intensity that the prudent planner cannot transgress if technical progress is biased.

Growth-limiting Factors

Given the planner's valuation about the intensity of "sacrificing the present for the future," his willingness to force a higher growth rate of output obviously constitutes only a necessary, but not sufficient, condition for achieving the target rate. As we have previously pointed out, when making the decision to raise the rate of growth of output, the planner must take into account the consumers' frustration barrier. But this is not all. He must also consider various physical barriers to growth acceleration emerging in a supply determined economy.

Kalecki studied at close range the growth-limiting factors in a planned economy and his generalization on the bottlenecks to development and a system's limited absorptive capacity is of great practical importance. Although in many respects pioneering, this clearly is not a "finished" work. A closer integration with the mainstream of his analysis would have been beneficial. Apart from stressing the "internal" ceilings to growth, of particular interest is his analysis of difficulties in foreign trade which may eventually make it impossible to exceed a certain level of the growth rate, and his relating of growth dynamics to the problems and benefits of foreign trade. This part of his work seems to be an extension and application of his prewar analysis regarding the relationship between movements of aggregate production and a balance-of-payments situation.

In an economy that neither grants nor receives foreign credits, increase in imports has to be reciprocated by increase in exports. During the course of economic development, import requirements, especially for raw materials and semifabricates, are accelerated; and export earnings must rise to pay for the growing imports. The higher the rate of growth, the more rapidly must exports be accelerated, and the greater will be (in all likelihood) the problems of securing foreign markets for effective exchange. Higher rates of growth require greater exports or a limitation on imports. Large physical volume will probably be sold only at reduced prices. Export drives are likely to be accompanied by price markdowns for particular products in some markets, and will force export activity to other markets offering less advantageous terms, and, in the process, will make exports less effective as foreign exchange earners (while still preempting goods from domestic advancement or consumption). Thus, owing to powerful pressures of supply, the prices received on foreign markets may decline to such an extent that it would become impractical to obtain the amounts of foreign currency necessary to cover import requirements. Even if the foreign currency earned would be sufficient to cover such needs, it will necessitate relatively high investment outlays in relation to the effect in terms of foreign currency. Therefore, *ceteris paribus,* a given level of investment will then yield a smaller increment of national income, and a given investment rate will yield a lower rate of growth. The dangers of unrealistic and ineffective selection of foreign trade plan variants cannot be underrated. But even if the foreign trade plan proves to be realistic, foreign trade efficiency calculus is required to ascertain the influence of expansion of exports or import-substitutions on investment outlays. The outlays necessary for securing a unit of imports or of domestic production of their substitutes would tend to rise because (1) they have to be imported at the sacrifice of a larger physical volume of exports, (2) a changed product mix of exports requires more inputs, or (3) the inputs required to produce import substitutes would be larger than those for producing the goods formerly exported to secure the foreign exchange to pay for the imports.

Difficulties in equilibrating the balance of payments are not confined to any limited ability to sell a large volume of products abroad at the prevailing terms of trade or to the deterioration of the efficiency of foreign trade accompanying the sharp increases in the volume of trade (especially under conditions of overheating, where bottleneck crises endangering plan fulfillment in priority industries must be compensated for with scant regard to the costs of the remedies). Another difficulty is encountered when the growth rates of some branches, mainly those producing raw materials, trail behind. This again requires higher imports of raw materials to be paid for by increasing exports, thus contributing to balance-of-payments difficulties.

With a certain rate of expansion of a given industry, the volume of projects in construction is proportional to the length of the construction period. With an extended period of gestation, and a high rate of expansion, the number of construction projects proliferates and the available technical and organizational staff is unable to cope with them. Thus the gestation periods expand and this leads to a "freezing" of capital in construction projects. (Kalecki 1957k, pp. 3-13.) In addition there are difficulties in recruiting labor for certain occupations (e.g., coal mining) and a time-lag in mastering new technologies.

It may be concluded that, at a certain rate of growth, no attempts at equilibrating imports and exports can yield positive results. Additional cuts in export prices are fruitless, for they increase volume of exports, but not their aggregate value in foreign currencies. A similar situation exists with investment in import-substitution. Thus foreign trade difficulties, together with technological and organizational factors constraining the growth of some industries, result in a ceiling for the acceleration of the growth rate. Difficulties in foreign trade increase the capital and labor outlays per unit increment in national output. Hence marginal efficiency falls and the rate of increase of average productivity trails behind α generated by technical progress.

Uncertainty in this area should lead to adopting rather cautious growth rates. In case of a relatively self-sufficient economy, these problems should disappear if not for the bottlenecks involved in raw materials and the investment barrier. Indeed, if with high growth rates of output some industries lagged behind demand, the constraining factors to development would be even more apparent in the absence of foreign trade. In such an economy it would not be possible to fill the gap by imports paid for by exports of goods whose output can be expanded without reaching technological and organizational barriers. Long-run bottlenecks would have to be mitigated then by producing import-substitutes, which would often be less efficient than expansion of exports.

With an eye to problems of greatest practical relevance, Kalecki attached cardinal importance to the question of development of criteria for investment and foreign trade efficiency analysis. Here his contributions have been many. His work has had immense impact not only on the development of theory, but also in the practice of investment efficiency analysis in Poland (socialist economies).[5] Only in the more general aspect, Kalecki commented that investment efficiency is evaluated in principle in a socialist economy for the purpose of (a) comparison of alternative technical variants for achieving the same effect; and (b) comparison of alternative possibilities for achieving the foreign currency necessary for acquiring indispensable imports either via exports or via import-substitution measures. Investment efficiency calculus could still be extended by the determination of the optimum structure of consumption, but at the present stage it is a very complex matter, as it requires the criterion of equivalence of two different consumption aggregates.[6]

Kalecki disputed the view held frequently in the West, and increasingly in some quarters in the socialist countries, that an application of investment efficiency analysis so conceived is too narrow in its scope, as it leaves out the major macroeconomic decisions about a growth pattern to the arbitrary political decisions of the central planner. He maintained that this argument is based on a misunderstanding. It is interesting to record here his position.

To begin with, consider the mythical but still instructive case. Take a closed system where there are only two technological variants; i.e. each output target can be produced by one method only. Moreover, in the perspective plan the planner has determined the growth path of national income over time (measured at constant prices); the composition of consumption; the structure of so-called unproductive investments; and the relations between these magnitudes each year of the plan period.

> It can be seen easily that in such conditions there exists only one balanced-plan variant. The volume and structure of investment are determined by the planned growth of national income, and so are the structure of consumption and unproductive investment, and the relation between these two magnitudes. Suppose for instance that consumption is at a level higher than in the plan so constructed. Then, since the relation between consumption and unproductive investment is given, the structure and volume of investment also have to be adjusted, and for a given national income less is left for productive accumulation and the increase in circulating capital. The lower level of these magnitudes, in turn, without the possibility of technical

> choice and the operation of international trade, and also for a determined structure of consumption and unproductive investment, cannot in any way be sufficient to achieve the increase of national income assumed in the plan.
>
> Not only cannot the volume of investment undergo change with respect to the plan constructed, but neither can its structure, because again the assumptions made would not allow the achievement of the assumed structure of consumption and unproductive investment. This means that in a situation where there is no problem of choice of production techniques nor of foreign-trade variants, once the planning authorities have determined the time path of national income, the structure of consumption and unproductive investment, the problem of evaluation of investment efficiency does not arise.
>
> Together with the possibility of choice of techniques and of various patterns of foreign trade, two degrees of freedom arise, and indeed it is within the framework of these degrees that the evaluation of investment efficiency can operate—given the assumptions made by the planning authorities about the growth rate of national income, the structure of consumption and unproductive investment. (Kalecki 1972b, pp. 120-21.)

Kalecki observed that exactly the same situation is encountered in practice. Plan variants should be constructed for several hypothetical paths of growth of national output. The resolution of the conflict that usually arises between short- and long-run consumption is, as we have seen, a decision of the central planner, containing "elements of a political nature." The task of efficiency calculus, as conceived by Kalecki, is to achieve a given increment of national income with the smallest possible investment resources, consistent with ensuring equilibrium in the labor market and the balance of payments. A saving of manpower can be achieved by a variety of means and, *ceteris paribus,* the variant with the lowest investment outlays is the one to select. No purpose is served by saving labor through costly automation if the equivalent can be achieved at smaller outlays through primitive mechanization of "yardwork." The often encountered opinion that the most sophisticated equipment is always preferable is fallacious. The best choice can be determined only by a calculation of investment efficiency and depends on economic circumstances. It is not necessarily true that what is profitable for a concern in the U.S.A. will also be profitable in Poland. Effective production does not only depend on a saving of labor, but also on a saving of investment resources. In this context an important role is played by modernization, which often assures both savings of labor and increased production capacity with relatively low investment outlays. "For a given value of exports that covers (together with possible foreign loans) the value of imports, investment should be fixed at the lowest level at which the full employment of the labour force is obtained. A lower level of investment would mean that the plan is unrealistic, given the unemployment of labour. A higher level of investment would in turn imply a waste of resources that would negatively affect consumption." (Kalecki 1972b, p. 122.)

Kalecki argued that efficiency calculus by itself cannot fully determine the profile of foreign trade or even production techniques. As noted above, the barrier for most effective formation of exports might manifest itself on the supply side through the technical and organizational factors limiting the rate of expansion of specific branches and on the demand side through insufficient absorptive capacity of foreign markets. Composition of exports is most effective when the rate of expansion is relatively low, for efficiency of exports is, *inter alia,* a function of its volume and rate of acceleration. Application of some more advanced techniques can meet long-term development bottlenecks (for example, the burning of oil is more effective than the burning of coal, but if a country has to import crude oil, while it possesses coal deposits, this aggravates foreign trade difficulties). When these considerations are taken into account, it becomes evident that the volume of necessary investments is, in fact, higher than that arrived at by applying a "pure" efficiency of investment calculus. Kalecki illustrates the argument by addressing himself to the warmly debated question in Poland and elsewhere:

> . . . whether manufacturing industries should not be developed, because of their lower capital intensity, rather than primary industries producing raw materials. If we treat the question independently of foreign trade considerations, it really makes no sense at all. We cannot produce machines rather than copper, since that leads to a surplus of machines and a deficit of copper.
>
> Only if this problem is considered within the context of foreign trade can an answer to it be found in the calculus of investment efficiency. This calculus can in fact show that it is more advantageous to produce machines for export and to import copper in exchange, rather than produce copper at home. But even this . . . still does not prejudge the issue. The point is that it is not necessarily feasible for the export of machines to be expanded in order to import copper, and we might have to sell the machines so cheaply that this becomes ineffective. Therefore the construction of a copper mine, regardless of its capital intensity, can turn out to be, in the end, an appropriate way of implementing the development plan of the economy.

> Generally speaking, the so-called problem of the 'directions of development' makes sense only when it is treated as the choice of the pattern of foreign trade (as well as the production technology), because only then does it not lead to plan imbalance. Once the problem is formulated in this way, it *can* be solved by means of the calculus of investment efficiency, provided allowance is made for the absorption capacity of foreign markets for different export goods, and for the technical-organizational barriers to the development of the production of particular branches. (Kalecki 1972b, pp. 122-23.)

We may add, *en passant*, that there seems to be no valid rule for every country to push the export of machinery. For example, there is the inherent danger that Poland might overexpand production of machinery (with rather gloomy prospects for export to capitalist countries), since such exports require increased imports of copper; and it is not always feasible or advantageous to increase export of equipment to procure copper indirectly. It is possible that machinery would have to be sold at such disadvantageous terms that production would be ineffective.

All this brings into the open the powerful system-made obstacles to disseminating technical progress and to maintaining a competitive position on foreign markets. Kalecki's model assigns a crucial role to the impact of technical progress and focuses on its type properties. Foreign trade plays an important role as an indirect way of producing goods. The question arises: To what extent does the planning system affect technical progress, its dissemination, and the quality of goods produced; to what extent is it conducive to a shift of the parameters of the production function; and to what extent does it lend itself to promoting innovations? While the centrally planned economy undoubtedly possesses many advantages for promoting technical progress, there appear to be obstacles and strong opposition to its dissemination in the existing institutional arrangements, especially at the lower echelons of economic activity. Here also there seems to be little motivation for innovational activity. The efficiency of investment, or more generally, the efficiency of the entire productive system hinges not only on the appropriate selection of macro-proportions and appropriate choice of technical forms in which the investment is embodied (at the central echelon or its extension), but also on the implementation of the investment project and on putting the final object into operation, where the system of functioning of the economy plays a significant role. (Cf. Feiwel 1971a, 1971b). Not only is the effect of the functioning system important for the existing potential but also for the dynamic efficiency of the system.

There seem to be sufficient grounds to suppose that correction of some of the flagrant system-made inefficiencies would constitute a significant source allowing for a reduction of the rate of accumulation. But there may not be sufficient grounds for reducing this statement to quantitative terms on tenable assumptions. Even if we cannot satisfactorily measure the effects, it does not mean that we should disregard them. As Kalecki emphasized in personal conversation, it should be borne in mind that even one percentage point rise in u—resulting from a better utilization of, say, underemployed capacity in the machine-building and construction industry—would produce "immediately" one percentage point increase in r—not an altogether inconsequential effect.

Kalecki's model contains the noninvestment variable and may be applied to situations where the variation in this variable (or in its further disaggregated form) plays a crucial role as an empirically quantitatively significant source of growth. Viewed from the perspective of its growth-setting, Kalecki's model circumscribes the likely impact of noninvestment sources of growth and eradication or mitigation of system-made obstacles.

From General to Institutionalized Growth Theories

In Kalecki's model there are two essential growth equations to provide a framework for analysis of growth processes and constraints in a centrally planned economy. In the application of the analytical framework, Kalecki chose to emphasize particular aspects or uses, partly guided by the exigencies of planning as he saw it. However, the content and implication of the theory is much richer than indicated by the choice of policy variables. Taking a narrower point of view, we have two equations and three unknowns.

It is useful to distinguish between relatively transitory or intermediate-run as compared with long-run growth, *stricto sensu.* Certain instruments or measures produce a relatively transient effect as compared with enduring long-run growth effects. This separation is not clear-cut, for the effects of certain measures that appear to be transient, like improvements in the economy's *modus operandi,* might have a cumulative effect and might affect the value of α. The economy is also "learning by doing" during the transitory or adjustment process. All said and done, the level of m affects here r_t only through the substitution effect. This effect is, however, transitory and, in the long-run, quite insignificant. In pursuing the study of long-term growth determinants our attention shifts to the first two terms in Kalecki's second growth equation. While definitely important, β is usually a small number and thus appears to be of smaller, empirically-relevant quantitative importance, especially at a higher level of industrialization. At least this seems to be the case in comparison with the potentially more powerful growth-generating factor α, broadly interpreted. For reasons stressed elsewhere, Kalecki does not concentrate in *Introduction* . . . on the determinants of α—but here his analysis can be extended.[7]

It appears that Kalecki's choice of presentation of the argument for deductive purposes, by keeping the capital-output ratio constant, in the first half of his book was not without its pitfalls. For instance, it gave rise to the misunderstanding that the basis for the entire analysis is solely equation 1, where m is a fixed capital-output coefficient.[8] There are clearly two equations and not one. (Cf. Kalecki 1969b, p. 26, chs. 8-10; 1966c, pp. 1269-78.) Kalecki focuses attention on equation 1 under the assumption of constant m. Once the assumption is relaxed, it is clear that it is the second equation that determines the growth rate of output and the first, *ceteris paribus,* the rate of investment. By way of summary the first equation tells us about the potential growth rate of output allowed by expansion of capacities. Obviously, this rate cannot be equal to the actual growth rate if we do not have enough labor to operate new vintage capital. At a given m, productivity of labor can be read from the production curve. We may, therefore, find the output that can be produced within a given supply of labor. In other words, we can find the potential growth rate of output allowed for by that labor force. The growth rate of output in the first equation is meaningful only if it is less than, or equal to, the growth rate determined by the second equation. Under conditions of full utilization of capital and full employment, both growth rates must be equal.

Whatever the merits, achievements, and failures of the growth-model-building industry, it has come under increasing criticism for "growth mania" and neglect of ecology and quality of life.[9] Kalecki can be criticized on similar grounds. Although the quality of life aspect figures prominently in Kalecki's work, he was not concerned with the dehumanizing aspects of an affluent society—rather with those of poverty.

On another plane, growth models reflect a pre-institutional type of analysis. (Cf. Koopmans 1967, p. 2.) Kalecki argued that the institutional framework of a social system is a fundamental component of its economic dynamics and, therefore, of the growth theory relevant to that system: "The idea sounds plausible but nevertheless there is a tendency in Western economics . . . to deal with something like a *general* theory of growth working on models fairly remote from the realities of the present capitalist, socialist or 'mixed' economies." Consequently, both our past and present have been riddled with the unfortunate situation where economic theoreticians were apt to spin out theories which were not particularly relevant to the world we live in, or even to the better world in which we should be living. (Kalecki 1970e, p. 311.)

In a centrally planned economy there is usually conflict between accumulation and consumption, together with a host of other knotty problems, but there is *no* problem of effective demand as such. Indeed, one of the principal advantages of the centrally planned (socialist) economy is, as Kalecki illuminated, that it can solve the perplexing problem of effective demand simply by fixing relative levels of prices and wages; at the same time it can resolve the problem of financing investments and other nonconsumption expenditures.

Kalecki posed the important question whether equation 1 could also be applied for analyzing the dynamics of a capitalist economy and answered in the negative for "the difference between the capitalist and the socialist system will make its appearance in the interpretation given to the coefficient u." Under socialism "the productive capacity is, at least in principle, fully utilized. Nevertheless owing to improvements in the organization of labour, to more economical use of raw materials, etc. a steady increase may be achieved in the national income through better use of existing equipment."

Under capitalism the rate of utilization of capacity depends "first and foremost on the relation between effective demand and the volume of productive capacity. Thus u is not an independent coefficient in this case but reflects changes in the degree to which it is possible to find a market for the output of the existing productive facilities." Under socialism utilization of capacity is (or should be) "safeguarded by the plan (first and foremost by fixing an appropriate relation between prices and wages) [so] that the coefficient u begins to reflect solely the effect of organizational and technical improvements which do not require significant capital outlays." (Kalecki 1969b, p. 13.)

Furthermore, in a socialist system, coefficients *m*, *a*, nd *u* "are determined, so to say, on the supply side: *m* and *a* depend on the decision of planning authorities as to technique of production (capital intensity of new production and policy of scrapping obsolete equipment); *u* represents the rate of growth of utilization of existing equipment as a result of organizational progress." Equation 1 "will remain entirely correct in a *laisser faire* capitalist economy but the interpretation of the coefficients is quite different." (Kalecki 1970e, p. 316.)

Par contre, Kalecki believed that to some extent "Western" models are applicable to the problems of the socialist economy. "Their problems and results are easily translatable into the categories of a socialist system and, what is of interest, they fit in better here than with capitalism but not quite well still, for they concentrate frequently on points which do not happen to be most essential." (Kalecki 1970e, p. 311.) In a socialist economy:

> Prices are fixed by *planning authorities* in relation to wages in such a way as to achieve full utilization of resources (and this is true not only in the long run but even in the short period).
>
> The trouble, however, arises out of the fact that the models to which we refer do not concentrate frequently on essential problems rooted in the realities of socialist economies. Two points of this character are worth emphasizing as examples.
>
> (i) Most of the stuff on long-run economic growth is written in terms of "comparative statics." For instance, the problem of what capital-output ratio secures in a uniformly expanding system the highest real wage, while full employment is maintained, may be of small practical importance; for if the initial capital-output ratio is less, the "retooling" of the stock of capital in order to achieve this paradise means a long period of higher investment, in the early part of which the real wage would fare *worse* than if no change in capital-output ratio were attempted. We have here a typical case of "sacrificing the present for the future" which I believe to be a political problem of first rank in the socialist economy. But the basis for political decisions on problems of this nature is a thorough economic inquiry into the *transition* from one curve of growth to another.
>
> (ii) Nowhere in Western models discussed here appears the problem of "long-run development bottlenecks." When national income grows at a high rate the expansion of certain industries lags behind that of demand for their products because of certain organizational or technological factors, for instance shortage of an appropriately trained personnel or difficulties in adaptation of technical improvements (the latter is especially the case in agriculture). The resulting

gaps have then to be made good by foreign trade and to maintain the balance of the latter either some exports have to be increased or some imports replaced by home production. These operations will be usually accompanied by higher outlays of capital and labour and in this way affect profoundly the problems of economic growth.

The contradiction between consumption in the short period and in the long run and the long-run bottlenecks, appearing under the guise of the difficulties in balancing foreign trade, are in fact the central problems of a realistic theory of growth in a socialist economy. (Kalecki 1970e, pp. 313-14.)

XV

CHOICE OF TECHNIQUES CONTROVERSY

•

UNDER CONDITIONS OF FULL EMPLOYMENT one of the fundamental questions of growth strategy is the feasibility and advisability of growth acceleration maneuvers via changing the capital intensity of investment and/or rejuvenating capital through intensified scrapping. The criteria adopted by Kalecki for answering this perplexing question are not so much how such growth acceleration maneuvers affect maximization of production over time, but the pattern of consumption over time, and thus the trade off between immediate and more distant consumption. The problem is that, in considering the optimum level of capital intensity for a given life span of equipment (and vice versa), the attainment of "paradise" may prove to be too costly in terms of sacrifice of current consumption during the course of reforging and rejuvenation of the vintage structures of capital. Under conditions of unlimited supply of labor, the rate of growth of national income can be accelerated without altering capital-output ratio (or rejuvenating the capital stock) by speeding up the expansion of employment. But this opens only a new opportunity, which does not necessarily mean that it is an optimal strategy to be followed. Thus under conditions of surplus labor, the planner's freedom of choice is clearly greater, but he also faces the problem of conflict between output and employment objectives and the existing capacity to produce which might be insufficient to employ the employable labor. Indeed, conditions of labor supply make such expansion necessary. What is the implication of the labor plethora spectrum for the choice of techniques (variability or modification of capital intensity)?

Prima facie, it would appear that, in an overpopulated economy where the surplus of labor has not yet been fully absorbed and whose employment cannot be solved in the foreseeable future by "financial tricks," the way to speed up, compatible with maximum employment and rational allocation of resources, is through adoption in the new investments of less capital- and more labor-intensive techniques. That is, the question may be asked whether a rational policy does not require that the capital-output ratio should be *reduced* by a fuller utilization of the existing labor force, at least to the extent that such possibilities of applying more primitive techniques, capable of reducing capital intensity of production, have not yet been exhausted.

It is entirely rational to advocate an *increase* of capital intensity even with a labor plethora? Given the assumed framework and subject to qualifications, Maurice Dobb and Amartya Sen and some other reputable economists answer affirmatively, while Kalecki is sceptical about the benefits of such a maneuver, if not opposed to it as a general proposition. He intends to show "that the idea of raising the capital-output ratio, given a reserve of labour, would probably yield no benefits even in the long run unless the rate of increase in labour productivity resulting from technical progress, α, is very small." (Kalecki 1969b, p. 93.)

According to Sen, "one of the major problems of development planning is that of choosing between alternative techniques of production. The number of alternatives that are open to a developing economy is often quite large . . . . Different techniques often imply quite different strategies of economic development with very different effects on the performance of the economy." (Sen 1968, p. 11.) And "the determination of the optimum *size* of total savings and that of the optimum *capital-intensity* of investment are interdependent problems . . . . The choice between projects of different degrees of capital-intensity depends, thus, on the relative weights to be attached to investment *vis-à-vis* consumption." (Sen 1968, p. xiii.)

The implied policy recommendation and the approach to the problem of choice of techniques when a reserve of labor exists, as in underdeveloped economies, appear to depend on the different weights accorded to the priorities of maximizing employment and consumption in the immediate future and to those of expansion of production and, therefore, future employment and consumption in the long run. Dobb and Sen seem to accentuate the requisites of growth of output and point out that wishing to absorb labor reserves as rapidly as possible and preferring more labor-intensive, capital-saving techniques of production may, in effect, postpone, rather than shorten, the period of achieving full employment. Kalecki tends to take the opposite view.

The problem of choice of techniques in an overpopulated economy cannot be reduced, of course, to selecting one objective and disregarding others. But the problem is really of relative weights. In Dobb's words:

> Manifestly there is a conflict between the humanitarian objective of providing employment to the maximum number of persons in the present or near future and the requirements of growth. It may well be that in any actual situation some compromise would have to be made between them and only a doctrinaire would insist on plumping for one objective. . . . Yet is this conflict between growth and employment, when we examine it, quite as real as superficially it appears to be? . . . If to give more employment can only be done by a change in the forms of investment that is harmful to the expansion of the investment-potential, then it will not be very long before such a course entails a *lower* level of employment than would have resulted had this course not been adopted. In other words, the conflict is a real one to the extent that one focuses attention on the near future; and it disappears the further one looks ahead. There will be some date in the future beyond which the two rival objectives will fuse, and the course which maximises growth (if pursued over the whole period from now to then) will also maximise employment at any given date. (Dobb 1960, pp. 42-43.)

Dobb also points out:

> It is as well to remember that a course of increasing total investment at the maximum possible rate may do more within the not-so-distant future to absorb any reserve army of rural unemployed into employment (as Soviet experience shows; employment has there increased to between 4 and 5 times what it was 25 to 30 years ago) than the minimum-capital-intensive use of the existing investment potential (at the expense of its growth rate) can do in the near future. In other words, maximising investment potential and maximising employment may only be in conflict as policy-objectives within a fairly narrow time-horizon; and discussion of such matters might be less at cross-purposes if the participants were careful to indicate the time-dimension to which their maximising propositions referred. (Dobb 1956, pp. 38-39.)

In order to present Kalecki's reasoning a fuller treatment of the Dobb-Sen argument is in order.[1] Kalecki adapted his presentation of the problem in order to facilitate comparison of the results. In Kalecki's restatement the problem of choice of the capital-output ratio in the case under consideration can, broadly speaking, be discussed in the following way: The growth speed-up maneuver under the conditions discussed here must encroach on immediate consumption. But the extent of such sacrifices during the course of the acceleration is a matter of fundamental importance that raises the question of constraints on shifting the burden to short-run consumption. The extent of the population's willingness to sacrifice the "present for the future" sets an upper limit to the increase of the accumulation rate. Generally, the adoption of any strategy which does not provide for a certain rate of increase of consumption per capita faces at least a floor below which the level of real wages cannot be depressed. Such a strategy is likely to be counterproductive, even if the humanitarian aspect of the problem be disregarded.

Clearly, a growth speed-up maneuver which provides only for a constant aggregate consumption fund would be inadmissible, for, with expanding employment, the real wage falls. Suppose then that the planner aims at the fastest possible rate of output expansion, but subject to the restriction that he cannot resort to a reduction in real wages. In such a case the planner resolves to stimulate output expansion by using the whole growth in productivity owing to technical progress for the purpose of raising the rate of capital accumulation. Thus the decision to maintain wages at a constant level for a long period determines the course of growth acceleration. The planner chooses also to raise the share of accumulation in national income by superimposing on the "normal" increase in the rate of accumulation, based on the rise in productivity resulting from technical progress during the transitional period, a shift to a higher captial intensity in new investment in order to get an "extra" increase in productivity in the relevant period.

Take again the simpler case of neutral technical progress. With no technical progress (the rate of increase of productivity owing to technical progress $\alpha = 0$ and is constant over time by definition) and with no changes in capital intensity of investment (the increase in productivity from higher capital intensity is equal 0 and remains stationary over time as assumed), the combined rise of national income over that period is obviously not propelled by technical advance and substitution. Relaxing the assumption of an economy without technical progress, but still supposing that the capital-output ratio is maintained by the planner at its initial level m_o, the accretion in national output, relative to consumption, after n years is enlarged [roughly in the proportion $(1+\alpha)^n$]. But should the planner decide to force higher mechanization which entails an increase in productivity owing to an increase in capital intensity from m_o to m, the combined effect of the two policy moves (fruits of α are used up almost exclusively for capital accumulation, with superimposition on this of the process of reforging to higher capital intensity), will be that, in the n years of the strategy, the national output will outdo consumption $(1+\alpha)^n(1+p)$, where p as before expresses the proportional rise in productivity in the newly commissioned capacity owing to a rise in capital intensity from m_o to m. If i_o, as before, stands for the initial rate of accumulation, but i_n is the rate of accumulation that would have been n years later had capital intensity remained invariant m_o, and i_n' is the accumulation rate n years later supposing the planner has adopted a policy of raising the capital intensity of the system via reforging to m, then: $i_o < i_n < i_n'$.

Applying the growth equation to the respective growth rates of national income, Kalecki shows that, whereas manifestly $r_n > r_o$ (for, *ceteris paribus*, including the coefficient of capital intensity, the rate of capital accumulation increases), it is not necessarily so in case of $r_n' > r_n$. For, while the accumulation rate i_n' is definitely larger than i_n, an increase in capital intensity $(m > m_o)$ has the opposite effect on growth dynamics.[2] Then, simply, the necessary condition for r_n' to be higher than r_n is that $(i_n'/m) > (i_n/m_o)$. In other words, the necessary condition to achieve a faster growth of national income, as a result of reforging to higher capital intensity, is the relative rise in the rate of accumulation, outpacing that of capital intensity.

Reiterating Kalecki's argument, "Even if such is the case, however, it is not by itself a conclusive argument for raising the capital-output ratio; in addition we must take into account (as we do throughout this essay) not only what happens in the long run—i.e, in this case, at the end of the n-year period of 'recasting'—but also what will occur in the near future." (Kalecki 1969b, p. 92.)

Kalecki reasons that, at the *outset* of the reforging period, the r_n' is lower than the initial rate $r_o = \alpha + \beta$, for the growth in productivity—either owing to technical progress or to increasing capital intensity—does not yet affect the accumulation rate. Thus in this period unemployment will go up, for the growth rate of national output moves slower than that of productivity plus the natural rate of growth of the labor force. Therefore, it is not at all certain that the prudent planner should opt for a rise in capital intensity of the system, even if such a decision should entail substantial increase in the stream of output at the later stages of the reforging period. Kalecki's contention is that most probably, in the final analysis, the strategy of raising the capital-output ratio, with unlimited supply of labor, would fail to produce a desirable effect also in the long run, unless one would postulate a relatively meager or zero rate of increase in productivity resulting from technical advance. But even a small α

compared with the likely values of an increase in productivity resulting from high capital intensity is decisive for the argument. Once the analysis shifts to an economy where technical progress is going on and shifts the production curve down, the argument that economic growth should be speeded up by raising the capital-output ratio—according to Kalecki—curiously weakens the Dobb-Sen case and their argument loses major practical significance for an economy with a labor plethora. Kalecki shows that even a small value of α may be decisive for the selection of a growth strategy and the result depends on the relative values assumed for the growth of productivity owing to technical progress α and that to increased capital intensity p. What the relative values are is a question of fact, relying on the dose of realism regarding the approximate strength of α and p under concrete configuration of factors in the actual case. *Ceteris paribus,* the lower the value of α (or zero as in the Dobb-Sen framework) or the higher the relative value of p, the relatively stronger (or less objectionable) is the argument in favor of raising capital intensity with an unlimited labor supply, and the opposite holds in the opposite case.

The analytical argument presented by Kalecki is relatively complicated. Here we shall examine only certain aspects of an optimal capital intensity, under the conditions of a labor plethora. In the presentation of the argument it is useful first to disregard technical progress and to assume $\alpha=0$, then to relax the assumption and compare the results.

Consider first the question of maximization of the growth rate of national income in a system characterized by the absence of technical progress and with labor plethora, under the condition that a given real wage is maintained over the reforging period, either because the initial level of the real-wage rate cannot be squeezed for political considerations, or because it is already so low that it would grossly depress the productivity of the system. Briefly, now Y_n at the end of the reforging period will be increased in relation to its initial size by $(1+p)$ only, for α equals zero by assumption; $Y_n=Y_o(1+p)$. Similarly, as a result of rising capital intensity, the national income will be increased in relation to consumption in the proportion $1+p$ only, as again $\alpha=0$. The initial ratio of national income to consumption is $Y_o/C_o=1/(1-i_o)$ as $C_o=Y_o[1-(I_o/Y_o)]=Y_o(1-i_o)$ and at the termination of the reforging period $Y_n'/C_n'=1/(1-i_n')$. The national output per man employed (productivity) derived here from adopting techniques of higher capital intensity in the new plants rises over the n years of the reforging period in the proportion $1+p$. And in conformity with the assumption about the behavior of the real-wage rate, consumption may rise only throughout the period as a result of expanding employment in the proportion $1+p$. Employment per incremental unit of national income is proportionate to the reciprocal of $1+p$; i.e., the index of productivity in the new plants characterized by higher capital intensity. Thus capital intensity is increased in such a way with respect to its initial level that, by keeping the initial level of the real wage nonaugmented, the gains in productivity resulting from the movement along the production curve to the right (increases in productivity α owing to technical progress equal zero) are used up for increasing capital formation. The real-wage rates remain rigid and do not increase with a rise in productivity. Kalecki then derives the following formula: $i_n' = 1-[(1-i_o)/(1+p)]$, for $[1/(1-i_n')]/[1/(1-i_o)] = 1+p$.

Reverting to a graphical exposition, in figure 10 the curve BT portrays simply the production curve. On the horizontal axis increasing values of the coefficient of capital intensity are plotted, but now on the vertical axis the term $(1-i_o)/(1+p)$ is plotted. The coordinates of point B represent the initial position; $m_o = OD$ and $1-i_o = BD$, and clearly p equals zero, for capital intensity has not yet been altered. In accordance with the last formula, for a given $m = OL$, the rate of accumulation i_n' is equal to the distance MN between the production curve BT and the horizontal line CN parallel to the horizontal axis representing capital intensity and drawn at a distance equal to 1 of that axis. The slope of the straight line connecting points C and M equals i_n'/m or $i_n' = MN$ and $m = OL = CN$. The ratio i_n'/m determines the growth pace of national income when the reforging process comes to an end.

This framework helps to tackle the question of selecting optimal techniques; i.e., how far should the planner push the capital-output ratio in order to maximize the growth rate of national income when the reforging process comes to an end, at a given wage rate, in the case considered in figure 10. The slope of the straight line connecting intercept C on the horizontal axis with any point on the curve BT has maximum absolute value at the point P, where the straight line CP is tangent to the curve BT. Thus, in the absence of technical progress and with a constant real-wage rate, the planner should increase capital intensity of investment up to point P, but should reject solutions characterized by higher capital intensity beyond

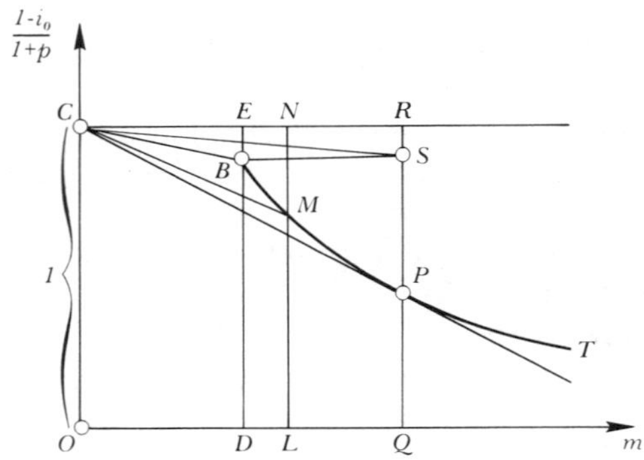

Fig. 10

that critical point which maximizes the rate of growth. Kalecki adds in a footnote: "The rate of growth equal to the slope of CP is closely akin to that yielded by J. von Neumann's model because it is the highest rate of growth under conditions of an unlimited supply of labor with a constant real wage."[3]

Kalecki argues that this is not a sufficient criterion for an optimal choice of capital intensity for it is necessary to take into account what happened in the early stages of the foregoing process. Had m_O remained unaltered, the growth rate would have been determined by the ratio i_O/m_O, which is portrayed in figure 8 by the slope of the line *CB*. The abscissa of point *B* corresponds to $OD = CE = m_O$, and the ordinate is represented by $BD = 1 - i_O$; $EB = 1-(1-i_O) = i_O$. But if the planner chooses to push capital intensity beyond the critical level $m = OQ = CR$, it would be counterproductive as it would lower the maximum obtainable rate of growth determined by the production technique. Following the rise of m_O to m at the outset of the period of reforging, the rate of growth is determined by the ratio i_O/m (represented in fig. 8 by the slope of the straight line *CS*) instead of the ratio i_O/m_O (represented by slope of the line *CB*). The "cost-benefit analysis" must take into account not only a higher rate of growth of aggregate output in a relatively long-term time horizon (represented by the difference between the slopes of the straight lines *CP* and *CB*), but also the impending sacrifices in the more immediate future, represented as the difference between the slopes of lines *CB* and *CS*.

Thus, *ceteris paribus,* Kalecki's planner will not adopt the criterion for choice of techniques corresponding to von Neumann's construction. Instead, he is likely to choose the capital intensity coefficient somewhere in the range between m_o and m, or between the levels *OD* and *OQ* in figure 10. He may even decide against any increase of capital intensity and to maintain the m_o level.

But this is within the confines of a von Neumann economy without technical progress. However, the answer to the question of what an optimal capital-output ratio under conditions of a labor plethora should be depends very much on the assumptions one makes regarding technical progress. Next, Kalecki shows that the situation is radically changed even when the rate of growth of productivity resulting from technical progress is rather slight. Take the case of neutral technical progress, in which the growth rate of productivity α is independent of the level of the capital-output ratio. Now the ratio of national income to consumption will expand over the n years reforging period in the proportion roughly $(1+\alpha)^n(1+p)$. Again the assumption that the real-wage rate is maintained unaltered throughout is essential. *Mutatis mutandis,* the formula now becomes $i_n' = 1-[(1-i_o)/(1+p)][1/(1+\alpha)^n]$, for $[1/(1-i_n)]/[1/(1-i_o)] = (1+\alpha)^n(1+p)$. Clearly, in the special case where $\alpha=0$, the formula reads as before. But the *differentia specifica* of the case now under discussion, compared with the previous one, is the presence of technical change; and here the whole argument hinges on it.

By the same route as before, it is clearly seen that, if capital intensity remains unaltered at the level m_o, $p=0$ and the growth rate after n years, determined from the "expanded formula," derives from the growth in productivity that is brought about exclusively by technical change, with unchanged real-wage rates throughout the period, $i_n = 1-[1-i_o][1/(1+\alpha)^n]$.

In what follows, Kalecki supposes that α has a value as low as 2.5 per cent, and that n stands for 20 years; thus $(1+\alpha)^n$ is valued at 1.65. To analyze the problem it is convenient to revert to graphical presentation (fig. 11), adopting the techniques used in the previous case. As before, in figure 11 we plot capital intensity along the horizontal axis, but now the vertical axis represents $[(1-i_o)/(1+p)][1/(1+\alpha)^n]$. If, to begin with, a curve identical to *BT* is drawn and then its ordinates are divided by $(1+\alpha)^n$, the curve *B'T'* is obtained, portraying the relationship between the values plotted along the ordinates and along the abscissas. If $m = OL = CN$, the rate of accumulation i_n' is represented by the distance *M'N* between the curve

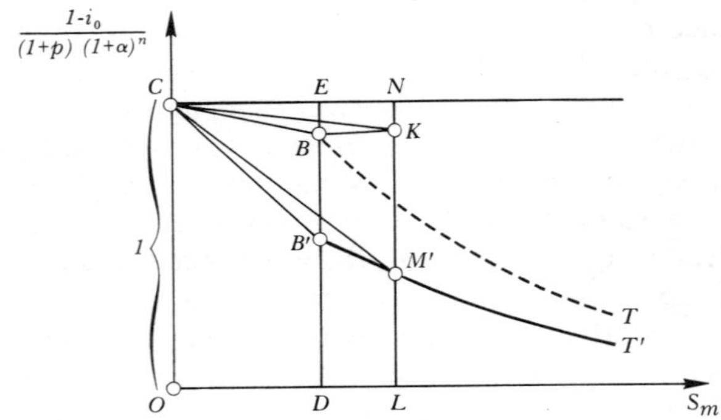

Fig. 11

$B'T'$ and the line parallel to the horizontal axis CN, drawn at a unit distance from such axis. With unaltered initial $m_o = OD = CE$ (thus $p = O$), the corresponding $i_n = 1 - [1 - i_o][1/(1+\alpha)^n]$, is represented graphically by $B'E$.

Let us draw a straight line connecting intercept C with points M' and B' on the curve $B'T'$ and points K and B on the plane. The slope CM' portrays the ratio i'_n/m. The slope of the straight line CB' represents the ratio i_n/m_o. The slope of the straight line CB is equal to the ratio i_o/m_o, and that of CK is equal to i_o/m. The point is that, in the case portrayed in figure 11, it is not beneficial for the planner to increase capital intensity above $m_o = OD$. Essentially, while the point M' moves in the curve $B'T'$ along to the right, the slope of the line CM' falls, which means that $i'_n/m < i_n/m_o$. Thus increasing capital intensity of investment entails a deceleration in the growth pace of national output at the end of the reforging process. Clearly, the same adverse effect takes place at the outset of the reforging period; the slope of the line CN is smaller than that of CB.

Here again the order of magnitudes assumed for technical progress is of crucial importance. For if it is supposed to be absent, as in figure 8, the growth pace of national income at the time when the reforging to higher capital intensity has come to an end is at its maximum value, with a capital coefficient about twice as large as that before the process of readjustment to higher capital intensity was initiated. But granted even a very modest growth of productivity owing to technical progress ($\alpha = 2.5$ per cent per annum), the rate of growth of national income deteriorates as a result of the postulated rise in capital intensity. Thus Kalecki's conclusion is that once technical change is allowed, this considerably detracts from the practical usefulness of the Dobb-Sen argument. Although the value of α (prevailing type of technical progress: movements of α in relation to p) is a question of fact, it would appear that Kalecki's approach is more relevant to the problem at hand in the real world, and that, prima facie, his criticism of the Dobb-Sen argument is justified. "Our analysis seems to lead ultimately to the conclusion that the theory that economic growth should be accelerated by increasing the capital-output ratio has probably no major practical significance in the case where there exists a reserve of labour; however, the fact that the theory demonstrated a new aspect of the problem of choice of production techniques considerably increased the scope of the discussion of this subject." (Kalecki 1969b, p. 100.)

So far the argument postulated a floor to the real-wage rate equal to the initial level. But the imposition of the floor here also amounts to a ceiling, as the rate is to remain unchanged over a very long period, and consumption may increase only due to expansion of employment. This type of restriction is untenable and politically dangerous. Assume next that the real-wage rate were allowed to increase over a long period, but at a rate lower than that of the growth of productivity owing to technical progress; i.e., the fruits of α would be used up over that period to increase both accumulation and consumption. Consequently, at the end of the n years the ratio of national income to consumption would be increased in the proportion $(1+\alpha-z)^n$ and $z<\alpha$. Now when capital intensity is changed from m_o to m, national income expands relative to consumption in the proportion $(1+\alpha-z)^n(1+p)$, and the formula is altered by now having in the denominator of the last term on the right-hand side $(1+\alpha-z)^n$ instead of $(1+\alpha)^n$.

This case is more favorable to the Dobb-Sen approach as it depresses the value of α. Indeed this case is equivalent to the preceding one subject to the change of the growth rate of productivity resulting from technical progress now assumed to be $\alpha-z$ instead of α. The slower the pace of α, the more probable that increasing capital intensity with a labor plethora would turn out to be an efficient undertaking. Reverting once again to a diagram similar to figure 11, and assuming that $\alpha-z$ is depressed now to 1.5 per cent per annum, Kalecki shows that even with the value of "net α" as low as that, the Dobb-Sen argument is of little practical usefulness. (Kalecki 1969b, pp. 99-100.)

Granted that there are opportunities to speed up growth by adopting more capital-intensive techniques, clearly the inquiry is not confined only to the question of whether, in view of the availability of labor reserves, such opportunities should be exploited and how far the substitution of capital for labor should be carried out, or should m remain unaltered; but also the other way round. In other words the dilemma facing the planner is not only whether to raise the capital-output ratio or to leave it unchanged, but also whether the capital-output ratio should not be *reduced,* i.e., whether, in new investments, less capital- and more labor-intensive techniques should not be chosen. This is not to say that there are no political, institutional, and technical constraints in moving in the "opposite" direction. For one, lowering capital intensity is likely to reduce the growth rate of production and the index of labor productivity—widely considered as cardinal performance criteria. There are well-known pressures to adopt sophisticated, advanced foreign techniques and to increase capital intensity for prestige and other reasons, to be discussed later. Clearly, technical reasons cannot be ignored. In any branch of industry there is usually some minimum capital-output ratio which may be fairly high. Application of less mechanized or more primitive techniques may not be capable of reducing capital intensity of production. Kalecki noted that it is difficult even to conceive reasonable primitive variants, for example, in the case of many chemical processes. Even if such variants do exist they are not always less capital intensive. True, the spinning wheel is more capital intensive than modern spinning machinery. But granted such technical limitations, there do exist various industries and processes, even in underdeveloped countries, where it is feasible to lower m by selecting techniques which entail both less investment and more labor. (Cf. Sen 1968, chs. 3,4; apps. A, C, D.)

To the extent that it is possible in an underdeveloped country with a large labor reservoir to lower the average capital intensity, such action may yield certain definite advantages.[4] Assume that it is possible to *reduce* to some extent m_o (thus $m_o > m$), neutral technical progress prevails, and initially foreign trade difficulties are not taken into account. The problem is analyzed with the aid of figure 12, similar to that employed in the analysis of a rising capital intensity. Now with a smaller capital coefficient m, and the same relative share of investment in national income, there is a higher r. In particular the abscissa of point $B = OA$ portrays the relative share of investment in national income i_o, which corresponded in the initial

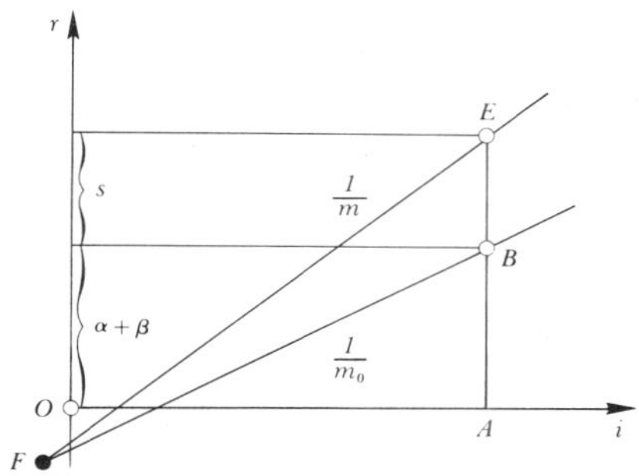

Fig. 12

position and was represented by the ordinate $AB = \alpha + \beta$. The same relative share of investment (abscissa of point $E = OA$) corresponds now to the higher growth rate as measured by the ordinate of point $E = AE = \alpha + \beta + s$. If, in the past, the growth rate of employment was below that of the natural rate of increase of the labor force, the problem is of exploiting the untapped reserve. The greater the rate of absorption of this reserve, the sooner full employment in a growing economy is approached. In an economy suffering from a deficiency of productive capacity, the problem of unemployment cannot be effectively solved unless the growth rate is raised above that determined by the natural growth rate (owing to technical progress α and the natural growth of the labor force β). Only if the rate of expansion of employment outpaces that of the natural growth rate of the labor force, the labor reservoir will be gradually absorbed. The distance *EB* indicates the extent to which the labor reserve has been drawn on to increase the rate of growth of national income above the level determined by the natural rate $\alpha + \beta = AB$ to the level $AE = \alpha + \beta + s$. Since one of the important factors is how employment is affected by the process of introduction of less capital-intensive techniques, it is important to note that the aggregate rate of increase of employment is above that determined by the natural increase of the labor force and the extent of absorption of the labor reservoir $\beta + s$. This is due to effects of the process of reforging capital to a lower capital intensity (symmetrical with reforging capital equipment to a higher level of mechanization) and the need to compensate the retardation of the growth rate of productivity during that period by an increase in the rate of expansion of employment by h—more about which presently. The aggregate growth rate of employment amounts to $\beta+s+h$, of which s and h are drawn from the labor reservoir.

Figure 13 shows how productivity, national income, and employ-

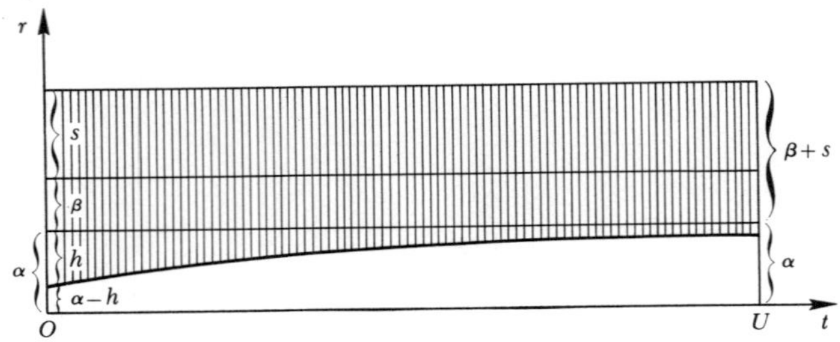

Fig. 13

ment change during the process of reforging to the lower capital intensity of production. Time t is plotted on the abscissa and the ordinate represents the growth rate of national income r. As before the initial growth rate of productivity owing to technical progress is α. After the reduction of capital intensity has been introduced by lowering m to m_O, the growth rate of productivity must drop, *ceteris paribus*, below that of α, for the new investment is characterized by lower capital intensity and thus, correspondingly, by a lower overall increase in productivity. At the outset of the process of reforging, the growth rate of productivity is $\alpha-h$, where h stands for the effect on the productivity of the system of the first batch of investment put into operation embodying a lower capital intensity than that of pre-existing stock. The adverse effect on productivity and output is, however, compensated by the employment-augmenting substitution effect h superimposed on $\beta+s$. In time as we move from O to U, the variance between the rate of growth of productivity of the system and α becomes smaller and smaller. As new investments embodying a lower capital intensity permeate the vintage structure of capital, the growth rate of average productivity of the system deviates less and less from α. After all capital has been rejuvenated and reduced to a lower capital intensity and old equipment has been retired, the growth rate of productivity will return to α. Thus, as portrayed in figure 11 the growth rate of productivity rises from $\alpha-h$ at the outset of the reforging period and to α at its termination. Conversely, the growth rate of employment decelerates from $h+\beta+s$ at the outset and to $\beta+s$ at the end of the reforging period as shown by the shaded area on the diagram.

What are the consequences of the process of reforging the system to a lower m, once the vintage structure has been saturated with less capital-intensive techniques? The gradual drawing on the labor reserve in the course of the period led to its extinction at the end of the period. Under such conditions, including maintenance of capital intensity at the m level, the growth rate of national income declines to the level determined by the natural rate $\alpha+\beta$, simply because untapped labor resources have been exhausted and $s=0$. If then the planner intends to speed up the growth rate of national production, it would be necessary, *ceteris paribus,* to reverse the process of reforging to lower capital intensity now by raising the system's productivity by selecting more capital-intensive techniques. Kalecki notes that such a shift in strategy appears to be paradoxical at first, for after the process of readjustment to lower capital intensity has been completed, the planner attempts to restore the initial position. But this is not so if more immediate effects of long-run strategies are taken into account. "In the meantime surplus labour has been absorbed and national income and consumption increased at a high rate. Having achieved full employment we may either go back to the initial rate of growth or if we desire a higher rate, we have to reverse the process and 'recast' equipment in order to increase its capital intensity because we no longer have the advantage of a labour reserve from which we benefited in the past." (Kalecki 1969b, p. 104.)

It is, therefore, possible for an underdeveloped country with a labor plethora to increase the rate of growth in a different way by drawing on labor reserves and without increasing the relative portion of accumulation in national income only because the availability of labor makes it possible to increase the rate of growth of employment by $h+s$ at the outset of the process of reforging to more labor-intensive techniques. It is this state of the labor supply that explains the "miraculous" capacities to speed up both national income and consumption. Thus, *ceteris paribus,* in the case of a labor plethora a prudent policy is, within the realm of possibility, to reduce capital intensity as discussed above. However, in pursuing such a maneuver the following restrictions must be imposed: The introduction of more labor-intensive techniques (lowering m) should not be pushed by the planner so far as to render the value of

h larger than α (a negative difference between $\alpha - h$), for that would be tantamount to an absolute fall in productivity at the outset of the reforging process. This would entail a reduction of real wages per worker that is highly undesirable and violates the condition imposed as to the floor of the wage level which should be observed in view of the bitter lessons of practice. If lowering of capital intensity were permitted to such an extent as to make $h > \alpha$, the growth rate of employment $(h + \beta + s)$ would outpace that of consumption and national income, with a resulting fall in real wage. But if $\alpha > h$, a more desirable path of consumption (accumulation) is pursued, the wage rate would be moving up, but at a slower pace than change of productivity owing to technical progress. Subject to the limitations stipulated, this kind of growth strategy pursued is a rewarding operation, for instead of deepening the problem of unemployment in the short run as does a policy of choosing more capital-intensive techniques, it makes possible a simultaneous increase of the growth rates of employment, national output, and consumption.

The strategy of reducing the capital coefficient with the labor plethora assumes new dimensions when difficulties of equilibrating the balance of foreign trade are admitted, and, if such foreign trade barriers are of sufficient quantitative importance, they must be taken into account in deciding on a growth strategy. Again it is convenient to resort to graphical presentation (fig. 14). Suppose that, sub-

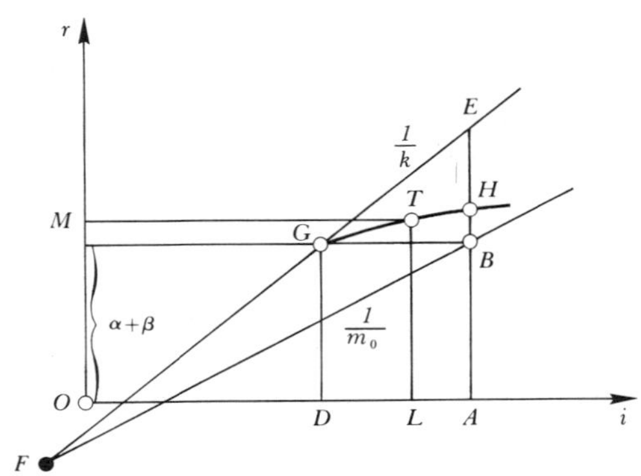

Fig. 14

sequent to a lowering of the capital coefficient from m_0 to m, as shown in figure 12, the slopes of lines FB and FE present the reciprocal of the capital coefficient in the initial and changed positions respectively, and the growth rate is maintained at its initial level $r_0=\alpha+\beta$. Owing to the reduction of capital intensity, the relative proportion of accumulation in national income required to support r_0 will fall from *OA* to *OD*. But had the planner instead embarked on the maneuver of raising the growth tempo over that initial level, this would have entailed adverse implications on the foreign trade balance which cannot be ignored. If no difficulties of equilibrating foreign trade were brought about by such acceleration, the relationship between the growth rate, and the accumulation rate could be presented by the straight line *FE* (or the segment *GE*). If the planner is conscious of the foreign trade barrier, the relationship between *i* nd *r* must reflect the implications of the open system. Here the movement is on a curve *GH* (instead of a straight line), and what matters now is that the slope changes as a consequence of variations in *i*. The whole argument presented in figure 14 rests on the essential assumption that curve *GH* is quite flat, and so again the growth pace of national output will be modest.

Under such conditions, Kalecki's planner decides to maintain the growth rate at $\alpha+\beta$, rather than forcing it up via an increase in the share of accumulation in national income. The obvious benefit is the smaller relative rate of accumulation and the higher relative rate of consumption in national income. If in this case the prudent planner lowers the capital intensity of investment from m_0 to m, a higher relative share of consumption in national income would be achieved, without affecting adversely the dynamics of national production. Here such a choice of less capital-intensive techniques is tantamount to an immediate rise in the level of consumption, without impairing the increase in the rate $\alpha+\beta$ thereafter, thus preventing the depression of the future growth rate of consumption below the level determined by the natural rate. The trend in the growth of productivity will be similar to that discussed in the case of reforging to lower capital intensity without taking into account foreign trade difficulties, but the increase in the growth rate of employment will now retard from $h+\beta$ at the outset of the reforging period, to that determined by the natural rate of increase β at time *U.* (Cf. Kalecki 1969b, p. 106, fig. 26.)

The existence of a labor surplus allows the planner to make up for the decline in the growth rate of productivity $(\alpha-h)$ at the outset of the reforging period by a corresponding absorption of potential labor force into the production process. The fruit of the expanded employment is the higher relative proportion of consumption in aggregate output which augments the *level* of consumption during the entire process, for the gains from lowering the capital output ratio are allocated to consumption. The *rate* at which consumption, as well as aggregate output, is growing remains steady throughout the period considered (constant at the level $\alpha+\beta$). At time *U*, extraction of surplus labor will stop, and the growth rate of productivity at that time becomes again α. If by that time the labor surplus has been eliminated, this, in contradistinction to the case considered before, will have no effect on the growth rate which is determined solely by the natural rate $\alpha+\beta$. Here the existence of labor surplus makes it possible to gain a once-and-for-all increase in the level of consumption, rather than a faster growth pace of consumption (national income) throughout the *OU* period.

The planner might find it opportune to resolve the conflict among growth, employment, and consumption by selecting a compromise solution between the two variants considered above; for instance as represented by point *T* on the curve *GH*. Such an intermediate variant will render a rise in both the growth rate of production and the relative share of consumption throughout the period *OU*. At *T* the corresponding rate of accumulation will be *OL* (i.e., lower than *OA* corresponding to point *E*) and the growth rate will be represented by the ordinate *LT* (i.e., higher than the natural rate). The speed-up in the growth rate will be slower than in the first variant, and the increase in the share of national income allocated to consumption will be smaller than in the second variant.

Kalecki's treatment of the problem of choice of the capital-output ratio under conditions of a labor plethora—elaborated in the second edition of his book—seems to be a significant contribution to the weighty controversy surrounding choice of techniques in underdeveloped countries. This is not only an interesting theoretical exercise, but has great practical importance, not only in the light of policies carried out in Eastern Europe.

XVI

PROBLEMS OF THE THIRD WORLD

KALECKI'S CONTRIBUTION to solving the economic problems of the third world really fits into three interrelated parts: (1) the interpretation of the sociopolitical environment and its relationship to the development of the economy; (2) the methods of financing development; and (3) his practical counseling work to various developing nations, in particular, Israel, India, and Cuba. The first two are fairly easy to present to the general reader. One of the problems encountered here is that the literature on developing economies is so large both in its model-building and in its empirical approaches that it is difficult to place Kalecki's position within the stream of current thought on the subject. His analysis of the sociopolitical situation is obviously radical, with a highly pragmatic and nondoctrinaire approach to solving some of the problems to smooth the way to development. The third part is far more difficult to present and analyze, for it involves a study of the countries in question, their background, and the road they have traveled since receiving Kalecki's advice. Obviously, such a presentation is far beyond the scope of this book. Kalecki was convinced that, generally, his advice was not heeded. He once ironically remarked that his only immediate impact was a negative correlation in the case of Israel, where the adopted policies were the exact opposite of what he had recommended. In fact in 1951 he had suggested, *inter alia,* that Israel adopt a very forceful and consistent set of measures for reducing imports and increasing exports to equilibrate the balance-of-payments, with considerably less reliance on direct foreign investment. Kalecki argued from the standpoint of (1) diversifying the industrial structure, making it independent of foreign powers, (2) preventing flight of capital, and (3) guarding political autonomy. (Kalecki 1951.)

Essentially, Kalecki became interested in developing economies as a result of the postwar emancipation of colonial states. However, his keener interest in the 1960s probably derived from the applicability of his theory of growth to the problems facing the third world. At the expense of oversimplification, one could condense Kalecki's views of economic development problems into the following outstanding issues: (1) Economic development should not be paid for by sacrifices of the lower income groups, hence the process of growth must be noninflationary. (2) Assuming noninflationary development, the principal ceiling on economic growth is the supply of necessities. (3) Consumption of luxuries (as a drain on national income that could be devoted to investment or consumption of necessities) should be restricted by indirect taxes and increased income taxes on the higher income groups. (4) The cutback on the consumption of luxuries should allow for some relaxation of the balance-of-payments difficulties and for larger imports of capital goods and raw materials. (5) The most effective type of foreign aid from the standpoint of the receiving country is in the form of long-term loans repaid, *in natura,* in goods which were not hitherto exported by the given country. (6) Direct foreign investments tend to limit the country's independence and are a drain (an upsetting factor) on the balance of payments.

Principal Differences Between Socialist and Mixed Economies

Economists concerned with the economic development of the third world generally agree that long-term development plans have to be constructed. However, the assumed content of these plans differs widely, ranging from mere forecasting through indicative to directive plans. Even within the latter concept there is a wide gamut of interpretation with more or less restrictive central decision-making. When constructing a central long-term development plan for a mixed economy, on the basis of his findings about growth processes in a socialist economy, Kalecki distinguished three specific areas of difference between such an economy and the existing socialist economies of Eastern Europe. (Kalecki 1963h, pp. 13-14; 1963d, pp. 21-22.) Thus in a mixed economy there are additional growth barriers that have to be taken into account in a long-term plan.

1. In a developing mixed economy owing to specific agricultural conditions (i.e., feudal land ownership and/or subjection of the peasantry to traders and moneylenders), agricultural output grows slowly. The snail-paced expansion of food supply imposes a ceiling on the growth of national income or gives rise to inflationary movements in the prices of wage goods. Although Kalecki does not mention it,

there is a certain similarity between the insufficient expansion of food supply in mixed economies and the experience of socialist economies, but for different reasons. This barrier appeared in the socialist economies (especially more forcefully in the U.S.S.R.) in the form of disincentives to agricultural production and the mass pumping over of "surplus product" from agriculture to capital formation in industry. Presumably, Kalecki disregards this barrier because it is not inherent in a socialist system. It is only a manifestation of a type of socialist system adopted in the U.S.S.R. and Eastern Europe.

2. In contrast with socialist economies where such a problem does not arise, the mixed economy has to influence investment in the private sector. Such investment might prove insufficient in certain branches crucial for plan implementation, whereas it might be excessive in others, such as the construction of luxury housing.

3. Having decided for better or for worse on the nagging question of intertemporal allocation of resources, the central planner of a socialist economy can tackle the issue of financing investment by an appropriate fixing of prices and wages. However, in a mixed economy, state investment is financed primarily by taxation. "Now direct or indirect taxation of the poor, as long as the very rich are in existence, is inequitable. But the very rich and the well-to-do and last but not least the foreign companies resist the imposition of taxes which affect them by their political influence upon the Government; and even if the respective laws are passed, they nevertheless manage frequently to evade them. The result is in part shifting of the burden of financing investment to the poor and in part restriction of the possibilities of accumulation." (Kalecki 1963d, p. 22).

The Social and Political Aspects of Economic Development

Despite the lack of historical precedents, Kalecki considered that, in many underdeveloped countries, there exist specific conditions encouraging the lower middle class and rich peasantry to perform the role of the ruling class (Kalecki 1965n, pp. 568-72; 1967c, pp. 1-5): (1) At the threshold of independence there is a numerous lower middle class, with a scant upper class and with large industry mostly foreign owned; (2) the socialist economies aside, there are numerous examples of state intervention in economic affairs of the developed countries; and (3) reliance on aid (from the capitalist or socialist blocs) is less inhibiting since the receiving country can play one benefactor against the other. In order to remain in power this ruling class must achieve (or at least make the motions of achieving) the following: (a) a certain independence from foreign economic domination; (b) a land reform; and (c) a sustained economic growth.

In carrying out the objectives under items *a* and *b* the lower middle class antagonizes the capitalists and feudal landlords, who are anyway too weak to promote economic development on a large scale. Development must depend on the state for basic investments. Hence the lower-middle-class interests are identified with state capitalism. The enlarged role of the state in economic decision-making obviously leads to a propensity for economic planning of one sort or another.

The development of state capitalism is not successfully checked by side conditions attached to foreign credits by the developed capitalist countries simply because the receiver can revert to credits from the socialist bloc. The "neutrality" of the developing country also strengthens its bargaining position in securing larger amounts of credits. In fact, "the 'intermediate regimes' are the proverbial clever calves that suck two cows: each bloc gives them financial aid competing with the other." (Kalecki 1965n, p. 572.)

Such a social system benefits the lower middle class and the rich peasants because (a) there is no danger that small firms will be forced out of business; (b) the development of state enterprises expands the managerial and technical employment opportunities for the young men of this class; and (c) the land reform usually maintains the dependence of poor farmers on the lower middle class and consolidates the strength of the rich farmer. This ruling class is supported by white-collar and skilled workers of large enterprises—usually a weak stratum in an underdeveloped country. Its chief antagonists are: (1) the upper middle class and feudal landowners, supported by foreign capital; and (2) the poor peasants (small landowners and the landless) and the urban poor (workers in small factories, occasionally employed migrants from the rural areas, and the unemployed).

1. The feudal landlords are virtually politically inactivated by the land reform. Big-business interests are almost deprived of power by means of a more or less far-reaching nationalization at compensation. At any rate, this power depends very much on the strength of big business at the time of political emancipation. Also the capital-

ists fear the urban and rural poor, who are effectively kept in check by the ruling lower middle class.

2. The urban and rural poor benefit little from the changes. The land reform benefits mostly the rich and the middle-class peasant, with little land going to the poor. The poor farmers remain at the mercy of moneylenders and traders, and the wages of farm laborers remain depressed. There is little hope for small farms to expand production. In view of the inflationary pressures on necessities, the aggregate real incomes of these strata do not increase as a result of the growth in employment. But these strata, controlled by some form of local oligarchy, are not really dangerous for the ruling class. The urban poor constitute a reserve army of workers constantly under the threat of unemployment. Moreover, they are difficult to organize.

Towards a Model of Economic Development

By contrast to a developed capitalist economy where the core problem is the adequacy of effective demand—as such an economy possesses a stock of productive capital which more or less matches the existing labor force, and, therefore, is capable of generating a rather high per capita income, provided that its resources are fully and effectively employed — the crucial problem of an underdeveloped economy is the deficiency of productive capacity, rather than its variable utilization. (Kalecki 1966o, p. 974; 1968b, pp. 9-18.) In all contemporary (anomaly of capacity underutilization) economies, governments tend to interfere more or less in economic processes. However, the type and extent of interference differs. Whereas in a developed capitalist economy the government resorts to more or less effective anticyclical and anti-inflationary policies ("financial tricks"), in a developing economy it must tackle the problem of expanding the productive potential.

In underdeveloped economies, even if productive capital is fully utilized, it is insufficient to absorb all available labor resources. Consequently, the broad masses continue to suffer a very low standard of living. Of course, even in such an economy there may be a deficiency of effective demand and underutilization of even meager capacities. But the core problem cannot be remedied by "financial tricks." There deficiency of productive capacity, rather than the anomaly of its underemployment, remains the pivotal issue. The spotlight shifts from the question of how to utilize capacity fully to how it could be considerably and rapidly enlarged, not for the sake of creating sufficient effective demand, but in order to accelerate expansion as a *conditio sine qua non* for a rapid rise in national income.

This basic proposition deserves special stress in order to place the problem in proper perspective and to focus on the crucial issue. It is especially important in that advisors from developed countries often recommend financial tricks to solve the problems of developing nations, without recognizing the basic difference between developed and developing nations as outlined above. Moreover, the financial tricks do not work because the institutions that are required are often nonexistent. When the advisors recognize the differences in institutions, they often recommend the organization of institutions that would facilitate application of financial tricks. One wonders which approach is less satisfactory from the standpoint of the developing country.

The increase of investment encounters three essential obstacles: (1) private investments might not be forthcoming at a sufficiently high rate; (2) a shortage of natural resources and human skills necessary for increasing the production of capital goods and for expanding the construction front; and (3) an inadequate supply of wage goods to satisfy the demand resulting from increased employment. The first obstacle may be partly overcome by supplementing private investments by state investments in order to achieve the required level. In the case of the second obstacle, one could assume that certain reserves exist, especially in construction. Furthermore, a significant share of investment goods is obtained through indirect production so that an increase of investment might be facilitated by additional exports or reduced imports of luxuries. Assuming the first two obstacles would be overcome, as soon as investment is increased, inflationary pressures for the limited necessities will build up. This difficulty cannot be overcome by financing additional investments through taxation of profits, for it would lead to a situation where profit after taxes will not rise and the capitalists' consumption will not tend to increase. Higher employment will spur pressures on the limited supply of necessities, and their prices will rise to a level where real wages of the enlarged wage bill will be equal to the unchanged supply of necessities. Profits before taxes will increase by the amount of additional investment, but this increment will be taxed away. Thus both profits after taxes and the real-wage bill will remain unchanged. However, with increased employment, more work will be executed at the same real wage; i.e., real wages per worker will fall. Consequently, a higher level of investment will be possible. But, as Kalecki emphasized, this would be a highly inequitable way of increasing investment for accelerating economic growth. (Kalecki 1966o, pp. 974-75.)

Another problem in developing economies is that of expanding the "pick and shovel" variety of employment; i.e., with very little additional capital goods. Such employment could be engaged easily in construction, in certain industries, and in services. But this again poses the problem of the supply of necessities, conditioned by the inelasticity of agricultural output. Thus the level of agricultural production imposes a ceiling on employment growth, irrespective of the expansion of capital goods. Direct or indirect taxation would be a highly inequitable way of mitigating inflationary pressures, for it would strike mostly at the poor, with little effect on the volume of necessities consumed by the rich.

Hence, the employment problem (and, for that matter, development) can be tackled successfully only by rapid expansion of agricultural production. The issue here is to implement techniques that would increase yield per unit of arable land, rather than productivity per agricultural worker. For example, large-scale mechanized farms would make a larger agricultural surplus available for the urban population, thus permitting increased employment in cities; but by cutting down on farm labor, it would also increase unemployment in rural areas. Yield per unit of arable land is the important index. It may be enhanced by such investments as small-scale irrigation, appropriate use of fertilizers, and improved seeds. (Kalecki 1960i, pp. 59-61.)

Financing Economic Development

Like most economists, Kalecki became interested in the problems of economic development after World War II, with the emancipation of former colonies and the avalanche of interest in uplifting their standard of living. Relatively early during this period (1953) he attempted to construct a model for financing economic development:[1]

1. Initially, Kalecki assumed a closed economy and insignificant government expenditure and revenue. This model distinguished

three social strata: capitalists, workers, and small proprietors. The latter two groups supposedly save little and their consumption is equal to their income. Hence total saving equals savings of capitalists. The economy is divided into two sectors: Department I, producing investment goods, and Department II, producing consumer goods. Investment also includes the accumulation of inventories in order to simplify the argument by making investment and consumption coincide respectively with production in Departments I and II.

The excess of goods produced in Department II, unconsumed by its workers and capitalists, is available to the respective groups in Department I. Thus consumption in Department I is equal to saving in Department II. The basic equation is inspired by Marx's reproduction schemes. Again, the argument is couched in terms of an equality between total saving and total investment.

Formally, the volume of investment is not financially constrained. The crucial issue is to what extent financing of investments promotes inflationary pressures. The answer inevitably hinges on whether or not, or to what extent, consumer goods production can grow in response to demand. If capacities in Department II are fully utilized and have not been expanded during the period in question, production of consumer goods cannot grow and increased demand for these goods in Department I will influence an increase in prices. Therefore, real wages will fall. The workers will react by demanding higher wages, inevitably leading to a price-wage spiral. If Department II disposes of sufficient capacities to expand production in response to demand, output of consumer goods will be pushed to a point where it will satisfy increased consumption in Department I, at constant prices.

2. The assumptions are relaxed by allowing for public investment financed by government loans. Here the equality between saving and investment will be maintained. Inflationary pressures will again hinge on the conditions of consumer goods supply.

3. The model is further complicated by relaxing the assumption of the elasticity of consumer goods. Usually in underdeveloped economies the supply of industrial consumer goods is elastic because of either sufficient idle capacities or ease of expanding them at a relatively low cost. On the other hand, supply of foodstuffs is usually rigid, owing principally to institutional factors. In underdeveloped countries the additional labor force will be drawn primarily from the disguised unemployment in agriculture, which will not diminish

production of agriculture. On the contrary it might augment per capita peasant consumption or leave a surplus of agricultural produce to be marketed in urban centers. Also consumption standards of urban workers usually exceed those of poor peasants. Hence, increased demand of a larger labor force will not be fully met by the surplus released by rural-urban migration.

Thus increased investment might create powerful pressures on food supplies, while production of industrial consumer goods could be increased. If the higher food prices benefit the peasants, the demand for industrial consumer goods will rise. But if these increased prices benefit only landlords, traders, or moneylenders, the larger incomes will be spent on luxuries or not at all.

Inflation can be prevented by an adequate food supply, and also by an increase in industrial productivity; with the important difference that the first tends to raise real wages at a given level of nonagricultural employment, whereas the second tends to raise real wages by reducing the level of employment compatible with a given level of nonagricultural production. If increased capital per worker is responsible for all growth of industrial output, the problem of inflation does not arise. However, it would prevent the rural-urban migration which, in a developing country, in many cases favors increased living standards.

4. Rapid economic development usually involves a strained balance of foreign trade. Imports will grow rapidly because increased investment will require a larger volume of capital goods that cannot be produced domestically; because growing production activity will require larger inputs of imported raw materials and semifabricates; and because food imports might be required to meet the increased demand. The growing domestic production of industrial consumer goods might not be sufficient for export purposes, to pay for the growing requirements for imports. Difficulties might be encountered in increasing exports in line with imports. One of the reasons might be that investment resources were primarily directed to increasing production for the domestic market. Another is the problem of entering foreign markets without causing a deterioration of the terms of trade. In view of all these intricacies in equilibrating the balance of trade, vigorous economic development is often accompanied by restrictions on the import of nonessentials.

The same volume of investment can be achieved, with a larger share of imported investment goods and with a smaller share of domestic goods, thus relieving pressure on consumer goods. Hence a smaller amount of saving is needed to finance a given volume of investment. The same holds true if, instead of investment goods, consumer goods are imported. In the first case the pressure is relieved from the demand side, and in the second, from the supply side. However, such activity adds pressure on the balance of payments, which is already increasingly strained.

Basically import of capital can take place in the form of grants, loans, or direct investments. Obviously grants would not encroach on the balance of payments, but their receipt might be conditioned by a number of political commitments, which might reflect on the whole course of development. Direct investments might not be necessarily those that the economy needs for a consistent long-term development, and they might also be a drain on the future balance of payments. Moreover, foreign concerns might acquire a measure of political power that, in the long run, would not necessarily be in the interests of the country's economic development. By process of elimination, loans seem to be the most suitable form of securing import of capital, especially if pressures on the future balance of payments can be eliminated by specifying that the loan be repaid by export of specific goods. Perhaps import of capital would become a less pressing issue if the developing country could prevent the flight of visible capital and some hidden transactions in the form of deflated export prices and inflated import prices. Similarly, foreign capital could be secured by restricting transfers of dividends by foreign enterprises. Although such action would have a disincentive effect on direct foreign investments, Kalecki does not consider it of great validity in view of his skeptical attitude to direct foreign investments. Finally, any improvement in terms of trade can be presumed to be equivalent to import of capital, without the strains on the future balance of payments. The government can impose export or import duties respectively when the improvement of terms of trade is manifested in a rise in export prices or a fall in import prices.

5. So far it has been assumed that the state budget was balanced and that state investment was financed entirely by loans. This assumption can be relaxed by allowing for part or full financing of government investment by taxation. There the amount of saving, corresponding to a given level of investment, will be cut by the amount of additional taxation. However, this does not necessarily mean a reduction of pressure on real wages. Indirect taxes or direct taxes on lower income groups will make inroads into real wages.

Such taxes on capitalists will only partly reduce their consumption and their savings.

Inflationary pressures will be partly mitigated by a taxation of profits, which will somewhat depress capitalists' consumption, although no wage goods will be released in this manner. However, a lower level of employment will correspond to a given level of investment because less will be produced for the capitalists' consumption, thus attenuating inflationary pressures. Reduced capitalists' consumption will also relieve some strains in the balance of payments in view of the reduced demand for imported luxuries. Taxation also reduces the creation of liquid assets. This might be a weapon to fight an inflationary spiral that had already set in and which might be aggravated by speculative hoarding stimulated by sufficient availability of liquid assets.

The idea is that only those profits created by state investments would be taxed away. If public investment is financed entirely by taxation, the resulting saving and profits are such as would prevail if public investment did not exist. Therefore, an increase in public investment, together with a correspondingly higher revenue from profits taxes, would not be a disincentive for private investment.

6. Banking credit restrictions can serve as an anti-inflationary tool by depressing the level of investment, thus decelerating the pace of development. But this can be done by more direct methods, such as reducing state investment or licensing private investment. Perhaps the most important anti-inflationary role of banking credit restrictions could be in counteracting hoarding—a secondary effect of an already developed inflation. However, such a system might be ineffective. Special-purpose credits might be used for speculative hoarding, simply by releasing the firm's own funds for such activity.[2]

Planning Economic Development

Kalecki suggested that the experience of East European economies with long-term economic planning could serve developing nations as a guide for constructing economic plans. In particular, he had in mind the Polish perspective plan which he and his staff prepared. Also most of his warnings about realistic and optimistic plan construction, which are discussed at length in chapter eighteen, apply equally to socialist and developing economies. Therefore, in what follows we shall concentrate exclusively on the special features of planning in developing economies.

The basic difficulties of developing economies can be significantly assuaged by mapping out a long-term plan of economic development, as contrasted with an abrupt acceleration of the expansion of productive capacities (takeoff). In constructing such a plan, both a gradual growth of investment in relation to national income and a gradual increase of the production of necessities can be taken into account. Inflationary pressures can be prevented by planning the increase of the supply of necessities to match the growth of demand for them resulting from the planned increase of national income.

A second and parallel problem is a gradual increase of the rate of investment. A larger share of investment is synonymous with a smaller share of consumption in national income. According to Kalecki, this end can be achieved equitably by taxing luxuries in order to restrict their consumption. This theoretical solution to the problem of noninflationary growth of developing economies meets in practice with serious political obstacles, of which Kalecki distinguishes three in particular:

1. Not only the size, but the structure of investment has to be planned, since investment has to be properly allocated among production of necessities, nonessentials, and capital goods. As previously mentioned, this requires greater state intervention than the countercyclical activity of governments in developed capitalist economies. On the one hand, the state must invest in all areas where private investment proves insufficient or unprofitable (external returns to investment), and, on the other, private investment has to be controlled in order to prevent it from exceeding the planned levels in certain branches possibly giving rise to a chain of bottlenecks.

2. The most difficult task is to ensure adequate growth of necessities. It would be fair to assume that, in order to ensure execution of the planned growth of foodstuffs, the planner has earmarked given investments for agriculture and for the fertilizer industry. But the point is that no matter how well endowed the agricultural and agriculture-supporting sectors, in an underdeveloped economy agricultural growth is constrained by a series of obstacles whose roots are in feudal or semifeudal property relationships, in the system of landlease, and in the subjection of poor peasants to traders and moneylenders. Thus agricultural development cannot be accelerated without adequate institutional changes. An agrarian reform by itself is

insufficient. The experience of many developing nations shows that, abstracting from the circumstances and mishandling of the reforms, it does not solve the poor peasant's domination by traders and moneylenders. (Kalecki 1966o, p. 976.)

Kalecki seems to have drawn these generalizations primarily from India where agricultural holdings fall mainly into three categories: (a) large or medium holdings, cultivated by owners or peasants with security of tenure; (b) small holdings of a similar type; and (c) relatively large holdings cultivated by a number of small tenants without security of tenure. In the second category, the peasants, owing to their inherent poverty, are under the domination of the trader and moneylender, and they are not in a position to take advantage of irrigation facilities, more fertilizers, improved seeds, etc. In the third category, the landlords are often disinterested in introducing improvements. The tenants suffer from a lack of security in addition to all the other disabilities of the small-scale peasant.

Kalecki suggested that a way of solving the dependence on the trader or moneylender would be to institute a government agency that would buy or sell agricultural produce at stable prices. Simultaneously, the government should grant short- and medium-term credits to counteract the activities of the moneylender. As to the question of leased large holdings, Kalecki proposed a scaled progressive land tax. The tax per marginal acre of relatively large holdings would have to be high enough to impel the owner either to sell a part of his land or to introduce the necessary improvements. In the former case a mortgage bank would purchase the land which would be resold to the tenant on installment, with annual payments not in excess of the rent paid to the landowner. According to Kalecki such an approach would afford a splendid opportunity for starting a forceful agricultural cooperative movement. (Kalecki 1960c, pp. 1119-21.)

3. A serious problem is the overcoming of the opposition of privileged groups nowhere more obvious than in the attempt to tax the well-to-do in order to finance increased investment. It is difficult to collect taxes in underdeveloped countries and tax evasion is common practice. This argument is often used by the privileged groups in combating tax regulations. As a result no essential progress can be expected in this area.

The three issues mentioned above—the state's investment function, the overcoming of institutional barriers for a rapid development of agriculture, and an adequate taxation of the higher income groups—clearly present essentially political problems. In theory most ruling groups will agree that such measures are an economic necessity. But when it comes to their implementation, undermining a whole gamut of privileges and vested interests, the situation changes radically and various forms of decisive opposition develop. (Kalecki 1966o, p. 977.) Indeed, a parallel could be drawn with the attempts to introduce economic reforms in Eastern Europe, where the bureaucracy—representing a new form of privileged group—fights tooth and nail to protect its vested interests.

Having examined briefly the institutional obstacles faced by economic planners in developing countries, Kalecki concentrated on a strategy for economic development that such planners could pursue in mapping out a medium-term plan (five or ten years) for financing development.[3] Kalecki's concept of financing is essentially reduced to ensuring equilibrium between supply of and demand for necessities and to searching for means of overcoming the foreign trade barrier which constrains the rate of economic growth.

1. The proposition largely hinges on a distinction between two kinds of consumer goods: necessities (wage goods) and nonessentials. The first largely consists of staple foods and goods consumed by a broad cross-section of the population. The second is chiefly consumed by the higher income groups. As the standard of living increases the list of the first will broaden to include some items hitherto classified as nonessentials. The two limiting assumptions accepted by Kalecki are: (1) Prices of necessities (especially staple foods) cannot be inflationarily propelled; and (2) the lower income groups and necessities should be exempt from taxation, with demand for consumer goods restricted by increased income taxes on the higher income groups or indirect taxes on nonessentials. These two assumptions fundamentally influence the process of economic development, for they subject it largely to the rate of increase of the supply of necessities. In fact, this is the central and recurring theme in Kalecki's writings on economic development.[4]

2. In constructing the medium-term plan, it becomes apparent that the rate of increase of supply of necessities entailed in the growth of national income at a given rate (r) is a definite increasing function of r. Assuming that aggregate personal consumption grows *pari passu* with national income, without major alterations in income distribution among various classes, then a definite rate of increase of demand for necessities (Cn) corresponds to r. If r is equal to the rate of increase of the population, per capita consumption

remains unaltered. If, however, r is higher than the rate of growth of population, per capita consumption increases. The average income elasticity of demand for necessities is influenced by the elasticities among the various income groups and by income distribution among these groups. Usually, throughout the medium-term plan the average income elasticity of demand for necessities will tend to decline as per capita consumption increases.

3. The assumption of proportionate growth of aggregate consumption with national income is relaxed. In fact, consumption might have to be moderated to permit investment to outpace national income. This should be accomplished by increasing taxes on higher income groups or nonessentials. As we have previously indicated, this move will not restrain consumption of necessities by the higher income groups. Hence the relation between r and Cn will remain fairly unaltered, and, therefore, Cn can be considered to represent approximately the rate of supply of necessities to support income growth rate r.

4. A higher rate of growth of national income entails a relatively higher share of investment in national income, so that the relative share of consumption will decline, and the average rate of growth of consumption will be below that of national income. The rates of growth of national income and consumption will grow further apart as the rate of growth of national income accelerates. An acceleration of the rate of growth of national income will require a curb on the rate of increase of consumption in the form of taxation to afford an increase in the relative share of investment in the national income. In case of an increase in private investment, the revenue from additional taxation is used as an "offsetting" budget surplus.

5. So far a constant capital-output ratio for the given period has been assumed. If the capital-output ratio rises, the average rate of growth of consumption will have to be checked since larger investment will be required to maintain a given rate of growth of national income. Hence even with an unchanged rate of growth the relative share of investment in national income will tend to increase, depressing that of consumption, and the average rate of growth of consumption will be lower than that of national income.

6. In examining the interrelationship among the rates of growth of aggregate consumption, national income, and supply of necessities, two can be determined if one is given. In underdeveloped mixed economies the rate of growth of supply of necessities can be considered as given. In such economies, the limit of the rate of

growth of supply of necessities conditions the rate of growth of national income. Making allowances for the necessary investment rate to support the growth of national income, the rate of increase of aggregate consumption can be determined. The latter is restrained, as previously mentioned, by appropriate taxation of higher income groups and nonessentials. It is here that Kalecki saw the main source of financing economic development in a mixed economy. However, the planners cannot determine a rate of growth of national income that would be so high as to present difficulties for financing by taxation of only the higher income groups and nonessentials. The overwhelming ceiling on noninflationary growth in a developing mixed economy appears to be the slow rate of development of agriculture.

7. If the rate of growth of national income exceeds that which could be supported by the rate of increase of supply of necessities, prices of necessities will go up;[5] real incomes of the broad masses will decline, thus restoring equilibrium. Increased profits do not raise demand for necessities; they are either spent on nonessentials or saved. The additional savings diminish the necessity of taxation for financing investment. The higher income groups definitely benefit from the kind of growth that involves inflationary price increases of necessities. The rate of growth of consumption of the lower income groups is the same as would be at a lower rate of growth of national income (matched with the actual rate of growth of supply of necessities). Employment is higher, but real wages decline correspondingly to the increase in the prices of necessities. Hence the lower income groups bear a proportionately higher burden of financing development.

8. The assumptions are relaxed to include foreign trade. Some countries endowed with ample natural resources (e.g., oil) are able to supplement significantly their supply of necessities by foreign purchases. If during a period import of necessities can grow faster than their domestic production, then the rate of growth of the latter can be below that of the total supply of necessities. As the rate of growth of national income is accelerated, there is increased demand for imports other than necessities. Under such conditions balancing imports by expanding exports becomes more intricate because of either difficulties in producing exportables or in finding and entering foreign markets. Therefore, an acceleration of imports of necessities, to fill the growing gap between domestic production and demand, becomes more and more unmanageable. If the rate of growth of national income is accelerated beyond the point where

domestic production and imports of necessities increase at the same rate, it seems that the rate of increase of domestic output of necessities would have to exceed that of the domestic demand for these goods, in order to pay for the increasing imports of goods other than necessities. If, as in the case of oil-producing countries, foreign trade contributes to accelerating the rate of increase of the supply of necessities, it will promote a higher rate of growth of national income. But with a less propitious foreign trade position, foreign trade might contribute nothing to achieve a higher noninflationary growth rate. In fact it might be detrimental by impinging on the supply of necessities (e.g., when necessities have to be exported to pay for imports of capital goods).

9. The assumption that import is fully covered by export is relaxed by acknowledging the possibility of the import of capital. The latter allows for a larger supply of necessities and for a higher rate of balanced growth. Foreign credits permit a decline in the rate of increase of domestic production of necessities and larger imports of other goods, such as machinery or raw materials to support a higher rate of growth.

10. Foreign credits also influence financing of investment per se. Government controls over the sale of goods imported by means of foreign credits increase investment funds and alleviate the need to tax higher income groups and nonessentials. As a result of foreign credits, the overall supply of goods will increase faster than national income during the period under consideration. Simultaneously, the share of investment in national income, which is dependent on the latter's rate of growth, will remain unaltered. The same time curve of investment, as when foreign credits were not available, will correspond to the given rate of growth of the national income. Aggregate consumption will grow at a higher rate than that warranted by a given rate of growth of national income without foreign credits. Since the rate of growth of necessities remains the same, the beneficiary is consumption of nonessentials, which will not have to be restricted to the same extent as before. Increased demand for nonessentials may raise their import. If demand is directed toward domestically produced nonessentials, the output of capital goods must be reduced in order to avoid inflationary pressures on necessities. In both cases foreign credits are wasted, while development is not accelerated. Indeed, even when foreign credits are used for accelerating the rate of economic growth, taxation of higher income groups or nonessentials does not have to be reduced. The proceeds can be

used for such purposes as housing, health, and education. By endowing the developing country with a given amount of foreign currency, the structure of production can be modified. By increasing the volume of domestic supply, without creating additional incomes, the foreign credit diminishes the corresponding need for accumulation. The above are the obvious advantages of foreign credits. Their obvious disadvantages become apparent when they (plus accumulated interest) have to be reimbursed.

Foreign Aid

Essentially, Kalecki's views on foreign aid to developing countries could be summarized as follows: (Kalecki and Sachs 1967n, pp. 35-80.) (a) increasing import possibilities and (b) augmenting the receiving country's financial resources, of which the former is more important, as it improves external growth conditions. The influence of foreign aid on the receiving country can only be assessed within the framework of a development plan. In the long run the receiving country's ability to repay the loan depends on how successfully it develops its export potential. The receipt of foreign aid is not a sufficient condition for sustained economic growth. The receiving country prefers long-term credits, repayable in goods. A positive change in terms of trade is comparable to a constant inflow of grants, without any side conditions. Other favorable forms of aid, without import of capital, are multilateral trade development, bilateral long-term export contracts at stabilized prices, and agreements on partial division of labor.

1. From the standpoint of the receiving country foreign aid represents additional foreign currency (or its equivalent in goods) beyond the import capacities achieved by means of export, at costs lower than those for "normal" credits and without the need of immediate reimbursement. These additional resources are used to raise the level of economic activity. But all inflow of capital is not foreign aid. Whether the inflow of capital can be viewed as aid depends on the comparative costs of obtaining it and the uses to which it is put. For example, economic activity of the receiving country will not be improved if the additional resources are used to increase consumption of luxuries.

2. The granting countries may be divided into two groups: (a) where the existing capacity is fully utilized, and (b) where there is

under-utilization of capacities owing to a deficiency of effective demand. In the first case, aid in the form of an export surplus is a sacrifice because the distributable national income (i.e., national income plus import less export) will be smaller than the national income produced, which cannot be increased above the maximum level determined by existing capacities. In the second, the export surplus is followed by the multiplier effect. By granting foreign aid, the developed country with free capacities raises itself to a higher level of activity.

3. From a quantitative standpoint, foreign aid is like an improvement in terms of trade. Better terms of trade or reduced transfers of profits on direct foreign investments would improve the external conditions of development of a given country similarly to quantitatively the same inflow of foreign aid, with the positive difference that indebtedness to foreign countries would not increase. Foreign aid may be instrumental in raising the rate of growth in an economy constrained by the foreign trade barrier. Whether foreign aid is used to advantage can be assessed only within the framework of a development plan. The experience of developing countries has shown that, by means of effective taxation and other institutional arrangements, the share of investment in national income can be raised considerably without infringing on consumption, thus overcoming to a certain extent the barrier of insufficient accumulation. However, the chief bottleneck in the growth of almost all underdeveloped countries is the inabsorbent world market for their traditional exports. Foreign aid should not be assessed on the basis of the structure of additional imports. Additional import of capital goods may be detrimental if it serves for expanding production of luxuries. But import of necessities, contributing to equilibrating effective demand and supply could promote a higher rate of investment without provoking inflationary pressures.

4. Theoretically the absorptive capacity of foreign aid is unlimited. However one of its limits is the repayment ability. Without new export possibilities repayment will become a serious problem especially when the country seeks successive loans. This is a cumulative process which cannot be solved by a steady flow of aid as long as the country's foreign trade remains in an impasse. The absorptive capacity also depends largely on the extent and qualifications of existing skilled personnel.

5. Developing countries usually prefer inter-government foreign aid, as it prevents powerful foreign concerns from interfering in the

internal affairs of the developing country. By granting aid to given private firms, the foreign country (or firm) is able to influence the developing country's investment (production) structure. Developing countries also prefer multilateral (from various UN agencies) to bilateral aid. Notwithstanding their justification, these arguments tend to abstract from the realities of the complex contemporary political situation. In addition bilateral aid requires no complicated bureaucratic apparatus, may be granted in new and more flexible ways, and is more easily coordinated and harmonized with foreign trade.

6. From a strictly economic standpoint grants are the best form of foreign aid, unentangled with either present or future repayments. But foreign aid is often a political instrument, and the more or less disguised conditions and intentions of certain grants cannot be disregarded. The political price of grants is difficult to assess, but they definitely cannot be evaluated on their outward economic merit alone.[6]

7. Very often foreign aid takes the shape of loans at more beneficial terms than the usual transactions. These loans often refer to concrete investment projects and certain forms of technical aid. Since the early 1960s the loan conditions have been changing in favor of the developing countries in view of the competition between the socialist and capitalist blocs in their lending (and influencing) capacities. The cost of the loan is more influenced by the cadence and period of reimbursement than by the interest rate. The more "commercial" the nature of the loan, the less probable are its disguised political conditions. Loan repayments can take place in (a) convertible currency; (b) nonconvertible domestic currency (soft loans); and (c) goods. In the first case the receiving country must bolster up its export potential. In the second, the situation is somewhat better, for the creditor becomes interested in acquiring new goods from the developing country. But here also indebtedness can accumulate, leading to repayment in convertible currency or foreign interference in the developing country's economic life. From the receiving country's standpoint, the most favorable is the third form of repayment. For example, when the construction of a factory is financed by a foreign loan, and when the loan is repaid by goods produced by this factory, there is mutually beneficial self-liquidating credit. The positive attributes of loans are that, in the interest of both parties, they intertwine elements of aid and trade.

8. U. S. foreign aid usually takes the shape of wheat supplies according to law PL480—shipping abroad agricultural surplus which anyway would be disposed of (dumped) within the framework of the agricultural support policy. These grants are partly repaid by the receiving country in domestic currency financing the operations of U. S. agencies in that country and partly in aid to promote U. S. companies in the country. The remainder are grants, which increase the supply of necessities and thus relieve inflationary pressures that would accompany higher growth rates and mitigate problems of financing investment. These wheat deliveries alleviate many tensions; but they may lead to neglect of domestic agriculture by the ruling elite or to cheap sales of wheat among the population to gain its support, without considering that such policy might influence domestic producers to restrict cultivation of arable land.

9. It has been argued that direct foreign investments are cheaper than credits since they do not have to be repaid. But profits transferred abroad might exceed the cost of the loan. Reinvested profits augment the book value of foreign investments without further inflow of capital. This is a cumulative process in contrast to loans which create an indebtedness for a specific period. In Kalecki's opinion direct foreign investments should not be considered as foreign aid. If such investments are to be at all beneficial for the developing country, certain minimum conditions should be met (although they might constrain the inflow of foreign investment): (a) private investments should be licensed to ensure an adequate branch allocation of resources; (b) foreign-owned firms should be subject to the same type of taxation as local firms; (c) all foreign transfers, license payments, etc., should be restricted and controlled; and (d) transfers abroad of profits on foreign investments and on reinvested profits should be forbidden during a given period of time.

10. Aid through foreign trade could mean improvement of existing terms of trade or creation of additional export markets. Such aid could take place both through multilateral and bilateral undertakings. Once again the latter seems more realistic. They could take shape mainly through: (a) long-term export agreements at stabilized prices; or (b) agreements about partial division of labor. In the first case, the contracts should stipulate increasing volumes of deliveries at stable or partially stable prices. Such agreements would permit the planners in developing countries to determine with a relative degree of certainty the volume of future exports and to make the

appropriate investment decisions. Generally, the developing economies suffer so from fluctuating revenues from exports, due both to volume and to price changes, that they would be inclined to sacrifice hypothetical profits for price stability. The controlled economies that deal with developing countries should also be interested in securing relatively stable sources of supply at a predetermined cost. At any rate economies where capacities are almost fully utilized should be interested in accepting stable prices for their imports from developing countries rather than granting credits which encroach on domestic investment or consumption. Long-term bilateral agreements could foresee changing structure of exports from the developing country in order to afford it the possibility to develop new industries. Mutual guarantee of stable and growing markets for new products seems to be the only realistic approach to regional integration and inclusion of the developing economies into the world division of labor.

Although Kalecki was not really a specialist on the third world and clearly lacked the same sure touch that he had for the unadorned facts of the capitalist and socialist economies, he was able to extract some of the realities of the situation during his brief visits to developing nations, in his contacts with foreign students, and in his experience as an international public servant. Instead of applying simple growth models elaborated for advanced economies, Kalecki paid particular attention to the peculiar institutional framework of the third world, which provided a fresh point of view for this aspect of his work.

XVII

WORKING ARRANGEMENTS IN A SOCIALIST ECONOMY

•

KALECKI ON THE SYSTEM OF FUNCTIONING? The idea is rather paradoxical in view of our previous warning that Kalecki was not overly interested in the reforms of working arrangements for resource allocation. Kalecki never developed a theory of the *modus operandi* of a socialist economy. He has made some observations on this subject which, in view of the later developments and aborted reforms, have proved to be extremely realistic. It is this very realism of Kalecki's evaluation of what could and could not be done, at a time when many other prominent economists were optimistic about the possibilities of reforming the functioning system, that gave the appearance of a certain reluctance toward reform.

In larger perspective, the solutions he offered to specific problems are not overly important. What matters is the inference that can be drawn from his germinal ideas about the relation between the pace and pattern of economic development and the economy's *modus operandi,* relating the planning system to the problems and pressures of the macrosphere and structure of the economy.

With his usual sense of realism, Kalecki suggested an improved system of incentives, factory prices, and quality control that would be in tune with the high-pressure demands of a fully employed economy. Although he consistently opposed breakneck industrialization that disregards the consumption-investment conflict, he was just as averse to allowing resources to lie idle in order to absorb the protracted adaptation maneuvers of enterprises gearing their output to market fluctuations.

In the final analysis any kind of meaningful economic reform that promotes enlarged decision-making of the lower echelons would require sizable reserve resources and would have to go hand in hand with a relaxation of the growth momentum. Realizing what the conditions for such a reform are, and the likely consequences, rightly or wrongly, Kalecki did not want to pay the price. He might have underrated the benefits of such an undertaking for long-term improvements in quality of output, in performance of the human agents of the economic process, and in the quality of life. But he drew attention to the highly relevant considerations that must be taken into account before embarking on such an undertaking.[1]

On the Polish Economic Model

In a nutshell the central theme of Kalecki's position during the model discussion was that tackling the problems of the functioning of the economy, without a clear-cut conception of the strategy of economic growth, was putting the cart before the horse. The difficulties and distortions that appeared during the Six-Year Plan resulted largely from the content of the plan and the continued accumulation of errors, with the system of functioning only as a contributing factor.[2]

1. According to Kalecki, with reference to Polish experience, central planning should embrace output, the wage fund, the larger investment projects, price control, and distribution of basic materials. Such central planning should be maintained primarily for the large enterprises, but not for local industry or cooperatives, whose management should run rather along the lines of the Yugoslav model.

Kalecki protested against the then prevalent opinion that central planning of output should be replaced by profit-sharing incentives to induce enterprises toward maximum exploitation of their productive capacity. In practice such a system falls prey to many difficulties and complications: (a) Since the relationship of profit to the wage fund differs in various enterprises, a percentage share of the personnel in the profits will have to be set on a uniform basis in order to avoid serious anomalies in rewarding employees in various industrial branches and even in various enterprises of the same branch. But if a given enterprise is badly managed and, therefore, reports a small profit, there is no reason for its employees to get a larger share in profit in order to equalize their rewards in relation to those of other employees. However, if a lower profit results from the technical backwardness of an enterprise, there is no reason for discrimination against these employees. Since this situation is subject to continuous change, the process of determining the share of the labor force in the profit with a modicum of social equity becomes a very complicated undertaking. He feared the proliferation of bureaucracy that this would engender. (b) The significance of the share in profits as a material incentive is limited since incomes from this source cannot be excessively high in relationship to basic salaries. Otherwise there would be extreme fluctuations in workers' incomes. However, if the share in profits is not an essential part of income, it would be difficult to expect such an incentive to improve significantly the functioning of the enterprise. (c) Finally, profit not only reflects the size of output, but also, and often to a larger degree, costs. One can expect the efforts of the enterprise to be directed not only to increasing production, but also to cost reduction. Under certain conditions this might be beneficial, but in others it might not. If, for example, with an existing "oversupply" of labor in relation to material supply, or productive capacity, the main attention would be directed to saving labor costs, a reduction of employment, rather than an increase in per capita income, would result. This would lead to an increase in unemployment instead of an increase in national income.

2. It has been proposed repeatedly that the central distribution of materials be replaced by a market system with flexible price policy conducted by central organs. According to this concept insufficient supply of some materials should be equilibrated with demand by means of an appropriate price increase, thus replacing bureaucratic direct allocation at all levels by "economic" methods.

Like many concepts of a similar type it sounds far better on paper than in practice. Assume, for example, that serious shortages of rolled steel have arisen. What could be expected from an increase in price? The prices of capital goods and of some consumer durables (e.g., automobiles) would have to be increased. With unchanged funds for investments, the increased prices of capital goods would reduce the physical volume of investment, but it would not be easy to predict to what extent such a reduction in investment would influence the curtailment of demand for rolled steel. The situation would be similar in consumer durables. Price increases would reduce demand for them, but again it would be difficult to predict to what extent and after what lapse of time. In order to equilibrate demand with the reduced supply of rolled steel, prices would have to be raised so that the reduction of demand from these two sources would be sufficient. This can only be achieved by trial and error. Moreover, should there be no considerable reduction in demand of the producer whose output is particularly "steel-intensive" (e.g., railroad cars or automobiles), the general reduction of investment and consumption would have to be very high. Such equilibrium would only be achieved with a time-lag, during which the use of steel would exceed supply, and stocks would be depleted.

For Kalecki a much simpler and more expedient procedure would be a limitation of investment that would take account of general priorities and their "steel-intensity" and a similar restriction on durables. In case of the latter, prices would also be increased (higher turnover tax) to the level where demand is more or less equilibrated with supply. As a result the distribution of steel among the various branches would be reduced, and the production plans would be modified. Even with this method an increase in prices of rolled steel would be indicated if the shortages were of a recurring nature. Kalecki assumes some form of incentive system which should induce savings in material inputs and in the investment process. Under such conditions, increasing prices of steel should stimulate its replacement by other materials whenever possible, or at least its economical usage.

3. Demands for centralization will be more vigorous with faster postulated rates of growth. In such a case, the level of the long-run standard of living would clash with the relatively low share of consumption in national income in the short run. In order to resolve this problem decision-makers would tend to mobilize all resources, creating a taut economic situation. With rapid economic development, there is far more danger of a lack of synchronization of individual sectors and branches, resulting in bottlenecks (e.g., the disparity between the growing import needs and export possibilities). An economy that has to cope with these problems requires more strict central planning than one developing at a more moderate pace.

4. A system consisting of a synthesis of central planning and workers' councils is desirable. But it is a delusion that such a system is free of contradictions and easy to steer. It will always contain tendencies, on the one hand, to curtail the prerogatives of workers' councils in favor of greater centralization and, on the other, to undermine central planning by workers' councils.

On the Administrative Apparatus

The economic reform measures undertaken in late 1956 and early 1957 were half-hearted. From the inception the necessary political prerequisites and fundamental institutional changes at all levels of the hierarchy were lacking. There was no basic reshuffling of the cumbersome, bureaucratic, and costly planning apparatus. In this context, in 1957, Kalecki offered a solution for rearranging the administrative apparatus, at least at the echelon overseeing the enterprise. (Kalecki 1957e.)

To a large extent the structure of directives and incentives, and especially the possibility of differentiating them for individual branches of industry, and the efficiency of supply depend on the nature of the intermediary echelon between the central authorities and the enterprise. The idea of associations of enterprises of given branches (even freely formed) has much in common with cartels. Kalecki proposed that, instead of associations, large vertical concerns be established as self-sufficient as possible, from the standpoint of the supply system (e.g., incorporating steel mills and machine-building plants). Furthermore, the existence of several concerns producing the same or similar final output might counteract monopolistic tendencies.

The central planner should not interfere in the concern's operational problems. All directives and incentives addressed to the concern by the central planner would deal with its outside activities, e.g., its marketable output and its profit or loss from total activity. The concern would manage its wards by means of directives and incentives, adapted to the specific conditions of these enterprises. The amount of profit left at the concern's disposal would be distributed to reward the individual enterprises and the managerial staff of the concern as a whole.

Some of the advantages of such a scheme include: (1) the creation of a community of interests between the management of the concern and the individual enterprises; (2) the differentiation of the structure of directives and incentives by the concern according to the enterprise's specific conditions with the nature of this structure depending solely on the concern's evaluation of the situation at its enterprises, and subject to periodic (e.g., annual) alteration to fit changing conditions; (3) the simplification and greater flexibility of economic administration where the central planner would deal exclusively with a restricted number of large units for which he could also vary the structure of directives and incentives to fit individual conditions; and (4) the simplification and streamlining of the supply and subcontracting system.

Again in the discussion on the Polish economic model which at times took some very sharp utopian turns, Kalecki showed his powerful practical reasoning which never strayed from the path of possibility. He contributed and inspired the development of investment and foreign trade efficiency criteria. He was one of the first in Eastern Europe to advocate use of world market prices in setting domestic prices. He also made a considerable imprint on the development of the incentive system and factory prices.

INCENTIVES AND FACTORY PRICES

On the subject of applying economic incentives, Kalecki maintained a good dose of reserve, mainly because (1) he did not conceive incentives as a panacea for all economic ills; and (2) he foresaw that, to manage the economy by means of incentives, seemingly so simple on paper, would prove to be extremely complicated in practice. (Kalecki 1962o, pp. 170-71.)

In 1957, Kalecki drafted an incentive scheme, which he later supplemented with some observations on factory prices and quality control. The basic elements of this scheme include: (1) value added as a main plan index of the enterprise's activity; (2) limit of the wage fund determined on the basis of value added; (3) the change of profit, i.e., the increment of profit over the previous period, as a basis for determining premiums; (4) the principles of factory price formation to calculate the wage fund and premiums; (5) quality control; (6) interest-bearing, nonrepayable investment credits.[3]

1. Value added is understood as the difference between gross output in factory prices and the value of materials, fuels, and semifabricates, computed in the actual purchasing prices (transfer prices). Each enterprise should receive from its superiors an output plan of value added, computed according to the prices of goods and materials of the preceding year. In calculating value added, Kalecki favored the method whereby the value of output is computed according to prices of the basic period; and the value of materials, etc., also in the prices of that period, is deducted from the former. He considered it preferable in view of the allowance for material savings. In this case, even with unchanged gross output, a material saving would increase the value added index. Although a directive value added index will be transmitted to the enterprise by its superiors,

plan fulfillment or overfulfillment will no longer be a basis for premiums.

2. To serve as a base, the wage fund of the enterprise in the preceding year is recomputed in terms of the wage rates in force in the given year. The limit of the wage fund is obtained by augmenting this base to the extent that value added of the given year exceeds that of the preceding year. A wage fund so computed should exceed that required to cover the increase of employment and piece-rate wages. This excess should serve for paying out all sorts of special premiums, determined by the enterprise. Such a method should induce increase of value added with a given employment. However, it provides no incentive for expanding value added by increasing employment, since it does not raise the wage fund per employee. An incentive providing benefits for the existing employees from increasing employment can be found in the share in the increment of profit.

3. Profit in the given year, computed in factory prices, is compared with profit in the preceding year, and the difference between the two is the basis for premiums.[4] The premium fund is a share of the increment of profit. The incentive stresses increase of value added as a whole and not only value added per employee. Essentially the increase of employment over the preceding year will create an increment of profit which will be a source of premiums for the staff as a whole.

4. In Polish economic literature and practice, a distinction is drawn between factory and transfer prices. The former are the prices for the producer and the latter those for the buyer.[5] Kalecki's argument in favor of different prices for producers and buyers can be briefly summarized as follows: Since transfer prices are supposed to equilibrate supply and demand, in view of a large demand for a given product, a transfer price would have to be set at a level above production costs. This higher price could be transmitted to the enterprise as an incentive for increasing the output of the given product. But, the enterprise could have limited production capacities, so that it would be unable to increase output. It could then be argued that this would be an incentive for demanding appropriate investments. However, the required investment outlays may be too high to warrant increasing output which would lead to a reduction of the transfer price to a level proportionate to costs.

The above might be an exceptional case, and essentially transfer prices could be set proportionately to factory prices. In the attempt to clear the market, the transfer price is set with a given, and in many cases rather high, profit margin which plays a significant role in the incentive system outlined previously. The increment of profit depends on the increase of output and the reduction of costs. If output expands by a given percentage, the absolute increment of profit is proportionate to the profit markup, whereas the increment of profit from cost reduction is insensitive to the profit markup. Therefore, if the profit markup is high, rewards are distributed primarily for increase of output, with relatively minor stress on cost reduction. A misconceived premium system could emerge in industries limited by the import of raw materials, with incentives required for material savings, rather than for increase of output. Hence for premium purposes the profit margin should not be identical with that included in transfer prices, but should be set at a relatively low level.

When determining the factory price, the profit margin should be differentiated, depending on whether the aim is to achieve an increase in output or a reduction in costs. Factory prices should include profit markups differentiated according to branches, but in principle they should be uniform for the products of a given branch, in order not to induce interenterprise manipulation of the product mix.

Assuming that, even if at the beginning of a five-year plan the profit markup in factory prices is set on these principles, it would soon be undermined by nonuniform changes in costs during the quinquennium. In order to avoid this situation, factory prices must be changed during the quinquennium at least to take into account changes in prices of certain inputs, or wage rates, but not necessarily the nonuniform influence of technical progress on cost reduction of different products that can be dealt with during the general price revision.

5. All learned discussions on incentives make sense only if the system of quality control is revised at least as long as a buyers' market is not the prevailing phenomenon. If adequate quality control is not introduced, the more effective the incentives, the lower will be the quality of output. The index of value added, which takes into account the necessary material savings, would provoke fictitious material savings, achieved by means of reducing output quality. Also with a lack of adequate control, superficially high labor savings can be reported by producing "trash." Any workable incentive system should be accompanied by quality control independent of the

enterprise's management, for, so far, Poland (and the other socialist countries) is far from such market satiation that these functions could be assumed by the buyer. Further, even under conditions of a satiated market, such control by the buyer may be misleading, for the shortcomings of the product could become apparent only after an extended period of usage (especially in the products of machine-building).

6. The interest of the enterprise in the increment of profit would become a stimulus for investment.[6] However, to stimulate parsimony in investment outlays, it is necessary to levy an interest rate on these expenditures. The previous investment subsidies should be treated as nonrepayable credits, bearing a given interest rate. A given share of depreciation would remain with the enterprise, with the balance transmitted to central funds. The part of depreciation that remains at the disposal of the enterprise should be earmarked for renewal and modernization. However, the state would pay to the enterprise an interest charge on the share of depreciation transferred to the central funds.

The above applies to investment outlays controlled by the central authorities. Aside from that, there would exist a decentralized investment fund from which the enterprise would receive bank credits on the basis of bank criteria of evaluation. These credits could also be nonrepayable, but would bear a higher interest rate than those distributed for centralized investments. In this case the interest rate would be an equilibrium rate between the amounts earmarked for decentralized investments and the demand for those credits. Such a rate would be subject to constant change.

The above observations deal with incentives and directives transmitted to individual enterprises by their superiors. Kalecki saw the system in a different light when dealing with enterprises grouped in concerns. In that case the enterprise's superior would be the management of the concern's head office. The incentives and directives emanating from central authorities would be addressed primarily to the concern as a whole, principally pertaining to its value added, the limits of its wage fund, and the premium of the entire group of enterprises.

It seems that Kalecki's most enduring contribution to the discussion on the system of functioning of a socialist economy is an indirect one. His practical proposals for change that I have outlined in this section are only a demonstration of his belief that the primary determinant of the development of an economy and increasing well-being of its people is the decision on the rate of growth. The system of functioning is a tool for implementing the main policy objective, and as such is subordinate to that objective limited by the barriers and ceilings under which the economy labors. By illuminating these constraints, Kalecki has shown indirectly the limits of decentralization in the functioning system.

Interdependence Between Growth Strategy and the System of Functioning

Essentially the economic reform problems that beset the Polish economy throughout the 1960s were of a dual nature: (1) the reform measures were timid, ill-synchronized, often contradictory, and at cross-purposes with many remnants of the traditional, centralized Soviet-type economy; and (2) the expected rate of growth required a huge transfer of resources to investment, generating an overheating in the economy which hindered significantly the introduction of reform measures. In the final analysis, it was the consumer (worker) who suffered from this situation. The planners had expected that the savings of resources derived from the greater efficiency induced by the reform would be used to improve the consumers' welfare. This did not materialize, and the consumer again bore a full share of planning errors.

The economic reform blueprints of Eastern Europe usually refer to increased efficiency derived from economic reform as an additional source of economic growth. At this juncture I should like to point out the inverse relationship between economic reform and the growth strategy whose roots can be found in Kalecki's theory of growth under socialism.[7] The essence of this inverse relationship is that, in practice, excessive overheating of the economy invalidates the general principle of economic calculation. The execution of an excessively taut plan is accompanied by increasing supply shortages in one area of production after another. Under such conditions economic calculation is forgone in favor of "production at all costs." The latter might be an expression of the "state of higher necessity," for the enterprise losses which it causes counteract even greater losses on the scale of the national economy. But this is no excuse for such a situation to arise, especially when there are no sufficient reserves to compensate the losses. Excessive tautness and the ensuing disturbances in the interbranch and interenterprise flows considerably weaken economic incentives.

An overheated economy, provoked by stipulating an excessive growth rate in relation to real possibilities, becomes the source of two mutually propelling difficulties: (1) the emergence and perpetuation of bottlenecks; and (2) the prevention and often impossibility of introducing and applying a set of economic instruments which could increase the economy's efficiency, take advantage of idle reserves, spur technical dynamism, and thus contribute to increasing the rate of growth without excessive strains.

In the final analysis, economic performance depends not only on the content of the plan chosen, but on the system of functioning. The latter will be a function of its inherent logic and the development strategy involved. There is then an obvious interactive relationship between the plan and model of *modus operandi* of the economy. One cannot be considered in abstraction of the other. Changes in the model of functioning are *not* a priori assumed to be inconsequential, *nor* is it assumed that growth is propelled *exclusively* by investment. Contrariwise, choice of *both* an appropriate growth rate and a more effective planning system would *jointly* produce better results than could be achieved by attacking the economic riddle on one front only.

XVIII

HOW TO PLAN AND HOW NOT TO PLAN

DIFFERENT APPROACHES TO PLANNING assign different scope to the capacity, limitations, and efficiency of deliberate decision-making to transform or control the course of economic life. Planning techniques and arrangements are influenced by planning philosophies, so to speak. The controversies about economic planning, at least within the socialist context, have been characterized by two principal lines of division: (1) the deterministic and (2) the voluntaristic approaches to the problem.

Although proponents of both approaches would agree that plan construction must start out with an assessment of the existing economic situation, the country's stage of development, and other domestic and foreign constraints, the principal difference between the two approaches is that the first is swayed in most of its decisions by the given situation and realistic possibilities of altering it, whereas the second allows for decisions which largely disregard the given conditions and aim at shaping the future as if the present almost did not exist. In its extreme, whereas the first approach is carefully and realistically guided by the set of existing constraints, the second optimistically tends to view "the sky as the only limit"—thus the first approach gives cognizance to the constraints of the existing economic structure, past economic trends and their projection into the future, feasible alternatives, investment efficiency calculus, "balanced relations" between sectors, and a "harmonious" growth pattern. The second, on the other hand, stresses choice of plan goals primarily on the basis of political and social considerations ("planner's arbitrariness") without due heed to extrapolating trends. The second approach is colored by the widespread fallacy that exhortative targets "mobilize" executants toward better performance. The underlying philosophy is that a taut plan is a *conditio sine qua non* for achieving higher targets. Such conditions have led in practice to a high degree of centralization and identification of "plan-satisfying" output with progress in economic performance.

Quite often proponents of one approach concede that some of the features of the other are necessary, and the finer lines of distinction may be blurred. However, they become more pronounced when policy makers have to choose between the realistic and optimistic plan targets.

The sharp contrast between the two positions became evident during the Soviet industrialization debate of the 1920s (which became known as the controversy between "teleologists" and "geneticists"). (Cf. Erlich 1960; Spulber 1964.) It has resurfaced at various times, whenever the traditional Soviet growth strategy—the embodiment of the voluntaristic approach—has been challenged. The vivid contrast between the two approaches was again strikingly delineated at the end of the 1950s in Poland when the perspective plan (1961-75) and its first quinquennium (1961-65), prepared under the guidance of Professor Kalecki, were found unacceptable by the authorities on the grounds that they were defeatist, and focused attention on limiting rather than mobilizing factors.

Essentially, the principal difference between Kalecki's concept of planning and the traditional concept of the leadership of a Soviet-type economy can be condensed as follows: Kalecki believed an economic plan to be a realistically conceived document to guide future activity taking into account present constraints and possibilities, projected into the future, with a healthy dose of pessimism. On the other hand, the leadership basically viewed the plan as a promise of a bright future, conceived with a good deal of optimism in possibilities to stimulate, motivate, and mobilize the efforts of the human agents of economic activity, and to "mobilize hidden reserves," but without providing conditions for doing so.

In response to the widespread criticism of the short-term approach of planning authorities, Kalecki and a staff of the Planning Commission were charged with elaborating a fifteen-year perspective plan (1961-75) of the Polish economy. This plan was never adopted, but ranks as one of the finest efforts at long-term planning in a socialist economy. The realistic approach makes it a model for all those who aspire at drafting a deterministic perspective plan for a developing economy. When its first segment (the 1961-65 five-year plan) was to be officially adopted, a heated controversy arose between determinism and voluntarism in planning. The voluntarists won, discrediting Kalecki's cautious approach and propelling the Polish economy into a new wave of investment. The adopted 1961-65 plan featured a particularly optimistic view of hidden reserves and increased efficiency. It relied on improvements of the functioning system which it did not provide for, nor afforded possibilities of introducing. Briefly all planning errors made further inroads into consumption. By that time Kalecki had been deprived of any real influence on the planning authorities. His pen remained his only weapon. In the midst of the economic havoc caused by the 1961-65 plan, he showed where overoptimistic planning can lead and counseled planners to revert to plan realism, in order to alleviate past blunders and to ensure future rationality.

Methodology of Perspective Plan Construction

The construction of the perspective plan was undertaken in an attempt to find some sort of viable alternative to the disastrous policies pursued during the Six-Year Plan. Obviously, an important, although often understated, part of the economic discussion that followed the "Polish October" centered on finding a satisfactory growth strategy and mapping out the development path. The central planning authorities were being criticized for giving insufficient weight to long-range planning, and for their preoccupation with current matters. In 1957 a Perspective Plan Institute of the Planning Commission and a Central Commission on the Perspective Plan were set up and entrusted with the preparation of the 1961-75 fifteen-year perspective plan. The chief architect and moving spirit of this plan was Michal Kalecki.

Before we describe the method of plan construction adopted by Kalecki, it might be useful to refer to his concept of a perspective plan. In contrast with a medium-term (five-year) plan which he saw as a directive to execute certain minimum tasks and a pledge of the authorities to the population of a socialist country to achieve a certain living standard, Kalecki viewed the perspective plan as a long-term development program to guide the planner in solving current problems and in constructing more detailed short- and medium-term plans. The perspective plan could be corrected during the construction and implementation of the more specific plans. It could also be envisaged as a sliding plan, moving ahead by five years at the end of each quinquennium. Of course, the perspective plan would be corrected continuously in accordance with new developments in technology, foreign trade relations, etc. Although its indexes cannot be conceived as immovable promises, the perspective plan should not be treated as a figment of fantasy—a Jules Verne novel. On the contrary: on the basis of the most reasonable assumptions, the authors of the perspective plan should attempt to construct a comprehensive, consistent, and realistic plan of long-term economic development. But one should not believe uncritically in a fifteen-year plan based in many respects on purely hypothetical assumptions. (Kalecki 1958j, pp. 27-28.)

The 1961-75 perspective plan prepared by Kalecki was not accepted by the authorities, and the controversy that surrounded it will be examined later. Perhaps at this juncture one should observe that so far this perspective plan remains the most consistent, complete, and scrupulously elaborated long-term (perspective) plan in the history of economic planning in socialist countries. As the practical embodiment of Kalecki's growth theory under socialism, the construction of the perspective plan differed *toto coelo* from the voluntaristic planning of the traditional Soviet-type economy.

Kalecki considered the average annual rate of growth of national income as the crucial parameter of a long-term plan.[1] The selection of an appropriate plan variant is treated as really tantamount to a selection of the appropriate growth rate and composition of national income. Decision-makers tend to choose the highest possible growth rate, in order to develop the economy rapidly. Such a decision encounters a number of constraints, the most obvious of which is that the higher the growth rate, the higher usually must be the relative share of productive investments in national income. In the short run, a higher relative share of productive investment in national income is bound to depress the share of consumption and nonproductive investment. Pushing this too far might arouse antagonism in the population despite the fact that, the cumulative effect of a high growth rate might raise the living standard. In addition, difficulties in equilibrating the balance of trade often follow such a move. "In its effort to achieve this equilibrium the country is forced down the path of investment requiring higher capital outlays in relation to the effect achieved in foreign trade and thus the relative share of productive investment in the national income (which we imagine to be adjusted for deterioration in terms of trade) will increase *pro tanto* more." (Kalecki 1963d, pp. 11-12.) It is quite possible that, at a given level of the growth rate, foreign trade can no longer be balanced, thus posing an absolute barrier to the growth rate. Another barrier is an emergent labor scarcity. This could be counteracted by increasing investment outlays, which will again raise the relative share of productive investment in national income.

The rough draft of the perspective plan starts out with a higher rate of growth than the country's past experience. Thus a high variant is deliberately chosen. Already at the first testing stage it might have to be scaled down. Then a capital coefficient is chosen (to relate the increment of national income and productive investment) on the basis of past experience and amended to fit changing conditions. This would still be only a very rough approximation, for the capital coefficient is largely influenced by the structure of the increment of output, which might not be the same as in the past.

Having chosen the capital coefficient, the first approximation of the annual productive investment in the beginning, middle, and end of the perspective plan is obtained together with the coefficient of increase in inventories. The total of consumption and nonproductive investment at the various periods of the perspective plan is obtained by deducting productive investment and increase in inventories from national income. Consumption is separated from nonproductive investment by comparing the resulting level of consumption with the capacity of fixed assets rendering consumer services. The decision thus obtained will still be largely arbitrary. By this time the plan might already prove to be untenable because the relative share of productive investment plus increase in inventories in national income infringes intolerably on consumption (and nonproductive investment) in the short run. Yet the variant may be entertained somewhat longer since it is as yet based on the hypothetical capital coefficient.

Before drawing a general outline of the industrial structure, we must make some reasonable assumption of the future structure of consumption.[2] This can be based on the structure of consumption of more developed countries, adapted to local conditions, or on domestic income elasticities of demand derived from family budgets. Then the industrial structure may be roughly determined. It is required both for testing the balance of trade and for reaching a second approximation of the capital coefficient.

Kalecki divides industry (including all branches of economic activity, such as agriculture, transport, etc.) into two groups: (1) supply-determined and (2) demand-determined.[3] The first includes industries whose output owing to certain technical and organizational reasons cannot grow in the long run beyond a certain ceiling, despite considerable increases in capital outlays. The second includes industries where such ceilings do not occur, at least within the range considered. Therefore, their output can grow in the long run in accordance with demand.

There is a wide range of technological and organizational factors which condition the growth rates of supply-determined industries. The best illustration is limited natural resources. The lapse of time needed to promote and to adapt new techniques is another. A third factor may be difficulties in attracting labor to certain industries or in training a sufficient number of skilled personnel. In particular, shortages of sufficiently skilled and experienced construction staff are the underlying factor of the extended construction (gestation) periods hampering expansion of particular industries. With a long construction period and a high rate of investment, the existing skilled personnel is incapable of mastering the large number of construction projects. Should the high rate of investment be maintained despite these circumstances, the construction period is further extended, resulting in frozen capital rather than in accelerated expansion of the given industry, as outlined in chapter fourteen.

Domestic demand for the goods of the various branches can be estimated as soon as the volume of productive and nonproductive investment, the increase in inventories, and the volume and structure of consumption are known. In supply-determined industries an estimate of what is left for export or what has to be imported can then be made. Imports will also include products that cannot be domestically produced. However, the import estimate will have to take into account domestic production of some substitutes. Thus the total import requirements can be estimated. By deducting from the latter the value of exportables provided by supply-determined industries, one obtains the necessary exportables to be covered by demand-determined industries. The output of demand-determined industries is thus established so as to cover domestic demand for the given goods and their contribution to exports.

Obviously, if the export plan is not realistic, the growth rate will have to be scaled down. The balance of trade is more likely to be equilibrated if the rate of growth of national income is pared down while the rate of growth of supply-determined industries is preserved. Thus demand for imports should fall considerably, together with a likely increase in the surplus of supply-determined industries released for export. Even if the foreign trade plan is quite realistic, such large investment outlays may be required to obtain the required exports, that the escalated rate of investment might cause rejection of a plan that would make excessive inroads into consumption in the short run.

Before investment can be estimated, a balance of and demand for labor is drafted. The supply of labor is estimated on the basis of demographic data. The demand for labor is estimated on the basis of the industrial structure of production with allowance for increased productivity owing to technical progress. With the assumed growth rate, an emerging labor shortage might require escalation of investment outlays to provide more mechanization.

At this point total productive investment can be estimated. The result can diverge materially from that arrived at by using the hypothetical capital coefficient. Despite the fact that the balance of foreign trade might be ensured at the assumed growth rate, the relative share of productive investment in national income so calculated might prove untenable. Then the rate of growth would have to be pared down further and the new variant re-examined as outlined above. In final analysis the highest rate of growth cannot be identified as a touchstone of economic advancement. "The variant finally adopted should be characterized by the highest possible rate of growth at which there is a realistic possibility of balancing foreign trade and at which the relative share of productive investment plus the increase in inventories in the national income is considered tolerable by the authorities from the point of the impact upon consumption and unproductive investment in the short run." (Kalecki 1963d, p. 19.)

To aim at excessively high rates by overinvesting is to invite flagrant disproportions, to court ample fluctuations in the rate of economic activity, to raise growth barriers, etc. "The obstacle to a very high rate of growth in a perspective plan is the high capital outlay required both directly and as a result of the difficulties in equilibrating the balance of foreign trade and possibly also of the shortage of labor; in fact the difficulties in foreign trade may make virtually impossible exceeding a certain level of the rate of growth." (Kalecki 1963d, p. 12.)

The Polish Perspective Plan and Its First Quinquennium

As Kalecki pointed out at the outset, the Polish perspective plan for 1961-75 was supposed to provide a firm basis for preparing the

1961-65 quinquennium.[4] In fact the fate of the perspective plan was sealed with the resumption of the investment momentum at the end of the 1950s as part of the second wave of investment which lasted with only short breathing spells throughout the 1960s.

The first approximation of the perspective plan rested on the following basic assumptions: The standard of living should be the "highest possible" throughout the period in question. By 1975 food consumption should approach the maximum norm stipulated by physiologists. Also by 1975 a relatively high standard of residential facilities should exist and full employment should be maintained throughout. The plan was to refrain from excessively taut or risky targets and from foreign credits. The distinctive features of the plan could be catalogued as follows:

1. The national income targets were gross, in factory prices, in order to avoid distortive inflation of the consumer goods sector due to turnover tax incidence in transfer (sale) prices of mostly consumer goods. Both productive and nonproductive investments were computed in gross investment outlays. In view of the lack of an adequate basis for computing depreciation, net investments were not calculated. Consumption was computed in transfer prices.

2. Productive investment was determined at a level that would assure the postulated rate of growth and replacement of fixed capital. The investment level depends not only on the growth of total national income, but also on changes in its structure and thus it had to be determined by means of successive approximations.

3. The nonproductive investment level was set so as to achieve by 1975 certain given goals in housing, public utilities, health and education, and culture. These investments would grow much faster than national income (3 times as against 2.6 times during 1961-75), but the stock of facilities created thereby would grow at a slower pace than national income.

4. The plan was not built on the expectation of foreign credits; it dealt only with credits already obtained. Therefore, the distributed national income differed only from the produced national income in that the former was computed in factory prices and the latter in transfer prices (including turnover tax). The plan accounted for repayment of credits which, even though quantitatively insignificant in the distributed national income, was particularly serious for the 1961-65 balance of payments.

5. Per capita consumption would almost double by 1975. Thus by 1975, Poland was slated to reach the 1957-58 standard of living of

the wealthier European countries. Yet despite the postulated growth of nonproductive investment, Poland would still lag in housing and public facilities.

The 1961-65 quinquennium was the most precisely elaborated part of the fifteen-year plan. Kalecki's concept of this quinquennium throws into sharper focus his approach to planning, especially in the light of the plan that was later adopted, the problems that arose during its implementation, and the reverberation of these blunders in the 1970s. Kalecki's interpretation of the economic situation at that time and his defense of the key features of the plan he prepared may be summarized as follows: (Kalecki 1959c, pp. 1-4.)

1. The 1961-65 plan was a sort of bridge between the initial period of postwar development of the Polish economy (1950-60) which constituted, as it were, a closed cycle, and the fifteen-year development plan. In particular the 1961-65 period differed considerably from its predecessor (1956-60). In the latter period significant economic successes were recorded, promoted, *inter alia,* by the retarded achievements of the Six-Year Plan and the mending of its errors. Investment activity centered primarily on completing projects which raised the overall index of investment efficiency. Changes in economic policy promoted intensified use of capacities, especially in agriculture, where cooperatives were disbanded and the collectivization policy was apparently renounced. The following five-year period would be essentially more difficult. It would start a new cycle of investment. Some of the projects would be in construction for more than five years. Moreover, 1961-65 would not provide as many opportunities of exploiting reserves.

In a way 1961-65 was not dissimilar from the Six-Year Plan period. Both followed on the heels of periods where output had grown considerably, hence the dangerous tendency of underestimating the difficulties of the following period. Moreover, both plans initiated large investment cycles, and Kalecki warned that a similar background might give rise to similar errors. His prophetic admonition resounds ominously to this day in the ears of the planners: "Someone once said jokingly that history teaches us only that it teaches us nothing. All efforts should be made that the plan for 1961-65 should not corroborate this gloomy joke." (Kalecki 1959c, p. 4.)

2. Output was to grow at a slower rate than in 1956-60. The difference was even sharper as regards growth of consumption—i.e., in 1961-65 consumption was expected to grow by 35 per cent, and the corresponding rate for 1956-60 was to be 48 per cent. A part of this

difference was directly attributable to the decelerated rate of growth of national income. Moreover, the 1965 distribution of national income assumed a certain reserve to direct to the growth of consumption. This reserve was to compensate for the possibility of underfulfillment of the national income target, or the absorption of a larger than the planned share of national income by accumulation. Finally the share of productive investment in national income was supposed to decline from 1955 to 1960, whereas from 1960 to 1965 it was slated to increase. Hence a somewhat slower rate of growth was to be achieved at the cost of a higher share of productive investment in national income.

3. In 1956-60, Poland benefited from a number of long-term foreign credits, which had to be reimbursed in 1961-65. Clearly, the inflow of credits in 1956-60 helped the balance of payments and the procurement of imported raw materials, which enabled the economy to exploit its productive capacities. The 1961-65 situation was bound to be much more difficult. Furthermore in 1956-60 the import of machinery declined rapidly, whereas exports grew thanks to the rapid development of machine-building. Although further steps in this direction were postulated in 1961-65, the role of this factor in the balance of payments was to be relatively smaller.

4. If the share of investment in national income were to be raised, in 1961-65, national income would increase only slightly until 1965, with the full effect achieved only in the latter part of the decade. A shift in the distribution of national income in favor of productive investment would infringe on consumption or nonproductive investment, which is as essential as growth of consumption for raising the standard of living. Since in 1961-65 per capita consumption was supposed to grow slower than in 1956-60 (by 25 per cent and 35 per cent, respectively), increase of the share of productive investment in national income was rather out of the question. Also, in certain areas, especially in the development of the raw materials base, a rise in investment would encounter technical-organizational barriers. However, this should not preclude the undertaking of additional, particularly effective investments which would also be beneficial from a consumption standpoint. Those are investments which render quick results alleviating bottlenecks and causing an increment of national income incommensurate with the expenditures. Although such possibilities did exist, their scope should not be exaggerated.

5. National income can grow faster when production reserves are used more intensively. However, when exploitation entails use of

raw materials in short supply, the issue is quite different. In practice this is often the case since reserves can be found chiefly in processing industries rather than raw materials branches. Import of additional raw materials is not readily available, in view of the difficulties in selling the finished goods on foreign markets. Kalecki concluded that the limited raw materials base and the circumscribed export possibilities of finished products make it difficult to increase growth of national income by taking advantage of production reserves in the processing industries.

6. Growth of national income can also be enhanced by savings in investment expenditures or in material inputs. Growth of national income would be accelerated if larger productive capacities are obtained from the same investment expenditures. But here again, in view of the long construction period, the full effect would only materialize after 1965. However, since in some areas planned investment outlays might be exceeded, the prospective investment savings might be absorbed.

Clearly, with an unchanged raw materials base, savings in material inputs that increase output without infringing on the foreign trade balance can largely enhance the growth of national income. However, reduced material input norms were already utilized in constructing the plan. The plan was criticized on the grounds that it did not postulate sufficiently taut savings targets. Kalecki retorted that such targets could be planned annually without endangering the realism of the entire quinquennium, which would be the case if possibilities were exaggerated. In the five-year period realistic savings could only be postulated on the basis of new techniques and additional investments of quick returns.

7. Kalecki considered that, on the whole, the targets postulated in the control figures would not be easy to implement. The targets in agriculture would require special efforts and considerable investment. This would have to be supported by adequate investment incentives, such as giving the peasant attractive tax exemptions for undertaking investment. In addition government policy would have to support land improvement and fertilization in order to promote an increase in plant and livestock production.

8. In conclusion Kalecki warned the decision-makers that those who aim at accelerating the rate of growth consent as it were to strains and pressures in various areas. On the other hand, those who aim at ensuring plan fulfillment search out the weak points and attempt to eradicate them, and only then reflect about increasing

the rate of growth. These laconic words essentially describe the positions of the contestants in the debate about the future of Polish economic development.

Voluntarism Versus Determinism

As previously stated, Kalecki's perspective plan was found unacceptable by the government. The main objection was essentially against the low growth rates envisaged. The official rejection came at the Twelfth Plenary Session of the Central Committee of the Polish United Workers Party, held in October, 1958, to approve the economic program for the period 1959-65. The most incisive attack was launched by Eugeniusz Szyr and Boleslaw Ruminski, whose arguments struck a familiar note for a student of the traditional Soviet-type growth strategy.[5]

Szyr contended that the growth rates of the 1959-65 period *can and should be* accelerated. He accused "the defenders of a slower growth rate" of unwisely magnifying the shortcomings of the 1949-53 period, and mistakenly claiming that higher growth rates infringe always on short-run consumption and are unavoidably accompanied by acute dislocations. In a typically voluntaristic fashion, Szyr bombastically proclaimed that it would be possible simultaneously to escalate growth rates of production, to increase capital formation, and to raise consumption markedly. The planners had been allegedly intimidated by the phantom of disproportions and sacrifices in living standards.

Szyr related Polish economic development to that of the socialist bloc. He pointed out that, from 1953 to 1957, these countries were alleviating disproportions, determining "adequate proportions" between industry and agriculture, and altering somewhat the functioning mechanism. However, by 1959 these countries had resumed the investment offensive. Szyr accused those who prepared the Polish plan draft of underestimating the possibilities for embarking on a similar industrialization rush. He complained that for "objective and subjective" reasons this plan understated the potential growth rate of production, rise in labor productivity, cost reduction, growth of investment efficiency, and reduction of planned gestation periods. The draft plan was, therefore, unacceptable. More strenuous targets would have to be adopted. A fixation on growth barriers and ceilings could not be allowed to determine the tempo of industrialization. Szyr proclaimed that Poland's commitment to accelerated industrialization in order to win the economic race with the capitalist world was the main goal, to which all else had to be subordinated. This was precisely the goal neglected by those who stressed factors limiting industrialization and therefore favored a slower growth rate.

In academic circles the perspective plan was debated at a session of the Economics Institute of the Polish Academy of Science and the program for 1959-65 was discussed at a plenary session of the Economic Council. The sharply delineated positions of the groups (1) favoring the voluntaristic approach and (2) defending the deterministic one were brought into focus at both discussions, although no names were mentioned.[6]

In short, the perspective plan and its first quinquennium were attacked on the grounds that they were defeatist, pessimistic, and relied on limiting rather than mobilizing factors, neglecting the great reserves and advantages of a socialist economy. Indeed, realistic planning might lead to a lower growth rate than the "mobilizing paper goal," but the actual growth rate would probably be higher than that resulting from the execution of plans that initially ignore such barriers and eventually have to be scaled down to alleviate unbearable strains. As a rule, analysis of growth barriers and ceilings does not claim that these obstacles cannot be overcome. It merely indicates the additional undertakings required to mitigate them. These usually make inroads into consumption. The issue is to avoid excessive tensions in order to further a more harmonious growth of production and consumption in the long run.

THE RENEWED INDUSTRIALIZATION RUSH

In 1959, Poland embarked on a new wave of investment and stepped up development of heavy industry.[7] I have already alluded to the similarities between 1961-65 and the Six-Year Plan. However, the return to forced industrialization was less extreme, and was somewhat more circumspect. Greater attention was paid to agriculture; attempts were made to check the departure of the labor force from agriculture; growth of investment was less pronounced; etc. On the whole, whereas both agriculture and the worker-consumer paid for the first wave of investment, the second was financed primarily at the cost of the urban worker-consumer.

Perhaps the single weakest feature of the approved 1961-65 plan was that it had been constructed by overoptimistic planners, who consistently overestimated possibilities on all fronts. The plan was constructed without reserves in the more susceptible areas (i.e., agriculture and foreign trade), while relying on undisclosed reserves and potential sources of growth outside investment (intensive growth), without providing the necessary and sufficient conditions to elicit them. The plan relied heavily on increased efficiency and competence in management. It banked on increased investment efficiency both as regards choice and execution. It estimated that the bulk of the increment of output would be derived from growth of productivity. Finally, the accumulation *v.* consumption dilemma was "solved" by postulating that the share of national income earmarked for the increase in inventories would fall drastically to allow for a considerable increase of productive investment without infringing on consumption. Obviously, a reduction of the share of increment in inventories would be possible only with a considerable, consistent, and lasting improvement in the availability, use, and flow of materials, and in the adaptation of output to the needs of users. This, in turn, would require an improved planning system, a reform of performance criteria and incentives, and a whole gamut of sensitive economic instruments.

As a result of the enormous tensions built into the plan and a disastrous harvest in 1962, the plan collapsed midstream. During the first two years of the plan, it became quite clear that the sanguine expectations of its designers would remain wishful thinking. Instead of diminishing, inventories grew at a very rapid rate, thus infringing on consumption. This did not mean a better supply, but rather an accumulation of unsuitable or unwanted goods and increased hoarding, while serious shortages of specific goods persisted. The labor productivity did not keep pace with the plan; instead there was a sharp, above-plan increase of employment, which cut into growth of nominal and real wages. Reduction of construction periods and costs did not materialize. In fact, although planned outlays were not cut, several projects had to be eliminated from the plan. The construction process was freezing a mounting volume of assets. Exports did not increase as expected. On the contrary, imports grew faster than exports, with above-plan imports and below-plan exports of machinery. To equilibrate the balance of foreign trade, the planners resorted to above-plan exports of food and agricultural produce, raw materials, and fuels.

In view of the weight attached to increased efficiency as a potential source of growth, one would have expected that the planners were preparing a well-rounded and consistent reform of the functioning system for the 1960s. This was not the case. Aside from the fact that they misjudged the length of time required for a system alteration to begin showing returns in the sense of improved efficiency (and probably the extent to which increased efficiency can replace real resources), they consented only to very haphazard, timid, and entirely inconsistent half-measure tinkering with the system.[8] Moreover, the strains and stresses built into the plan, resulting in a generally overheated economic situation, did not provide the necessary and sufficient conditions to implement an economic reform. (Cf. Brus 1962; 1963.) In this particular case the overoptimism of Polish planners is blatantly obvious: They expected short-run miracles, while providing neither a blueprint for consistent reforms, nor the conditions for their introduction. In the end, the industrialization momentum again made significant inroads into consumption. The latter remained the shock absorber of planning errors and miscalculations.

ON ROMANTICISM AND REALISM IN PLANNING

Kalecki's reaction to the colossal blunders of the 1961-65 plan was compressed in a sharp and caustic comment on fanciful and "mobilizing" planning. He also showed how the romantic propensities could be moderated. In essence it is probably the most sober and clear-cut assessment of how to plan and how not to plan:

1. A realistic plan must be balanced; otherwise various shortages and surpluses will undermine the plan. The point is to apply a method of plan construction that would avoid both shortages and useless surpluses.

As in the case of a perspective plan, construction of a medium-term plan should start out by assuming a certain rate of growth of national income. Then certain assumptions are made as to future structure of consumption and to the relationship between consumption and nonproductive investment. These assumptions roughly determine the distribution of national income into productive investment, nonproductive investment, increase of inventories, and consumption. They also determine largely the branch structure of national income and of productive investment. The branch structure further depends on the choice of (a) technology and (b) the direction of foreign trade (e.g., import *v.* domestic production of a given good). In essence, the branch structure of national income is determined by (1) the rate of growth; (2) the structure of consumption and its relationship to nonproductive investment; and (3) efficiency analysis of alternative production techniques and foreign trade variants.

By implication, the traditional method of plan construction, which starts out by assuming target rates of expansion of various branches of the economy, is incompatible with complex balancing of the plan. With this method shortages in some branches and surpluses in others can be expected. Attempts will usually be made to eliminate the shortages. But there might appear a dangerous tendency to preserve the high indexes of "surplus" branches, if the latter are identified with economic and technical progress. This is a fallacious approach, for it leads to a swelling of planned requirements for the products in question, or to the classification of the surplus as a reserve. Plan reserves should be formed in susceptible areas, but not arbitrarily wherever the planner desires to maintain high growth indexes. In practice such surpluses are wasteful, either because they provoke excessive demands already at the planning stage, or because useless reserves tempt careless use of resources during plan execution. The growth index of a certain branch should only be raised with a general alteration of expansion indexes of various other branches, which would then be compatible with the higher rate of growth of national income. In no case should it take place on the basis of an arbitrary determination of growth rates of specific branches, which follows from measuring the advance of civilization, for instance, by increase in tons of steel or growth in the volume of machinery.

2. A realistic plan must be based on the efficiency of investment calculations. Analysis of investment efficiency from the standpoint of the balance of foreign trade concentrates on both pro-export and anti-import investments. The latter are subdivided into investments (a) for substituting domestic production for imported goods, (b) for replacing imported raw materials by substitutes, and (c) for savings of raw materials. The calculation should show the most effective method of obtaining the foreign currency required to pay for indispensable imports. In practice it is not always possible to concentrate on the most effective exports because of limited foreign markets and growth barriers of certain branches as previously discussed.

Hence the planners must increasingly consider effective anti-import investments. (Kalecki 1963c.)

3. In analyzing the consequences of an increase in labor productivity, two specific cases should be distinguished: (1) a growth of labor productivity leading to an increased output, with the same employment; and (2) a growth of labor productivity leading to reduced employment, with the same output. If, for example, in some factory the run of machinery is accelerated, with a given employment, production increases owing to a more intensive utilization of the existing productive capacity. But if growth of labor productivity involves a smaller number of workers servicing the same machinery (working at the same speed), the same output corresponds to a reduced labor force. In the first case national income is directly increased; in the second case, savings are obtained in manpower, which could be more or less propitious for the national economy, depending on the labor situation.

After distinguishing those two cases, one should note that the more advantageous case of increased production through better utilization of capacity and labor may also cause all sorts of disturbances in practice. An indispensable condition for such a solution is the additional supply of raw materials. As we have seen, such an interaction of the production effort (and of the export effort in order to make up the shortages in foreign trade) will not always be possible, and at any rate it will not take place automatically as a result of the realization of the general "slogan" of increasing labor productivity. If the increase of production has to be forgone as a result of a deficiency of additional raw materials, the first case is transformed into the second case; i.e., instead of an increase of production, a reduction of employment will take place.

Expansion of output might not always be desirable even when there are no technical limitations on expansion of supply. Difficulties in increasing production cannot be considered without regard to demand conditions. One could always counter that such a danger does not exist, for an increase of marketable output is followed by an appropriate increase of real wages through a rise in wages or a decrease in prices. But again this is not always a simple matter. With an increase of real wages, demand increases not only for the consumer goods that are in surplus as a result of additional production, but also for those (e.g., food and clothing) whose supply does not change (the Allen-Hicks-Slutsky income effect of price change).

Theoretically, this difficulty could be counteracted by a price maneuver, i.e., a sufficient price reduction of surplus goods in comparison to the prices of other consumer goods. However, in order to ensure partial equilibriums in the consumers' market, it might be necessary to increase somewhat the prices of other goods at the same time. In this case the increase of real wages would take place as the difference between the effect of price reductions on surplus goods and the effect of price increases on other consumer goods. However, if the price hike affected necessities, such a maneuver would meet with difficulties in practice, since the population would adversely evaluate and react to an increase in real wages that was derived in this manner. Moreover, the level of the lower real wages could actually decrease as a result of such a price maneuver. If, owing to the aforementioned difficulties, real wages were not increased in relation to the increased production of consumer goods, stockpiling would result.

Obviously, when an economy suffers from general labor shortages, increasing labor productivity is essential for a full use of the productive apparatus. Otherwise, the additional savings of the labor force can only allow for a shortened working time, and if working time is not shortened the outflow from agriculture will be curbed, employment of married women and young people will decrease, and some form of unemployment will result. In such a case, the increase of productivity is hardly beneficial, as it is compensated by a lower level of employment.

However, even though the entire labor force could be completely sufficient for manning the productive apparatus, there might be labor shortages in certain areas. In such cases, pressures on savings of the labor force in the activities where there are shortages can be of significance, but should not entail any exaggerations about the necessity of such pressures in the entire economy.

The likely results are different if the assumption of a given productive apparatus is relaxed and we allow for enlargement of capacity and face the familiar choice-of-techniques problem. The increased productivity obtained from an existing plant and equipment entails savings of investments necessary for carrying out a given production program. In turn, such savings in investment will result in either a reduction of the volume of investment and a corresponding increase of consumption or in the achievement of a larger increment of national income with a given volume of investment. In both cases, the procurement and sales difficulties that were discussed above will be alleviated or even eliminated, for required changes in the structure of production can be largely achieved by appropriate alterations in the investment structure. In this context *modernization* of old factories is of particular significance because it promotes a better use of the labor force and the productive apparatus, with relatively small investments. (Kalecki 1960j.)

Generally, regarding the choice of techniques, we see again the application of Kalecki's familiar argument that more or less capital-intensive techniques are, per se, neither superior nor inferior. The choice of a correct capital intensity of production depends on the state of the labor supply; on the prevailing trends of technical advance, after allowance for technical imitations of substitution; and on imposition of a condition of minimum rate of increase of real wages over time.

4. Then there is the question of plan realism per se. With so-called mobilizing plan indexes, despite "on paper" balancing, execution of the plan becomes vulnerable—to say the least. Planners' optimism can appear in assessing various areas: material input norms, utilization of existing capacity, construction and gestation periods, export possibilities, and investment cost estimates. In effect, mobilizing indexes, which are not based on some concrete undertakings, usually mobilize plan executants toward ingenious product-mix manipulations, more or less discernible quality deterioration, etc. Thus arises the phenomenon of a taut plan—an ambitious, but risky, if not totally unrealistic, plan. If such a plan misfires, as it often does, it involves great losses: the growth rate is far below that which could have been achieved had a more cautious plan been adopted. Essentially, plan realism means a choice of a plan variant that would minimize the risk of nonfulfillment.

Plan reserves should be determined in areas where it is particularly difficult to forecast the future. An obvious example is the development of exports to capitalist countries which largely depends on world market fluctuations. However, reserves should not replace detailed calculations of material balances and investment costs. Here uncertainty and hence reserves could be reduced to a minimum. In practice the following misconceived procedure is often followed: A "heroic" index is accompanied by a reserve which, at least partially, compensates this "heroism." This only obfuscates the plan for, under the circumstances, even a large reserve might prove insufficient.

Aside from reserves in the form of surpluses in balances, a significant role is played by reserves of resources, such as fuels, raw materials, foreign currency, etc. Such reserves are particularly of service in short-term perturbations. The fuels reserve, for example, should be sufficient to endure even a severe winter. The foreign currency reserve should be rather substantial, for foreign trade is subject to all sorts of acute short-term fluctuations. This includes, *inter alia,* the problem of poor harvests necessitating additional imports. The foreign currency reserve cannot be accumulated rapidly, for it would provoke a temporary reduction of the growth rate or tensions. Until such a reserve is accumulated, short-term credit and drastic markdowns on exports, etc., have to be accepted.

5. One should always remember the negative repercussions of a steep rate of growth on consumption in the short run. Very often it is the difficulty of this decision that is at the roots of unrealistic and overoptimistic plans, which are a sort of escapism from the hard realities of short- and long-run consumption dilemma. If the principle of a realistic plan is observed and consumption in the short run is considered, a moderate rate of growth will be set. The latter can be maintained at a relatively high level if waste is avoided, attention is paid to investment and foreign trade efficiency, and the *modus operandi* of the economy is streamlined. (Kalecki 1963c.)

In final analysis, the unfulfillment of an unrealistic plan reflects mainly on consumption. There is a natural penchant to maintain the continuity of the investment process to avoid freezing of capital in unfinished projects. The damages caused by unfulfilled consumption plans cannot be underestimated. The apathy and discouragement of the population not only affects detrimentally the motivation and performance of the human agents of economic activity, but generally aligns the worker-consumer against the socialist ideals.

XIX

VOLUNTARISM ON TRIAL

•

THE CALAMITIES THAT BEFELL THE POLISH ECONOMY in 1966-70 fully vindicated Kalecki's position. But he would not have gotten any satisfaction from "I told you so." He did his utmost to prevent the "laboratory experiment." He not only disapproved of the economic policies promulgated for the second half of the 1960s and demonstrated how disastrous the implementation of such a plan would be, but took a constructive and positive stand by elaborating a concrete alternative proposal.

In his 1971 lecture at the Gramsci Institute in Rome, Wlodzimierz Brus reported the so-called official public pre-Congress discussion of the 1966-70 plan as a most glaring example of muffled criticism, suppressed dissent, and rising costs of disobedience. As Brus puts it, "one of the most illustrious Polish economists of international repute" expressed his views in writing, offering concrete alternative solutions. The allusion is obviously to Kalecki. The negative reaction from the powers that be was immediate and exceptionally violent. (Brus 1971, pp. 27-28.) A further illustration of repressed dissent was offered by deposed Premier Jozef Cyrankiewicz, who revealed that, several years before, a distinguished economist (the allusion again seems to be to Kalecki) handed over to him a substantial and illuminating report on the conflict between consumption and investment. Cyrankiewicz passed the report to Gomulka, who was outraged by the "revisionist" ideas and peremptorily rejected the findings. (Cyrankiewicz 1971.)

Kalecki's realistic counterproposal for the 1966-70 plan, keenly sensitive to the usual constraints, and aiming at gaining a measure of acceptability without compromising in principle, represents an important and final chapter in his articulation of a prudent and sober policy and his courage and determination to fight voluntarism in planning. For a man who identified the socialist economy with the largest possible rate of increase of living standards (subject to maintenance of a prudent growth rate), and whose primary concern was full employment, the meager increase or even retrogression of living standards in the second half of the 1960s and deliberate policy of creating unemployment were gloomy events.[1]

Modification of Production Techniques: Kalecki's Counterplan

At the outset of his alternate proposals to the promulgated pre-Congress thesis, Kalecki called attention to the specific economic issues facing the system's directors when drafting the 1966-70 plan:

1. The second half of the 1960s followed a five-year period during which a meager average rate of increase of the living standard was recorded. It would seem, therefore, that one of the overriding tasks of the 1966-70 plan should have been to redress this deplorable state of affairs.

2. In comparison to the first half of the 1960s, the labor force was to increase considerably, with a slight deceleration of population growth.

3. The rate of growth could not be accelerated because of difficulties in balancing foreign trade. Throughout the development of postwar Poland, the balance of payments has been a major bottleneck. There was every indication that, in 1966-70, difficulties in equilibrating it would become more acute. While means of limiting imports and forcing exports had to be an integral part of the plan, it was, of course, irrational to eliminate those imports which, in one way or another, contributed to producing the necessary exportables.

It could be deduced from these basic characteristics of the period in what direction the 1966-70 plan would have to lean. The ample increase of the labor force would have to be not only fully employed, but also utilized effectively to raise consumption standards and to achieve other goals of the national economy. Only if such an approach had been adopted would the increase of the primary factor of production cease to be a quandary and become a source of national wealth. The relative abundance of manpower should have been utilized *to reduce the capital intensity of investment, thereby decreasing outlays for achieving a given increment of national income and releasing additional funds for consumption.* To the extent that the labor force could contribute not only to savings on investment, but also to savings of raw materials (for example, greater use of by-products), its relative abundance should have promoted a relaxation of tensions in foreign trade. *The same effect could have been achieved indirectly by earmarking a part of the investment outlays saved by adopting the more labor-intensive variants for achieving raw materials savings.* For example, by adopting less capital-intensive processes in the textile industry, the resources thus saved could be diverted to investment in finishing and increasing the durability of textiles, resulting in reduced requirements for imported raw materials. *Thus, the demographic situation clearly dictated a shift toward a mode of development generally featuring labor-intensity and savings on productive investments and materials.*

This approach could have served to achieve the supreme end of the 1966-70 plan which, according to Kalecki, should have been the highest possible growth rate of consumption, compatible with other desiderata and constraints. The pre-Congress thesis promulgated the goal of full employment, but left loopholes for introducing a number of measures incompatible with full employment policy.

As Kalecki pointed out, pronouncements that investment outlays per job should be as low as possible left wide room for interpretation. In his counterproposal, Kalecki interpreted the statement as the choice of less capital-intensive and more labor-intensive techniques of achieving a given production effect. This could be achieved, *inter alia,* by improving the utilization of the existing stock of capital, thus increasing output without investment and with labor productivity remaining essentially unchanged. The labor-intensive and capital-saving variant could also be found for new investments (for example, variants of less expensive mechanization). The adoption of such investment variants does not mean that the index of labor productivity would not be higher than in the old plan, but merely that the increase would not be as large as it would have been, had labor shortages compelled the planners to choose a more capital-intensive variant. It cannot be overemphasized that technical progress could be geared not only to increasing labor productivity, but also to reducing capital and material intensity of production.

The pre-Congress thesis accentuated the structure of production rather than the modification of production techniques. The stress was on the shift in the branch structure of employment. It was promulgated that employment should increase in the more labor-intensive branches, like the service sector, haberdashery, clothing, and toys. However, such restructuring could only be limited if it were not to involve major imbalances. If such shifts would be consequential they would affect directly the structure of exports and/or domestic consumption. In case of exports, the problem becomes immediately one of finding new markets on a large scale and the effectiveness of such exports. Also there is restricted freedom for modifying the structure of sales on the domestic market. On a large scale eggs cannot be replaced by toys. On the whole, this method is dangerous because it can prove to be unrealistic or can lead to grave distortions of the structure of consumption and consumers' discontent. A more appropriate method would be the aforementioned modification of production techniques. (Kalecki 1963k, pp. 3-7.)

Particularly in agriculture it was apparent that production techniques were not adapted to the labor situation. With the assumed unchanged number of those engaged in private farming, investment outlays for mechanization were clearly excessive. A contributing factor, accentuating the disproportion, was the small planned increase of livestock production, which is relatively less capital intensive. Kalecki attacked the mechanization drive aimed at forcing increased domestic grain production in order to restrict gradually the import of grain—slated to cease by 1970. As a result of the agricultural policy adopted, there was an extraordinarily high ratio of investment outlays to the increase of value added.

Although the qualitative differences in the approach of the planners and Kalecki's counterplan were probably more important, the key quantitative difference between the control figures and Kalecki's counterproposal lay in the average annual rate of increase of consumption (stipulated at 4.8 per cent by the control figures, and at 5.5 per cent by Kalecki). Prima facie, the difference does not seem to be strikingly high, but the crux of the matter lies in the realism of underlying assumptions—i.e., safeguards that plan blunders will not be shifted onto the consumers.

In Kalecki's counterplan, which he endeavored to make more palatable to the planners, there is a strikingly divergent approach to the structure and size of investment. To begin with, he stressed that he did not propose to decelerate the rate of expansion of raw materials branches to produce raw materials indirectly in exchange for less capital-intensive export of final products. As it was, the export plan would be difficult to meet, and its further expansion would be terribly risky. However, it was possible to save on investments for a *given* increase of raw materials production. The four-shift system (including one repair shift) in the new coal and copper mines was of utmost importance. Moreover, a substantial role could be played by the modernization of obsolete plants to achieve the increments of output. Such savings of investments could be used for producing the output stipulated by the planners for the selected labor-intensive branches. Thus the structure of this output would not be initially restricted by imposing limiting conditions of labor intensity. Imported materials could be secured by shifting a part of the saved investment outlays to material savings. Consequently, the additional output would be less labor intensive and more capital and material intensive than stipulated in the control figures, whereas the opposite changes would take place in the rest of the economy. Thus the assumed plan of employment and consumption would become more realistic, palatable, and harmonious. Again Kalecki opposed the undiscriminatory folklore of technology. The investment profile he suggested would require smaller import of machinery from convertible-currency countries.

Even taking into account the postulated machinery for state farms, cooperatives, and agricultural circles to execute the plant production targets, the agricultural state investments on mechanization could be reduced considerably, and overall productive investments could be cut accordingly. The planner's propensity to save on the so-called nonproductive investments, affecting consumers' welfare, were attacked by Kalecki. (He proposed that nonproductive investments be raised mostly for housing construction.)

The planned low rate of growth of livestock production contributed considerably to the very slow planned rate of increase of the national income originating in agriculture. Kalecki propounded that a more rapid increase in livestock production was desirable. It would increase national income and consumption by almost the entire surplus of final produce over feed because it would not require consequential investment outlays. It would also enhance consumer welfare, contributing to an improvement in the structure of consumption. Finally, the small private farmers would largely benefit from the rapid increase of livestock production. The basic difficulty was to persuade planners to give up the goal of cessation of grain import by 1970. Kalecki argued strongly that the additional import of grain required to increase the growth index of livestock production would be a prudent undertaking and could be financed even without foreign credits. Three alternatives could be used: (1) import of grain could be covered by additional export of pork; (2) if the world market could not absorb this volume of export, beef (whose production was planned to increase considerably) could be sold abroad and replaced by pork on the domestic market; and (3) since the large grain exporters have difficulties in selling their products, some of them would probably be willing to enter into long-term agreements for the exchange of grain for other products.

Kalecki emphasized that the realism of the control figures and of his variant of the 1966-70 plan depended to a large extent on implementing certain envisaged organizational changes: (1) planning of investment; (2) material savings; and (3) import policy.

1. It is a sad, but true, state of affairs that, thus far, investments had not been prepared in several variants and calculation of investment efficiency played a subsidiary role. More generally, are the elaborate studies on investment efficiency calculation of practical importance? Can equivalent results be achieved in this way by means of much smaller expenditures? This depends entirely on the number of different project variants being submitted for every investment undertaking considered. Regretfully, this method cannot be substituted by any theory of the efficiency of investment, however elaborated. If in practice different variants are not submitted, investment efficiency calculations are useless, for there is simply no problem of choice where there is only a single variant. Calculations of investment efficiency can ensure considerable savings when substantially different production variants are taken into account. There is little chance for a shift from capital- to labor-intensive variants without accustoming decision-makers to thinking in terms of variants. Kalecki emphatically rejected the proposition that the prevailing investment practice prevents adoption of his proposal about choice of techniques. Contrariwise, there is no more urgent reform than that of a system that prevents attempts to allocate resources efficiently. He doubted that this problem could be satisfactorily solved by an appropriate formulation of the incentive system. At any rate, it could not be the only factor in refurbishing the existing inefficient system. It might be necessary to create a central institution whose skilled engineers and economists would not only evaluate investment projects submitted, but would elaborate at least general counterproposals. The work conducted at such an institution should also raise the level of elementary verification of investment projects. Even perusal of the initial projects could show at least the deficiencies of the projects submitted. Clearly the problem of comparing the efficiency of investment is extremely complicated. Nothing must be accepted uncritically. But a study of the manifold alternatives and their yields is of paramount importance.

2. Savings of raw materials can be derived from modified production processes or induced by incentives for more economical use of materials with the same equipment. A material-saving investment policy can be supported by the central investment institution described above. But material incentives could help in initiating such investments from below. Considerable current savings could also be achieved by applying forms of value added for computing output. As previously stipulated all incentives aimed at reducing material inputs would prove useless, if they were not accompanied by a reform of the system of quality control independent of the enterprise's management. Moreover, a policy of promoting material-saving investments should be supported by a share of investment funds granted the ministries exclusively for investments that would reduce raw materials and fuel inputs.

3. Poland's export policy toward developing nations mainly centered on selling complete plants at long-term credits. These credits did not help solve short-term balance-of-payments perturbations. They burdened the national economy in the same manner as investments. It might be much more reasonable to attempt to enter into such contracts with only short- or medium-term credits. Not only raw materials, but also some semifabricates and finished goods, could be imported from these underdeveloped countries. Such contractual arrangements could be made attractive by offering not only fixed volumes of goods, but also fixed prices, because developing countries aim at assured outlets for their raw materials at fixed prices. (Kalecki 1964w.)

In June, 1964, the Fourth Congress of the PUWP was held, and the basic control figures of the 1966-70 FYP that were adopted did not significantly differ from the pre-Congress thesis. In conformity with the experience of Polish industrialization, the main targets of the 1966-70 five-year plan featured a growing share of industry in the production of national income, a one-sided development of the raw materials base, an accelerated growth of the machine-building and chemical industries, increased export of machinery, and a faster rate of growth of investment than national income. The development of the economy was supposed to rely increasingly on infusion of technical progress in all areas of the economy, without any measures to ensure that technological advancement would be an integral part of the working arrangements. Again, rhetoric aside, no real reserves were provided. While in some respects greater caution was evinced in formulating the targets, this was definitely not the case in allocating resources to consumption, in increasing real wages, and generally in measures affecting the population's welfare. The planners underestimated the potential powder keg of the population's discontent with its lagging living standards, earnings, employment, the size and composition of the consumption fund, etc., which eventually proved to be the instrument of their undoing.

Overall Performance

During the second half of the 1960s, Poland registered the *lowest* rate of increase in real wages of all CMEA countries. According to official sources, in the 1960s, the real wages rose only very slightly, if at all. Admittedly, some groups actually suffered a decline. Real wages are calculated on the basis of the official average cost of living index. But the weighty component is occupied by food prices, which grew rapidly. This particularly affected the lowest paid workers. The real wages were lower than the average published statistical indexes, not only because of disguised price increases. The lowest nominal wage set in July, 1966, at 850 zl. was kept at this level until the end of 1970. This was the longest period during which the lowest earnings remained at an unchanged level in Poland. While during the 1966-68 period average wages grew annually by over 2 per cent, in 1969-70, they remained virtually unchanged. ("Materialy IV . . ." 1971.) The targets of the 1966-70 five-year plan, albeit very modest, were not implemented.

As Kalecki predicted, considerable strains and stresses prevailed during the implementation of the 1966-70 plan, especially on the consumers' market, in construction, and in foreign trade. The factor primarily responsible for the dislocations was overexpansion and direction of investment activity. The investment expenditures target was considerably overfulfilled. As a whole, during the 1960s Poland's rate of growth of investment was higher than that of the U.S.S.R., Czechoslovakia, and East Germany. In Poland, as a result of the very high rate of investment activity, the share of accumulation in national income increased from 25.9 per cent in 1965 to 26.9 per cent in 1970, that of investment from 17.6 per cent to 20.6 per cent, and that of productive investment from 10.5 per cent to 12.7 per cent. The share of national income devoted to increase in stocks declined from 8.3 per cent to 6.3 per cent. Thus the share of consumption declined from 74.1 per cent to 73.1 per cent, and that of personal consumption from 65 per cent to 62.8 per cent. (*ZG* No. 45, 1971.)

Clearly the figures do not illustrate the dimensions of the formidable economic problems. Progress in the vital field of technical dynamism was very disappointing. The perennial problems of malstructure of production (including that of plan-satisfying output), foreign trade, and consumption haunted the planners. The record of how policies misfired and the "textbook case how not to plan" cannot be scrutinized here. (Cf. Feiwel 1971a, pp. 333-476, and 1971b, pp. 261-367.)

In the 1960s the delicate agricultural situation was greatly mismanaged. The policy pursued in the latter part of the 1960s was to limit livestock breeding in order to ensure self-sufficiency in grain production. Almost prophetically, Kalecki pointed out, before the 1966-70 plan was put into execution, that the all-out stress on domestic plant production was bound to encroach on livestock breeding and result in meat shortages. As he predicted, the misconceived agrarian policy proved to be one of the key blunders of the economic improvisation of Gomulka's regime. After the fall of Gomulka, Kalecki was vindicated and given full credit for the courage and tenacity with which he waged the battle for a sober agricultural policy. (Mieszczankowski 1971.) But it took bloodshed and a violent shake up of the regime to redress the policy.

Self-sufficiency in grain production could be aimed at by increasing procurement of grain from the farmers. This was done not only by increasing the supply of fertilizer to raise yields, but also by increasing purchase prices of grain to encourage the farmers to sell more grain to the state. By manipulating the relative state purchase prices of grain and livestock, i.e., by increasing the purchase prices of grain, while leaving prices of livestock at about the same level, the planners induced the farmers to sell more grain to the state, while leaving less for livestock breeding. Had the planners reconciled themselves to the previous average imports of grain, they would not have had to induce farmers to dispose of their grain to such an extent, and would not have unwittingly discouraged livestock breeding. This misconceived policy was aggravated by the decision to undertake mass production of fodder mixtures, which claimed large quantities of grain and vast investment resources. Probably better results could have been achieved if the grain had been left with the farmer to mix albumen concentrates for feed and the resources used for larger production and subsidy for fertilizers.

In the end, the planners were forced to increase substantially prices of fodder mixtures (at the end of 1970) in order to make up state deficits on this production, while raising the purchase prices of livestock for slaughter.

Purchasing power was above that planned, with systematic overfulfillment of the plan of producer goods and underfulfillment of consumer goods, with foreign trade aggravating, rather than mitigating, the situation. Even if the plan of consumer goods had been realistically determined and implemented, the above-plan increase of the population's spending power would still have been an undermining factor. Understating the disposable income at the planning stage, the planners were able to balance projected income flows with relatively smaller flows of consumer goods. This "paper balancing" enabled the planners to earmark more resources for the production of producer goods. If for no other reason, a plan so constructed was bound to provoke strains and imbalances. The plan failed to foresee the full disposable income effect of the marked expansion of investment activity. The application of stringent administrative control compressed only temporarily the rate of increase of employment. The new construction projects and the new capacities in the producer goods sector had to get a work force. But not only did the demand for labor condition expansion of employment, but the meager increases, rigidity, or fall of real wages stimulated increased labor supply. The planners understated the intensity and potency of social and political pressures to raise the level of real wages, especially when they were artificially held down.

By 1969 full employment policies were blamed in many quarters as the main obstacle to increased productivity. Unemployment was advocated as a disciplinary measure—the unemployment scare was supposed to overcome the lax attitude toward work. Apart from the social significance of such a policy, it should be noted that, under actual conditions prevailing in Poland, all attempts to reduce employment cut down on the employment of women and not on the undisciplined labor force (loafers, etc.)—a phenomenon mainly encountered among the male labor force. The planners were fascinated by the slogan of intensifying production and forcing growth of labor productivity at the expense of the primary factor of production, seemingly unaware of the seething social tensions that their actions might provoke. Kalecki was again proven right in predicting that the policies pursued were consistently leading to unemployment—a situation which he had dreaded all his life and devoted most of his energies to combat and which he considered incompatible with the very objectives of the socialist economy.

THE LESSONS OF DECEMBER 1970

Bitterness caused by higher prices, their manner of introduction, and the income and employment policy pursued were the direct but not ultimate causes of the tragic events of December 1970.[2] The Gomulka regime was toppled primarily, if not exclusively, on the grounds of the economic debacle—as a result of the harsh policies featured by the second wave of industrialization (since the late 1950s), the mismanagement of the economy, and the failure to undertake radical refurbishing of the economic system. It took a dramatic manifestation of workers: protest in the form of bitter street fighting, strikes, destruction of property, and loss of life to bring about *some* economic concessions to the worker-consumer. Faltering and modest concessions were gained under strong pressure from below. The new regime did not face an enviable task. No doubt political expediency dictated some of the measures adopted. After some hesitation, the Gierek regime had to rescind the price increases, to unfreeze wages, to abandon the "new" incentive system that was geared to freezing earnings, and to reappraise the deliberate creation of unemployment. Such action required expanded production and imports of consumer goods, and a radical turn in the disastrous agricultural policy. The planners' maneuverability in placating the consumer was severely circumscribed and conditioned by the investment program started in the 1960s. There were powerful constraints on reshuffling resources, not only due to indivisibilities, technical rigidities, and resistance of the production system to change, but also because of system-made impediments to change.

Clearly, the lessons to be drawn from December 1970 are not only specific to the particular configuration of conditions in Poland at that time. They have a more universal significance. Without repeating some of the other broader issues, at least one point should be underlined: One of the great advantages of the socialist economy was apparently the ability of the planner to set and manipulate the rate of accumulation, largely irrespective of consumers' intertemporal preferences. The Polish experience indicated that the planner's range of maneuverability is considerably narrower than is usually conceived. The conflict between the intertemporal preferences of planners and consumers (workers) takes many forms. A socialist economy is not free from powerful institutional constraints in response to the reduction of money (real) wages or to the reduction of the normal (expected) rate of their increase.

Higher prices of consumer goods and services relative to nominal wages entail lower real consumption by workers. There is a lower limit, or rather a maneuverable range, of the level to which real wages can be depressed without provoking pressures to restore (or raise) their level. There is a conflict between the desire of the planner to step up capital formation and the refusal of workers to accept the given level of real wages compatible with the postulated shifts to nonconsumption. Indeed, the socialist economy suffers from what Joan Robinson called the inflationary barrier—the lower limit below which real wages cannot be reduced without evoking political and social disturbances and depressed productivity. Something must give way: either the system explodes or some check operates to curtail the propensity for capital formation. (Cf. Joan Robinson 1966a, pp. 48-49, 356; Sulmicki 1957, pp. 127-52.)

The toppling of Gomulka's regime is ample proof of the lower limit below which compression of real earnings provokes outward political and social disturbances. With some oversimplification, the simultaneous clamp-down on the increase of employment and earnings (deliberate policy of creating unemployment) and the sharp increase of foodstuff prices activated powerful forces of resistance against shifting the cost of blunders in economic policy onto the worker-consumer (especially onto the lower income groups or households with only one breadwinner).

The Gierek leadership that took over in 1971 has shown a certain concern for living standards and the well-being of the population. But this concern is not novel in recent Polish history. The 1956-60 plan ushered in by Gomulka (especially in its first two years) was distinguished by its solicitude for raising real wages, which in the quinquennium went up by almost 30 per cent over an extremely depressed level. But the pressures from below were increasingly weaker and the reversion to old methods, neglect of the population's needs, and repression by the top leadership were increasingly stronger. The point is that, if the Gierek leadership is not to fall into a similar pitfall, it would have to become continuously sensitive to the aspirations and pressures from below. Whether the lessons have been learned remains to be seen. By nature, Kalecki was a pessimist. If experience is to be any guide, it is difficult to refrain from a similar tendency.

EPILOGUE

The Last Years

MICHAL KALECKI DIED ON APRIL 17, 1970, a broken and totally despondent man. His pessimistic view of humanity and its frailties had been completely justified by the events and aftermath of a new wave of repression in the late 1960s. The spring of 1968 was the crisis point, for Poland and for Kalecki himself, and thereafter he merely existed, bitter and lonely to the end.

Until that fateful year of 1968, however, Kalecki led a relatively happy life, pursuing his teaching and research interests and surrounded by the general esteem of colleagues and students. Despite his general irritation with the irrational economic policy of Poland, with the state of affairs in the world at large, and with the direction economics was taking, he could still find satisfaction in being able to influence a group of respected Polish economists and able students. Although he hoped that they might take over where he left off, he did not live to see the hope fulfilled.

Poland has had a long history of repressions, but since the days of World War II alone, it has experienced a series of catastrophic pogroms of intellectuals. First came the mass murders in Hitler's camps, next the Stalinist purges, and then, in 1968, the purge of "revisionists" and "Zionists," the latter a euphemism for Jews. In this last event, Poland lost a good portion of its intelligentsia, which had been built up from a very narrow base at the end of the war. It lost a large number through emigration and a smaller, but no less significant or irretrievable one, that chose to remain but was effectively muzzled.[1] The latest purge did not relate as personally to Kalecki as it did to others, but many of his students and followers were affected, which made a tremendous impact on their friend.

The most recent anti-intellectual campaign started building in the early 1960s. The leash on the freedom of expression, dissent, and criticism, which had been relatively loose since 1956, was progressively tightened. Gomulka's regime was becoming less secure; as promises of better living standards, greater freedom, and all-around improved social conditions went unfulfilled, the regime faced steadily diminishing support from its original backers—the working class and the intellectuals. Because the government leadership viewed its greatest threat from the recalcitrant intellectuals, it proceeded to decimate them.

The overt repression began in 1964 when, on October 14, about twenty university teachers and students in Warsaw, Lodz, and Lublin were arrested. This occurrence, together with ensuing dismissals of other university students and teachers, set into motion a process of growing opposition to the government, and increasingly repressive response, which culminated in the first events that were to make 1968 an especially tragic year: in January of that year the authorities closed Mickiewicz's play *Dziady*. The play was a rather innocuous criticism of Russia, and of the Tsarist period at that, but the audience, showing its dislike of anything Russian, applauded roundly at every critical thrust. Although the audience's reaction and the immediate closing of the play seem to have been minor incidents in themselves, and though the student protests that followed were relatively mild, the government apparently used the occasion to build its case against its chosen scapegoats, the "revisionists" and "Zionists." Playing on the basest of human characteristics—prejudice, envy, and fear—the authorities believed that they could capitalize on the workers' apprehension and inbred dislike of intellectuals and on traditional anti-Semitism.

The real witch hunt began in March of 1968. On March 8, the students demonstrated at Warsaw University, an event followed by similar student protests or demonstrations at many other institutions of higher learning. In some cases when students prepared to disperse they were prevented from doing so by university gates being closed in their faces, allowing the representatives of "law and order" to beat and maul the demonstrators. It has been suggested that the student protests were in part provoked, as a means of providing an escape valve for popular unrest and dissatisfaction (cf. Bauman 1968, p. 16), but the extent of such provocation is difficult to ascertain. Jewish students, whether they participated in the demonstrations or not, were dismissed along with the protesters. University professors—all of whom were branded as revisionists or Zionists—were likewise dismissed; and they included many of Kalecki's followers. Among the academics who fell victim to the purge were Kazimierz Laski, professor at SGPiS, a younger colleague of Kalecki who was greatly influenced by him and who became a leading exponent of the theory of growth in a socialist economy; Professor Ignacy Sachs, a prominent authority on economic development, influenced by Kalecki's ideas in that field; and Professor Wlodzimierz Brus, who derived from Kalecki's work the integration of growth and functioning theory and who was probably his moral heir. One of Kalecki's leading students, the mathematical economist Stanislaw Gomulka, left Poland, along with many others. Laski and Sachs emigrated; Brus chose to remain, having been given a research post at the Housing Institute, but he was not allowed to publish.

The dismissals and purges affected people in all walks of life: students and professors at universities, teachers in other schools, party and government functionaries at all levels, literary and artistic people, management personnel in industry and trade, and even the humblest clerks. An especially severe blow was the almost complete destruction of the once-famous film school and film industry in Lodz. The sociopolitical sciences were particularly hard hit. Professor Leszek Kolakowski was dismissed and his philosophy department at Warsaw University disbanded. Zygmunt Bauman, the sociologist, also lost his post; and there were countless others.

Even so, economics may have been the hardest hit of all. It lost the brightest stars in a firmament that, for about a decade, had included some of the most progressive economists in Eastern Europe. Since the mid-1950s, in fact, there had been a veritable renaissance of Polish economic thought. Poland could boast of two internationally famous theoreticians—Michal Kalecki and Oskar Lange—and a sizable number of students and followers whom they had trained. New ideas were being advanced and tested in many quarters. Bright young men were eager to shed the shackles of dogmatism and to learn. Serious schools of thought developed, and the recognized scholars soon had a wide following. New theories of growth and functioning of a socialist economy were spun out. Warsaw was sometimes called the "Socialist Cambridge." (Lipinski 1970c.) Students came from abroad to study planning and theory, and Polish economists were listened to at international meetings. All of this came to an end in 1968. Two major schools of thought—the study of development economics and that of growth economics in a socialist economy—were mercilessly decimated, so that today they are of secondary importance. Kalecki became a voluntary recluse, and his ablest students and followers, as well as those of Lange, who had died in 1965, were dispersed to the four corners of the world or else effectively silenced at home. Polish economics became a wasteland.

Many explanations and theories have been advanced to account for the 1968 events. Even a tentative analysis is beyond the scope of this work, but some of the possible reasons should be mentioned. As already implied, the government's desire to liquidate nests of independent thinking—represented most visibly by the universities—has been suggested as one of the immediate and underlying goals. (Bauman 1968, p. 12.) Until March 1968, Polish university professors were nominated for life and, unless they committed a crime, could not be discharged; hence, university circles were the last stronghold of relatively independent thought. In the eyes of the ruling group, this was a basic sin. Furthermore, the intellectuals were restless, and there was a growing friction between their ranks and those of the regime.

As background for this focus on intellectuals, it should be remembered that a tense atmosphere had pervaded Poland since the Israeli War of June 1967. Although the evidence is very inconclusive, it would appear that the historically anti-Russian Poles, rendered even more so by the recent experience of Soviet domination, were sympathizing with the Israelis because their own government was taking a pro-Arab (pro-Soviet) stand.[2] Such antigovernment sentiment was sufficient justification for reprisals against various sectors of the population, but the purge, as might be expected, was aimed primarily at eliminating dissidents and "revisionists" from positions of power and influence. The Polish paradox was that some of the one-time orthodox Marxists had, since 1956, been at the forefront of decentralization and revisionist movements. In 1968 they were part of the nucleus of the liberal left wing of party intellectuals. Chance would have it that many of them were Poles of Jewish origin, and most of them showed a spirit of independence that Gomulka could ill afford to tolerate.

There were other reasons as well, including the intraparty factional struggle for the seat of power; the need, previously mentioned, for diversionary action from the mounting economic and social ills with which the authorities could not cope; the increasing sensitivity of the regime, especially during and after the Prague spring, to the dissidents within its own ranks; and that haunting factor, traditional anti-Semitism. The last two points are related and merit further elaboration.

Within the party, the middle-class, middle-aged population was getting restless for advancement; a purge was needed to make room at the top, and the most obvious targets were the Jews. Yet it seems that the regime miscalculated about arousing the anti-Semitic feelings of the population at large. Whereas before the war anti-Semitism had deep economic foundations, in postwar Poland it was generally weakened because (1) few Jews were left, and (2) the new generation was brought up on socialist egalitarian slogans. Thus the sympathy with anti-Semitism unleashed by the state was found mostly among the frustrated and ambitious middle-class whose envious eyes turned toward the higher positions occupied by Jews. The witch hunt failed to create the necessary room at the top because there were not enough Jews occupying high posts. (Bauman 1968, pp. 19-20.)

Kalecki was emotionally shaken by the wave of repression. He opposed vehemently the dismissal of his colleagues, but, as has been noted, he himself was not an overt target of the purge. One can only speculate on why. Was it because the government was afraid of international opprobrium if it touched a man of his reputation and standing? Was it because he was nearing retirement age? Or was it because he resigned, choosing voluntary retirement to protest the action against his colleagues rather than give the authorities an opportunity to dismiss him later? There is very little that one man can do to fight officially organized tyranny and repression, but Kalecki did what he could to remove himself from any association with those responsible. In addition to resigning his teaching post at SGPiS, he relinquished all of his other remaining official duties, and he refused thenceforth to contribute to Polish economic journals. Reportedly, he said: "You have accused the 'revisionists' of having monopolized the scholarly publications; now try to fill the pages yourselves." He also refused to represent Poland at international meetings.

Aside from criticism of Kalecki's views that appeared here and there in the press, the one instance of direct attack on Kalecki took place at the June 18 and 19 conference organized by the party cell at SGPiS. The main speaker at the conference, representing the official position, was Dymitr Sokolow, a mediocre economist who had been prominent during the Stalinist period. In his report, which received full press coverage (*TL* June 21-22, 1968; *ZG* June 23-30, 1968), Sokolow accused Kalecki of not being a Marxist. Specifically, he deplored the fact that, instead of being influenced by his "Marxist disciples," Kalecki managed to instill in them his "non-Marxist" research methods. In Kalecki's courageous and provocative riposte, which was not published, he defended his former colleagues by pointing out the irrationality of the indictments and by disarming, point by point, the accusations. In his own case he did not dignify the indictment with a defense. His only retort was that, if Sokolow were the epitome of a Marxist, he (Kalecki) wanted nothing to do with Marxism.

It seems just as unnecessary here to defend Kalecki against the slanders that appeared in the press. One of the principal accusations repeated in several instances even after Kalecki's death was that the investment wave of the 1960s was traceable to the influence of Kalecki's growth theory on economic policy makers. (Cf. Florek 1970; Kozlowski and Waszczynski 1971.) This nonsense would not even be worth repeating if I had not met with similar misconceptions in the West.[3] To one who has studied Kalecki's work, the fallacy is obvious; he consistently opposed at all times and whenever possible adventurous raising of the growth rate to the detriment of consumption,[4] always pointing to the conflict between consumption and investment and perpetually warning against the dangers of overinvestment, the consequent spreading of bottlenecks throughout the economy, and the adverse effects on the quality of life and performance. For instance, his growth theory in a socialist economy was developed as an antithesis to the dogma that the producer goods sector should always grow faster than the consumer goods sector. Kalecki's perspective plan was rejected by the authorities because it assumed a slower rate of growth (and investment) than that desired by the leaders. In his analysis of the 1961-65 plan, Kalecki pointed to the lack of realism with which it was constructed. He warned planners that they could not build a plan that would assume a rapid increase of investment and a considerable increase in consumption by relying on improvements in efficiency (which might, or might not, materialize) as an additional source of growth, unless they provided necessary conditions; for in the final result, consumption will come out the loser. He urged that more attention be paid to consumption in the short run and to moderation in the rate of growth. Again, in his counterproposal for the 1966-70 plan, Kalecki urged forcefully an increase in real wages, reduction of the investment impetus, and a more realistic foreign trade and agricultural policy. To speak of Kalecki as being responsible (even in part) for the investment drive of the 1960s, which sapped the energy of the Polish economy and was so dearly paid for by the workers, shows ignorance of Kalecki's work, to say the least.

Kalecki's remaining two years, following his resignation, were tragically unhappy ones, in the sense of being totally empty. He had seen his ideals shattered and he lost faith in his fellow man. Although he was a skeptic by nature and did not expect much of humanity, he was bitter that it did not even measure up to his modest vision for it. He was lonely in more ways than one, for his hopes for his native land departed at about the same time that many of his followers, colleagues, and friends left Poland. Except for a trip to Cambridge in the spring of 1969, he led a forlorn, day-to-day existence—especially for a man who had always been active, accustomed to getting out of the house early in the morning and not returning until night. During these last two years, when he performed no activities other than personal research and writing, he would arise early in the morning and march out with his briefcase under his arm as though going to the office. His destination, however, since he had no other place to go, was only a neighboring reading-room. His former expectations for socialism in his native land were sorely disappointed.

It seems to me that his expectations were based, not so much on socialism as it *was*, as on socialism as it *could be.* Although he lamented the losses in progress owing to wrong policies and fully recognized and disapproved of the repression of totalitarian regimes, he often pointed out that living and working conditions of the lower income group were better in postwar than in prewar Poland. When he had returned to Poland in 1956, it was a time of hope for better living standards, greater freedom for intellectual and artistic pursuits, and generally a better life. Slowly thereafter, he saw these hopes eroded, often in piecemeal fashion, but steadily and in ever-widening areas of the society. Still, there was no reason to turn away in horror—until, that is, the witch hunt of 1968 was launched. To Kalecki, it was inconceivable that a so-called socialist regime could appeal to the basest sentiments of a population and stage a pogrom against a handful of Jews only a quarter century following the previous holocaust.

The actions of some of his friends, associates, and acquaintances contributed in large measure to his loss of faith in his fellow man. His grain of pessimism notwithstanding, he was sorely disillusioned that not more of them had the moral stamina to stand up for what they professed to believe and to disapprove overtly of the official course. Dark ages are conducive to degradation of the human spirit, and those individuals of "flexible integrity," concerned primarily with their own safety or even advancement, are not apt to exhibit laudable qualities. The party-line approvers, even those who tried to avoid personal involvement in repressive programs, might be expected to act as they did, but the so-called dissenters were another matter. Although some of them had professed similar sentiments and ideals to Kalecki's in freer and better times, now they seemed to be expressing contrary views or else they remained mute. Some of them apologized to Kalecki in private for their public stands. With him, however, self-respect could not be bought back so easily; he was a harsh judge. He was not reluctant to voice his contempt when he met these erstwhile colleagues, and I was told that many whose conscience troubled them would go to great length to avoid confronting him.

With his considerable contacts abroad, Kalecki was in a good position to help many of those who chose to emigrate, and he was full of compassion for their lot. Having been an émigré himself, he understood and sympathized with their untenable position at home and the difficulties they would encounter abroad. He spoke fondly and respectfully of those who chose to remain in Poland, bearing the brunt of the regime's malignancy and bravely withstanding the *déclassement.* He was especially proud of the moral fortitude evinced by Professor Brus, who elected to stay in Poland although the authorities had shunted him to the ranks of nonpersons. Kalecki admired Brus's exemplary and dignified behavior in the face of crass and vicious attacks, but he was also greatly distressed that an economist of Brus's abilities should be thwarted in his research and teaching pursuits. The waste was incalculable.

The trip to Cambridge for the Easter Term of 1969 was Kalecki's single escape from the depression of his final years. Appointed as Overseas Fellow of Churchill College, he renewed old friendships and was enthusiastically greeted by Cambridge students, who had been brought up on his economic theories. The reception to his University Lecture on the theories of growth under various social systems must have been gratifying, for the hall was packed to capacity, with many in the audience crouching on the steps and floor. To those in attendance it seemed that the ovation he received was the response to an incisive and logical analysis of a very timely topic even more than it was homage to a wise old man.

Even so, these few months in Cambridge were not happy ones. Kalecki could not seem to unburden his heavy heart. Unlike many travelers, he brought his sorrows with him, brooding constantly about the state of affairs in his native land. Few at Cambridge understood his despondency, although many knew that he was quite ill at the time, which undoubtedly contributed to his dejection. Upon his return to Warsaw, however, his health improved, and plans were made for him to become visiting professor at the University of Rome in 1970 and to attend in June of that year the Conference on National Economy Modeling in the U.S.S.R. (Novosibirsk). The engagements were not fulfilled, for Kalecki died in April. Professor Lawrence R. Klein told me that Kalecki's place on the printed program at the Conference was delicately framed in black, and that the sessions opened with a moment's silence in his honor. Kalecki's Soviet colleagues held him in high esteem, confessing to Klein that they were pleased he had not actually "defected," despite rumors to the contrary that were circulated in the U.S.S.R.

With Michal Kalecki's death, the world lost a unique individual of extremely high principles, powerful energy, and brilliant mind, and economics lost a model and inspiration. His legacy, however, cannot be erased. He left it in written form and as an imprint on students, colleagues, and homeland—the latter a particularly ironic twist in view of Poland's failure to capitalize on his thought during his lifetime. It is unfortunate that the life of so productive a man should have been plagued with crises and bitter disappointments, even acknowledging that many of his problems were self-created. He demanded perfection, or at least an unalloyed commitment to that goal, he could not tolerate slovenly thought or superficial minds, and, most significant, he simply would not compromise his principles. Looking back over his troubled years, Kalecki once made the sad but true observation that the story of his life could be compressed into a series of resignations in protest—against tyranny, prejudice, and oppression.

NOTES*

•

(Notes to pages 5-15)

Prologue: Portrait of the Man and Scholar

[1]One evening in Cambridge in 1969, when he was preparing to watch on television one of the Apollo flights, I asked him whether he was interested in these achievements. As usual, he was not overly enthusiastic. However, he admitted that he would rather see money spent on the Apollo missions than on the production of armaments. His point was that the competition in space was partly a substitute for the arms race.

[2]A leading British Marxist recalls that, in discussing Soviet policy before the war, Kalecki was highly critical. He advanced the view that this policy reflected the interest of the skilled industrial workers; i.e., of the more privileged minority strata of the industrial proletariat, rather than of the class as a whole.

[3]See Kalecki's stand at the United Nations Conference on the Application of Science and Technology for the Benefit of the Less Developed Areas, "Summary Report of Specialized Session held on February 9, 1963" Geneva: United Nations, E/Conf. 39RR.86 (H) (Apr. 3, 1963), p. 3.

[4]On the other hand, Maurice Dobb exclaimed surprise at the fact that Kalecki's highly concentrated and austere writings did not attract as much attention as they deserved: "Apart from their classic quality, what has especially struck this reviewer in reading (or re-reading) these essays, is the great economy as well as lucidity and directness of exposition—a quality which should have made his ideas more widely known than they are." Dobb 1972, p. 217.

[5]Indeed, "great economists usually discover their leading ideas rather than excavate them from the literature." Stigler 1955, p. 294.

[6]This and the quip about Israel were Professor Kalecki's favorite sayings about his experience as economic advisor.

* All references to Kalecki's works are to the latest editions.

[7]This was true even in relatively inconsequential matters; e.g., I was told that he would get quite upset if he felt that he was not being paid (by his employer or publisher) according to his worth.

[8]At the same time, Kalecki was prompt to retract if, after deliberation, he felt that he was in the wrong. I was told that at a meeting in Zakopane he mercilessly attacked a position taken by one of the students. After some deliberation he realized that the student had been right and he wrong. The following day he combed through Zakopane to find the student and apologize to him.

THE PREWAR PERIOD (1899-1939)

[1]Mrs. Ada Kalecki, his widow, informs me that all pre-World War II correspondence was lost during the Nazi occupation. Kalecki was not fond of writing letters. Again, according to Mrs. Kalecki, most of his letters are brief statements, generally concerned with a narrow subject comprehensible only to the addressee and not particularly useful to a biographer.

[2]However, as we shall see in chapter 2, in a review of Keynes's *General Theory* (1936c), Kalecki did point out that he had arrived at similar conclusions in his 1933f.

[3]Kalecki 1971d, p. vii. Abba P. Lerner told me recently that, although he had been one of the first outside-of-Cambridge converts to the Keynesian Revolution and saw Kalecki frequently in London in 1936-37, Kalecki never told him of his priority of publication. Only many years later did Lerner become aware of this fact. Similarly, Maurice Dobb recalls that, although he knew Kalecki in his early Cambridge days and was aware of the independence of Kalecki's discoveries, he did not realize that they pre-dated 1936.

[4]"As Robert Merton has pointed out in his important researches on the sociology of science, one should not be surprised that there is great sensitivity among scientists concerning issues of priority, issues which must inevitably arise because of the great probability of nearly simultaneous discovery. For, as Merton points out, reputation for originality is the only coin that the scholar can work for: who robs me of my theorem steals not trash but all that there is to steal. Nor have the greatest scientists been immune to this (even though they are in the favored position of being able to create a new theorem if one is snatched from them)." Samuelson 1972, p. 688. A glimpse of Kalecki's reaction to official recognition can be had from

the following incident, related to me by Dobb. During one of his postwar lectures at Cambridge, Kalecki was introduced by Guillebaud, who acknowledged that, in fact, Kalecki had anticipated the main ideas of the General Theory, so that it could have been called the Kaleckian Revolution. Kalecki, although inclined to be expressionless on such occasions, looked as if this pleased him distinctly.

[5]Kalecki does not even appear in the name index. In the notes to the unfinished portion of the *History* the following can be found: "The most successful of all the theoretical systems that have been inspired by this wish to simplify the structure of economic theory is the static system that is associated with the name of the late Lord Keynes. Many others have also been constructed, for example, by Amoroso, Frisch, Kalecki, Pigou, Tinbergen, Vinci." Schumpeter 1954, pp. 1143-44. We can only speculate here whether Schumpeter knew of Kalecki's contribution and intended to incorporate it in the final version of his book, or whether he was simply unaware of it. It is inconceivable that, had he known and understood its import, he would have neglected it.

One explanation might be that, since Schumpeter was no great admirer of Keynes, he did not attach much importance to an anticipation of Keynes. Another might be that Schumpeter missed the very important ways Kalecki differed from Keynes, as we shall see in chapter 2.

Chapter I

[1]Klein 1966, p. 225. On the Swedish school, see also Lundberg 1957; Shackle 1967, ch. 10; Frisch 1958 and 1933; Myrdal 1939; and Ohlin 1937a, pp. 53-67, and 1937b, pp. 221-40.

[2]The background of the Keynesian Revolution and the new economics are only sketched in here for obvious reasons. Of course, many arguments are subject to important qualifications that had to be forgone in this oversimplified form.

[3]On Kalecki's view of the fallacy of Say's Law of the Market, see, *supra,* pp. 10-11. For a summary statement and criticism of Say's Law and classical monetary theory, see Schumpeter 1954, pp. 615-25; Fellner 1960, ch. 8; Lange 1942; Joan Robinson 1971a, ch. 6; and Samuelson 1972, pp. 529-43. Blaug 1968, ch. 5, on Say's Law contains comprehensive references to the literature. Patinkin 1965 provides extensive commentary on the literature on this subject. On pp. 193 ff. he discusses the ambiguity in the meaning of Say's Law

and the implication of Say's Identity. Patinkin argues that Say's Identity is not a logically necessary and basic component of the classical and neoclassical position. See n.L and *passim.* See also Leijonhufvud 1968, pp. 91-102.

[4]Kalecki 1944d, pp. 131-32. Cf. Pigou 1943, pp. 343 ff. Patinkin hailed Kalecki for being the first to point out "that the stock of money relevant for the real-balance effect was not the usually defined concept of hand-to-hand currency plus demand deposits, but the monetary base alone." Patinkin 1969, p. 1140. On Kalecki's contribution to this field, see also Patinkin 1965, p. 296, and 1971, *passim.* Cf. Leijonhufvud 1968, pp. 315-31.

[5]For a different interpretation, see Leijonhufvud 1968 and Johnson 1972a.

[6]On the need to strike a balance between fiscal and monetary policies rather than treating them as alternatives, see Kahn 1972, pp. 125 ff. The manipulations to expand deficient and to contract excessive demand to the level that spending is neither too little nor too great and the inclusion of monetary policy need to be emphasized, for Keynes has frequently been misunderstood by people who took his recipe for the special conditions of a deep depression to be the general case.

[7]Kalecki first presented the argument in complete form in 1933f. A shortened and more formalized version was presented in Oct. 1933 at the meeting of the Econometric Society in Leyden and appeared as 1935h, pp. 327-441.

[8]Kalecki's articles of that period are rich in policy prescriptions and analyses of current economic situations. These themes are barely touched upon here.

[9]The argument is drawn more or less verbatim from Kalecki 1935e, pp. 1320-24. In some cases the source is other pre-*General Theory* articles. In those cases appropriate references are given. Some of these essays have been translated and published in part or in full in 1966h.

[10]Kalecki 1932e, pp. 1413-14, where Kalecki also discusses brilliantly the intricacies of creation of purchasing power and the financial process, pp. 1412-13.

[11]Kalecki 1933d, p. 10. Kalecki elaborated the theoretical argument in support of "domestic exports" (deficit financing) in 1933c, pp. 27-35, trans. and rpt. in 1966h, pp. 16-25.

[12]Schumpeter 1954, p. 41. See also pp. 1170-84. On the recent marked decline of interest in the General Theory, see Leijonhufvud 1968, pp. 3 ff.

[13]". . . personalities were not spared in Keynes' sarcastic attack upon the classical economists . . . Professor Pigou was cited in the *General Theory* as a particular exponent of the theory which Keynes was attacking . . . Pigou returned the blow with a bitter argument against the *General Theory.* It is not difficult to see that Keynes was the winning economist but the losing gentleman; he hardly observed the rules of the academic game." Klein 1966, pp. 93-94.

CHAPTER II

[1]For a complete rendering of Keynes's life, see the standard biography by Harrod 1951 and the thoughtful review article by Klein 1951a. See also E.A.G. Robinson 1964, pp. 13-98; Samuelson 1964, pp. 315-47; and Schumpeter 1965, Essay 10.

[2]For Keynes's position, see Keynes 1936, ch. 24; Keynes's letter to Hayek (Harrod 1951, pp. 436-37); Klein 1966, ch. 7.

[3]Klein 1966, p. 131. Keynes's attitude toward capitalism is perhaps best illustrated by contrasting it with that of Marx and Marshall—as Joan Robinson does. She shows Marx trying to understand the system in order to destroy it, Marshall trying to present it in a favorable light, and Keynes trying to discover the tools for saving the system from self-destruction. Along these lines Marx claimed that the system was bound for self-destruction and workers should combine to accelerate the downfall. Marshall countered that, notwithstanding its faults, capitalism worked toward the good of all. And Keynes found the system permeated by flaws which, he believed, could be eliminated. Marx argued that the capitalist system is pernicious for the workers, who will revolt against it. Marshall claimed that the system promotes the largest possible growth of wealth in which all classes share and enjoy. Keynes showed that growth of wealth can only be assured if the system is reformed. Joan Robinson 1960, pp. 1, 3, and 5.

[4]The relation of Keynes to his predecessors has been the subject of great controversy. See, *inter alia,* Klein 1966, chs. 1 and 2; Hansen 1953, ch. 1; Harris, ed. 1947, ch. 6. Clearly, other writers who influenced Keynes were concerned with the question of effective

demand. For a summary of views by Lauderdale, Malthus, Hobson, and Wicksell, see Hansen 1964, chs. 14 and 17. See also Schumpeter 1954, *passim;* and Leijonhuvfud 1969.

[5]This is not to say that all writers treated Say's Law as a self-evident proposition. More sophisticated argumentation was advanced. See Schumpeter 1954, pp. 615-25; and Patinkin 1965, especially n.L.

[6]As Kalecki wrote in a foreword to his prewar essays, republished in English after the war: "It is worth noticing that there is a certain affinity between these theories of mine and those of Rosa Luxemburg." (1966h, p. 1.)

[7]Joan Robinson 1964, p. 338. On Keynes and Marx, see also Joan Robinson 1951, pp. 133-45; 1960, pp. 1-17; Klein 1966, pp. 130-34.

[8]The problem was that Ricardo was concerned with the theory of distribution between classes under conditions of long-run equilibrium (long-run accumulation of capital requires savings, and higher profits would raise the growth rate of capital stock and foster a long-run growth rate of employment). Malthus was preoccupied with the determinants of short-run variations in the volume of output in the real world (short-run profitability requires spending). Ricardo indicated the source of the dispute when he wrote: "It appears to me that one great cause of our difference in opinion on the subjects which we have so often discussed is that you have always in your mind the immediate and temporary effects of particular changes, whereas I put these immediate and temporary effects quite aside, and fix my whole attention on the permanent state of things which will result from them. Perhaps you estimate these temporary effects too highly, whilst I am too much disposed to undervalue them. To manage the subject quite right, they should be carefully distinguished and mentioned, and the due effect ascribed to each." Quoted after Keynes 1963a, p. 116. See also Malthus's reply, *ibid.*

[9]Keynes 1963a, pp. 117, 120-21. For a masterful introduction to Ricardo, see Sraffa 1951. On Ricardo and Malthus, see Blaug 1968, chs. 3, 4, and 5, where extensive references to the literature may be found. Again, Schumpeter 1954 is worth consulting.

[10]Schumpeter 1954, p. 623. Schumpeter charged that Keynes suffered from a Ricardian vice—"the habit of piling a heavy load of practical conclusions upon a tenuous groundwork." *Ibid.*, p. 1171.

[11]"The difficulty lies, not in the new ideas, but in escaping from the old ones, which ramify, for those brought up as most of us have been, into every corner of our minds." (Keynes 1936, p. viii.)

[12]"Thus Say's law . . . is equivalent to the proposition that there is no obstacle to full employment. If, however, this is not the true law relating the aggregate demand and supply functions, there is a vitally important chapter of economic theory which remains to be written and without which all discussions concerning the volume of aggregate employment are futile." Keynes 1936, p. 26. Remarkably, Keynes himself wrote about the revolutionary character of the book he was writing. He believed that this new economics would undermine Marxism. "I believe myself to be writing a book on economic theory which will largely revolutionize—not, I suppose, at once but in the course of the next ten years—the way the world thinks about economic problems. When my new theory has been duly assimilated and mixed with politics and feelings and passions, I can't predict what the final upshot will be in its effect on action and affairs. But there will be a great change, and, in particular, the Ricardian foundations of Marxism will be knocked away." Keynes to George Bernard Shaw, Jan. 1, 1935. Quoted by Harrod 1951, p. 462.

[13]For a Marxist evaluation of Rosa Luxemburg, see Sweezy 1942, pp. 202-209 and *passim.* For a more sympathetic treatment, see Kowalik 1964b, pp. 203-19. For a good introduction to Luxemburg's economic writings, see Joan Robinson 1960, pp. 59-73, and the biographical study by Nettl 1966.

[14]"Under-consumption theories have been associated with an appeal for reform rather than revolution—with the view that capitalism *might* be made to work satisfactorily—and for this reason they are uncongenial to the Marxist creed." Joan Robinson 1966b, p. 72.

[15]For a fuller and more sophisticated presentation of the argument and discussion of the effects of various methods of financing, see the 1933 article on stimulating recovery by "export surplus" and "domestic exports" (government deficit). (Kalecki 1966h, pp. 16-25.)

[16]Tugan-Baranovsky 1901. On rival interpretations of Marx's theory of crisis, see, *inter alia,* Dobb 1939, *passim;* Sweezy 1942, pp. 156-213. See also Hansen 1964a, pp. 277-92.

[17]Sweezy 1942, pp. 158-59. Schumpeter called Tugan-Baranovsky the most eminent Russian semi-Marxist. The Russian economists of the beginning of the twentieth century were trained on Marx. The Marxist influence is obvious even in those who criticized their master. See Schumpeter 1954, p. 878. On the history of ideas of European socialism, see Landauer 1959; and Gerschenkron 1970, pp. 1-17.

[18]I plan to translate and edit several prewar Polish articles by Kalecki, including the complete review.

[19]Kalecki pointed out in this review that, in his 1933f, similarly to Keynes, he had shown that investment is a determinant of the overall size of production (pp. 20-21).

[20]Again, Kalecki noted the similarity with his concept in 1933f, pp. 22 and 23.

[21]Kalecki noted that he also indicated the independence of the size of output from nominal wages in 1933f, pp. 45-46.

[22]On the distinction between marginal efficiency of capital and marginal efficiency of investment, see Lerner 1944.

[23]Kalecki's answer draws upon his 1933 model. "He took risk over from the demand side (where it lies rather uneasily in Keynes' scheme) to the supply side, and postulated that the amount of finance that each individual enterprise will commit to investment is an increasing function of the prospective rate of profit, depending upon the ratio of borrowing to its own capital. Then, with any given distribution of capital amongst enterprises, there is a particular relation between the total amount of investment plans being drawn up at any moment and the level of prospective profits. The second difficulty was that, though Keynes himself attached great importance to the idea that the present is always over-weighted in forming a view about the future, he treated his schedule of prospective profits as though it was independent of the *actual rate of* investment." (Joan Robinson 1964, pp. 338-39.)

[24]This debate and broader aspects of the role of interest in the economic process were lucidly surveyed by Shackle 1966, pp. 108-53. Patinkin 1965 (a sophisticated and thought-provoking treatise) and the already referred to incisive and highly praised reappraisal of the Keynesian Revolution by Leijonhufvud 1968 are important items in the literature on the subject. See also Conard 1959; and Grossman 1972, pp. 26-30; and Johnson 1972a, pt. 2. Cf. Hansen 1953, p. 27.

[25]Cf. Kalecki 1937a, pp. 440-47; 1939a, Essay 4; and 1943k, Essay 2. Examination by Behrman of selected data concerning cash balances held by certain large manufacturing companies and the short-term rate of interest in the U.S. during 1919-40 seems to substantiate Kalecki's theory about the close connection between the velocity of circulation and the short-term rate of interest. (Behrman 1948, pp. 185-90.) This study was undertaken on Kalecki's suggestion.

[26]Klein 1964, p. 191; cf. Klein 1966, pp. 37-38. See also Joan Robinson 1966c, p. xi. For a reflective discussion of liquidity preference

and critique of Kalecki's formulation of the "antibootstrap view," see Kahn 1972, pp. 72-96.

[27]"We take as given the existing skill and quantity of available labour, the existing quality and quantity of available equipment, the existing technique, the degree of competition, the tastes and habits of the consumer, the disutility of different intensities of labour and of the activities of supervision and organization, as well as the social structure including the forces, other than our variables set forth below, which determine the distribution of the national income. This does not mean that we assume these factors to be constant; but merely that, in this place and context, we are not considering or taking into account the effects and consequences of changes in them." (Keynes 1936, p. 245.)

[28]Joan Robinson 1951, p. 155. Since then, Harrod acknowledged Kalecki's seminal contribution to economic dynamics. Cf. Harrod 1964, p. 179. " . . . the groundwork that Keynes and Kalecki laid out for the generalisation of the *General Theory* must be fully recognized. There is little doubt that had English writers had earlier reference to Kalecki's work their task of applying Keynes's theories to long-run growth would have been greatly eased. The point of emphasis here is that modern Keynesian growth theory is in no sense an original creation of modern writers. The basic relations that underlie the systems of modern Keynesian theorists are traceable directly to the work of both Keynes and Kalecki." Kregel 1971, pp. 101-102.

[29]Klein 1966, p. 68; cf. Domar 1957, Essay 4 and *passim*. The role of capital stock in the investment function follows from the traditional theory of the firm, based on the principle of profit maximization. Also econometric research suggests a strong negative correlation between investment and the capital stock. Klein 1966, p. 68 and app.

[30]"*A reduction in money wages is usually accompanied as a result of price 'rigidity' by an increase in 'the degree of monopoly' and consequently leads to a reduction in real wages as well. However, this decline is accompanied by a fall rather than by a rise in employment. The slump in employment in question affects the wage good industries while employment in industries producing investment goods and capitalists' consumer goods remains unchanged. The real income of the capitalists does not rise but the real income of the workers declines.*" (Kalecki 1966h, p. 56.)

[31]Joan Robinson 1966c, p. xi. On Keynes's reliance on "a rather vague sort of Marshallian concept of competition," see Joan Robinson 1964, p. 339. Cf. Hansen 1953, chs. 10 and 11; Harris, ed. 1947, pt. 8; and Keynes 1939b, pp. 34-51.

[32]Keynes 1936, p. 265 and *passim*. It should be noted that Keynes wrote much about money and trade in other contexts.

[33]Whereas the U. S. and U. K. are good examples of this, other countries have been enjoying "export-led growth."

[34]See, for example, Samuelson 1970. "Kalecki's statement of the theory avoids the problem of the equality of saving and investment, which plagued us so much, by relying simply on the fact that the equivalent of investment outlay is added to profits. He cuts through another passage where Keynes made heavy weather by taking it for granted that the rate of interest is a monetary phenomenon. When investment, income and saving increase, it is necessary for the supply of the medium of exchange to be increased also; otherwise the rate of interest would rise and a drag be set upon investment." Joan Robinson 1964, p. 337.

[35]Joan Robinson 1964, p. 337. On Keynes as an outsider in the pure theory of business cycle, see Metzler 1947.

[36]Klein 1951a, pp. 450-51. In Samuelson's view, the critic of Tinbergen reveals that he "did not really have the necessary technical knowledge to understand what he was criticizing. How else are we to interpret such remarks as his assertion that a linear system can never develop oscillations?" Samuelson went even as far as to argue that "there is reason to believe that Keynes himself did not truly understand his own analysis." Samuelson 1964, pp. 327, 316.

[37]To mention just a few others: the mathematical restatement and extension of Keynes's system by Lange, Meade, Hicks, Harrod, and Domar; the celebrated Tinbergen-Klein econometric extension of Keynesian analysis; Kuznets's seminal work on national income accounting; and Leontief on input-output.

[38]Schumpeter made the distinction between Marx's vision and analysis. He gave Marx a very high grade on the former, but maintained that Marx's analysis was often faulty: "Through all that is faulty or even unscientific in his analysis runs a fundamental idea that is neither—the idea of a theory, not merely of an indefinite number of disjointed individual patterns or of the logic of economic quantities in general, but of the actual sequence of those patterns or of the economic process as it goes on, under its own steam, in historic time, producing at every instant that state which will of itself

determine the next one. Thus, the author of so many misconceptions was also the first to visualize what even at the present time is still the economic theory of the future for which we are slowly and laboriously accumulating stone and mortar, statistical facts and functional equations." Schumpeter 1942, p. 43.

[39]Again, Schumpeter called the broader implications of Marx's economic interpretation of history as doubtless "one of the greatest achievements of sociology to this day." Schumpeter 1942, p. 10. Historical materialism "explains the entire development of human society as a complex of dialectical processes in which the primary, incessantly repeated stimulus is the interaction between man and his material environment in the social process of production. . . . The historic importance of this discovery was appraised by Engels in the following words: 'Just as Darwin discovered the law of development of organic nature, so Marx discovered the law of development of human history.' " Lange 1963, pp. 44-45. Incidentally, Kalecki believed that one of Lange's most important lines of thought was his work on historical materialism. Kalecki considered Lange's 1936 paper on Ludwik Krzywicki a brilliant presentation of the gist of theory of historical materialism. See Lange 1961a, pp. 71-88. On historical materialism and modern sociology, see also the illuminating paper by Hochfeld 1964, pp. 207-32.

Chapter III

[1]Kalecki originally formulated his argument in 1938b, pp. 97-112. An amended version appeared in 1939a. Important alterations were made in the version which became Essay 1 in 1943k. While the gist of the argument remained, substantial modifications were introduced in 1954c and 1965l. He then returned to the subject in 1968j, pp. 263-76, and 1971a, pp. 1-9.

[2]As Kaldor remarked, referring to what he called the Ricardian-Marxian, the Keynesian, and the Kaleckian theories of distribution, "I am not sure where 'marginal productivity' comes in, in all this." Kaldor 1960, p. 236.

[3]Once the assumption of perfect competition is abandoned, "the production function approach is useless and other means must be found to analyze the distribution of income." Hahn 1972, p. 35.

[4]Hahn 1972, p. 37. Mitra praised Kalecki's pathbreaking theory as "certainly the only significant attempt in contemporary economics

to answer directly the problem of macro-economic income distribution." Mitra 1954, p. 88. Cf. Rothschild 1961, pp. 173-79. On the importance of Kalecki's theory of distribution and its marked contrast to alternative approaches to the theory of distribution, see Nell 1972, pp. 450-52. The significance of Kalecki's contribution in light of other approaches to distribution is stressed, *inter alia,* by Davidson 1959 and Kregel 1971, p. 101.

[5]Keynes was vastly impressed by the "stability of the proportion of national dividend accruing to labor," irrespective of the level of aggregate output and of the phase of business fluctuations, which he considered an "undisputed fact" of economic statistics. He spoke of it as a "bit of miracle." The only explanation of this phenomenon, Keynes wrote in 1939, was offered by Kalecki "in the brilliant article which has been published in *Econometrica*" (1938b). In that article, Kalecki "employs a highly original technique of analysis into the distributional problem between the factors of production in conditions of imperfect competition, which may prove to be an important piece of pioneer work." (Keynes 1939b, p. 49.)

[6]Interesting comments on the great constants, with particular reference to Bowley's Law, may be found in Kuznets 1959, p. 56; Klein and Hosobud 1961, pp. 173-98; and Feinstein 1972, *passim.*

[7]As Sraffa authoritatively comments, in the course of an investigation of the laws which govern the distributive shares, Ricardo was troubled by the fact that the size of the national product appears to alter when the division changes. Ricardo conceived the need to measure the aggregate that was to be distributed. The "problem of value which interested Ricardo was how to find a measure of value which would be invariant to changes in the division of the product; for, if a rise or fall of wages by itself brought about a change in the magnitude of the social product, it would be hard to determine accurately the effect on profits." (Sraffa 1951, p. xiii.) On this intricate subject, see Sraffa 1960.

[8]For criticism of Ricardo's approach see, *inter alia,* Knight 1935, pp. 3-15, 171-96; Schumpeter 1954, pp. 472-83; and Blaug 1968, pp. 92-144, and references therein. For an authoritative and brilliant analysis of Ricardo's economic system, see Sraffa 1951. The work of one of Sraffa's foremost students, Garegnani 1960, English ed. in preparation, is highly recommended. Recently, Milton Friedman, *inter alia,* questioned the emphasis placed by some economists on the relative class distributive shares. Friedman sees the sole concern of the theory of distribution with factor price determination (micro-

distribution) and finds it inconceivable that anyone could be interested "in the particular figure of the percentage of aggregate income that goes to wages." Wright, ed. 1951, p. 306.

[9]In the neoclassical or marginalist theories, as contrasted with Ricardian, Marxian, and what Kaldor called the Keynesian theories of distribution, "the problem of distribution . . . has no particular theoretical significance apart from the importance of the question *per se.* Nor do these theories yield a 'macro-economic model' of the kind that exhibits the reaction-mechanism of the system through the choice of a strictly limited number of dependent and independent variables." Kaldor 1960, p. 211.

[10]For a brief account of some of the neoclassical theories of distribution, see Kaldor 1960, pp. 210-11, 218-23; and Davidson 1959, pp. 36-43. Pt. 4 of Marchal and Ducros, eds. 1968, contains interesting papers on theories of distribution. For a sympathetic exposition of the marginal productivity theory, see pp. 476-501; and for critical comments, pp. 501-50. An expanded treatment could be found in Bronfenbrenner 1971, where a strong preference is evinced for the neoclassical theory, but where some of the major objections to it are analyzed in depth. See also the controversial Ferguson 1969 and the review by Joan Robinson 1970b, pp. 336-39.

[11]Walras 1954, p. 422. Or, in the Austrian version, prices of goods of "higher order," hence factor prices are imputed from the prices of goods of "first order."

[12]A leading representative of the marginal productivity school, Clark, emphasized the supreme importance of the distribution of wealth (income) among the different claimants participating in its creation. He asked whether there is a "natural law" according to which the income of society is distributed into wages, interest, and profit, and if so, what is that law? His answer was that, where "natural laws have their way, the share of income that attaches to any production function is gauged by the actual product of it." His aim was to demonstrate that unhindered competition, in terms of the product which the agent produces, tends to "give to labor what labor creates," to capital what capital produces, and to entrepreneurs what the coordinating function contributes. To each agent of production "a distinguishable share in production, and to each a corresponding reward—such is the natural law of distribution." The welfare of labor and other social classes depends on whether they get much or little of the national product, but the relationship between classes chiefly depends on whether the amount accruing to

labor, be it large or small, is what labor produces. If it could be shown that exploitation exists, i.e., that labor produces an identifiable ample amount of produce and gets only a part of it, conditions would be created for social unrest. The maldistribution would breed revolutionaries. Clark adds, with his usual ethical overtones, that laborers "would have the right to do so." Clark 1899, pp. 1-4. For instance, such critics of neoclassical theory as Joan Robinson argue that the notion of "productivity and capital" is to justify the income of its *owners*, i.e., the neoclassical system was to justify the *owning* of capital as a productive activity. Joan Robinson 1965, pp. 36-47; for an opposing view, see Solow 1965.

[13]For a critique of the approach, see Pasinetti 1968, pp. 501-503. This is not the place to review the sharp controversy concerning the very foundations of neoclassical economics started by Sraffa's *magnum opus*. Noteworthy, the book is subtitled *Prelude to a Critique of Economic Theory*, which, in itself, gave rise to heated outbursts of controversy and emotion. Sraffa is not actively engaged in the debate that he started. The meaning of the "Sraffa Revolution" and the real substance of the controversy do not need to detain us here. Harcourt, who sympathizes with the Robinson-Kaldor-Pasinetti position, surveyed the growing body of literature in 1972. Some of the contributions to the controversy, including several of those criticized, were reprinted by Harcourt and Laing, eds. 1971. Joan Robinson's position is stated in 1971a. Among many other contributions, see especially the Symposium 1966, pp. 508-83; Pasinetti 1965; and Samuelson 1972, pp. 187-229.

[14]Cf. Kaldor 1960, pp. 222-23. For a brief discussion of the conditions necessary for the validity of the neoclassical theory of income distribution, see Nuti 1970b, pp. 336-39; and Joan Robinson 1970a, pp. 309-17.

[15]For his elaborate argument, see Solow 1968a, pp. 449-50.

[16]For a brief account of the above argument, see Hunt and Schwartz eds. 1972, pp. 222-23. The rationale of the critique is defended on pp. 205-21, 233-44, and 245-91. Also the crucial objection is raised, if capital is nonmeasurable as a quantity (i.e., nonmeasurable theoretically) the notion is as inapplicable at the micro-level as at the macro-level.

[17]For an exposition and scrutiny of the dissenting economists, see Bronfenbrenner 1971, pp. 407-44. Bronfenbrenner distinguishes (1) Kalecki's monopoly theory; (2) Boulding's accounting identities; (3) Kaldor's saving-investment and magic constancy theories; and (4)

sociological and institutional theories. See also Krelle 1968, pp. 413-49. In his review of Bronfenbrenner's book, Nell distinguished among the main rivals in approaches to the theory of distribution: the neoclassical (aggregate production function), neoclassical (social rate of return), neo-Keynesian (Kaldor) and neo-Marxian (Kalecki), Kalecki's "approach stands out in marked contrast to all the rest." Nell 1972, p. 450.

[18]Bronfenbrenner 1971, p. 408. According to Solow, the main contributions since Paul Douglas's pathbreaking macroeconomic function were: the work of Kalecki in original and reformulated versions and the subsequent writings of Boulding, Kaldor, and Hahn. Solow 1958, p. 618.

[19]As contrasted with the price-taking, quantity-adjuster behavior of the entrepreneur. Under competitive conditions in order to sell a larger output, the firm does not have to lower its price or to incur increased selling promotion costs. With imperfect competition, there is a degree of freedom and an element of judgment in price formation, sales promotion, and prevention of potential competitors. The entrepreneur can make a profit while operating at less than full capacity.

[20]For criticism of Kalecki's assumption of excess capacity (depression economics), see Hahn 1972, pp. 40-41. For Kalecki's defense in his latest writings of his contention that underutilization of productive capacity is a *typical* condition of the modern capitalist economy, see, *inter alia,* 1968j, pp. 261-66; 1971a, pp. 2-8; and 1970e, pp. 311-14. It is true that the prevalence of surplus capacity has much sharper relevance to a prewar, depression-ridden economy than to the postwar period. It cannot be overemphasized that Kalecki considered his explanation of determination of investment decisions only as a first attempt to advance somewhat toward a plausible solution in this complex field. See also Kalecki 1950, pp. 62-64; and on empirical evidence, Klein and Preston 1967, pp. 34-58.

[21]Kalecki's assumptions about the elasticity of supply and approximate constancy of unit prime costs over the relevant range are incompatible with perfect competition. For, under perfect competition, the occurrence of surplus of the price over *MC* would drive the entrepreneur to expand production up to the full capacity output. Any firm staying in business would operate up to the point of full capacity, and the price would be pushed down to the level which equilibrates demand and supply. The excess of price over *MC* would disappear under the action of the forces of competition (the mark of

the absence of monopolistic price formation is the equality of price to *MC*).

[22]The study of the National Bureau of Economic Research 1943 tentatively concluded that, contrary to the customary assumptions in economic theory that marginal costs describe a smooth, U-shaped curve, marginal costs must necessarily rise from a certain point on (by cause of the law of variable proportions); and empirical studies indicate a linear cost-output relationship over large ranges of output in the majority of manufacturing industries, at least over the broad interval of output which the producer considers relevant. However, this seems to be the case largely under conditions of depression-ridden economy. On the rationale of the assumption of a U-shaped marginal cost curve and scrutiny of results of empirical research, see Machlup 1952, pp. 513-16 and *passim;* and Machlup 1967, pp. 1-33. The empirical evidence on the shape of the cost curve was scrutinized by Johnston 1960, and Gold 1966, pp. 161-94.

[23]For a summary of the pertinent literature on price-fixing behavior, see the survey by Silberston 1970, pp. 511-82.

[24]Kalecki's assumptions of constancy of marginal cost were also criticized, *inter alia,* by Bauer 1941, p. 201.

[25]Kalecki 1965l, p. 12. On the controversial assumption of profit maximization and its critique, see, in particular, Silberston 1970.

[26]The full-cost pricing principle, at least in its original version, maintains that the price which a manufacturer will normally quote for a particular product will equal the estimated average prime cost per unit taken as the base; a percentage addition is made to cover overheads, and a further addition is made for "customary profits." Cf. Andrews 1949, especially ch. 5. The essence of the problem is how the margin is determined, or how the "standard" volume of output and "something for profit" or the "customary profit" are arrived at. For Kalecki's criticism of the full-cost principle, which he contended has no precise theoretical meaning because the amount that is added for profit makes quite a lot of difference to the price and more still to the gross margin, see Kalecki 1943k, p. 27. He remarked that the manager of a modern cotton-spinning mill described once to him at great length the elaborate work of the cost-calculating department. To Kalecki's question whether the results were used in price-setting, the manager replied: "Oh, the prices were fixed by the market." *Ibid.*, p. 27. Interestingly, Keynes admitted that, in practice, producers often follow a full-cost pricing policy and thus rising *MC* may not be reflected in rising prices. Keynes

1939b, pp. 46-48. The full-cost principle is analyzed at great length by Sylos-Labini 1969, especially pt. 1.

[27]It was suggested that Kalecki's theory of distribution, against its author's intention, was used to support the popular belief that all gross profits are suspect as the result of a monopolistic racket, cunning, and exploitation; and that it gives the wrong impression that the entire difference between price and average prime costs represents the share of national income going to businessmen and shareholders, notwithstanding that a substantial part of the labor force constitutes nonmanual labor which is not actually employed directly in the process of production, and the margin includes normal capital cost allowances. Andrews 1949, p. 26. Cf. Whitman 1941, p. 265. Kalecki 1942m, pp. 125-27. Pen stressed more recently that very many factors influence distribution, and that Kalecki oversimplified the problem. Pen 1971, pp. 177-79.

[28]In his original formulation, Kalecki employed Lerner's measure of the firm's degree of monopoly power. In subsequent reformulations, Kalecki abandoned this measure. He also relaxed the assumption of profit maximization. If equality of (rising) *MC* and price is taken as a criterion of perfect competition (mark of an absence of monopoly), the inequality of *MC* and price is prima facie evidence of the presence and extent of monopolistic power to fix prices and to restrict output. Lerner suggested that the relative size of the variance $(p-MC)/p$ was an index of the degree of monopoly, often written as $1/n$. According to the fundamental theorem of imperfect competition, also known as the Amoroso-Robinson Relation, $MR=P[1-(1/n)]$, Lerner's formula resembles the inverse of the formula of the elasticity of demand for the product of an enterprise. It differs from this formula only in that the term *MC replaces the term marginal revenue.* Since in equilibrium $MC=MR$, Lerner's measure becomes identical with the inverse of elasticity of demand.

Kaldor argued that, on closer scrutiny, the elasticity of the demand curve facing an individual firm turns out to be no less a broken reed than its counterpart, the elasticity of substitution between factors. That, indeed, the very concept of a demand curve confronting an individual producer is illegitimate, or nonexistent, as such a curve is indeterminate since it depends on mutual interaction of rivals; the action of one seller depends on the anticipated reaction of others, who are mutually interdependent. Thus, under the prevailing conditions of oligopoly, the "theory of games" becomes relevant, and prices charged by different sellers cannot be assumed to be independent of each other; i.e., demand curves for individual sellers must not be drawn on the assumption that shift parameters, including rivals' prices, are held invariant, to the extent that oligop oly is dominant in industry, and probably the analysis could be applied to other sectors, say, services. Kaldor cites a lack of evidence to support the assertion that firms operating in imperfect markets fix their prices by reference to the elasticity of their demand function, or that short-period pricing is the result of any deliberate attempt to maximize profits by reference to an independent revenue and cost function. As Professor Kaldor informs me, this and similar arguments, first expressed in personal interchanges at the London School of Economics, were responsible for a shift in Kalecki's position.

Kalecki's degree of monopoly is still often linked with the elasticity of demand curve which probably adds to the confusion about Kalecki's analytical construct. True, the original formulation appears to be clearer than the successive presentations, especially that in 1965l. This probably is the reason why even the scant accounts of Kalecki's theory draw on his original presentation as slightly amended in 1939a. For instance, the latest account by Bronfenbrenner is based on Rothschild 1961 which, in turn, is based on Kalecki 1938b. Students in Cambridge tend to read 1939a rather than 1965l. As it often happens in economics, and with Kalecki in particular, successive reformulations are closer to reality, but not without expense of the elegance of the presentation. Kalecki always displayed a strong preference to sacrifice the second for the first. While the very essence of Kalecki's argument remained fundamentally unchanged over the years, substantial modifications were introduced. His latest formulations cannot be disregarded, and it is advisable to refer to 1965l or even subsequent reformulations, as we have attempted to do.

Kalecki was also criticized for misusing Lerner's measure by Bauer 1941, pp. 197-200; Whitman 1941, p. 262; and Machlup 1952, p. 517. Comprehensive references to the literature on oligopoly can be found in Sylos-Labini 1969, pp. 224-32. See also Boulding and Stigler, eds. 1952.

[29]Kaldor 1960, pp. 224-25, where he refers to Kalecki's original formulation. However, in personal conversation, he contended that the same applied to Kalecki's subsequent formulations. While I share Professor Kaldor's feeling about the complexity of the problem and agree that there are formidable problems of measurement

and conceptual refinement, this is a different matter from tautology. Kalecki's theory was also criticized for being tautological, *inter alia,* by Machlup 1952, pp. 517-18; and more recently by Pen 1971, pp. 175 ff. Bronfenbrenner 1971 also tends to support this position, pp. 410-11. For opposite views, see Joan Robinson 1960, pp. 97-98; and the valuable contributions by Rothschild 1961, and Riach 1971.

[30]Riach argued that, in a modern corporation one would expect long-run planning and profit objectives to be in terms of profit on capital invested, rather than in terms of "gross margin." He suggested that a plausible interpretation of the degree of monopoly involves, in the long run, substituting the rate of return on capital invested for the ratio of gross profit to sales revenue "as dependent variable thus creating the need to incorporate technical progress as an additional determinant of distribution." Riach 1971, p. 59

[31]This is a more general formulation than that presented in the pricing formula ($p=mu+nP_a$, where both m and n are positive coefficients, and n is postulated to be smaller than unity) describing semimonopolistic price formation in Kalecki 1965l, pp. 12-16, where the coefficients m and n, reflecting the degree of monopoly of the firm's position, specify linear relationship.

[32]For a treatment of price formation in an industry with differences in unit prime costs, see Kalecki 1965l, pp. 14-16.

[33]Completely identical products with uniform transportation costs, but different delivery dates may have different prices.

[34]Appropriately weighted and aggregated for an industry. Capital letters refer to the magnitudes of an industry as a whole.

[35]For simplification, subscripts are avoided, but Y is identified in order to avoid confusion with the value added of the system as a whole.

[36]In 1943k, Kalecki speaks of changes in the state of imperfect competition and oligopoly, in the ratio of prime selling costs, and in bottlenecks of available manufacturing capacities, p. 17.

[37]Andrews noted that, as a consequence of Kalecki's theory of distribution, there "has been the spread of an unjustified belief that the extent of actual monopoly in our economic system holds constant the share of the national income going to labour. Mr. Kalecki is not responsible for this—the misconceptions that have arisen come from sources where the terminology and the argument have been loosely repeated, . . ." Andrews 1949, p. 26.

[38]Sweezy praised Kalecki's contribution: "One of the first big steps toward a real theory of monopoly capitalism was taken by

Kalecki when he introduced what he called 'the degree of monopoly' into an analysis of the capitalist accumulation process." Sweezy 1972, p. 13; see also Baran and Sweezy 1966, especially p. 56.

[39]In agriculture and extractive industries, the outputs are raw materials and the relative share of wages in the value added depends primarily on the ratio of prices of raw materials produced to their unit wage costs. In communications, public utilities, trade, real estate, and finance, the relative share of wages in value added is rather small.

[40]Alterations in industrial composition depend not merely on variations in the volume of industrial components, but also on the relative movements of the respective prices. Kalecki 1965l, p. 30.

[41]See Kalecki 1939a, p. 32, and 1965l, pp. 17 and 34. Weintraub noted that Kalecki insisted first on a systematic long-run rise in monopoly power and only in the revised account (in 1965l) did he qualify his conclusion somewhat. Weintraub 1958, pp. 82-82. The offsetting factors were already stressed in 1939a, but their importance was accentuated in 1965l.

[42]Until recently the evidence does not seem to support this statement. Cf. Baran and Sweezy 1966; and M. A. Adelman 1951, pp. 269-96.

[43]Cf. Galbraith 1952a, pp. 101-102. For forms of nonprice competition, see Joan Robinson 1960, pp. 228-29; Silberston 1970; Baran and Sweezy 1966, ch. 5; Mansfield, ed. 1964; Cowling, ed. 1972; and Marris 1964.

[44]Kalecki 1965l, p. 19. Kalecki emphasized that his approach to this subject is in contradiction with the widely held contention that, in consequence of rising capital intensity of production, there is necessarily a continuous rise in the ratio of price to unit prime cost. This argument is based on the quite arbitrary assumption that the sum of overheads and profits (gross profits) varies in the long run roughly proportionately with the value of capital. Rising capital intensity of production is translated into a higher ratio of gross profits to proceeds and, thus, into an increase in the ratio of prices to unit prime costs. Kalecki argued that, not only are the underlying assumption and the above argument untenable, but he cited evidence (pertaining to capital intensity and the ratio of proceeds to prime costs in the American manufacturing industry for the period 1899-1944) indicating that, despite the fact that fixed capital rose continuously in relation to output (the value of production fell in relation to the value of fixed capital—both in relation to its "book value" and in

relation to valuation in current prices), the ratio of proceeds to prime costs remained roughly invariant over the period considered. This is so since gross profits indicated long-run decline in relation to the value of capital. Consequently, the ratio of prices to unit prime costs remained roughly stable, despite steady and considerable rise in capital intensity. 1965l, pp. 19-20, and for Kalecki's criticism of the underlying assumptions and objections raised against the above argument, see 1943k, pp. 28-30.

[45]One of the objectives of the trade unions is to secure a larger share of national income for labor. Pressure for higher wage rates is one of the devices to achieve this end. Opinions sharply differ on the following pregnant questions: Did labor gain in the long run by manipulating wages above the level that would have been achieved without the trade unions' powerful pressures? To what extent can the trade unions affect the overall long-run rate? Findings on the effects of unionization on raising real wages are inconclusive. Not surprisingly, some researchers claim that unions succeeded in raising real wages above the level at which they otherwise would have been, while others blame organized labor for artificially escalating wages and tampering with the resource allocation mechanism of the market. For contrasting points of view, see, *inter alia,* Rees 1957; Reynolds and Taft 1956; and Lewis 1963. Bronfenbrenner recently argued that, on the whole, studies on the impact of American trade unions on labor's share of national income concluded that there does not seem to be any significant correlation between increases in union strength and changes in labor's relative share. Bronfenbrenner 1971, p. 87.

[46]"For Marxists, the problem of the relation of the price level to movements in money-wage rates has been a stumbling block. It was easy enough to accept the argument that cutting wages in a slump will only lower prices and increase unemployment. But then how could Marx be right in asserting that raising money wages will not raise prices? On the other hand, to preach to the trade unions that raising wage rates does their members no good is clearly a deception. . . . Kalecki works out the consequences of continuously raising money-wage rates, and shows that while the main effect is to raise prices, yet it may also to some extent raise real wages. It is of no use to advocate 'incomes policy' as a remedy for inflation, without taking account of its political content." Joan Robinson 1971b, p. 2.

[47]1965l, p. 18. Pigou also observed that, in practice, monopolists frequently decide to exercise their monopolistic power *more fully*

during periods of depression than in periods of prosperity. Pigou 1929, pp. 189-90. Cf. Keynes 1939b, pp. 38 ff; Neild 1963; Tsiang 1947; Sylos-Labini 1969; and Godley and Nordhaus 1972, pp. 853-82.

[48]For instance, statistics of changes in the relative share of wages in the U. S. and Great Britain during the Great Depression seem to show that the adverse effect on labor's share of the rise of the degree of monopoly and changes in industrial composition were roughly counterbalanced by the impact of the fall of prices of raw materials in relation to unit wage costs. Data for recovery from 1933-37 indicate an increase in the relative wage share, reflecting the relatively great reduction in the degree of monopoly resulting from the increased power of trade unions. Of course, this is not meant to suggest that the results pertaining to the Great Depression (recovery) periods can be generalized as having universal validity.

[49]Kalecki 1965l, pp. 36-38. One of the problems in ascertaining the distributive shares is the fact that, in the postwar period, an increasing part of profits is paid out in the form of salary supplements or salary-type payments. And statistically, surely, "salaries" is a very heterogeneous, even quite dubious, category, with its upper boundary not easily distinguishable from profit. Cf. Feinstein 1968, pp. 115-39.

[50]Nearly all empirical research indicates that domestic prices of manufactured products are rather sticky and tend to remain unchanged for months or even years at a time. An important exception is when a raw material, which fluctuates widely in price, constitutes a high share of costs. Under such circumstances, the prices of final products are likely to change when costs of raw materials change appreciably. The above case excepted, short-run price stability is the general case, and short-run demand variations do not normally lead to price changes. Silberston 1970; cf. Kalecki 1943k, pp. 19-20.

[51]Kalecki's essential role as a critic of monopoly capitalism was stressed, *inter alia,* by Paul M. Sweezy and Maurice H. Dobb. Commenting on an earlier draft, Sweezy assessed Kalecki's influence in these terms: "I myself would tend to stress much more strongly than you do the breakthrough he scored by introducing the degree of monopoly into his dynamic model. I think he himself underestimated the importance of this, but it was the beginning of what I can only consider a significant new departure. Steindl was certainly directly influenced by Kalecki, and Baran and myself, among others,

were influenced by both Kalecki and Steindl in attempting a more full-dress analysis of monopoly capitalism. . . . This may even have been Kalecki's single most original contribution." (Letter dated Feb. 7, 1971. Cf. Dobb 1973, ch. 8)

CHAPTER IV

[1]Kalecki's theory of profits is akin to Keynes's. The following note by Kalecki is of interest: "The theory of profits presented here is closely allied to Lord Keynes' theory of saving and investment. It has been, however, developed independently of Lord Keynes in my 'Essai d'une théorie du mouvement cyclique des affaires,' *Revue d'economie politique,* Mars-Avril, 1935, and 'A Macrodynamic Theory of Business Cycles,' *Econometrica,* July 1935," *Studies,* p. 47. The exposition of Kalecki's theory of profits can be found in 1939a, Essay 2; and updated versions in 1943k, pp. 47-58; 1965l; and 1968j, pp. 263-76.

[2]The proposition that "workers spend what they earn and capitalists earn what they spend" was Kalecki's own saying, but he did not put it exactly in this form in print in English. Cf. Kalecki 1966h, pp. 44-49. Kaldor restated it as "capitalists earn what they spend, and workers spend what they earn" and propagated it as Kalecki's theory of profit. Kaldor acknowledged that in the development of his own theory of determination of aggregate profits—apart from Joan Robinson's work—"I owe a great deal of stimulus to a paper by Kalecki 'A Theory of Profits' (*Economic Journal,* June-September, 1942) whose approach is in some ways reminiscent of the 'widow's cruise' of Keynes' Treatise." Kaldor 1960, pp. 227-30.

[3]Kalecki 1965l, pp. 45-46. Obviously, the difficulty is that, in economics, we are dealing with interdependencies or simultaneous relations. Admittedly, some economists would give a different meaning to the term *determine* than that used by Kalecki and followed here. At any rate, it seems that what is of particular importance is that Kalecki set up a new approach which he used as a "model." But he really intended it as a set of hypotheses to be worked out.

[4]The time-lag in consumption expenditures is of lesser importance, and particular attention is focused rather on the time-lag between investment decisions and execution.

[5]Kalecki 1965l, p. 46. For presentation of the argument, employing the Marxian reproduction schemes, see *ibid.*, pp. 46-47; and 1971a, pp. 1-9.

[6]Relaxing the assumption of zero workers' savings, balanced budgets, and foreign trade, the currently nonconsumed part of GNP—i.e., total gross savings—is composed of capitalists' gross savings and workers' savings. The total is equal to the sum of gross investment, export surplus, and budget deficit.

[7]See in particular the discussion on extension of the simplified model to real conditions in Kalecki 1965l, pp. 56-74.

[8]Again, profits at the time $(t-v)$ are determined by investment during that period and by profits in the preceding period $(t-2)$, and so on. Thus profits at time t are a linear function of current and past investment and coefficients of investment in this relation will be 1, b, b^2, and so on, respectively. Since b is assumed to be considerably smaller than unity, the series of coefficients will be decreasing quite rapidly, only those relatively "recent" could be considered as consequential determinants of profits, and the more distant in time can simply be disregarded. To simplify the exposition, profits are treated as a function of both current investment and of investment in the near past. Roughly, profits ensue from investment with a time-lag, hence $P_t=f(I_{t-w})$, where w is the postulated time-lag.

[9]For Kalecki's derivation, modification, and generalization of the profit equation, see the sophisticated argumentation and formulation in 1933c, pp. 27-35, trans. in 1966h, pp. 16-25; and 1937c, pp. 444-50.

[10]If the budget is balanced and exports equal imports, and workers do not save, gross profits again equal gross investment, plus capitalists' consumption. But in the general case, gross savings are composed of capitalists' gross savings, plus workers' savings, and the aggregate gross savings equal the sum of gross private investment, export surplus, and budget deficit.

[11]Here there is a disregard of complications that arise from treatment of gross profits before and after taxes and the difference between gross income of the private sector and the gross national income. Cf. Kalecki 1965l, pp. 59-60 and 29-30; and 1937c, pp. 445-50.

[12]See Kalecki 1965l, pp. 46-47. For a presentation of the argument in terms of the Marxian schemes of reproduction, see Kalecki 1968e, pp. 73-77.

[13]If the assumptions of workers' zero savings, balanced foreign trade, and government balanced budget are relaxed, the general income determination equation becomes more complicated, but the basic principles hold. See Kalecki 1965l, pp. 60-65.

[14]The multiplier works in both directions, magnifying either increases or reductions in investment. The backward motion takes place during a slump in which a reduction in investment activity is not only equal to the primary effect on national income, but also sets into motion the entire chain of secondary effects of reduced consumption spending, so that the final fall of output, income, and employment is amplified compared to the original decline in investment.

[15]An interesting passage referring to a war-type economy is contained in Kalecki 1943k, pp. 19-20. While Kalecki maintained that the position in an "ordinary" boom is different in that bottlenecks in plant capacity and labor are not very significant (but raw material supply is sometimes inelastic), such bottlenecks in manufacturing become predominant in modern capitalist economies during a war-type mobilization of resources or in the postwar reconstruction periods. In such periods employment and the wage fund expand, while output of consumer goods is substantially reduced, mainly owing to shortages of materials and labor in the industries concerned. Consequently, "if the consumption of non-wage earners is not reduced sufficiently by increased propensity to save, taxation, and rationing to offset this divergency, prices will rise in relation to wage rates, i.e., the real wage rate will fall. This may happen in two ways: by the increase in prices of raw materials relative to wage rates and by the rise in the percentage gross margins of the manufactured products. Usually both these changes go hand in hand, although, if prices of raw materials are controlled and they are distributed among enterprises by a quota system, the equilibrium between demand for and supply of consumption goods is achieved only by the rise in percentage gross margins. The rise in money wage rates enforced by the workers who try to restore the 'old' real wages cannot remedy the situation, and results only in a new rise in prices; for at the root of the trouble lies the fall in the ratio of production of consumption goods to total employment. It is this that is the actual cause of the 'vicious spiral.' "

[16]Kalecki 1965l, pp. 62-63. In a footnote to this passage, Kalecki remarked that, in a growing socialist economy, a fall in the price-

cost ratio will reflect a relative, rather than an absolute, shift from *I* to *C*.

Chapter V

[1]Among the outstanding expositions, see Tinbergen 1951a, pp. 61-86; Goodwin 1964; Klein 1966, ch. 9; Samuelson 1965, pp. 335-49; and Gordon and Klein, eds. 1965, especially pts. 1-3.

[2]The economic mechanism is defined as a system of relations existing between variables describing the system. For the system to be dynamic, at least one of these relations determining it must involve different periods of time (lagged variables pertaining to previous time periods or derivatives) which create business fluctuations. Samuelson 1965, p. 336; Tinbergen 1935, pp. 241-42, and 1951b, pp. 22-26; Christ 1966, pp. 10 ff. See Also I. Adelman and F. L. Adelman 1959.

[3]As the reader will note, there is a wide difference between Harrod and Kalecki; for one, Harrod's lags do not in any sense make for a dynamic theory (see Harrod 1966; and Kregel 1971, *passim*).

[4]As Frisch has shown, only essentially dynamic theory can explain how one situation follows out of the preceding one (Frisch 1933, 1965, pp. 155-56).

[5]On the very definition of business cycle and varieties of business fluctuations, see Hansen 1964, pp. 4 ff.; Tinbergen and Polak 1950, *passim;* Klein 1950; Lundberg, ed. 1955; and Zarnowitz, ed. 1972.

[6]See footnote to title in Kalecki 1935h, p. 327.

[7]On the subject matter of econometrics and the relation between mathematical and econometric models, see Christ 1966; Frisch 1936, p. 95; Goodwin 1964; Klein 1962; Klein 1955, pp. 222-45; Tinbergen 1951b and Beach 1957. The reader would be advised to consult the exposition of mathematical trade-cycle theory, ch. 7, devoted to Samuelson and Hicks; ch. 8, devoted to Goodwin, Kalecki, and Phillips, in Allen 1965. The mathematical properties of Kalecki's model were analyzed by Lange in lecture notes at the University of Warsaw, Lange 1961b, pp. 264-86.

[8]Tinbergen 1935, p. 268. In presenting the argument, Kalecki was influenced by Tinbergen 1931. Cf. Kalecki *op. cit.,* 1935h, p. 333.

[9]Tinbergen 1935, p. 270. Referring to econometric models of the general business cycle movement, Tinbergen wrote later: "The first few of these models—e.g., Frisch's—have been set up mathemati-

cally and are consequently sharply outlined, but they are still rather distant from reality, as they are only based on measurement of a few magnitudes. Kalecki's model, likewise, although adapted to reality to a greater extent, is still relatively simple in its assumptions, nor is it based on elementary equations which have all been tested statistically. Nevertheless it is very instructive." "Annual Survey," Tinbergen 1951b, pp. 148-49.

[10]Kalecki noted on p. 116 of 1939a: "This essay is an altered version of the article published in *Review of Economic Studies*, February, 1937. The essential ideas in it were developed already in my 'Essai d'une Théorie du Mouvement Cyclique des Affaires,' *Revue d'Economie Politique,* March-April 1935, and in mathematical form in 'A Macrodynamic Theory of the Business Cycle,' *Econometrica,* July, 1935."

[11]Lange noted, however, that while the treatment of the relation between investment decisions and actual investment was "simplified and improved in clarity" in one respect (the fundamental diagram explaining fluctuation mechanism on p. 145), "Mr. Kalecki has changed the exposition of his theory definitely for the worse." (Lange 1941, p.284.)

[12]Kalecki 1939a, p. 117. For the pure business cycle, see Kalecki 1943k, pp. 59-79. On trend and cycle, see Tinbergen and Polak 1950, pts. 1 and 2; Hansen chs. 22 and 23; Fellner 1956; Gordon and Klein, eds. 1965, pt. l; Kaldor 1960; and Joan Robinson 1966a, chs. 22 and 27.

[13]Phillips 1955, p. 364. See also the interesting review by another distinguished contributor to the field, Goodwin, who dwells on the relative merits and contrasting intellectual temperaments of Kalecki's and Kuznets's contributions. Goodwin 1956, pp. 508-509. See also Goodwin 1955, pp. 203 ff.

[14]"In fact, it appears that, to any theory of the business cycle of a fairly broad category, there corresponds an unstable rate of growth which is devoid of practical significance." Kalecki 1962h, p. 134.

[15]Kalecki implicitly assumed that his zero rate of balanced growth is stable and therefore not "ephemeral." Stanislaw Gomulka suggested that the zero rate is unstable, too.

[16]The distinction between endogenous (generated from inside) and exogenous (generated from outside) theories of business cycles will be discussed in the next section.

[17]In Kalecki's model "the relationship between orders and deliveries of capital goods is also remarkable in anticipating a later development" of modern econometric models. Klein 1964, p. 191.

[18]On the dynamic features of Kalecki's model, see Tinbergen 1935, pp. 269 and 297-301. For other devices of making a system dynamic, see Christ 1965, p. 309, and Christ 1966, *passim*; Samuelson 1965, pp. 338 ff. Cf. Goodwin 1964; and Samuelson 1972, pt. 11.

[19]In his 1933 essay, Kalecki emphasized three distinct stages in the investment activity process: investment decisions and placing of investment orders, production of investment goods, and deliveries of finished equipment. For a discussion and graphical exposition of the relations among the three stages of investment, see Kalecki 1966h, pp. 5 and 6. Cf. 1939a, pp. 1-4.

[20]Clearly, there is a large variety of investment goods with widely different construction periods. Kalecki devoted much attention to the manner of calculating the average period for different projects.

[21]Kalecki attempted to estimate the time-lag for the U.S.A. for the period 1929-40 (1965l, pp. 109-16. Cf. 1935h, pp. 337-38).

[22]In his original essay, Kalecki arrived at the linear business cycle equation which, in simplified and reformulated form, reads: $D=aI-bK$. The decisions to invest taken at time t are directly dependent on the rate of investment I and inversely on the existing stock of capital K, and a and b are the corresponding positive coefficients of the linear dependence on I and K. Given the other relations to be discussed later, Kalecki derived by a longer mathematical argument the "business cycle equation." He justified the original equation in 1966h, pp. 6-10. The argument presented at the Leyden conference was summarized by Tinbergen, who showed that the equations lead to a mixed difference and differential equation. Tinbergen 1935, pp. 268-69. For a treatment of Kalecki's business cycle theory as a mixed-difference differential equation model, see Allen 1965, pp. 251-52, and Allen 1969, pp. 369-78. For a discussion of the mathematical properties of Kalecki's model, see Lange 1961b, pp. 264 ff. Cf. Samuelson 1965, pp. 340-42.

[23]Kalecki remarked that his treatment has a certain affinity with "the type of treatment which Mr. Lundberg has called 'model sequences.'" (See 1939a, p. 127.)

[24]On the superficial resemblance between Marx's treatment of the falling rate of profit and Kalecki's theory of the cycle, see Joan Robinson 1966b, pp. 40-41.

[25]For a graphical exposition, see Kalecki 1939a, pp. 136-45.

[26]See Kalecki 1966h, pp. 10 ff.; 1939a, pp. 135 ff.; and for explicitly taking changes in profits into account, see 1943k, pp. 69 ff.

[27]This is a weak point in Kalecki's theory.

[28]During depressions, deliveries of new investment goods are below replacement requirements, and thus the existing stock of capital shrinks. This reduction in capital initially moderates the reduction in investment orders and subsequently causes their increase. This is followed by a rise in output of investment goods, expansion of income, and so forth.

[29]For an illuminating treatment of the famous Schumpeterian innovation theory as partly fitting into the exogenous disturbance pattern, see Goodwin 1955, pp. 204 ff.

[30]J. M. Clark distinguished the originating factors and the responses of the business system. In the former, exogenous factors generate business fluctuations or play a part in producing them because they are acting in a particular kind of business system which acts on them in a particular way. He considered the responses of the economic system as being more important in determining the outcome than the particular character of the original disturbance from outside. Clark 1934, pp. 18 ff.

[31]Klein 1962, p. 211. On the limitations of linear models and on "the qualitative richness of non-linear systems," see Samuelson 1965, pp. 337-40. On the two ways of explaining the maintenance of oscillations—shocks and nonlinearities, see Goodwin 1964 and 1955. See also Ichimura 1954, pp. 192-226; and Allen 1965, pp. 242-51.

[32]"Imagine a motor-car proceeding along a horizontal road with an irregular surface. The car is fitted with springs which permit it to oscillate to some extent but are designed to damp out the oscillations as soon as the comfort of the passengers will permit. If the car strikes a bump or pothole in the road the body will oscillate up and down for a time but will soon come to rest so far as vertical motion is concerned. If, however, it proceeds over a continual succession of bumps there will be continual oscillation of varying amplitude and distance between peaks. The oscillations are continually renewed by disturbances, though the distribution of the latter along the road may be quite random. The *regularity* of the motion is determined by the internal structure of the car; but the *existence* of the motion is determined by external impulses." Kendall 1948, p. 423.

[33]As quoted by Frisch 1933, 1965, p. 178; Pigou made the important distinction between impulses that initiate the motion and the

conditions that determine the way in which the economic system responds to the originating impulses. Pigou 1927.

[34]Samuelson argued that, in order to obtain maintained oscillations, specification of a trade cycle model which is neither damped nor anti-damped and which does obey the law of conservation of energy in a physical system leads astray. This is so because the economic system does not correspond to a conservation law. It is "infinitely improbable that the coefficients and structural relations of the system be just such as to lead to zero damping." Moreover, the system is not an isolated one, but subject to exogenous disturbances. It may be said to be stable only in a nonstochastic case, but if random disturbances impinge on the economic mechanism, it becomes unstable in the sense that the (expected) amplitude of its oscillations increases with time and its variance approaches infinity in the limit. Realism requires that exogenous, stochastic, or probability disturbances be added to the endogenous economic system. Samuelson considered it ill-advised that Kalecki in his 1933 model "in an empirical determination of the coefficients of an assumed mixed-difference differential equation system should have imposed the conditions that the motion have zero damping. One can sympathize with his aim of deriving a system with constant amplitude of fluctuation, whatever one thinks of the empirical foundation for this hypothesis. But after imposing a highly improbable constraint, he did not achieve what he was looking for: namely a system with constant amplitude of fluctuation." Samuelson 1965, p. 337.

[35]Lange noted that someone jokingly remarked that, for instance, the Napoleonic Wars could be the cause of cycles as described by Kalecki's initial model. Lange 1961b, p. 271.

[36]Tinbergen 1935, p. 269.

[37]The subject is explored at greater length in the following chapter.

[38]In other words, this is a special case of the investment determinants function. Thus investment decisions will be determined only by the current internal savings. This is so because the remaining two determinants of investment decisions are inoperative, as, given the scaffolding, the rate of change of profits and the rate of change in capital stock are equal to naught.

[39]In early models with zero net accumulation of capital as the base, there are no exogenous forces. When they are introduced, trend is introduced as well, which explains some of the changes in approach. There is much to be said for Kalecki's view of innovation

and population change as in no sense exogenous—but at best "semiexogenous."

[40]Innovations in the sense of gradual adjustment of a producer to the current state of technology are assumed to be included under the category of "ordinary" investment as determined by the "normal" factors in the investment determinants equation.

[41]Influenced by Kalecki's work, Steindl expanded the thesis in Steindl 1952. For an evaluation of Steindl's work, see Kregel 1973. For some other views on stagnation, see Hansen 1964, pp. 615-16; Higgins 1968, pt. 1; Baran 1957; and Sweezy 1942.

[42]Kalecki 1965l, p. 156. A qualification is added in the footnote that if capital intensity, defined as the ratio of real value of capital to industrial capacity (potential output) rises sufficiently, the rate of capacity utilization may not be reduced. The fall in the output-capital ratio would then merely reflect the rise in capital intensity of production.

[43]On the concept of productive capacity and the problem of trend, degree of utilization of capacity, and the phenomenon of chronic underutilization in developed capitalist economies, see Kalecki 1968j, pp. 275-76, and 1962h, pp. 150-52.

Chapter VI

[1]For Kalecki's approach to the complex problem of depreciation and the treatment of net investment, see 1968j, pp. 273-75. Cf. Domar 1957, ch. 7; and Lange 1965, ch. 5.

[2]Kalecki 1965l, p. 97. For a generalization of the business cycle formula based on Kalecki's own theory, the acceleration principle, and Harrod's theory, where the net investment decision is an increasing function of saving, not of depreciation, see Kalecki 1962h, pp. 135-40.

[3]Kalecki noted that the variant of the acceleration principle introduced by Hicks does not suffer from this shortcoming, since Hicks assumed explicitly the lagged relation in consumption outlay to be equal to investment time-lag—a highly unrealistic supposition. Cf. Armstrong 1952.

[4]The rate of change in the volume of fixed capital equipment is equal to net investment in fixed capital in the same period; i.e., the

excess of deliveries of new equipment over the depreciation of equipment due to wear, tear, and obsolescence. Since $dK/dt = I' - U$, the equation can be rewritten: $I_t' + 1 = aS_t + b(dP_t/dt) - c(I' - U) + e$. By transferring cI' to the right side and dividing both sides of the equation by $1+c$, we obtain: $(I_t' + 1 + cI')/(1+c) = aS_t/(1 + c) + [b/(1 + c)][dP_t/dt] + (cU + e)/(1 + c)$. The left-hand side of the equation represents a weighted average of $I_t' + 1$ and I'. Kalecki assumed as a good approximation that it is equal to an intermediate value $I_t' + 1$, with some simplifying adjustments as to the duration of different time-lags than r. As c (the coefficient of the rate of change in the stock of capital) is a fairly small fraction, O is of the same order as r. Then: $I_t' + 1 = [a/(1+c)] S_t + [b/(1+c)][dP/dt] + (cU+e)/(1+c)$. To simplify the form of the equation, let the abbreviation b' stand for $b/(1+c)$ and e' for $(cU+e)/(1+c)$. Therefore, $I_t' + 1 = [a/(1+c)]S_t + b'(dP_t/dt) + e'$.

5 Relative cyclical fluctuations in the stock of capital tend to be rather small. Therefore, changes in the rate of profit resulting from this factor are small also. Generally, the reaction of investors to changes in stock of capital is considerably weaker than to changes in the rate of savings. Thus fluctuations in investment are accounted for to a much greater degree by changes in savings and the rate of change in profits than by variations in the stock of capital, though changes in the latter may be of considerable importance in certain phases of the trade cycle. This is to say that the amplitude of fluctuations in $c(dK/dt)$ is considerably smaller than that in investment gross of depreciation. Since dK/dt represents net investment and the cyclical variation of depreciation U are relatively small (in the long run depreciation varies with the size of capital), this means that c is a small fraction. Cf. Kalecki 1943k, pp. 6-7; 1965l, pp. 104 and 121-31; 1962h, p. 138; and restated in 1968j, pp. 266-75.

6 Strictly the rate of change of aggregate output or demand of the private sector. Kalecki distinguished between output and income. If O stands for real-gross output of the private sector, E for real value of total indirect taxes, then, $O = Y + E$. For simplicity, let $O = Y$. Since by the multiplier formula $Y_t = I_t/(1 - MPC)$, the inventory formula may also be rewritten in the form: $I'' = 1\{[dI/dt][1/(1 - MPC)]\}$.

7 Accumulation of unsold stocks is partly accounted for by the inventory time-lag. According to the "inventory equation," when the volume of sales stops rising and begins to fall, stocks will continue to

rise for a time, but the increase in stocks may be larger than implied by this relation. Kalecki observed that this deviation from the equation is not likely to have important bearing on the overall business cycle since this above normal stock accumulation tends to be completely liquidated. Kalecki 1943k, pp. 76-79 and 1965l, pp. 106-107.

[8]Again the formula for aggregate investment expresses functional relation with time-lags: (1) Between investment in fixed capital on the one hand the level of savings, the *rate of change* in profits (both S and dP/dt affect decisions to invest directly); on the other the effect of *changes* in the stock of capital; (2) between investment in inventories and the *rate of change* in aggregate demand (output), subject to qualifications. Changes in the rate of output influence investment in inventories directly. Evidently, in this formulation, investment decision is a function of (1) the level of economic activity and (2) the rate of change in this level allowing for certain time-lag.

[9]In addition to the investment equation, the relevant equations here are: (1) The profit determination equation ("multiplier equation") where profits after taxes are a function of investment with a time lag: $P_t=(I_{t-1}+A)/(1-MPC)$, where A is the stable part of capitalists' consumption. This equation is based on the equality between profits and the sum of investment and consumption by the capitalist sector and on the relation between consumption of the capitalist sector and profits at some earlier time—the equation reflecting the factors determining distribution. (2) The relation between gross output O and profit after taxes: $O_t=(P_t+B')/(1-\alpha')+E$, where the constant E denotes aggregate indirect taxes, gross income (Y), plus indirect taxes (E) equal gross output (O). The constant B' and the coefficient α' reflect the factors determining distribution of income and the system of profit taxes.

[10]Kalecki argued that the actual dynamic process can be separated into (1) a cyclical fluctuations pattern which is the same as that in a "static" system where the parameters—subject to long-run changes—are assumed invariant; and (2) smooth, long-run trend. To render the system static, except for cyclical fluctuations, Kalecki postulated that the parameters A, B', and E in the profit and distribution of income factors equations (see preceding note) are strictly constant for "pure" business cycle discussion. Thus the profit determination equation was transformed to represent the rate of change and trends (the stable part of capitalist consumption was assumed strictly constant) $dP_t/dt=[1/(1-MPC)][dI_{t-1}/dt]$. Similarly, by

differentiation and substitution we obtain: $dO_t/dt=[1/(1-MPC)(1-\alpha')][dI_{t-1}/dt]$. Cf. Kalecki 1968j, pp. 271 ff.

[11]With the results arrived at in the preceding note, we can substitute these expressions of dP/dt and dO/dt in the investment equation. We get:

$$I_{t+1}=\frac{a}{1+c}I_t+\frac{b'}{1-MPC}\frac{dI_{t-1}}{dt}+\frac{l}{(1-MPC)(1-\alpha')}\frac{dI_{t-1}}{dt}+e'=$$

$$\frac{a}{1+c}I_t+\frac{1}{1-MPC}\left(b'+\frac{l}{1-\alpha'}\right)\frac{dI_{t-1}}{dt}+e'.$$

Again the first term on the right-hand side expresses the strength of influence on investment decisions of current savings (coefficient a) and also the retarding effect or increase in capital stock [coefficient $1/(1+c)$]. The second term indicates the influence of the rate of change in profits [coefficient $b'/(1-MPC)$] and in output [coefficient $l/(1-MPC)(1-\alpha')$].

[12]In order to render the system trendless, not only the parameters of a, b', and e must be postulated strictly constant, but the same must be assumed about e'. Here additional conditions must be satisfied: such a system must be capable of being at equilibrium at the level of investment I, equal to depreciation U. For this state investment is stabilized at the level of depreciation and the rate of change of investment is equal to zero. Under these circumstances the business cycle equation is reduced to: $I_{t+1}=[a/(1+c)]I_t+e'$; and since $I=U$, it can be rewritten as: $U=[a/(1+c)]U+e'$. This is the condition e' must fulfill for the system not to be subject to long-run growth. By subtracting the "reduced equation" from the expanded equation of the business cycle, we get:

$$I_{t+1}-U=\frac{a}{1+c}(I_t-U)+\frac{1}{1-MPC}\left(b'+\frac{l}{1-\alpha'}\right)\frac{dI_{t-1}}{dt}$$

To simplify, let us denote the coefficient of the second term on the right-hand side of the equation by u. For depreciation, U constant: $d(1-U)/dt=dI/dt$. Hence $I_{t+1}-U=[a/(1+c)]\ [I_t-U]+u(dI_{t-1}/dt)$.

[13]As noted, U is constant; $di/dt=dI/dt$.

[14]However, it may be asked here whether there is a lower limit imposing a floor to the downward movement of the economy in the sense that there is a ceiling imposed by the limits of productive

capacity. Kalecki noted that such a floor is certainly set up in the case of investment in capital goods because its gross amount cannot fall below zero. But there is no analogous limit that prevents disinvestment in inventories.

[15]For an outline of Kalecki's earlier model by graphical presentation, see 1939a, pp. 135-45, and 1966h, pp. 5-12. On "conditional equilibrium," stability, and instability, see 1939a, pp. 139-40. Cf. Samuelson 1965, pp. 258 ff; Morishima 1964; and Baumol 1970.

[16]"Just as Ehrenfest and other physicists had to add probability to the causal systems of physics to get around the time-reversibility feature of classical mechanics that was so inconsistent with the time asymmetry of the Second Law of Thermodynamics, so we must, in the interests of realism, add stochastic or probability disturbances to our economic and biological causal systems." Samuelson 1972, p. 451.

[17]Kalecki 1965l, p. 140. The random disturbances give rise to continuing and irregular oscillatory movements *à la* trade cycle in an autoregressive scheme (stochastic equation which involves lagged variables). On the Yule-Slutsky effect and autoregression model see, Yamane 1964, pp. 726-29. To repeat, nonlinearities are another way of explaining maintained fluctuations.

[18]Equations containing random or chance happenings (and clearly, thus a randomly determined pattern of disturbances) are called stochastic equations; for in statistics the term *stochastic* refers to a quantity which can assume a number of values with given probabilities of events happening. Economic problems are frequently of a stochastic nature or at least probabilistic rather than deterministic as the data and the unknowns of the problem are not precisely predictable magnitudes, but rather subject to error; e.g., stochastic disturbances to economic mechanism in the form of innovation subject to whatever probability laws are appropriate for such events.

One of the great difficulties in discovering the facts in economics and in other fields is owing to the random elements in a large number of pertinent events. A successful attack of these problems requires the cooperation or skill of econometricians well versed in probability theory. "In econometrics, as distinct from mathematical economics, one cannot neglect the random variables in the relationships being considered. Econometrics does not deal with exact relationships; probabilistic considerations are fundamental throughout." (Klein 1962, p. 28; see also pp. 135-39 and 236-69. Cf. Tinbergen

1967, pp. 52-53; Samuelson 1972, pp. 466-69; and Wallis and Roberts 1963, p. 8.)

[19]Kalecki 1965l, p. 129. Kalecki noted in a footnote that, if the cyclical mechanism gives rise to fluctuations of constant amplitude (zero damping), erratic shocks will produce explosive-type fluctuations. But the system will be prevented from exploding as sooner or later the ceiling is reached and from then on the amplitude of fluctuations is constant.

[20]"Although these results still require a mathematical explanation, the phenomenon itself is virtually certain: the cycle generated by shocks with a normal frequency distribution shows a considerable stability with respect to changes in the basic equation which involve substantial increases in damping. Thus, even with relatively heavy damping such shocks generate fairly regular cycles.

"This result is of considerable importance. It shows that a semi-regular cycle may be in existence even though the 'business cycle equation' involves substantial damping. It thus dispenses with the necessity of accepting the explosive cycle as the general pattern of economic fluctuations which we considered unrealistic." Kalecki 1965l, p. 142.

Chapter VII

[1]Kalecki expounded on full employment in many articles written in the 1930s. These contributions include: 1929m, pp. 1295-97; 1931g; 1932a, pp. 1-3; 1932c, pp. 1-2; 1932l, p. 4; 1933b, pp. 1111-15; 1933c, pp. 27-35; 1933d, pp. 9-11; 1934b, pp. 1531-34; 1934c, pp. 637-40; 1935b, pp. 1574-76; 1935e, pp. 1320-24; 1935b, pp. 1385-87; 1935g, pp. 701-703; 1936b; 1937c, pp. 444-50. The most comprehensive treatment of the subject is to be found in 1944g, pp. 39-58. His other interesting contributions to this subject include 1944h, pp. 131-35; 1943c, pp. 2-7; 1945a, pp. 83-92; 1945b, pp. 449-64; 1946a, pp. 81-84; 1946b, pp. 322-27.

[2]On the confusion, see the particularly lucid comments in Kahn 1972, p. 124. Tinbergen's standard formulation of aims and means of economic policy can be found in 1967, pp. 11-26 and *passim;* cf. Robbins 1935.

[3]Thus, Kalecki noted that it is frequently maintained that the government spending program should be fully appropriated to public investment in the strict sense of the term (roads, hospitals, schools,

etc.) While there is no objection to this view from the standpoint of creating sufficient effective demand, the deflationary gap may be so large that public investment, at least in absence of sensible programing, will tend to become largely useless. (The principle of social priorities should "eliminate such projects as building five bridges over one stretch of the river for the mere purpose of providing employment.") In such a situation it is pernicious to restrict government spending to public investment when consumption standards could be improved by channeling part of this spending to consumer oriented activities, although opposition to such direction of the government spending program may be powerful. Kalecki 1944g, p. 50.

[4]The compilation *The Economics of Full Employment* contains a background paper by F. Burchardt on the causes of unemployment, Kalecki's theoretical paper, G. D. N. Worswick's work on stability and flexibility of employment, E. F. Schumacher's paper on relations of public finance to full employment. T. Balogh's paper on the international aspects, and K. Mandelbaum's contribution on Nazi Germany's experience. Here and later in this chapter I shall be concerned only with Kalecki's contribution, and, for obvious reasons, cannot review the other works.

[5]In his analysis of the White Paper, Beveridge referred to Kalecki 1944h. See Beveridge 1944, p. 272.

[6]In his critique of the White Paper, Kalecki also strongly underlined that it was not a full-employment program. 1944h, p. 135.

[7]"The White Paper (Cmd 6527) marks an important stage in the development of economic policy. For the first time an official document acknowledges the responsibility of the Government for preventing large fluctuations in output and employment. This represents a great advance upon the creed that slumps are natural and even salutary which has hitherto prevailed, but it does not amount to a complete programme of full employment. For even if deep and lasting depressions are overcome by Government intervention, it does not mean that unemployment will be reduced to the bare minimum." Kalecki 1944h, p. 131.

[8]For a summary program, philosophy, and main objectives of Beveridge's proposal, see Beveridge 1944, pp. 274, 272-73, 30-31.

[9]Harrod 1951, p. 534. Although the volume of Keynes's collected papers pertaining to that period has not yet been published, I understand from one of the editors that there is no evidence that Keynes favored more radical steps to full employment.

[10]Kalecki was more convinced that it would than was Keynes.

[11]Cf. Kalecki 1937c. As a more general point one might note the relation between the existence of the debt, and structure of financial markets, and the greater scope for monetary policy that this implies. In the absence of debt, central banks would be restricted to playing with the currency issue. But owing to the debt they hold all kinds of government assets with which to operate, possibly exerting an implicit influence in favor of monetary policy as the preferred technique.

[12]Malthus 1836, p. 409. For a survey of the views of leading economists in historical perspective, see Burkhead 1954, pp. 191-216. On the "burden" of the debt, see Domar 1957, pp. 350-69; Buchanan 1958; Lerner 1943, pp. 38-51, and 1961, pp. 139-41; Modigliani 1961, pp. 730-55.

[13]"Ever since Sir Kingsley Wood's Budget of April 1941, about eight months after Keynes entered the Treasury, the Chancellor of the Exchequer, in presenting his Budget proposals, has dealt not only with the financial resources of the Exchequer but also with the physical resources of the nation. Dr. Hugh Dalton has told us that this 'new approach to budgetary policy owes more to Keynes than to any other one man'; he says that 'what he launched was one of the intellectual revolutions of our time.' " Kahn 1972, p. 107.

[14]Cf. Musgrave 1959; Lerner 1951; Kaldor 1955. Even if it is oversimplified, Lerner's contention that taxes are levied only to prevent inflationary forces from gathering momentum is very revealing. Many modern theorists hold that "the primary function of taxes is to bring about a release of command over resources in what is regarded as an optimal and equitable pattern." Samuelson 1966, vol. 2, p. 1282.

[15]Kalecki 1943b, pp. 76-80; 1944g, pp. 44-46; 1946a, pp. 81-94; 1941p, pp. 159-64. On new fiscal policy norms (cyclically balanced budget) and techniques of deficit financing and surplus disposal, as well as fiscal policy in practice, see Heller 1967. On the fiscal gauge and the "full employment surplus" and fiscal draw, see Okun 1970, pp. 44 ff.; Committee for Economic Development 1947; Heller 1957, pp. 634-51; Levy 1963; Myrdal 1939, pp. 183-93; Stein 1969; and Caves 1968, pp. 21-67. On the concepts and measures of fiscal policy and the full employment budget, see Okun 1972, pp. 76-82.

[16]Shares and debentures are to be excluded from the valuation of wealth to avoid a double taxation of the capital of private firms.

[17]On the probable order of magnitude of such a tax and its administration in Britain, see Kalecki 1943b, pp. 78-79; 1944g, p. 45.

[18]Kalecki, in common with other writers of that period, probably underestimated the strategic role of tax rate variations as a stabilization policy device. This is, of course, not meant to underrate the formidable difficulties of affecting tax changes, *inter alia,* because once taxes are lowered, it is difficult to raise them when necessary.

[19]Kalecki adds that, to the extent that changes in net profits will ensue from a deliberate income redistribution policy, appropriate compensatory measures will have to be taken to neutralize the negative effect upon investment.

[20]Kalecki noted: "If the working population is decreasing, but the rise in productivity is higher than the decline in population, the resulting full employment output will rise more slowly than the productivity of labour. The capacity of equipment must expand in this case also proportionately to full employment output." 1944g, p. 47. Cf. Domar 1957, pp. 24-26; Worswick 1944b, pp. 59-84.

[21]According to Kalecki one of the principal features of a developed capitalist economy was that productive equipment is adequate to achieve full employment. If unemployment does not arise as a result of inadequate productive capacity, and if in the first approximation frictional and seasonal unemployment is neglected, and if actual employment E is less than full employment E_f, the unemployment $E_f - E$ is assumed to be accounted for by deficiency of effective demand (sometimes called "Keynesian unemployment") in the sense that, with sufficiently high effective demand, E would reach the full-employment level E_f. If E_d stands for demanded employment characterized by the level of employment which would be reached at a given level of effective demand, provided that there is no labor shortage, when actual employment E is below the full employment level, E_f, the "demanded employment," $E_d = E$. This is the case of inadequacy of effective demand, which is characterized by the inequality $E_f > E_d = E$. The case of full employment arises when $E_f = E_d = E$. If $E_d > E_f$; $E = E_f$. This is the case of labor shortage (overemployment), which is thus characterized by the inequality $E_d > E_f = E$. Cf. Kalecki 1950, pp. 62-63.

[22]It appears that in Britain after a remarkable advance in productivity during the first years following nationalization, the subsequent period was marked by a long stagnation in the nationalized industry, while during the 1960s growth of productivity in the nationalized sector outpaced that in the private manufacturing sector. Moreover, it is claimed that the record of the British nationalized industries in the 1960s was better than that of their counterparts on

the European Continent, while the comparative performance of private manufacturing industry in Britain and other West European countries is unfavorable. Of course, a number of factors were at work and the politics of nationalization makes any assessment tentative, not to speak of the particular prejudices of the investigator for or against nationalization. Cf. Pryke 1971; Coombes 1971.

[23]A preferable method is to substitute a part of the existing profit tax by a modified profit tax, as it removes the adverse effects of profit tax on the expected net profitability of investment. *Ceteris paribus,* the larger the shift from typical to modified profit tax, the larger are the stimuli imparted to investment.

[24]On the serious difficulties entailed in regulating private investment by varying the interest rate (or profit tax) and the critical comments on the efficacy of monetary policy and its distributive effect, see Kalecki 1946a, pp. 81-84; 1940a, pp. 2-5; 1944g, pp. 49-51. Cf. Kahn 1972, pp. 72-96.

[25]On Kalecki's subsequent work in this field, see the part on growth and planning.

[26]Whether income redistribution will significantly raise consumption is an important question. Research findings, admittedly inconclusive, differ regarding the likely effect. Early postwar estimates tended to show that increases in consumers' outlays as a result of redistribution of current income are small. According to one source, "if the present data are correct, too much emphasis should not be placed on income redistribution for the solution of the savings-investment problem. However, the data are inadequate to arrive at a definite conclusion." Lubell 1947, p. 157. More recent research suggests that the consumption function is moderately affected by the income distribution. Klein 1966, pp. 59, 188, and 245-48.

Chapter VIII

[1]For a feeling of the times, see Joan Robinson 1969b, pp. ix-xvi.

[2]On the "unemployment-inflation dilemma," see Okun, ed. 1972, pt. 1; and Tobin 1972, pp. 1-18, and references therein.

[3]"In any case the experimental demonstration of the Phillips curve has failed." Joan Robinson 1972, p. 6.

[4]On the relevance of the Phillips curve, see Johnson and Nobay 1971, pt. 2, and references therein. For an opposing view, see the review of the above by Lomax 1972, pp. 716-18.

[5]Kalecki 1941p, pp. 159-61. On the British wartime experience, see Sayers, *passim;* Hancock and Gowing 1949; and Kalecki 1943l, pp. 137-42; 1940i, p. 7.

[6]Kalecki's analysis of the budget deficit and inflation was developed in connection with his basic work on the war economy and finance at the Oxford Institute of Statistics, whose various other aspects will be discussed at length in subsequent chapters of this study. The dissatisfaction with the state of inflation theory at the beginning of World War II led Kalecki to a brief review of the most important definitions of inflation and to develop a concept of inflation that would provide a basis for its measurement.

[7]For a comprehensive survey of sources and definitions of inflation, see Bronfenbrenner and Holzman 1966, pp. 46 ff. See also Haberler 1960; Johnson 1967; Joan Robinson 1951, pp. 89-98; Schultze 1959; Johnson and Nobay 1971; Phelps 1972.

[8]At any moment, the price level is mainly influenced by the level of money wage rates. A once-and-for-all rise in the level of prices occurs unless wages begin to go up.

[9]But it seems that the corollary that, under conditions of postwar recessions the power of trade unions should have been appreciably weakened, is at variance with the facts.

[10]Kalecki 1941p, pp. 161-63. Recently, Samuelson and Solow, *inter alia,* argued that, to explain possible cost-push inflation, it is better to recognize that imperfect competition is the essence of the problem and to drop the perfect competition assumption. In the same way that wages and prices may be sticky, in the case of unemployment and underutilization of capacity, so may they be pushing upward beyond what can be explained in terms of levels and shifts in demand. In a partial market, price may increase either because of the rise in demand or fall in supply as a consequence of cost increases. In the first case output should increase, while in the second it should decline. However, if prices rise, sector by sector, it cannot be concluded with certainty that demand-pull inflation must be at work. It is possible that certain sectors face excess demand, without there being aggregate pressure. Those sectors will produce sharp price increases and increases in production or pressure on capacity. In the real sense, the source of inflation is the failure of other sectors, in which underutilization of capacity develops, to reduce prices sufficiently. This may be the result of market imperfections, of administered prices, market power, rigid markups, sticky wages, and all the paraphernalia of new inflation. Prices in the modern

industrial economy tend to be more flexible upward in response to a rise in demand than downward to its fall. Prices tend to be rigid in a downward direction. This is likely to impart an upward bias to the rise in the general price level. Not only the aggregate level of demand, but also its composition plays a central role in generating inflation. Solow 1968b. The argument is pursued by Schultze, 1959. Cf. also Means 1962; Bronfenbrenner and Holzman 1966, pp. 80-88; Phelps *et al.* 1970; and the review by Fisher 1972, pp. 718-21; Hall 1972, pp. 65-66.

[11]A distinction is usually made between open and repressed inflation. The former refers to outright, uncontrolled, "laissez faire" type conditions of a rise in the price level, while the latter describes a situation where measures are taken to suppress the symptoms of inflation by applying controls (price, rationing, foreign exchange allocations). The terms *repressed* and *suppressed* are often used synonymously, as opposed to open inflation. Some differentiate the terms, e.g., when direct controls remain effective only in the short run, the inflation is termed repressed, but when these controls are in force indefinitely, inflation is designated as suppressed. See Bronfenbrenner and Holzman 1966, pp. 50-51; Charlesworth 1956.

[12]Kalecki's scheme of rationing is to be explored in pt. 2.

[13]In what follows, the material is drawn very closely from United Nations 1949a.

[14]In a centrally planned economy the equilibrium would be reached through the rise in government receipts ensuing from the rise in prices. Thereby, the initial increase in NNCP would disappear. Such a case is analogous to that of a rise in government expenditures financed by indirect taxation (turnover tax).

[15]For a discussion of situations in which an inflationary spiral may develop despite the existence of unemployment, see United Nations 1949a, pp. 11-20.

[16]Kalecki 1935b, p. 1574; 1935g, p. 702. "The stimulation of the business upswing in Germany in the last two years supplies empirical data essential for the understanding of economic processes. The mechanism of the upswing is in this case exceptionally clearcut. Since it is the government that finances investment by means of credit, it is easy to discern the cause and effect and analyze precisely the process of creating purchasing power.

"Moreover, the German experiment clearly shows the limits of the business upswing in the area of balance of payments if this upswing is not accompanied by an influx of foreign capital. Finally, we may observe in Germany a specific process—one not devoid, however, of general significance—the process of using for armament purposes those results of the business upswing which should be reflected in the increased consumption of the broad masses of the population." Kalecki 1935b, trans. and rpt. in Kalecki 1972a, p. 65.

CHAPTER IX

[1]Recently, Professor Wassily Leontief acknowledged that the income and size of "wealth controlled by any one group, in relation to other groups, determines decisively the power it can wield in influencing, not to say in directing, all government activities." Thus, "it is not surprising that by exercising a decisive influence on government policy, particularly in the economic sphere, a small group of citizens controlling a disproportionately high share of the national income and still greater share of the national wealth has been capable of defending its economic and political dominance against all assaults." Leontief 1972, p. 7. Cf. Bronfenbrenner, 1971.

[2]Whatever the differences between Kalecki and Keynes, clearly the policies adopted by modern capitalist economies (strictly speaking in the U.K. and U.S.A. on which my preliminary research was based) differed considerably from those Kalecki, Keynes, and Kahn had in mind. The actual policies were partly an expression of political forces at work.

[3]It is not suggested here that, in reality, fluctuations in the rates of economic activity can be completely eliminated, but rather that they can be significantly damped or moderated. Cf. Tinbergen 1967; Klein 1971a; Hickman 1972; and Zarnowitz 1972.

[4]Actually, Kalecki envisaged opposition to government-stimulated prosperity in his writings in the early 1930s, but he did not then enunciate the pattern of the political business cycle.

[5]Kalecki 1943g, pp. 322-31. The main tenets were first presented in the spring of 1942 at a lecture given to the Marshall Society in Cambridge.

[6]Galbraith wrote about the revolutionary times when the Employment Act gave qualified support to government intervention for maintaining full employment, and when the Council of Economic Advisors was created: "And there was some effort at counter-revolution. Nobody could say that he preferred massive unemployment to Keynes. And even men of conservative mood, when they under-

stood what was involved, opted for the policy—some asking only that it be called by some other name. The Committee for Economic Development, coached by Ruml on semantics, never advocated deficits. Rather it spoke well of a budget that was balanced only under conditions of high employment. Those who objected to Keynes were also invariably handicapped by the fact that they hadn't (and couldn't) read the book. It was like attacking the original Kama Sutra for obscenity without being able to read Sanskrit." Galbraith 1965.

[7]Interestingly, Keynes was troubled by the same disquietude, although he presented his fears less forcefully and, to my knowledge, he did not predict the regime of the political business cycle. As Lord Kahn pointed out, toward the end of the war, Keynes wrote in a letter to T. S. Eliot "that the maintenance of full employment required that we should be 'not only good but clever. . . . It may turn out, I suppose, that vested interests and personal selfishness may stand in the way. But the main task is producing first the intellectual conviction and then intellectually to devise the means.'" Kahn 1972, p. 103.

[8]For objections in the United States business community, see the very interesting article by Alexander 1948, pp. 177-98, which in many cases reads exactly like Kalecki's prediction, except that Alexander based himself on actual occurrences and, it seems, was unaware of Kalecki's article, published five years before his.

[9]On the concept of economic power and the classification of the noneconomic forms of power (physical, personal, social, administrative, organizational, state, legal, and political), see Rothschild, ed. 1971, especially pp. 7-17 and 77-116, and references therein.

[10]Samuelson correctly pointed out that, when fiscal policy is accepted as an instrument of countercyclical measures, it is necessary, *inter alia,* to: (1) relax vigilance over inefficiency in government; (2) relax vigilance against invasion by government of private consumption and personal liberty; and (3) accept unnecessary and wasteful projects as a necessary evil at any time. Samuelson 1966, vol. 2, p. 1274.

[11]The sophisticated argument about the self-exclusiveness of planning and freedom is argued most clearly and vehemently by Hayek and Friedman, and in the case of developing countries by Bauer. See, *inter alia,* Hayek 1944 and 1972; Friedman 1962; Bauer 1971. On the contention that Keynesian economics is incompatible with basic freedom, see, *inter alia,* Hazlitt 1965. For a critique of this

notion, see Samuelson, 1963. For an attack on Friedman's position, see MacPherson 1968, pp. 95-106.

[12]Kalecki 1943g, p. 326. Kalecki emphasized that businessmen "seem, however, still to be consistently opposed to creating employment by subsidizing consumption"—a policy that he strongly advocated. *Ibid.*, p. 329. Thirty years later this sounds like a very cogent criticism of Nixon's New Economic Policy.

[13]Interestingly, in socialist Poland, at the threshold of the 1970s, full-employment policies were blamed as the main obstacle to an increase in productivity and the basic reason for the lax attitude toward work. It was widely held that the only way to deal effectively with the use of manpower was to create unemployment, as only the fear of losing one's job might increase productivity and strengthen work discipline. On the advocacy of greater unemployment as a measure of raising efficiency in Britain, see Caves 1968, pp. 277-78.

[14]It is in this context that income policies are strictly limited. They are called upon when something must be done, but they must appear to be "income distribution neutral." Robert Heilbroner claims that, in the U. S., the super corporations now accept government regulation of aggregate demand and alleviation of poverty. But they will fight tooth and nail, and successfully so, any incursion into income distribution in favor of the underprivileged strata of society. Cf. Heilbroner 1966; and Lekachman's review 1967, p. 114.

[15]Indeed, the Hoover administration, faced with an intolerable economic disaster, used a number of accounting gimmicks to increase spending, while paying lip service to a balanced budget. But a more relaxed attitude toward budget-balancing did not appear in government policy until the Roosevelt administration. See Stein 1969, *passim.*

[16]See Kalecki 1964g. This and other papers written over a span of thirty years, reflecting Kalecki's observations on political and economic situations in modern capitalism, are available to the English reader in a collection of essays, 1972a.

[17]There are germs of truth, even if one-sided, in John Stuart Mill's observation that it is only in the backward countries of the world that increased production is still an important object; in those most advanced, what is economically needed is a better distribution. Mill 1900, p. 749. Cf. Lundberg 1968; Mermelstein 1973; Nordhaus and Tobin 1972; and Weintraub, Schwartz, and Aronson, eds. 1973.

THE WAR YEARS

[1]I was present just a few years ago at an altercation between a noted wartime government economist and a former member of the OIS when the latter contended that many of the institute's proposals served as a basis for the governmental options. This provoked an unexpected and wholly "un-British" outburst of vehemence on the part of the distinguished and usually very calm former government economist.

[2]See Kalecki's restrained and moving eulogy of Rothbarth, 1945d, pp. 121-22.

[3]I have heard it said that one of the reasons Kalecki was not offered a more permanent position after the war was that he did not apply for British citizenship.

CHAPTER X

[1]The need for productivity incentives during the war was confirmed by the findings of the Stamp Survey, conducted in June 1940, which found "patriotism and peril curiously transient as complete substitutes for the old incentives" and evidence of intolerably serious waste in production. Hancock and Gowing 1949, p. 340. "To the majority of the population military sanctions were not applicable, yet patriotism was not enough; the ordinary economic incentive of the pay-packet at the end of the week remained in use." Sayers 1956, p. 2.

[2]See Steindl 1941a, p. 165. Indeed, in Britain during the war wage earnings were of much greater importance in augmenting purchasing power than a rise in wage rates. In July 1941, earnings were 43 per cent above the Oct. 1938 level, while wage rates were only 18 per cent higher. Hancock and Gowing 1949, p. 339. The total number of persons employed in industry, the armed forces, auxiliary services, and full-time civil defense, at the peak of the war, in 1943, was 25 per cent greater than in 1938. For a general account of changes in employment, incomes, consumption, and prices in Britain during the war, see Nicholson 1945, pp. 230-44. For a summary of the changes in earnings and hours of labor between 1938 and 1945 and a discussion of the different factors responsible for these changes, see Nicholson 1946, pp. 146-63. Cf. Kalecki 1943j, pp. 173-78.

[3]For an exposition, evaluation, and criticism of what Robbins called the "fiscal theory of war controls," see Robbins 1947, pp. 31 ff., and Scitovsky, Shaw, and Tarshis 1951, pp. 133-39; cf. Keynes 1940b, *passim.*

[4]Kalecki 1943a, pp. 96-97. On the composition of the cost of living index, see Hancock and Gowing 1949, p. 166.

[5]Moggridge 1971, pp. 424-25. In Feb., 1941, Churchill attacked high taxation as destructive of incentives. In his reply to Sir Kingsley Wood's proposal to increase income tax rates, Churchill considered them incompatible with national thrift or enterprise: "If you suppose you can collect at these high rates without waste or great diminution of effort, without striking a deadly blow at good housekeeping and good management in every form, you are mistaken . . . . The same spirit of deference not to sound financial canons but to harping and insatiable left-wing propaganda has led to folly of 100% excess profit tax, with all the waste and carelessness that arises therefrom." Quoted after Sayers 1956, p. 557, from unpublished documents of Sir Winston Churchill.

[6]See Sayers 1956, pp. 118-26 and *passim;* Hancock and Gowing 1949, pp. 163 ff. On some of the controversies surrounding the EPT, see Sabine 1970, pp. 211-12 and *passim;* and Hancock and Gowing 1949, pp. 118-26 and *passim.*

[7]On the rapid growth of the size of contract and a survey of the major problems of war contract policy, see Worswick 1945, pp. 79-90.

[8]Three types of remuneration were used in government contracts: (1) Fixed price contract where the contract price was agreed prior to placing the order and the contractor bore the risk of subsequent changes in costs. A variation clause might modify the contract by stipulating that adjustments would be made with subsequent changes in prices of inputs. The price was usually arrived at by competitive tender or based on cost estimates. (2) Cost plus contract, where the government agreed to cover all costs whatever they were and the contractor bore no risk, accompanied by the general incentive to inflate costs. To constrain the producer, a maximum cost limit or possibility of disallowing extraneous costs might be introduced. The profit surcharge was stipulated either as a percentage on actual costs or as a fixed amount. (3) Target cost contract where in principle a target cost was to be fixed prior to the commencement of work (but in practice was often fixed much later), with reference to similar work done and included a fee. If actual

cost was below target, the contractors got a certain share of the variance. If it exceeded the target, various arrangements were stipulated so as to distribute the additional burden between the government and the contractor. In practice, the risk of additional costs to the contractors was often limited. For a more detailed treatment of the subject, see Steindl 1941a, pp. 164-69.

[9]Clearly, if the firm produces only one type of product, the standard profit is earned when the target output is reached and $u=1$, and proportionately less when the actual output falls short of that targeted.

[10]Applying the principle developed by Kalecki, Steindl suggested that the subsidy should be calculated so as to permit the producer operating with reasonable efficiency and full utilization of the available labor supply to earn standard profit under EPT, but no more than that. Steindl 1942, p. 274.

[11]For a discussion of the content of the budget, see Sabine 1970, pp. 181-201; and Sayers 1956, pp. 84-90.

[12]Sayers 1956, pp. 58-67. For the list of market prices of the main foodstuffs which were subsidized in the latter part of the war and estimates of what the prices would have been if subsidies had been removed, see Nicholson 1945.

[13]The spiral of wages and prices in 1939 and early 1940 was rapid. The wholesale price index (August, 1939=100) jumped to 128 in Jan., 1940, to 142 in July, 1940, and to 156 in July, 1941. The cost of living index rose respectively to 112, 121, and 128, and wage rates to about 104, 113, and 122, respectively. Not until mid-1941 was the rate of price increases contained. After 1941 wage rates and prices of goods outside the subsidized cost of living index continued to rise. Expenditures spilled over on smoking, drinking, and entertainment. There were queues, under-the-counter transactions, and black markets. But the last were not so alarming as to cause widespread social discontent. On the movement and composition of the cost of living index, see Hancock and Gowing 1949, pp. 166 and 201. The subject is dealt with at length and relevant data are analyzed by Nicholson 1945, pp. 230-44.

[14]In support of his argument for the impossibility of further taxation of the rich as a serious contribution to revenue, Sir Kingsley Wood estimated that taxing 100 per cent of income above £2,000 would bring additional revenue and reduce purchasing power merely by £30 million. However, Nicholson's estimates indicated that the excess of net incomes of those who in 1941-42 earned more

than £1,200 after taxes, yielded taxation in the order of £80 million per annum and, therefore, remained a significant source of budgetary revenue. Nicholson 1944a, pp. 23-29.

[15]In the 1941 budget excise duty on beer was raised by 45.5 per cent. In 1942 the flat increase in the average rate of customs duty on tobacco was 53 per cent, the average rate of excise duty on beer was 40 per cent higher in 1942-43 than the rate prevailing in 1941. It was anticipated that, as a result of expected price increases (tobacco by some 36 per cent and beer by some 22 per cent), consumption in both cases would fall by about 8 per cent. Goldmann 1943, pp. 35-39.

[16]The more general results of Goldmann's inquiry about the likely impact of increased indirect taxes on tobacco and beer consumption and cinema attendances were: (1) In a period of rising income, indirect taxes are unlikely to bring about an enduring reduction in consumption. (2) In the 1924-38 period there was a close correlation between the real wage bill on the one hand and consumption of tobacco and beer on the other, with variations in income accounting for a very large part in the variations in consumption. (3) Both absolute and relative changes in the price of tobacco and beer have an appreciably smaller influence on consumption than variations in real income. Goldmann 1943, pp. 35-39; cf. Sabine 1970, pp. 294 ff.

[17]Nicholson recalculated the cost of living which had been grossly underestimated on the basis of official indexes which took insufficient account of the consumption of beer and tobacco by the British worker.

[18]The chancellor justified the switch in price stabilization policy, not only on the grounds that such an upward revision of prices would contribute to the solution of domestic problems, but also that it would help alleviate the balance of payments and external finance problems. Kalecki took an opposite stand arguing that it would only induce a rise in wages and, as a consequence, lead to further price advances. In his budget speech, Anderson commented that subsidies were necessitated, not only by rising costs of wages, but were also occasioned by increasing costs of imports. He warned against increasing "beyond a certain limit" the gap between domestic and world market prices. Kalecki retorted that the dangers involved in such a situation are by no means clear. The relatively low level of domestic prices could not in any way impair the position of exports. To the extent that it increased the population's real income, it raised the demand for imports. The chancellor explicitly committed

the government to the policy of full employment. Under laissez faire, higher prices in relation to wages would depress effective demand, output, and employment, and thus reduce the demand for imports. But in the regime of full employment, the deficiency in effective demand would be compensated by countermeasures, and thus the demand for imports would be roughly maintained. In case of particularly unfavorable conditions for exports, the full employment regime might lead to difficulties in equilibrating the balance of foreign trade, thus causing bottlenecks in the supply of imported goods. Such problems would have to be attacked by rationing and controls. Kalecki 1944a, pp. 101-104.

[19]Keynes showed that dependence on the method of voluntary savings during World War I resulted in putting some £2,500 million into the pockets of the capitalists. Harder work was not recompensed. Britain ended up with a national debt vastly greater than was required and very inequitably distributed throughout society.

[20]Other provisions of Keynes's scheme included maintenance of adequate consumption of the lowest income groups and special relief of the poor, a scheme of family allowances, a general capital levy to be enforced after the war to ensure sufficient budgetary receipts to discharge the liability with respect to deferred income. Some of the proposed measures were dictated by Keynes's intent to redress the inequalities of income distribution. He objected to comprehensive rationing and price control as a pseudo-remedy. Nevertheless, some measure of rationing and price control was to play a part in his more comprehensive scheme and was to be a valuable adjunct to his major proposal. To meet the demand of trade unions for some security against the risk of price increases outstripping the level of wages even if the deferred income plan should be adopted, Keynes suggested that a minimum ration of consumption articles, restricted to a limited list of necessities, be made available at a low fixed price (but no undertaking should be given about future price), but even such a safeguard might involve subsidies. As an absolute condition for the acceptance of the limited rationing arrangement, Keynes insisted that his deferment-of-income scheme be simultaneously adopted, and that the trade unions should undertake not to press for any further wage increases due to increases in the cost of living. Without such conditions, the spending power would render any attempt at price fixation very illusive. The low price for the minimum ration would merely exert an "income effect" and would release

greater purchasing power to chase goods in other directions, which would drive prices up.

[21]According to the authoritative report by Sir Roy Harrod, Keynes "hoped that he could persuade the Trade Union world to accept, in the form of compulsory saving or deferred pay scheme, what it would not have accepted in the form of direct taxation or taxes on standard articles of consumption. Thus the scheme was in essence to woo Labour to accept voluntarily an ordered plan for preventing a rise in purchasing power in lieu of the disorderly and unjust method of open inflation, which would undoubtedly ensue if something like his scheme were not accepted. Thus, at the outset, it was in essence a political device." Harrod 1951, pp. 491-92.

CHAPTER XI

[1]The original scheme devised by Kalecki was published as 1940c and elaborated as 1941d. In introducing Kalecki's final version of the scheme the editor of *OISB* prefaced it as follows: "A year ago one of the most important topics of discussion in the Press was the first draft of Mr. Keynes' plan of compulsory savings. . . . Important objections were made against the Keynes plan . . . and last June we published in the typed Bulletin an alternative scheme, for the rationing of expenditure in shops, devised by Mr. Kalecki. Although this scheme received some attention we consider it important that it should reach a wider public. In nearly all newspapers and journals recently there has been a demand for wide-spread rationing, but few concrete suggestions have been made as to how this object can best be achieved. Mr. Kalecki has now elaborated the original scheme, paying particular attention to problems of administration, and we publish here the amplified version." *OISB* (Jan. 11, 1941), p. 1.

[2]Rules would have to be elaborated determining the number of coupons of various categories to be surrendered for various types of meals. This would be indicated in the menus. The general principle is that total coupon value of a meal must be equal to the retail value of the ingredients and thus be lower than the price of the meal by the cost of services involved. In this manner the restaurant customers would be treated equally with the rest of the population.

[3]For a description of rationing in Britain and the controversies surrounding the introduction of various schemes, see Hancock and

Gowing 1949, pp. 49-52, 173-76, 209-23, and 325-32. See also Keezer 1943, pp. 264-82. Burchardt and Worswick 1941, pp. 184-189; and Worswick 1942, pp. 44-52.

[4]The discussion about rationing of consumer goods began in Nov. 1940. Many proposals were presented. Economists in the Treasury and the War Cabinet favored a rather comprehensive rationing scheme. They argued that rationing of individual or group foodstuffs would be insufficient, and that entire food consumption should be rationed by value or by the points system. The economists from the War Cabinet tried to convince the administrators of the advantages of points rationing. Such a scheme would contain aggregate demand for foodstuffs covered by it and approximately balance the supply and demand for a large number of foods by a points price system. Moreover no registration would be required. In contrast the Ministry of Food preferred schemes dealing with specific foods (a straight ration for cheese was put into effect). The Ministry of Food rejected any system of food rationing in aggregate either by value or by points. In Mar. 1941, the Committee of the War Cabinet came out in favor of a wider extension of rationing and deliberated on the desirability of a value or points scheme for food. Notwithstanding objections from the Ministry of Food, the Committee objected to the instigation of a piecemeal rationing and expediency measures to deal with particular foods only as acute shortages arose. It was held that such an approach would result in excess demand shifted to unrationed goods, rampant inflation, and dissatisfaction with the inequitable distribution of goods. Hancock and Gowing 1949, pp. 325-32.

[5]After prolonged controversy, the Ministry of Food agreed to the experiment with points rationing of canned meat, fish, and beans, and to extend the experiment pending on its results. Some practical difficulties in launching the scheme were encountered. New ration books had to be produced and distributed. The procedure for passing the coupons back had to be elaborated, and an initial schedule of points prices had to be drawn up. Stores had to be provided with inventories. But the difficulties were overcome without grave problems, and the points rationing began to function on Dec. 1, 1941. Reportedly, the "public's approval was instantaneous. The Government had achieved one of its big home front successes of the war." Preparations for a points rationing of clothes went off smoother than for food. At the time the points scheme for foodstuffs was only ready, a points system for clothes rationing was already operating

satisfactorily. Hancock and Gowing 1949, p. 332. According to Lord Robbins, the points rationing had re-established, at least on the demand side, the essential features of the price system, since point values were prices and point allotments cash. Robbins argued that the difference was solely that the initial distribution of power to demand was altered. Robbins 1947, pp. 6-7. For an illuminating discussion, see Worswick 1944a, pp. 33-39. An American observer who conducted a first-hand study of the British points system remarked: "The point system of rationing . . . is generally recognized as introducing into the economic life of Great Britain something in the nature of a new currency, having social, political, and economic implications which are not likely to vanish at the close of the war." Keezer 1943, p. 243.

[6]Kalecki 1941n, p. 269. Early in 1942 the government decided that it would have adverse effects on war production to impose further reduction of food and tobacco. However, further cuts were imposed on some goods. In the spring of 1942 a decision was reached to reduce the general clothing ration of 1942-43 by about one quarter. In effect, the adult clothing purchases were cut to about half the prewar level, and the volume of children's clothing to about 60 per cent. (This rate was maintained until Feb. 1945). Hancock and Gowing 1949, p. 493.

[7]Obviously, under a regime of rationing, the consumption of certain articles is restricted and the consumer, facing the decision of how to spend his money, is more constrained in exercising his freedom of choice than he was prior to the institution of rationing. It cannot be assumed that, at the prevailing prices, the individual would purchase the same commodities and in the same quantities as he would in the absence of the rationing constraint. In estimating changes in real income, some allowance should be made for the effects of such limitations on the consumers' freedom of choice. J. L. Nicholson developed a method by which the loss in real income ensuing from rationing may be approximately estimated. Basing himself on fragmentary data and realizing that the estimate gives only some idea of the probable order of magnitude involved, he obtained an estimate of the effects of rationing on the cost of living of the working class during the first few years of the war in Britain. He considered only rationed foods, since the rationing of clothing was assumed to have probably a negligible effect on most working-class households. Family budget studies in 1937-38 relating to industrial working-class households indicated that expenditures on ra-

tioned foods amounted to about one-quarter of total outlays. For the period between 1938 and 1941, estimates, allowing for goods which were not included in the official index, showed that the cost of living of wage-earners increased by 33 per cent. The average reduction in the consumption of rationed goods, including foodstuffs, no longer obtainable, was somewhere between one-half and one-third. Allowing for the elasticity of substitution between rationed and all other goods (between 0.6 and 0.8), Nicholson estimated the additional increase in the cost of living, on account of rationing, at between 4 and 11 per cent. Consequently, the final index for the period from 1938 to 1941 was raised from 133 to between 137 and 144. Allowing only for the rationing of food, the rough results indicated that rationing had indeed an appreciable effect on real income. J. L. Nicholson 1942, pp. 68-72; Cf. Worswick 1942.

[8]By this procedure rationing by value would function similarly to allotments by points and could be organized along the same lines as the rationing schemes then operating.

[9]Since the statistics on food imports and production were unavailable, it would have been very difficult to make even a very rough estimate of the expenditure ration in question. Clearly, it might have been difficult to estimate it even with more reliable statistics, and thus it might have been necessary to determine it by trial and error. Kalecki 1941n.

[10]In consequence the fall of prices of certain goods might render their production unprofitable, and might require granting appropriate subsidies to the producers.

[11]"In discussing rationing problems with those trying to solve them in Great Britain, I was frequently told emphatically that the British people are so constituted that they will stand almost any degree of rationing if they are convinced that everyone is being treated equally, but that they decisively resent any arrangement which smacks of discrimination." Keezer 1943, p. 271.

[12]"To suggest that the heavy worker can remain really efficient, happy, and healthy on the same diet as the sedentary worker plus a little extra bread, is like suggesting that a Rolls Royce can run on the same petrol as a seven h.p. car with the addition of a little coal." A. V. Hill, *Hansard* (Oct. 2, 1941), quoted after Goldmann 1945.

[13]For percentage of household expenditures on food in 1938 and 1943 together with the corresponding percentages in industrial working-class households and middle-class households, see Nicholson 1942.

[14]Kalecki 1942c, pp. 215-17. Goldmann, who investigated the application of differential rationing, concluded that there seemed to be a tendency to overrate the difficulties connected with any scheme that differentiated between various strata of the population. Actually, such differential rationing already existed in Britain in the case of clothing and cheese, and the schemes did not meet with opposition. Another attempt at differential rationing was made in the preferential treatment of canteens. Such democratic countries as Sweden and Switzerland had, to a large extent, adopted the differential rationing of foodstuffs during the war. Heavy workers benefited under these arrangements; for example, they received twice the ration for meats and fats as the ordinary consumer. Experience gained in Britain and elsewhere suggested that differential rationing according to needs combined with compulsory surrender of appropriately weighted coupons for meals taken out was equitable and helpful in intensifying the war effort. Goldmann 1945.

[15]One of the main aims of the shipping policy was to avoid cutting essential military requirements. However, the heavy military demands on cargo shipping arose partly from the inflated requirements and extravagance of the military for transport and equipment. The War Office was pressed to strive for economies in transport. The most pronounced source of shipping economies was in food imports. Among other measures, bread rationing was seriously considered, but the War Cabinet was reluctant to adopt such a drastic step, fearing that such a basic change in food policy, fraught with so many dangers, would not be worthwhile unless it was going to save an appreciable volume of wheat imports. The minister of food envisaged no prospect of such a saving, and the bread rationing scheme was abandoned in Aug. 1942. Hancock and Gowing 1949, pp. 417-26.

[16]Doubts, hesitancy, and lack of a clear-cut program characterized some of the government's actions in the early years of the war. This was clear in the case of coal, where, after the outbreak of the war, production was kept steady at the depressed prewar level. For example, in the summer of 1940, coal miners were allowed to move freely to armed forces or to the munitions factories. When, in the later years of the war, demand for fuel sharply increased, it had to be sustained with an inferior work force. Throughout the later years of the war there was a continuous and intense fear of coal shortages' hindering the war effort. But the anxiety did not begin until 1942. The coal question was brought once more to the fore when, by the

spring of 1942, the situation was very threatening. Between Nov. 1941 and Mar. 1942 the average weekly output of coal declined significantly while the war was gathering momentum and war industries' demands for coal rose sharply. It was estimated that the 1942-43 coal budget would show an intolerably large deficit. It was recognized that the gap could be bridged: (1) by allocation of coal to industry in the same manner as other raw materials, but it was argued that instituting such a system involved very intricate administrative problems; (2) by reorganization of the coal industry to increase production (e.g., arresting the exodus from coal mining, measures to remedy manpower shortages, improving recruitment of juvenile labor, remedies to contain the decline in labor productivity, extension of mechanization, greater reliance on technical advice, concentration of manpower in most productive mines and seams, increase in government control over mines, etc.); and (3) by reduction of consumption by rationing domestic fuel. "Out of the proposals for the rationing of fuel to domestic consumers there blew one of the biggest storms of the war in the sphere of home politics." Hancock and Gowing 1949, p. 471.

In mid-1941 when the government began vaguely to realize that something had to be done about the impending shortages of coal, maximum monthly deliveries of household coal to each civilian user were prescribed. The measure was inequitable and fundamentally unsound, for households with gas and electricity could simply use them instead of coal. Moreover, despite the restrictions imposed, the consumption of household coal in the winter of 1941-42 rose appreciably above that of the previous year. In the meantime, the Mines Department was preparing a rationing scheme covering all types of fuel. Out of several proposals the government favored the most comprehensive scheme, and William Beveridge was asked to elaborate the details forthwith. The scheme was to make all types of fuel interchangeable on a points system and to have a ration, based on the number of rooms in a house (but not in excess of seven habitable rooms) and a personal ration. At first public opinion did not resist fuel rationing. The government, however, departed in this case from its usual custom never to announce any new development of rationing in advance (this practice has been regarded as one of the main reasons for the smooth functioning of food- and clothes-rationing schemes). The plan to ration fuel was made public and discussed in Parliament prior to the introduction of the scheme, stirring violent opposition. While those opposed stressed the manifold practical difficulties of the scheme, the real outrage was that the scheme would have imposed particular hardships on those with larger houses. The government was anxious to avoid a widespread controversy and requested re-examination. The discussion on the rationing of fuel was resumed in the fall of 1942 as the coal situation worsened. The Ministry of Fuel and Power argued that rationing was out of the question as uncertainty about coal production and transport facilities made it unfeasible to guarantee the rations and proposed to continue relying on the existing restrictions on coal deliveries and voluntary economy on the part of the population. After some controversy, in the end rationing of coal was definitely set aside, and the restrictions on the consumption of gas and electricity were nominal. In reaching the final decision, not only factors of political expediency and considerations of intricate administrative complexities far greater than those in case of food and cloth-rationing were weighed, but what really tipped the scale against rationing was the apprehension that, if a severe winter brought severe transport bottlenecks, fuel-rationing would break down due to the inability of ensuring deliveries. Fuel-rationing never again became a bone of contention during the war. But, as was pointed out by Hancock and Gowing, the government took grave risks. The wisdom of these decisions was not really tested in practice. "Fortunately, rather exceptionally mild winters cooperated," but without the cooperation of Mother Nature, the mining and transport of coal would have probably severely hindered and virtually damaged the war effort. Hancock and Gowing 1949, pp. 466-79.

[17]Prewar preparations had been made for rationing gasoline, fuel, and essential foods. To conserve stocks, rationing of gasoline and fuel was announced on the first day of the outbreak of war. While reportedly the scheme for gasoline was effective, that for coal, gas, and electricity was "very loose and operated only in name." Hancock and Gowing 1949, p. 175.

[18]Opinions about the possibility of an appreciable increase in the production of coal differed. But whatever increase in output may have been achieved, the need to build up large and dispersed inventories was urgent. In view of the deteriorating fuel situation, the curtailment of domestic fuel consumption was necessary. It was increasingly agreed that the only equitable way of distributing the shrinking supplies was by rationing.

[19]On utility policy and utility schemes and prices, see Kalecki 1942i, p. 326; Ady 1942, pp. 281-87.

[20]The institution of the rationing of clothing and footwear in Great Britain during the war was a case in point of rationing unaccompanied by price control. After rationing went into effect in June 1941, the retail price index of the Ministry of Labour continued to climb until Mar. 1942, registering an overall rise from June 1941 to Mar. 1942 of about 10 per cent. While some increases of prices of raw materials and labor inputs occurred, they were not of such order as to justify the rise of prices of finished goods by 10 per cent. Simultaneously, a shortage of cheaper (lower quality) products was noticeable. Probably, it was chiefly prices of the cheaper assortments that pushed the increase in the price index. The increase in prices after the institution of rationing might have been partly owing to the allowed rations' being too high in relation to the available supply. However, the prevailing shortages of cheaper assortments pointed to an influence of a factor which appears to be more weighty in this context, viz, a *relative* shift in demand. The introduction of the rationing of food and clothing reduced drastically the consumption of the higher income groups, while that of the lower income groups was little or not affected. The composition of output did not adapt itself to the shift in the structure of demand for some time. (The quota of producers specializing in manufacturing cheap and expensive clothing was probably reduced in the same proportion initially.) As a consequence, prices of cheaper products tended to rise, while those of the more expensive assortments did not decline. The increased market imperfections resulting from rationing and reduced buyers' sensitiveness to price differentials between alternate sources of supply (especially for products purchased by the richer segments of the population whose consumption was reduced considerably by rationing, below the level they could afford with their incomes) may have been an important contributing factor here. Thus the price index of clothing tended to increase independently even of the possibility that the rations might have been fixed somewhat higher in relation to the available supply. After some time, in order to promote change in the composition of output, price-controlled utility goods were introduced. In order to meet essential needs, standard utility articles were manufactured in a simple design and were moderately priced, so as to bring them within the range of the lower income groups. Consequently, after Mar. 1942, the price of clothing ceased to increase, and in September of that year it started to decline. Kalecki 1944e, pp. 31-32.

POSTWAR

[1]*World Economic Report 1953-54,* published in 1955, was initiated by Kalecki, but published after his resignation.

[2]Subsequently, he objected to similar treatment of the nature of growth of labor productivity. Such a treatment in various industries should depend on the nature of this growth and the general economic conditions. (Kalecki 1960j, p. 1.)

CHAPTER XII

[1]In studying the development of Kalecki's theory of growth in a socialist economy, the first indication in print of Kalecki's ideas can be found in the analysis presented in United Nations 1954. Noteworthy, the formula used therein helped Kalecki to systematize and present the argument. United Nations 1954, p. 44. The reader's attention is also called to Kalecki's analysis of costs of shifts in economic policy (United Nations 1955).

[2]The tenet of priority of heavy industry found among its defenders some of the leading Western Marxist economists. For example, the late Professor Paul Baran treated it as an axiom for achieving a high and rapid rate of economic growth. Baran 1957, p. 284. For a sophisticated rationalization of the tenet and some aspects of the Soviet mode of development, see Dobb 1967, pp. 110-16. Cf. Feiwel 1968, pp. 592-95.

CHAPTER XIII

[1]The basic outline of Kalecki's theory of growth in a socialist economy was contained in his paper "Z zagadnien teorii dynamiki gospodarki socjalistycznej" [Problems of the Theory of Dynamics of a Socialist Economy] delivered at the Second Congress of Polish economists, and published as 1956a. It was later developed in 1963m and 1968l. It was corrected and supplemented by an appendix on the production curve and evaluation of investment efficiency in a socialist economy—an excerpt from the paper published in 1967a. The second edition was translated into English and published as 1969b. For a panoramic view of the state of growth theory in the West, see Hahn and Matthews 1964, pp. 779-902, and the invaluable

bibliography therein. See also Meade 1964; Morishima 1969; Burmeister and Dobell 1970; and Kregel 1972.

[2]While Kalecki does not deal with these factors directly in 1969b, he has dealt with them in his earlier writings when discussing technical progress and population growth.

[3]See Kalecki 1969c, pp. 257-64. For a good exposition of the production function in neoclassical theory, see Bronfenbrenner 1971; Hicks 1965, ch. 24; Brown 1966; and Meade 1968. Cf. Johansen 1972.

[4]For Kalecki's approach to how to deal with such difficulties by approximations, see 1969b, pp. 5 ff. Cf. Kalecki 1970c.

[5]On multisector growth models, see Burmeister and Dobell 1970, ch. 7; Lange 1965. In an interesting study, Laski claims that Kalecki believed that his production curve was applicable only to a centrally planned socialist economy. Laski 1972, p. 90. Cf. Kalecki 1968e.

[6]In an article written in 1941, Kalecki described the effects of technical progress on economic development. 1941l, pp. 178-84. See also the survey article by Kennedy and Thirlwall 1972, pp. 11-72; Stiglitz and Uzawa, eds. 1969.

[7]In case of the familiar neoclassical production function, it is assumed that, as a mathematical abstraction, it is legitimate to describe the technical production process by a function $Y=F(K, L, t)$, where the increment of the rate of aggregate production, Y, capital, and labor inputs are all functions of time; and where t explicitly stands for the shifting techniques. Constant returns to scale (production function homogeneous of first degree) are implied by Kalecki, but the assumption is not explicitly stated. Cf. Chilosi and Gomulka 1969a, pp. 271-98; and 1969b, pp. 22-23.

[8]Kalecki illustrates the capital intensity encouraging variety of technical progress by the following example: Suppose that each group of products can be produced by two variants: (a) of lower and (b) of higher capital intensity. Moreover, assume a new variant that came into existence as a result of the latest technical advance. Capital intensity is in all cases equal to that of *b*. Thus absolutely ineffective variants, i.e., involving no lower investment, but higher labor costs, are discarded. Clearly, the level of productivity is higher in the variant reflecting the newest technology. Therefore absolutely technically inefficient former variants *b* for individual groups of products are eliminated and replaced by newly discovered combi-

nations. However, there is no a priori reason for eliminating the variants *a,* for their capital intensity is lower than that of the new combination made possible by the advent of technology. Take the case of this type of technical progress where the capital coefficient is given. At time *t* there corresponds to a given level of *m,* a definite combination of variants for individual groups of products, in some cases it is the variant *a* and in others *b.* In the following period, as a result of new invention, and in conformity with the assumption made, in all cases where new inventions take place the variants *b* are substituted by the latest techniques. However, variants *a* must remain unchanged, for if they were replaced by the newly invented techniques, the value of *m* would have to change. Here technical progress is of the variety promoting capital intensity because the higher *m,* the higher is the share of more capital intensive variants *b* for individual products, thus the greater the degree of freedom for replacement by newly discovered combinations, and the greater is the rate of increase in productivity.

[9]Again, Kalecki's illustration helps to clarify the rationale of his classification. Suppose the newly discovered variants have a capital intensity equal to that of the less capital intensive variants *a,* and that their index of productivity, although rising, remains below that of the variants *b* in the periods considered. Thus whenever new variants are discovered, *a* must be discarded as absolutely inefficient and replaced by the variants representing the newly invented techniques. However, there is no a priori reason to eliminate variants *b,* for by assumption, they feature higher productivity than those newly invented. By time $t+1$ a combination of variants for individual products which correspond to a given coefficient *m* at time *t,* has been altered by replacing variants *a* by the newly invented ones, keeping variants *b* unchanged. Clearly, had variants *b* been replaced by the new variants, production methods corresponding to the capital intensity of *a,* the coefficients *m* would have to be altered. The larger is *m,* the smaller the share of less capital intensive variants *a.* Thus there is lesser opportunity for replacement by newly invented techniques, and the lower is the increase in productivity.

[10]Chilosi and Gomulka 1969b, p. 21. For another demonstration of the correspondence between Kalecki and Harrod's classifications, see Laski 1972, pp. 88-90.

[11]Kalecki 1969b, p. 26. To simplify the exposition, Kalecki has assumed that the increase of inventories is proportionate to the increase of national product (of unchanged composition). Admittedly, the assumption is particularly invalid in cases where the redistribution of national product in favor of investment takes place. Significant diversion from consumption to investment generally raises considerably the volume of gestating investments (included, in accordance with the definition adopted, as constituents of working capital). As the share of gestating investments in current investment expenditures in construction is usually preponderant, under such circumstances the capital output ratio of increase in stocks would materially increase. As in his trade cycle theory, to focus attention on both constituents of productive accumulation, Kalecki has presented a more expanded version of equation 1. The growth equation may be rewritten relating the growth rate to the aggregate productive capital formation, composed of fixed productive investments and additions to the stock of inventories per annum. The significance of the "expanded version" lies in its focus on inventories as a crucial growth determinant, and in its indication of how the equation can be profitably employed by further decomposing the elements or introducing new ones. To simplify the exposition, proportionality of the increase of stocks to the increase in national product is postulated. Thus it is of no major significance for the argument presented whether the expanded or simpler versions are employed.

[12]For graphical presentation, see Kalecki 1969b, p. 26. If, for convenience, the difference between u and a would be assumed as 0, then, oversimplifying, $r=(1/m)I=\alpha+\beta$, and the straight line representing the linear function, given a simplified growth equation, is the slope equal to the reciprocal of the capital coefficient and intersects the r axis at origin.

[13]Phelps 1961, pp. 638-43; and 1965, pp. 793-814. A good exposition of the Golden Rule can be found in Branson 1972, ch. 21; and Burmeister and Dobell 1970, pp. 49-53.

[14]In a similar vein, the higher the "social rate of discount" set, the lower is the present value of the stream of future gains in consumption, and conversely in the opposite case. Cf. Feldstein 1965, pp. 277-87; Horvat 1964; Marglin 1963, pp. 95-111; Sen 1961, pp. 479-96, and 1967, pp. 112-29.

[15]For developments in Soviet economics, see Zauberman 1967.

CHAPTER XIV

[1]In other words, at the end of the reforging period the national income will be $(1+r_o)^n(1+p)$ of the level it was in the initial period, for productivity over n years is increased $(1+p)$ times by raising the capital coefficient. Kalecki argues that labor released by retiring the old plant and by new accrual to the labor force is the same as it would have been had m not been changed. Thus new investment generates output which is $(1+p)$ times larger than if m had remained constant. After the reforging process is completed, the aggregate stock of capital produces an output which increases in these proportions. Beyond the reforging, the system is poised for steady growth at a rate determined by growth of productivity owing to technical progress and the natural growth of the labor force.

[2]*Ceteris paribus,* it does not make sense for the planner to embark on the process of reforging up to the higher capital intensity of the aggregate productive capacity unless the increase in consumption will be greater, the greater is the rise in p, brought about by raising the capital-output ratio from m_o to m. The result of recasting depends on the effect of the rise in capital intensity on labor productivity.

[3]Rewriting the expression on the left of the inequality given in the text, we get $\{1+p\}\{1-[(i_n-i_o)/(1-i_o]\}$. Now the initial rate of growth r_o is equal to the terminal rate r, $r_o+a-u=i_o/m_o$, $r=(i_n/m)-a+u$, and $r+a-u=i_n/m$. By simple algebraic manipulation: $i_n-i_o=(r_o+a-u)(m-m_o)$, where i_n and i_o stand for terminal and initial accumulation rates, respectively. Coefficients m and m_o designate final and initial capital-output ratios.

[4]The accumulation rate and the growth rate of consumption are significantly lower than under conditions of unlimited supply of labor. For in an overpopulated economy, the accumulation rate is determined by the point of intersection of the planner's decision curve with the straight line *B'N'*; the growth of consumption, given that, after some protracted time, it returns to its initial level, by projecting this point onto the straight line *BN.* Kalecki 1969b, pp. 32-33.

[5]For an illuminating account, see Zauberman 1962, pp. 234-54; Laski 1972; and Nuti 1970a. See also Rakowski, ed. 1961.

[6]Kalecki suggested a method of determining the consumption structure in the perspective plan, but he himself considered his work as preliminary, as neither having reached a general solution to

the problem, nor being ready for application in practice. Writing in 1963, he observed: "... it is clear even at this stage that there is still quite a lot to be done before mathematical machines will begin to compute the optimum consumption structure. Both with regard to theory and availability of statistical data, we are still very remote from being able to "feed" the electronic computers adequately. And until we shall have made substantial progress in these directions, the machines—as in many other problems—will merely be reducing to absurdity our immature ideas." Kalecki 1965, p. 16—a translation of 1963k.

[7]We must note here a promising development by a student of Kalecki. Gomulka 1971.

[8]See the interesting review of Kalecki's 1972b by Horvat 1972, pp. 255-58. I benefited from an exchange of views with Stanislaw Gomulka on some of the misconceptions to which this review might lead.

[9]Mishan 1967, p. 3. In a footnote, Mishan adds: "Like a national flag and a national airline, a national plan for economic growth is deemed an essential item in the paraphernalia of every new nation state." An indication of the change can be found in the 1946 statement by Domar that the concept of the rate of growth "has been little used in economic theory, and in which I put much faith as an extremely useful instrument of economic analysis," Domar 1957, p. 82. The Soviet economist, G. A. Feldman, writing in the late twenties, appears to have been the first among Marxist economists to have concentrated on growth *rates.* For illuminating discussion of the Feldman growth model, see Domar 1957, pp. 223-261. Cf. Horvat 1964. The reader's attention is drawn to the growing literature on the fundamental issue "to grow or not to grow." One should stress here the importance of the controversy about the desirability, possibility, and necessity of economic growth. See, *inter alia,* Weintraub, Schwartz, and Aronson, eds. 1973; Nordhaus and Tobin 1972; Passell and Ross 1972.

Chapter XV

[1]For fuller treatment, see a critical survey of literature by Sen 1969, pp. 45-58; Laski 1969, pp. 59-78; Chenery 1965, pp. 125-55; and Meyer, ed. 1970, pp. 333-70.

[2]Disregarding the effect of growth speed-up on the reduction of the average vintage age structure of capital, if i_o, i_n, and i'_n are respectively 0.15, 0.21, and 0.3; $m_o=3$ and $m=4$; then $r_o=5\%$, $r_n=7\%$, and $r'_n=6\%$.

[3]Kalecki 1969b, p. 95. The English translation of von Neumann's pathbreaking 1938 paper appeared in 1945, pp. 1-9. For an excellent exposition and evaluation, see, *inter alia,* Hahn and Matthews 1964, pp. 853-68; Koopmans 1964, pp. 355-94; Hicks 1965, pp. 208-37; Morishima 1969; and Burmeister and Dobell 1970, pp. 210-27.

[4]Kalecki considered this as the gist of the Chinese concept of the "Big Leap." He believed that the experiment failed mainly owing to the fallacious implementation of the idea, which is not an indication of the fallacy of the idea itself. 1966i, pp. 1269-78.

CHAPTER XVI

[1]The model was expounded in his lectures at the Centro de Estudios Monetarios Latino-americanos (Mexico City) in Aug. 1953, and published as 1954a, pp. 381-401, English trans. 1955, pp. 1-22.

[2]Indeed, the experience of Eastern European economies in financing current activity (bank credit *v.* self-financing) is very instructive in this case. See Feiwel 1965, pp. 182-87.

[3]Kalecki 1963f; 1963j, pp. 1114-24; Kalecki and Sachs 1966n, pp. 11-32. A shorter version appeared in English, 1965i, pp. 37-50. The propositions advanced in the paper are graphically presented, and formal proofs are derived. In what follows I have restricted myself to exposing only the general line of reasoning.

[4]His advice to the Indian government regarding the Third Five-Year Plan (1961-65) started out exactly from those assumptions. See 1960c, p. 1119.

[5]In his advice to the Indian government at the threshold of the 1960s, Kalecki pointed out that, in case of semimonopolistic price increases of given products, the demand for them will be restrained, with some capacities remaining idle. The result will be similar to physical shortage. Hence besides providing adequate capacities, the state will have to control prices of necessities. 1960c, p. 1121.

[6]For an interesting assessment of political leverage in foreign aid, see the controversial study by Hayter 1971.

Chapter XVII

[1]The strong points and limitations of Kalecki's work on the system of functioning can be fully appreciated only in the light of the decentralized systems developed by Lange, Brus, and others. The interested reader is referred to Feiwel 1965, ch. 1.

[2]The following synthesis of Kalecki's proposals is based primarily on his 1956c; reprinted in 1964aa, pp. 11-23; and 1957f.

[3]The following synthesis of Kalecki's incentive scheme is based primarily on his 1957h and 1964a, pp. 226-30.

[4]For an exposition of the premium system that functioned in Poland from 1960 to 1964 which was, to a certain extent, inspired by Kalecki's proposals and those of Brus 1957a and 1957b, see Feiwel 1965, pp. 220-31.

[5]For the consequences of the rift between the producer and the market for his product when using separate prices for producers and buyers, see, *inter alia,* Brus 1958. On the practical application of factory prices, their shortcomings, and reforms, see Feiwel 1965, pp. 80-88, and 1971b, pp. 23-30.

[6]For an outline of Polish practical experience with investment financing, see Feiwel 1965, pp. 187-96, and 1971b, pp. 73-121.

[7]This trend of thought has been pursued by Brus in 1959 and 1962 and Feiwel 1971a and 1971b, where the reader will find copious references to the literature on the subject.

Chapter XVIII

[1]My description of the methodology used by Kalecki draws primarily on Kalecki 1963c; 1963l, pp. 3-12; 1964p, pp. 15-16; and 1963d, pp. 9-21.

[2]For sophisticated treatment, see Kalecki 1963k, pp. 3-7, trans. as 1965h, pp. 3-16.

[3]It might be preferable to speak of different elasticities of supply and demand so that we have a spectrum, rather than just two types. This would avoid the suggestion that industries divide into those with an absolutely inelastic supply and those with an absolutely inelastic demand.

[4]For an examination of the Polish perspective plan, see Kalecki 1958j, pp. 27-44; 1958f; 1959b, pp. 53-58; 1958a, pp. 1-5.

[5]Very scant coverage was given to this debate, which, by all accounts, was quite fiery. The account of Szyr's position is based on a stenographic (mimeographed) report of the Plenary Session that was never published in full. "Materialy XII" 1958, pp. 66-76 and 102-108. Szyr's views were also expressed in a number of published statements, the most elaborate of which is Szyr 1959.

[6]Among the defenders of the perspective plan, one could probably find Kalecki, Oskar Lange, Wlodzimierz Brus, and Czeslaw Bobrowski, whereas the opponents probably included Bronislaw Minc, Kazimierz Secomski, and Jan Zygmunt Wyrozembski. See Frankel 1958.

[7]For a more complete discussion of the 1961-65 plan, which is outside the scope of this study, see, *inter alia,* Feiwel 1971a, pp. 291-332.

[8]For an analysis of the Polish reforms of that period, see Feiwel 1965, especially chs. 2, 4, and 5.

CHAPTER XIX

[1]The record of performance of the 1960s and some of the economic events that precipitated the Polish December, 1971, were discussed in greater detail in Feiwel 1971a and 1971b.

[2]According to official sources, a total of 45 people were killed during the riots, or died later in hospitals of wounds; 1,165 were injured, including 564 civilians, 524 policemen, and 70 soldiers and officers of the Polish army. But, of course, the magnitude of the dramatic events is not confined to the accounting of casualties of bitter street-fighting.

EPILOGUE: THE LAST YEARS

[1]At the time of writing (1973), almost three years after Gomulka's downfall, there is no sign that the muzzle on the remaining "revisionists" has been lifted. The personal venom and animosity have slackened, but the regime still does not trust these recalcitrants.

[2]The current joke in Warsaw then was: "*Our* Jews beat up *their* Arabs."

[3]In fact, I was stimulated to pursue a more thorough study of Kalecki's contribution to the economics of socialism after a discus-

sion in which my interlocutor expressed similar views. See, in particular, Feiwel 1970b, pp. 122-34; and 1971a and 1971b.

[4]I would like to call the reader's attention to a courageous letter to the editor of *ZG* (No. 38, 1970) written in defense of Kalecki's views by Tadeusz Kowalik, an admirer of Kalecki who also became *persona non grata* after 1968. He deplored the fact that such nonsensical attacks have not stopped despite the officially toned-down antirevisionist campaign—"a sad and also instructive commentary on the times and their legacy."

BIBLIOGRAPHICAL ABBREVIATIONS*

•

Journals and Newspapers

AA	*Acta Arithmetica*
AEP	*Australian Economic Papers*
AER	*American Economic Review*
BNWEPUW	*Biuletyn Naukowy Wydzialu Ekonomii Politycznej Uniwersytetu Warszawskiego*
BPEA	*Brookings Papers on Economic Activity*
CE	*Co-existence*
CJE	*Canadian Journal of Economics*
CJPS	*Canadian Journal of Political Science*
CR	*Cambridge Review*
DE	*De Economist*
Ec	*Economica*
EDCC	*Economic Development and Cultural Change*
EEE	*East European Economics: A Journal of Translations*
EI	*Economia Internazionale*
EJ	*Economic Journal*
Ek	*Ekonomista*
Em	*Econometrica*
EMM	*Ekonomika i Matematicheske Metody*
Enq	*Enquiry*
ER	*The Economic Record*
ES	*Economie et Sociétés*
EW	*The Economic Weekly*
GP	*Gospodarka Planowa*
Ha	*Harper's*
IB	*Inwestycje i Budownictwo*
IER	*International Economic Review*
IERev	*Indian Economic Review*
IJLE	*Indian Journal of Labour Economics*
ILR	*International Labour Review*
JEH	*Journal of Economic History*

*All diacritical marks have been omitted.

JEL	*Journal of Economic Literature*
JIE	*Journal of Industrial Economics*
KG	*Koniunktura Gospodarcza*
KS	*Kultura i Spoleczenstwo*
Kul	*Kultura (Paris)*
KwS	*Kwartalnik Statystyczny*
Ky	*Kyklos*
MG	*Mysl Gospodarcza*
MR	*Monthly Review*
MS	*Manchester School of Economics and Social Studies*
MSES	*Mathematical Studies in Economics and Statistics in the USSR and Eastern Europe: A Journal of Translations*
NC	*La Nouvelle Critique*
ND	*Nowe Drogi*
NP	*Nauka Polska*
NR	*National Review*
NYRB	*The New York Review of Books*
NYTBR	*New York Times Book Review*
OEP	*Oxford Economic Papers*
OISB	*Oxford University, Institute of Statistics, Bulletin*
PE	*Politica ed Economia*
PG	*Przeglad Gospodarczy*
PH	*Przemysl i Handel*
PIBKGC	*Prace Instytutu Badania Koniunktur Gospodarczych i Cen*
PK	*Przeglad Kulturalny*
PM	*Prace i Materialy Miedzyuczalnianego Zakladu Problemowego Gospodarki Krajow Slabo Rozwinietych*
PMat	*Prace Matematyczne*
PoG	*Polska Gospodarcza*
Pol	*Polityka*
PP	*Polish Perspectives*
PPo	*Przeglad Polityczny*
PQ	*Political Quarterly*
PS	*Przeglad Socjologiczny*
PSo	*Przeglad Socjalistyczny*
QJE	*Quarterly Journal of Economics*
REP	*Revue d'Economie Politique*
RES	*Review of Economic Studies*
ReStat	*Review of Economics and Statistics*

Rin	*Rinascita*
RPAS	*Review of the Polish Academy of Sciences*
RPE	*Rivista di Politica Economica*
RPTM	*Roczniki Polskiego Towarzystwa Matematycznego*
SC	*Socialist Congressman*
SD	*Spoljnopoliticka Dekumentacja*
SJPE	*Scottish Journal of Political Economy*
SR	*Social Research*
S&S	*Science and Society*
SSI	*Social Science Information*
SSt	*Soviet Studies*
TB	*The Banker*
TE	*El Trimestre Economico*
TL	*Trybuna Ludu*
WA	*Weltwirtschaftliches Archiv*
WM	*Wiadomosci Matematyczne*
ZG	*Zycie Gospodarcze*
ZM	*Zastosowania Matematyki*
ZNUL	*Zeszyty Naukowe Uniwersytetu Lodzkiego*
ZPAN	*Zhurnal Polskoy Akademii Nauk*
ZW	*Zycie Warszawy*

Publishers and Institutions

CMEA	Council for Mutual Economic Assistance
FAO	Food and Agricultural Organization
IBKGC	Instytut Badania Koniunktur Gospodarczych i Cen
IGS	Instytut Gospodarstwa Spolecznego
ILO	International Labour Office
ISM	Instytut Spraw Miedzynarodowych
KiW	Ksiazka i Wiedza
OIS	Oxford Institute of Statistics
PTE	Polskie Towarzystwo Ekonomiczne
PWE	Panstwowe Wydawnictwo Ekonomiczne
PWN	Panstwowe Wydawnictwo Naukowe
SGPiS	Szkola Glowna Planowania i Statystyki [Central School of Planning and Statistics (Warsaw)]
UN	United Nations
UNESCO	United Nations Educational, Scientific, and Cultural Organization

BIBLIOGRAPHY OF KALECKI'S WORKS

•

1927

"Zblizenie gospodarcze amerykansko-rosyjskie" [American-Russian Economic Rapprochement], *PG* No. 23 (1927), p. 1029.

1928

a. "Amerykanski kartel miedziany" [American Copper Cartel], *PG* No. 14 (1928), pp. 732-34.
b. "Dalszy rozwoj brytyjsko-sowieckich stosunkow gospodarczych" [Further Development of British-Soviet Economic Relations], *PG* No. 6 (1928), p. 260.
c. "Europejski trust linoleumowy" [Linoleum Trust in Europe], *PG* No. 7 (1928), pp. 329-30.
d. "Kauczuk" [Rubber], *PG* No. 22 (1928), pp. 1154-55.
e. "Konsekwencje gospodarcze zatargu angielsko-sowieckiego" [Economic Consequences of British-Soviet Conflict], *PG* No. 1 (1928), pp. 19-20.
f. "Metale" [Metals], *PG* No. 17 (1928), pp. 886-87; No. 19, pp. 981-82; No. 21, pp. 1100-1102; No. 23, pp. 1202-1204.
g. "Monopolistyczne tendencje niemieckiego przemyslu zelaznego" [Monopolistic Trends of the German Iron Industry], *PG* No. 11 (1928), pp. 542-44.
h. "Szwedzki trust zapalczany" [Swedish Match-Trust], *PG* No. 3 (1928), pp. 101-104.
i. "Swiatowa wytworczosc aluminum" [World Production of Aluminum], *PG* No. 10 (1928), pp. 503-504.
j. "Swiatowa wytworczosc cyny" [World Production of Tin], *PG* No. 13 (1928), pp. 678-79.
k. "Swiatowa wytworczosc olowiu" [World Production of Lead], *PG* No. 15 (1928), pp. 777-78.
l. "Trust zapalczany a Sowiety" [Match-Trust and the Soviet Union], *PG* No. 20 (1928), pp. 1027-28.

m. "Trust zapalczany w I-ej polowie 1928 r" [Match-Trust in the First Half of 1928], *PG* No. 13 (1928), pp. 661-63.
n. "Walka o niemiecki rynek weglowy" [Struggle for the German Coal Market], *PG* No. 6 (1928), pp. 274-75.
o. "Wojna naftowa" [Petroleum War], *PPo,* No. 1-2 (1928), pp. 77-85.
p. "Zniesienie angielskich restrykcyj kauczukowych" [Cancellation of English Restrictions on the Rubber Market], *PG* No. 9 (1928), pp. 451-53.

1929

a. "Bawelna" [Cotton], *PG* No. 12 (1929), pp. 609-11; No. 14, pp. 698-99; No. 16, pp. 788-90; No. 18, pp. 871-72; No. 20, pp. 976-78; No. 22, pp. 1070-71; No. 24, pp. 1179-80.
b. "Bawelna: Swiatowy rynek bawelny" [Cotton: World Cotton Market], *PG* No. 10 (1929), pp. 509-11.
c. "Bawelna: Wytworczosc i spozycie swiatowe" [Cotton: Production and World Consumption], *PG* No. 8 (1929), pp. 417-19.
d. "Brytyjsko-sowieckie stosunki gospodarcze" [British-Soviet Economic Relations], *PG* No. 5 (1929), pp. 237-40.
e. "Europejski kryzys weglowy" [Coal Crisis in Europe], *PH* No. 26 (1929), pp. 1154-55.
f. "Francuska polityka naftowa" [French Petroleum Policy], *PH* No. 22 (1929), pp. 972-74.
g. "Kauczuk" [Rubber], *PG* No. 4 (1929), p. 207.
h. "Kauczuk: Z miedzynarodowego rynku kauczuku" [Rubber: On the International Rubber Market], *PG* No. 10 (1929), pp. 511-12.
i. "Koniunktury przemyslu wlokienniczego w okresie 1927-1929" [Business Fluctuations of the Textile Industry During the 1927-1929 Period], *PH* No. 43 (1929), pp. 1823-26.
j. "Metale" [Metals], *PG* No. 1 (1929), pp. 36-37; No. 3, pp. 161-63; No. 5, pp. 259-61; No. 7, pp. 365-67; No. 9, pp. 462-65; No. 11, pp. 561-63; No. 13, pp. 655-57; No. 15, pp. 751-53; No. 17, pp. 827-28; No. 19, pp. 919-22; No. 21, pp. 1017-20; No. 23, pp. 1122-24.
k. "Miedzynarodowe wspolzawodnictwo weglowe" [International Coal Competition], *PPo* No. 1-2 (1929), pp. 49-53.
l. "Opanowanie przemyslu przez kapital zagraniczny" [Control of Industry by Foreign Capital], *PH* No. 40 (1929), pp. 1710-11.
m. "W sprawie aktywizacji bilansu handlowego" [Activating the Balance of Trade], *PH* No. 30 (1929), pp. 1295-97.

n. "Wyniki dzialalnosci miedzynarodowego kartelu stalowego" [Consequences of the International Steel Cartel], *PH* No. 14 (1929), pp. 612-14.
o. "Zakonczenie wojny naftowej" [The End of the Petroleum War], *PG* No. 6 (1929), pp. 301-302.

1930

a. "Bawelna" [Cotton], *PG* No. 2 (1930), pp. 95-96; No. 4, pp. 183-84; No. 6, p. 288.
b. "Dynamika spozycia pieczywa pszennego oraz miesa w Polsce" [Dynamics of Consumption of Wheat Baking and Meat in Poland], *KG* No. 6 (1930), pp. 181-82.
c. "Marza zarobkowa drewna tartego" [Profit Rate in Lumber], *KG* No. 5 (1930), pp. 157-58.
d. "Metale" [Metals], *PG* No. 1 (1930), pp. 40-42; No. 3, pp. 140-41; No. 5, pp. 237-39; No. 7, pp. 330-32; No. 9, pp. 423-24; No. 11, pp. 502-504; No. 13, pp. 593-94; No. 15, pp. 670-72; No. 17, pp. 749-50; No. 21, pp. 911-12; No. 23, pp. 1001-1002.
e. "Wplyw znizki cen artykulow przemyslowych dla konsumpcji na przebieg koniunktury" [Influence of Price Reduction of Industrial Consumption Goods upon the Course of the Business Cycle], *PoG* No. 48 (1930), pp. 2089-90.
f. "Wskaznik cen polfabrykatow inwestycyjnych" [Price Index of Semifabricates for Investment Goods], *KG* No. 3 (1930), pp. 106-107.
g. "Wskaznik wysokosci opodatkowania towarow" [Index of Goods Taxation], *KG* No. 12 (1930), p. 330.
h. "Wskazniki symptomatyczne dochodow mas konsumentow oraz ruchu inwestycyjnego" [Symptomatic Indexes of Consumer Incomes and Investment Activity], *KG* No. 12 (1930), pp. 327-29.
i. "Zbyt wapna jako wskaznik ruchu budowlanego" [Sales of Lime as an Index of Building Activity], *KG* No. 8 (1930), pp. 227-29.

1931

a. "Ankieta o handlu hurtowym" [Enquiry about the Wholesale Market], *KG* No. 7 (1931), pp. 202-207.
b. Wisniewski, J. [co-author] "Eliminowanie sezonowosci z odsetka bezrobocia" [Elimination of Seasonality from the Rate of Unemployment], *KG* No. 3 (1931), pp. 82-83.

c. "Kauczuk: Sytuacja na rynku kauczuku" [Rubber: Situation on the Rubber Market], *PG* No. 8 (1931), pp. 364-65.
d. "Konsekwencje dumpingu" [Consequences of Dumping], *KG* No. 4 (1931), pp. 108-12.
e. "Metale" [Metals], *PG* No. 1 (1931), pp. 42-43; No. 3, pp. 132-33; No. 5, pp. 234-35; No. 7, pp. 328-30; No. 9, pp. 408-409; No. 11, pp. 495-96; No. 13, pp. 372-73; No. 15, pp. 642-43; No. 19, pp. 793-94; No. 21, pp. 864-65; No. 23, p. 949.
f. "Szacunek rozmiarow ruchu inwestycyjnego w Polsce" [Estimation of Size of the Investment Activity in Poland], *KG* No. 11 (1931), pp. 276-85.
g. Braun, Henryk [pseud.] "Swiatowy kryzys finansowy" [The World Financial Crisis], *PSo* No. 1 (1931), pp. 1-3.
h. "Zbyt nici jako symptomat koniunktury wlokienniczej" [Thread Sales as a Symptom of Textile Market Fluctuations], *KG* No. 2 (1931), pp. 56-59.

1932

a. Braun, Henryk [pseud.] "Czy mozliwe jest 'kapitalistyczne' wyjscie z kryzysu?" [Is "Capitalist" Crisis Overcoming Possible?], *PSo* No. 10 (1932), pp. 1-3
b. Landau, L. [co-author] "Handel wlokienniczy w Polsce" [Textile Trade in Poland], *PIBKGC* No. 3-4 (1932), pp. 30-42.
c. Braun, Henryk [pseud.] "Inflacja i wojna" [Inflation and War], *PSo* No. 13 (1932), pp. 1-2.
d. ———. "Ivar Kreuger" [Ivar Kreuger], *PSo* No. 9 (1932), pp. 5-6.
e. "Koniunktura a inflacja" [Business Cycles and Inflation], *PoG* No. 48 (1932), pp. 1411-15.
f. "Metale" [Metals], *PG* No. 1 (1932), pp. 35-36; No. 3, pp. 125-26; No. 5, pp. 203-204; No. 7, pp. 293-94; No. 9, pp. 376-77; No. 11, pp. 468-69; No. 13, pp. 537-38; No. 15, pp. 607-608; No. 19, pp. 742-43; No. 21, pp. 814-15; No. 23, pp. 894-95.
g. "Na marginesie planu Papena" [On the Margin of the Papen Plan], *PoG* No. 39 (1932), pp. 1157-58.
h. Braun, Henryk [pseud.] "Na marginesie wydarzen niemieckich" [On the Margin of the German Events], *PSo* No. 15 (1932), pp. 4-5.
i. " 'Nowe' przemysly a wyjscie z kryzysu" ["New" Industries and Issue from Crisis], *PG* No. 31 (1932), pp. 907-908.

j. Braun, Henryk [pseud.] "Obnizka plac w czasie kryzysu" [Reduction of Wages During Crisis], *PSo* No. 2 (1932), pp. 1-2.
k. ———. "Podstawy konfliktu mandzurskiego" [Bases of the Manchurian Conflict], *PSo* No. 2 (1932), pp. 6-8.
l. ———. "Przewidywania p. Keynes'a" [Mr. Keynes's Predictions], *PSo* No. 6 (1932), p. 4.
m. "Szacunek rozmiarow ruchu inwestycyjnego w Polsce i wskaznik kwartalny inwestycji" [Estimation of Investment Activity in Poland and the Quarterly Index of Investment], *PIBKGC* No. 1 (1932), pp. 7-10.
n. Braun, Henryk [pseud.] "Tandeta w produkcji kapitalistycznej" [Shoddiness in Capitalist Production], *PSo* No. 11 (1932), p. 5.
o. ———. "Uwagi o hitleryzmie i 'sferach gospodarczych' " [Remarks about Hitlerism and "Economic Spheres"], *PSo* No. 3 (1932), pp. 5-6.
p. ———. "Wojna na Wschodzie" [War in the East], *PSo* No. 5 (1932), pp. 1-3.
q. "Wplyw dewaluacji funta sterlinga na ceny swiatowe" [Influence of Devaluation of the Pound Sterling upon World Prices], *PG* No. 2 (1932), pp. 67-68.
r. "Wplyw kartelizacji na koniunkture" [Influence of Cartelization upon Business Cycle] *PG* No. 32 (1932), pp. 932-33.
s. "Wskazniki spozycia i ich analiza" [Indexes of Consumption and Their Analysis], *PIBKGC* No. 1 (1932), pp. 3-6.
t. Braun, Henryk [pseud.] "Zmierzch Deterdinga" [Deterding's Decline], *PSo* No. 12 (1932), pp. 4-5.

1933

a. "Metale [Metals], *PG* No. 1 (1933), pp. 30-31; No. 4, pp. 144-45; No. 6, pp. 225-26; No. 8, pp. 316-17; No. 10, pp. 387-88; No. 12, pp. 459-60; No. 16, pp. 614-15; No. 18, pp. 681-82; No. 20, p. 757; No. 22, pp. 833-34; No. 24, pp. 912-13.
b. "Nakrecanie koniunktury swiatowej" [Stimulating a World Upswing], *PoG* No. 37 (1933), pp. 1111-15.
c. "O handlu zagranicznym i 'eksporcie wewnetrznym' " [About Foreign Trade and "Internal Export"], *Ek* No. 3 (1933), pp. 27-35.
d. "Obecna faza kryzysu swiatowego" [The Present Phase of World Crisis], *PoG* No. 1 (1933), pp. 9-11.
e. "Odpowiedz na: 'Uwagi krytyczne o jednej z matematycznych teoryj koniunktury' Aleksandra Rajchmana" [Reply to "Critical

Remarks about One of the Mathematical Theories of Business Cycle" by Alexander Rajchman], *KwS* No. 4 (1933), pp. 497-502.
f. *Proba teorii koniunktury* [Essays on Business Cycle Theory]. Warsaw: IBKGC, 1933, 55 pp.
g. "Udzial karteli w dzialalnosci przemyslowej na rynku polskim" [Share of Cartels in Industrial Activity on Polish Market], *PIBKGC* No. 3 (1933), pp. 3-6.
h. "W sprawie wskaznika wytworczosci skartelizowanej" [On the Index of Cartelized Production], *PG* No. 23 (1933), pp. 872-73.

1934

a. Landau, L. [co-author] *Comparabilité internationale des indices de la production industrielle.* Warsaw: Druk "Kadra," 1934, 16 pp.
b. "Koniunktura a dobrobyt" [Business Cycle and Welfare], *PoG* No. 50 (1934), pp. 1531-34.
c. "Losy eksperymentow" [The Fate of Experiments], *PoG* No. 21 (1934), pp. 637-40.
d. "Metale" [Metals], *PG*, No. 2 (1934), pp. 70-71; No. 4, pp. 153-54; No. 6, pp. 229-30; No. 8, pp. 313-14; No. 10, pp. 389-90; No. 12, p. 459; No. 16, pp. 587-88; No. 18, pp. 656-57; No. 20, pp. 723-24; No. 22, pp. 807-808; No. 24, p. 884.
e. "Nowy wskaznik inwestycyj" [The New Investment Index], *PIBKGC* No. 1 (1934), pp. 10-15.
f. "Odpowiedz na art. A. M. Neumana: O 'trzech ukladach' " [A Reply to Paper of A. M. Neuman: "Three Agreements"], *Ek* No. 4 (1934), pp. 97-100.
g. Landau, L. [co-author] Porownywalnosc miedzynarodowa wskaznikow produkcji przemyslowej i proba jej porownania" [International Comparability of Industrial Production Indexes and an Attempt at Comparison], *PIBKGC* No. 2-3 (1934), pp. 3-8.
h. ———. *Szacunek dochodu spolecznego w r. 1929.* [Estimation of Social Income in 1929]. Warsaw: IBKGC, 1934, 54 pp.
i. "Trzy uklady" [Three Agreements], *Ek* No. 3 (1934), pp. 54-70.
j. Landau, L. [co-author] "Wahania produkcji przemyslowej a wahania konsumpcji" [Fluctuations of Industrial Production and Fluctuations of Consumption], *PIBKGC* No. 4 (1934), pp. 3-6.

1935

a. Landau, L. [co-author] *Dochod spoleczny w r. 1933 i podstawy badan periodycznych nad zmianami dochodu* [Social Income in 1933 and Bases of Periodical Investigations of Income Fluctuations]. Warsaw: IBKGC, 1935, 48 pp.
b. "Eksperyment niemiecki" [The German Experiment], *PoG* No. 49 (1935), pp. 1574-76.
c. Landau, L. [co-author] "Encore sur la comparabilité internationale des indices de la production industrielle," *Travaux de l'Institut des Recherches sur le Mouvement General des Affaires et sur la Formation des Prix* No. 3-4 (1935), pp. 108-10.
d. "Essai d'une théorie du mouvement cyclique des affaires," *REP* No. 2 (1935), pp. 285-305.
e. "Istota poprawy koniunkturalnej" [The Essence of the Upswing], *PoG* No. 43 (1935), pp. 1320-24.
f. "Koniunktura a bilans platniczy" [Business Cycle and Balance of Payments], *PoG* No. 45 (1935), pp. 1385-87.
g. "Koniunktura a zbrojenia" [Business Cycle and Armaments], *PoG* No. 32 (1935), pp. 701-703.
h. "A Macrodynamic Theory of Business Cycles," *Em* No. 3 (July 1935), pp. 327-44.
i. "Maszyny krajowe i importowane a charakter inwestycyj przemyslowych" [Domestic and Imported Machines and the Nature of Industrial Investments], *PIBKGC* No. 2 (1935), pp. 68-69.
j. "W sprawie porownywalnosci miedzynarodowej wskaznikow produkcji przemyslowej" [On the International Comparability of Indexes of Industrial Production], *PIBKGC* No. 3-4 (1935), pp. 108-10.
k. Landau, L. [co-author] "Wahania cen i kosztow a wahania produkcji przemyslowej w Polsce" [Price and Cost Fluctuations of Industrial Production in Poland], *PIBKGC* No. 2 (1935), pp. 51-61.
l. "Wskaznik zbytu produktow przemyslowych" [Index of the Sale of Industrial Goods], *PIBKGC* No. 3-4 (1935), pp. 105-107.

1936

a. "Comments on the Macrodynamic Theory of Business Cycles," *Em* No. 4 (1936), pp. 356-60.
b. *Mechanizm poprawy koniunkturalnej* [The Mechanism of the Upswing]. Warsaw, 1936, 34 pp.

c. "Pare uwag o teorii Keynesa" [Some Remarks on Keynes's Theory], *Ek,* No. 3 (1936), pp. 18-26.

1937

a. "The Principle of Increasing Risk," *Ec* (Nov. 1937), pp. 440-47.
b. "A Theory of the Business Cycle," *RES* (Feb. 1937), pp. 77-97.
c. "A Theory of Commodity, Income, and Capital Taxation," *EJ* (Sept. 1937) pp. 444-50.

1938

a. "Mr. Kalecki's 'Principle of Increasing Risk': A Reply," *Ec* (Nov. 1938), pp. 459-60.
b. "The Determinants of Distribution of the National Income," *Em* (Apr. 1938), pp. 97-112.
c. "The Lesson of the Blum Experiment," *EJ* (Mar. 1938), pp. 26-41.
d. [Review of] Havas, F.: *Grundgedanken zu einer Theorie der störungs freien Geldschöpfung.* Jena, 1936. *EJ* (Dec. 1938), pp. 713-14.
e. [Review of] Lukas, E.: *Die Aufgaben des Geldes.* Stuttgart 1937. *EJ* (Mar. 1938), pp. 76-77.
f. [Review of] Manoilesco, M.: *Die Nationalen Produktivkrafte und der Aussenhandel.* Berlin, 1937. *EJ* (Dec. 1938), pp. 708-11.

1939

a. *Essays in the Theory of Economic Fluctuations.* London: Allen and Unwin, 1939, 154 pp.
b. *Place nominalne i realne* [Money and Real Wages]. Warsaw: IGS, 1939, 59 pp.
c. [Review of] Landau, L.: *Gospodarka swiatowa, produkcja i dochod w liczbach* [World Economy, Production and Income in Figures], Warsaw, 1939. *EJ* (June 1939), pp. 513-15.

1940

a. "The 'Mysteries' of Money Market," *OISB* (Oct. 1940), pp. 2-5.
b. Tew, B. [co-author] "A New Method of Trend Elimination," *Em* (Apr. 1940), pp. 117-29.

c. "A Scheme of Curtailment of Consumption," *OISB* (June 30, 1940) pp. 7-9.
d. "The Short-Term Rate and the Long-Term Rate," *OEP* (Sept. 1940), pp. 15-22.
e. "A Supplement," *OISB* (Aug. 31, 1940), pp. 10-13.
f. "The Supply Curve of an Industry Under Imperfect Competition," *RES* (Feb. 1940), pp. 91-112.
g. "The Third Quarter," *OISB* (Dec. 1940), pp. 1-5.
h. "Wage Bill and Cash Circulation," *OISB* (Aug. 10, 1940), pp. 2-6.
i. "War Finance in the First Half of 1940," *OISB* (Sept. 1940), pp. 7-10.
j. [Review of] Guillaume, G., and Guillaume, E.: *Economique Rationelle.* Paris, 1937. *EJ* (June-Sept. 1940), pp. 276-78.

1941

a. "The Budget and Inflation," *OISB* (Apr. 26, 1941), pp. 112-13.
b. "Changes in Stocks of Commodities in 1940," *OISB* (Nov. 1, 1941), pp. 335-38.
c. "The Financial Position on the Eve of the Budget," *OISB* (Mar.15, 1941), pp. 61-65.
d. "General Rationing," *OISB* (Jan. 11, 1941), pp. 1-6.
e. "Inflation, Wages and Rationing," *TB* (Oct. 1941).
f. Tew, B. [co-author] "A New Method of Trend Elimination: A Correction," *Em* (Jan. 1941), pp. 93-94.
g. "Notes on Finance," *OISB* (Feb. 22, 1941), pp. 51-53.
h. "Notes on General Rationing," *OISB* (Apr. 5, 1941), pp. 103-105.
i. "Recent Trends in the Financial Situation," *OISB* (Dec. 31, 1941), pp. 389-93.
j. "The Share of Wages in the National Income," *OISB* (June 28, 1941), pp. 196-98; erratum (Aug. 9, 1941), p. 262.
k. "The Short-Term Rate of Interest and the Velocity of Cash Circulation," *REStat* (May 1941), pp. 97-99.
l. "A Theorem on Technical Progress," *RES* (June 1941), pp. 178-84.
m. "The Theory of Long-Run Distribution of the Production of Industry," *OEP* (June 1941), pp. 31-41.
n. "Towards Comprehensive Rationing," *OISB* (Aug. 30, 1941), pp. 51-53.
o. "Wartime Changes in Employment and the Wage Bill," *OISB* (Sept. 20, 1941), pp. 294-98.
p. "What is Inflation?" *OISB* (June 7, 1941), pp. 159-64.

1942

a. "The Budget," *OISB* (Apr. 25, 1942), pp. 129-32.
b. "The Burden of War. B: The Burden on Wages and Other Incomes," *OISB* (Jan. 10, 1942), pp. 10-11.
c. "Differential Rationing," *OISB* (Aug. 8, 1942), pp. 215-17.
d. "Employment, Wage Bill, and Cash Circulation," *OISB* (Feb. 21, 1942), pp. 67-70.
e. "Excess Profits Tax and Government Contracts," *OISB* (Jan. 10, 1942), pp. 40-43.
f. "The Fall in 'Small' Savings," *OISB* (Oct. 31, 1942), pp. 290-93; erratum (Jan. 9, 1943), p. 22.
g. "The Financial Situation in the First Half of 1942," *OISB* (Sept. 19, 1942), pp. 247-52.
h. "The Problem of Profit Margins," *OISB* (Apr. 4, 1942), pp. 114-17.
i. "Some Problems of Non-Food Rationing," *OISB* (Dec. 12, 1942), pp. 325-26.
j. "A Theory of Profits," *EJ* (June-Sept. 1942), pp. 258-67.
k. "Wages and the National Income in 1940 and 1941," *OISB* (May 16, 1942), pp. 150-53.
l. "War Finance in 1940 and 1941," *OISB* (June 6, 1942), pp. 161-66.
m. "Mr. Whitman on the Concept of 'Degree of Monopoly,' A Comment." *EJ* (Apr. 1942), pp. 121-27.

1943

a. "The Budget," *OISB* (Apr. 24, 1943), pp. 96-97.
b. "The Burden of the National Debt," *OISB* (Apr. 3, 1943), pp. 76-80.
c. "Economic Implications of the Beveridge Plan," *OISB* (Feb. 20, 1943), suppl. 4, pp. 2-7.
d. "The Financial Situation in the First Half of 1943," *OISB* (Sept. 18, 1943), pp. 216-20.
e. Schumacher, E. F. [co-author] "International Clearing and Long-Term Lending," *OISB* (Aug. 7, 1943), suppl. 5, pp. 29-33.
f. "Labour in the War Industries in Britain and USA: A. Sources of Manpower in the British War Sector," *OISB* (Jan. 9, 1943), pp. 2-11.
g. "Political Aspects of Full Employment," *PQ* No. 4 (1943), pp. 322-31.

h. "The Problem of 'Small' Savings," *OISB* (Nov. 20, 1943), pp. 260-65.
i. "Profits, Salaries and Wages," *OISB* (June 5, 1943), pp. 125-29.
j. "Sources of Manpower in the British War Sector in 1941 and 1942," *OISB* (Aug. 7, 1943), pp. 173-78.
k. *Studies in Economic Dynamics.* London: Allen and Unwin, 1943, 92 pp.
l. "War Finance in 1940, 1941 and 1942," *OISB* (June 26, 1943), pp. 137-42.
m. "The War-Time Trend of Deposits," *OISB* (Mar. 13, 1943), pp. 63-66.

1944

a. "The Budget: A. The Stabilisation Policy," *OISB* (May 20, 1944), pp. 101-104.
b. "Employment in the United Kingdom During and after the Transition Period," *OISB* (Dec. 4, 1944), pp. 265-87.
c. "Excess Profits Tax and Post-War Re-equipment," *OISB* (Mar. 18, 1944), pp. 58-61.
d. "Prof. Pigou on 'The Classical Stationary State.' A Comment," *EJ* (Apr. 1944), pp. 131-32.
e. "Rationing and Price Control," *OISB* (Feb. 5, 1944), pp. 29-32.
f. *Studies in Economic Dynamics.* New York: Farrar and Rinehart, 1944, 92 pp.
g. "Three Ways to Full Employment." In *The Economics of Full Employment.* Oxford: Basil Blackwell, 1944, pp. 39-58.
h. "The White Paper on Employment Policy," *OISB* (June 10, 1944), pp. 131-35.
i. "The White Paper on the National Income and Expenditures in the Years 1938-1943," *OISB* (July 1, 1944), pp. 137-44.

1945

a. "Full Employment by Stimulating Private Investment?" *OEP* (Mar. 1945), pp. 83-92.
b. "The Maintenance of Full Employment in the Transition Period," *ILR* 5 (1945), pp. 449-64.
c. "On the Gilbrat Distribution," *Em* (Apr. 1945), pp. 161-70.
d. "The Work of Erwin Rothbarth," *RES,* No. 2 (1945), pp. 121-22.

1946

a. "A Comment on 'Monetary Policy,'" *REStat* (May 1946), pp. 81-84.
b. "Multilateralism and Full Employment," *CJE* (Aug. 1946), pp. 322-27.

1947

a. "The Maintenance of Full Employment after the Transition Period. A Rejoinder to Mr. Woytinsky's Note," *AER* (June 1947), pp. 391-97.
b. "Labour in the War Industries of Britain and U.S.A."; "What is Inflation?"; "The Budget and Inflation"; "The Budget (1942-1943)"; "The Budget (1943-1944)"; "The Budget (1944-1945)"; "The White Paper on the National Income and Expenditure in the Years 1938-1943"; "The Problem of 'Small' Savings"; "The Fall in 'Small' Savings"; "The Burden of the National Debt"; "General Rationing"; "Rationing and Price Control"; "Inflation, Wages and Rationing"; "Differential Rationing"; "Measuring the Cost of the War"; "The Problem of Profit Margins"; "Excess Profits Tax and Government Contracts." Rpt. in *Studies in War Economics.* Oxford: Basil Blackwell, 1947.

1948

a. "Determinants of the Increase in the Cost of Living in the United States," *REStat* (Feb. 1948), pp. 22-24.
b. "Further Comments on the Department of Commerce Series," *REStat* 3 (1948), pp. 195-97.

1949

a. Contribution to the Discussion on "The Practice of Economic Planning and the Optimum Allocation of Resources," *Em* 17 (1949) suppl., pp. 176-77.
b. "A New Approach to the Problem of Business Cycles," *RES* No. 2 (1949), pp. 57-64.

1950

"A Note on Long-Run Unemployment," *RES* No. 1 (1950), pp. 62-64.

1951

Report of Main Current Economic Problems of Israel. Tel-Aviv: Israel Government Printing Office, 1951, 23 pp.

1954

a. "El problema del financiamento del desarollo economico," *TE* No. 4 (1954), pp. 381-401.
b. [Contribution to] "Fluctuations Economiques," *Analyses de Théories.* Paris: Ed. D. Montchrestien, 1954, 402 pp.
c. *Theory of Economic Dynamics: An Essay on Cyclical and Long-Run Changes in Capitalist Economy.* London: Allen and Unwin, 1954, 178 pp.

1955

"The Problems of Financing of Economic Development," *IERev* No. 3 (1955), pp. 1-22.

1956

a. "Dynamika inwestycji i dochodu narodowego w gospodarce socjalistycznej" [The Dynamics of Investment and National Income in Socialist Economy], *Ek* No. 5 (1956), pp. 61-70.
b. "Investments and National Income Dynamics in Socialist Economy," *Enq* No. 3 (1956), pp. 6-20.
c. "Rady robotnicze a centralne planowanie" [Workers-Councils and Central Planning], *ND* No. 11-12 (1956), pp. 38-45.
d. "Sytuacja gospodarcza Stanow Zjednoczonych w zestawieniu z okresem przedwojennym" [The Present Economic Situation of the U.S.A. as Compared with That of the Prewar Period], *Ek* No. 4 (1956), pp. 3-13.
e. *Theoria de la dinamica economica.* Mexico City: Fondo de Cultura Economica, 1956, 184 pp.
f. *Teoria della dinamica economica.* Torino: Edizioni Scientifiche Einaudi, 1956, 217 pp.

g. "Zagadnienie finansowania rozwoju ekonomicznego" [The Problem of Financing Economic Development], *Ek* No. 1-2 (1956), pp. 181-202.
h. [Trans. of] Keynes, J. M.: *Ogolna teoria zatrudnienia, procentu i pieniadza* [The General Theory of Employment, Interest and Money]. Warsaw: PWN, 1956, pp. xviii, 532.

1957

a. "Les conseils ouvriers et la planification centrale," *NC*, 83 (1957), pp. 85-96.
b. Polaczek, S. [co-author] "Dyskusja o cenach surowcow podstawowych" [Discussion on Prices of Basic Raw Materials], *GP* No. 9 (1957), pp. 66-68.
c. Szeworski, A. [co-author] "Ekonomiczne problemy automatyzacji produkcji w krajach kapitalistycznych" [The Economic Problems of Automation in Capitalist Countries], *Ek* No. 3 (1957), pp. 105-15.
d. "Jak lagodzic sprzecznosc: inwestycje—konsumpcja" [How to Moderate the Contradiction Between Investment and Consumption], *ZW* No. 117 (1957), p. 3.
e. "Koncern pionowy? Propozycje ekonomiczne" [A Vertical Concern? The Economic Proposals], *Pol* No. 8 (1957), p. 1.
f. "Nie przeceniac roli modelu: Jak wyobrazam sobie polski model gospodarczy" [Let Us Not Overestimate the Role of the Model: How I Imagine the Polish Economic Model], *TL* No. 33 (1957), p. 3.
g. "Rady robotnicze a centralne planowanie" [Workers' Council and Central Planning]. In *Dyskusja o polskim modelu gospodarczym* [Discussion on the Polish Economic Model]. Warsaw: KiW, 1957, pp. 31-45.
h. "Schemat nowego systemu bodzcow i nakazow" [Scheme of a New System of Incentives and Orders], *ZG*, No. 27 (1957), p. 1.
i. Szeworski, A. [co-author] *Studia z zakresu koniunktury wspolczesnego kapitalizmu.* [Studies on Business Cycles of Contemporary Capitalism]. Vol. 1. Warsaw: PWN, 1957, 136 pp.
j. Polaczek, S. [co-author] "Uwagi w sprawie metody ustalania cen surowcow podstawowych" [Remarks on the Method of Fixing Prices of Basic Raw Materials], *GP* No. 4 (1957), pp. 18-22.
k. "Wplyw czasu bodowy no wspolzaleznosc inwestycji i dochodu narodowego a wspolczynnik zamrozenia" [The Influence of the

Time of Construction on the Interdependence of Investment and National Income and the Coefficient of Freezing], *Ek* No. 1 (1957), pp. 3-13.

1958

a. "Czynniki okreslajace tempo wzrostu dochodu narodowego w gospodarce socjalistycznej" [Factors Determining the Rate of Growth of the National Income in Socialist Economy], *GP* No. 8 (1958), pp. 1-5.
b. "Dynamika inwestycji i dochodu narodowego w gospodarce socjalistycznej" [Dynamics of Investment and National Income in Socialist Economy]. In *Zagadnienia ekonomii politycznej socjalizmu* [Problems of Political Economy of Socialism]. Warsaw: KiW, 1958, pp. 145-75.
c. Polaczek, S. [co-author] "Dyskusja o cenach surowcow podstawowych" [Discussion on the Prices of Basic Raw Materials]. In: *Spor o ceny* [Controversy about Prices]. Warsaw: KiW, 1958, pp. 121-35.
d. "Iz teoreticheskikh problemov perspektivnogo planirovania," *ZPAN* No. 3-4 (1958), pp. 1-5.
e. "Kilka uwag na marginesie organizacji koncernu angielskiego" [A Few Remarks on the Organization of an English Concern], *GP* No. 6 (1958), pp. 43-45.
f. "Kilka uwag o planie perspektywicznym 1961-1975" [A Few Remarks on the Perspective Plan, 1961-1975], *ZW*, No. 25 (1958), pp. 3-4.
g. "Model mechanistyczny zjawiska losowego" [Mechanistic Model of a Random Phenomenon], *ZM*, 2 (1958), pp. 113-29.
h. "O canach surowcow podstawowych" [On the Prices of Basic Raw Materials], *Ek* No. 3 (1958), pp. 574-78.
i. "O wspolczynniku zamrozenia" [On the Coefficient of Freezing], *Ek* No. 6 (1958), pp. 1393-1400.
j. "Plan perspektywiczny na lata 1961-1975" [The 1961-1975 Perspective Plan], *ND* No. 8 (1958), pp. 27-45.
k. "Radnicki saveti i centralno planiranje," *SD* No. 9 (1958), pp. 6-9.
l. "Some Theoretical Problems of Long-Run Planning," *RPAS* No. 3-4 (1958), pp. 1-6.
m. *Teoria dynamiki gospodarczej* [Theory of Economic Dynamics]. Warsaw: PWN, 1958, 237 pp.

n. *Theory of Economic Dynamics* [Title and text in Japanese]. Tokyo: Shin Hyoron, 1958, 254 pp.
o. "Uwagi w sprawie metody ustalania cen surowcow podstawowych" [Remarks on the Method of Fixing Prices of Basic Raw Materials]. In: *Spor o ceny* [Controversy about Prices]. Warsaw: KiW, 1958, pp. 62-75.
p. [Ed.] *Studia z zakresu koniunktury wspolczesnego kapitalizmu* [Studies on Business Cycles of Contemporary Capitalism]. Vol. 2. Warsaw: PWN, 1958, 157 pp.

1959

a. "Lata 1961-1965" [The 1961-1965 Years], *PK*, No. 4 (1959), pp. 1, 5.
b. "O waskich gardlach planu perspektywicznego" [On Bottlenecks in the Long-Run Plan], *NP* No. 1 (1959), pp. 53-58.
c. "Powdstawowe zagadnienia planu pieciolетniego na lata 1961-1965" [The Main Problems of the 1961-65 Five-Year Plan], *GP* No. 1-2 (1959), pp. 1-4.
d. "The 1961-1975 Long-Run Economic Plan," *PP* No. 3 (1959), pp. 3-19.
e. "Uogolnienie wzoru efektywnosci inwestycji" [Generalization of the Investment Efficiency Formula], *Prace i Materialy Zakladu Badan Ekonomicznych Komisji Planowania*, No. 17 (1959), pp. 1-16. Also *GP* No. 11 (1959), pp. 4-7, and *IB* No. 11 (1959), pp. 6-9.
f. "Wypowiedz w dyskusji nt.metodologii badan efektywnosci inwestycji" [A Contribution to the Discussion on the Methodology of Investment Efficiency Analysis]. *IB* No. 7-8 (1959), pp. 9-10.
g. "Z zagadnien teorii dynamiki gospodarki socjalistycznej" [On Problems of Theory of Dynamics of a Socialist Economy]. In *Zagadnienia ekonomii politycznej socjalizmu* [Problems of Political Economy of Socialism]. 2d ed. Warsaw: KiW, 1959, pp. 145-75.
h. [Ed.] *Studia z zakresu koniunktury wspolezesnego kapitalizmu* [Studies in Business Cycles of Contemporary Capitalism]. Vol. 3. Warsaw: PWN, 1959, 96 pp.
i. [Interview] Rozmawiamy z prof. . . . [A Talk with Prof. . . .], *ZG* No. 25 (1959), p. 1.

1960

a. "Consigli operai e pianificazione centralizata." In: *Vecchia e nuova pianificazione economica in Polonia.* Milan, 1960, pp. 127-37.
b. "Dinamica degli investimenti e del reddito nell' economia socialista." In: *Vecchia e nuova pianificazione economica in Polonia.* Milan, 1960, pp. 299-312.
c. "Financial Problems of the Third Plan," *EW* No. 28 (1960), pp. 1119-23.
d. *Hypothetical Outline of the Five Year Plan 1961-1965 for the Cuban Economy.* 1960, FAO, 45 pp. [mimeographed].
e. *Measures to Expedite the Increase in Agricultural Production in the Third Five Year Plan.* New Delhi, 1960, 4 pp. [mimeographed].
f. *An Outline of Financial Policy for the Third Five Year Plan.* New Delhi, 1960, 13 pp. [mimeographed].
g. "Pitanja tempa rasta socjalisticke privrede." In *Poljski ekonomisti o problemi na socjalisticke privrede.* Belgrade, 1960, pp. 71-108.
h. "Rozwoj sytuacji gospodarczej w Stanach Zjednoczonych w okresie 1956-1959" [Development of Economic Situation in United States During 1956-1959]. In *Studia z zakresu koniunktury wspolczesnego kapitalizmu* [Studies on Business Cycles of Contemporary Capitalism]. Vol. 4. Warsaw: PWN, 1960, pp. 5-19.
i. "Unemployment in Underdeveloped Countries," *IJLE* No. 2 (1960), pp. 59-61.
j. "Uwagi na temat wydajnosci pracy" [Remarks about Labour Productivity], *ZG* No. 31 (1960), pp. 1, 3.
k. "Uwagi o problemach finansowych trzeciego planu piecioletniego w Indiach" [Remarks on the Financial Problems of the Third Five-Year Plan of India], *Ek* No. 6 (1960), pp. 1278-84.
l. "Z zagadnien teorii dynamiki gospodarki socjalistycznej." [On Problems of the Theory of Dynamics of a Socialist Economy]. In *Zagadnienia ekonomii politycznej socjalizmu.* [Problems of the Political Economy of Socialism]. 3d ed. Warsaw: KiW, 1960, pp. 145-75.
m. [Ed.] *Studia z zakresu koniunktury wspolczesnego kapitalizmu. Zmiany w strukturze gospodarki USA i Francji* [Studies on Business Cycles of Contemporary Capitalism: Changes in the Economic Structure of the U.S.A. and France]. Vol. 4. Warsaw: PWN, 1960, 194 pp.

1961

a. "Gospodarcze aspekty militaryzacji Niemiec Zachodnich" [Economic Aspects of the Militarization of West Germany], *Ek* No. 6 (1961), pp. 1245-50.
b. "Mechanistic Model of a Random Phenomenon," *Sankhya.* Series A, No. 1 (1961), pp. 11-24.
c. "Polityczne aspekty pelnego zatrudnienia" [Political Aspects of Full Employment], *Ek* No. 5 (1961), pp. 1072-76.
d. "W odpowiedzi A. Swiecickiemu" [A Reply to A. Swiecicki], *Ek* No. 5 (1961), pp. 1173-77.

1962

a. "Akumulacja a maksymalizacja spozycia" [Accumulation and the Maximization of Consumption], *Ek* No. 3 (1962), pp. 706-708.
b. "Les aspects économiques de la remilitarization de l'Allemagne Occidentale," *Annuaire Polonais des Affaires Internationales* (1962), pp. 73-82.
c. "Economic Aspects of West German Rearmament," *EW* (May 12, 1962), pp. 775-80.
d. "Efektywnosc 'programu' inwestycyjnego" [Effectiveness of the Investment "Program"], *GP* No. 3 (1962), pp. 9-12.
e. Rakowski, M. [co-author] "Generalization of the Pattern for Effectiveness of Capital Investment," *EEE* No. 1 (1962), pp. 20-25.
f. "Kilka uwag o 'Gospodarce Planowej' i planowaniu" [Some Remarks on the Polish Monthly "Planned Economy" and on Planning in General], *GP* No. 1 (1962), pp. 6-7.
g. "A Model of Hyperinflation," *MS,* Vol. 72, No. 3 (1962), pp. 275-81.
h. "Observations on the Theory of Growth," *EJ* (Mar. 1962), pp. 134-53.
i. "Outline of a Method of Constructing a Perspective Plan." In *Four Papers Prepared for International Conference to Be Held in Geneva, 1963.* Warsaw, 1962, pp. 1-15.
j. *Prace z teorii koniunktury 1933-1939* [Studies in the Theory of Business Cycles 1933-1939]. Warsaw: PWN, 1962, 103 pp.
k. "Proba wyjasnienia zjawiska przestepczosci gospodarczej" [An Attempt at Explaining the Economic Crime Phenomenon], *KS* No. 3 (1962), pp. 73-77; also in *ZW* No. 236-37 (1962), p. 3.

l. "Short Papers on Economic Growth," *The Higher Course in Economic Planning.* Teaching Materials, Vol. 1. Warsaw: SGPiS, 1962, p. 89.
m. *Szkice o funkcjonowaniu wspolczesnego kapitalizmu.* [Essays on the Functioning of Contemporary Capitalism.]. Warsaw: PWN, 1962, 68 pp.
n. "Uwagi o teorii wzrostu" [Observations on the Theory of Growth]. In *Teorie wzrostu ekonomicznego a wspolczesny kapitalism* [Theories of Economic Growth and Modern Capitalism]. Warsaw: PWN, 1962, pp. 49-76.
o. "W sprawie dzialania bodzcow ekonomicznych" [On the Performance of Economic Incentives], *ND* No. 2 (1962), pp. 170-71.

1963

a. *Investment and National Income Dynamics in a Socialist Economy.* Dept. of Economics, Univ. of Ghana, 1963, 16 pp.
b. "Model hiperinflacji" [A Model of Hyperinflation], *Ek* No. 2 (1963), pp. 312-16.
c. "O podstawowych zasadach planowania wieloletniego" [On the Fundamental Principles of Long-Term Planning], *ZG* No. 24 (1963), pp. 1, 2.
d. "An Outline of a Method of Constructing a Perspective Plan. [Based on Polish Experience]." In *Essays on Planning Economic Development.* Vol. 1. Warsaw: PWN, 1963, pp. 9-22.
e. *The Problem of Financing Economic Development.* Dept. of Economics, Univ. of Ghana, 1963, 27 pp.
f. "Problems of Financing Economic Development in a Mixed Economy." Paper presented at the UNESCO Seminar in Sao Paulo, Jan. 1963. Sao Paulo, 1963, pp. 37-50.
g. "Przedmowa" [Foreword to] *Efektywnosc inwestycji* [Efficiency of Investment]. Warsaw: PWE, 1963, pp. 5-8.
h. "Roznice miedzy planowaniem perspektywicznym w socjalistycznych i mieszanych gospodarkach" [Differences Between Perspective Planning in the Socialist and Mixed Economies]. *PM* No. 2 (1963), pp. 13-14.
i. *Unemployment in Underdeveloped Countries.* Dept. of Economics, Univ. of Ghana, 1963, 3 pp.
j. "Zagadnienie finansowania rozwoju gospodarczego w malorozwinietych krajach kapitalistycznych" [The Problem of Financing

Economic Development in Underdeveloped Capitalist Countries], *Ek*, No. 6 (1963), pp. 1114-24.

k. "Zagadnienie optymalnej struktury spozycia" [The Problem of Optimum Structure of Consumption], *GP* No. 7 (1963), pp. 3-7.

l. "Zarys metody opracowania planu perspektywicznego" [An Outline of a Method of Constructing a Perspective Plan], *PM* No. 2 (1963), pp. 3-12.

m. *Zarys teorii wzrostu gospodarki socjalistycznej* [Outline of the Theory of Growth of a Socialist Economy]. Warsaw: PWN, 1963, 119 pp.

1964

a. "Ceny, mierniki, kontrola" [Prices, Yardsticks, Control]. In *Mierniki oceny dzialalnosci przedsiebiorstwa przemyslowego* [Yardsticks for Evaluating the Activity of an Industrial Enterprise]. Warsaw: PTE, 1964, pp. 226-30.

b. "Dinamika kapitalovlozheniya i natsionalnogo dokhoda v sotsialisticheskom khozyaistve." In *Ocherki po teori sotsialisticheskogo vosproizvodstva i tsen.* Warsaw: 1964, pp. 9-29.

c. "Dlaczego ekonomia nie jest dotad nauka scisla?" [Why Is Economics Not an Exact Science?], *ZG* No. 25 (1964), p. 2.

d. "Dochod narodowy: definicje i zalozenia" [National Income: Definitions and Assumptions]. In *Materialy do studiowania ekonomii politycznej socjalizmu.* [Materials for Studying the Political Economy of Socialism]. Ed. by W. Brus. Warsaw: PWN, 1964, pp. 175-79.

e. "Econometric Model and Historical Materialism." In *On Political Economy and Econometrics: Essays in Honour of Oskar Lange.* Warsaw: PWN, 1964, pp. 233-38.

f. "Faktory opredelyayushche temp rosta natsionalnogo dokhoda v sotsialisticheskoy ekonomike." In *Ocherki po teori sotsialisticheskogo vosproizvodstva i tsen.* Warsaw: 1964, pp. 271-88.

g. "Faszyzm naszych czasow" [Fascism of Our Times], *Pol* No. 46 (1964), pp. 1, 9.

h. Rakowski, M. [co-author] "Generalized Formula of the Efficiency of Investment." In *Studies on the Theory of Reproduction and Prices.* Warsaw: PWN, 1964, pp. 191-201.

i. "Glos w dyskusji" [A Voice in the Discussion]. In *Dalsze uwagi o kierunkach perspektyw rozwoju rolnictwa* [Further Comments about the Direction of Development of Agriculture]. Warsaw: PWN, 1964, pp. 98-99.

j. "Glos w dyskusji o kierunkach perspektyw rozwoju rolnictwa" [A Voice in the Discussion about the Perspectives of Agricultural Development]. In *O socjalistyczny rozwoj wsi: Dyskusja* [About the Socialist Development of Agriculture: A Dicussion]. Warsaw: PWN, 1964, pp. 504-508.

k. "Konferencja o miernikach—Fragmenty dyskusji" [Conference about Yardsticks—Parts of the Discussion], *ZG* No. 1 (1964), p. 5.

l. "Ludwik Landau—ekonomista i statystyk" [Ludwik Landau—Economist and Statistician], *ZG* No. 11 (1964), pp. 1, 2.

m. "Model ekonometryczny a materialistyczne pojmowanie dziejow" [The Econometric Model and Historical Materialism], *Ek* No. 4 (1964), pp. 724-29.

n. "O pewnych sumach rozciagnietych na liczby pierwsze lub czynniki pierwsze" [On Certain Sums of Prime Numbers or Prime Factors], *RPTM* Series 1: *PMat,* 8 (1964), pp. 121-29.

o. "O podstawowych zasadach planowania wieloletniego" [About the Basic Principles of Long-Term Planning]. In *Materialy do studiowania ekonomii politycznej socjalizmu* [Materials for Studying the Political Economy of Socialism]. Ed. by W. Brus. Warsaw: PWN, 1964, pp. 654-61.

p. "An Outline of a Method of Constructing a Perspective Plan. A Polish View," *SC* (July 4 and Sept. 1, 1964), pp. 15-16.

q. "Plan perspektywiczny na lata 1961-1975" [The Perspective Plan for 1961-1975]. In *Materialy do studiowania ekonomii politycznej socjalizmu.* [Materials for Studying the Political Economy of Socialism]. Ed. by W. Brus. Warsaw: PWN, 1964, pp. 702-19.

r. "Porownanie dochodu robotnikow i pracownikow umyslowych z okresem przedwojennym" [Comparisons of Blue- and White-Collar Workers' Incomes with the Prewar Period], *KS* No. 1 (1964), pp. 35-40.

s. [Contribution to:] *Programacion del desarrollo economico.* Buenos Aires: Fondo de Cultura Economica, 1964, p. 191.

t. "Przemowienie" [Speech]. In *Biuletyn IGS 1964, Zeszyt Specjalny: W dwudziesta rocznice zgonu Ludwika Landaua (1901-1944)* [Bulletin of the Institute of Social Economics, 1964, Special Issue Commemorating the Twentieth Anniversary of the Death of Ludwik Landau (1901-1944)], pp. 9-12.

u. "Short Papers on Economic Growth," *The Higher Course in National Economic Planning.* Teaching Materials, Vol. 1. Warsaw: SGPiS, 1964, 89 pp.

v. "Uwagi o cenach fabrycznych, miernikach produkcji i kontroli jakosciowej" [Remarks about Factory Prices, Production Yardsticks, and Quality Control], *GP* No. 5 (1964), pp. 26-28.

w. "Uwagi o planie gospodarczym na lata 1966-1970" [Remarks about the Economic Plan for 1966-1970], *ZG* No. 15 (1964), pp. 1, 2.

x. "Uwagi o spoleczno-gospodarczych aspektach ustrojow posrednich" [Remarks about the Socio-Economic Aspects of Intermediate Regimes], *PM* No. 4 (1964), pp. 55-61.

y. Polaczek, S. [co-author] "Uwagi w sprawie metody ustalania cen surowcow podstawowych" [Remarks about the Methods of Setting Prices of Basic Raw Materials]. In *Materialy do studiowania ekonomii politycznej socjalizmu.* [Materials for Studying the Political Economy of Socialism]. Ed. by W. Brus. Warsaw: PWN, 1964, pp. 624-30.

z. "Why Economics Is Not an Exact Science," *PP* No. 9 (1964), pp. 62-65.

aa. *Z zagadnien gospodarczo-spolecznych Polski Ludowej* [Socio-Economic Questions of People's Poland]. Warsaw: PWN, 1964, 100 pp.

bb. "Z zagadnien teorii dynamiki gospodarki socjalistycznej"[Questions of the Theory of Dynamics of a Socialist Economy]. In *Materialy do studiowania ekonomii politycznej socjalizmu* [Materials for Studying the Political Economy of Socialism]. Ed. by W. Brus. Warsaw: PWN, 1964, pp. 235-53.

cc. [Review of] "Landau L.: *Kronika lat wojny i okupacji.t.1-3"* [Review of L. Landau's *Chronicle of the War and Occupation Years,* Vols. 1-3], *ND* No. 2 (1964), pp. 116-17.

1965

a. "Dlaczego ekonomia nie jest nauka scisla?" [Why Is Economics Not an Exact Science?], *BNWEPUW* No. 16 (1965), pp. 3-7.

b. "Dzielo Oskara Langego" [The Work of Oskar Lange], *ZG* No. 41 (1965), p. 1.

c. "Krzywa produkcji a rachunek efektywnosci inwestycji" [The Production Curve and the Investment Efficiency Calculation], *Ek* No. 1 (1965), pp. 3-14.

d. *Nacrt teorie rustu socialisticke ekonomiky.* Prague: Nakl. Politicke Literatury, 1965, 157 pp.
e. "O liczbach bedacych sumami liczb pierwszych pewnego typu" [On Numbers Which Are Sums of Prime Numbers of a Certain Type], *RPTM* Series 1: *PMat,* 9 (1965), pp. 193-200.
f. "On Paul Baran's Political Economy of Growth," *MR* (Nov. 1965), pp. 58-60.
g. *Outline of Theory of Growth of a Socialist Economy* [Title and text in Japanese]. Tokyo: Nihon Hyoronsha, 1965, 148 pp.
h. "The Problem of the Optimum Structure of Consumption." *Mathematical Studies in Economics and Statistics in the USSR and Eastern Europe. A Journal of Translations,* No. 4 (1965), pp. 3-16.
i. "Problems of Financing Economic Development in a Mixed Economy." In *Essays on Planning and Economic Development.* Vol. 2. Warsaw: PWN, 1965, pp. 37-50.
j. "Problemy optimalnoy struktury potrebleniya." *EMM* No. 1 (1965), pp. 54-61.
k. "Tempo bezinflacyjnego wzrostu i import kapitalu" [The Rate of Non-Inflationary Growth and Import of Capital], *PM* No. 1 (1965), pp. 5-10.
l. *Theory of Economic Dynamics.* 2d rev. ed. London: Allen and Unwin, 1965, 178 pp.
m. "Twierdzenie o sumach typu Σa (N_r) i jego zastosowanie" [A Theorem Concerning Sums of the Type Σa (N_r) and Its Application]. *RPTM.* Series 1: *PMat,* 9 (1965), pp. 129-35.
n. "Uwagi o spoleczno-gospodarczych aspektach 'ustrojow posrednich' " [Remarks about the Socio-Economic Aspects of "Intermediate Regimes"], *Ek,* No. 3 (1965), pp. 568-72.

1966

a. Sachs, I. [co-author] "Forms of Foreign Aid: An Economic Analysis," *SSI* No. 1 (1966), pp. 21-44.
b. "Krivaya proizvodstva i raschet effektivnosti kapitalovlozhenia." *EMM* No. 4 (1966), pp. 510-19.
c. "O 'Ekonomii politycznej wzrostu' Paula Barana" [About Paul Baran's *Political Economy of Growth*], *ZG* No. 6 (1966), p. 1.
d. Introduction to *Efficiency of Investment in a Socialist Economy.* Warsaw: PWN, 1966, pp. ix–xi.
e. "Oskar Lange, 1904-65," *EJ* (June 1966), pp. 431-32.

f. "Roznice w wezlowych problemach gospodarczych miedzy wysoko rozwinieta i zacofana gospodarka kapitalistyczna" [Differences Between the Crucial Economic Problems of Highly Developed and Backward Capitalist Economies], *PM* No. 1 (1966), pp. 5-13.

g. "Some Remarks on the Socio-Economic Aspects of 'Intermediate Systems.'" *Polish Round Table,* Warsaw: ISM, 1966, pp. 97-100.

h. *Studies in the Theory of Business Cycles 1933-1939.* With intro. by Joan Robinson. Oxford: Basil Blackwell, 1966, xii, 71 pp.

i. "Tempo wzrostu gospodarki socjalistycznej w warunkach nieograniczonej podazy sily roboczej a kapitalochlonnosc" [The Rate of Growth of a Socialist Economy under Conditions of Unlimited Labor Supply and Capital Intensity], *Ek* No. 6 (1966), pp. 1269-78.

j. *Théorie de la dynamique économique.* 2d ed. Paris: Gauthier-Villars, 1966, 158 pp.

k. *Theorie der wirtschaftlichen Dynamik.* Vienna: Europa Verlag, 1966, 206 pp.

l. "Ustroje posrednie" [Intermediate Regimes], *Pol* No. 41 (1966), pp. 1, 8, 9.

m. "Uwagi o postopie technicznym i jego typach" [Remarks about Technical Progress and its Types], *ZNUL* 10 (1965), pp. 5-6.

n. *Vallalatvezetes Tervezes Gazdasagi Novekedes.* Budapest: Kozgazdasagi es Jogi Konyvkiado, 1966, 203 pp.

o. "Wysoko rozwinieta i zacofana gospodarka kapitalistyczna: Roznice w wezlowych problemach gospodarczych" [Highly Developed and Backward Capitalist Economy: Differences Between the Crucial Economic Problems], *Ek* No. 5 (1966), pp. 971-77.

p. "Zagadnienie okreslania stopy wzrostu gospodarki socjalistycznej w warunkach nieograniczonej podazy sily roboczej" [The Problem of Determining the Rate of Growth of a Socialist Economy under Conditions of Unlimited Labor Supply], *PM* No. 2 (1966), pp. 5-17.

1967

a. "The Curve of Production and the Evaluation of the Efficiency of Investment in a Socialist Economy." In C. H. Feinstein, ed., *Socialism, Capitalism and Economic Growth.* Cambridge: Cambridge Univ. Press, 1967, pp. 87-100.

b. *Introduction to the Theory of Growth of Socialist Economy.* Teaching Materials, Vol 29. Warsaw: SGPiS, 1967, p. 132.

c. "Observations on Social and Economic Aspects of 'Intermediate Regimes,'" *CE* No. 1 (1967), pp. 1-5.
d. "Das Problem der Wachstumsrate einer sozialistischen Wirtschaft unter der Bedingung unbegrenzten Arbeitskrafteangebots," *Jahrbuch für Wirtschaftsgeschichte 1967.* Berlin, 1967. Pt. 2, pp. 51-64.
e. Sachs, I. [co-author] Introduction to *O gospodarce mieszanej w krajach "trzeciego swiata"* [About the Mixed Economy in the Countries of the "Third World"]. Warsaw: PWN, 1967, pp. 7-8.
f. "Remarks on Factory Prices, Production Indicators, and Quality Control," *EEE* No. 1 (1967), pp. 28-30.
g. "Robinson, J." *Wielka Encyklopedia Powszechna* [Large Universal Encyclopedia]. Warsaw: PWN, 1967, Vol. 10, p. 5.
h. "Roznice w wezlowych problemach gospodarczych miedzy wysoko rozwinieta i zacofana gospodarka kapitalistyczna" [Differences Between the Crucial Economic Problems of Highly Developed and Backward Capitalist Economies]. In *O gospodarce mieszanej w krajach "trzeciego swiata"* [About the Mixed Economy in the Countries of the "Third World"]. Warsaw: PWN, 1967, pp. 9-21.
i. "A Simple Elementary Proof of $M(x)=\sum_{n \leq x} u(n)=o(x)$," *AA* 1 (1967), pp. 1-7.
j. *Teoria dello sviluppo di una economia socialista.* Rome: Editori Riuniti, 1967, 151 pp.
k. "Uogolnienie postulatu Bertranda" [A Generalization of the Bertrand Postulate], *RPTM* Series 2: *WM* 9 (1967), pp. 219-20.
l. "Uwagi o ostatnim podejsciu M. Rakowskiego do problematyki efektywnosci inwestycji" [Remarks about M. Rakowski's Latest Approach to the Problem of Investment Efficiency], *GP* No. 7 (1967), pp. 15-17.
m. "Wietnam przez pryzmat USA" [Vietnam Through the Prism of the U.S.A.], *Pol* No. 3 (1967), pp. 1, 10.
n. Sachs, I. [co-author] *Z zagadnien finansowania rozwoju krajow o "gospodarce mieszanej"* [Questions of Financing the Development of "Mixed Economies"]. Warsaw: PWN, 1967, 146 pp.
o. "Zagadnienie realizacji u Tugana Baranowskiego i Rozy Luksemburg" [The Question of Realization in Tugan-Baranovsky and Rosa Luxemburg]. In *Wokol teorii ekonomicznych "Kapitalu"* [About Economic Theories of *Capital*]. Warsaw: PWN, 1967, pp. 7-21; and in *Ek* No. 2 (1967), pp. 241-49.

1968

a. "Determination of the Rate of Growth of a Socialist Economy under Conditions of Unlimited Supply of Labour." In *Essays on Planning and Economic Development,* Vol. 3. Warsaw: PWN, 1968, pp. 19-34.

b. "The Difference Between Crucial Economic Problems of Developed and Underdeveloped Non-Socialist Economies." In *Essays on Planning and Economic Development.* Vol. 3. Warsaw: PWN, 1968, pp. 9-18.

c. *El desarrollo de la economia socialista.* Mexico City: Fondo de Cultura Economica, 1968, 123 pp.

d. "Krivaya proizvodstva i teori effektivnosti kapitalovlozheni." In *Tempy i proportsi sotsialisticheskogo vosproizvodstva.* Moscow, 1968, pp. 116-27.

e. "The Marxian Equations of Reproduction and Modern Economics," *SSI* No. 6 (1968), pp. 73-79.

f. "O wyborze technik produkcji w gospodarce socjalistycznej" [About the Choice of Techniques of Production in a Socialist Economy]. Abstract in *Bilanse gospodarki narodowej* [Balances of National Economy]. Warsaw, 1968, p. 165.

g. "On the sum $\sum_{n \leq x} \left\{ f\left(\frac{x}{n}\right) \right\}$," *RPTM* Series 1: *PMat* 11 (1968), pp. 189-91.

h. "Problemy teori dinamiki sotsialisticheskoy ekonomiki." In *Tempy i proportsi sotsialisticheskogo vosproizvodstva.* Moscow, 1968, pp. 25-47.

i. *Theory of Economic Dynamics.* New York and London: Modern Reader Paperbacks, 1968, 176 pp.

j. "Trend and Business Cycles Reconsidered," *EJ* (June 1968), pp. 263-76; corrigendum (Sept. 1968), p. 729.

k. *Z ostatniej fazy przemian kapitalizmu* [From the Last Phase of Transformation of Capitalism]. With foreword by W. Brus. Warsaw: PWN, 1968, 67 pp.

l. *Zarys teorii wzrostu gospodarki socjalistycznej* [Outline of a Theory of Growth of a Socialist Economy]. 2d corrected and supplemented ed. Warsaw: PWN, 1968, 140 pp.

1969

a. Kowalik T., and K. Secomski [co-authors] "Ekonomia Edwarda Lipinskiego" [The Economics of Edward Lipinski], *Ek* No. 2 (1969), pp. 329-65.
b. *Introduction to the Theory of Growth in a Socialist Economy.* Oxford: Basil Blackwell, 1969, 125 pp.
c. "On the Choice of Techniques of Production in a Socialist Economy," *ZM* 10 (1969), pp. 257-64.
d. "A Short Elementary Proof of the Prime Number Theorem," *RPTM.* Series 1: *PMat* 13 (1969), pp. 51-55.
e. Polaczck, S. [co-author] "Uwagi w sprawie metody ustalania cen surowcow podstawowych" [Remarks about Setting Prices of Basic Raw Materials]. In *Efektywnosc handlu zagranicznego* [Efficiency of Foreign Trade]. Warsaw: PWN, 1969, pp. 276-84.

1970

a. "Courbe de production et calcul d'éfficacité des investissements," *ES* No. 1 (1970), pp. 65-80.
b. *Théorie de la croissance en économie socialiste.* Paris: Editions Sirey, 1970, 133 pp.
c. "Ob osnovnykh problemakh teori effektivsnosti kapitalovlozheni," *EMM* No. 5 (1970), pp. 683-94.
d. *Ocherk teori rosta sotsialisticheskoy ekonomiki.* 2d ed. Moscow: Progress, 1970, 141 pp.
e. "Theories of Growth in Different Social Sytems," *Scientia* (May-June 1970), pp. 311-16.
f. "Zakres zastosowania rachunku efektywnosci inwestycji w gospodarce socjalistycznej" [The Applicability of Investment Efficiency Calculation in a Socialist Economy]. In *Problemy teorii gospodarki socjalistycznej* [Theoretical Problems of a Socialist Economy]. Warsaw: PWN, 1970, pp. 111-16.

1971

a. "Class Struggle and the Distribution of National Income," *Kyklos* No. 1 (1971), pp. 1-9.
b. Kowalik, T. [co-author] "Osservazioni sulla 'riforma cruciale,'" *PE* No. 2-3 (June 1971), pp. 190-96.
c. "On an Inequality in the General Additive Theory of Numbers," *PMat* 15 (1971), pp. 133-34.

d. *Selected Essays on the Dynamics of the Capitalist Economy 1933-1970.* Cambridge: Cambridge Univ. Press, 1971, 198 pp.

1972

a. *The Last Phase in the Transformation of Capitalism.* With intro. by G. R. Feiwel and foreword by W. Brus. New York: Monthly Review Press, 1972, 124 pp.

b. *Selected Essays on the Economic Growth of the Socialist and the Mixed Economy.* Cambridge: Cambridge Univ. Press, 1972, 176 pp.

GENERAL BIBLIOGRAPHY

•

Abramovitz, M. *The Role of Inventories in Business Cycles.* New York, 1948.

Adelman, I., and F. L. Adelman. "The Dynamic Properties of the Klein-Goldberger Model," *Em* (Oct. 1959).

Adelman, M. A. "The Measurement of Industrial Concentration," *REStat* (Nov. 1951).

Ady, P. H. "Utility Goods," *OISB* (Oct. 31, 1942).

Aftalion, A. *Les crises periodiques de surproduction.* 2 vols. Paris, 1913.

———. "The Theory of Economic Cycles Based on the Capitalist Techniques of Production," *REStat* (Oct. 1927).

Alexander, S. S. "Opposition to Deficit Spending for the Prevention of Unemployment." In *Income, Employment, and Public Policy: Essays in Honor of Alvin H. Hansen.* New York, 1948.

Allen, R. G. D. *Mathematical Economics.* London, 1965.

———. *Macro-Economic Theory.* London, 1967.

Andrews, P. W. S. *Manufacturing Business.* London, 1949.

Armstrong, D. E. "The Acceleration Principle." Ph.D. diss.,AMcGill Univ., 1952.

Arrow, K. J. "The Economic Implications of Learning by Doing," *RES* (June 1962).

Bain, J. S. *Barriers to New Competition.* Cambridge, Mass., 1956.

———. *International Differences in Industrial Structures.* New Haven, 1965.

Balogh, T. "Money, Incentive and the Production Drive," *OISB* (Oct. 11, 1941).

Baran, P. A. and P. M. Sweezy. *The Political Economy of Growth.* New York, 1957.

———. *Monopoly Capital.* New York, 1966.

Bauer, P. T. "A Note on Monopoly," *Ec* (May 1941).

———. *Dissent on Development.* London, 1971.

Bauman, Z. "O frustracji i o kuglarzach" [About Frustration and Jugglers], *Kul* No. 12 (1968).

Baumol, W. J. *Economic Dynamics.* New York, 1970.
Beach, E. F. *Economic Models.* New York, 1957.
Behrman, J. N. "The Short Term Interest Rate and the Velocity of Circulation," *Em* (Apr. 1948).
Beveridge, W. H. *Fuel Rationing: Report by Sir W. Beveridge, to the President of the Board of Trade.* Cmd. 6352. n.d.
———. *Full Employment in a Free Society.* London, 1944.
Blaug, M. *Economic Theory in Retrospect.* Homewood, Ill., 1968.
Bliss, C. J. "On Putty-Clay," *RES* (Apr. 1968).
Boulding, K., and G. Stigler, eds. *Readings in Price Theory.* Homewood, Ill., 1952.
Bowen, I., and G. D. N. Worswick. "The Controls and War Finance," *OEP* (Sept. 1940).
Branson, W. H. *Macroeconomic Theory and Policy.* New York, 1972.
Bronfenbrenner, M. *Income Distribution Theory.* Chicago, 1971.
———, and F. D. Holzman. "A Survey of Inflation Theory." In *Surveys of Economic Theory.* Vol. 1. New York, 1966.
Brown, M. *On the Theory and Measurement of Technological Change.* Cambridge, 1966.
Brus, W. "Koncepcja bodzcow opartych na zysku" [The Concept of Incentives Based on Profit], *ZG* No. 25 (1957a).
———. "Proba konstrukcji systemu bodzcow z zysku" [An Attempt at Constructing an Incentive System from Profit], *ZG* No. 26 (1957b).
———. "Zysk, ceny i zjednoczenia" [Profit, Prices and Associations], *ZG* No. 9 (1958).
———. "Wzrost a model" [Growth and the Model], *ZG* No. 2 (1959).
———. "O pewnych warunkach postepu gospodarczego" [About Certain Conditions for Economic Progress], *ZG* No. 45 (1962).
———. "Rozwazania na polmetku" [Reflections on the Half-Way Mark], *PK* No. 21 (1963).
———. "Sei mesi dopo la crisi del Baltico," *Rin* No. 26 (1971).
———. *The Market in a Socialist Economy.* London, 1972.
Buchanan, J. H. *Public Principles of Public Debt.* Homewood, Ill., 1958.
Burchardt, F. "Shipping, the Bottleneck," *OISB* (July 18, 1942).
———, and G. D. N. Worswick. "Point Rationing," *OISB* (June 28, 1941).
Burkhead, J. "The Balanced Budget," *QJE* (May 1954).
Burmeister, E., and A. R. Dobell. *Mathematical Theories of Economic Growth.* New York, 1970.

Burns, A. F. *Economic Research and Keynesian Thinking of our Times.* New York, 1946.

Byrd, H. F. In *Congressional Record,* Vol. 101, pt. 4, 84 Cong., 1 sess., May 4, 1955. Rpt. in P. A. Samuelson, ed., *Readings in Economics.* New York, 1970.

Caves, R. E., ed. *Britain's Economic Prospects.* Washington, D. C., 1968.

Charlesworth, H. K. *Economics of Repressed Inflation.* London, 1956.

Chenery, H. B. "Comparative Advantage and Development Policy," in *Surveys of Economic Theory.* Vol. 2. New York, 1965.

Chilosi, A., and S. Gomulka. "Alternatywne klasyfikacje postepu technicznego oraz asymptotyczne scieszki wzrostu" [Alternative Classifications of Technical Progress and Asymptotic Growth Paths], *Ek* No. 1 (1969a).

———. "Technical Progress and Long-Run Growth," *RPE* No. 3 (1969b).

———. "Technical Conditions of Balanced Growth: Criticism and Restatement." Mimeo. London, 1973.

Christ, C. F. "Aggregate Econometric Models," *AER* (June 1956). Rpt. in R. A. Gordon and L. R. Klein, eds., *Readings in Business Cycles.* Homewood, Ill., 1965.

———. *Econometric Models and Methods.* New York, 1966.

Clark, J. B. Introduction to K. Rodbertus, *Overproduction and Crises.* London, 1898.

———. *The Distribution of Wealth.* London, 1899.

Clark, J. M. *Strategic Factors in Business Cycles.* New York, 1934.

Committee for Economic Development. *Taxes and the Budget.* New York, 1947.

Conard, J. W. *An Introduction to the Theory of Interest.* Berkeley, 1959.

Coombes, D. *State Enterprise.* London, 1971.

Cowling, K., ed. *Market Structure and Corporate Behaviour.* London, 1972.

Cyrankiewicz, J. Speech at the Feb. 1971 Plenary Session of the Polish United Workers' Party, *ND* Special Issue (1971).

Davidson, P. *Theories of Aggregate Income Distribution.* New Brunswick, N. J., 1959.

Dillard, D. "Keynes and Proudhon," *JEH* (May 1942).

———. *The Economics of John Maynard Keynes.* Englewood Cliffs, N. J., 1964.

Dobb, M. H. *Political Economy and Capitalism.* New York, 1939.

———. "Second Thoughts on Capital-Intensity of Investment," *RES* No. 1 (1956).

———. *An Essay on Economic Growth and Planning.* London, 1960.

———. *Papers on Capitalism, Development and Planning.* New York, 1967.

———. "Review of *Selected Essays in the Dynamics of the Capitalist Economy,*" *EJ* (Mar. 1972).

———. *Theories of Value and Distribution.* Cambridge, 1973.

Dobrska, Z., and A. Szeworski. "Wiedza i charakter" [Knowledge and Character], *Pol* (May 2, 1970).

Domar, E. *Essays in the Theory of Economic Growth.* New York, 1957.

Duesenberry, J. S. *Business Cycles and Economic Growth.* New York, 1958.

Durant, H., and J. Goldmann. "The Distribution of Working-Class Savings," *OISB* (Jan. 13, 1945).

Economic Report of the President. Washington, D. C., 1963.

Edwards, R. C., M. Reich, and T. E. Weisskopf, eds. *The Capitalist System.* Englewood Cliffs, N. J., 1972.

Erlich, A. *Soviet Industrialization Debate 1924-1928.* Cambridge, Mass., 1960.

Feinstein, C. H. "Changes in the Distribution of the National Income in the United Kingdom Since 1860." In J. Marchal and B. Ducros, eds., *The Distribution of National Income.* London, 1968.

———. *National Income, Expenditure and Output of the United Kingdom, 1885-1965.* Cambridge, 1972.

Feiwel, G. R. *The Economics of a Socialist Enterprise.* New York, 1965.

———. "Review of *Papers on Capitalism, Development and Planning,*" *AER* (June 1968).

———. "The Economics and Life of Michal Kalecki (1899-1970)," *EI* (Nov. 1970a).

———. "Towards a Theory of Growth of a Centrally Planned Economy," *SSt* (July 1970b).

———. *Poland's Industrialization Policy: A Current Analysis.* Vol. 1 in *Industrialization and Planning Under Polish Socialism.* New York, 1971a.

———. *Problems in Polish Economic Planning.* Vol. 2 in *Industrialization and Planning Under Polish Socialism.* New York, 1971b.

———. *The Soviet Quest for Economic Efficiency.* New York, 1967 and 1972.

Feldstein, M. S. "The Derivation of Social Time Preference Rates," *Ky* No. 2 (1965).

Fellner, W. *Trends and Cycles in Economic Activity.* New York, 1956.

———. *Modern Economic Analysis.* New York, 1960.

———, and B. F. Haley, eds. *Readings in the Theory of Income Distribution.* Homewood, Ill., 1951.

Ferguson, C. E. *The Neoclassical Theory of Production and Distribution.* Cambridge, 1969.

———. "Two Books on the Theory of Income Distribution," *JEL* (June 1972).

Fisher, M. R. "Review of *Microeconomic Foundations of Employment and Inflation Theory,*" *EJ* (June 1972).

Florek, H. *Dywersja w ekonomice* [Diversion in Economics]. Warsaw, 1970.

Frankel, S. "Napiecie czy dynamika?" [Pressure or Dynamics?], *ZG* No. 48 (1958).

Friedman, M. *Capitalism and Freedom.* Chicago, 1962.

Frisch, R. *Sparing og cirkulasjons regularing.* Oslo, 1933.

———. "Propagation Problems and Impulse Problems in Dynamic Economics." In *Economic Essays in Honour of Gustav Cassel.* London, 1933. Rpt. in R. A. Gordon and L. R. Klein, eds., *Readings in Business Cycles.* Homewood, Ill., 1965.

———. "Note on the Term Econometrics," *Em* (Jan. 1936).

———. *Knut Wicksell.* Oslo, 1958.

———, and H. Holme. "The Characteristic Solutions of a Mixed Difference and Differential Equation Occurring in Economic Dynamics," *Em* 3 (1935).

Galbraith, J. K. *American Capitalism.* Boston, 1952a.

———. *A Theory of Price Control.* Cambridge, Mass., 1952b.

———. "How Keynes Came to America," *NYTBR* (May 1965).

———. *The New Industrial State.* Boston, 1967.

Garegnani, P. *Il capitale nelle teorie della distribuzione.* Milan, 1960.

Gerschenkron, A. "Reflections on European Socialism." In G. Grossman, ed., *Essays in Socialism and Planning: In Honor of Carl Landauer.* Englewood Cliffs, N. J., 1970.

Godley, W. A. H., and W. T. Nordhaus. "Pricing in the Trade Cycle." *EJ* (Sept. 1972).

Gold, B. "New Perspectives on Cost Theory and Empirical Findings," *JIE* (Apr. 1966).
Goldmann, J. "Taxation of Tobacco, Beer and Cinema Attendances," *OISB* (Jan. 30, 1943).
———. "Differential Rationing in Practice," *OISB* (Oct. 10, 1945).
Gomulka, S. *Inventive Activity, Diffusion and the Stages of Economic Growth.* Arhus, Den., 1971.
———. "Business Cycles and Trend: On the Growth Proposition of Michal Kalecki." Mimeo. Arhus, Den., 1973.
Goodwin, R. M. "The Non-Linear Accelerator and the Persistance of Business Cycles," *Em* (June 1951).
———. "A Model of Cyclical Growth." In E. Lundberg, ed., *The Business Cycle in the Postwar World.* London, 1955.
———. "Review of *Theory of Economic Dynamics,*" *EJ* (Sept. 1956).
———. "Econometrics in Business Cycle Analysis," ch. 22 in A. H. Hansen, *Business Cycles and National Income.* New York, 1964.
Gordon, R. A., and L. R. Klein, eds. *Readings in Business Cycles.* Homewood, Ill., 1965.
Grossman, H. I. "Was Keynes a Keynesian?" *JEL* (Mar. 1972).
Haberler, G. *Prosperity and Depression.* New York, 1941; Cambridge, Mass., 1958.
———. *Inflation.* Washington, D. C., 1960.
Hahn, F. H. "Some Adjustment Problems," *Em* (Jan. 1970).
———. *The Share of Wages in the National Income.* London, 1972.
———, ed. *Readings in the Theory of Growth.* London, 1971.
———, and R. C. O. Matthews. "The Theory of Economic Growth: A Survey," *EJ* (Dec. 1964).
Hall, R. E. "Review of *Microeconomic Foundations of Employment and Inflation Theory,*" *JEL* (Mar. 1972).
Hamberg, D. *Business Cycles.* New York, 1951.
Hancock, W. K., and M. M. Gowing. *British War Economy.* London, 1949.
Hansen, A. H. *A Guide to Keynes.* New York, 1953.
———. "Was Fiscal Policy in the Thirties a Failure?" *REStat* (May 1963).
———. *Business Cycles and National Income.* New York, 1964a.
———. *The Postwar American Economy.* New York, 1964b.
Harcourt, G. C. *Some Cambridge Controversies in the Theory of Capital.* Cambridge, 1972.
———, and N. F. Laing, eds. *Capital and Growth.* Harmondsworth, U. K., 1971.

Harris, S. E., *The Economics of the Kennedy Years.* New York, 1964.
———, ed. *The New Economics.* New York, 1947.
Harrod, R. F. *The Trade Cycle.* London, 1936.
———. "Review of *Essays in the Theory of Employment,*" *EJ* (June 1937).
———. *The Life of John Maynard Keynes.* London, 1951.
———. "Optimum Investment for Growth." In *Problems of Economic Dynamics and Planning: Essays in Honour of Michal Kalecki.* Warsaw, 1964.
———. *Towards a Dynamic Economics.* London, 1948, 1966.
———. "Imperfect Competition, Aggregate Demand and Inflation," *EJ* (Mar. 1972), supplement.
Hayek, F. A. *The Road to Serfdom.* Chicago, 1944.
———. *A Tiger by the Tail.* London, 1972.
Hayter, T. *Aid as Imperialism.* Harmondsworth, U. K., 1971.
Hazlitt, H. "The Development of Economic Thought," *NR* (Nov. 1965).
Heller, W. "CED's Stabilizing Budget Policy After Ten Years," *AER* (Sept. 1957).
———. *New Dimensions in Political Economy.* New York, 1966.
Heilbroner, R. L. *The Limits of American Capitalism.* New York, 1966.
Hickman, B. G., ed. *Econometric Models of Cyclical Behavior.* 2 vols. New York, 1972.
Hicks, J. R. *A Contribution to the Theory of Trade Cycles.* Oxford, 1950.
———. *Capital and Growth.* Oxford, 1965.
Higgins, B. "The Theory of Increasing Underemployment," *EJ* (June 1950).
———. *Economic Development.* New York, 1968.
Hochfeld, J. "Oskar Lange as a Theoretician of Historical Materialism." In *On Political Economy and Econometrics: Essays in Honour of Oskar Lange.* Warsaw, 1964.
Horvat, B. *Towards a Theory of Planned Economy.* Belgrade, 1964.
———. "Review of *Selected Essays on the Economic Growth of the Socialist and the Mixed Economy,*" *EJ* (Mar. 1973).
Hunt, E. K., and J. G. Schwartz, eds. *A Critique of Economic Theory.* Harmondsworth, U. K., 1972.
Hutchison, T. W. "Some Questions About Ricardo," *Ec* (Nov. 1952).

Ichimura, S. "Toward a General Nonlinear Macrodynamic Theory of Economic Fluctuations." In K. Kurihara, ed., *Post-Keynesian Economics.* New Brunswick, N. J., 1954.
Johansen, L. "Substitution Versus Fixed Production Coefficients in the Theory of Economic Growth," *Em* (Apr. 1959).
———. *Production Functions.* Amsterdam, 1972.
Johnson, H. G. "A Survey of Theories of Inflation." In H. G. Johnson, ed., *Essays in Monetary Economics.* Cambridge, Mass., 1967.
———. *Macroeconomics and Monetary Theory.* Chicago, 1972a.
———. *The Theory of Income Distribution.* London, 1972b.
———, and A. R. Nobay, eds. *The Current Inflation.* New York, 1971.
Johnston, J. *Statistical Cost Analysis.* New York, 1960.
Kahn, R. *Essays on Employment and Growth.* Cambridge, 1972.
Kaldor, N. *Expenditure Tax.* London, 1955.
———. *Essays on Value and Distribution.* London, 1960.
———. "Capital Accumulation and Economic Growth." In F. A. Lutz and D. C. Hague, *The Theory of Capital.* London, 1961.
Kaplan, A. D. H., J. B. Dirlam, and R. F. Lanzilotti. *Pricing in Big Business.* Washington, D. C., 1958.
Keezer, D. M. "Observations on Rationing and Price Control in Great Britain," *AER* (June 1943).
Kendall, M. G. *Advanced Theory of Statistics.* London, 1948.
Kennedy, C., and A. P. Thirlwall. "Technical Progress," *EJ* (Mar. 1972).
Keynes, J. M. *General Theory of Employment, Interest and Money.* London, 1936.
———. "Professor Tinbergen's Method," *EJ* (Sept. 1939a).
———. "Relative Movements of Real Wages and Output," *EJ* (March 1939b).
———. "Comment: On a Method of Statistical Business-Cycle Research," *EJ* (Mar. 1940a).
———. *How to Pay for the War.* London, 1940b.
———. *Essays in Biography.* London, 1933; New York, 1963a.
———. *Essays in Persuasion.* London, 1931; New York, 1963b.
Klein, L. R. *Economic Fluctuations in the United States.* New York, 1950.
———. "The Life of John Maynard Keynes," *JPE* (Oct. 1951a).
———. "Studies in Investment Behavior." In National Bureau of Economic Research, *Conference on Business Cycles.* New York, 1951b.

———. "Statistical Testing of Business Cycle Theory." In E. Lundberg, ed., *The Business Cycle in the Postwar World.* London, 1955.

———. *Introduction to Econometrics.* Englewood Cliffs, N. J., 1962.

———. "The Role of Econometrics in Socialist Economics." In *Problems of Economic Dynamics and Planning: Essays in Honour of Michal Kalecki.* Warsaw, 1964.

———. *The Keynesian Revolution.* New York, 1947, 1966.

———. *An Essay on the Theory of Economic Prediction.* Chicago, 1971a.

———. "The Role of War in the Maintenance of American Economic Prosperity." In *Proceedings of the American Philosophical Society,* No. 6 (Dec. 1971b).

———, and R. F. Hosobud. "Some Econometrics of Growth: Great Ratios in Economics," *QJE* (May 1961).

———, and R. J. Preston. "Some New Results in the Measurement of Capacity Utilization," *AER* (Mar. 1967).

Knight, F. H. "The Ricardian Theory of Production and Distribution," *CJE* (Feb. and May 1935).

Koopmans, T. C. "Measurement Without Theory," *RES* (Aug. 1947).

———. "Economic Growth at a Maximal Rate," QJE (Aug. 1964).

———. "Objectives, Constraints, and Outcomes in Optimal Growth Models," *Em* (Jan. 1967).

Kowalik, T. "Biography of Michal Kalecki." In *Problems of Economic Dynamics and Planning: Essays in Honour of Michal Kalecki.* Warsaw, 1964a.

———. "R. Luxemburg's Theory of Accumulation and Imperialism." In *Problems of Economic Dynamics and Planning: Essays in Honour of Michal Kalecki.* Warsaw, 1964b.

Kozlowski, S., and J. Waszczynski. "Elementy polityki ekonomicznej" [Elements of Economic Policy], *ZG,* No. 35 (1971).

Kregel, J. A. *Rate of Profit, Distribution and Growth.* Chicago, 1971.

———. "Marx, Keynes and Social Change: Is Post-Keynesian Theory Neo-Marxist?" Mimeo. Working Paper No. 7214. Louvain, Belg., 1973.

Krelle, W. "The Laws of Income Distribution in the Short and Long Run," in J. Marchal and B. Ducros, eds., *The Distribution of National Income.* London, 1968.

Kuznets, S. *National Product Since 1869.* New York, 1946.

———. "Quantitative Aspects of Economic Growth of Nations," *EDCC* (Apr. 1959).

———. *Modern Economic Growth.* New Haven, 1966.

———. *Economic Growth of Nations.* Cambridge, Mass., 1971.

———. *Quantitative Economic Research.* New York, 1972.

Landauer, C. *European Socialism.* 2 vols. Berkeley, 1959.

Lange, O. "On the Economic Theory of Socialism." In *On the Economic Theory of Socialism.* Minneapolis, 1938.

———. "Review of *Essays in the Theory of Economic Fluctuations,*" *JPE* No. 2 (1941).

———. "Say's Law: A Restatement and Criticism." In *Studies in Mathematical Economics and Econometrics.* Chicago, 1942.

———. "W sprawie doraznego programu" [About an Immediate Program], *ZG* No. 14 (1956).

———. *Pisma ekonomiczne i spoleczne 1930-1960* [Papers in Economics and Sociology 1930-1960]. Warsaw, 1961a.

———. *Teoria rozwoju gospodarczego* [Theory of Economic Development]. Warsaw, 1958. Partly rpt. in *Pisma ekonomiczne i spoleczne 1930-1960.* Warsaw, 1961b.

———. *Political Economy.* Vol. 1. New York, 1963.

———. "Michal Kalecki," *PP* (Sept. 1964).

———. *Teoria reprodukcji i akumulacji* [Theory of Reproduction and Accumulation]. Warsaw, 1965.

Laski, K. "Investment Criteria in Developing Countries." In *Planning for Advanced Skills and Technologies.* New York, 1969.

———. *The Rate of Growth and the Rate of Interest.* Vienna, 1972.

Leijonhufvud, A. *On Keynesian Economics and Economics of Keynes.* London, 1968.

———. *Keynes and the Classics.* London, 1969.

Lekachman, R. "Review of *The Limits of American Capitalism,*" *Ha* (Oct. 1967).

Leontief, W. "Theoretical Assumptions and Nonobserved Facts," *AER* (Mar. 1971).

———. "Introduction to George McGovern, 'On Taxing and Redistributing Income,' " *NYRB* (May 4, 1972).

Lerner, A. P. "The Concept of Monopoly and the Measurement of Monopoly Power," *RES* (June 1934).

———. "Functional Finance and the Federal Debt," *SR* (Feb. 1943).

———. *Economics of Control.* New York, 1944.

———. *Economics of Employment.* New York, 1951.

———. "The Burden of Debt," *REStat* (May 1961).

———. "The General Theory," *ILR* (Oct. 1936). Rpt. in R. Lekachman, ed., *Keynes' General Theory: Reports of Three Decades.* New York, 1964.

———. "Employment Theory and Employment Policy," *AER* (May 1967).

Levy, M. E. *Fiscal Policy, Cycles and Growth.* New York, 1963.

Lewis, H. G. *Unionism and Relative Wages in the United States.* Chicago, 1963.

Lipinski, E. "Wiernosc sobie: Wspomnienia o Michale Kaleckim 1899-1970" [Truthfulness to Oneself: Reminiscences about Michal Kalecki 1899-1970], *KS* No. 4 (1970a).

———. "Wspomnienia o Michale Kaleckim" [Reminiscences about Michal Kalecki], *Ek* No. 4 (1970b).

———. "Z dziejow madrosci w Polsce" [From the History of Wisdom in Poland], *Pol* No. 29 (1970c).

Lipsey, R. G. *Introduction to Positive Economics.* London, 1966.

Lomax, K. S. "Review of *The Current Inflation,*" *EJ* (June 1972).

Lubell, H. "Effects of Redistribution of Income on Consumers' Expenditures," *AER* (Mar. 1947).

Lundberg, E. *Studies in the Theory of Economic Expansion.* London, 1937.

———. *Business Cycles and Economic Policy.* London, 1957.

———. *Instability and Economic Growth.* New Haven, 1968.

———, ed. *The Business Cycle in the Postwar World.* London, 1955.

Luxemburg, R. In F. Mehring, *Karl Marx: The Story of His Life.* London, 1936.

———. *Die Akkumulation des Kapitals.* Berlin, 1913. *Accumulation of Capital.* New York, 1968.

McFarlane, B. J. "Michal Kalecki's Economics: An Appreciation," *ER* (Mar. 1971).

Machlup, F. *Political Economy of Monopoly.* Baltimore, 1952.

———. *Essays on Economic Semantics.* Englewood Cliffs, N. J., 1963.

———. "Theories of the Firm: Marginalist, Behavioral, Managerial." *AER* (Mar. 1967).

MacPherson, C. B. "Elegant Tombstones: A Note on Friedman's Freedom," *CJPS* (Mar. 1968).

Malthus, T. R. *Principles of Political Economy.* London, 1836.

Mann, H. M. "Sellers Concentration, Barriers to Entry and Rates of Return in Thirty Industries, 1950-1960," *REStat* (Aug. 1966).

Mansfield, E., ed. *Monopoly Power and Economic Performance.* New York, 1964.

Marchal, J., and B. Ducros, eds. *The Distribution of National Income.* London, 1968.

Marglin, S. "Social Rate of Discount and the Optimal Rate of Investment," *QJE* (Feb. 1963).

Marris, R. *The Economics of 'Managerial' Capitalism.* London, 1964.

Marx, K. *Capital.* Trans. by E. Untermann. 3 vols, Chicago, 1906 and 1909.

"Materialy XII Plenum KC PZPR" [Materials of the Twelfth Plenary Session of the Central Committee of the Polish United Workers' Party]. Mimeo. Warsaw, Oct. 1958.

"Materialy IV Plenum KC PZPR" [Materials of the Fourth Plenary Session of the Central Committee of the Polish United Workers' Party], *ND* (Special Issue, Feb. 1971).

Matthews, R. C. O. *The Business Cycle.* Chicago, 1959.

Meade, J. E. *The Theory of International Economic Policy.* Vol. 1. London, 1951.

———. *A Neo-Classical Theory of Economic Growth.* London, 1964.

———. *The Growing Economy.* London, 1968.

Means, G. C. *Pricing Power and the Public Interest.* New York, 1962.

Meier, G. M., ed. *Leading Issues in Economic Development.* New York, 1970.

Mermelstein, D., ed. *Economics: Mainstream Readings and Radical Critiques.* New York, 1973.

Metzler, L. A. "Keynes and the Theory of Business Cycles." In S. Harris, ed., *New Economics.* New York, 1947.

———. "The Nature and Stability of Inventory Cycles." In R. A. Gordon and L. R. Klein, eds., *Readings in Business Cycles.* Homewood, Ill., 1965.

Meyer, J. R., and E. Kuh. *The Investment Decision.* Cambridge, Mass., 1957.

Mieszczankowski, M. "Wbrew ekonomice i potrzebom spolecznym" [Despite Economics and Social Needs], *ZG* No. 9 (1971).

Mill, J. S. *Principles of Political Economy.* Ed. by W. Ashley. London, 1900.

Minc, B. *Ekonomia polityczna socjalizmu* [The Political Economy of Socialism]. Warsaw, 1961.

———, and W. Przelaskowski. "Rownanie akumulacji, akumulacja a maksymalizacja spozycia" [The Accumulation Equation, Accumulation and Maximization of Consumption], *Ek* No. 6 (1961).
Mishan, E. J. *The Costs of Economic Growth.* New York, 1967.
Mitra, A. "The Share of Wages in National Income." Ph.D. diss., Netherlands School of Economics, 1954.
Modigliani, F. "Long-Run Implications of Alternative Fiscal Policies and the Burden of the National Debt," *EJ* (Dec. 1961).
Moggridge, D. E., "Review of *British Budgets in Peace and War 1932-1945,*" *EJ* (June 1971).
Morishima, M. *Equilibrium, Stability, and Growth.* London, 1964.
———. *Theory of Economic Growth.* Oxford, 1969.
———. *Marx's Economics.* Cambridge, 1973.
Musgrave, R. A. *The Theory of Public Finance.* New York, 1959.
Myrdal, G. "Fiscal Policy in the Business Cycle," *AER* (Mar. 1939a). Supplement.
———. *Monetary Equilibrium.* London, 1939b.
National Bureau of Economic Research. *Cost Behavior and Price Policy.* New York, 1943.
Neild, R. R. *Pricing and Employment in the Trade Cycle.* Cambridge, 1963.
Nell, E. J. "Two Books on the Theory of Distribution," *JEL* (June 1972).
Nettl, J. P. *Rosa Luxemburg.* 2 vols. London, 1966.
Nicholson, J. L. "Rationing and Index Numbers," *RES* No. 1 (1942).
———. "The Distribution of Incomes," *OISB* (Feb. 5, 1944a).
———. "The Distribution of the War Burden," *OISB* (July 22, 1944b).
———. "Employment and National Income During the War," *OISB* (Oct. 13, 1945).
———. "Earnings, Hours and Mobility of Labour," *OISB* (May 1946).
Nordhaus, W., and J. Tobin. "Is Growth Obsolete?" In *Economic Growth.* New York, 1972.
Nuti, D. M. "Problems of Investment Planning in Socialist Economies." Ph.D. diss., Univ. of Cambridge, 1970a.
———. " 'Vulgar Economy' in the Theory of Income Distribution," *DE* 118 (1970b).
Oderfeld, J., and A. Schinzel. "O pracach matematycznych Michala Kaleckiego" [About the Mathematical Works of Michal Kalecki]. Mimeo. Warsaw, n.d.

Ohlin, B. "Some Notes on the Stockholm Theory of Saving and Investment," *EJ* (Mar. 1937a).

———. "Some Notes on the Stockholm Theory of Saving and Investment," *EJ* (June 1937b).

Okun, A. M. *The Political Economy of Prosperity.* New York, 1970.

———. "Have Fiscal and/or Monetary Policies Failed?" *AER* (May 1972).

———, ed. *The Battle Against Unemployment.* New York, 1972.

Panski, A. "Teorie ekonomiczne Marksa z perspektywy czasu" [Marx's Economic Theories from a Time Perspective], *PS* 5 (1937).

Pasinetti, L. *A New Theoretical Approach to the Problem of Economic Growth.* Vatican City, 1965.

———. "Comment on Neo-Classical Distribution Theory." In J. Marchal and B. Ducros, eds., *The Distribution of National Income.* London, 1968.

Patinkin, D. *Money, Interest, and Prices.* New York, 1965.

———. "Money and Wealth: A Review Article," *JEL* (Dec. 1969).

———. *Studies in Monetary Theory.* New York, 1971.

Passell, P., and L. Ross. *The Retreat from Riches.* New York, 1972.

Pen, J. *Income Distribution.* New York, 1971.

Phelps, E. S. "The Golden Rule of Accumulation: A Fable for Growthmen," *AER* (Sept. 1961).

———. "Substitution, Fixed Proportions, Growth, and Distribution," *IER* (Sept. 1963).

———. "Second Essay on the Golden Rule of Accumulation," *AER* (Sept. 1965).

———. *Inflation Policy and Unemployment Theory.* New York, 1972.

———, *et al. Microeconomic Foundations of Employment and Inflation Theory.* New York, 1970.

Phillips, A. W. "Review of *Theory of Economic Dynamics,*" *Ec* (Nov. 1955).

Pigou, A. C. *Industrial Fluctuations.* London, 1927.

———. *Employment and Equilibrium.* London, 1929.

———. "Real and Money Wage Rates in Relation to Unemployment," *EJ* (Sept. 1937).

———. "The Classical Stationary State," *EJ* (Dec. 1943).

———. *Keynes's General Theory.* London, 1951.

Poole, W. "Thoughts on the Wage-Price Freeze," *BPEA* No. 2 (1971).

Pryke, R. *Public Enterprise in Practice.* London, 1971.
Rakowski, M., ed. *Efektywnosc inwestycji* [Investment Efficiency]. Warsaw, 1961.
Rees, A. *Wage Inflation.* New York, 1957.
Reynolds, L. G., and C. H. Taft. *The Evolution of Wage Structure.* New Haven, 1956.
Riach, P. A. "Kalecki's 'Degree of Monopoly' Reconsidered," *AEP* (June 1971).
Ricardo, D. *The Works and Correspondence of David Ricardo.* Ed. by P. Sraffa, with the collaboration of M. H. Dobb. 8 vols. Cambridge, 1951.
Robbins, L. *Essays on the Nature and Significance of Economic Science.* London, 1935.
———. *The Economic Problem in Peace and War.* London, 1947.
Robertson, D. "Mr. Clark and the Foreign Trade Multiplier," *EJ* (June 1939).
Robinson, E. A. G. "John Maynard Keynes 1883-1946," *EJ* (Mar. 1947). Rpt. in R. Lekachman, ed., *Keynes' General Theory: Reports of Three Decades.* New York, 1964.
Robinson, Joan. *Collected Economic Papers,* Vols. 1, 2 and 3. Oxford, 1951, 1960, 1965.
———. *Economic Philosophy.* Chicago, 1962a.
———. *Essays in the Theory of Economic Growth.* London, 1962b.
———. "Kalecki and Keynes." In *Problems of Economic Dynamics and Planning: Essays in Honour of Michal Kalecki.* Warsaw, 1964.
———. *The Accumulation of Capital.* New York, 1956, 1966a.
———. *An Essay on Marxian Economics.* New York, 1942, 1966b.
———. Introduction to *Studies in the Theory of Business Cycles 1933-1939,* by M. Kalecki. Warsaw, 1966c.
———. *The Economics of Imperfect Competition.* London, 1933 and 1969a.
———. *Introduction to the Theory of Employment.* London, 1947, 1969b.
———. "Review of *On Keynesian Economics and the Economics of Keynes,*" *EJ* (Sept. 1969c).
———. "Capital Theory Up to Date," *CJE* 3 (1970a).
———. "Review of *The Neoclassical Theory of Production and Distribution,*" *EJ* (June 1970b).
———. *Economic Heresies.* London, 1971a.
———. "Michal Kalecki," *CR* (Oct. 22, 1971b).

———. "The Second Crisis of Economic Theory," *AER* (May 1972).

Rothschild, K. "Some Recent Contributions to a Macro-Economic Theory of Income Distribution," *SJPE* No. 8 (1961).

———., ed. *Power in Economics.* Harmondsworth, U. K., 1971.

Sabine, B. E. V. *British Budgets in Peace and War 1932-1945.* London, 1970.

Salant, W. A. "Taxes, Income Determination, and the Balanced Budget Theorem," *REStat* (May 1957).

Salter, W. E. G. *Productivity and Technical Change.* Cambridge, 1960.

Samuelson, P. A. "Interactions Between the Multiplier Analysis and the Principle of Acceleration," *REStat* (May 1939).

———. "Fiscal Policy and Income Determination," *QJE* (Aug. 1942).

———. *The Economic Role of Private Activity: A Dialogue on the Proper Economic Role of the State.* Chicago, 1963.

———. "The General Theory," *Em* (July 1946). Rpt. in R. Lekachman, ed., *Keynes' General Theory: Reports of Three Decades.* New York, 1964.

———. *Foundations of Economic Analysis.* Cambridge, Mass., 1947; New York, 1965.

———. *The Collected Scientific Papers of Paul A. Samuelson.* 2 vols., Cambridge, Mass., 1966.

———. *Economics.* New York, 1970.

———. *The Collected Economic Papers of Paul A. Samuelson,* Vol. 3. Cambridge, Mass., 1972.

Sayers, R. S. *Financial Policy 1939-45.* London, 1956.

Schinzel, A. "O pracach Michala Kaleckiego z teorii liczb" [About Michal Kalecki's Works in the Theory of Numbers], *Ek* No. 5 (1970).

Schultze, C. L. "Recent Inflation in the United States." In U. S., Congress, Joint Economic Committee, Study Paper No. 1. *Study of Employment, Growth and Price Levels.* Washington, D. C., 1959.

Schumpeter, J. A. *Capitalism, Socialism and Democracy.* New York, 1942.

———. *History of Economic Analysis.* New York, 1954.

———. *The Theory of Economic Development.* New York, 1934, 1964.

———. *Ten Great Economists.* New York, 1951, 1965.

Scitovsky, T. "Review of *Studies in Economic Dynamics,*" *EJ* (Sept. 1946).

———, E. Shaw, and L. Tarshis. *Mobilizing Resources for War.* New York, 1951.

Secomski, K. "Michal Kalecki 1899-1970," *NP* No. 1 (1971).

Sen, A. "On Optimizing the Rate of Saving," *EJ* (Sept. 1961).

———. "Solution, Assurance, and the Social Rate of Discount," *QJE* (Feb. 1967).

———. *Choice of Techniques.* Oxford, 1960, 1968.

———. "Choice of Technology." In *Planning for Advanced Skills and Technologies.* New York, 1969.

———, ed. *Growth Economics.* Baltimore, 1970.

Shackle, G. L. S. "Recent Theories Concerning the Nature and Role of Interest." In *Surveys of Economic Theory,* Vol. 1. New York, 1966.

———. *The Years of High Theory.* Cambridge, 1967.

Sheshinski, E. "Balanced Growth and Stability in the Johansen Vintage Capital Model," *RES* (Apr. 1967).

Sichel, W., ed. *Industrial Organization and Public Policy.* Boston, 1967.

Silberston, A. "Price Behaviour of Firms," *EJ* (Sept. 1970).

Solow, R. M. "A Skeptical Note on the Constancy of Relative Shares," *AER* (Sept. 1958).

———. "Investment and Technical Progress." In K. J. Arrow, S. Arlin, and P. Suppes, eds., *Mathematical Methods in the Social Sciences.* Stanford, Calif., 1960.

———. *Capital Theory and the Rate of Return.* Chicago, 1965.

———. "Distribution in the Long and Short Run." In J. Marchal and B. Ducros, eds., *The Distribution of National Income.* London, 1968a.

———. "Recent Controversy on the Theory of Inflation." In S. W. Rouseas, ed., *Inflation: Its Causes, Consequences, and Control.* Wilton, Conn., 1968b.

Spulber, N. *Soviet Strategy for Economic Growth.* Bloomington, Ind., 1964.

———, ed. *Foundations of Soviet Strategy for Economic Growth.* Bloomington, Ind., 1965.

Sraffa, P. "The Laws of Returns Under Competitive Conditions," *EJ* (Dec. 1926).

———. Introduction to *The Works and Correspondence of David Ricardo.* Ed. by P. Sraffa, with the collaboration of M. H. Dobb, 8 vols. Cambridge, 1951.

———. *Production of Commodities by Means of Commodities.* Cambridge, 1960.

Stans, M. H. "The Need for Balanced Federal Budgets." In *Annals of the American Academy of Political and Social Science,* 1959. Rpt. in P. A. Samuelson, ed., *Readings in Economics.* New York, 1970.

Stark, W. "A Note on Rosa Luxemburg," in R. Luxemburg, *Accumulation of Capital.* New York, 1968.

Stein, H. *The Fiscal Revolution in America.* Chicago, 1969.

Steindl, J. "Economic Incentive and Efficiency in War Industry," *OISB* (June 7, 1941a).

———. "The Production Executive's Regional Boards," OISB (Aug. 30, 1941b).

———. "Rationing and Surplus Goods," *OISB* (Nov. 1, 1941c).

———. "The Problem of Price and Wage Control," *OISB* (Oct. 10, 1942).

———. *Maturity and Stagnation in American Capitalism.* Oxford, 1952.

Stigler, G. J. *Production and Distribution Theories.* New York, 1946.

———. "The Nature and Role of Originality in Scientific Progress." *Ec* (Nov. 1955).

Stiglitz, J., and H. Uzawa, eds. *Readings in Modern Theory of Economic Growth.* Cambridge, Mass., 1969.

Strumilin, S. "Socjalistyczna metoda produkcji" [The Socialist Method of Production], *Ek* No. 2 (1959).

Studies in War Economics. Oxford, 1947.

Sulmicki, P. "Pojecie inflacji w gospodarce socjalistycznej" [The Concept of Inflation in a Socialist Economy], *MG* No. 5 (1957).

Sutton, F. X. *et al. The American Business Creed.* Cambridge, Mass., 1956.

Sweezy, P. M. *Theory of Capitalist Development.* New York, 1942.

———. "John Maynard Keynes," *S&S* No. 4 (1946). Rpt. in R. Lekachman, ed., *Keynes' General Theory: Reports of Three Decades.* New York, 1964.

———. "On the Theory of Monopoly Capitalism," *MR* (Apr. 1972).

Sylos-Labini, P. *Oligopoly and Technical Progress.* Cambridge, Mass., 1969.

Symposium on "*Paradoxes in Capital Theory,*" *QJE* (Nov. 1966).

Szyr, E. *Niektore problemy rozwoju gospodarki narodowej w latach 1959-65* [Some Problems of the Development of the National Economy in 1959-65]. Warsaw, 1959.

Tinbergen, J. "Ein Schiffbauzyklus," *WA* No. 1 (1931).

———. "Annual Survey: Suggestions on Quantitative Business Cycle Theory," *Em* 3 (1935).

———. "On a Method of Statistical Business-Cycle Research," *EJ* (Mar. 1940).

———. "The Significance of Keynes' Theories from the Econometric Point of View." In S. Harris, ed., *New Economics.* New York, 1947.

———. "Econometric Business Cycle Research," *RES* 3 (1940), pp. 73-90. Rpt. in G. Haberler, ed., *Readings in Business Cycle Theory.* Philadelphia, 1951a.

———. *Econometrics.* New York, 1951b.

———. *Economic Policy.* Chicago, 1967.

———, and J. J. Polak. *The Dynamics of Business Cycles.* Chicago, 1950.

Tobin, J. "Inflation and Unemployment," *AER* (Mar. 1972).

Tsiang, S. C. *The Variations of Real Wages and Profit Margins in Relation to the Trade Cycle.* London, 1947.

Tugan-Baranovsky, M. *Studien zur Theorie und Geschichte der Handelkrisen in England.* Jena, 1901.

United Nations. *Inflationary and Deflationary Tendencies, 1946-48.* New York, 1949a.

———. *World Economic Report 1948.* New York, 1949b.

———. *World Economic Report 1952-53.* New York, 1954.

———. *World Economic Report 1953-54.* New York, 1955.

Von Neumann, J. "A Model of General Economic Equilibrium," *RES* No. 1 (1945).

Wallis, W. A., and H. V. Roberts. *Statistics.* New York, 1963.

Walras, L. *Elements of Pure Economics.* Paris, 1926; London, 1954.

Weintraub, A., E. Schwartz, and J. R. Aronson, eds. *The Economic Growth Controversy.* White Plains, N. Y., 1973.

Weintraub, S. *An Approach to the Theory of Distribution.* Philadelphia, 1958.

Whitman, R. "A Note on the Concept of 'Degree of Monopoly,' " *EJ* (June-Sept. 1941).

Wicksell, K. *Lectures on Political Economy.* Ed. with intro. by L. Robbins. London, 1934.

Worswick, G. D. N. "Notes on Rationing," *OISB* (Jan. 10, 1942).

———. "Dual Capacity," *OISB* (Apr. 3, 1943).

———. "Points, Prices and Consumers' Choice," *OISB* (Feb. 26, 1944a).

———. "Reliability and Flexibility of Full Employment." In *The Economics of Full Employment.* Oxford, 1944b.
———. "A Survey of War Concept Procedure," *OISB* (Apr. 7, 1945).
Wright, D. Mc., ed. *The Impact of the Union.* New York, 1951.
Yamane, T. *Statistics.* New York, 1964.
Zarnowitz, V. *The Business Cycle Today.* New York, 1972.
Zauberman, A. "The Soviet and Polish Quest for a Criterion of Investment Efficiency," *Ec* (Aug. 1962).
———. "A Few Remarks on Kalecki's Theory of Economic Growth Under Socialism," *Ky* No. 3 (1966).
———. *Aspects of Planometrics.* New Haven, 1967.
Zimmerman, L. J. *The Propensity to Monopolize.* Amsterdam, 1951.

INDEX